A POLITICAL AND SOCIAL HISTORY OF MODERN EUROPE

BY

CARLTON J. H. HAYES

ASSOCIATE PROFESSOR OF HISTORY IN COLUMBIA
UNIVERSITY

VOLUME II

New York
THE MACMILLAN COMPANY
1918

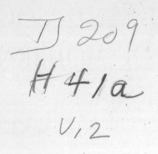

Norwood Press
J. S. Cushing Co. — Berwick & Smith Co.
Norwood, Mass., U.S.A.

CONTENTS

VOLUME II

PART IV

DEMOCRACY AND NATIONALISM

PART V

NATIONAL IMPERIALISM

MAPS

VOLUME II

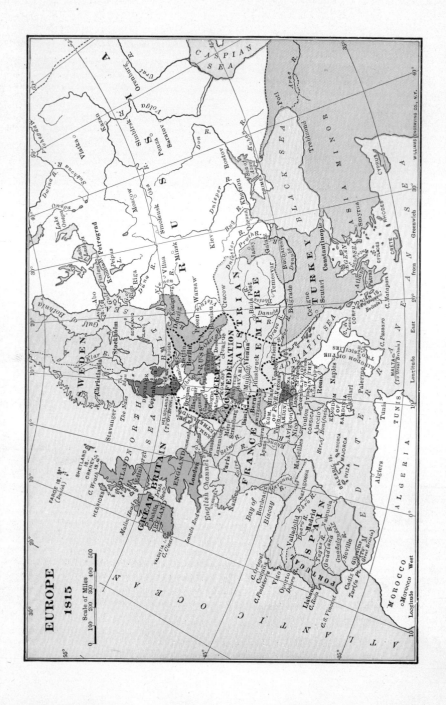

EUROPE
1815

Scale of Miles
0 100 200 300 400 500

CHAPTER XVII

THE ERA OF METTERNICH, 1815–1830

REVOLUTION OR REACTION?

CERTAIN basic principles in society and in politics were proclaimed by the French Revolution. The Napoleonic Era served to communicate them to Europe. The ensuing period was marked by a bitter struggle within nearly every European state for their general acceptance or for their wholesale rejection.

To all Frenchmen liberty, equality, and fraternity already meant definite facts or rights: those who espoused them were inherently revolutionaries — radicals or liberals — Continued while those who repudiated them were reactionaries or Conflict conservatives, intent upon maintaining or restoring Revolution the political and social institutions of the old régime. and the Old The Bourbon settlement of 1814 in France was in Régime the nature of a compromise, a nice balancing of the forces of revolution and reaction. Outside of France the sovereigns of Europe were almost without exception reactionaries, determined to bolster up the theories and practices of the eighteenth century, but many of their subjects who, in the years between 1789 and 1814, had learned from the French in one way or another the significance of popular sovereignty, individual rights, and national patriotism, gave unmistakable signs of a contrary determination. The question resolved itself into this: should revolutionary or reactionary doctrine henceforth shape the society and politics of the European nations? It was a question fraught with the most momentous consequences to succeeding generations. Another fifteen years would pass before the outcome could be indicated — the fifteen years (1815–1830) of conflict between liberals and conservatives which we shall now proceed to treat as the Era of Metternich.

Throughout the period the distinction between liberals and conservatives was everywhere based largely on differences among

The Reactionaries and Conservatives

social classes and in geographical location. The princes whose divine authority to rule was questioned; the nobles whose lands and privileges were confiscated or threatened with confiscation; the ecclesiastics whose consciences were violated or activities abridged: these pillars of the old régime were uniformly conservative. On the other hand, the great bulk of the bourgeoisie, — the professional classes, business men, traders, and shopkeepers, — whose traditional repugnance to nobles and clergymen was sharpened by an ambition to secure complete control of national policies and finance; the generality of the Continental universities — professors and students — together with other "intellectuals" drawn from many walks of life, who were intensely patriotic

The Revolutionaries and Liberals

and who dreamed of the perfectibility of mankind; the workingman of the town and many a day-laborer in the fields, who felt that any change might add to the contents of his dinner-pail: these groups, restless under the old régime, were solidly liberal. The peasantry who still constituted the majority of European population were swayed between the contending parties: still respectful of authority in state and church, sincerely religious, and innately skeptical of the fine phrases which were on liberal lips, they could at times and in places be reckoned conservative; but there was one important respect in which many of them doggedly resisted alliance with the reactionaries, and that was their fanatical attachment to the social achievements of the Revolution — they were done forever with feudalism and serfdom, they would own their own lands.   As a general rule it may be observed that the further west one went and the nearer to revolutionary France one came, the larger proportion of liberals one found, and that, conversely, the further east one went and the more remote from France, the larger proportion of conservatives one encountered.

For several years after the downfall of Napoleon the con-

Religious Revival

servatives enjoyed throughout Europe an influence perhaps out of proportion to their actual numbers. There was a renewed loyalty on the part of patriots to the monarchs who had headed the great national uprisings against

Napoleonic despotism. There was a marked revival of devotion to the Catholic Church, whose supreme pontiff, the venerable Pius VII, in the face of insults and injuries from Napoleon, had set a noble example of Christian charity and fortitude. Above all, there was universal horror at the bloodshed and wretchedness which the Revolutionary and Napoleonic wars had entailed. Thousands upon thousands of human beings, drawn from every nation and from every social class, had been butchered. Famine, pestilence, crime, and indescribable disease, — the attendant miseries of war, — had walked abroad in every land. Small wonder that prince, priest, and people united in extoll- **Desire for** ing the blessings of peace! Even the liberal bour- **Peace** geoisie perceived that the revival of Continental industry and trade was a concomitant of peace. With some justice Metternich was able to avow that "what the European peoples want is not liberty but peace." To prevent the recurrence of such insurrections as the Revolution had witnessed and of such wars as the career of Napoleon had involved, — in a word, to preserve domestic and foreign peace, — became the watchword and countersign of reactionary Europe.

Among the host of figures who crowd the stage from 1815 to 1830, Prince Metternich stands out most prominently, not indeed in any such unique way as did Napoleon Bona- **Prince** parte from 1799 to 1815, but still conspicuously **Metternich** enough to justify the common use of his name in designating the era. A contrast more striking than that between Metternich and Napoleon can hardly be imagined.

Count Clemens Metternich was born at Coblenz on 15 May, 1773, of a very distinguished family which ranked high among the oldest nobility of the Rhenish Germanies and which **His Early** had furnished several electors to the great ecclesias- **Career** tical sees of Trier and Cologne in the sixteenth and seventeenth centuries. His father had entered the diplomatic service of the Holy Roman Empire, and in the social setting of the old régime and the aristocratic atmosphere of the punctilious Habsburg court young Clemens was reared. He was a sixteen-year-old student at the University of Strassburg when the vigor of the town mob gave him his first knowledge of, and distaste for, the French Revolution, a distaste which the seizure of his princely family estates by Napoleon fourteen years later was not likely to counteract. Following his father's career, he soon attracted the favorable attention of the veteran Austrian chancellor, Count Kaunitz, whose grand-daughter he married in 1795. This alliance not only brought him large estates in Austria, but made him heir to the prestige of the great diplomat of the eighteenth century and introduced him into the most exclusive circles of Viennese society. Henceforth his rise was rapid. He served as representative of the Habsburg emperor successively at Dresden (1801), Berlin (1803), Petrograd (1805), and Paris (1806). Despite his country's embarrassment during the years immediately following the catastrophe of Austerlitz, and although he was now pitted against Talleyrand, in many ways as great a master of subtlety as himself, his remarkable good looks, his clever wit, and his charm of manner won him high favor at Napoleon's court, and gained for him an extraordinary diplomatic experience. Although he urged his sovereign to undertake the premature war of 1809, he was one of the first to counsel peace after the defeat of Wagram.

In 1809 Metternich became the actual head of the Austrian government, under the nominal rule of the well-intentioned but **Austrian** procrastinating Emperor Francis I, a position he was **Minister** able to retain for nearly forty years. The statesman could not but be impressed with the need of reformation within his country, and he at once made a few proposals for national betterment. But his detestation of revolution from below made him fearful of reforms from above, and he preferred to bring honor and prestige to Austria by means of successful foreign diplomacy rather than through what always seemed to him the more uncertain means of internal changes in society and political organization.

In foreign affairs, Metternich's hatred of Napoleon was conditioned by his fear of Russian aggrandizement in the event of **His Rela-** the French emperor's downfall. Accordingly, from **tions with** 1810 to 1813 his policy was to play off Napoleon and **Napoleon** Alexander against each other. He pressed forward with alacrity the negotiations for the marriage of an Austrian archduchess to the Corsican adventurer. He watched with glee the herculean combat of 1812 between Napoleon and the tsar, promising to the former the assistance of an army corps of 30,000 men, while assuring the latter that the Austrian forces would not be employed on the offensive. All the time he was actually keeping the whole Austrian army on a war footing and maintaining an armed neutrality, ready to throw his weight upon whichever side might finally be in a position to bestow the greater benefits upon Austria. Such was the success of his well-laid plans that the intervention of Austria was the decisive factor in the Battle of the Nations (October, 1813) and in the campaign of 1814: Napoleon's power collapsed and Austria became the dominant Power among the victorious allies. Metternich was hailed as the most astute statesman of his age — he hobnobbed with the Russian and Prussian monarchs, he was fêted by Talleyrand and Louis XVIII, he was given a fulsome welcome on a visit to England, he was named a magnate of the kingdom of Hungary and a count and hereditary prince of the Austrian Empire.

THE CONGRESS OF VIENNA AND THE RECONSTRUCTION OF EUROPE

The most important problem which confronted European diplomacy, after the restoration of the French Bourbons, was that of general territorial readjustments. Napoleon had badly mutilated the ancient map of Europe. How far could, or should, his victors mend it? To what extent were they justified in rewarding themselves territorially for their efforts and sacrifices? What punishment should they mete out to his late allies? It was a recognition of the decisive part played by Austria and of the commanding personality of Metternich that Vienna was chosen as the scene of the great international congress convened (September, 1814) for the purpose of answering these questions and of reëstablishing the balance of power in Europe.

International Problems Created by Napoleon

Never had Europe beheld such a galaxy of gold lace and titled dignitaries of the old régime as gathered at Vienna. Six monarchs attended: the Tsar Alexander, a curious mixture of shrewdness and mysticism, of ambition and compassion; the polite and cautious Emperor Francis I[1] of Austria; King Frederick William III

The Congress of Vienna, 1814–1815

[1] Francis II, Holy Roman Emperor from 1792 to 1806, known as Francis I, emperor of Austria, after 1804.

of Prussia, who was at once timid and obstinate, and quite fascinated by the Christian-like benevolence of the tsar; and the kings of Denmark, Bavaria, and Württemberg. German dukes, princes, and electors were present in crowds, while among the special envoys were two Irish noblemen, the sagacious Lord Castlereagh and the "Iron" Duke of Wellington, who in turn represented Great Britain; Hardenberg and Baron von Humboldt from Prussia; Nesselrode from Russia; Stein, now a personal agent of the Tsar Alexander; the insinuating Talleyrand from France, with his new discovery of "legitimacy"; and last but not least Metternich himself, who discharged the obligations that devolved upon him as host of the imposing congress with becoming grace and dignity. With the possible exception of Alexander, whose predilections for French liberalism and for the "free" institutions of England were still sincere if somewhat vague, the Congress of Vienna in its personnel as well as in its actions was one grand pageant in celebration of the defeat of revolution and the triumph of reaction.

In conformity with the best usages of eighteenth-century diplomacy, the divine-right monarchs and their splendid representatives who assembled at Vienna interspersed their negotiations with a round of banquets and balls. This fact, together with the inherent difficulty of many of the problems handled, protracted the deliberations for several months. Almost from the outset differences in claims developed between Russia and Prussia on one hand and Austria, backed by Great Britain and France, on the other, so that for some time neither the stubbornness of the tsar nor the machinations of Metternich proved sufficient to solve the vexatious problems of the disposition of Poland and Saxony. It required the shock of Napoleon's return from Elba to bring the statesmen together, to smooth out the rough places, and to arrange a compromise. The Final Act of the Congress of Vienna was signed (9 June, 1815) only a few days before the battle of Waterloo.

The general principle underlying the Viennese settlement was the restoration so far as practicable of the boundaries and of the reigning families of the several European countries as they had been prior to the outbreak of the French Revolution and the advent of Napoleon Bonaparte. It was the very principle of "legitimacy" which Talleyrand exploited in order to save France from further territorial spoliation and to enable his vanquished country still to play an influential rôle in the counsels of Europe, and which Metternich adopted from him as a valuable asset of Austrian policy and of general reaction.   In accordance with the theory of "legitimacy," France was not compelled to pay heavily even for the Hundred Days: the second treaty of Paris, concluded in November, 1815, guaranteed her approximately the boundaries of 1789 and obliged her only to restore the art-treasures which Napoleon had pilfered from other countries, to pay an indemnity of 700,000,000 francs, and to submit for a term of five years to foreign occupation of her chief fortresses.   Likewise consonant with the doctrine of "legitimacy," the treaties of Vienna recognized the restoration of the Bourbons in Spain and in the Two Sicilies, of the house of Orange in Holland, of the house of Savoy in Sardinia and Piedmont, of the pope to his temporal possessions in central Italy, and of the various German princes whose territories had been included in the Confederation of the Rhine. Still in the name of "legitimacy," Austria recovered the Tyrol and the Illyrian provinces; the Swiss Confederation was restored under a guarantee of neutrality; and Poland was again dismembered, much the same as in 1795, by Russia, Austria, and Prussia, although the tsar promised to treat his lion's share as a separate kingdom with its own constitution.

" Legiti-macy " and the Vienna Settlement

The principle of "legitimacy" was somewhat compromised by the necessity of providing more or less arbitrary "compensations."   In the course of the Napoleonic wars, Great Britain, as we have already seen, appropriated, along with Malta, Mauritius, Tobago, St. Lucia, Trinidad, and part of Honduras, the important Dutch colonies of Ceylon, South Africa, and Guiana.[1]   These colonies were now confirmed to the British, but as compensation to the Dutch, and also in order to erect a strong state on the northern frontier of France, the Austrian Netherlands — what is present-day Belgium — were joined with Holland, to form the United Kingdom of the Netherlands under the rule of the Dutch king, despite the fact that nearly two and a half centuries of political separation

" Compen-sations " in the Vienna Settlement

[1] A part of Guiana was retained by the Dutch.

had augmented the racial and religious antipathies between the two regions. To compensate Austria for the surrender of her claims on the Belgian Netherlands, she was given a commanding position in Italy: the territories of the ancient republic of Venice and of the duchy of Milan were transferred to her outright, and members of the Habsburg family were seated upon the thrones of the small central states of Tuscany, Parma, and Modena. Sweden, as compensation for the cession of Finland to Russia and of Pomerania to Prussia, secured Norway from Denmark, whose protracted alliance with Napoleon seemed to merit a severe punishment. Prussia was similarly allowed to annex two-fifths of Saxony and, as a further safeguard against France, to enlarge her former provinces in the lower Rhine valley. On the southeastern frontier of France, the king of Sardinia was permitted to possess himself of the former republic of Genoa.

In the territorial and constitutional settlement of the Germanies neither Austria nor Prussia found it advantageous to **Reconstruction of the Germanies** insist too rigorously upon "legitimacy." There was no thought of reviving the two-hundred-odd ecclesiastical states and petty principalities which had been suppressed in 1803. There was no serious intention of restoring to life the Holy Roman Empire which had expired in 1806. There was certainly no favor shown by the German kings and diplomats to the popular agitation for a strongly knit national state. Baron vom Stein, it is true, proposed the unification of all Germany under the supremacy of a single Power, but King Frederick William III displayed no ambition to assume the leadership, and Metternich had already promised the princes of south Germany that Austria would respect their sovereign rights. Instead of adopting a frankly national policy, the governments of Prussia and Austria, as well as the smaller German states, were bent on safeguarding their respective interests against possible encroachments by others. The outcome of this particularist, or states-rights, feeling was the creation of the Germanic Confederation, a loose organization of the remaining thirty-eight states, with a Diet consisting of delegates of the reigning princes, presided over by Austria. The members might not enter into alliance with a foreign Power either against the Confederation as a whole or against a fellow-member. The constitution was placed under the guarantee of Europe, and, by means of the traditional and interested support which the lesser princes gave to Austria, the Confederation soon came to be directed from Vienna.

Thus did the foremost reactionaries of Europe refashion their map. Thus in the name of legitimacy was France saved and at the same time so hemmed in that she would not be able again to dictate to the Continent. Thus, too, were the allies rewarded who had certainly overthrown Napoleon and had possibly stayed the Revolution. Thus, finally, under Metternich, had the leadership of Europe passed from France to Austria. Great indeed was the power and prestige of Austria at the close of the Congress of Vienna. Metternich now found himself in charge of the affairs of an enormous state. With the exception of the distant Belgian Netherlands, which had always been a source of weakness, the Habsburg dominions of 1763 were again intact, and to them had been added the richest and most prosperous districts of neighboring Italy. In fact, throughout the entire Italian peninsula, French influence was replaced by Austrian. Then, too, within the Diet of the new Germanic Confederation the Austrian emperor, backed by the weight of the Habsburg power beyond the borders of Germany, exercised a greater influence than had ever the Holy Roman Emperor.

Commanding Position of Austria

In all these territorial readjustments there was little that was permanent and much that was temporary. The union of Sweden and Norway lasted ninety years; that of Holland and Belgium, fifteen; and the Italian and German settlements survived but fifty years. The fatal mistake of the Congress was the willful disregard of the principle of nationality. Howsoever the reactionary monarchs and diplomats might combat liberty and equality, they could ill afford to be oblivious of the patriotic, nationalistic movements that had recently stirred the French, the Poles, the Portuguese, the Spaniards, the Italians, and the Germans. Yet they calmly set aside all national considerations, and, true to the international usages of the seventeenth and eighteenth centuries, they proceeded once more to treat the European peoples as so many pawns in the game of dynastic aggrandizement. That was why the princes were left all-powerful in the Germanies, why the Italian states passed

Disregard of Nationalism

under the domination of Austria, why the Belgians as well as the Dutch were handed over to the house of Orange, why Swedes and Norwegians were given a joint sovereign. The longing for nationality was already a very real fact throughout Europe; failure to satisfy it was the chief defect in the work of the Congress of Vienna.

The harking back of the plenipotentiaries at Vienna to the days of territorial rivalry among the Great Powers also prevented

Paucity of Other Achievements of the Congress of Vienna them from fulfilling the expectations which the Tsar Alexander and enlightened public opinion had entertained of a wider and more fundamental scope for the labors of the Congress. To these altruistic souls, the termination of a terrible period of revolution and warfare, of bloodshed and misery, and the rapid development of a sense of solidarity among all European princes and peoples seemed a particularly auspicious opportunity for effecting a permanent settlement of the balance of power, for the discovery of safeguards against its future disturbance, for general disarmament and assurance of international peace, for the suppression of the slave trade and of piracy, and for the solution of social problems. Such subjects were actually broached at Vienna by the tsar, but their reception, though polite, was essentially chilly and most of them were suffered to drop quite out of sight: even Alexander was soon absorbed in the ambition of securing Finland and Poland for the Romanov dynasty. Largely through British representations, a declaration was appended to the final treaty to the effect that the slave trade should be abolished, although each Power was left free to fix such a date as best suited its own convenience. Provisions respecting the free navigation of international rivers and regulating the rights of precedence among diplomatists, — minor modifications in the recognized content of international law, — were also adopted. But the more serious questions of the future

Metternich's Policy: the Maintenance of the Status Quo were not perceived or were left unheeded.

Metternich was certainly desirous of rendering the Viennese settlement permanent. He was henceforth a stanch advocate of the maintenance of international peace. But he believed that the peace of Europe could best be maintained not by a central tribunal resting upon the consent of the European peoples, which would recognize the

hateful principle of democracy and which might seriously interfere with the hegemony of Austria, but rather by the vigi-
lant benevolence of allied sovereigns. The treaty of Paris (20
November, 1815), which formally renewed the treaty **The**
of Chaumont, bound the Quadruple Alliance — **Quadruple**
Austria, Russia, Prussia, and Great Britain — to **Alliance**
the future convocation of diplomatic congresses for the preservation of peace and of the *status quo*, and this was sufficient
for Metternich.

But the Tsar Alexander, in his dreamy, mystical way, had
already gone further. While loyally adhering to the Quadruple
Alliance as an effective means of maintaining the **Tsar Alex-**
treaties of Vienna by physical force, he had felt that **ander and**
the great Christian principles of peace, forbearance, **the Holy**
and mutual good will, solemnly subscribed to by all the **Alliance**
European monarchs, would supply the underlying and sacred spiritual motives for preserving modern society as well as boundaries
and governments. Accordingly he had induced the pious king of
Prussia and the obliging emperor of Austria to join with him in
forming (26 September, 1815) the celebrated Holy Alliance, by
which the three sovereigns solemnly declared their "fixed resolution, both in the administration of their respective states, and in
their political relations with every other government, to take for
their sole guide the precepts of that Holy Religion, namely, the
precepts of Justice, Christian Charity, and Peace, which, far
from being applicable only to private concerns, must have an
immediate influence on the councils of Princes, and guide all their
steps, as being the only means of consolidating human institutions
and remedying their imperfections." They mutually promised
to "remain united by the bonds of a true and indissoluble fraternity, and, considering each other as fellow-countrymen, they will,
on all occasions and in all places, lend each other aid and assistance; and, regarding themselves towards their subjects and
armies as fathers of families, they will lead them, in the same spirit
of fraternity with which they are animated, to protect Religion,
Peace, and Justice." Their Majesties consequently recommended to their people, "with the most tender solicitude, as the
sole means of enjoying that Peace which arises from a good
conscience, and which alone is durable, to strengthen them-

selves every day more and more in the principles and exercise of the duties which the Divine Saviour has taught to mankind."

Alexander was the only sovereign who took the Holy Alliance very seriously. The pope upbraided the Catholic emperor of **Weakness** Austria for making a Christian declaration in union **of the Holy** with a schismatic Russian and an heretical Protestant. **Alliance** A brilliant Catholic apologist discovered in the document the "spirit of visionaries who opposed religiosity to religion." The Catholic emperor of Austria frankly told Alexander that he did not know what it meant: "if it was a question of politics, he must refer it to his chancellor, if of religion, to his confessor." Metternich scornfully called it "verbiage," and Lord Castlereagh pronounced it "a piece of sublime mysticism and nonsense." Nevertheless, with the exception of the sultan, the pope, and the prince-regent of Great Britain, all the European rulers out of deference to the tsar and doubtless influenced in many instances by the religious revival of the time, signed the treaty and were duly admitted to the Holy Alliance. The British prince-regent in his letter announcing his inability to become a signatory hypocritically expressed his "entire concurrence with the principles laid down by the august sovereigns" and stated that it would always be his endeavor to regulate his conduct "by their sacred maxims."

To the liberals of the nineteenth century the Holy Alliance became the embodiment of a diabolical conspiracy to stamp out democracy, nationalism, and social justice. But such an estimate of its significance is derived from a confusion of terms and is quite mistaken. The eventual failure of the Holy Alliance to ameliorate political and social conditions was not due to a want of sincerity in its author or to any criminal character in its purposes, but rather to the very fact that few of its signatories made any serious attempt to live up to it. It is a fact that the political ideas of the tsar underwent a profound change, but from the outset Alexander's Holy Alliance, with its lofty idealism, was confused in the popular mind with the actual workings of the more worldly and selfish Quadruple Alliance under the masterful direction of Metternich.

So far we have dealt with the general European situation in 1815. We have seen that immediately after the overthrow of

Napoleon the population of every country was roughly divisible on political and social questions into the two camps of liberals and conservatives, that territorial settlements were made at Vienna by conservatives on the basis of "legitimacy" and "compensations," a more or less actual return to pre-revolutionary times, and, finally, that a powerful Quadruple Alliance existed for the maintenance of treaty engagements and the preservation of peace. Incidentally, we have witnessed the exaltation of Austria paralleled by the rise of Metternich. From 1815 to 1830 this faithful chancellor of the Habsburg emperor was at once the conservative patriot of Austria and the reactionary genius of Europe. He employed the influence and might of Austria to control Europe; he sought to control Europe in order that the old régime might not be disturbed in Austria. And peace and quiet were always his goal in domestic and foreign affairs. *Metternich's Rôle in the New Era, 1815–1830*

During the period of Metternich's mastery, it was by no means the rivalries of rulers that endangered the peace of Europe, but rather the unrest of liberals who threatened their reactionary sovereigns with revolution or incited oppressed nationalities to insurrection. The career of peace-loving Metternich became a ceaseless warfare on liberalism. Throughout the first seven years of his predominance he was completely successful. It was in the years from 1815 to 1822 that under the auspices of the Quadruple Alliance[1] he convoked the four great congresses of Aix-la-Chapelle (1818), Troppau (1820), Laibach (1821), and Verona (1822), and prevailed upon the plenipotentiaries of Europe thus assembled to authorize what amounted to the policing of the whole Continent for the suppression of liberalism. So far did he realize his ambition that even Alexander was won to the cause of reaction and signed with the other Holy Allies the memorable protocol of Troppau: "States which have undergone a change *Systematic Repression of Liberalism* *The Concert of the Great Powers and the International Congresses, 1815–1822* *Protocol of Troppau*

---

[1] The Quadruple Alliance, strictly speaking, included Austria, Russia, Prussia, and Great Britain. Frequently after 1818, however, the Concert of the Great Powers is referred to as the Quintuple Alliance from the fact that from the Congress of Aix-la-Chapelle was supposed to date the formal restoration of France to her position as a legitimate member of the European family. French representatives were admitted to the congresses of the allied Powers.

of government due to revolution, the results of which threaten other states, *ipso facto* cease to be members of the European Alliance and remain excluded from it until their situation gives guarantees for legal order and stability. . . . If, owing to such alterations, immediate danger threatens other states, the Powers bind themselves, by peaceful means, or if need be by arms, to bring back the guilty State into the bosom of the Great Alliance." Under Metternich it thus became the duty of the Powers to stamp out revolution, even to the extent of intervention in the domestic concerns of a friendly state. During the last seven years of his supremacy, Metternich was obliged, through force of circumstances, to recede from the rigorous execution of the protocol of Troppau, but not until the stirring events of the year 1830 was his commanding influence in central Europe shaken, and not until the more momentous events of 1848 did he lose his hold on Austria.

Some idea of the politics of the Era of Metternich may now be gathered from a review of the principal public happenings within the chief European states. In every country conservatives will be found in control of the government; liberals will be in opposition and sometimes in rebellion; and Metternich will be noticed concerting measures of repression with the Quadruple Alliance. All the time, however, the number of liberals will be steadily growing, until, by 1830, they will be in possession of several governments in western Europe; the Quadruple Alliance will be dissolved; Metternich, shorn of his weapons of offense, will be on the defensive; and the principles of liberty, equality, and fraternity will finally be in the ascendant.

Chief Political Characteristics of the Era: Liberals vs. Conservatives

THE BOURBON RESTORATION IN FRANCE

It will be illuminating to begin the review with France — the nation of the most striking political contrasts. France in the middle of the eighteenth century afforded the typical illustration of the old régime; at the close of that century she was the storm-center of revolution; and during the first half of the nineteenth century, conservatives and liberals — heirs respectively of the old régime and of the Revolution — were more evenly balanced in France than in any other European country.

Waterloo put the Conservatives definitely into office. Only twenty days after that battle Louis XVIII reëntered his capital and resumed the reins of government. France was not in such unfortunate condition as one who has followed in detail the last great campaigns of Napoleon might imagine. She was defeated but not crushed. The economic advantage of having millions of sturdy, thrifty peasants as small landed proprietors was already displaying itself. The emperor, too, had waged his wars almost to the last at the expense of his conquered foes, and it was certainly a tribute to his foresight and to his genius for finance that the French national debt in 1815 was only one-sixth as large as that of Great Britain. The middle class took immediate advantage of the return of peace to extend their trade and to expand their business-interests. For these reasons, France rapidly rose under the restored Bourbons to a position of strength and prosperity hardly equaled in all Europe, despite bad harvests, political unrest, and foreign military occupation which continued three years after Waterloo.

Restoration of Louis XVIII, 1815

Louis XVIII was confronted upon his restoration by two bitterly irreconcilable political parties. On one hand were the Liberals, comprising not merely theorists of the rights of man, but close-fisted peasants and businesslike bourgeois who had been beneficiaries of the abolition of serfdom and the confiscation of church lands, together with numerous old soldiers who had fought gloriously under the tricolor and the "Little Corporal," all of them now stung by defeat and obstinate in their principles. On the other hand were the reactionaries, or Ultra-Royalists, nobles and clergy, and old-fashioned folks in the southern and western provinces who, in loving remembrance of the old régime, had fought stubbornly against the Revolution from its very inception, dispossessed of their goods and expelled from their fatherland, or silenced by oppression, now brought back in victory by the turn of events, eager for vengeance and retaliation. Between these two extreme factions Louis XVIII counted upon the bulk of the French people to aid him in steering a middle course. Although he clung tenaciously to the forms of the ancient monarchy and the white flag of his family, he had common sense

French Liberals

French Ultra-Royalists

Compromise of Louis XVIII with the Revolutionary Ideas

enough to retain Napoleon's legal and administrative reforms and the Napoleonic institutions of the Legion of Honor, the Bank of France, the Concordat, and the University. He recognized the imperial nobility as on an equal footing with that of the old régime. He confirmed the charter which the year before he had granted to France.

The royal charter of 1814 made provision for a constitutional government, modeled in part after that of Great Britain. There was to be a parliament of two chambers: the upper, composed of peers nominated by the king; and the lower, elected by Frenchmen paying a heavy direct tax. The Chambers could not initiate legislation, but could approve or reject measures proposed by the crown, and no measure could be promulgated without their consent. The king was to govern by means of ministers, but the relation of the ministry to parliament was left vague. The charter also recognized liberty of worship and of the press, and the inviolability of sales of land made during the Revolution. Surely this was unlooked-for clemency and concession from the brother of Louis XVI, but France had traveled a long way since 1793, and Louis XVIII never dreamed of suffering martyrdom for his principles.

A fierce complaint went up at once from the Ultra-Royalists. They besought the king, now that his very clemency had proved Ultra-Royalist Reaction: the " White Terror " incapable of preventing the wretched episode of the Hundred Days, to revoke the charter, and when he turned a deaf ear to them they wreaked their vengeance on what Liberals they could. For several months in 1815 there was a good deal of rioting and bloodshed, which, instigated by the enraged Royalists, has passed into history under the designation of the "White Terror." The reactionaries prevailed upon Louis XVIII, in spite of his promise to punish only those who were declared by the Chambers to be traitors, to proscribe nearly sixty persons who had deserted to Napoleon during the Hundred Days. It was the irony of fate that the list was drawn up by the same crafty Fouché who had voted for the death of Louis XVI and had subsequently been the right-hand man of Napoleon in ferreting out Royalist conspiracies. Thirty-eight of the proscribed were banished and a few were shot, among the latter being the illustrious Marshal Ney. In southern France hundreds of Liberals fell victims to reactionary mobs. At Nîmes, where Protestants had espoused the cause of Napoleon, the murders took the form of a crusade for the extirpation of heresy. The dispatch of an army into the affected regions was required to reëstablish order and security.

In the midst of the White Terror, elections for the new Chamber were conducted : the terrified Liberals absented themselves from the polls, and the result was the return of a parliament of Ultra-Royalists, more conservative than the king himself. The questionable Talleyrand and Fouché were at once turned out of their ministerial posts, and for a year the so-called *chambre introuvable* directed affairs of state in a bitterly reactionary spirit. Laws were passed shackling the press, excepting several classes from amnesty, creating special arbitrary courts for trying cases of treason, and repealing the divorce provisions of the *Code Napoléon*. In 1816 Louis XVIII, fearing the effect of his furious friends upon the country at large, dissolved the *chambre introuvable*, and ordered new elections. This time the bulk of the representatives were Moderate Royalists, loyal to the charter and the settlement of 1815 and in full sympathy with the conciliatory efforts of the king, while Ultra-Royalists and Liberals constituted two small but warring minorities.

The years of the Moderate Royalists' control, from 1816 to 1820, were marked by consistent progress. Reorganization of the public finances was effected. The preparation of an annual budget of estimated expenditure and income, which had been largely farcical under the empire, now became an important part of the routine work of the Chambers. Large loans were floated in order more rapidly to pay off the indemnity to the allied conquerors of France, with such success that, in accordance with arrangements made at the European Congress of Aix-la-Chapelle, the last foreign troops were withdrawn from French soil in 1818, and France was once more recognized as a Great Power with a stable government. A new electoral law assured the preponderance of the bourgeoisie in the Lower Chamber by instituting a comparatively simple system of elections and requiring the payment of a sum of at least three hundred francs a year in direct taxes

Moderate Royalists in Control, 1816–1820

as a qualification for the exercise of the suffrage. Another measure based the recruiting of the French army for the ensuing fifty years upon the principle of national conscription. Finally, a generous press law, modeled after that in vogue in England, was enacted. Such legislation and the concurrent maintenance of peace were gradually winning the business classes to the support of the Bourbon dynasty.

The period of liberal legislation was rudely interrupted early in 1820 by the assassination of the king's nephew by a fanatical Liberal. The Ultra-Royalists, who were swept into power on the wave of popular indignation at this outrage, promptly returned, as might have been expected, to a policy of reaction and repression. They suspended the charter guarantees of individual liberty : they reëstablished a strict censorship of the press; they intrusted the whole educational system to the Catholic clergy; and, in order to retain their majority in the Chamber, they modified the electoral law, by introducing a highly complicated scheme of election, by giving double suffrage to citizens who paid 1000 francs annually in direct taxes, and by lengthening the duration of a parliament to seven years. They elaborated a system of espionage and employed the army to crush opposition and to root out such secret revolutionary societies as that of the "Charcoal-Burners" which was spreading from Italy among the French Liberals. With the approval of Metternich and the Continental Powers they went to the length in 1823 of sending a French military expedition into Spain under command of the king's nephew to restore the tyrannical government of the Bourbon king of that country. Strange irony of fate that French arms, which had so recently carried the message of liberty, equality, and fraternity to the peoples of Europe, should now be the weapon of divine-right monarchs against the liberties of a nation! Yet so unreasoning was the patriotic emotion that accompanied military success that the Spanish expedition actually strengthened the hold of the Ultra-Royalists upon the hearts and minds of the French nation. When Louis XVIII died in 1824 the Bourbon dynasty seemed firmly reëstablished upon the throne of France and reaction the permanent rule of French society and politics.

Ultra-Royalists Restored, 1820

The leader of the Ultra-Royalists ever since the restoration had been the count of Artois, the late king's brother, who now, as next of kin, succeeded to the throne under the title of Charles X. No family history can be more interesting or instructive than that of the three Bourbon brothers who at different times and under varying circumstances were obliged to deal with revolutionary forces in France — Louis XVI, Louis XVIII, and Charles X. The first-named was well-intentioned, religious, but fatally weak and influenced by others, so that he lost his life by the guillotine. The second was hard-hearted, unprincipled, but so clever and astute a politician that in the midst of the struggles of irreconcilable factions he rounded out a not inglorious reign of ten years. The last-named had the political misfortune to resemble more closely the first than the second, save only that he possessed great strength of will and a dogged determination quite distinctive of himself. It had been the count of Artois who, with Marie Antoinette, had engineered the court intrigues against the Revolution in its earliest stages. It had been he who had headed the emigration of the nobles and clergy when their privileges were threatened by the Revolution. He it was who never tired of agitation against the revolutionaries and against Napoleon; and he it was who, on the triumphant return of his family and of the émigrés, encouraged the Ultra-Royalists in acts of retaliation. Yet personally he was courteous and kindly, a loyal friend, and sincerely devoted to the cause of religion. Principles he had and cherished : union of the altar and the throne; revival of the institutions of the old régime, political, religious, social, and intellectual; detestation of revolutionary doctrines. "It is only Lafayette and I," he said, "who have not changed since 1789."

With ostentatious pomp becoming the dignity of a divine-right monarch, Charles X was solemnly crowned. With the assistance of the Ultra-Royalist majority in the Chambers he set to work to achieve his purposes. Further restrictions were imposed upon the freedom of the press. Many privileges were restored to the clergy. The Jesuits were allowed to return to France. The penalties for sacrilege and blasphemy were increased. An indemnity amounting to a billion francs was guaranteed to the

Accession of the Ultra-Royalist King Charles X, 1824

Continued Reaction in Favor of Clergy and Nobility

émigrés for the Revolutionary confiscation of their lands and privileges. Even a bill tending to undermine equality of inheritance and to reëstablish the practice of primogeniture was debated. Certainly, in France, during the Era of Metternich, the Ultra-Royalists appeared to be taking long strides toward the complete realization of the reactionary program which was defined by a faithful minister of Charles X as "the reorganization of society, the restoration to the clergy of their weight in state affairs, and the creation of a powerful aristocracy surrounded with privileges."

THE BOURBON RESTORATION IN SPAIN

In Spain during the same period neither the reaction nor the opposition to it was so veiled. When Ferdinand VII was restored to his throne in 1814, not through any efforts on his part but The Liberal rather through the efforts of Wellington and the Constitution British and of his own loyal and heroic subjects, he of 1812 found a robust sense of nationalism and a constitutional government. It will be recalled that in 1812 the provisional *junta*, which was directing the national revolt against Joseph Bonaparte, adopted a written constitution that resembled the French instrument of 1791 both in its arrangements for limiting the power of the king and in those for abolishing feudal rights and privileges and class distinctions. This constitution, which was largely the work of middle-class business-men, scholars, theorists, and army officers — of the classes particularly influenced by the French Revolution and inclined toward anti-clericalism — had been tolerated by the other classes in the community so long as it was necessary for the whole nation to present a united front against the French. But as soon as peace was restored and the national independence of the country assured, the nobles and clergy protested vehemently against the constitution. Taking advantage of these protests and of the ignorance or indifference of the mass of the peasantry, Ferdinand VII immediately declared the Constitution of 1812 null and void, and abolished the Cortes.

Surrounding himself with advisers drawn exclusively from officials of the old régime, the king at once instituted a thorough reactionary policy. With him there would be no compromise with revolutionary principles. The old system of absolute government was restored with all its inequalities and injustices. The privileges of the clergy and no- bility, including exemption from taxation, were re- affirmed. Monasteries were reopened. The Jesuits were allowed to return. The Inquisition was reëstablished. Individual liberties were taken away, and the press was placed under the strictest censorship. Liberals who had assisted in making the royal restoration possible were now arbitrarily arrested and banished or thrown into prison. That not much blood was shed was due partly to the urgent entreaties of Wellington.

Ferdinand VII (1814–1833) and Reaction

The sordidness of the Spanish reaction in 1814 is traceable largely to the character of the king himself. Ferdinand VII was rancorous, cruel, ungrateful, and unscrupulous. Moreover, he did not possess the compensating qualities of ability or foresight. Instead of steering a middle course between extremist factions and seeking to consolidate the whole nation, he threw all his weight on the side of the reactionaries, while against the Liberals he continued to take such harsh measures that even Metternich in far-away Vienna, apprehensive of consequences, urged modera- tion. Instead of striving to repair the injuries inflicted by the Peninsular War and to husband his country's resources, he actu- ally hampered trade and industry and, in addition, squandered enormous sums of money upon himself and his favorites. Instead of adopting a conciliatory attitude toward the Spanish colonies in America, which already were maintaining governments prac- tically of their own making, instead of redressing their grievances, and bringing them once more into the bond of a great national empire, he sorely neglected them at the outset, and, when it was too late, he endeavored to subjugate them by force of arms. The results of Ferdinand's mistaken policies were apparent within five years of his restoration: a Spain hopelessly divided into the two camps of Conservatives and Liberals, each with its group of irreconcilables, respectively reactionaries and revolu- tionaries; grave scandals and abuses in administration; an army honeycombed with disaffection; a bankrupt treasury; and the American colonies in open, and apparently successful, revolt.

Throughout these five years, Liberal agitation against the royal tyrannies grew apace. Deprived of a free press and of the

Liberal Opposition to the King right of public meeting, the agitators gradually gravitated to such secret societies as the Carbonari and the Freemasons. The lodges were convenient centers of revolutionary propaganda, and their close affiliation and nation-wide extent enabled the Liberals, by means of signs and grips and mysterious passwords, to communicate the teachings of liberty, equality, and fraternity to all the brethren. Among the irreligious or anti-clerical element of the middle class, the movement spread, — and likewise among the army officers, — until Spain faced civil war.

In 1819 a mutiny in the army which the king had assembled at Cadiz for the subjugation of the American colonies was the

Revolt in Spain, 1820 signal for a general insurrection which in the first two months of 1820 broke out in such distant places as Seville, Barcelona, Saragossa, and the Asturias. In March, 1820, Ferdinand, quaking with fear, gave his royal oath to support the Constitution of 1812 and appealed to the Liberals in a pompous declaration: "Let us advance frankly, myself leading the way, along the constitutional path." The insurgents took him at his word and laid down their arms.

The king's conversion was merely the reaction of cringing fear upon a thoroughly cowardly and hypocritical nature. Ferdinand had no serious intention of keeping his pledges, and, although for two years (1820–1822) he was obliged to rule in accordance with the statutes of the newly convened Cortes and under the direction of Liberal ministers, he was busied, almost from the outset, in countenancing reactionary revolts against the new régime and in inditing confidential letters to the Great Powers, especially to his Bourbon cousin, the king of France, imploring foreign aid against the very government which he had solemnly sworn to uphold. Success soon crowned his intrigues. The Liberals fell to quarreling among themselves; the clergy and nobles resisted the execution of reform legislation; the sincere and ardent Catholics — in Spain a goodly number and well disciplined — treated as sacrilege and blasphemy the anti-clerical tendencies of the new Cortes. In many districts spasmodic riots became chronic and anarchy prevailed, betokening the advent within Spain of a counter-revolution against liberalism.

In the Spanish revolt of 1820, the reactionary Powers of Europe perceived the haunting specter of revolution. Despite the fact that they had been disgusted with Ferdinand's impolitic behavior, they were now terrified by the thought of what the success of the king's enemies might mean to the whole Continent. The Tsar Alexander, whom Metternich had just won over to the policy of international suppression of liberalism, volunteered, with that sudden and quixotic zeal which characterized his attachment to every newly found principle, to lead a great Russian army across Europe in order to reinstate Bourbon absolutism in Spain. But the French king at once conceived a most violent distaste for the employment of Russian troops even in his own cousin's cause, for he rightly feared the effect on the French nation of the reappearance of foreign troops. Metternich, too, was loath to allow Russian soldiers to cross Austrian territories, and he at once sought to moderate the tsar's enthusiasm. Nevertheless, something must be done. Consequently, in 1822, after protracted international negotiations, the members of the Quadruple Alliance, together with France, held the Congress of Verona. It was the opportunity of the reactionaries then in power in France : they proposed that a French army, acting on a general European mandate, should intervene in Spain. Thus by a single stroke France would be spared the humiliation of seeing foreign troops cross her borders ; a Bourbon king would be reinstated in absolutism ; the cause of reaction would triumph in Spain ; and whatever glory might attend French arms would redound to the credit of reaction in France. Metternich gladly accepted the proposal. Great Britain alone objected.

Attitude of Europe toward the Spanish Revolt

Early in 1823, acting on the recommendation of the Congress of Verona, the governments of France, Austria, Russia, and Prussia presented separate notes to the Liberal ministry of Spain, expostulating on the anarchical conditions, which they greatly exaggerated, and demanding the abolition of the Constitution of 1812 and the liberation of the king from the restraints that had been imposed upon him. The Spanish Liberals naturally refused and protested against what they deemed an unwarranted interference with the purely domestic affairs of their country ; and

French Intervention in Spain, 1823

the French army, under the duke of Angoulême, promptly crossed the Pyrenees.

The French invaders encountered no such difficulties in 1823 as had faced them in 1808. No united nation now opposed them. Indeed, the majority of the Spaniards actually abetted or applauded them, so great was the popular distrust of, or indifference toward, the Liberal régime. In May, Angoulême was in possession of Madrid, and the Liberal ministry and Cortes had fled to Cadiz, taking Ferdinand with them as a hostage. From June to October Cadiz was closely besieged by the French. On 1 October, the Liberals released the king on the understanding that he should grant a general pardon and guarantee the establishment of a "moderate government." Of course Ferdinand promised — no man was ever more facile with promises than he — and Cadiz immediately capitulated and the Liberals again laid down their arms.

No sooner was the king safe within the French lines than he characteristically annulled his promises and pronounced sentence of death upon all constitutionalists. In vain Angoulême counseled moderation and conciliation: the representatives of Metternich, of the Tsar Alexander, and of timid Frederick William of Prussia urged vigor to the royal arm, and in cruelty Ferdinand could always be vigorous. There followed in 1824 a reaction throughout Spain far more blind and bitter than that of 1814. Not only were the recent Liberal measures abrogated and the old régime again restored in its entirety, but the revolutionaries and the sympathizers with constitutional government were sought out with cunning ingenuity; hundreds were arbitrarily put to death; hundreds more were exiled or confined in noisome dungeons. By the time the French expedition withdrew from the country, Ferdinand VII had mercilessly broken the back of Spanish liberalism.

Restoration of Ferdinand VII and Absolutism

From that time till his death in 1833, Ferdinand ruled Spain as sovereign autocrat, irresponsible apparently either to man or to God. Abuses which had disfigured the earlier part of his reign now increased ten-fold, until general corruption prevailed at home and disgrace abroad. It was a sorry legacy that the contemptible Ferdinand VII bequeathed to his successor.

The decisive reason why the British government did not support the intervention of its Continental allies in Spain was not any lack of sympathy with reaction, for, as we shall presently see, the Tories then in authority in Great Britain were themselves sufficiently reactionary in internal policies to satisfy the fastidious taste of a Metternich: it was rather a consideration of trade. So

The Revolt in the Spanish Colonies: British Attitude

long as Spain owned and controlled the bulk of South America, Central America, and Mexico, she attempted to monopolize commerce with those territories to the exclusion of the British. As soon, however, as the Spanish colonies set up governments of their own, they opened their ports to British merchantmen. The British government rightly argued that European intervention in Spain in 1823 might serve not only to restore Ferdinand VII but to enable him to recover the Spanish colonies and thereby to close to Great Britain a lucrative trade. In the United States Great Britain found a valuable ally. Of course the purpose of the United States was different from Great Britain's, for the former was actuated not so much by commercial consid- erations as by apprehension lest the extension of the system of Metternich should endanger American polit- ical and social institutions, but both desired the same object : the freedom of the Spanish colonies. In 1821 the United

Attitude of the United States: the Monroe Doctrine

States had purchased the Spanish claims to Florida. In 1822 she recognized the national independence of Colombia, Chile, Argentina, and Mexico. And on 2 December, 1823, at the very time when French troops at the behest of the allied Powers were in possession of Spain, President James Monroe, acting with the foreknowledge and friendly assurances of the British govern- ment, made to the American Congress a celebrated pronounce- ment, which has since been known as the Monroe Doctrine. "In the wars of the European powers," he said, "in matters relating to themselves we have never taken any part, nor does it comport with our policy so to do. It is only when our rights are invaded or seriously menaced that we resent injuries or make preparations for our defence. With the movements in this hemisphere we are of necessity more immediately connected, and by causes which must be obvious to all enlightened and impartial observers. The political system of the allied powers is essentially different in this respect from that of America. . . . We owe it, therefore, to candor, and to the amicable relations existing between the United States and those powers, to declare that we should consider any attempt on their part to extend their system to any portion of this hemisphere as dangerous to our peace and safety. With the existing colonies and dependencies of any European power we have not interfered and shall not interfere. But with the governments who have declared their independence and maintained it, and whose independence we have on great consideration and on just principles acknowledged, we could not view any interposition for the purpose of oppressing them or controlling in any other manner their destiny by any European power in any other light than as the manifestation of an unfriendly disposition towards the United States. . . . It is impossible that the allied powers should extend their political system to any portion of either [American] continent without endangering our peace and happiness; nor can anyone believe that our Southern brethren, if left to themselves, would adopt it of their own accord. It is equally impossible, therefore, that we should behold such interposition in any form with indifference." The year following this remarkable declaration, Great Britain formally acknowledged the independence of Mexico and Colombia; and her recognition of the other Spanish American states was only postponed until they should have given proof of their stability.

Failure of Metternich's Project of Intervention in America
In the face of these facts, Metternich abandoned any hope he might have cherished of employing the Quadruple Alliance for the suppression of liberalism beyond the seas, and Spain made no further efforts to subdue her colonies, although she long withheld formal recognition of their freedom. The ambition of Napoleon Bonaparte, the fatuity of Ferdinand VII, the commercial interests of Great Britain, and the political principles of the United States, lost to Spain forever her continental empire in America.

REACTION IN PORTUGAL

A similar combination of circumstances vitally affected Portuguese history during the Era of Metternich. The Napoleonic incursion of 1807 sent the royal family of Portugal fleeing across the Atlantic to their distant colonial dependency of Brazil. Great Britain, whose trade relations with Portugal had long been intimate, avenged the insult, chased out the French, and erected a provisional government at Lisbon.

When finally in 1815 peace settled down upon Europe and the period of Metternich's predominance began, the British, in view of the protracted residence of Portuguese royalty in Brazil, found it of great advantage to their own economic interests to prolong their military occupation of the mother-country. It was soon obvious that Portugal was being treated as a mere appendage to Great Britain; and patriotic reactionaries, who demanded the return of the king and the expulsion of the foreigners, commenced to make common cause with the Liberal faction, which was recruited from much the same classes as that in Spain and which had learned the revolutionary doctrines of liberty, equality, and fraternity in much the same way. Lord Beresford, the British governor, crushed several incipient rebellions, but in 1820, during his absence from the country, the Portuguese army, following the example of their Spanish neighbors, overthrew the regency, and the Liberals, who thereupon gained the upper hand, promulgated a radical constitution similar in almost every respect to the Spanish Constitution of 1812. The next year King John VI, intrusting the government of Brazil to his elder son, Dom Pedro, returned to Portugal and in 1822 swore obedience to the constitution.

Revolution of 1820 and Return of Royal Family from Brazil

The Brazilians, on their side, incensed by the departure of the king, now rebelled and, finding themselves supported by the regent, proclaimed him Emperor Pedro I of the independent Empire of Brazil (1822). In Portugal, the reactionaries who opposed constitutional government found a leader in Dom Miguel, the king's younger son, whose cause received additional popular support as a protest against the loss of Brazil. For twelve years after 1822 Portugal was a prey to constant factional strife.

Independence of Brazil

Factional Strife in Portugal

In 1823 King John, relying upon the presence of a reactionary French army in Spain, revoked the constitution, but even this concession did not stay Dom Miguel's followers from attacking him, so that the united action of the European Powers was re-

quired to restore the king. On the death of John VI in 1826,
Pedro I of Brazil, who now became Pedro IV of Portugal, granted
to the Portuguese people a charter which provided for moderate
parliamentary government on the model of the French charter
of 1814, and then surrendered his Portuguese crown to his
daughter Maria, a little girl seven years of age, on the understanding that she should become the wife of her uncle, Dom Miguel.
Accordingly Miguel swore allegiance to Pedro, to Maria, and to
the constitutional charter, but on his arrival at Lisbon in 1828
he promptly repudiated his promises and, with the support of the
clerical and reactionary majority in the country, he reigned as
sole and absolute king until 1834. Miguel was dissipated, illiter-
ate, and cruel, and the admiration for Metternich, which he
had conceived during a three years' residence in Vienna, gave a
particularly rigid character to his warfare against liberalism.

In the family struggle between the absolutist Miguel and the
more liberal-minded Pedro, Austria, Russia, and Prussia
naturally sympathized with the former, while Great Britain,
again not through any excess of enthusiasm for the cause of
liberalism but rather for the sake of trade, abetted the latter.
Sentiment in the United States was undoubtedly unanimous in
favoring the separation of Brazil from Portugal, and British warships actually intervened to prevent Portuguese troops from attempting to subjugate the Brazilians by force of arms. Thus the
Portuguese colonial empire was disrupted, and though still under
monarchical institutions, Brazil became, like the United States
and the neighboring Spanish colonies, an independent American
nation.

TORY REACTION IN GREAT BRITAIN

The Power which above all others was to profit by the reactionary régimes in Spain and in Portugal was Great Britain —
the Power which to contemporary Continental statesmen seemed the least reactionary in Europe. But if,
during the Era of Metternich, the British government
appeared repeatedly to check the efforts of Continental
reactionaries to suppress liberalism, it was due rather
to commercial considerations or fortuitous circumstances than
to love of democracy and devotion to the "rights of man."

The British Government Liberal Abroad and Conserva- tive at Home

Certainly at home British statesmen were just as insistent upon maintaining the eighteenth-century institutions of their country as was Metternich in preserving the Austrian, or Charles X in restoring the French. Whatever else they may have been, the Tory leaders who dominated Great Britain throughout the period were neither revolutionaries nor liberals.

Some confusion is likely to arise from the fact that in the eighteenth century British political institutions differed from those on the Continent. To a Montesquieu or a Voltaire they seemed "liberal" and therefore worthy of praise. Naturally, in the first half of the nineteenth century the term "liberal" was still applied to them even by Metternich. But that they were not liberal in our present-day sense will be obvious to any one who takes the trouble to peruse again the account of them as given in a preceding chapter.[1] It will be seen that Great Britain was then ruled nominally by a king and by a representative Parliament, but that the king's actual power had been transferred to a ministry or cabinet and that the Parliament, powerful though it was, really represented only the merest fraction of British citizens, a fraction composed largely of great landowning aristocrats and of clergymen of the Anglican Church.

On the eve of the French Revolution, an agitation to reform Parliament in a democratic direction had been fostered by British statesmen of such divergent characters and views as the Younger Pitt and Charles James Fox. But the memory of Blackstone's laudation of the ancient, self-developing British constitution and the scathing strictures passed by Edmund Burke on liberty, equality, and fraternity as exemplified by the French radicals, combined with the long, weary, revolutionary and Napoleonic wars between France and Great Britain to create in the minds of British statesmen a most lively distrust of French political and social experiments. Reform was indefinitely shelved in England. Everything was subordinated to the exigencies of conducting a vast foreign war. The only noteworthy and permanent acts of Parliament from 1793 to 1815 were the Union of Ireland (1800) and the abolition of the slave-trade (1807).

Great Britain Seemingly Unaffected by the French Revolution

[1] See Vol. I, ch. xiv.

Attempts on the part of small groups of more or less unpractical philosophers and poor workingmen to keep alive the demand for parliamentary and social reform by means of revolu-

Reactionary Character of the British Government tionary organizations like the "London Corresponding Society" were sternly discountenanced by the governing classes; and the very titles of such parliamentary acts as those on Treasonable Practices (1795), Seditious Meetings (1795), and Corresponding Societies (1799), are unmistakable indications of the government's determination to abridge all those rights of public meeting, free speech, and free press, which might serve to acquaint Englishmen with hateful novelties from across the Channel. And the results of the long war seemed to enhance the reputation and prestige of the Tory government. The United Kingdom almost alone of all European states suffered no French invasion. A series of brilliant naval victories confirmed English maritime supremacy. The actual operation of the Continental System was less disadvantageous to the British than to the Continental peoples. The conduct of the Peninsular campaign and the crowning triumph at Waterloo attested the bravery of British armies and the genius of British generals. Finally, the diplomatic successes of British statesmen at Vienna added materially to the extent and importance of the British colonial empire. The British governing classes could afford to be proud and boastful. Not only was England practically exempt during the Napoleonic Era from the infiltration of French revolutionary ideas, but the political and social institutions of a country which had been instrumental in humiliating a Napoleon appeared to deserve hearty commendation and loyal preservation.

It was natural, therefore, that in 1815 the Tory ministers and the Tory majority in Parliament should set their faces resolutely against any reform in politics or society. Represent-

The Reactionary Tory Leaders ing, as they did, the aristocratic agricultural and ecclesiastical interests, and standing for the patriotic instincts of the kingdom, they would conserve existing institutions. In this sense they were conservatives and reactionaries. Head and shoulders above their fellow-Tories in championing such a policy stood Castlereagh, Wellington, and the Prince Regent. From 1811 when hopeless insanity finally overtook the narrow-minded King George III, the influence of the crown was exercised by his son, the Prince Regent, an unpopular fop whose rigid support of conservatism was as unwavering as his father's, but whose cynical, sensual immorality was in glaring contrast to his father's simple domestic virtues. The accession of the prince regent to the throne on his father's George IV, death in 1820 changed the form but not the fact: 1820–1830 George IV remained until his death in 1830 the stout advocate of reaction. In Castlereagh and Wellington, two Castlereagh Irish noblemen and landowners, he possessed powerful allies. Castlereagh (1769–1822),[1] though never technically prime minister, wielded from 1812 till his suicide in 1822 an influence such as few ministers have ever exercised: gifted and affable, he directed the foreign policy and controlled the House of Commons. Wellington (1769–1852),[2] though not in conspicuous civil employment until after Castlereagh's death, Wellington contributed the renown of his military exploits and the prestige of his soldierly, blunt, outspoken personality to upholding as far as possible in England the reactionary cause he had so ably headed on the Continent. Such were the men who guided the destinies of Great Britain during the greater part of the Era of Metternich.

How deserving they were of the epithet of "reactionary" becomes clear when one considers the twofold character of their domestic policies: first, the legislation in behalf of the British landed aristocracy which they themselves directly Reaction represented; and secondly, the stern measures of Favorable to the repression which they directed against every attack Landed upon that aristocracy. Aristocracy

It was at this time that the process of "inclosure" reached its culmination. Long ago the process had begun of depriving the British peasants of their common arable-, pasture-, Inclosures and wood-lands and of reducing large numbers to the position of agricultural tenants on great "inclosed" estates of noblemen. The chief purpose of these inclosures, as we have seen, had been to enable the landowners to raise sheep and thereby to engage on a large scale in the wool business. Now at the close

---

[1] Robert Stewart, Lord Castlereagh, second marquess of Londonderry.
[2] Sir Arthur Wellesley, first duke of Wellington.

of the eighteenth and the beginning of the nineteenth century, the system advanced by leaps and bounds. During the single reign of George III, Parliament passed as many as 3209 private inclosure acts, affecting over six and a quarter million acres. Of course the avowed object was now not to reinvigorate the expiring trade in wool but to put the country under closer cultivation. The general result, however, was the same. The number of landowners was greatly diminished and the wealth and influence of the landed aristocracy were perceptibly increased.

Also, despite the fact that the war already had raised the cost of living, Parliament persevered in its policy of subsidizing the

Corn Laws

landholding class by maintaining and strengthening the Corn Laws, which levied high import duties on foreign foodstuffs. A new corn law in 1815 actually forbade the importation of grain into the country so long as the price for home-grown wheat was under 80 shillings a quarter (twenty dollars for eight bushels).

Against this narrow class legislation and against the political

Sources of Opposition to the Tory Reaction

and social circumstances that rendered it possible, a many-sided opposition arose and gained strength between 1815 and 1830. The resultant conflict was the parallel in Great Britain to the struggle between liberals and conservatives on the Continent.

Several factions or classes, for one reason or another, and in this or that respect, opposed the Tory régime. There was first

The "Intellectual" Radicals

of all the group of "Intellectual Radicals" who, like William Godwin (1756–1836),[1] entertained elaborate theories of a complete social readjustment, or, like Thomas Paine, were indoctrinated with the somewhat more practicable teaching of the French revolutionaries. This group lived on, despite governmental attempts to suppress it, recruited mainly from middle-class theorists, small shopkeepers, and self-educated artisans: at one extreme its radicalism appeared in the

[1] Godwin's chief writing — *The Inquiry Concerning Political Justice* (1793) — taught the perfectibility of man, the inherent evil in every form of government, and the right of every man to the use of the soil. He has been hailed as an early Socialist, and, more justly, as the father of modern anarchism. His wife was Mary Wollstonecraft (1759–1797), one of the earliest advocates of feminism. His influence was noteworthy on such men-of-letters as Shelley, Byron, and Bulwer-Lytton.

passionate pleas for liberty and freedom of a Shelley and a Byron, and at the other in the coarse invective of a pugnacious, egotistical pamphleteer like William Cobbett. Of these "Intellectual Radicals" hardly any two were exactly agreed upon a full scheme of reform, but all were of one mind in assailing existing institutions. Many of them advocated a few simple measures in the direction of political democracy such as would seem commonplace if not antiquated to present-day Englishmen and Americans. But by the governing classes and patriotic masses of Great Britain during the Era of Metternich, the Radicals were deemed unpatriotic and dangerous, and radicalism became almost synonymous with treason. Radicalism is a "spirit," wrote the vicar of Harrow in 1820, "of which the first elements are a rejection of Scripture, and a contempt of all the institutions of your country; and of which the results, unless averted by a merciful Providence, must be anarchy, atheism, and universal ruin."

A second British faction arrayed against the Tory régime was that of the Roman Catholics, who for centuries had been the victims of bigotry and persecution. Reduced to a small minority in England and Scotland, they still Roman Catholics constituted a large majority of the inhabitants of Ireland, yet throughout the kingdom they were denied political and civil rights. Few Roman Catholics entertained any sympathy for the doctrines of the French Revolution, but in agitating for their own emancipation they found themselves in temporary alliance with the Radicals. The Protestant Dissenters too, although by no means in such a plight as the Dissenters Catholics, protested vigorously against a government which forced them to pay tithes for the support of the Anglican Church and which not only discriminated against them in officeholding but, always in the interests of the same Anglican Church, refused them a university education.

It might have been possible for Castlereagh, Wellington, the Prince Regent, and their friends to have maintained indefinitely the cause of reaction in Great Britain against the intellectual protestations of a handful of "Radicals" and against the religious opposition of disorganized Catholics and Dissenters, but in the face of amazing economic transformations the Tories might have perceived

The New and Unrepresented Industrial Classes

their eventual doom. It was during the Revolutionary and Napoleonic periods that the Industrial Revolution produced its first great results in England : the mechanical inventions in weaving and spinning, the development of new motive power, the building of factories, the marvelously increased production, the shift of population from the country to the towns. These phenomena speedily substituted industry and trade in the place of agriculture as the chief source of Great Britain's wealth, and enhanced the numbers, the prosperity, and the ambition of the new "business man," — in fact, of the whole middle class. Yet not the middle class but the landed aristocracy controlled Parliament and determined the policies of the realm. The interests of these two groups were quite incompatible : a struggle was inevitable; and the final outcome, in view of the fateful circumstances, could not admit of doubt.

From 1815 to 1822 the Tory ministers maintained their system in seemingly undiminished strength. Reaction was supreme.

Period of Extreme Reaction, 1815–1822

The noble landholders continued to "inclose" the commons by leave of the Tory Parliament, and to reap large profits from the Corn Laws. The Anglican clergy continued to enjoy ecclesiastical supremacy : no redress of Nonconformist grievances was forthcoming, and the depraved Prince Regent mouthed "the principles of his revered and excellent father" in order to justify his resistance to Catholic emancipation. Parliament in 1818 took five million dollars from the public funds to build Anglican churches. Parliamentary reform seemed dead and individual liberties appeared to be dying.

Yet throughout England there was the liveliest economic distress. The use of machinery in industry had already thrown

Economic Distress and Riots

many hand-laborers out of employment. Now in 1815 the conclusion of foreign war, by breaking the trading monopoly of Great Britain, seriously decreased the market for British manufactures and thereby threw thousands of British wage-earners out of work. The poorest classes, thus condemned to forced idleness, avenged themselves by destroying the machinery to which they naturally attributed their unemployment. These so-called Luddite [1] riots, which had begun as

[1] "The name [Luddite] had a curious origin. More than thirty years before there lived in Leicestershire one Ned Ludd, a man of weak intellect, the village

early as 1811, reached their climax in 1816 when social disturbances and wanton destruction of property occurred in every part of the country. The riots were economic rather than political in character, and, being precipitated by poor, ignorant, and unorganized people in the frenzy and despair of the moment, they were in every case suppressed by the middle-class factory-owners acting in harmony with the Tory government, and leading rioters were put to death. Not in the severity, however, with which they suppressed these riots, was to be discovered the chief fault of the British reactionaries, but rather in their willful blindness to the true causes which produced economic distress.

Economic distress was at once utilized by the Radicals to attract the lowest working class to the support of their political programs — and with considerable success. For a number of years after 1816, workingmen gave numerical strength to intellectual radicalism. An attack made on the Prince Regent at the opening of Parliament in 1817 led to an official inquiry which revealed the existence of an elaborate secret organization for the overthrow of the existing order. Earlier repressive measures were at once revived and extended, and, in the midst of the aristocratic alarm, a bill suspending for a year the venerable right of Habeas Corpus was passed through both Houses by large majorities. Arbitrary arrest and arbitrary punishment were restored in England, at least temporarily. At the same time the government opened a campaign against the traditional freedom of the press by instructing the justices of the peace to issue warrants for the arrest of any person charged on oath with publishing blasphemous or seditious libels. Prosecutions followed so thick and fast that William Cobbett, now the most influential of the Radicals, in order to avoid arbitrary imprisonment, suspended his newspaper — the fiery, twopenny *Political Register* — and, "deprived of pen, ink, and paper," sailed for America.

butt. Irritated by his tormentors, the unhappy fellow one day pursued one of them into an adjoining house. He could not find the lad who had been mocking him; but in his fury he broke a couple of stocking frames which were on the premises. When frames were afterwards broken, it was the common saying that Ludd had broken them; and thus Ned Ludd, the village idiot, gave a name to one of the most formidable series of riots of the [nineteenth] century." (Sir Spencer Walpole.)

In demanding parliamentary reform the Radicals found interested supporters not only in Roman Catholics and in work-ingmen, but in the middle class, who in the rapidly growing manufacturing towns of northern and central England were without any representation in the House of Commons. Monster mass meetings were held at Smithfield, at Leeds, at Stockport, and at Birmingham, and in the last-named city a "legislatorial attorney and repre-sentative" was duly elected. A similar mass meeting, convened on St. Peter's Field at Manchester, in August, 1819, was charged by royal troops with drawn swords and broken up after six bystanders had been killed and many injured. The "Man-chester Massacre" showed the determination of the governing classes of Great Britain to employ soldiery for the suppression of liberty of speech, in the true spirit of Metternich and of the other Continental reactionaries.

"Man-chester Massacre," 1819

The Tories quickly followed up the lamentable scene at Man-chester with Six Acts of Parliament (November, 1819) — the capstone and crown of reaction in Great Britain. The first prohibited unauthorized persons from prac-ticing military exercises. The second provided for the speedy trial of offenders. The third empowered magistrates to issue warrants to search private houses for arms. The fourth authorized the seizure of every seditious and blas-phemous libel and the banishment of the author for a second offense. The fifth regulated and restricted the right of public meeting. And the sixth subjected all publications below a certain size to the heavy stamp duty on newspapers. With the exception of the third and fifth, the whole six were designed as permanent acts.

Repressive Measures: the Six Acts, 1819

Now that every peaceful demonstration against the reac-tionary régime was prohibited, a handful of violent Radicals formed in London the Cato Street conspiracy (1820) to massacre the whole Tory cabinet. The plot was discovered and five of the conspirators were hanged. Force had failed to shake conserva-tism, and for the moment Great Britain settled down into a state of external calm.

Reaction continued to hold sway in Great Britain throughout the remainder of the Era of Metternich, although after 1822 its foundations were slowly but surely undermined. All the forces of opposition took breath and renewed the attack. William Cobbett (1766–1835) returned to England and injected new energy into the Radicals. The Catholics found an heroic and gifted champion in Daniel O'Connell (1775–1847). Everywhere the middle classes were clamoring for parliamentary representation and for

Period of Less Rigorous Reaction, 1822–1832

legislation favorable to the new industry, and in their clamors they were drawing assistance from the British working classes. On the other side, the scandalous domestic difficulties, culminating in attempted divorce, between George IV and the unhappy Queen Caroline cost the king whatever patriotic devotion he might otherwise have been able to inspire for reactionary principles; and the death of Castlereagh in 1822 transferred the actual management of the Tory régime to younger colleagues who soon came to differ from the master in essential matters. Through the foreign policy of George Can-

Canning

ning (1770–1827), Great Britain formally repudiated the Quadruple Alliance and definitely opposed the intervention of any government in the internal affairs of another state for the suppression of liberalism. Through the efforts of men like William Huskisson (1770–1830) and Sir Robert Peel (1788–1850), who were identified with industrial and commercial interests rather than with those of the unprogressive landed aristocracy, new remedial legislation was gradually inaugurated toward the close of the decade of the 'twenties. Even the reactionary Tories were eventually pushed by an inexorable fate upon the highway of liberal reform. The inexorableness of this fate, which by 1832 rendered old-fashioned reaction no longer possible in Great Britain and established in its place the real political supremacy of the business middle class, will be comprehended later when we study in some detail the genesis and course of the Industrial Revolution.

TRIAL AND ABANDONMENT OF LIBERAL ADMINISTRATION IN RUSSIA

Strange as it may seem, the European Power which in 1815 supported the cause of reaction least loyally was not England but

Russia. It was with the tsar that Metternich had at first his most serious difficulties.

Of the character of Alexander I (1801–1825) enough has already been said to make clear that it was paradoxical. Carefully

Tsar Alex-
ander I,
1801–1825

trained under the auspices of his despotic grandmother, the Tsarina Catherine the Great, in the traditions of Russian autocracy, he had also imbibed from a Swiss tutor many of the democratic ideas of the time. Convinced that he was truly a "little father" to the Russian people, he had meditated the introduction of English political and social institutions. A lover of peace, he had been the chief instrument in effecting Napoleon's military downfall. Sincerely religious, he had dreamed of federating all Europe into one Christian family.

During the early part of his reign Alexander gave repeated proofs of his attachment to liberalism. He surrounded

Early
Attachment
of Alex-
ander to
Liberalism

himself with reforming advisers.[1] He seemed to desire that Russia should supplant France as the champion of constitutional liberties, for he was in part responsible for the charter which Louis XVIII granted to the French people in 1814; he confirmed the independent constitution of Finland; and to the Poles he freely accorded a constitution which established a form of representative government and guaranteed individual liberties. At the Congress of Vienna he endeavored, with the aid of Baron vom Stein, to further German regeneration; he strongly favored the immediate abolition of the slave-trade; and in the Holy Alliance he provided what he thought would be a most beneficent agent in securing the triumph of his own generous and humane aims throughout Europe.

In the meantime Alexander was planning reforms for Russia in the time-honored manner of a benevolent despot rather than

Experiments
of Alexander

after the fashion of the French revolutionaries. Some of the earlier and more rigid restrictions on personal freedom were removed; the clergy, the nobles, and the middle-class merchants were exempted from corporal punishment; the bureaucratic system of administration was reorganized; an advisory Council of the Empire was created; a reform ministry

[1] Notably, Prince Adam Czartoryski (1770–1861) and Count Mikhail Speranski (1772–1839).

was established, responsible, however, to the tsar; and the idea of granting a written constitution for all Russia was seriously discussed. Moreover, great schemes for promoting popular education were entertained; parish schools, normal schools, and ecclesiastical seminaries were founded; the existing universities of Moscow, Vilna, and Dorpat were reorganized and new ones were erected in Petrograd, Kazan, and Kharkov. Elaborate reports were prepared on the ways and means of abolishing serfdom throughout the Russian Empire, and a small beginning of the vast work of emancipation was actually made in the Baltic provinces.

Almost all of these liberal schemes were conceived prior to 1815. That few of them were fully realized was due to the distractions of the Napoleonic Wars and to ignorance or downright hostility on the part of the bulk of the Russian people. After 1815 Alexander continued for some time to cherish his reforming plans, but gradually his ardor cooled. He perceived the glaring lack of education among his subjects and how unfitted they were for a democratic régime. Little by little he shifted his enthusiasm from political reform to religious revival. And most portentous of all developments, he eventually came under the influence of Metternich. *Gradual Conversion of Alexander from Liberalism to Reaction*

The Austrian chancellor never neglected an opportunity to impress upon the kind-hearted tsar the dangers of abetting liberalism: that the more concessions Liberals and Radicals received, the more they would demand; the more they were allowed to agitate, the greater violence and disorder they would incite; and that, therefore, the only sure means of maintaining Christian peace and charity would be the stern, unrelenting suppression of liberalism. A series of events soon alarmed Alexander and played into the hands of Metternich: a revolutionary conspiracy among the officers of the tsar's guard (1818); the murder of a Russian agent, Kotzebue, by a German Liberal (1819); the assassination of a nephew of the French king (1820); and the ensuing uprisings in Italy and Spain. At the Congress of Troppau (1820), Alexander confessed to Metternich his full and complete conversion. "Today," said the repentant tsar, "I deplore all that I said and did between the *Alexander and Metternich*

years 1815 and 1818. I regret the waste of time, which we must
try to retrieve. You have correctly judged the state of affairs.
Tell me what you desire and what you wish me to do, and I
will do it."

Thenceforth Alexander was a steadfast ally of Metternich
in devising and executing reactionary measures against the
revolutionary movements in Germany, Italy, and
Spain. The Holy Alliance was practically transformed into an organization for policing Europe in the
interest of a most worldly conservatism. In the
affairs of his own country Alexander henceforth refrained from
extending or perfecting the liberal institutions which he had
already called into being.

*Abandon-
ment of
Liberalism
in Russia*

The immediate result in Russia of the tsar's conversion was a
feeling of profound disappointment in the Liberal section of
the cultured classes and especially among young army
officers who had learned a good deal of French revolutionary doctrine during their campaigns in western
Europe. Secret societies sprang up and Liberal agitation assumed a character strikingly similar to that in Spain and
Italy.

*Opposition
of Russian
Liberals*

When Alexander died suddenly in December, 1825, the new
revolutionary societies made an attempt to halt the reaction.
They opposed the late tsar's directions that he be succeeded by his second brother Nicholas in preference
to his first brother, the erratic but liberal-minded
Grand Duke Constantine, and organized a mutiny among the
troops quartered in Petrograd. "Constantine and Constitution" became the motto of the revolt, but Constantine
speedily repudiated his friends, and Nicholas encountered no
great trouble in restoring order and obtaining general recognition for himself. How superficial as yet was the Liberal propaganda in Russia may be inferred from the well-attested fact
that many of the mutinous soldiers believed that "Constitution"
was Constantine's wife! The ringleaders of this December
revolt, who were subsequently known as Decembrists, were
severely punished by the new tsar.

*The
Decembrist
Revolt, 1825*

Nicholas I (1825–1855) had never entertained any sympathy
for liberalism, and the unfortunate circumstances of his acces-

sion could but strengthen his conservatism. Of all opponents of revolution and reform, Nicholas was the most determined, the boldest, and the most successful. During the thirty years of his reign he employed the most rigorous measures to prevent liberal ideas from germinating spontaneously among his own people and from being transplanted from abroad. For this purpose he established an extremely strict censorship of the press, an expensive system of passports, which made it very difficult for Russians to visit foreign countries or for aliens to enter Russia, and an elaborate secret police in order to discover and punish sedition. If, at the beginning of the Era of Metternich, Russia had seemed a noxious and dangerous bog of liberal enthusiasms, it was no longer such at the close of the period : to thoroughgoing reactionaries it had become a political paradise.

Continued Reaction under Nicholas I, 1825-1855

MAINTENANCE OF AUTOCRACY IN CENTRAL EUROPE

Between the countries of western Europe, where liberals struggled most valiantly and most hopefully against conservatives, and the huge eastern empire of Russia, in which conservatism definitely triumphed, lay the extensive lands that were owned or controlled by Austria, the veritable lodestone of reaction.

Strategic Position of Metternich in Austria

Metternich's first and greatest care was to employ the whole force of the Habsburg government to keep things precisely as they were within the Austrian dominions. He would have no change, not even a compromise with reform. To check the bitter racial rivalries which perpetually threatened the disintegration of his hodge-podge state, he relied upon a large and well-trained army, advantageously scattered : Hungarian regiments garrisoned Italy; Italian regiments guarded Austrian Poland; Germans occupied Bohemia; Czechs defended Austria proper; and southern Slavs restrained Hungary. To combat the danger of the infiltration of revolutionary ideas from abroad, a wall of tariffs and censors was erected around the Austrian lands. To guard against the peril of incipient liberalism at home, the press was rigidly supervised, clerical control of education was reëstab-

Reaction in the Austrian Dominions under Metternich

lished, and only music escaped governmental interference. This administrative policy was accompanied, as might have been expected, by economic stagnation. Agriculture, still by far the most important pursuit of all the Habsburg peoples, was hampered, as in France before the Revolution, by the surviving feudal privileges of a proud landed aristocracy which no longer gave any equivalent service to the public weal; trade languished on account of the system of high tariffs at the frontier and of special customs at interior points; and inequality of assessment, waste in collection, and extravagance in expenditure made the imperial taxes positively crushing. Yet such a régime Metternich was able to maintain within the Austrian lands until his own downfall in 1848.

Next to his solicitude for the immediate dominions of the Habsburg crown was his anxiety so to dominate Italy and Germany as to stamp out any political or social movements which might spread into Austria and tend to subvert the institutions which he worshiped. And the territorial settlements of 1815 were such as to enable him to exercise the desired domination.

Metternich's Policy in Germany and Italy

Particularly in his relations with the Germanies, Metternich encountered little trouble. Austria had the presidency of the new Germanic Confederation and could always count upon the support of the princes of the smaller states who were instinctively jealous of Prussia. By this means Metternich effectively blocked repeated attempts to fulfill the promise of article XIII of the Confederation's constitution that "a representative form of government shall be adopted in the federative states." In several states of southern Germany, where the tradition of alliance with France kept liberalism very much alive, the princes, it is true, deemed it expedient to grant charters [1] somewhat like that accorded by Louis XVIII of France, and they continued the Napoleonic code of laws, but in almost every case harsh game-laws, restrictions on the press, and maintenance of many social ills kept up a smoldering discontent; and Metternich used his influence to prevent further reforms. In northern and central Germany affairs were more reactionary:

The Germanic Confederation

---

[1] Notably in Bavaria (1818), Baden (1818), Württemberg (1817, but soon suspended), and in the small Thuringian states of central Germany.

with the exception of the high-minded duke of Saxe-Weimar, every prince in those regions now evaded whatever promises of constitutional government he had made during the patriotic period of the War of Liberation. An often-cited case was that of the old elector of Hesse-Cassel, who, after spending eight years in banishment, returned with the phrase, "I have been sleeping these years," and, with the aid of his soldiers in their old-fashioned powder and pigtails, proceeded to restore all the antique abuses. Perhaps King Frederick William III of Prussia was quite sincere in his promise to grant a charter to his people, but he was a timid soul, easily frightened by the slightest difficulties, and always considered it an honor to defer to the superior judgment of Metternich or of the tsar. Besides, Prussia had immediately to deal with the task of improving her finances, bettering her military system, and welding together the new territories which the Congress of Vienna had secured her.

Nevertheless, within all the Germánies the spirit of liberalism evoked by the Revolutionary and Napoleonic storms was still alive. The bourgeoisie desired to participate in the government. The lower classes wanted social reform. Patriots in every walk of life yearned for a great and glorious, united Germany. No coercion availed to stamp out the embers of unrest. Especially in the universities radicalism throve. Students formed secret societies, which, under the names of *Tugendbund* and *Burschenschaft*, made noisy demonstrations that caused uneasiness alike in Berlin and in Vienna. Thus the Wartburg festival in October, 1817,[1] which was attended by nothing more dangerous than undergraduate hilarity and a solemn burning, in imitation of Martin Luther, of various odd emblems of the old régime, was magnified by Metternich into a rebellion and drew down upon the grand-duke of Saxe-Weimar the joint protest of the reactionary Powers. Two years later, the assassination of the dramatist Kotzebue, a prominent reactionary and spy in the service of Russia, by a fanatical student named Karl Sand, clinched the matter. Metternich, assured of Prussian aid, convoked an extraordinary

Persistence of Liberal Agitation in the Germanies

[1] The 300th anniversary of the publication of Luther's theses against indulgences (see Vol. I, p. 131), and the fourth anniversary of the Battle of the Nations (see Vol. I, p. 564).

meeting of German statesmen at Carlsbad to take steps to crush Liberal agitation.

The result was the promulgation of the famous Carlsbad Decrees by the German federal Diet (September, 1819). These

Attempted Repression of Liberalism: the Carlsbad Decrees, 1819
contained detailed provisions for supervising university professors and students and muzzling the press, declaring that no constitution "inconsistent with the monarchical principle" should be granted, and establishing a central committee at Mainz to investigate "the origin and manifold ramifications of the revolutionary plots and demagogical associations directed against the existing constitution and the internal peace both of the union and of the individual states."

The years that directly followed the Carlsbad Decrees were uneventful in Germany. The Mainz Committee, though hampered by the mutual jealousies of some of the princes, proved effective enough in preventing all free expression of opinion, and the official "curators" of the universities kept Liberal enthusiasts in order. Metternich's hold on the Germanies was complete.

Hardly less complete was Metternich's influence in the Italian states. Not only were Venetia and Lombardy administered as

Metternich's Influence in the Italian States
integral parts of the Habsburg Empire but Austrian princes ruled in the duchies of Tuscany, Parma, and Modena; the Austrian chancellor was on intimate terms with the pope; and Ferdinand, the despicable king of the Two Sicilies, reinstated in Naples by an Austrian army, had bound himself by a secret article in the treaty of 1815 not to introduce methods of government incompatible with those in force in Austria's Italian possessions. In all these states, throughout the whole Era of Metternich, the conduct of public business, thoroughly reactionary, gave rise to abuses. A system which was burdensome when applied in Austria by natives to a traditionally contented populace, was well-nigh intolerable when exercised in Italy by foreigners over a people who had drunk deeply of an effervescent revolutionary stimulant imported from France. Victor Emmanuel I, the king of Sardinia, was the only ruler in the peninsula with exclusively Italian interests. But although he was joyfully acclaimed upon his restoration in Turin, he speedily yielded to his own inclinations and to

the menacing representations of Metternich: he disavowed French reforms, and restored, as far as possible, conditions as they had been prior to 1789. Officially all Italy was reactionary.

Yet here, too, beneath the surface, liberalism seethed. The peasantry, ignorant and influenced by the clergy, were generally indifferent, but among the educated classes, the pro- *Liberalism* fessional and business men, and many day-laborers, *in the* the double demand for constitutional government and *Italian* for national independence grew ever louder. As in so *States* many other countries, the Radicals employed underground means of agitation, and various secret societies like the *Carbonari* (Charcoal-Burners) and the Freemasons found fertile soil in Italy for revolutionary propaganda. The *Carbonari* in Naples alone numbered thousands. Against the nationalist and constitutionalist aspirations of these Italians, Metternich was always able to use powerful Austrian armies. The history of his Italian domination is in fact but an alternation of popular riots and military suppression.

The seeming success of the Spanish revolution of 1820 was the signal for a Liberal uprising in Naples against the tyrannical Ferdinand I.[1] The king, deserted by his army, sub- *Suppression* scribed to a constitution modeled after the Spanish *of Uprising* instrument of 1812. But hardly had he taken the *in Naples,* oath with gratuitous solemnity, when Metternich *1820* assembled the Congress of Troppau and prevailed upon the Prussian king and the Russian tsar to sanction the principle of intervention,[2] to denounce revolution, and to summon Ferdinand to appear before them; the next year, at the Congress of Laibach, King Ferdinand dishonorably repudiated his oath and formally "invited" an Austrian army to march into Naples "to restore order." The campaign that followed was eminently satisfactory to Metternich. Neapolitan opposition collapsed; the constitution was abrogated; and Ferdinand, protected by Austrian bayonets, inaugurated an era of savage persecution. The Two Sicilies long maintained the reputation of being the worst governed state in Christian Europe.

---

[1] Ferdinand (1751–1825) IV of Naples, III of Sicily, I of the Two Sicilies; the third son of Charles III of Spain.

[2] See Troppau Protocol, pp. 13 f., above.

Following closely upon the heels of the Neapolitan revolt came a Liberal uprising in Piedmont. In 1821 soldiers mutinied and seized Turin; King Victor Emmanuel abdicated in favor of his brother Charles Felix, and named Prince Charles Albert, next in line of royal succession, as regent.

Suppression of Uprising in Piedmont, 1821

Charles Albert, who was in open sympathy with liberalism and a bitter opponent of Austria, at once proclaimed a constitution similar to the Spanish document of 1812, but the speedy intervention of Austrian troops enabled Charles Felix to expel the liberal-minded regent and to reëstablish absolutist government. Metternich endeavored at the Congress of Verona (1822) to punish Charles Albert by depriving him of the right of succession to the throne of Piedmont, but Charles Felix successfully interposed the doctrine of "legitimacy," and Charles Albert soon manifested conversion to orthodox Metternichian reaction by enlisting in the French expedition to restore the impossible Ferdinand VII to the throne of Spain. Italy like Germany was bound hand and foot to the triumphant reactionary chariot of Austria.

FAILURE OF METTERNICH'S POLICIES AND PARTIAL TRIUMPH OF LIBERALISM, 1822-1830

From 1815 to 1822 Metternich's supremacy throughout Europe was unquestioned. After 1822 several factors contributed to weaken his position, so that by 1830 the cause of reaction was definitely doomed, at least in the western countries. For another eighteen years the Austrian chancellor continued to dominate Germany and Italy, but his efforts to unite all sovereigns for the extirpation of liberalism were already in 1830 marked with failure.

Decline of Metternich's Fortunes, 1822-1830

Three main elements in the decline of Metternich's fortunes were (1) the foreign policy of Great Britain, (2) the Greek insurrection, and (3) a wave of revolutionary movements in the year 1830. A few words must be said about each one of these.

It will be recalled that in 1822 George Canning succeeded Castlereagh as British foreign secretary. Canning felt no personal horror of liberalism; on the other hand, he was quite willing to coöperate with Liberals if it would promote the economic interests of Great Britain. Hence against the activities of Metternich he urged a policy of non-intervention. To the international congress assembled at Verona in 1822, **The Policy** he sent word that "while England was no friend to **of Canning:** revolution, she did emphatically insist on the right of **Non-Inter-** **vention** nations to set up for themselves whatever form of government they thought best, and to be left free to manage their own affairs, so long as they left other nations to manage theirs." The coöperation of Canning with the government of the United States, as has already been explained, checkmated every plan to reimpose autocracy on the rebellious Spanish colonies. Canning, in the words of his own proud boast, had "called the New World into existence to redress the balance of the Old." Such an attitude on the part of a British foreign secretary meant the defection of Great Britain from the Quadruple Alliance and serious damage to Metternich's chief instrument for the suppression of liberalism. Within a few years public opinion in France forced the government of that country to concur with Great Britain in the policy of non-intervention. Thenceforth the Concert of Europe was a mere fiction.

Metternich might still have been able to count on a powerful triple alliance — Austria, Russia, and Prussia — to uphold the noble cause of "legitimacy," had not a more disconcert- **The Greek** ing event transpired — the revolt of Christian Greeks **Insurrec-** against their "legitimate" but Mohammedan masters, **tion:** **Ypsilanti** the Ottoman Turks. While the European diplomats were assembled at Laibach in 1821, news came that a Greek, Prince Alexander Ypsilanti, had raised the standard of revolt among his countrymen in Moldavia and was confidently expecting aid from Russia. Metternich at once perceived the danger and prevailed upon the Tsar Alexander to disown Ypsilanti. The rising in Moldavia was easily put down by the Turks; and Metternich had the pleasure of confining the Greek leader in an Austrian prison for seven years.

But this was not the end of the Greek revolt—it was only a premature beginning. The Greeks, though long deprived by the Turks of their independence as a nation, had never been obliterated as a people. The Greek Orthodox Church had been a strong bond of union; and the seafaring and business propensi-

ties of the Greeks had given them an important commercial
and financial position in the Ottoman Empire.   Traditionally

The
National
Uprising in
Greece

democratic and patriotic they had recently been
aroused to action by the example of the French
revolutionaries.   A secret society — the *Hetairia
Philike*—founded in 1815, now numbered 200,000
members, pledged to labor for the overthrow of the Moslems
and the restoration of the Greek Empire at Constantinople.
What had been a theatrical display of an adventurer in Moldavia
was now rapidly succeeded by a national uprising in the Morea
and in the Ægean Islands (1821).   The Turks, this time taken
unprepared and badly beaten, had recourse to savage reprisals.
The Orthodox patriarch of Constantinople was murdered, and
a wholesale massacre of Christians was ordered in Macedonia
and Asia Minor.   The utmost ferocity marked the struggle on
both sides.   Metternich remained obdurate, cynically remark-
ing that the revolt should be allowed "to burn itself out
beyond the pale of civilization."

Yet the Greek revolt proved too serious even for Metternich.   It
appealed to the enthusiasm and imagination of Europe as nothing

General
European
Sympathy
for the
Greeks

else could.   The educated saw in it a revival of the
ancient glories of Hellas.   Patriots perceived in it a
war for national independence.   Liberals beheld in it a
struggle for liberty and democracy.   Pious Christians
of every creed witnessed with deepest sympathy a
modern crusade.   Volunteers flocked to the Greek standard
from every country of Europe.   Victor Hugo praised the rebels
in martial poems, and Lord Byron gave pen, fortune, and life
for Greek independence.

Popular sentiment was unanimously in favor of the Greek
insurgents not only in France and Great Britain, but, omen even

Concern of
Russia

more portentous, in Russia also.   Political ambition
of the tsars and a succession of wars had made Russians
and Turks hereditary enemies, while community of religion and
culture linked the Russian and Greek nations together.   Consequently, it was with some difficulty that Alexander, now a
faithful henchman of Metternich, restrained his own subjects
from giving aid to revolutionaries; yet until the tsar's death in
1825, Russia was steered in "legitimist" channels.

Meanwhile the Greeks, contrary to foreign expectation and despite chronic domestic feuds, were more than holding their own against the Turks. But just about the time of Alexander's death, the sultan, resolving upon a final drastic effort to subjugate his rebellious subjects, called to his assistance Ibrahim Pasha, the son of his vassal, Mehemet Ali of Egypt. Then for three years Ibrahim operated in the Morea with energy and ferocity. He easily defeated the Greeks in the open field, and, when hostile bands harassed his army, he took revenge by desolating the country and sending thousands of the Christian inhabitants into slavery in Egypt. The resulting indignation throughout Europe decided the new Tsar Nicholas to close his ear to the counsels of Metternich : in July, 1827, representatives of Great Britain, France, and Russia signed the treaty of London, agreeing to demand an armistice as preliminary to settlement of the Greek question; and in October, after the sultan had refused to accept mediation, the combined fleets of the new allies destroyed the Turco-Egyptian squadron in the harbor of Navarino. The battle of Navarino was decisive in that it rendered hopeless any further efforts of the Turks to suppress the Greek revolt and also in that it dealt a hard blow to Metternich's European system. Even the Russian tsar was openly backing rebels against "legitimately" constituted authority.

The War of Greek Independence, 1821–1829

Battle of Navarino, 1827

Tsar Nicholas now gave free rein to the sympathies and patriotism of his subjects. In 1828 he formally declared war against Turkey, and the next year a Russian army fought its way almost to Constantinople, and obliged the Porte to sign the treaty of Adrianople — a treaty of first-rate importance in the history of the dismemberment of the Ottoman Empire. By the settlement, Turkey virtually acknowledged the independence of Greece; granted practical autonomy to Serbia [1] and to the principalities of Moldavia and

Russo-Turkish War, 1828–1829

[1] The fame of the Greek War of Independence should not obscure the importance of the parallel Serbian War of Independence. From 1804 the Serbs under the leadership successively of two patriots — Karageorge and Milosh Obrenovich — waged almost constant war with their Turkish overlords until 1817, when they finally won autonomy, though still nominally under the suzerainty of the sultan. This autonomy was placed on an international basis by the treaty of Adrianople (1829).

Wallachia (modern Rumania); surrendered claims on Georgia and other provinces of the Caucasus to Russia; and recognized the exclusive jurisdiction of Russian consuls over Russian traders in Turkey.

An international conference in London subsequently fixed the Greek frontier at a line running from the Gulf of Volo [1] on The Greek the east to Arta on the west, and in 1832 Prince Otto Kingdom of Bavaria became the first constitutional king of Greece. The new kingdom embraced a comparatively small minority of the Greek-speaking people, but in spite of its diminutive size and of the poverty and political feuds which long afterwards distracted it, it was a very real example of how, even despite Metternich's fulminations, nationalism and liberalism might bear fruit. It was an ironical aftermath of the Greek revolt, which might have appealed to the cynical nature of Metternich, that the Tsar Nicholas should join in 1832 in forming a league of the three eastern monarchies — Russia, Austria, and Prussia — for the support of "divine-right" against the two Powers — France and Great Britain — which had "the courage to profess aloud rebellion and the overthrow of all stability."

The definite triumph of liberalism in France, the resulting cleavage in political principles between the governments of western Europe and those of the east, and the narrowing of Metternich's influence, were the achievements of the revolutionary movements of 1830.

General Revolutionary Movements of 1830

In France the reactionary rule of Charles X was becoming more and more unpopular. As it became increasingly obvious that the king was bent upon being an absolute sovereign in fact as well as in name and that Ultra-Royalist control meant additional class legislation in behalf of the clergy and the nobility, the bourgeoisie and many of the workingmen gave louder utterance to grumbling and fault-finding. The less well-to-do bourgeois were excluded from participation in government by the heavy property qualifications; the numerous irreligious bourgeois were angered by the exaltation of the Catholic Church; and, to cap the climax,

Middle-class Opposition in France to the Government of Charles X

---

[1] In 1832 the frontier was pushed still further south, to a line drawn from the Gulf of Arta to the Gulf of Lamia.

the wealthy bourgeois had a most galling economic grievance against the Ultra-Royalists. It will be recalled that the Chambers had authorized in 1825 the indemnifying of the émigrés to the amount of one billion francs for the losses which they had sustained during the Revolution. The means employed for paying the indemnity were amazing. Knowing that it would be impossible to restore such a huge capital sum to the nobles, the government hit upon the plan of funding the entire public debt of the nation at a materially lower rate of interest and of paying the amount thereby saved in the form of annuities to the émigrés. In other words, the middle-class holders of government bonds suddenly found their annual income reduced by a third for the benefit of a crowd of " grasping and traitorous aristocrats." It was this financial transaction more than any other fact which sealed the doom of divine-right monarchy in France. Men of business were henceforth arrayed with Napoleonic veterans and Liberal idealists against the régime of Charles X.

After the elections of 1827 had reflected the public feeling by depriving the Ultra-Royalists of their majority in the Lower Chamber, the king temporarily made personal concessions by appointing moderates to office. But that he was steadfast against making any concession of principle was fully apparent in 1829 when, in the face of an adverse vote of the Chambers, he intrusted the premiership to Prince de Polignac, one of the émigrés, a person as obstinate as he was ignorant and visionary.

The issue was clear : it was a conflict between the king and his reactionary minister on one side, and the Chambers, supported by the bourgeoisie, on the other. In vain did the government endeavor to make the nation forget the domestic conflict by intervening in behalf of Greek independence and by sending an expedition to seize Algiers and to chastise the Barbary pirates. The Chamber simply persisted in voting "lack of confidence" in the ministry and in referring to the rights guaranteed by the Charter of 1814; Liberal newspapers applauded the Chamber and openly criticized the king.

In the spring of 1830 Charles X dissolved the Chamber which still demanded the dismissal of the Polignac ministry, but the new elections returned a Chamber even more hostile to reaction than its predecessor. The king, thoroughly incensed that the

nation could have and express a will different from his own, replied on 26 July, 1830, with the publication of four arbitrary
The July   ordinances: (1) the rights of the press were to be
Ordinances   most carefully restricted; (2) the newly elected
Chamber, which had not as yet assembled, was dissolved;
(3) a new electoral law was promulgated which disfranchised
at least three-fourths of the electors, mostly troublesome
bourgeois; and (4) new elections were called for September.

On the very day of publication of these ordinances, the Liberal
printers and journalists, eager to reassert the sovereignty of the
              people against that of the Bourbons, incited all classes
The July   of Paris to armed insurrection. After three days of
(1830)
Revolu-   street-fighting against a mere handful of royalist troops
tion in   who were ill-prepared and feebly led, the Parisian
Paris   workingmen, driven to the barricades by the deliberate
closing of Liberal workshops, gained the victory: Charles X
abdicated in favor of his ten-year-old grandson, the count of
Chambord, and took refuge in England.

The "July Days" of 1830, with slight bloodshed, put an end
to divine-right monarchy in France. What political system
Overthrow   should take its place became at once a subject of heated
of Charles X debate. On the one hand there still survived a Republican party, recruited chiefly from among the students and the
Parisian workingmen, led by Godefroi Cavaignac, and desirous of
reëstablishing the republic of 1795; they had small support in
the country districts or among persons of prominence in Paris.
On the other hand were the Liberal bourgeoisie, admirably led by
the journalist Thiers and the great banker Laffitte (1767–1844),
quite willing to accept royalty, provided it should be constitutional rather than divine-right and should permit them actually
to rule the country, and counting on the sympathy of all Frenchmen who desired "order" as well as "liberty." An armed con-
Louis   flict between the two parties was at one time im-
Philippe,   minent, but was averted by the aged Lafayette, who
"King of
the   once more appeared on the scene and exerted his in-
French,"   fluence with the Republicans to have them accept
1830–1848   the system which the Liberal Monarchists had already formulated. The plan was the accession to the throne by
popular acclaim of Louis Philippe, duke of Orleans, a member,

of course, of the Bourbon family, but, as the son of that Philippe Égalité who had voted in Convention for the death of Louis XVI, far removed from Bourbon political principles. Louis Philippe had taken an eager part in the Revolution of 1789; he had been present at the capture of the Bastille; he had been enrolled in the Jacobin Club and had held military office under the republic; he had fought at Valmy and in the Netherlands; he had learned lessons of sturdy self-reliance during a long and adventurous exile in Europe and America; more recently he had made himself popular with the middle class by sending his sons to middle-class schools and by avowing his own faith in the opinions of Voltaire and Rousseau.

Early in August, 1830, Louis Philippe accepted the invitation of the Chamber to become "King of the French." The revolutionary tricolor at once replaced the white flag of the Bourbons, and popular sovereignty supplanted the theory of monarchical absolutism. But the most momentous result of the July Revolution in France was the triumph of the bourgeoisie: it was that class which had shaped the course of the great revolution of 1789, which had saved its conquests from the lower classes in 1794, and which had been again endangered by the privileged orders from 1815 to 1830; it was the same class which now put a reactionary king to flight, which stilled a revolutionary proletariat, and which definitely seized the reins of government itself. To the question asked in 1814 whether French political and social institutions were to be restored as they had been before the Revolution, the movement of 1830 constituted a categorical answer in the negative.

The suddenness and success of the July Revolution in France sent an immediate tremor throughout Europe: reactionaries were alarmed, and liberals took heart. In Belgium, in the Germanies, in Italy, in Poland, and in Switzerland, the shock of the movement was felt. Confronted with such widespread disturbances, Metternich had to abandon all thought of uniting Europe and forcing "legitimacy" once more upon France. *Effects of the July Revolution in Europe*

Friction between Belgians and Dutch had been acute since the Congress of Vienna had arbitrarily joined them into one state. They had divergent interests, they spoke different languages, and

they were proudly conscious of separate nationality.   The Dutch
were traditionally hostile to the French, mainly Protestant, and
Situation in largely engaged in agriculture and commerce, while
Belgium   the Belgians were French in sympathy, overwhelmingly Catholic in religion, and industrial in occupation.   The
pig-headed Dutch king, William I, contrived to annoy all classes
of his Belgian subjects.   He outraged their patriotism by imposing upon them Dutch law, Dutch language, and Dutch officials.
He irritated the Catholics by placing education under the control
of Protestant inspectors.   He alienated the Liberals by restricting the freedom of the press.   He angered the business men by
forcing them to contribute a disproportionately large amount of
taxes towards the interest on the heavy Dutch debt.

Matters came to a crisis in Brussels when the success of the
Parisian insurrection was appreciated.   Barricades were thrown
The Belgian up in the streets, unpopular ministers were assailed,
Insurrec- and a national guard was formed.   At first the rioters
tion   demanded only a separate legislature under the com-
mon king, but, when they found William stubbornly determined
to subdue them, they proclaimed the complete independence of
Belgium (October, 1830).

International politics at the time favored the Belgian cause.
Palmerston, the new British foreign secretary, who followed in
Independ- the steps of Canning as a promoter of advantageous
ence of   commercial treaties and consequently as a champion of
Belgium   small nationalities, recommended to the foreign repre-
sentatives in London that Belgian freedom be promptly confirmed.
The government of Louis Philippe, itself reposing on a revo-
lutionary basis, was naturally quite favorable to such a course;
Metternich was so occupied with disorders in Italy and in the
Germanies, and the Tsar Nicholas with a formidable Polish
uprising, that neither could interpose any serious objection,
while the Prussian king was duly intimidated by French threats.
Under these circumstances an international agreement was
reached at London in 1831, whereby Belgium was erected into an
independent state, with a constitutional king in the person of
Leopold of Saxe-Coburg.   It still required a naval blockade of
Dutch ports by the British fleet and the capture of Antwerp by
a French military expedition before the House of Orange could

be induced to evacuate Belgium, and it was not until 1839 that King William I assented to the final treaty of peace and amity. In that year the independence and neutrality of Belgium were guaranteed by Great Britain, France, Russia, Austria, and Prussia.

In the Germanies, neither Austria nor Prussia was directly affected by the revolutionary wave of 1830. In several of the lesser states, however, — Hanover, Brunswick, Sax- *The* ony, and Hesse-Cassel, — popular movements in imi- *Germanies* tation of the French and Belgian insurrections led *in 1830* to the grant of moderate constitutions, and in states which already enjoyed constitutional government further Liberal concessions were made or promised.

Of the Italian states, both Naples and Piedmont, which had suffered the discomfiture from Austrian intervention in 1821, now remained quiet, but the Liberals in the central *The Italian* states, counting on the support of the new French king, *States in* rebelled against their autocratic and foreign rulers. *1830* In the Papal States they raised a new tricolor of Italian unity and democracy (the red, white, and green, which subsequently became the flag of the kingdom of Italy) and readily shook off (1831) the temporal rule of the newly elected Pope Gregory XVI, an ardent reactionary and friend of Austria.   There were similar outbreaks in Parma and Modena against the Habsburg sovereigns who, thinking discretion the better part of valor, betook themselves hurriedly to Vienna.   Under Metternich's auspices Austrian troops were promptly rushed into Italy: the old governments were easily reëstablished, and many patriots were hanged. Louis Philippe, who had grandly declared that not only would he refrain from meddling in the affairs of other countries, but he would not permit other Powers to intervene, limited his protection of Italy against Metternich to stationing a French garrison in the papal town of Ancona.[1]

Thus the revolutionary movements of 1830 in Germany and in Italy were not very fruitful.[2]   As soon as the storm had sub-

---

[1] This French force, which gave umbrage to the pope as well as to the Liberals, was not withdrawn until 1838.

[2] Otherwise was the result in Switzerland.   The July Revolution in Paris gave a marked impetus to the tendency, already apparent, of small towns and villages

sided a little, Metternich was able, in one case with the aid of
the Federal Diet, and in the other with Austrian bayonets,
Continued   to resume his task of holding the revolutionaries in
Predom-   check.   Yet the movements were not without sig-
inance of
Austria in   nificance : they showed a slow but steady growth
Germany   of liberalism in central Europe, and they served
and Italy   to prevent Metternich from arresting the victory
of bourgeois liberalism in western Europe.

A particularly tragic aspect of the revolutionary movement
of 1830 was its communication to Poland.   It was almost incon-
Futile   ceivable that a Russian autocrat could be a Polish con-
Revolt of   stitutional king, and since the accession of Nicholas I
Poland, 1831 difficulties had increased.   The long-standing sympathy between Poles and Frenchmen, and the spread of a rumor
that the tsar intended to use his Polish regiments to coerce Louis
Philippe and the Belgian insurgents, inspired a mutiny in Warsaw
(November, 1830), accompanied by the murder of a number of
objectionable Russian officials and the expulsion of the viceroy,
Grand Duke Constantine.   The resulting war lasted from January till September, 1831.   The Poles fought gallantly, but their
defense was paralyzed as usual by the entire lack of natural
means of fortification and by bitter intestine feuds.   They were
overwhelmed by numbers, moreover, and no foreign assistance
was forthcoming : the fact that both Prussia and Austria had
Polish subjects rendered those Powers hostile to an independent
Poland, and neither Louis Philippe nor the British government
did anything more than to expostulate with the tsar concerning
alleged "cruelties."

As soon as the revolt was crushed, Nicholas proceeded to
inflict exemplary punishment upon the unfortunate Poles.   He
abrogated the constitution which his brother had granted in 1815
and incorporated the Polish kingdom as a conquered province
into the Russian Empire.   He put hundreds of patriots to death
and exiled other hundreds.   He filled the land with Russian
soldiers and sought in every way to extirpate Polish nationality.

to rise against the somewhat oppressive rule of the head-cities and to establish new
cantonal institutions on a more democratic basis.   The Swiss cantons, whose
political differences were embittered by religious disputes, remained in almost
constant commotion until 1848.

No remnant of Poland's separate political existence henceforth remained.[1]

At this point the era of Metternich's European supremacy closes. Ever since the downfall of Napoleon he had given masterful support by subtlety of diplomacy and by force of arms to every effort of divine-right monarchs, of clergy, and of nobility, to restore antique institutions in society and in government; but a series of recent events, — the disruption of the Spanish colonial empire, the Greek revolt, the successful uprisings in France and Belgium, and increasing unrest in Germany and Italy, — clearly indicated that he had been fighting for a lost cause. The old régime was doomed. Already in western Europe the victorious bourgeoisie were trampling on its ruins; and, in order to preserve its fabric in central and eastern Europe, Metternich with his Russian and Prussian allies was reduced to a strictly defensive policy.

Significance of the Era of Metternich

The real significance of this Era of Metternich was the assured triumph of the principles of the French Revolution, the permanence of the ideas of "liberty, equality, and fraternity," and the substitution, at least in western Europe, of the political and economic supremacy of the bourgeoisie for that of the older privileged classes. Until 1848 Metternich managed to keep his grasp on central Europe, but the struggles of those last years were everywhere fundamentally different from those which marked the era that we have reviewed in this chapter. After 1830 social and political conflicts were waged not only between the bourgeoisie and the old privileged orders but also between the bourgeoisie and the workingmen. If Metternich may serve as a fitting close to the period of noblemen's privileges, the Industrial Revolution will provide a convenient starting-point for the story of the workingmen's slow and painful emancipation.

ADDITIONAL READING

Brief Texts on the History of the Nineteenth Century. In addition to the textbooks and manuals on the general history of modern times mentioned in the preceding volume (pp. xxiii f.), the following are specially valuable

[1] Except the minute republic of Cracow which continued to be a center of Polish national agitation until 1846, when it was annexed by Austria.

to college students for the whole, or greater part, of the nineteenth century:
C. D. Hazen, *Europe since 1815* (1910), reliable and very readable, largely
political, and provided with excellent bibliographies; Charles Seignobos,
A Political History of Europe since 1814, Eng. trans. ed. by S. M. Macvane
(1900), dealing with events country by country, burdened with excessive
political detail, more an encyclopedia than a textbook though containing
good chapters on social conditions and international relations; C. M.
Andrews, *The Historical Development of Modern Europe, 1815–1897*, 2 vols.
in 1 (1900), interesting and informing, particularly on the political aspects
of the conflict between revolutionaries and reactionaries; C. A. Fyffe,
A History of Modern Europe, 1792–1878, popular ed. (1896), almost wholly
political; Oscar Browning, *History of the Modern World, 1815–1910*, 2 vols.
(1912), a well-written narrative displaying much knowledge but marred
by lack of proper proportion; C. E. M. Hawkesworth, *The Last Century
in Europe, 1814–1910* (1913), political and military, with glimpses of economic phenomena; R. W. Jeffery, *The New Europe, 1789–1889* (1911),
devoted almost exclusively to wars and rumors of war; W. A. Phillips,
Modern Europe, 1815–1899, 2d ed. (1902), useful for the diplomatic history
of Europe prior to 1878, very weak on the period after that date; Wilhelm
Müller, *Political History of Recent Times, 1816–1875, with special reference
to Germany*, Eng. trans. by J. P. Peters (1882), breezy and suggestive as
showing Germany's relation to the general European history of the period;
F. A. Kirkpatrick (editor), *Lectures on the History of the Nineteenth Century* (1902), comprising seventeen brief résumés by such scholars as Mantoux on France, Marcks on Germany, and Vinogradoff on Russia; E. H.
Sears, *An Outline of Political Growth in the Nineteenth Century* (1900),
concerned chiefly with the development of representative government
throughout the world, already somewhat out-of-date; L. C. Jane, *From
Metternich to Bismarck, 1815–1878* (1910), a dry summary of political,
diplomatic, and military happenings; Édouard Driault and Gabriel Monod,
Évolution du monde moderne: histoire politique et sociale, 1815–1909 (1910),
an excellent French manual; Paul Feyel, *Histoire politique du XIXe
siècle*, 2 vols. (1913–1914), a suggestive manual written in French and
from a Roman Catholic standpoint. A convenient and inexpensive atlas
of the nineteenth century is C. G. Robertson and J. G. Bartholomew, *An
Historical Atlas of Modern Europe from 1789 to 1914* (1915).

General Works on the Era of Metternich. Brief summaries: C. D.
Hazen, *Europe since 1815* (1910), ch. i–v, xviii, xix; J. H. Robinson and
C. A. Beard, *The Development of Modern Europe* (1907), Vol. I, ch. xvi,
and Vol. II, ch. xvii; C. E. M. Hawkesworth, *The Last Century in Europe,
1814–1910* (1913), ch. i–xiii; Oscar Browning, *A History of the Modern
World, 1815–1910*, Vol. I (1912), Book I; W. A. Phillips, *Modern Europe,
1815–1899* (1902), ch. i–ix; Charles Seignobos, *A Political History of
Europe since 1814*, Eng. trans. (1900), ch. i, xxv; C. A. Fyffe, *A History
of Modern Europe, 1792–1878* (1896), ch. xiii–xvii; Wilhelm Müller, *Political History of Recent Times, 1816–1875*, Eng. trans. (1882), ch. i–xiv.

More detailed treatises: *History of All Nations*, Vol. XVIII, by Theodor Flathe, *Restoration and Revolution; Cambridge Modern History*, Vol. IX, *Napoleon* (1906), ch. xix, and Vol. X, *The Restoration* (1907); *Histoire générale*, Vol. X, ch. i–ix, xv, xvii, xxiii; Alfred Stern, *Geschichte Europas seit den Verträgen von 1815 bis zum Frankfurter Frieden von 1871*, Vols. I–IV (1894–1905), the most exhaustive and undoubtedly the best single work on the period, should be translated into English; Constantin Bulle, *Geschichte der neuesten Zeit, 1815–1885*, 4 vols. (1886–1887); Antonin Debidour, *Histoire diplomatique de l'Europe, 1814–1878*, 2 vols. (1891), Vol. I on the Holy Alliance, Vol. II on the revolutionary movements; Émile Bourgeois, *Manuel historique de politique étrangère*, Vol. II, *Les révolutions, 1789–1830*, 4th ed. (1909); Sir Edward Hertslet, *The Map of Europe by Treaty*, Vol. I (1875), an indispensable collection of documents relating to the Congress of Vienna; Baron Descamps and Louis Renault, *Recueil international des traités du XIXᵉ siècle*, Vol. I, *1801–1825* (1914); W. A. Phillips, *The Confederation of Europe* (1914), a valuable study of the European alliances, 1813–1823, as an experiment in international pacifism; Claude Roget (pseud. E. Muhlenbeck), *Étude sur les origines de la Sainte-Alliance* (1888). On Metternich: G. B. Malleson, *Life of Prince Metternich* (1895); *Memoirs of Prince Clemens Metternich*, ed. by Prince Richard Metternich and in part trans. into English by Mrs. Alexander Napier, 4 parts in 5 vols. (1881–1882); Charles de Mazade, *Un chancelier d'ancien régime: le règne diplomatique de M. de Metternich* (1889). On Talleyrand at the Congress of Vienna: his *Memoirs*, Eng. trans., 5 vols. (1891–1892); and *Correspondance inédite de Talleyrand et du roi Louis XVIII pendant le congrès de Vienne*, ed. by G. Pollain, 3d ed. (1881), also in English translation. Likewise, for both Metternich and Talleyrand, see the justly celebrated Albert Sorel, *Essais d'histoire et de critique*, 12th ed. (1884).

The Restoration in France, 1815–1830. *Cambridge Modern History*, Vol. X, ch. ii, iii; J. R. Hall, *The Bourbon Restoration* (1910); G. L. Dickinson, *Revolution and Reaction in Modern France* (1892), essays on the various schools of political thought in France from 1789 to 1871; Georges Weill, *La France sous la monarchie constitutionelle, 1814–1848*, rev. ed. (1912), topical, not narrowly political, but social and economic as well; Émile Levasseur, *Histoire des classes ouvrières et de l'industrie en France de 1789 à 1870*, Vol. I (1903), Book III, excellent on social conditions; Jean Jaurès (editor), *Histoire socialiste*, Vol. VII, by René Viviani, *La restauration, 1814–1830* (1906); Pierre Rain, *L'Europe et la restauration des Bourbons* (1908), an intensive study of the years 1814–1818; Henry Houssaye, *1815*, 3 vols. (1896–1905), an able detailed account of the troublous year of transition, especially valuable Vol. III, *La seconde abdication, la terreur blanche;* Louis Michon, *Le gouvernement parlementaire sous la restauration* (1905), a study in constitutional government under the Charter of 1814; Paul Thureau-Dangin, *Le parti libéral sous la restauration*, 2d ed. (1888), useful for a proper understanding of the opposition to the restored divine-right Bourbons.

Spain and Portugal. The Revolt of the Spanish Colonies. *Cambridge Modern History*, Vol. X (1907), ch. vii–x; Butler Clarke, *Modern Spain, 1815–1898* (1906), ch. i–iii, full but jejune; M. A. S. Hume, *Modern Spain, 1788–1898* (1900), ch. v, briefer but more interesting than Clarke's narrative; Gustave Hubbard, *Histoire contemporaine de l'Espagne*, 6 vols. (1869–1883), of which Vols. I, II treat of the reign of Ferdinand VII, exhaustive and scholarly; Hermann Baumgarten, *Geschichte Spaniens vom Ausbruch der französischen Revolution bis auf unsere Tage*, 3 vols. (1865–1871), especially Vol. II. On the revolt of the American colonies: W. R. Shepherd, *Latin America* (1914), pp. 69–80, a very brief but clear introduction; Bernard Moses, *South America on the Eve of Emancipation* (1908); F. L. Paxson, *The Independence of the South American Republics, a Study in Recognition and Foreign Policy* (1903), valuable for the policies of Great Britain and the United States; Bartolomé Mitre, *The Emancipation of South America* (1893), the condensed Eng. trans. of an important work by a former president of Argentina; F. L. Petre, *Simon Bolivar* (1910), a good biography; A. H. Noll and A. P. McMahon, *The Life and Times of Miguel Hidalgo y Costilla* (1910), an account of the revolutionary movement in Mexico; W. F. Reddaway, *The Monroe Doctrine* (1898), the work of an English scholar; F. J. Turner, *Rise of the New West, 1819–1829* (1906), ch. xii, the best brief statement of the genesis and early application of the Monroe Doctrine; J. H. Latané, *The Diplomatic Relations of the United States and Spanish America* (1900), ch. i, ii, a valuable contribution.

Great Britain under the Tories, 1800–1830. Textbook summaries: Gilbert Slater, *The Making of Modern England*, new rev. ed. (1915), ch. i–iv; A. L. Cross, *History of England and Greater Britain* (1914), ch. xlvi–xlix; C. W. Oman, *England in the Nineteenth Century* (1900), ch. i–iv. Somewhat longer political narratives: *Cambridge Modern History*, Vol. X (1907), ch. xviii; A. D. Innes, *History of England and the British Empire*, Vol. IV (1914), ch. i, ii; J. A. R. Marriott, *England since Waterloo* (1913), ch. i–iii; Sir Herbert Maxwell, *A Century of Empire*, Vol. I, *1801–1832* (1909); G. C. Brodrick and J. K. Fotheringham, *Political History of England, 1801–1837;* J. F. Bright, *History of England*, Vol. III, *Constitutional Monarchy, 1689–1837;* Sir Spencer Walpole, *History of England since 1815*, rev. ed., 6 vols. (1902–1905), a standard work, reaching down to 1858, by a famous Whig-Liberal; Harriet Martineau, *History of the Peace: being a History of England from 1816 to 1854, with an Introduction, 1800–1815*, 4 vols., treats of the period through most of which the authoress lived, thus an important original source. On special phases of the period in English history: H. D. Traill and J. S. Mann (editors), *Social England*, illus. ed. (1909), Vol. VI, for the ordinary life of the times; C. G. Greville, *Journal of the Reigns of George IV and William IV*, ed. by Henry Reeve (1888), an illuminating source compiled by an influential clerk of the Privy Council; W. O'C. Morris, *Wellington, Soldier and Statesman* (1904); Sir Herbert Maxwell, *The Life of Wellington*, 2 vols. (1899); E. and A. G. Porritt, *The Unreformed House of Commons*, new ed., 2 vols. (1909); T. E.

Kebbel, *History of Toryism* (1886), covering the years 1783–1881; Gilbert Slater, *The English Peasantry and the Enclosure of the Common Fields* (1907); John Ashton, *Social Life under the Regency*, 2 vols. (1890), dealing with the years 1810–1820; R. M. Garnier, *History of the English Landed Gentry* (1893), and, by the same author, *Annals of the British Peasantry* (1895); E. C. K. Gonner, *Common Lands and Inclosure* (1912); J. S. Nicholson, *The History of the English Corn Laws* (1904); C. B. R. Kent, *The English Radicals* (1899); Oliver Elton, *A Survey of English Literature, 1780–1830*, 2 vols. (1912); and, on the career of *Canning*, the biographies by J. A. R. Marriott (1903) and H. W. V. Temperley (1905), and *George Canning and his Friends*, ed. by J. F. Bagot, 2 vols. (1909).

Russia, 1801–1831. *Cambridge Modern History*, Vol. X (1907), ch. xiii, xiv, a good account, by S. Askenazy, of Alexander I and of the Polish revolt of 1831; Alfred Rambaud, *Histoire de la Russie depuis les origines jusqu'à nos jours*, 6th rev. ed. (1914), ch. xxxiii–xxxvi, perhaps the best brief narrative, also in English translation; W. R. A. Morfill, *History of Russia from the Birth of Peter the Great to the Death of Alexander II* (1902), a dry account, and, by the same author, *Poland* (1893); C. Joyneville, *Life and Times of Alexander I*, 3 vols. (1875), a standard detailed work, now superseded in large part by Grand Duke Nicholas Mikhaïlovitch, *L'Empereur Alexandre Ier*, 2 vols. (1913); Prince Adam Czartoryski, *Memoirs and his Correspondence with Alexander I*, ed. by A. Gielgud, in Eng. trans., 2 vols. (1888); Theodor Schiemann, *Geschichte Russlands unter Nikolaus I*, Vol. I (1904), deals with the reign of Alexander I, Vol. II (1908) with the years 1825–1830, and Vol. III (1913) with the Polish insurrection of 1830–1831; W. A. Phillips, *Poland* (1915), ch. vii, viii, a useful synopsis of Polish history, 1801–1846, in the "Home University Library."

Central Europe during the Era of Metternich. On the Germanies: G. M. Priest, *Germany since 1740* (1915), ch. viii; *Cambridge Modern History*, Vol. X (1907), ch. xi; E. F. Henderson, *A Short History of Germany*, Vol. II, ch. viii; Ferdinand Schevill, *The Making of Modern Germany* (1916), ch. iv; Heinrich von Sybel, *The Founding of the German Empire*, Eng. trans., 7 vols. (1890–1898), a famous "national" history, of which Vol. I treats of the period of Metternich; Heinrich von Treitschke, *History of Germany in the Nineteenth Century*, trans. by Eden and Adar Paul, Vol. I (1915), strongly Prussian, a full account of political happenings to 1819; Karl Biedermann, *Geschichte Deutschlands, 1815–1871* (1891); M. L. Deventer, *Cinquante années de l'histoire fédérale de l'Allemagne* (1870), a history of the German Confederation from 1815 to 1866; Louis Leger, *History of Austro-Hungary from the Earliest Times to the Year 1889*, trans. by Mrs. B. Hill (1889); Anton Springer, *Geschichte Oesterreichs seit dem Wienerfrieden 1809*, Vol. I (1863); C. M. Knatchbull-Hugessen, *The Political Evolution of the Hungarian Nation*, Vol. I (1908), ch. ix–xi. On the Italian States: *Cambridge Modern History*, Vol. X (1907), ch. iv; R. M. Johnston, *The Napoleonic Empire in Southern Italy and the Rise* *of the Secret Societies*, 2 vols. (1904); Bolton King, *A History of Italian Unity*, Vol. I (1899); W. J. Stillman, *The Union of Italy, 1815–1895* (1898); W. R. Thayer, *Dawn of Italian Independence*, Vol. I (1893).

Greek Independence. *Cambridge Modern History*, Vol. X (1907), ch. vi, an excellent account by W. A. Phillips, and, by the same writer, *Greek War of Independence* (1897); Lewis Sergeant, *Greece in the Nineteenth Century: a Record of Hellenic Emancipation and Progress, 1821–1897* (1897); Sir Richard C. Jebb, *Modern Greece*, 2d ed. (1901); George Finlay, *History of the Greek Revolution*, being Vols. VI and VII of his *History of Greece*, rev. ed. by H. F. Tozer, 7 vols. (1877), the standard work by a scholarly contemporary; *Letters and Journals of Samuel Gridley Howe*, Vol. I, *The Greek Revolution*, ed. by Laura E. Richards (1906), interesting memoirs of an American college student who served as a volunteer in the War of Greek Independence; Lord Byron, *Letters and Journals*, Vol. VI, ed. by R. E. Prothero (1904).

On the revolt of the Serbs against the Ottoman Empire, see Prince and Princess Lazarovich-Hrebelianovich, *The Servian People, their Past Glory and their Destiny*, Vol. II (1910), and Grégoire Yakschitch, *L'Europe et la résurrection de la Serbie, 1804–1834* (1907).

For the revolt of the Belgians against the Dutch, see *Cambridge Modern History*, Vol. X (1907), ch. xvi, and P. J. Blok, *History of the People of the Netherlands*, Vol. V, Eng. trans. by Ruth Putnam (1912).

PART IV

DEMOCRACY AND NATIONALISM

PART IV

DEMOCRACY AND NATIONALISM

WITHIN the eighty years from 1750 to 1830 a new Europe had been in process of creation. It was a Europe which laid violent hands upon the traditions and institutions of the past. Ancient privileges of churchmen and of titled landowners tended to disappear before the onrush of a wealthy, intelligent bourgeoisie. Doctrines of popular sovereignty and of the rights of man were supplanting the practices and precepts of divine-right monarchy. Allegiance to dynasties was waning, and nations were becoming acutely self-conscious.

What finally determined the issue of the conflict between revolutionaries and reactionaries and the triumph of the ideas of Liberty, Equality, and Fraternity, was not a little revolutionary wave in politics, such as that of 1830, but a great revolution in industry — a revolution which threw all its strength and weight into the balance against the reactionaries.

Within the eighty-odd years from 1830 to 1914, the Industrial Revolution worked wonders for the new Europe. It afforded all men — priests, and noblemen, and bourgeois, and workingmen, and peasants — marvelous and novel ways of living, and working, and traveling. It made democracy the dominant and all-powerful political ideal in Europe. It rendered nationalism a widely contagious and fiercely effective force in European society, whether in the British Empire, or in Latin Europe, or in the countries of Teutons and Slavs. It stimulated science and most variant speculation. It caused Europe to reach out faster and farther than ever before to colonize the uttermost parts of the world or to impress upon them the stamp of her own peculiar civilization. It created the gravest problems both in domestic affairs and in international relations. With all these matters Parts IV and V of this volume attempt to deal.

CHAPTER XVIII

THE INDUSTRIAL REVOLUTION

THE collapse of divine-right monarchy and of feudal privilege had been foreshadowed by the French Revolution; and new ideals had been established of political democracy and civil equality. Yet after all, such a revolution made little direct change in everyday life. The taxes might be borne by all alike; all might obey the same laws; one might not fear the lord of the castle as formerly; and a far-away legislative assembly might debate ever so eloquently; — but the farmer still goaded on the slow-moving oxen before the wooden plow; the cobbler still pegged away at his shoes; the thrifty housewife still sat by her spinning wheel. Manners had changed slightly: in France men wore long trousers instead of satin knee-breeches. But the peasant ate the same food, the artisan worked at the same rough bench, the traveler execrated the same lumbering stage-coach, and the same small sailing vessel took weeks to cross the Atlantic. That was at the beginning of the nineteenth century.

Daily Life Little Altered by the French Revolution

Since then the world has changed! The farmer now possesses a sharp steel plow and he has thrown his hand-flail away; our clothes and shoes are turned out by whirring machines in great factories. In his evening paper, the tired business-man reads how his wares are selling in far-away China. The artisan now trudges, dinner-pail in hand, to the noisy factory; the traveler leans back in a luxurious chair as his train speeds through the country; and tourists play tennis on deck during their five-day passage of the Atlantic.

All this has been brought about by a great change in industry, a transformation so sudden and so complete that we call it the "Industrial Revolution." Its two basic elements were: (1) the

67

invention and application of machines and engines to facilitate
mining, manufacturing, agriculture, and transportation, (2) the
building of factories.   This revolution took place in
Great Britain approximately between 1770 and 1825.
Since 1815 it has spread throughout Europe, to the
New World, and to the Old.   Everywhere it
has brought machines, engines, factories, rich men,
trade-unions, slums; it has planted sky-scrapers where apple-
trees grew, and put pounding locomotives where the creaking
stage-coach used to roll.

The "Industrial Revolution" in Great Britain, 1770-1825

Before we narrate the story, let us pause to ask ourselves why
it was in eighteenth-century England that the revolution first
occurred.   We cannot tell surely why machines had
never been made before — perhaps the people of the
middle ages were too "old-fashioned," too conservative, too much bound by gild restrictions, and too
little occupied with thinking out better ways of doing
things.   Nevertheless the French had made many
improvements in method long before 1770.   But in the England of the eighteenth century conditions were ripe for the
great change.   The newer industries were not shackled by gild
regulations; manufacturers were relatively free to apply new
methods.   Not only was England fortunate in possessing the
damp climate requisite to textile manufacture, but her swift
streams would offer an abundant supply of water power for
the new machinery and beneath her soil lay rich stores of coal
and iron, which would prove indispensable to the growth of
modern industry.   Moreover, England had come out of the commercial and colonial struggles of the sixteenth, seventeenth, and
eighteenth centuries with a thriving commerce and promising industries.   Even after the seeming set-back of the War of American Independence, Englishmen had continued to increase their
trade and industry, and during the Revolutionary and Napoleonic
Wars their country might have been called justly the "work-
shop of the world."   England's merchants could sell all the goods
that her manufacturers could make.   Every one wanted to be
rich, and the surest way to gain wealth was to make things more
cheaply and rapidly than other manufacturers.   Capitalists
were ready to spend fortunes for inventions, in the hope of reap-

England Prepared in the Eighteenth Century for Industrial Revolution

ing still greater fortunes. The smiths, and carpenters, and metal-workers, more skillful than before, were able to construct the machines which the inventors devised. And many thoughtful men were busy thinking how the science of the century might be turned to practical use. England was ready for inventions.

THE MECHANICAL INVENTIONS

Not a few great geniuses, but hundreds of obscure workers, were responsible for the inventions. Where thousands of active minds were searching for easier and better ways of doing things, there were sure to be many inventors and many inventions. And the number of inventions has steadily increased since the Industrial Revolution, until nowadays machines get out of date within a few years. Among the many, a few inventors stand out, whose names have become connected with revolutionary changes: Kay, Hargreaves, Arkwright, Crompton, Cartwright, Whitney, Watt, Fulton, and Stephenson.

The first six of these men introduced improvements in the making of cotton cloth. At the beginning of the eighteenth century, most cloth was made of wool, although cotton cloth was much in demand. A few English manufacturers had begun to make cloth of the down — "cotton wool," it was called — which grew on the cotton bushes of Asia and the West Indies. The work was still done in a very simple and painfully slow manner. First the seeds had to be picked out of the cotton by hand. Then the tangled fibers had to be brushed out straight (*i.e.*, "carded") with a wire brush, and spun into thread on a spinning-wheel such as our grandmothers used. It took all day to spin the thread which we can now buy for a few cents.

Machinery for Spinning and Weaving

Weaving was done on a wooden frame called a "loom." Parallel threads were strung across the loom, and then the "shuttle," an enlarged wooden needle attached to the end of a ball of thread, was woven back and forth between the parallel threads (the "warp"). At first a man could make cloth only as wide as he could reach across to weave the shuttle back and forth; but in 1738 a certain John Kay invented a simple device — the "fly-shuttle" — by which the weaver

John Kay's Fly-Shuttle, 1738

had only to pull a string in order to push the shuttle back and forth, and could make his cloth as wide as desired.

With the aid of the fly-shuttle weavers could now work twice as fast as before, and they, therefore, called for twice as much thread. But the old hand-spinners and spinning-wheels were as slow as ever, and could not supply the demand for cotton thread. Prizes were offered for an invention that would make spinning easier.

More than thirty years went by, but at last in 1770 a weaver in Lancashire by the name of James Hargreaves patented a spin-

Hargreaves's Spinning Jenny, 1770

ning "jenny." In the jenny eight spinning wheels were combined and turned by one crank, so that in effect one person could spin eight threads simultaneously. The device was so cheaply made and easily operated that by 1788 some 20,000 were in use in England, the largest forming eighty threads at once, and even the smallest doing the work of six or eight spinning-wheels.

Almost at the same time, Richard Arkwright, a shrewd, ambitious business-man, patented a "water-frame," or water-

Arkwright's Water-Frame, 1769

power machine, for spinning. The water-frame consisted of four pairs of rollers, between which the thread was drawn out, all rotated by a belt from a water-wheel. A few years later Arkwright patented machines which brushed out the raw cotton ready to be spun.

Arkwright's machines were so heavy, costly, and complicated that special buildings had to be erected for them. But

Arkwright, Father of the Factory

it was worth while, for once the machines were set up and connected with a water-wheel, water-power did most of the work and less money had to be paid out in wages. Arkwright's spinning-mills soon made him a millionaire, and he became so famous that King George III made him *Sir* Richard Arkwright.

The third great improvement in spinning was made by Samuel Crompton in 1779. Crompton combined certain features of the

Crompton's Mule, 1779

jenny with Arkwright's water-frame in such an ingenious way that the new machine, the spinning "mule," not only made fine and strong thread, but produced it more rapidly than had hitherto been possible. By 1812 Crompton estimated that there were spinning mules in several hundred establishments, with a total of 5,000,000 spindles.

With the help of these inventions, the spinners were now producing more thread than the weavers could make into cloth, and it was now the turn of the weavers to improve their methods. The great invention which revolutionized weaving was made by a clergyman, Edmund Cartwright, in 1785. Although at the outset he knew almost nothing about weaving, Cartwright managed to construct a loom which worked itself and received its motion from water-power. Three of these power-looms, with a boy of fifteen to mend broken threads, could do the work of four skillful hand-loom weavers.

Cart-wright's Power-Loom, 1785

The spirit of invention made itself felt in all branches of the cotton industry. In 1792 Eli Whitney, an American, made the first cotton gin, a machine which would pick the seeds out of raw cotton more rapidly than fifty negroes could do it. Another invention made it possible to bleach cloth in a day or two by chemicals instead of in a month by the sun and to dye it a hundred times more speedily than before. The spinning mule and the power-loom were improved and improved; until in 1913 the machines of Great Britain were producing for export alone some 7,000,000,000 yards of cotton cloth every year — enough to make 175 yard-wide belts for the earth.

Whitney's Cotton Gin (1792) and Other Inventions for Cotton Manufacture

The great value of machines is not that they enable a man to do work more expeditiously but that they enable man to make horses, or water-wheels, or steam-engines do the work. For steam-engines are stronger than men, and work without asking wages, and without fatigue. Our machines are like so many black, iron slaves, eating coal and performing our work. Long before the Industrial Revolution windmills had been in use, but too often the wind was lazy. Water-power also was utilized, and many a turbulent stream turned the water-wheel which moved the mill which ground the grain. Water-power, indeed, worked Arkwright's first spinning-mills, and between 1780 and 1800 numerous mills were built along the swift streams of western England.

Motive Power for the New Machinery

But where rivers were slow, it was necessary to make artificial rapids by building a high reservoir from which the water would fall with some force upon the water-wheel. To fill the reser-

voir a powerful pump was needed. Pumps were also needed
in the mines to drain out the water which flowed in from un-
The Steam- derground springs. It was to satisfy these demands
Engine   for pumps that the steam-engine was invented. The
first steam-engines were simply pumps; the application of
steam-power to machinery came later.

Crude steam-engines had been constructed as early as 1698
by Captain James Savery, and even earlier (1690) by a French-
Early   man, Denys Papin. A much better engine was pa-
Attempts   tented in 1705 by Thomas Newcomen. Improved
Newcomen "fire-engines," as they were called, doing the work
of fifty horses at one-sixth the cost, were used extensively to
pump water from English mines in the first half of the eighteenth
century, but the engine was not yet a complete success. At every
stroke of the piston the steam cylinder had to be heated and
chilled, and this alternate heating and chilling consumed too
much coal and too much time.

The steam-engine first became worth while in the hands of
the Scotchman James Watt, whom, therefore, we call the inventor
James   of the steam-engine. Watt was a philosopher, scien-
Watt's   tist, engineer, mechanic, and born inventor, all in one.
Steam-   While employed to make astronomical instruments for
Engine, 1769 the University of Glasgow, he was asked to repair
an exhibition model of Newcomen's engine. Observing how
wasteful the engine was, he soon hit upon a remarkable improvement which he patented in 1769. The steam was condensed in a
separate condenser, always kept cold, while the cylinder remained
hot, instead of being chilled and heated alternately; by this
means three-fourths of the coal was saved. But the steam-
engine was still only a pump. Watt next invented devices by
which the back-and-forth motion of the piston could be made
to turn machine wheels, as the piston of a locomotive turns the
driving wheels. The improved steam-engine could then be
applied to Cartwright's loom and to Arkwright's spinning-ma-
chines. Watt's work was (1) to make the steam-engine more
efficient, and (2) to apply it directly to machinery.

To invent steam-engines is one thing, to construct them for the
market is another. Iron was expensive; only the most skillful
workmen could be trusted to do the work; and it required con-

siderable capital as well as business ability.   Fortunately, Watt
was able to induce a wealthy manufacturer by the name of
Matthew Boulton to finance the enterprise, and the steam-
engine was thereby made a paying proposition. After 1775, mine-
owners began to buy Watt engines for pumping; mill-owners
installed steam-engines to run their looms, spinning-mules, or
grindstones; purchasers came to Watt's factory even from France
and Germany.   The first steam spinning-mill was established
in 1785; in 1790 Arkwright used the steam-engine for his cotton-
mills; and the application of steam to industry went on until a
foreigner, traveling through England in 1802, could write:
"It is hardly an exaggeration to say that in England these machines are as common as water-wheels and wind-mills in our
country."

Since a great deal of iron and coal was needed to make steam-
engines, and since the steam-engine facilitated mining, coal
and iron were produced in unprecedented quantities. **Iron**
New methods of smelting iron ore were discovered. **Industry**
James Watt in 1783 constructed a steam-hammer weighing 750
pounds and striking 300 blows a minute.   Great blast furnaces
then began to appear, lighting up the sky by night, while in the
foundries titanic steam-hammers beat the iron into shape.   Engines, looms, and even ships were constructed of iron.   The
"iron age" had dawned.

Of the many uses to which the steam-engine was put, three
in particular deserve mention: the steamboat, the steam locomotive, and the steam printing press.   Robert Fulton, **The Steam-**
an American, although not the first to construct a **boat**
steamboat, was the first to make the steamboat pay.   His side-
wheeler, the *Clermont*, equipped with a Watt engine, in 1807 made
the trip up the Hudson River from New York to Albany (150
miles) in 32 hours, startling the farmers by its noise, and seeming
to them "a monster moving upon the waters, defying wind and
tide, and breathing flames and smoke."   In 1838 the first
"ocean greyhound," the *Great Western*, steamed across the
Atlantic from Bristol to New York in 15 days — half the time
usually demanded by sailing packets.

Land travel also felt the influence of the steam-engine.   In
1808 Richard Trevithick built a railway in London on which

the *Catch-me-who-can*, one of the first steam locomotives ever built, made from twelve to fifteen miles an hour. A miner's son,

The Steam Locomotive George Stephenson, became interested in the idea, experimented with it, and in 1825 turned out an engine capable of drawing ninety tons at twelve miles an hour. Railways were opened — the railway from Stockton to Darlington in 1825, and the Liverpool-Manchester Railway a few years later.

It was long considered dangerous to ride on the "steam-waggons," and many preferred the good old stage-coach.

The Steam Press But even the timid could profit by the steam-engine in another way, for newspapers were now printed by steam-power. The first steam printing press was installed by the London *Times* in 1814. Benjamin Franklin, with his old hand-press, might have turned out with great effort some 2000 printed sheets in one day. The new press of the *Times* in 1814 could print the same number in less than two hours.[1] The rapidity and cheapness of printing enabled publishers to sell books, pamphlets, and newspapers so cheaply that even the poorer classes could buy reading matter. Had there been no Industrial Revolution it would have been useless to teach the poor to read, for they could not have afforded to buy books. Cheap newspapers, moreover, informed the workingman on political questions. In this way the steam printing press became the invaluable ally of universal education and of democracy.

The steam printing press, the steam locomotive, and the steamboat were only a few of the children of Watt's steam-engine.

Continuity of the Industrial Revolution For with every new generation, new uses for machinery and new applications for power were discovered. The nineteenth century was indeed the age of steam.

But the age of steam is passing, and a more powerful force which we call electricity is being harnessed to our streetcars and trains, is turning our machines and printing our newspapers. This new servant of man, since the invention of the telegraph (1832), the telephone (1876), and the wireless (1895), will carry messages for him with lightning speed across continents and over wide oceans.

[1] So great has been the advance of printing during the last hundred years that in 1914 a sextuple Hoe Perfecting Press, run by electricity, would print, fold, and count 24,000 twenty-four-page newspapers per hour.

Flying-machines, submarines, sky-scrapers, — the unreal dreams of a century ago, — are the common realities of to-day. When in the thirteenth century Roger Bacon talked about the possibility of flying-machines, he was laughed at. But his fancy has become fact. The "Little Lame Prince" flying through the air on his enchanted carpet, once existed only in the land of fairy-tales, but to-day one does not have to be a prince to possess an aëroplane as good as any enchanted carpet. It is the spirit of invention which has made dreams and fairy-tales come true. And it is the spirit of invention which marks us off from the savages. The Australian aborigine has used his boomerang for many centuries, but the American sportsman may buy an improved rifle every year. Ever since the Industrial Revolution we have gone on, inventing machines to wash our clothes, to churn our milk, to play our pianos, steam-shovels to dig our canals, and vacuum cleaners to sweep our floors. Mechanical invention is the order of the day.

ECONOMIC EFFECTS OF THE INDUSTRIAL REVOLUTION

Direct results of the mechanical inventions appeared in an expansion of industry and commerce, in a growth of cities, and in an increase of wealth.

Machines made it possible to manufacture, to mine, and to farm on an enormous scale. For example, only 17,350 tons of iron were taken from English mines in 1740; but in 1910 the iron produced amounted to more than 10,000,000 tons. The value of British cotton manufactures increased from $1,000,000 in 1760 to $600,000,000 in 1910. If every man and woman in the New World were set to work at an old-fashioned spinning-wheel, all together could not make as much thread as is now made by machinery. Even agriculture has become more fruitful — with scientific methods and with improved plows, self-binders, and automatic churns. Moreover, entirely new industries have grown up. Canned fruit, phonographs, photographs, automobiles, torpedoes, telephones, matches, patent-medicine, — these are a few of the new manufactures.

Commerce has expanded with industry, for there are now more commodities to sell than ever before. And it is easier **Increase of** to sell them. Ocean-liners, railways, macadamized **Commerce** roads, telegraphs, telephones, and cheap postal service make the world seem very small and very compact. Transportation is now so cheap and rapid that fruit can be shipped without spoiling from South America to Europe. Easy communication enables different countries to specialize in particular products — enables Great Britain to make cloth and cutlery for other nations, while relying upon Russia and Canada for its wheat supply. The increase in commerce can perhaps best be expressed in figures. For instance, the cotton trade trebled in fifteen years (1788–1803). The United States exported 275 bales of cotton in 1792, and 9,256,000 bales in 1913. The commerce of the United States and Europe increased 800 per cent in half a century (1830–1880).

The development of commerce and industry has been attended by remarkable increases of population — for clothes **Growth of** could be made and food produced more easily than **Population** ever before in the world's history. In the first half of the nineteenth century, the population of England was doubled. During the nineteenth century the population of Europe, roughly speaking, grew from 175,000,000 to 392,000,000.

This increased population has been largely concentrated in cities. The tendency of allied industries to locate in the same **Growth of** place, the demands of commerce, and the natural at- **Cities** tractiveness and conveniences of urban life, may be ascribed as causes for the growth of cities. Most of the people of Europe once lived in the country, but now three-fourths of the population of England is urban. The London of the seventeenth century, with its half a million inhabitants, has become the metropolis of the world with some seven millions of human beings. At the opening of the nineteenth century Europe possessed fourteen cities of more than 100,000 inhabitants; at the close of the century there were 140 such cities.

Rapid as the increase in population has been, the multiplication of wealth has been more phenomenal. The myriad iron fingers of machinery are able to produce much more than enough wealth to support the added millions of people. That is why the savings banks' deposits mount up in the United States alone to five billions of dollars. Surplus wealth would be sufficient to support more millions of people, or to give comforts Increase of and even luxuries to the present population. But in Wealth large part, it is accumulated in the hands of relatively few very rich men, whose mansions, yachts, and touring cars put to shame the palaces and coaches of a Louis XIV. At first sight it seems strange that the greatest benefits of the Industrial Revolution should be monopolized by a minority. The reason is not to be discovered in the mechanical inventions themselves, but in a second aspect of the Industrial Revolution — the formation of the factory system.

CAPITALISM AND THE FACTORY SYSTEM

Up to this point we have been studying the Industrial Revolution as a transition from hand-labor to machine-labor; we now regard it as a transformation of the independent Labor and home-laborer into the wage-paid factory laborer. Capital Before the Industrial Revolution, most work had been before the done in the home of the worker: the cobbler lived Revolution over his shop, the weaver had his loom in his own attic, the spinning-wheel stood by the cradle. The shoemaker bought his leather from the tanner, and with his own tools made it into shoes, which he sold directly to his customers.

Even before the invention of machinery this medieval system began to give way, and the independent workman became partially dependent on the capitalist. The richer master-shoemakers ceased working themselves and hired more journeymen; the journeymen practically became day-laborers. In the woolen industry there were arising rich merchants who paid weavers so much a yard for converting the yarn into cloth. The beginnings of the factory-system were already to be seen, where the merchant manufacturer had gathered half a dozen looms in a shed or attic, and hired weavers to work therein for wages.

Thus the separation of labor and capital, of worker and employer, had already begun before the invention of machinery. But the true revolution did not come until the adoption of

power-machinery — and then factories sprang up like mushrooms.   For heavy machinery has to be set up in special
Factories   buildings, and it does not pay to erect a water-wheel
and   or to purchase a costly steam-engine, unless its power
Machines   can be transmitted to a large number of machines.
In order to run a number of machines, there must be many at-
tendants who will work at regular hours, for the machine must
not be left to rust whenever the workman feels lazy or tired.
The result is the erection of great factories, into which hundreds
and thousands of workmen file every morning at the sound of
the whistle, to work until the whistle shall blow again at the
close of the day.   And as machines are grouped together in
factories, so factories are collected in factory-cities, the cloth-
mill beside the thread-factory, the gun-shop beside the blast-
furnace.   The weaver now spends his days in the factory, and
goes home to sleep in the tenement house.   Home labor and the
cottage have largely disappeared before the factory-city.

Wherever the factory has appeared, it has brought with it
two new social classes — the capitalist and the wage-earner.
New   The old régime had its nobles and serfs, its gild-
Divisions of masters and journeymen, its merchants, shopkeepers,
Society   and clerks; but the factory-city knows neither gild-
masters nor journeymen, nobles nor serfs, but only capitalists
and wage-earners.   The wage-earning class we call the proletariat; the factory-owners form a new subdivision of the bourgeoisie,
which now consists of industrial capitalists, bankers, merchants,
shopkeepers, and professional men.

The first industrial capitalists were men like Arkwright
— Sir Richard Arkwright, inventor of the water-frame and
Capitalists   "father of the factory-system."   He was what we
            might now call a "promoter," a man who pushes
new business enterprises.   It was his part to erect factories, to
install machines, to hire workers, to organize the business.   In
addition, he acted as superintendent of his factories.   Speeding
along from mill to mill in his "coach and four," he saw that each
mill was running properly, that the workmen were not idle, that
the machines were in good order.   And finally, he purchased the
raw cotton and disposed of the finished thread.

These three functions of promoter, superintendent, and salesman were at first fulfilled by most factory-owners. But as the factory-system became more complex, the factory-owner or capitalist became less and less active. Especially as larger business enterprises were undertaken, the capitalist often became a mere investor: he furnished the money to start with, but salaried employees, acting as superintendents and salesmen, did the organizing, the directing, and the buying and selling. Nevertheless, the capitalist still claimed the major share of the profits, which he called the "interest" or "return on his capital." A man who had money to spare would deliver it to a broker for investment in some business and would thenceforth receive annual dividends without serious expenditure of mental or physical energy. In this manner shrewd investors — the new capitalists — easily acquired great wealth, which in turn gave them weight in politics, exalted them in popular appraisal as well as in their own self-esteem, and enabled them to purchase the *châteaux* of the old feudal nobility.

While the factory raised the capitalist to a position of wealth and power, it reduced the worker to dependence and poverty. After the invention of the power-loom, cloth could **Wage-** be made so rapidly and cheaply by machine [1] that **Earners** the price of cloth fell and the hand-loom weaver could no longer make a living. He was too poor to buy expensive machinery, and, in order to escape starvation, he found himself obliged to work in some capitalist's factory. In the factory, the weaver became merely a human machine — he neither bought his raw materials nor sold his finished product. Experience and skill counted for little, when one had simply to pull levers on a machine, to brush away dirt, and to mend broken threads. All he could sell was his labor. And that had to be sold cheaply. For there were always plenty of poor people ready to work for almost nothing, and naturally no employer would pay high wages when he could avoid it.

Nor was factory-work as pleasant as home-work. The old

[1] "A very good hand-weaver 25 or 30 years of age will weave two pieces of shirting per week. In 1823 a steam-loom weaver about fifteen years of age attending 2 looms could weave 9 similar pieces. In 1826 a steam-loom weaver about fifteen could weave 12 similar pieces in a week, some 15. In 1833 a steam-loom weaver from fifteen to twenty, assisted by a girl of twelve, attending to four looms could weave 18 pieces " (Porter, p. 183).

hand-weaver had been able to hear his children laugh as he plied the shuttle; he could choose his own hours, and divide his time between the garden and the loom. The factory-worker heard the buzz and hum of machinery, instead of children's laughter; he came and went at the sound of the whistle; his work was monotonous, repeating the same trivial operation for ten, twelve, or even eighteen hours a day. Moreover, he had to keep pace with the machine, no matter how tired he might be, for the machine never slackened its speed. It was nervous unhealthy work, and it made nervous unhealthy men.

Yet it was not the grown man who suffered most, but rather the woman and child. Machines could be tended by weak hands as well as by strong, and broken threads were mended more deftly by the nimble fingers of children. So the women left their homes, and the children left their play, to work in the factories and mines. They did not earn much — wife and children together could hardly earn enough to support the family, even though they worked from six in the morning till ten at night. Meanwhile the grown man could seldom find any work to do.

Labor of Women and Children

"No work to do" — that indeed has been the bitter and constant complaint of workingmen ever since the Industrial Revolution first began, and the unemployment problem is still one of the gravest problems resulting from the factory-system. The first machines were looked upon with fear and hatred by the hand-worker — it seemed as if the machine was taking away his work. And often machines were smashed by jealous artisans. But machines were made faster than they could be smashed, and the riots against machinery gradually ceased. The problem of unemployment remained, however, not that there was less work to do than before, — there was on the contrary much more; but the women and children were doing the work, while many men stood idle, unable to find employment. Moreover, "hard-times" were frequent, when factories were closed down for months, and the factory-hands left without work or food.

New Problems: Unemployment

A second great problem was the draining of sturdy farmers into city slums. English statesmen were deeply perturbed when they beheld the disappearance of the independent farmer-class — the "yeomen" — before whose valor foreign armies anciently had fled. The process of inclosure, by which, as we have seen, rich farmers in the eighteenth and early nineteenth centuries were buying up the land for large-scale cultivation, led, in connection with the Industrial Revolution, to the general removal of the yeomen from the land to the factories, there to become wage-earners with hardly a spark of their old independent spirit.

New Problems: Disappearance of the Yeomanry

The greatest problem was the deterioration of the working-class under the capitalistic system. Hours were too long, wages too small, and conditions unhealthful and insanitary. The once independent and home-loving yeoman had lost home and independence. His shoulders stooped from bending long hours over machines. Constant indoor work had driven the ruddiness from his cheeks. Worst of all, the employment of women and children seemed to have the most terrible results. The babies of factory-women, weak and without proper care, died in alarming numbers. The children, breathing the close air of the mill, were pale and sickly, and developed into stunted and deformed men and women. And to cap the climax, there seemed to be a shocking increase of vice in the great factory and mining towns. Men who had spent their days in the dark, damp mines spent their hours of rest in the saloon instead of in their cheerless homes. Young boys became drunkards, and working-women, who had no homes to enjoy, and who were separated from their children by the factory, easily fell into immorality and vice.

New Problems: Degradation of Factory-Hands and Miners

What would become of the nation whose workers were in such condition? Of what good were schools if the children were in the factories? Of what good was democracy if the voters were ignorant and depraved? Never had statesmen been confronted with such problems, never had they been forced to answer such questions. Let us see how they responded.

The first impulse was to make laws restraining the undesirable tendencies of factory-industry, or, rather, to enforce the old laws. It will be remembered that mercantilist statesmen of the sixteenth and seventeenth centuries (like Colbert) had issued elaborate regulations for industry. France in 1789 had

eight bulky volumes of rules, prescribing just how work should
be done, with what tools, with what materials, how wide cloth
should be woven, how large buttons should be. In
England the rules were not so elaborate, but the government had felt the same impulse to regulate industry.   Queen Elizabeth, for instance, had a law
passed limiting the number of iron-furnaces, because
the furnaces burned too much wood and destroyed the forests.
Then, there was the celebrated Elizabethan Statute of Artificers, of 1563, which decreed that workmen should serve an
apprenticeship of seven years.   Moreover, the number of apprentices was limited, it being provided in some industries that
there must be at least one grown workman to every three apprentices.   This last measure, if enforced, would have checked
child labor; and the other laws would have rendered factory
industry practically impossible.

Attitude of Government: Era of Repression

In addition to these royal laws in restraint of industry, there
were gild regulations to be obeyed, especially on the Continent, —
regulations which made innovation next to impossible.   And,
finally, there were many restrictions on trade, chartered companies which hampered commerce, customs duties on raw materials,
and tariffs on imported grain, all of which rendered it more difficult for manufacturers to procure cheap materials and cheap
food for their workmen.

We have already observed how the theory and practice of industrial regulation came to be denounced as ruinous by numerous
progressive philosophers of the eighteenth century.
In France Turgot and the other advocates of the
new "political economy" cried *"laissez-faire"* — or
"hands off."   And in 1776 the British citizen, Adam
Smith, published his learned treatise on the *Wealth
of Nations*, in which he held that industry and commerce should
be largely free of restrictions and taxes.   The true strength of a
nation lies in the wealth of its citizens, Adam Smith argued, and
individual wealth is promoted best by liberty.   Restrictions are
useless and even harmful.   Each man knows best how to make
himself rich, and if each man in the nation were rich, the nation
would be rich.   Therefore, each individual should be allowed
freedom in business, unhampered by laws or restrictions.

Era of Non-Interfer-ence: " Laissez-faire "

Other philosophers went even further, to show that interference with industry was not only unwise, but positively immoral and contrary to man's "natural rights." The "Economic idea that there were certain natural rights of man Individualism" had become a favorite one with eighteenth-century philosophers; and had not only exercised an influence over philosophical speculation but had found its way even into documents of state, such as the American Declaration of Independence and the French "Declaration of the Rights of Man." From the dogma enshrined in the latter, that "private property is an inviolable and sacred right," it was an easy step to the conviction that each human being had a sacred and inviolable "right" to make money in whatever way he chose. The "liberty" of the French Revolution was promptly and successfully applied to economics. Manufacturers and capitalists must be "free."

This belief in "natural rights" was fortified by another product of eighteenth-century philosophy — the popularity of "natural laws." Since physical laws had been for- "Economic mulated for the movements of the stars, why could not Laws" "laws" be found which would explain why a nation is prosperous, or why some people are rich while others are poor? The problem seemed fairly simple, and many political economists, especially in Great Britain, came forward with solutions. There must always be poverty, said one,[1] because there is not enough wealth to go around. If the poor men were given larger wages, they would have larger families and so there would be more mouths to feed, and as much poverty as before. Rent, said another, is not determined by the greed of the landlord, but by a natural law. Government can do nothing to relieve misery, vice, and suffering, which are referable in last instance to the inexorable operation of the eternal natural laws of sound political economy. The best results and the greatest prosperity, therefore, are not to be obtained by man-made laws. But how then? By "enlightened self-interest." According to the political economists of the time, each man should be concerned only with his own gain, and should let others shift for themselves, for each man knows best how to take care of

[1] Malthus.

himself, and if all are well taken care of (by themselves individually), the state will be prosperous.   The golden rule and the command to love one's neighbor appeared now as pretty sentiments which it would be folly to practice.   "He helps others who helps himself."   "Private interest is the great source of public good."

Such a justification of selfishness found ready acceptance as the Industrial Revolution progressed.   The old interpretation of Christianity which taught unselfishness and humility seemed to be passing away before the rise of a new school of moral philosophers, who believed, in the words of Emerson, that "a man contains all that is needful to his government within himself . . . all real good or evil that can befall him, must be from himself."   And as the prosperous mill-owner looked back on his own life, it seemed to him indeed as if his success had been won simply by his own thrift, enterprise, and brains.   If others had been as sober, industrious, and intelligent as himself, they, too, would have been wealthy, respected, and good citizens.   And so it came to be asserted in many so-called Christian countries that each man should fight for himself, and "the devil take the hindermost."

The application of the new theories of individualism and liberty demanded three things.   (1) The abolition of all govern-

Demands of the New Economics mental restrictions on industry.   The state should be merely a big policeman to prevent robbery, murder, and sedition.   (2) The abolition of all gilds, chartered companies, and monopolies, which might obstruct free competition.   (3) The prohibition of workingmen's unions. Each individual workingman should be allowed to make his own bargain or "free contract" with the employer.   Unions, in attempting to compel employers to raise wages or to shorten hours, interfered with this right of "free contract."   It was rank tyranny, said the champions of industrial liberty, to interfere with any workingman's sacred right freely to sell his labor as cheaply as he pleased.   Let each wage-earner make his separate bargain with his employer, and if the worker wants more wages than the employer will pay, let him be free to seek employment elsewhere or to go without work.

The demands of economic "liberty" were achieved in most

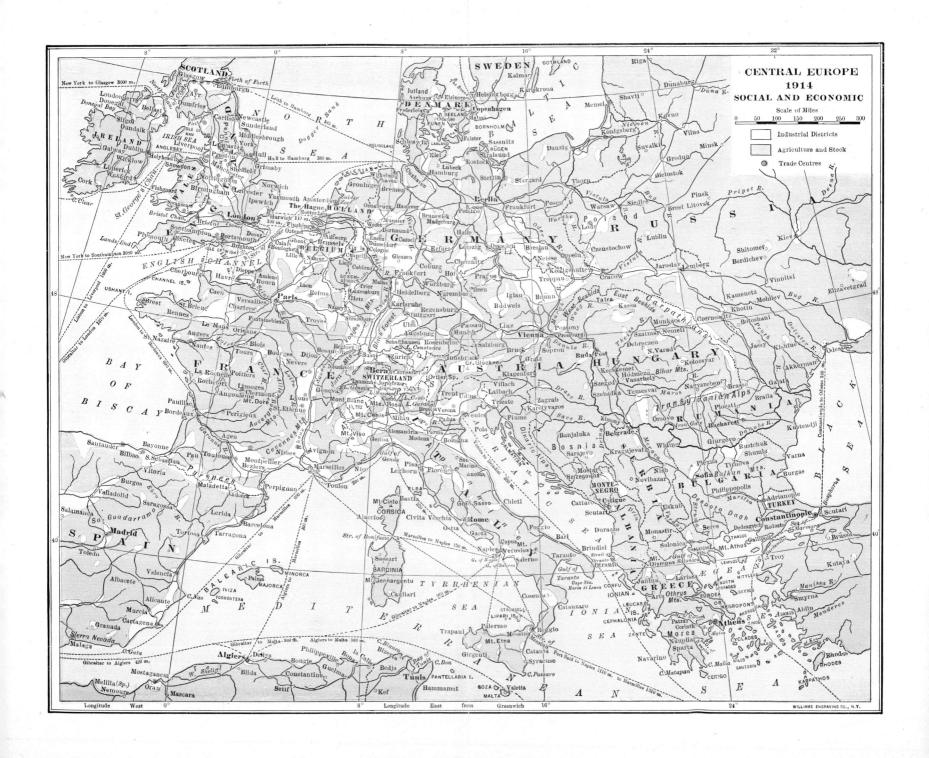

CENTRAL EUROPE
1914
SOCIAL AND ECONOMIC

Scale of Miles

0   50   100   150   200   250   300

☐ Industrial Districts
☐ Agriculture and Stock
◉ Trade Centres

WILLIAMS ENGRAVING CO., N.Y.

countries during the nineteenth century, as the influence of the industrial capitalists became strong in politics. In Great Britain during the first thirty or forty years of the century, Emancipation, industry and commerce were rendered almost entirely free of restriction. Similarly in France and in Industry the United States manufacturers were allowed great freedom. For example, in France in 1791 and in Great Britain in 1800, combinations of workingmen were forbidden. Industrial liberty became the order of the day in every industrial state.

It was expected that with the achievement of liberty, happiness and prosperity would be attained. And truly Great Britain, whose industry was most completely emancipated, "Liberty" grew very wealthy; her capitalists were more pros- and the perous, and her factories and ships more numerous Capitalists than those of any other nation. The fruits of liberty seemed to be as precious as the golden apples of ancient fable.

Yet along with the golden apples, the tree of liberty brought forth bitter and unsightly fruit for the workers. The early factories were ugly, ill-ventilated, poorly lighted, and in- "Liberty" sanitary buildings, hastily and cheaply built. "In and the these dingy buildings, choked with dust and worn with Wage-Earners overwork, the English freemen enjoyed to the utmost the blessed privilege of freedom of contract." In the mines, too, women and children worked along with the men. Women and girls were harnessed to coal-carts, creeping on all fours through the low-roofed galleries of the coal mines.

In the early nineteenth century a great crusade was preached in England against negro slavery, and slave owners in British colonies were forbidden to work their slaves more than nine hours a day, or six hours for children. But the white citizens of Great Britain received no such protection. There was a law by which pauper children could be forced to work, and under this law thousands of poor children, five and six years old, were taken from their homes, sent from parish to parish to work in factories, and bought and sold in gangs like slaves. In the factories they were set to work without pay, the cheapest of food being all they could earn. If they refused to work, irons were put around their ankles, and they were chained to the machine, and at night they were locked up in the sleeping-huts. The working day was long — from five or six in the morning till nine or ten at night. Often the children felt their arms ache with fatigue and their eyelids grow heavy with sleep, but they were kept awake by the whip of the overseer.   Many of the little children died of over-work, and others were carried off by the diseases which were bred by filth, fatigue, and insufficient food.

When the attention of factory-owners was drawn to these conditions, they replied that business would not pay if employees worked less or received larger wages, that no employer would intentionally misuse his employees, and that anyway it was wrong for government to meddle with a man's private business. With this answer they dismissed the problem, and would do nothing to relieve the suffering of the workers in factory or mine.   What few measures were enacted to restrict child labor and to improve factory conditions in the first half of the nine-teenth century were the work of Tory landowners, not of Liberal factory-owners.   The reforms were trifling, however, and the working classes everywhere seemed to be sinking into abject poverty.   Instead of a boon to mankind, machinery appeared to be but a cruel instrument of oppression in the hands of con-scienceless capitalists.

Bourgeois economists might explain that poverty resulted from inexorable economic *laws;* but during the nineteenth century

Opposition to Economic Individual-ism: the Socialists

a new class of theorists was arising to predict better things for the workingman.   The economists had emphasized the rights of the individual; the new theorists thought more about the betterment of so-ciety than about the enrichment of a few individuals; they exhorted men to be social, not selfish.   It was quite natural, then, that such reformers should be styled Socialists.

Robert Owen (1771–1858) was one of the best-known early Socialists.   As manager and part owner of large cotton mills at New Lanark in Scotland, Owen was well acquainted with the evils of the factory-system.   He first tried to make New Lanark a model community.   How well he succeeded may be judged from his own words : "For 29 years we did without the neces-sity for magistrates or lawyers ; without a single legal punish-ment ; without any known poor rates ; without intemperance or religious animosities.   We reduced the hours of labour, well

educated all the children from infancy, greatly improved the condition of the adults, diminished their daily labour, paid interest
on capital, and cleared upwards of £300,000 of profit." The
success of the New Lanark experiment made Owen famous as a
social reformer. He believed that communities like New
Lanark should be formed all over the world and federated in a
great world-republic. Each community should consist of about
1200 people, combining farm and factory life, all living in one
large building, and sharing the profits of their work. Many
people were antagonized by Owen's attacks on Christianity, and
by his loose views on the question of marriage. Moreover,
several attempts to set up Owenite communities [1] met with discouraging failure. When Owen died in 1858, it was already clear
that society would not be reorganized according to his scheme.[2]

While Owen was attempting to reform society in Great Britain,
Saint-Simon and Fourier were advocating visionary schemes in
France. Comte Henri de Saint-Simon (1760–1825) Saint-Simon
appealed to Louis XVIII to establish a new régime and Fourier
in which men of science would rule in the interests of industry.
François Marie Fourier (1772–1837), on the other hand, elaborated a system more like that of Robert Owen, based upon independent industrial communities (*phalanges*) of 1800 persons, in
which earnings should be distributed $\frac{5}{12}$ to labor, $\frac{4}{12}$ to capital,
and $\frac{3}{12}$ to talent. For ten years Fourier waited in his rooms at
noon every day, awaiting the arrival of some wealthy man who
might take up his scheme. Needless to say, he was disappointed. After his death a *phalange* was instituted at Brook
Farm in Massachusetts, but without permanent success.

Saint-Simon and Fourier were prominent in the first quarter
of the nineteenth century. In the next generation Socialism was
represented in France by Louis Blanc (1811–1882), Louis Blanc
a brilliant Parisian journalist, who vigorously condemned industrial competition and proposed that the state should

---

[1] At Orbiston (Scotland); at New Harmony (Indiana, U. S. A.); at Ralahine
(Ireland); and at Tytherly (England).

[2] One important result of Owen's work was the establishment of coöperative
stores, in which the profits were divided among the members of the coöperative
society. There were more than 1400 such stores in the United Kingdom in 1906,
with about 2,250,000 members. Owen is likewise remembered as an early and
vigorous advocate of trade-unionism.

create "social workshops." Each of these social workshops was to be independent and the workingmen themselves were to choose managers and divide the profits.

Louis Blanc's ideas appealed directly to many of the working-men, whereas Fourier and Saint-Simon had been able to interest only a few philanthropists or faddists of the upper classes. But Louis Blanc was hardly more successful in regenerating society.[1] Owen, Saint-Simon, Fourier, Blanc, — all dreamed of ideal *systems* which were never realized. It was not until 1848 that the Socialist movement appeared as an organized party, with a political program.[2]

Although the early Socialists — Owen, Saint-Simon, Fourier, Blanc — failed to organize permanent socialistic parties, and failed to realize their dreams, they at least forced people to think about social problems, and to react against the *laisser-faire* philosophy. The socialistic theories of Robert Owen in England, and of Louis Blanc in France, were reflected in the be-lief of many workingmen that the capitalist made large profits at the wage-earner's expense.[3] Hoping to obtain justice, the work-ingmen turned to trade-unions and to democratic agitation and to all sorts of visionary schemes. This growing unrest on the part of the lower classes in the cities, with the demand for democracy and for economic equality, was destined to exercise a profound influence upon the history of the later nineteenth century.

IMMEDIATE EFFECTS OF THE INDUSTRIAL REVOLUTION UPON POLITICS

During the first half of the nineteenth century the problems of the working classes were overshadowed by the rise of the middle classes. For the immediate effect of the In-dustrial Revolution was to weaken and impoverish the lower classes while it strengthened and enriched the bourgeoisie or middle classes. The expansion of industry, the growth of commerce, the increase of wealth, and the rise of cities, which we have just reviewed, meant

The Bourgeoisie and its Political Ambitions

---

[1] See below, p. 255.   [2] See below, p. 257.

[3] Making toward much the same end was the agitation in England of the group of so-called "Christian Socialists," including such distinguished clergymen and writers as J. F. D. Maurice (1805–1872) and Charles Kingsley (1819–1875).

that thousands of wholesale merchants, bankers, and promoters were acquiring wealth, and that thousands of shops were being opened up to supply food, clothing, shoes, and luxuries to the new urban population. The financial and commercial bourgeoisie, and the shop-keeping class (which was between the bourgeoisie and the lower class), were, therefore, more important and more powerful than ever before. Allied with these older middle classes, there was a new class — the class of industrial capitalists created by the Industrial Revolution. To the industrial bourgeoisie belonged the men who owned factories, mines, foundries, machine-shops, mills, and railways.

It was inevitable that these men of the middle classes, the favored children of the Industrial Revolution, should exercise a powerful influence upon politics. Men who by their energy and determination had forced themselves ahead in the world of business were not likely to rest until they had won a place for themselves in politics. They were the "captains of industry," and they were more important to the nation than old-fashioned feudal nobles. Why then should they not be given positions of power and dignity in the government? Why should not they be the trusted advisers of the king? Why should they not be the upper class instead of the middle class?

Over and above natural ambition, the middle class, and especially the factory-owners, had economic motives for political activity. (1) The burdensome royal regulations, Economic inherited from mercantilist legislators, interfered Motives for with the new methods of machine-production and Activity must be abolished. Cloth must be made in the of the cheapest way possible, not as some ancient statute Bourgeoisie prescribed. Industry must be set free. (2) In the second place, the factory-owners wanted political power in order to prevent the factory-hands from forming trade-unions or demanding higher wages. (3) Moreover, there were customs duties on grain, which increased the cost of living, and thus made it necessary to pay higher wages; there were often customs duties on the raw materials for manufacture; and there were many vexatious hindrances to commerce, such as tolls, interior customs lines, etc. All of these must be done away with. In making their demands, the middle class relied not so much on

numerical strength as on other sources of influence. After
all, the bankers, factory-owners, and merchants were few compared with the great mass of the population. But they were
wealthy and could afford to buy votes or seats in Parliament.

Political
Influence
of the
Bourgeoisie

They were energetic, domineering, and self-reliant.
They claimed, moreover, to represent "industry";
since the greatness of a nation depended upon the
prosperity of its industries, these men who represented
industry had to be taken into consideration. It was felt that if
business were prosperous, the government would have plentiful
resources. The rate of wages was also said to depend upon prosperity, and capitalists, then as now, could say that if business
was disturbed, many would be thrown out of work. By dwelling
upon this argument the bourgeoisie could usually obtain the
support of the workingmen and of the shopkeepers in times of
stress, and threaten revolution in order to enforce bourgeois
demands.

The effect of the Industrial Revolution in strengthening the
political influence of the middle classes can be seen most clearly

Middle-
class
Political
Achieve-
ments in
England:
Repre-
sentation in
Parliament,
1832

in England. Parliament, as we have noticed in an
earlier chapter,[1] had come under the control of a
small group of Tory landlords and Whig nobles, and
therefore afforded practically no direct representation
to the middle classes. Great industrial towns like
Manchester and Birmingham were without representatives in the House of Commons, while scores of
little villages sent two members each to Parliament.
Reform had often been talked of before, but in 1832 the bourgeoisie had become strong enough to carry a Reform Bill which
gave representation to the larger factory towns and enfranchised the richer classes in town and country.

Of this Reform Bill of 1832 we shall speak at greater length
in the following chapter; for the present we are interested in it
only as a political result of the Industrial Revolution. We shall
be content at this point to observe (1) that the towns enfranchised were predominantly factory-towns, (2) that the people
who demanded parliamentary reform most zealously, and
profited most by it, were the members of the industrial bour-

[1] See Vol. I, ch. xiv.

geoisie. In Manchester, for instance, the reform gave votes to 6726 "ten-pound" householders out of a total population of 187,022 persons; that is, the well-to-do business men, who could afford to live in fine houses, were enfranchised. The middle class had gained a voice in the House of Commons.

When the factory-owners tried to use their new power, however, they discovered that Parliament was only half-reformed. The House of Lords, aristocratic in its very constitution, could set at naught the demands of the House of Commons. A test case came up in 1835. The men who had championed parliamentary reform were then advocating a reform of municipal corporations, and had a majority for the reform in the Lower House, but encountered stubborn opposition in the House of Lords. In their anger some of the Reformers even threatened to abolish that ancient and honorable institution. Finally, the bill was passed, doing away with the oligarchic town corporations which had tyrannized over many of the cities, and allowing all ratepayers to vote for aldermen and mayor. This was a second triumph for the middle class, and allowed the newly-rich factory-owners to supplant the old cliques in municipal politics. It also dealt a blow at the prestige of the aristocratic House of Lords.

Control of Municipal Government, 1835

The greatest achievement of the middle class in England was the repeal of the Corn Laws in 1846. The "Corn Laws"[1] were parliamentary statutes forbidding the importation of foreign wheat unless the average price of wheat in the United Kingdom was 70s. per quarter.[2] If wheat was scarce and sold for over 70s., foreign wheat was admitted under a heavy duty, which became lighter as the price of wheat rose. The effect of this duty was to make bread very expensive and in hard times to cause untold misery to the poor. Nevertheless, the landowners defended the Corn Laws, because high prices meant high rents, and because they thought that England ought to raise her own grain. The new manufacturing class, however, believing in the theories which Adam Smith had formulated, complained that the

Middle-class Opposition to the Corn Laws

---

[1] "Corn" meant grain, not simply maize.

[2] In 1815, the normal price had been fixed at 80s. per quarter. It was changed to 70s. in 1822.

Corn Laws increased the cost of living, and thus not only caused much suffering but made it necessary for manufacturers to pay higher wages. Many of the bourgeoisie were opposed to any kind of a protective tariff. They thought the duty of 6*d*. a pound on raw wool handicapped the British textile industries. Such duties, it was claimed, prevented free exchange between nations, and, if other nations were not free to sell their products to England, how could England expect other nations to buy her manufactures? For these reasons the leading merchants of London as early as 1820 asked Parliament to repeal the protective tariff. The protective system gave way little by little: duties on silk were reduced in 1824; on raw wool, in 1825. But the landlords would not surrender the Corn Laws without a severe struggle.

The agitation against the Corn Laws was determined, persistent, and well-organized. In 1838 the Anti-Corn Law League was formed to work for the free importation of wheat, and found gifted leaders in Richard Cobden and John Bright, two remarkable manufacturers. Richard Cobden owned cotton-printing works at Manchester and at Sabden. John Bright was the son and partner of a Rochdale mill-owner. Cobden supplied the arguments, Bright the passionate oratory. They well knew that cheaper flour would benefit their own class, the factory-owners, and they eloquently demonstrated to the workmen that the Corn Laws were responsible for the sufferings of the poor. Other factory-owners generously contributed to the campaign funds, while Cobden, Bright, and others harangued mass-meetings throughout the country, and pamphlets were given out by the million.

Nature assisted the Free Traders. The harvest of 1845 was seriously injured by rain, and the potato crop, upon which

Repeal of the Corn Laws, 1846 Ireland depended, was ruined by the blight. Thousands died of starvation. To prevent thousands more from falling victims to famine, the Corn Laws had to be repealed. Although a majority of the Conservatives, representing the landed interests, were anxious to maintain the tariff, a Corn Law Repeal Bill was proposed by Sir Robert Peel, the Conservative prime minister, whose father, by the way, owned a cotton mill. The bill was carried by a combination of the 223 Liberals with 104 Conservatives against 129 Conservatives. By its provisions all duties on grain were to be abolished within three years; and in the same year duties on foreign manufactures were greatly reduced. Soon after the Corn Laws were repealed, Sir Robert Peel had to resign the leadership of the Conservatives, since he had defied his party in advocating the repeal. Richard Cobden, it is interesting to notice, received nearly £80,000 as a spontaneous and grateful tribute from his friends and followers.

The repeal of the Corn Laws in 1846 marks the triumph of the middle classes in England over the old aristocracy. By the Reform Act of 1832 they had secured representation in Parliament; by the Municipal Reform of 1835 they had gained control of municipal politics; and they had defeated the landowners on the tariff issue. The next phase of the struggle in England was to be characterized by the attempts of the workingmen to gain political power and to better themselves.

In France the Industrial Revolution did not get thoroughly under way until after the end of the Napoleonic Wars, and indeed not until 1825, when the prohibition on the ex- **The New** port of machinery from England was removed. France, **Industry** moreover, had a larger number of small farmers than **in France** England, who represented the agricultural interests as over against the industrial classes of the cities. Throughout the greater part of the nineteenth century, the majority of the French people lived entirely by agriculture.

French industry, though less important than English, nevertheless grew rapidly. In 1789 only 250,000 tons of coal were mined in France; in 1830, 1,800,000 tons were produced. In 1822 France exported to the United States and England 99,000,-000 francs' worth of silk; in 1847 the figure had risen to 165,000,-000 francs. In 1788 the value of woolen exports was 24,000,000 francs; in 1838, 80,000,000. The cotton industry tripled in the 25 years from 1815 to 1840.

This industrial expansion was partly the cause and partly the result of the increasing political power of the French middle classes. During the reign of Charles X the bourgeoisie had been offended by the reassertion of the old aristocratic spirit, and had suffered financial injuries. For instance, the interest on government bonds was cut down from 5 per cent to 3 per cent in 1825; in the following year, moreover, the duty on wool was raised to 30 per cent and that on steel to 100 per cent, while the tariff on grain remained at a high level. The manufacturers thus were forced to pay dearly for the steel of which their machines were made, for the raw wool of which they made cloth, and for their food.

All this was changed, however, by the Revolution of 1830, which put Louis Philippe on the throne as a constitutional mon-

The Bourgeoisie and the Revolution of 1830

arch. The aristocratic Chamber of Peers was now weakened and subordinated to the middle-class Chamber of Deputies, elected by 200 franc tax-payers. From 1830 to 1848 France was a middle-class monarchy. Yet the king and the bourgeoisie were not completely in harmony. While on the one hand the

The Middle-class Monarchy of Louis Philippe, 1830–1848

middle classes defended Louis Philippe against the supporters of the old régime, against the working-class Republicans, against any kind of social revolution; on the other hand jealousy betrayed them into many quarrels with the king and with each other.

During the first part of Louis Philippe's reign the bourgeoisie feared that the "Legitimists," as the supporters of Charles X were called, would dethrone Louis Philippe, and that the Republican agitators would incite the people of Paris to revolt against the monarchy. Consequently newspapers were forbidden to print attacks upon the existing government, and fines were imposed on journals which sympathized too strongly either with Legitimist or Republican views. The business men demanded peace and order: they were satisfied with things as they were, and became a "party of resistance" to further change. When the danger from Legitimists and Republicans passed, the ruling party itself split up. One faction under Thiers held that the ministry should be responsible to the Chamber, not to the king. "The king reigns and does not govern." This group would have made the king a figurehead for the rule of the middle classes. Thiers was prime minister in 1840, but he lost his popularity because, by appealing to the Napoleonic tradition of military glory, he almost involved France in war. The business men were afraid war would disturb industry, and Guizot, the chief of the rival faction, who succeeded Thiers, and was minister from 1840 to 1848, steadfastly endeavored to maintain peace abroad and order at home. He made sure of a majority in the Chamber by purchasing the support both of electors and deputies with government offices, tobacco licenses, and other pecuniary favors. When a newspaper censured the government, he brought suit against the editor. When Radicals demanded that the number of voters should be increased, Guizot retorted: "Work and grow rich, and you will become voters."

What reforms were made during the "July Monarchy" were essentially middle-class reforms, and strongly resembled the contemporaneous reforms in England. There was a municipal reform in 1831, by which the municipal councils were made elective, only the largest taxpayers and professional men being allowed to vote. There was a tariff reform, moderating some of the most burdensome duties, though little was done along this line till after 1848. There was an educational reform (1833), providing primary schools in the communes; the number of pupils increased 75 per cent during the reign of Louis Philippe.

Middle-class Political Achievements in France under Louis Philippe

The immediate political results of the Industrial Revolution were strikingly similar in France to those in England. In both countries the middle classes became rich, and obtained an influence in the legislature under a constitutional monarchy. In France it was by the Revolution of 1830. In England it was by the almost revolutionary reform agitation of 1832. In both countries, the middle class, having acquired power, supported middle-class reforms, and refused to extend political rights to the lower classes. In both countries, the lower classes were restless, and many workmen listened readily to democratic and socialistic agitators.

In Germany, or rather in the Germanies, the Industrial Revolution was even more backward than in France. While the Continent had been disturbed by wars (1793–1815), English manufacturers had been perfecting their machinery until now they could undersell German producers. The first political result of the Industrial Revolution in Germany was, therefore, a demand for a protective tariff. Each little state placed duties on imported manufactures,

The New Industry in the Germanies

in order to encourage domestic industry. There were so many German states, however, that this multiplicity of customs duties seriously interfered with commerce. Hoping to overcome this difficulty, Prussia in 1818 established a uniform tariff for all parts of the Prussian kingdom, with a 10 per cent duty on manufactured goods, and 20 per cent on colonial products. Prussia then invited other German states to adopt the same regulations and to unite their customs administrations with hers. After much

The hesitation most of the German states joined with
Zollverein Prussia, and on 1 January, 1834, the *Zollverein*, or Customs Union, went into effect between Prussia, Saxony, Bavaria, and fourteen other German states. Hanover, Baden, Nassau, Brunswick, Luxemburg, and Frankfort-on-Main entered the union later; Austria remained outside. German merchants might now trade as freely within the *Zollverein* as though Germany were a united nation, and still German manufacturers were protected against their British and French competitors by the common customs tariff.

This economic union, brought about in the interests of merchants and manufacturers, with Prussia at its head, paved the way for political union. The business men learned to disregard state boundaries and to think of the *Zollverein* as a nation. Railways were built — 400 miles between 1835 and 1840 — and bound the country more closely together. The rulers and the nobility of each petty principality might resent any attack upon the independence of their realm, and the quarrels between Austria and Prussia might disturb the German Confederation; but behind the scenes, the Industrial Revolution was preparing the stage-setting for the political unification of Germany.

Under the auspices of the *Zollverein*, German industry increased by leaps and bounds, and machine-production rapidly took the place of hand-labor. In the years 1836–1840 the raw cotton annually used by German manufacturers amounted only to 185,000 cwts.; fifteen years later more than 500,000 cwts. were being spun every year. And the spinning machines were so improved that in 1852 each spindle was working twice as rapidly as in 1836. The industrial class increased in numbers; the bourgeoisie grew richer and more powerful; and by 1848 the middle class in Germany was following the example of the middle class in

France and England, in demanding a voice in the government. The effect of the Industrial Revolution in Germany was primarily to unify the country, and then to bring about political reform.

ADDITIONAL READING

General. Brief accounts: J. H. Robinson and C. A. Beard, *The Development of Modern Europe*, Vol. II (1907), ch. xviii; Archibald Weir, *An Introduction to the History of Modern Europe* (1907), ch. vii–ix; Gilbert Slater, *The Making of Modern England*, new rev. ed. (1915), introductory chapter; A. D. Innes, *England's Industrial Development* (1912), Book III; G. H. Perris, *The Industrial History of Modern England* (1914), ch. ii–v; E. P. Cheyney, *An Introduction to the Industrial and Social History of England* (1901), ch. vii, viii; G. T. Warner, *Landmarks in English Industrial History*, 11th ed. (1912), ch. xv–xvii; William Cunningham, *An Essay on Western Civilization in its Economic Aspects*, Vol. II (1910), pp. 225–267; W. J. Ashley, *The Economic Organization of England: an Outline History* (1914), lect. vii, viii. More detailed treatments: Paul Mantoux, *La révolution industrielle au XVIIIᵉ siècle* (1906), probably the best general work, unfortunately not translated into English; H. de B. Gibbins, *Industry in England*, 6th ed. (1910), ch. xx–xxvi, and, by the same author, *Economic and Industrial Progress of the Century* (1903), containing chapters on France and Germany as well as England, perhaps the best general narrative in English; William Cunningham, *The Growth of English Industry and Commerce in Modern Times*, 5th ed., 3 vols. (1910–1912), Vol. III covering the years 1776–1850; Arnold Toynbee, *Lectures on the Industrial Revolution of the Eighteenth Century in England*, new ed. (1913), fugitive lectures, originally published in 1884, by the scholar who is responsible for the phrase "Industrial Revolution"; *Cambridge Modern History*, Vol. X (1907), ch. xxiii on economic changes at the opening of the nineteenth century, and ch. xxiv on the early British economists; R. H. I. Palgrave, *Dictionary of Political Economy*, 3 vols. (1910–1913), a reference work on topics connected with the Industrial Revolution in Great Britain, and Johannes Conrad, *Handwörterbuch der Staatswissenschaft*, 3d rev. ed., 8 vols. (1909–1911), a similar work, valuable for its scholarly articles on German industry.

Inventions and Inventors. C. H. Cochrane, *Modern Industrial Progress* (1904), a popular description; E. W. Byrn, *The Progress of Invention in the Nineteenth Century* (1900); *Dictionary of National Biography*, for lives of such famous inventors as Kay, Arkwright, Hargreaves, Cartwright, Crompton, Newcomen, Watt, Stephenson, etc.; Sir Edward Baines, *History of the Cotton Manufacture in Great Britain* (1835), a celebrated old history of the subject; M. S. Woolman and E. B. McGowan, *Textiles: a Handbook for the Student and the Consumer* (1913), affording up-to-date illustrations of technical processes; R. H. Thurston, *History of the Growth* *of the Steam Engine,* new ed. (1902), in the " International Scientific Series," an admirable popular account; Samuel Smiles, *Lives of the Engineers Boulton and Watt* (1904), and, by the same author, *George and Robert Stephenson* (1904); R. L. Galloway, *History of Coal Mining in Great Britain* (1882), and, by the same author, *Annals of Coal Mining and the Coal Trade* (1898); H. W. Dickinson, *Robert Fulton, Engineer and Artist: his Life and Works* (1913), an excellent study; E. A. Pratt, *A History of Inland Transportation and Communication in England* (1912); A. T. Hadley, *Railroad Transportation, its History and its Laws* (1903); A. W. Kirkaldy and A. D. Evans, *The History and Economics of Transport* (1915), an admirable work; Henry Fry, *History of North Atlantic Steam Navigation, with Some Account of Early Ships and Shipowners* (1896); G. R. Porter, *Progress of the Nation in its Various Social and Industrial Relations,* ed. by F. W. Hirst (1912), a new and convenient edition of a well-known work first published in 1851; Arthur von Mayer, *Geschichte und Geographie der deutschen Eisenbahnen von ihrer Entstehung bis . . . 1890,* 2 vols. (1891), an exhaustive study of the history of railway construction in the Germanies. Popular treatments of more recent inventions are to be found in the " Romance of Reality " Series.

Social and Economic Effects of the Industrial Revolution. D. H. Macgregor, *The Evolution of Industry* (1912), a handy little volume in the " Home University Library "; J. A. Hobson, *The Evolution of Modern Capitalism: a Study of Machine Production,* new rev. ed. (1912), excellent, especially ch. i, v, xvi, xvii; Leone Levi, *History of British Commerce and of the Economic Progress of the British Nation, 1763–1870* (1872), a standard treatise; A. F. Weber, *The Growth of Cities in the Nineteenth Century* (1899), a valuable statistical survey; M. G. Mulhall, *The Dictionary of Statistics,* 4th rev. ed. (1899), together with the supplementary volume of A. D. Webb, *The New Dictionary of Statistics* (1911), an indispensable work of reference; J. L. and Barbara Hammond, *The Village Laborer, 1760–1832: a Study in the Government of England before the Reform Bill* (1911); R. W. C. Taylor, *The Modern Factory System* (1891), uncritical but still useful; Allen Clarke, *The Effects of the Factory System* (1899); Charles Watney and J. A. Little, *Industrial Warfare, the Aims and Claims of Capital and Labour* (1912); A. L. Bowley, *Wages in the United Kingdom in the Nineteenth Century* (1900); A. C. Pigou, *Unemployment* (1914), a brief sketch of one of the gravest problems intensified by the Industrial Revolution, in the " Home University Library." Famous contemporary pictures of the life of the industrial proletariat: Friedrich Engels, *The Condition of the Working-Class in England in 1844;* Benjamin Disraeli, *Sybil, or, The Two Nations;* Charles Kingsley, *Alton Locke;* Charles Dickens, *Oliver Twist;* and for French factory-life the painstaking study of L. R. Villermé, *Tableau de l'état physique et moral des ouvriers employés dans les manufactures de coton, de laine et de soie,* 2 vols. (1840). Later studies of the condition of the working class in France: M. R. L. Reybaud, *Rapport sur la condition morale, intellectuelle et matérielle des* *ouvriers qui vivent de l'industrie de la soie* (1860), *le coton* (1862), *la laine* (1865), *le fer et la houille* (1872), all in the *Mémoires de l'académie des sciences morales et politiques;* Paul Leroy-Beaulieu, *La question ouvrière au XIXe siècle,* 2d ed. (1881), and, by the same author, *Le travail des femmes au XIXe siècle* (1888); Émile Levasseur, *La population française,* 3 vols. (1889–1892); Octave Festy, *Le mouvement ouvrier au début de la monarchie de juillet,* 2 vols. (1908). With special reference to the rise of the factory-system in the Germanies: Werner Sombart, *Der moderne Capitalismus,* 2 vols. (1902), and, by the same author, *Die deutsche Volkswirtschaft im neunzehnten Jahrhundert* (1903).

Economic Individualism. The best guide for the study of the classical economists — the *laisser-faire* advocates of the time — is Charles Gide and Charles Rist, *A History of Economic Doctrines from the Time of the Physiocrats,* Eng. trans. (1915), Book I, ch. iii, Books II–IV. Strong pleas for individualism are made by Herbert Spencer in several of his works, especially in *Man versus the State* (1884), and by Wordsworth Donisthorpe, *Individualism, a System of Politics* (1889).

Beginnings of Modern Socialism. John Spargo, *Socialism: a Summary and Interpretation of Socialist Principles,* new rev. ed. (1909); Thomas Kirkup, *A History of Socialism,* 5th rev. ed. (1913); Werner Sombart, *Socialism and the Social Movement in the Nineteenth Century, 1750–1896,* trans. by A. P. Atterbury (1898); W. D. Guthrie, *Socialism before the French Revolution: a History* (1907); Frank Podmore, *Robert Owen, a Biography,* 2 vols. (1906); Robert Owen, *Life, written by himself,* 2 vols. (1857); J. Tchernoff, *Louis Blanc* (1904), a French biography in the " Bibliothèque socialiste "; Gaston Isambert, *Les idées socialistes en France de 1815 à 1848: le socialisme fondé sur la fraternité et l'union des classes* (1905).

Immediate Political Effects. For the establishment of free trade in Great Britain, see Gilbert Slater, *The Making of Modern England,* new rev. ed. (1915), ch. xi; Bernard Holland, *The Fall of Protection, 1840–1850* (1913); *Cambridge Modern History,* Vol. XI (1909), ch. i; John (Viscount) Morley, *Life of Richard Cobden,* 2 vols. (1881); G. M. Trevelyan, *The Life of John Bright* (1914); Lord Rosebery, *Sir Robert Peel* (1899); C. S. Parker, *Life of Sir Robert Peel,* 3 vols. (1891–1899); *Memoirs of Sir Robert Peel,* 2 vols. (1856–1857). For the establishment of the *Zollverein* in Germany: W. H. Dawson, *Protection in Germany, a History of German Fiscal Policy during the Nineteenth Century* (1904), ch. i, ii; Benjamin Rand, *Selections illustrating Economic History since the Seven Years' War,* 5th ed. (1911), ch. viii; Wilhelm Oncken, *Das Zeitalter des Kaisers Wilhelm,* Vol. I (1890), Book I, *Das deutsche Bürgerthum und sein Eintritt ins Staatsleben.* For the reign of Louis Philippe in France, and for additional results of the Industrial Revolution in western and central Europe, consult the bibliography appended to Chapter XIX.

CHAPTER XIX

DEMOCRATIC REFORM AND REVOLUTION, 1830–1848

DEMOCRACY AND THE INDUSTRIAL REVOLUTION

HAD the social influence of the Industrial Revolution stopped short with the exaltation of the moneyed class, the lot of the working classes to-day would have been wholly miserable; but while with one hand the Industrial Revolution dealt the masses untold injury, with the other it held out a bright promise of the future. To offset the evils of the factory-system it offered a political remedy, a remedy which had never before been seriously tried, — democracy.

Inasmuch as political democracy is both a novel experiment and a fundamental principle of modern government, it is well worth while to make sure of its meaning. "Democracy" is derived from a Greek word meaning the rule of the people. The Greeks, however, meant not the rule of all the people, but only of the free citizens: the slaves who constituted a considerable part of the population in ancient times were absolutely deprived of political power, and were not accounted among "the people." Modern times have given to democracy a wider signification, and to the conception of "the people" a larger scope, including all men, rich and poor alike, and perhaps even women. How to give practical effect to the will of the people was discovered neither in the nineteenth nor completely as yet in the twentieth century; but political democracy has come to mean a fairly definite thing: obedience in political affairs to the will of the majority of the people, as that will is manifested through regular political channels.

Real political democracy in Europe was first made possible, as we hope presently to demonstrate, and first made imperative, by the Industrial Revolution. Spasmodic gropings after democratic government appeared during the period from 1830 to

1848, in Great Britain, France, Belgium, Germany, Austria, Italy, Hungary, in turn as these countries felt the influence of the Industrial Revolution. Those years might be called the period of democracy's infancy. Ever since, the peoples of Europe have gone on, experimenting with the ballot, the *plébiscite*, electoral reform, and all the machinery of majority rule, and have discovered hitherto unsuspected possibilities as well as perils in popular sovereignty.

Political democracy has a very definite meaning as an ideal of government and it is possible to trace its development step by step. But back of political democracy there is a certain faith in human nature, a spirit commanding "the rights of the people to be observed," a profound belief that all men should have, so far as possible, equal opportunities and equal privileges, a feeling which for lack of a better name we call the democratic spirit. In this democratic spirit may be detected, perhaps, several diverse elements. First of all we must acknowledge its debt to Christianity. By placing emphasis on the equality of all men in the sight of God, regardless of rank or wealth, and by enjoining all Christians to love their neighbors as themselves, Christianity gave Europe a great and lasting lesson — a lesson however slowly learned — in true democracy. In the second place, the French Revolution had given to the world the ringing watchwords of "liberty, equality, fraternity," with the ideas of economic liberty, equality before the law, and denial of titled aristocracy, although few outside the middle classes were immediately admitted to a full share in those blessings. Finally, the democratic movement received its great impetus, and bitterness, from the economic grievances created by the Industrial Revolution. The horrifying conditions in mine, in factory, and in sweatshop aroused the pity of the philanthropist, while the workmen were goaded to desperation. With more or less coöperation, the philanthropist on one hand, and the more intelligent workmen on the other, set about to end the economic oppression of the masses, sometimes by factory laws, sometimes by bloody and futile insurrections. Since the middle class had won liberty, why should not the working classes go one step farther and demand that *all* men should be truly free and equal, and brothers indeed! The

The Democratic Spirit

democratic spirit speedily expressed itself (1) in the agitation
for political democracy, (2) in the anti-slavery movement, (3) in
various attempts to relieve the distress of the lower classes,
(4) in various reforms in the direction of religious toleration,
universal education, and the reform of the criminal law.

If democracy was needed as never before to modify the results of the Industrial Revolution, it was also more easy of
attainment than ever before. Feudalism and divine-right
monarchy had practically ceased to be obstacles in the way of
political democracy, having been seriously impaired by the
bourgeoisie. The working classes were congregated in great cities,
where they were easily swayed by public opinion and easily
collected into mobs. A hundred workers in one factory were
more conscious of their common interests than a hundred men
working independently at home. Newspapers could be printed
so cheaply, since the invention of the steam printing press,
that political news might circulate rapidly; pamphlets sold at
a penny apiece or were distributed *gratis*, and reached thousands
who would not have been influenced by speeches. Most important of all, during the early part of the nineteenth century education began to make its way among the masses, enabling workmen to read their newspapers and to learn strange new political
doctrines from the pamphlets of radical philosophers. By all
these circumstances the democratic movement profited. We
shall now study the fruits of that movement, from 1830 to 1848,
in political reform and social legislation in Great Britain, and in
the revolutionary movements of 1848 throughout the Continent.

POLITICAL AND SOCIAL REFORMS IN GREAT BRITAIN

At the opening of the nineteenth century the government of
Great Britain and Ireland conflicted violently with the demo-

Lack of Democracy in Great Britain at Opening of Nineteenth Century
cratic principle in three ways. In the first place,
large classes of the population were excluded from
political rights on account of religion; secondly, the
majority of the people had no voice in electing the
members of Parliament; and thirdly, Parliament was
badly in need of reform. In this section we shall see
how the first of these defects was almost completely remedied
before 1830 and how a start was made on the other two in 1832.

Religious toleration made slow progress among the English people. True, since the Toleration Act of 1689, the Dissenters were no longer imprisoned for their theological con- Religious victions. Even the Roman Catholics were not per- Disabilities secuted as fiercely as two centuries before. But on the statute-books remained laws which, had the authorities executed them rigorously, would have doomed all Roman Catholic priests to perpetual imprisonment, would have fined Catholics (and actually did fine them as late as 1782) for not attending the Anglican Church, would have forced Catholic laymen to pay double land-taxes, and prevented them from inheriting land. Dissenters and Catholics alike hated the Corporation Act (1661), which aimed to exclude all but Church of England men from the municipal corporations, and the Test Act (1673), which prevented Roman Catholics who refused to renounce the doctrine of transubstantiation, and any who had scruples against receiving communion as administered by the Church of England, from holding office under the government Repeal of either in the civil service, in the army, or in the the Test and navy. After long agitation, the Test and Corporation Corporation Acts were at last repealed in 1828. Acts, 1828

The Catholics were not yet satisfied, for they were still excluded from Parliament by an act of 1678 which obliged the members of both Houses to subscribe to a declaration that Roman Catholic worship was idolatrous. In Ireland a determined and well-organized movement to obtain equal polit- Daniel ical rights for Roman Catholics was conducted under O'Connell the leadership of Daniel O'Connell, a lawyer whose boisterous enthusiasm and ready wit won him the whole-hearted support of the Irish peasantry. The serious character of this propaganda was demonstrated by the Clare election of 1828, when O'Connell was put forward against the governmental candidate for the House of Commons. Between forty and fifty thousand excited Catholic peasants, in defiance of their angry Protestant landlords, marched to the polls behind green banners. Priests and politicians helped to keep the rank and file sober and law-abiding. O'Connell received an overwhelming majority, but was excluded from Parliament because he refused to take the required oath. The Clare election convinced the Tory ministry, however, that Ireland was not in a mood to be dallied with, and Sir Robert Peel, the prime minister, was about to yield to O'Connell's demands when King George IV was seized with obstinacy, and dismissed the ministry after a six-hour harangue, in which brandy and passion prevailed over royal discretion. But on second thought the king gave way, and that very night recalled his ministry. Peel then proceeded

Catholic Emancipation, 1829 to put through Parliament a Catholic Emancipation Bill, which received the royal assent on 13 April, 1829, and Roman Catholics were admitted to all offices, excepting those of Guardian or Justice of the United Kingdom, Lord Lieutenant or Lord Deputy in Ireland, Lord High Chancellor, Lord Keeper of the Great Seal, and all those of ecclesiastical and collegiate establishment. The jubilation of the Catholics over this victory was chastened by the simultaneous disfranchisement of almost 200,000 "forty-shilling freeholders" in Ireland.

The first step was taken toward the accomplishment of the other reforms, — *i.e.*, the enlargement of the suffrage and the

Parliamentary Reform reform of Parliament, — in the Reform Bill of 1832. With that bill, as exemplifying the triumph of the bourgeoisie, we already have made some slight acquaintance; in the present chapter the bill receives more extended treatment as an important incident in the struggle for political democracy. The Reform of 1832 dealt chiefly with two great evils: the unrepresentative character of Parliament, and the narrowness of the franchise.

These evils, it will be remembered, had existed in Great Britain throughout the eighteenth century.[1] Efforts to eradicate them had been frustrated by the hostile reaction of English public opinion against the French Revolution, and, yet, simultaneously the Industrial Revolution had brought them into most glaring light. The Industrial Revolution gradually did for democracy in Great Britain what the French Revolution was prevented from doing. That the Parliament was reformed in 1832 and the franchise broadened, was due to a tremendous agitation on the part of the industrial middle class.

[1] From the "Glorious Revolution" of 1689 to the Reform Act of 1832, the British state was essentially aristocratic rather than democratic. For the nature of the "unreformed" Parliament, see Vol. I, pp. 292 f., 433 ff.

From a review of the facts of British history recorded in the two preceding chapters, it is obvious (1) that the Industrial Revolution greatly increased the numbers, wealth, and prestige of the middle classes, (2) that these middle classes believed their future prosperity, and, therefore, the general welfare of the whole country, depended upon their ability to remove mercantilist restraints on trade and industry, to destroy the special privileges of the land-owning aristocracy, and to establish complete *laisser-faire*, (3) that the same classes, largely unrepresented in Parliament, demanded the ballot for themselves in order to realize their economic and political program. While the Tory reaction, headed by the duke of Wellington, was in full swing against "Revolution," Lord John Russell, a Whig, came forward in 1819 as the champion of moderate middle-class reform. Lord Macaulay, though prophesying that universal suffrage would ruin the nation, wrote magazine articles to prove that a little parliamentary reform would do much good. Earl Grey, leader of the Whig party, stately aristocrat as he was, used parliamentary reform as a war-cry against the Tory ministry and as a means of consolidating his own party and attracting the middle classes to the support of the Whigs. Despite the fact that a small group of Radicals won some favor with workingmen by advocating thorough political democracy, — universal manhood suffrage, — the reform advocated by the Whigs was of distinctly moderate character and never embraced any proposal more radical than the extension of the suffrage to the fairly well-to-do middle class. It is interesting to note, however, that many of the more ignorant workingmen joined with their employers in shouting for the Reform Bill of 1832, stupidly believing that it contained provision for universal manhood suffrage, or would lead directly to it.

The margin note: **The Reform Championed by the Whig Party and the Middle Classes**

The Reform controversy began its acute stage in the midst of the excitement occasioned by the news of the successful revolt of the French middle classes in 1830. With heroism worthy of Waterloo, the duke of Wellington, who was then premier, declared emphatically that the old scheme of representation was not only without flaw, but perfectly "satisfactory" to the country at large. The duke's declaration caused his fall, however, and Earl Grey formed a Whig ministry pledged to Reform. The first Reform Bill proposed by the Whigs was defeated early in 1831. Strengthened by the elections of that year, the Whigs in the House of Commons, now a majority, proceeded to pass a second Reform Bill. The House of Lords, stanchly Tory, rejected it. After a short recess the Commons passed a third Reform Bill, somewhat altered from the others in detail; but the Lords were still opposed. The ministry decided to resort to an extreme measure, the creation of enough **Coercion of** new peers, pledged to support the bill, to outvote the **the Lords** obstinate Tory peers. But King William IV, who had been willing to consider Reform until it had become associated with popular violence, refused to create the peers, accepted the resignations of his angry Whig ministers, and invited Wellington again to take command. The people knew what brand of Reform that battle-scarred veteran was likely to give them, and would have none of it. In Birmingham a monster mass-meeting was held, and the Reformers declared their dogged determination to pay no more taxes until the bill was passed — a threat which was repeated throughout the realm. In London, Francis Place, a philosophical tailor who by his own efforts had made a fortune and educated himself, and who stood midway between the whole-souled democrats of the lower class and the middle-class Reformers, now exerted himself on the one hand to keep the masses from actual insurrection, while on the other he threatened the government with revolution and urged middle-class bank-depositors to create a financial panic by withdrawing their gold from the banks. It seemed as if the Whigs were ready to precipitate a civil war, and the victor of Waterloo, unable to command the support of his more timid fellow Tories in further opposing the bill, reluctantly informed the king that it was impossible to form a Tory ministry. Even more reluctantly the king then sent for Earl Grey (15 May, 1832) and promised, as the Whig leader demanded, to create enough new peers to assure the passage of the bill through the **Passage of** House of Lords. The threat proved sufficient, for **the Reform** thereupon the Lords yielded, though somewhat un-**Bill, 1832** graciously, and the Reform Bill received royal assent on 7 June, 1832.

The precise manner in which the Reform Bill of 1832 approached the political evils in the old régime of Great Britain was as follows. (1) *Redistribution of seats.* Certain boroughs containing less than 2000 inhabitants were entirely disfranchised; and boroughs containing between 2000 and 4000 inhabitants lost one of their two seats. Of the 143 seats thus set free, 65 were given to the larger English counties, 8 to Scotland, 5 to Ireland, and 65 to large towns, some of which, including Manchester, Birmingham, Sheffield, and Leeds, had never before been represented. (2) *Reform of the franchise.* In the counties, copyholders and leaseholders of lands worth £10 a year, and tenants-at-will of lands worth £50 a year, were entitled to vote. In the boroughs, the old irregularities were abolished, and a uniform requirement established, namely, that of owning or renting a building worth £10 a year. By this means the number of county electors in England was increased from 247,000 to 370,000, and the borough electors from 188,000 to 286,000; but the proportion of electors to the population was still only 1 to 22, whereas it had been 1 to 32. The workmen in the city and the laborers in the country were still unenfranchised. (3) A third reform was effected by the Reform Bill of 1832, in the *manner of voting.* Hitherto the voting had occupied as many as fifteen days, and the prolonged excitement had been responsible for scandalous bribery, rioting, and drunkenness. Henceforth polling was to be limited in each constituency to two days.

In the Reformed Parliament elected at the close of 1832, the Whigs appeared with a triumphant majority; the Tories were sadly beaten. Both parties were profoundly affected by the Reform. During the recent conflict, the Whig aristocrats—for it must be remembered that the old Whigs were quite as aristocratic as the Tories, being dominated by a group of wealthy peers—had won the allegiance of the iron and cotton princes of Birmingham, Manchester, and London, by posing as the liberal, reforming element. The pose became permanent, and the Whigs, continuing to pride themselves upon their advocacy of whatever "liberal" ideas might be current among the bourgeoisie, began to call themselves Liberals. The Tories, for their part, recog-

Provisions of the Reform Bill of 1832

Appearance of Liberal and Conservative Parties

nized the altered situation by rallying around the new standard
of "Conservatism" erected by Sir Robert Peel, who accepted
the Reform, but wished to proceed in future in a conservative
manner. The new principles won the adherence of many traders
and manufacturers whose loyalty to the Anglican Church, or
to the protective tariff, inspired them with distrust of Liberalism.
Only the more obstinate champions of the old régime were still
branded as "Tories."

Besides Liberals and Conservatives there sat a score or more
of Radicals, for whom neither Liberals nor Conservatives were
The   progressive enough, — men who had borne a leading
Radicals   part in the Reform struggle, and who were now come
into their reward as Members of Parliament. Their ideas of
what constituted true progress they had learned in large part
Jeremy   from Jeremy Bentham, who died at the age of 84 in
Bentham   the very year of the Reform Act. From his father,
a successful lawyer, Bentham had inherited a fortune sufficient
to enable him to gratify the taste for study which he had acquired when he began to read history and to study Latin at
three years of age. In his great work, *Principles of Morals and
Legislation* (1789), Bentham declared that existing institutions
should be valued, not for their antiquity, but simply for their
utility in promoting "the greatest happiness of the greatest
number." Few institutions satisfied this utilitarian test, and
Bentham's vigorous denunciation of the old régime so pleased
the French people that they conferred upon him the honor of
French citizenship in 1792. To him is due much of the credit
for having destroyed the complacent self-satisfaction with which
most Englishmen regarded themselves and their "matchless
Constitution." The Utilitarian philosophy, as Bentham's system was called, was less successful on its constructive side.
Although he himself was a very pleasant gentleman, who delighted in entertaining his many friends at dinner, and who spent
a good deal of his time at the piano — he had a piano in each
room of his house — Bentham believed the average man to be
actuated by purely selfish motives. Since each man acted for
himself alone, and since the good of the majority was to be attained, Bentham would say, the majority must be supreme in
politics. Political democracy, therefore, was justifiable and

desirable. These views led him to advocate such radical measures as the establishment of universal suffrage, vote by ballot, and annual Parliaments. Similar Radical Reforms had been advocated in 1780 by Charles James Fox and in 1776 by John Wilkes; but the philosophic justification of Radicalism was provided by Bentham. His *Catechism of Parliamentary Reform* (1817) provided Radical Reformers with a wealth of argument. Many other ideas teemed within his brain — schemes for revising the criminal law, for codifying the civil law, for prison reform, and for a Panama Canal, many of which have since been realized. Yet at heart Bentham was not democratic. In him, as in his disciples, the Philosophic Radicals, there was a strange paradox. While arguing for democracy, he had little faith in men. Furthermore, the man who accepted from Parliament £23,000 for inventing a scheme of prison construction which was never used, the man who leased a fine mansion and deer park for his own use, could hardly be accused of an inordinate love of democratic simplicity.

Among the political reformers who came under Bentham's influence, and adopted the Benthamite paradox, Francis Place (1771–1854) was the most interesting figure. By his Francis own superlative perseverance and sagacity he had Place fought his way up from the poverty of a journeyman tailor to a comfortable position as a small capitalist. While starving in a garret, he had painfully deciphered Euclid's geometry, and by other difficult studies had prepared his mind for Benthamite radicalism. Theoretically he believed in complete democracy; but in the great Reform agitation of 1830–1832 his tailor shop became the *rendezvous*, not of the champions of universal suffrage, but of the middle-class reformers who were backing the utterly inadequate Reform Bill. In his endeavor to thwart the demand for universal suffrage, he counseled his lieutenants to speak at mass-meetings as if in favor of universal suffrage, but to persuade the ignorant people to vote resolutions in favor of the bill.

Francis Place was one of the few Radicals not to enter Parliament after the Reform. Once represented in the House of Commons, Radicalism rapidly revealed its inherent weakness. Many laudable reforms were suggested, such as free trade, com-

pulsory education, disestablishment of the Anglican Church in
Ireland, land reform, milder game laws, abolition of flogging in
the army; and weak pleas were still made for a wider
electoral franchise, for the secret ballot, for restriction
of the legislative power of the House of Lords. But
the Radicals did little to accomplish the reforms they
planned. The veteran Radical William Cobbett was
laughed at in the House of Commons when he proposed the
immediate withdrawal of all paper money and the cessation
of interest payments on the national debt. After 1837 the
Radical group was no longer in evidence. Some of the Radical
ideas, such as free trade, the extension of education, the disestablishment of the Irish Church, and abolition of flogging in
the army, were taken up by the progressive wing of the Liberal
party. But the Liberals would have nothing to do with the
extension of the suffrage, introduction of the secret ballot, or
curtailment of the prerogatives of the Upper House. Had not
Lord John Russell, the sponsor of the Reform of 1832, declared
(1837) that that Reform was "final"?

*Weakness
of the
Philosophic
Radicals in
Parliament*

The people were by no means satisfied. The promises made
in 1832 had not been fulfilled. The middle classes, now comfortably fortified in the House of Commons, showed no sign of
extending the benefits of political enfranchisement to the lower
classes. The Reformed Parliament had done little to better
the lot of the workingman; worse than that, it had devised a
new Poor Law, by which indigent workmen were no longer
aided by the parish, but bundled off to workhouses. The picture drawn in Dickens's *Oliver Twist* was no exaggeration of the
bitter misery endured in those workhouses. Workmen were
supposed to have no human feelings; the sexes had to be separated,
even if a couple had lived together for half a century. To
add to the despair of the poor, the price of bread rose in 1837.
What could be done? Robert Owen's schemes of voluntary
associations among workingmen had been tried on a small
scale in 1834 and seemingly had failed. Parliament was deaf
to entreaty. Perhaps if workmen could sit in Parliament, there
would be some hope of relief.

So the workmen turned to a movement for political democracy
as a step towards economic relief. This was the Chartist move-

ment, which appeared in England from 1838 to 1848.   The
Chartists derived their name from a charter of liberties which they
proposed to obtain: just as *Magna Carta* had been for   Chartism
the barons, the Bill of Rights for the merchants, and
the Reform Bill for the factory-owners, so now there should be a
Charter guaranteeing six points for the workingmen. The famous
Six Points had been demanded before by Radicals, "The Six
but never so earnestly. They were: (1) universal Points"
manhood suffrage, (2) annual Parliaments, (3) equal electoral
districts, (4) vote by ballot, (5) removal of property qualification for members of Parliament, (6) payment of members.

The movement gathered rapid headway. It appealed to
half-fed and overworked men, as the only way to save themselves and their children from the terrible life in the tenements.
In 1839 a National Convention or "Workingmen's Parliament"
met in London to present Parliament with a petition for universal suffrage. Parliament refused the petition. Another
petition was presented in 1842, after a season of falling wages,
with the same outcome. Discouragement increased internal
divisions within the Chartist ranks. The better organized and
more prosperous artisans, who had all along insisted on legal
methods, now seceded,[1] leaving the more violent element, "the
party of physical force," in command. Feargus O'Connor, a
giant Irishman with a powerful voice and violent temper kept
up the enthusiasm of the party by heated oratory. The high
prices of 1847, a season of slack work, and news of a revolutionary movement in France in February, 1848, excited the
Chartists to a final effort. They planned to form an enormous
army to carry a third petition to Parliament; and whispered
threats bespoke the determination of some to use force, if the
petition failed.   In alarm, the government called upon   Chartist
the aged but still courageous Wellington. In addi- Demonstration to regular troops he armed 170,000 shop-keepers' tion, April,
sons as special constables, to shoot down any unruly   1848
Chartists.   10 April, 1848, the appointed day, arrived at last,
and with it a heavy rain which dampened the spirits of the

[1] Many were diverted from the charter by the promise which the middle-class
Anti-Corn Law agitators were making at about this time, of "cheap bread for
the workingmen."

scantily clad demonstrators. The parade was called off; O'Connor bundled the monster petition into five cabs and hurried it to Parliament, where it was discovered not to contain the boasted five million signatures but less then two millions, including such remarkable ones as "the Queen," "Wellington," and "Pug Nose." Chartism was worse than a failure, — it was a joke.

After the final fiasco, many Chartists relapsed into sullen despair, others threw themselves into the trade-union move-
Failure of Chartism as an Organized Movement, but Persistence of its Principles ment, still others turned to coöperative enterprises. A few Anglican clergymen, while they disapproved of Chartism as too bitter and too revolutionary, were very anxious to help the ex-Chartists to establish voluntary coöperative workshops. Of such clergymen, Charles Kingsley was an eminent example, and of their intentions a fair sample is afforded in Kingsley's book *Alton Locke*. As Carlyle said, in his essay on *Chartism*, the workman failed to gain "one ten-thousandth part of a speaker in the national palaver at Westminster," but it was the strength and selfishness of the middle classes rather than falsity of principle which made the charter a failure. For we shall see in subsequent chapters that a majority of the Six Points have since been recognized as desirable, and in large part they have been incorporated into the British Constitution.

As a general rule, a demand for political democracy springs more from social unrest than from abstract philosophical con-
Social Legislation in Great Britain viction. Votes are worth while only because they change laws. In the England of the early nineteenth century this was certainly true: the middle class obtained political power because it had middle-class social reforms to effect, and the Chartist movement meant that millions of workingmen desired Parliament to relieve their misery. Accompanying the movement for democracy there was a movement for social reform, and the social legislation enacted during
Tory Reforms, 1820-1829 the period, we shall now consider. Even before the Reform Act, three great reforms had been accomplished under the Tory ministry of Lord Liverpool (1812-1827), in which Sir Robert Peel, George Canning, and William Huskisson formed a trio of progress.

Canning, it will be recalled, revolted against a reactionary foreign policy. Peel was the son of a cotton manufacturer, who owed his fortune to Hargreaves's spinning-jenny. Huskisson had married a fortune of £100,000. Both Huskisson and Peel were interested in the new economic doctrine of *laisser-faire*, and inclined towards free trade.

The three reforms achieved under the auspices of these Tories were as follows. (1) The criminal code was revised (1821) in an humanitarian spirit, and in about 100 cases (such as shoplifting, picking pockets, poaching) the death penalty was replaced by a milder punishment. *Revision of Criminal Law* (2) Under a law of 1800, workingmen's combinations had been prohibited. This law was repealed in 1824,[1] and in 1825 a new law was framed allowing workmen to combine *Trade Unions* "to determine the scale of wages or hours of labour," but not to organize strikes. Trade unions were thus recognized, although restricted in their operations. (3) The third measure has already been mentioned — the removal of religious disabilities in 1828–1829. Besides introducing these reforms, the Tory administration had made a *Removal of Religious Disabilities* start in the direction of free trade and of factory legislation. About the latter we shall speak presently. The former was the outcome of the *laisser-faire* doctrines held by Peel and Huskisson, who secured a modification of the old customs tariff, and a lowering of the import duties on wheat.

When the liberal industrial bourgeoisie found itself enfranchised by the Reform Act of 1832, it set about accomplishing two class measures, — municipal reform and the emancipation of industry. The former meant that they gained control of local politics in cities like Liverpool and Leeds; the latter signified chiefly the abolition of the old protective tariff, especially of the Corn Laws. How the former was achieved in 1835, and how the Corn Laws were repealed in 1846, has been set forth in Chapter XVIII. Suffice it here to repeat that although the Liberals carried on the agitation, the actual repeal of the Corn Laws was the work of Sir Robert Peel, who, though a Conservative in politics, was the son of a cotton-manufacturer and was personally identified *Work of the Reformed Parliament*

[1] Largely through the efforts of Francis Place.

with the industrial bourgeoisie rather than with the landed aristocracy.

A great part of the minor legislation of the Reformed Parliament was dedicated to the twofold ideal of bourgeois thrift and business efficiency. A central Highways Bureau was established to improve the roads, over which merchandise had to be transported. Boards of health were nominated in the interest of public cleanliness. The county registrar, a new civil officer, took over from the clergy the registration of births, marriages, and deaths. Before the postal reform of 1839, one paid the postman a money fee for delivering a letter, the fee varying with the distance; after 1840 a penny stamp would carry a letter anywhere in the United Kingdom. But the greatest economy was effected by the revision of the Poor Law in 1834, under the ministry of Earl Grey. Under the old régime justices of the peace and church wardens had been empowered to impose rates (taxes) on the parish in order to dole out allowances to the aged or infirm, and even to those able-bodied laborers whose earnings were below a certain standard. It had cost England £8,600,000 in 1833. Under the new Poor Law, however, (1) no help was given to people living at home, except to sick and aged; (2) able-bodied paupers were put to work in the work-house; (3) several parishes might form a union, with a single "board of guardians" and a uniform poor-rate. The poor people detested the grim work-houses, and with good reason; and many families, which had relied on their few shillings a week from the poor-rates, were now destitute. But the new system was less extravagant than the old, and the middle class was satisfied.

Bourgeois Thrift and Efficiency

Poor Law Reform, 1834

Another group of Liberal laws was the outcropping of bourgeois idealism. Education had always been one of the ideals of the middle classes. Prior to 1833 the mass of Englishmen were uneducated, and schools were private affairs. In that year Parliament granted £20,000 to private societies for schools, and, after investigating the subject thoroughly, appointed a committee of bishops to name school inspectors; by 1851 the appropriation amounted to £164,000, and by 1861 to £800,000. Bourgeois idealism again

Bourgeois Idealism

Education

found vent in prison reform, in the abolition of whipping-post
and pillory, but most of all in the anti-slavery campaign. To
English business men of liberal views it seemed in- Prison
comprehensible that one man should *own* another. It Reform
was downright immoral. The dignity of man forbade it. William Wilberforce, a business man's son and a clergyman, was
chief of the anti-slavery orators, and as long ago as Anti-Slavery
1807 he had prevailed upon Parliament to abolish the Agitation
slave traffic. In 1833 the Reformed Parliament completed the
work by ordaining that negro slavery should gradually cease
in the British colonies, and that £20,000,000 should be paid
as compensation to the slave-owners.

It was wrong that white men should own negroes; yet a more
cruel evil existed in the factories of some of the anti-slavery
orators, where, as Sir Robert Peel said in 1816, Industrial
white children, "torn from their beds, were com- Legislation
pelled to work, at the age of six years, from early morn till late
at night, a space of perhaps fifteen to sixteen hours." Audiences
wept at hearing how cruel masters lashed their cowering negro
slaves in Jamaica; but in their own England little Englishmen
and Englishwomen ten years old were being whipped to their
work. The righting of this wrong was not inaugurated by
Liberal factory-owners, but by Tories. As early as 1802 the
Tory Parliament passed a well-meant but ineffectual law forbidding cotton manufacturers to work their apprentices (as the
pauper children were called who had been taken by the parish
authorities and bound over to the factory-owner) more than
twelve hours a day. After a parliamentary inquiry into factory
conditions, a Tory reformer, Lord Ashley, subsequently known
as the earl of Shaftesbury, induced Parliament to pass the
Factory Act of 1833 limiting the working-day to nine hours for
children and twelve hours for young persons.[1] The Mines Act
of 1842 prohibited underground labor for children under ten
years and for women. Incomplete and inadequate as these
acts were, they constituted the first attack on the old Liberalism
— the Liberalism that demanded the vote for factory-owners
and denied it to factory workers, the Liberalism that freed the
negro and allowed white children to endure a blacker slavery,

[1] In 1844 these hours were still further restricted.

the Liberalism which gave the poor man liberty to slave or starve and called it "freedom of contract."

The old Liberalism, in its first tentative efforts to clear away the mass of hoary political abuses in Great Britain, had sadly neglected to care for the welfare of the working classes. Nevertheless, the men who abolished slavery and wiped out the rotten boroughs must not be too severely censured for their disregard of the new social problems; as yet they were but groping blindly in the path of political democracy.

THE DEMOCRATIC REVOLUTION OF 1848 IN FRANCE

Louis Philippe reigned as "king of the French" from 1830 to 1848. In theory his government was based upon the doctrine of popular sovereignty — of democracy. But in practice, both through the close restriction of the parliamentary franchise and through the paramount influence which the middle class exerted upon legislation and administration, it was far from democratic. As the years progressed, the king and his advisers became increasingly cautious and conservative, and the opposition grew correspondingly more numerous and more determined, until by the year 1848 nearly all classes in France were arrayed solidly against the bourgeois compromise monarchy of Louis Philippe, and a considerable number were resolved to attempt the establishment of real political democracy.

Growing Opposition to Louis Philippe, 1830-1848

Between 1830 and 1848 one group after another was alienated by Louis Philippe. From the outset, he was hated by the Legitimists, who still adhered to Charles X, and later to his grandson, the count of Chambord, as the rightful king of France and as the natural champion of the privileges of the ancient aristocracy and Church. In the second place, he was held in even greater detestation by the Republicans, who had engineered the July (1830) Revolution, and to whom, therefore, he indirectly owed his crown. At the beginning, Louis Philippe had curried favor with the common people, but, as time went on, he appeared more and more clearly as the enemy of popular Republican principles. An anarchist's unsuccessful attempt to abolish the monarchy by bomb (1835) was followed by

Legitimists

Republicans

repressive laws which placed the press under as severe surveillance as in the worst days of Charles X, with 10,000 francs as the minimum fine for insulting the king. This, and the stern punishment of Republican rioters, earned the July Monarchy its most active enemies.

Then, too, all patriots who wished to see France great and glorious were disgusted with the pusillanimous foreign policy of Louis Philippe. The merchants who were interested in trade with Great Britain induced him constantly to **Patriots** adopt a cringing attitude toward that nation. Because Britain objected, he refused to allow his son to assume the crown of Belgium. French Liberals sympathized strongly with the struggle of the Poles against Russia, but Louis Philippe would not forcibly intervene. And he sat calmly by while Austria suppressed revolution in Italy, although his minister, Laffitte, had declared that France would not tolerate Austrian intervention in Italy. It was much the same with intervention in Spain. Adolphe Thiers, the journalist and Liberal Monarchist, who had played a prominent part in the Revolution of 1830, and who was the partisan of a vigorous foreign policy, was head of the cabinet in 1840 long enough to commit France to the support of Mehemet Ali, pasha of Egypt, who had victoriously rebelled against the Turkish sultan. Great Britain, Russia, Prussia, and Austria took the other side, and Louis Philippe, ever fearful, discharged his bellicose Thiers and abandoned Mehemet Ali. For the remaining eight years of the July Monarchy, 1840–1848, François Guizot, bourgeois and Huguenot, a minister after the king's own heart, devoted himself to "the preservation of peace, in all places, at all times," and advised his countrymen to turn their attention from the glory of France to her prosperity. "Business before honor!" Guizot lent himself to Louis Philippe's disgraceful intrigue, by which the king sought to secure the Spanish crown for his family. The middle-class monarchy had humiliated France, and well might the patriot ask: "Where are our friends? What positions remain to us in Europe? Poland is in exile, we have frustrated Italy, and oppressed Switzerland; Russia menaces us, Holland hates us, Belgium despises us, Germany shuns us, Portugal ignores us, Spain escapes us, Great Britain dominates us, and the conjuration of the powers has barred us from the Orient."

Hardly less scandalous was the domestic policy of the bourgeois king. At first, while the Revolution of 1830 was still in
the air, he had intimated that universal suffrage
Democrats would be granted. The electoral qualification was indeed lowered so that voters had to pay only 200 francs instead of 300 francs a year in taxes, and only 100 francs if they were magistrates, lawyers, doctors, or professors ; but believers in democracy could hardly be satisfied with a law which debarred all but 200,000 Frenchmen from the polls. All the lower middle classes, the shop-keepers, bakers, and plumbers, were at one with the masses in condemning the July plutocracy. Even the moneyed aristocracy itself was offended when in the last eight years Guizot reduced bribery to a fine art and converted the Chamber of Deputies into an employment bureau for dishonest politicians. At the outset the middle class had pretty unanimously supported Louis Philippe, but now it was sharply divided against itself as rival factions formed about the persons of those two bitterly antagonistic historians and politicians — Guizot and Thiers. And meanwhile the king, good business man that he was, realized that he must "make hay while the sun shone," and bent every effort to enrich his family while he had the opportunity. This was not constitutional monarchy, it was cynical mockery of government ; and even peace and prosperity seemed to have been purchased too dearly at such a price.

In the old days, Bourbon monarchs had often counted on the support of the Roman Catholic Church, but Louis Philippe could
look for no favor in that quarter. Since the great
Catholics French Revolution, there had been a remarkable religious revival in France, with noticeably democratic tendencies. The religious phase of the movement was inaugurated by Chàteaubriand (1768–1848), who maintained that Catholic Christianity alone satisfied man's romantic, artistic, and rational natures, and by Joseph de Maistre (1754–1821), who defended the authority of the pope. And the Democratic tendencies of this so-called "Neo-Catholic" movement were manifest when the brilliant leader Antoine Frédéric Ozanam (1813–1853) founded the Society of St. Vincent de Paul to relieve the poor, when Alphonse de Lamartine (1790–1869), abandoning

liberal-royalist for democratic sentiments, wrote a history to glorify the Girondists of 1792, and when Robert de Lamennais (1782–1854) insisted that from Catholic Christianity must be learned the spirit of true democracy — Christian democracy. Permeated by democratic doctrine, scandalized by the corrupt practices of Guizot, incensed by the favor which that Huguenot minister showed to the anti-clerical university, and determined to secure liberty of Christian education, the Catholic party denounced the July Monarchy.

And finally, the Socialists and other extremists raised their voices in protest. When the Lyons silk-weavers, rather than work at the starvation wages of 11 sous for a day of 15 to 16 hours, rebelliously raised the battle-cry "Live working Socialists or die fighting!" there could be no doubt that society needed reform. As to the nature of that social reform no unanimity of opinion existed between the Socialist disciples of Saint-Simon's doctrines, of Fourier's communistic scheme, or of Louis Blanc's coöperative associations, and the anarchistic followers of Proudhon, who condemned all government; but as to the necessity of reform all were agreed. Louis Blanc, the most influential of the Socialists, and editor of *The Reform*, declared in ringing words : "To the able-bodied citizen the state owes work; to the aged and infirm it owes aid and protection. This result cannot be obtained unless by the action of a democratic power. A democratic power is that which has the sovereignty of the people for its principle, universal suffrage for its origin, and for its goal the realization of this formula : 'Liberty, Equality, Fraternity.'"

By the year 1847 all these factions were at odds with the government, and most of them could agree in demanding electoral reform. In that year the party of constitutional The monarchy, the dynastic Left, *i.e.*, the Liberal and Roy- Banquets, alist middle class, began to hold public banquets to 1847–1848 promote the cause of electoral reform. A more revolutionary tone was gradually imparted to the banquets by Republicans and Socialists. Banqueters in Paris raised their glasses "to the amelioration of the lot of the working classes." Lamartine predicted the fall of the monarchy. In alarm the government prohibited an unusually large banquet which was to be held in Paris on

22 February, 1848. But it was too late. On the appointed day, angry workingmen and reckless students crowded the Place de la Concorde, shouting for Reform. There was nothing alarming in this, or in the bonfires that evening, and the Marseillaise was as yet sung only half in earnest. On the next day, however, the middle-class National Guards joined in the cry, "Down with Guizot," and Guizot resigned from the ministry. The

The February (1848) Revolution in Paris

insurrection might have stopped there, had not a detachment of soldiers, guarding Guizot's residence, rashly fired on a crowd of boisterous demonstrators. Twenty-three French citizens lay dead on the street and thirty wounded, some of them women and children. For a moment the crowd was stunned. Then in rage it bore the bodies on a wagon, blood-stained and ghastly in the glaring torch-light, for all Paris to behold. Reform could not now suffice. The dawning day of 24 February showed barricades blocking the narrow streets of the slums, and behind them workmen who shouted "Long Live the Republic!" Everywhere were the placards: "Louis Philippe massacres us as did Charles X; let him go join Charles X." Like the prudent man he had always been, Louis Philippe tarried only long enough to abdicate in favor of his grandson, the count of Paris, and then drove off as "Mr. Smith" in a closed carriage to follow Charles X to England, the asylum of superfluous French royalty.

The count of Paris was forgotten, however, while the republic was proclaimed simultaneously in two places: in the Chamber

The Second French Republic, 1848–1852

of Deputies at the Palais-Bourbon in the western part of Paris, and at the Hôtel de Ville in the east. At the Palais Bourbon were the bourgeois Republicans, whose flag was the tricolor, and whose aim was political democracy; at the Hôtel de Ville were the working-class Republicans whose banner was the red flag, and whose aim was political and social democracy. Those at the Palais-Bourbon set up a government representing middle-class Liberalism; those at the Hôtel de Ville nominated men who intended to bring about a social revolution in the interests of the working classes. Temporarily the two governments combined; the one at the Palais Bourbon joined the other at the Hôtel de Ville, and Louis Blanc himself was given a voice in the fusion government.

The provisional government thus established was composed of two irreconcilable elements, the middle class and the working class. At first, under the terror of the armies of the slums, the bourgeois faction gave unwilling attention to the problems of the poor and to Louis Blanc's socialistic remedies. On 25 February, while a mob waited in the hall, the provisional government assented to Louis Blanc's decree: that "the Government of the French Republic undertakes to guarantee the existence of the workingman by labor and to provide labor for all citizens." As a first installment on its promise, the government established "national workshops" for the unemployed. Louis Blanc had advocated "national workshops" or coöperative industrial associations established by the aid of the state and managed by the workingmen themselves; the "national workshops" created by the Second Republic were a pitiable parody on the idea, predestined to failure by the minister who had them in charge, a bourgeois who detested Louis Blanc's theories. The riff-raff of the town and the thousands of skilled artisans who had been deprived of work by the business crisis attending the Revolution, were herded together and set to work digging trenches. For such work, the state was paying, in May, an army of 100,000 men at the rate of 2 francs a day. Meanwhile Louis Blanc with his fellow-Socialist Albert had been delegated by the provisional government as a committee to hear the workingmen's grievances at the Luxembourg. The two worked faithfully at their task: they ordered the reduction of the working day from eleven to ten hours in Paris, and from twelve to eleven in the country; they proposed other desirable reforms; they held conferences and established a committee of labor-delegates; but they had no power to enforce their decrees, and the middle-class members of the government were congratulating themselves upon having found so harmless an occupation for their Socialist colleagues.

First Phase: Problems of the Working Class

The republic entered its second phase, its middle-class phase, on 23 April, the date set for the election by universal suffrage of a Constituent Assembly to formulate a constitution for the republic. Louis Blanc and his party could hope for little weight in the new body; their subversive principles were distrusted by the clergy, their working-class sympathies were repellant to business and professional men, and an increase in taxes helped

Second Phase: The Republic of the Middle Classes to persuade the parsimonious peasant that Louis Blanc had wasted the nation's funds employing Parisian ne'er-do-wells in the "national workshops." In the new Assembly there were but few Socialists, a great number of middle-class Republicans, and a considerable group of reactionaries. The "abomination of abominations," — the institution of national workshops, — was first attacked by the Assembly. The workshops were abolished and the workmen were offered their choice of service in the army, or earth-work construction in the country. But the workmen had tasted power too recently, and were too fiercely inflamed with revolutionary ideas to submit tamely. They again tore up the pavement to build barricades in the slums of Saint-Antoine. General Cavaignac, intrusted with dictatorial power by the Assembly, directed the bourgeois National Guards and the regular troops — an overwhelming force — to crush the working-class rebellion.

The "June Days," 1848 The archbishop of Paris lost his life in a futile but noble attempt to avert bloodshed. Three days the sanguinary street-fighting lasted, — the terrible "June Days" (24-26 June, 1848). There could be but one result: the armies of "order" triumphed, some of the revolutionaries were shot, and 4000 were transported to the colonies. The memories of the June Days, rankling in the breast of the Parisian workingman, made him hate the "bourgeois" republic; the peasant, on the other hand, was confirmed in his distrust of republicanism, which always seemed to bring bloodshed in its train.

In the Constituent Assembly the middle-class Republicans now had things all their own way. By insisting on "the family,

The Constituent Assembly, 1848 rights of property, and public order" as the "foundations" of the republic, they repudiated Socialism and Anarchism; but at the same time they favored social reforms, and even declared that the state must "with fraternal aid, assure the existence of needy citizens either by procuring them work . . . or by assisting those who are unable to work." Slavery, the censorship of the press, and capital punishment for political offenses, they declared to be inconsistent with the principles of Liberty, Equality, and Fraternity.

Free primary education, they warmly espoused. After promising these typical bourgeois reforms, they drew up a constitution closely modeled after that of the United States, with a president elected by universal suffrage for four years, and a cabinet chosen by him, but with a Council of State chosen by the Assembly instead of a separately elected Senate.

The Constitution of the Second French Republic

In the presidential election which took place on 10 December, 1848, the factions which had combined to effect the February Revolution were arrayed against one another, — and in that disunion was the weakness of the democratic republic. The Socialist Ledru-Rollin, the Catholic Lamartine, and the bourgeois Republican Cavaignac, defeated each other; while a fourth candidate, an adventurer with a great name, profiting by the confusion of the democratic parties, carried the day by appealing to nationalism. The career of this adventurer — a new Bonaparte — we must leave to the next chapter.

THE REVOLUTIONARY MOVEMENTS OF 1848 IN ITALY, GERMANY, AND AUSTRIA–HUNGARY

In the French Revolution of 1848 we have seen three elements — patriotic shame at a disgraceful foreign policy, economic unrest resulting from the Industrial Revolution, and bourgeois aspirations after political democracy — combining in February to establish the republic, conflicting in the tragic days of June, and eventually by their disagreement bringing an adventurer to the presidency of the republic. Throughout the rest of Europe the same three ingredients of revolution were present in varying degree, according as national sentiment had been violated by the settlements of Vienna, or the working classes degraded by the Industrial Revolution, or the Liberal class infuriated by the reactionary policies of Metternich. As the match to the powder, the sudden news of Louis Philippe's deposition came to touch off the Revolution in Italy, in the Germanies, and in Austria-Hungary. Within a few months half the monarchs of Europe had been either deposed or forced to concede constitutions. Even across the English Channel, the revolutionary uproar awakened a faint response

Three Elements

among the Chartists and gave them heart to shout more loudly,
if unsuccessfully, for their charter. We shall first discover the
elements of unrest — national, democratic, economic — in Italy,
in the Germanies, and in Austria-Hungary, which made possible
in those countries the revolutionary movements of 1848.

What national patriotism the Italians possessed rebelled
against the presence of the domineering Austrians, and dreamed
Nationalism of uniting all the petty principalities of the penin-
in Italy sula in order to expel the foreigner. The Lombardo-
Venetian kingdom, as we know, was directly subject to Austria;
the duchies of Tuscany, Modena, and Parma were ruled by Habsburg sovereigns, and the remainder of Italy was fearful of Austrian intervention. Patriots in Lombardy-Venetia longed to
drive out the hated Austrian soldiery; patriots in the other
Italian states strove to weld into a nation the kingdom of Sardinia, the kingdom of Lombardy-Venetia, the duchies of Parma
and Modena, the grand-duchy of Tuscany,[1] the Papal States,
and the kingdom of the Two Sicilies. Already three strong
movements were on foot. The anti-clerical secret society
founded by Mazzini, a Genoese lawyer, cherished the idea of
an Italian republic based on Jacobin principles. The Clericals
hoped to form a federation under the headship of the liberal-
minded Pope Pius IX, whose name was cheered all over Italy.
Thirdly, many looked to Charles Albert, the Liberal king of
Sardinia, as the strongest and safest leader. All talked of the
Risorgimento, the "resurrection" of Italy.

Liberalism in Italy meant a return to such a constitution as
had been framed by the Spanish revolutionaries in 1812. Only
Liberalism the boldest spirits of the middle class — the Young
in Italy Italy society — desired a republic; most Liberals
would content themselves with constitutional monarchy. Beginning with the Liberal concessions of Pius IX in 1846-1847,
— political amnesty, freedom of the press, a national guard,
and a council of state, — Liberalism made rapid headway. The
grand-duke of Tuscany granted identical reforms. Charles
Albert of Sardinia not only granted his people the privilege of
parliamentary government, by the Fundamental Statute (*Statuto*)
of 4 March, 1848, but suppressed feudal jurisdictions, constructed

---

[1] The duchy of Lucca was incorporated into Tuscany in 1847.

railways, founded agricultural societies, organized a customs
union with Tuscany and Rome, and provided for an army of
61,400 men, — for he knew that Liberalism involved also a
struggle with Metternich.

Very much the same situation prevailed in the Germanies.
There was strong popular feeling that the various states must
be firmly federated into one Fatherland; that Austria- Nationalism
Hungary must be expelled; and that Liberal con- in Germany
stitutions must be obtained. The Germanic Confederation of
1815 was a loose alliance of some thirty-eight sovereigns, in
which the king of Prussia and the Austrian emperor disputed
for precedence among a motley host of potentates: kings of
Bavaria, Hanover, Saxony, and Württemberg; grand-dukes,
dukes, princes, and even burgomasters of the free towns of
Hamburg, Lübeck, and Bremen. The emperor of Austria had
Italian and Slavic subjects, as well as Germans; the king of
Prussia had Polish possessions, and the king of Denmark (as
duke of Holstein) and the king of the Netherlands (as duke of
Luxemburg) boasted membership in the "Germanic" Confederation. To construct a national state out of such a hodge-podge
seemed a prodigious task. Nevertheless German professors in
the universities clung to their patriotic ideals. And an economic foundation for German unity had been laid in 1833 when
the *Zollverein* was established under the leadership of Prussia.
A common customs administration, the beginnings of a railway
system, and the relationships of commerce, were physically
unifying the country. Merchants with commercial interests at
stake were even more eloquent nationalists than the professors.

Notwithstanding repressive laws, a powerful Liberal sentiment had developed among the bourgeoisie and was reflected by
the lower classes. It demanded, on the one hand, Liberalism
constitutional liberties in the separate states, and, on in Germany
the other, a federal parliament more democratic than that
assembly of reactionary diplomats — the Diet of the Germanic
Confederation. The Liberals counted much on Frederick
William IV, who succeeded to the throne of Prussia in 1840;
but, by criticizing his tardiness in effecting reforms, the Liberals
so irritated the monarch that he insisted the more firmly upon
the fullness of his royal prerogative, and refused to yield an inch

to the United *Landtag* or Estates-General of the whole Prussian Kingdom, which he had created by a decree of 3 February, 1847.

Besides the bourgeois advocates of constitutional government and national unification, the king of Prussia had now to reckon The Berlin with the Berlin proletariat — the mob of discontented Proletariat workingmen, underpaid or unemployed, some of them Poles, ready to support any democratic movement, even to the length of violence.

In Austria-Hungary, nationalism tended not to union, as in Italy and in Germany, but to disunion. The realms of the Habs-burg emperor were truly a curious complex of nation-Conflicting alities, held together only by allegiance to the sover-Nationali-ties in eign. The majority of the population was made up of Austria-Hungary five Slavic nations: (1) the Czechs in Bohemia and Moravia, and their neighbors, the Slovaks, in north-western Hungary; (2) the Poles in northwestern Galicia; (3) the Ruthenians in eastern Galicia; (4) the Slovenes in Carniola and southern Styria; (5) and the Serbo-Croats in Croatia and Slavonia. Dominating the Slavic groups were (1) the German population, solid in the Austrian provinces, a strong minority in Bohemia, and scattering colonies throughout Hungary; and (2) the Magyars — the predominant people of Hungary. To add to the confusion of nations, there were Italians in Lombardy-Venetia and in the southern cities of Croatia-Slavonia, and Rumans in Transylvania and Bukowina. It is easy to perceive what havoc the spirit of nationalism would play with the Habs-burg dominions, especially when we remember that many of the subject peoples still cherished traditions of former inde-pendence.

During the reign of Ferdinand I (1835–1848), five different nationalist movements menaced the empire. (1) With the Nationalist Italian movement, we are familiar. (2) The deter-Movements mination of the Poles to restore their ancient king-under Emperor dom caused simultaneous conspiracies in Prussian Ferdinand Posen, in the diminutive republic of Cracow, and in I, 1835–1848 Galicia in 1846. The rebellious Polish nationalists were in turn confronted with a counter-revolution in eastern Galicia of the Ruthenian serfs who had both nationalist and economic reasons to revolt against their Polish landlords. The Ruthenians gained nothing by their insurrection, but simply helped the Austrians to crush the Polish revolt so effectually that Polish patriotism was practically paralyzed for the next dozen years.[1]   (3) The Czechs in Bohemia, remembering the national independence and the free constitution which had been theirs until 1627, were stirred in the 'forties by a revival of Bohemian (Czech) literature, by a campaign to introduce the Bohemian language in the schools, and by a demand for reunion with Moravia and Silesia. In 1845 the Diet of Bohemia appealed to national sentiments by asserting its tax-voting power against the Vienna bureaucracy, and to Liberalism by proposing that the towns be better represented in the Diet. But the Czechs, in asserting their own nationalism, naturally came into violent conflict with the nationalism of the numerous Germans who were settled among them. (4) The most formidable national movement was that of the Magyars or Hungarians, descendants of the savage Asiatic invaders who in the ninth century had crossed the Carpathians into the valley of the Danube and had reduced the adjacent Slavs to the position of subject peoples. Magyar patriotism had two phases: first, a fierce resentment of Austrian attempts to override Hungary's right to be ruled through an Hungarian Diet; and secondly, an ardent desire to force the Magyar language and nationality upon the Slovaks, upon the Rumans of Transylvania, and upon the Slavs of Croatia-Slavonia. (5) The attempt of the Magyars to force their language upon the Serbo-Croats inflamed the latter people with a nationalistic hatred of Hungary. Hitherto the Croats had been governed by a Hungarian "ban," or viceroy, and an elected Diet. Now they began to agitate for the erection of Dalmatia, Croatia, and Slavonia into a Triune Illyrian kingdom, subject to the Austrian emperor but independent of Hungary. (6) Finally, the most powerful national group of all, the Germans, although at present occupied mostly with Liberalism, might, by the success of any of the foregoing movements, be galvanized into patriotic energy.

Sometimes identical, and sometimes at odds with these nationalist aspirations, Liberal demands for more or less radical

[1] Cracow was incorporated in the Austrian Empire in 1846.

democratic institutions were attracting the attention of the middle and lower classes.   In Hungary, for instance, while István Széchenyi, an aristocrat of exceptional fore-sight, sought to make Hungary great and prosperous without introducing political democracy, the more famous Louis Kossuth (1802–1894), a popular journalist and an eloquent orator, though of noble rank, had already spent some three years in prison for passionate preaching of Liber-alism and of such democratic reforms as that the feudal nobles should be stripped of their privileges and forced to pay their share of taxes, that the criminal code should be revised, and trial by jury introduced.   But these democratic demands occupied only half of Louis Kossuth's attention; with the other he was planning to exalt his nation.   He was both a Liberal and a nationalist.   Similarly in Bohemia were to be found patriots no less desirous of Liberal than of national prog-ress — men who insisted that the Bohemian Diet should be made at once more representative of the people and more inde-pendent of Vienna.   In Croatia much the same connection be-tween Liberalism and nationalism obtained.   Among the Ger-mans in the Austrian provinces, however, the Liberal propaganda was both more advanced and less entangled with nationalism. Even the Assembly of Estates in Lower Austria — organ of the nobility as it was — favored moderate reforms in repre-sentation, legislation, and taxation.   The bourgeoisie of the cities, and preëminently the bourgeoisie of Vienna, went further and demanded liberty to publish revolutionary doctrines bor-rowed from French or English writers, and a constitution guaranteeing a representative legislature.   The university students, almost two thousand in number, were probably the most radical as well as the most reckless of Liberals.

Liberalism in Austria-Hungary

Nationalist and Liberal ideas no doubt exercised a powerful influence upon the minds of the lower classes, but keener still was the economic motive.   In Vienna were thou-sands of artisans who had been thrown out of work by machinery, for the Industrial Revolution was beginning to make itself felt even in the stronghold of "reaction"; other thousands starved on insufficient wages. In the rural districts hard-driven serfs longed to blot out the

The Industrial Revolution in Austria

feudal and manorial system — the system by which the bulk of their labor went to support some nobleman. The artisans of the city and the serfs of the country needed but an excuse to rise in rebellion against the economic system which ground them down.

That everywhere the people were murmuring against the established order, even Metternich, the main prop of that order, could not deny. For the very reason that the discon- *The Last* tent was everywhere prevalent, revolution, once in- *Years of* flamed, was bound to spread like wildfire. The "inter- *Metter-* national police" would find it more difficult to keep *nich's* *Régime in* the peace of the Continent than in 1830, for now each *Austria,* Power would be occupied at home. In two other *1830–1848* respects the situation by 1848 was far more perilous than in 1830. First of all, since 1830 numerous railways had been constructed, — one from Paris to Vienna, for example, — and by rail the news of revolutionary successes traveled from one country to another in hours instead of weeks. In the second place, commerce and the infant industrial revolution had increased the number of prosperous and ambitious business men, who were the middle-class Liberals; and at the same time the ranks of discontented workingmen had been swelled. Both of these classes, congregated in the cities, continually agitated by radical clubs and secret societies, rallied to revolution more readily than the slow peasants in their scattered villages.

The white-haired old gentleman of Vienna, Prince Clemens Metternich, now in his seventies, felt the reins slipping from his hands. In spite of a nominal censorship, revolu- *Precursors* tionary doctrines were being printed and published; *of the Revo-* notwithstanding his precautions, the universities were *tionary* becoming hotbeds of Liberalism. Peace could not *Movements* *of 1848* much longer be preserved. There was the Polish revolution of 1846. That had fortunately been suppressed. So had short-lived insurrections in Sicily and Naples during 1847. But in Switzerland, Metternich had failed to prevent a revolutionary upheaval of the Radicals in the northern cantons from overwhelming the defensive alliance (the *Sonderbund*) of the seven Catholic cantons (1847), and, although the democratic principle was disregarded in coercing the cantons of the *Sonder-*

bund, the Radicals professed to believe in republicanism, universal suffrage, and other "dangerous novelties." The year 1848 opened ominously with a desperate uprising in Palermo, on 12 January, which soon mastered the entire island of Sicily and led to the restoration of the Constitution of 1812. To ward off a like revolution in Naples, King Ferdinand voluntarily granted a constitution on 29 January. Meanwhile in Lombardy-Venetia, the Italians, having resolved to consume no more cigars while the Austrian government derived a profit from the sale of tobacco, stoned the Austrian soldiers who dared to smoke in the streets, and thereby precipitated "smoking riots" in Milan and Padua. Perhaps the rest of Europe would have revolted, even had France not given a spectacular example by her February Revolution.

The news of the proclamation of the Second French Republic (24 February, 1848), traveling through Europe, gave a clear signal for widespread revolution. In the train of the tidings from France, came information that the grand-duke of Baden had granted reforms; that Charles Albert of Sardinia had promulgated a constitution (*Statuto*); that the Frankfort Diet had appealed to the German nation; that Louis I had convoked the Bavarian Estates; that Pope Pius IX had appointed a Liberal ministry. Already, Metternich was beginning to fear that these rumblings portended the collapse of the old structure of absolutism. His forebodings were confirmed when Louis Kossuth, in a furious speech before the Hungarian Diet on 3 March, demanded a separate responsible ministry for Hungary. On 12 March a popular petition was presented to the emperor by two Viennese professors. On the following day a turbulent mob of students and workingmen in Vienna clashed with the troops. Later that day the middle-class civic guard, called out by Metternich, refused to suppress the riots, and great crowds collected about the imperial palace. A civic deputation demanded the dismissal of the detested chief minister. Assured that his hour had at last arrived, the white-haired old gentleman, still very courtly in his blue swallow-tail coat, and still suavely ironical, requested of the emperor that, since his presence was no longer required, he "might be allowed" to

Tidings of the February (1848) Revolution in France

Downfall of Metternich, 1848

resign. His palace was already sacked and burning. On 14 March an elderly "Englishman" and his wife departed quietly for London. Metternich, the veteran foe of revolution, was fleeing for his life before a revolution.

When Metternich reached London a little more than a month later, he learned that insurrections had broken out in Berlin and Milan; that Venice was a republic; that Sardinia was at war with Austria, that written constitutions had been exacted from the rulers of Tuscany, Sardinia, the Papal States, Austria, and Holland; and that the grand-duke of Baden, the king of Bavaria, the king of Saxony, the king of Prussia, and the king of Hanover had either convoked parliaments, or appointed Liberal ministries, or decreed other reforms. *Immediate Spread of the Revolutionary Movement*

In the independent Italian states, the revolutionary movement was at first chiefly Liberal in character, and was devoted to the acquisition of constitutions. In Lombardy-Venetia, however, the revolution was violent and nationalist. Transported with joy by news of the flight of Metternich, Milan began on 18 March a bloody five-days street-battle with General Radetzky's 18,000 Austrian troops. On 22 March, while Radetzky was retiring from Milan to his stronghold in Venetia,—the Quadrilateral,—the Venetians rebelled and proclaimed their independence as the republic of St. Mark. The Sardinian army of 23,000 under Charles Albert, and contingents of troops from Tuscany, from the Papal States, and from Naples, marched to emancipate all Italy from the Austrians. *1. March (1848) Revolutions in Italy*

Almost all of the German states experienced disturbances during March, 1848, and in almost all the demand was for limited monarchy, free press, and the unification of Germany. In Baden an extremist attempt to set up a republic was thwarted by timely concessions on the part of the grand-duke. In Bavaria, King Louis, having failed to stay the revolt by promises, abdicated in favor of his son, Maximilian II, who swore to observe a constitution. In Hesse-Cassel, freedom of the press and constitutional government were gained. Saxony and Württemberg were pacified by the nomination of Liberal ministries. The duke of Nassau was forced by a powerful peasant uprising to cede his private domains to the public. In Hanover, a public demonstration was followed *2. March (1848) Revolutions in the Germanies* by a change of ministry and a constitutional revision. In the petty Thuringian states the rulers retained their popularity by granting reforms. In Mecklenburg-Schwerin, freedom of the press and equal electoral rights were secured. In the three Hanse towns—Bremen, Hamburg, and Lübeck,—disturbances emphasized the demand for democratic reform.

In Prussia the king was so panic-stricken at the disloyalty of his people that he resisted the revolution but weakly. Dis-

3. March (1848) Revolution in Prussia quieted by the rioting and the erection of barricades in Berlin (13–16 March, 1848), Frederick William IV consented to call the combined Prussian Diet and to press for a national constitution for all Germany. Hearing of these royal concessions, crowds of workingmen and foreigners flocked to the palace-square, where they were received by musket-shots from the Royal Guards. Again barricades were erected and during that night upwards of two hundred were killed in the street-fighting; but on the morrow the king called off the troops, and completed his surrender by appointing a Liberal ministry.

Taking advantage of the almost universal sentiment in favor of German unification, a *Vorparlament*, or preliminary parlia-

Nationalist Movement in Germany ment, supposed to represent all German states, met at Frankfort on 31 March, and exercised so powerful an influence upon the German Diet that the latter body regularly convoked a parliament, or rather a Constitutional Convention, composed of one deputy for every 50,000 inhabitants throughout the Germanic Confederation. This was the famous Frankfort Assembly which was solemnly opened in St. Paul's Church, Frankfort, on 13 May, 1848.

Meanwhile the revolution had so altered the aspect of the Habsburg Empire that Prince Metternich, now leading a re-

4. The Revolution in Austria, March–May, 1848 tired life in Brighton (England), would not easily have recognized his country. On the very day after Metternich's flight (*i.e.*, on 15 March, 1848) an imperial manifesto had recognized freedom of the press, had authorized the formation of a National Guard, had called the Austrian Estates to meet on 3 July, and had promised a constitution for Austria. The new National Guard, the students, and a committee of 24 citizens, were thenceforward the real rulers of Vienna. On 25 April the emperor promulgated the promised constitution for all of his dominions, except Hungary and Lombardy-Venetia, granting civil and religious liberty, a National Guard, and a bicameral Diet. Even this was not fully satisfactory to the revolutionaries; a Constitutional Assembly, based on universal suffrage, must needs be convoked. The emperor again yielded, and then, terrified by fresh demonstrations in Vienna, fled to Innsbruck. In his absence, the ministry, by attempting to dissolve the students' organization, brought on a new popular revolt (26 May), and Vienna became a city of barricades, governed by a revolutionary Committee of Safety.

While the imperial government was paralyzed by the turmoil in Vienna, the Hungarians secured their autonomy by establishing a separate, responsible, Hungarian ministry, with a Liberal-Nationalist at its head. The Liberal character of the Magyar movement displayed itself in reforms of the Liberal type, effected in March and April, 1848. The press was freed, a National Guard was organized, feudal servitudes and titles were abolished, nobles were forced to share in the tax-burdens, Diets were to be held annually at Budapest and to be elected by the nobility plus the newly enfranchised middle classes ($150 property-holders). *5. March (1848) Revolution in Hungary*

The revolutionary wave of March–April, 1848, mildly nationalist, moderately Liberal, and widely successful, having overwhelmed Metternich and gained constitutional liberties for almost every central-European state, began to break up in the summer of 1848, as nationalist sentiments emerged more prominently. By its fatal entanglement with discordant nationalist ambitions, the democratic-nationalist revolution was doomed to destroy itself in a conflict of nations. *Nationalist Phase of All the Revolutionary Movements of March, 1848*

It was this nationalist element which made the new constitutional settlement impracticable for Austria-Hungary. Had Magyars, Slavs, and Germans harmoniously demanded constitutional government, their demand could not have been gainsaid. Unhappily, the Liberals, who desired democracy, were at the same time, and even more strenuously, insisting upon the separate national claims of their own people, and these national claims could not be satisfied for the Slavs without hurting the *The New Austrian Constitution Stultified by Nationalism*

pride of Germans and Magyars, or for the Magyars without
arousing the jealousy of the Slavs and Germans, or for the
Germans without incurring the resentment of the Slavs.

For this very reason the Austrian Constitution of 25 April,
1848, was unsatisfactory: it left Hungary entirely out of consideration, and at the same time fell short of the de-
1. National-
ism in the   sires of the other nationalities. To prepare a better
Reichstag   constitution, a *Reichstag* (Imperial Diet) representing
by universal suffrage all of the Habsburg territories except
Lombardy-Venetia and Hungary, assembled at Vienna on 22 July,
1848. Racial animosities divided the deputies, less than half
of whom were Germans, into distinct and discordant groups,
and stultified the deliberations. One great reform was accomplished, however, at the instance of the peasants, who composed a fourth of the Assembly, and by the acquiescence of the
middle-class majority, — namely, the abolition of the peasants'
servile obligations to their feudal lords.

Shortly before the meeting of the *Reichstag*, the Slavs had
held a congress of their own in June, 1848, in Prague, where the
2. The Pan-   Liberal movement had already secured a National
Slav Con-   Guard, the convocation of the Provincial Estates,
gress   and a responsible government. Czech, Polish, Russian, and Serbian delegates here met as brother Slavs, and
sounded the praises of their great and valorous race in unity
of spirit but with a Babel of dissonant tongues. Eloquent
manifestoes, proclaiming loyalty to the Habsburgs, appealing
to all branches of the Slav race, and calling for a general congress of all the nations, were the only achievements of the unpractical congress. But the excitement of the Czech populace
of Prague led to more tangible, if less desirable, results, — rioting
on 13 June, the erection of barricades, and an assault upon
the residence of Prince Windischgrätz, the Austrian commander,
and the shooting of his wife as she stood at the window. Fighting ensued, from which Prince Windischgrätz emerged as the
victor on 17 June, 1848. The Liberal reforms were hastily
withdrawn, Bohemia was put under martial law, and the Czech
movement expired.

Not so the movement of the southern Slavs. The Serbo-
Croats of Croatia and Slavonia, fearing rather the domineering

Magyars than the German Austrians, had secured the appointment as *ban* (viceroy of Croatia) of Count Joseph Jellachich von
Buzim, a Croatian nobleman who had inherited from
his father, a veteran of the Napoleonic Wars, and   3. Jel-
                                                         lachich,
manifested in border warfare against the Turks, the   Ban of
spirit of a patriot and of a fighter.   The new *ban*   Croatia
alarmed the imperial court and angered the Magyars by con-
voking a Croatio-Slavonic Diet (June, 1848).   The presence
of Slovenes from Styria and Carniola, Slovaks from northern
Hungary, and Czechs from Bohemia made the Diet virtually
a pan-Slavic congress, like the one simultaneously sitting at
Prague.   Mistrusting that Jellachich purposed to set up a
Croatio-Slavonic kingdom, the imperial government suspended
him from office.   Thereupon he hastened to visit the emperor
at Innsbruck with assurances that his innocent intent was
loyally to serve the house of Habsburg, and to overcome the
rebellious Magyars.   He was given a hearty welcome, for the
imperial government was daily becoming more hostile to the
Magyars, who had made Hungary practically independent, with
separate national flag, army, ambassadors, and ministry.   Moreover, Austrian financiers were frenzied by the emission of Hungarian paper money, which supplanted the notes of the National
Bank of Vienna.   Austria might very well encourage the Croatian movement so long as that movement was directed against
the troublesome Magyars.   So thought the emperor when early
in September, 1848, he reinstated Count Jellachich as *ban* of
Croatia.   The armed conflict of nations in Austria-Hungary
was at hand.

During the same eventful summer of 1848, all eyes in Germany, and in the German provinces of Austria, were focussed
on the Frankfort National Assembly, the living   4. The
embodiment of German national aspirations.   Here Frankfort
                                                   Assembly
again, there was woeful lack of unanimity.   Although
the Assembly, after long deliberation, announced [1] equality before the law, freedom of person, of press, of petition, of meeting,
to be the rights of Germans, it came to grief in attempting
to construct a national government.   The first essential, a
central executive, it hoped to secure by electing Archduke

[1] 27 December, 1848.

John of Austria, a prince who had openly derided Metternich's conservatism, to be *Reichsverweser* (Vicar of the Empire). By this step offense was given alike to the Republicans, who detested princes, to the jealous state governments, which feared eclipse, and to the Prussian nationalists, who hoped to build up the Fatherland around Prussia. The *Reichsverweser* was to govern through a ministry responsible to a democratic assembly. The extent of the new empire was a still more delicate question ; for it would not be a *German* Empire if Prussia brought in her unwilling Polish subjects, and Austria-Hungary her rebellious Czechs, Poles, Magyars, Slovaks, etc. On the other hand, the empire would be sadly mutilated if the German population of either Prussia or Austria should be excluded. There was, moreover, the problem of the Schleswig-Holsteiners whose German nationality Denmark was attempting to override, and Prussia was fighting to defend. Prussia's inglorious discontinuation of the Schleswig-Holstein War in September, 1848, provoked nationalist riots and outrages in Frankfort, which served only to incense the partisans of law and order.

In the Swiss cantons alone was the federating movement entirely successful. The Federal Constitution of 1848, on the one hand, gave to Switzerland at large a permanent

Success of Federalism in Switzerland federal unity, and, on the other, accorded to the people of the several cantons democratic-republican governments.

We left Italy in April, 1848, with the troops of Sardinia, Tuscany, the Papal States, and Naples hastening to emancipate

Failure of Federalism in Italy the peninsula from Austrian domination, and with constitutional governments in all the states except Venice — the republic of St. Mark. Patriots believed the resurrection of Italy — the *Risorgimento* — to be at hand : Italy would become a free federation of constitutional monarchies. To that glorious promise of freedom, facts soon gave the lie. On 29 April the pope repudiated the War of Liberation. In May, after a wild Republican outbreak in Naples, the king of the Two Sicilies dissolved his Chamber, abrogated the constitutional régime, and recalled the Neapolitan troops from the north. Thus abandoned, the northern nationalists, nevertheless, persisted in proclaiming the annexation of Lombardy-Venetia,

Parma, and Modena to the constitutional monarchy of Sardinia. The union was short-lived, however, for the poorly generaled, ill-organized forces of the Italians, unable to prevent a fresh Austrian army from reënforcing Radetzky, were defeated at Custozza (24 July, 1848); and the victorious Radetzky restored the former *status quo*. Only the city of Venice, defiantly Republican, refused to submit.

The summer of 1848 had been encouraging for the imperial Austrian government. The pan-Slav propaganda of the Czechs had evaporated before General Windischgrätz's musketry (June); General Radetzky had crushed the rebellion in Italy (July–August); the German situation was not threatening; and the still successfully insubordinate Magyar state was menaced by rebellious Rumans in Transylvania, and by truculent Serbo-Croats in the southwest. It was a favorable opportunity. In September, 1848, Jellachich was allowed to cross the Drave River into Hungary at the head of an army of invasion. At first he was repelled. Then the Austrian government dissolved the Hungarian Diet, declared Hungary in a state of war, made Jellachich commander of the troops in Hungary, and attempted to send part of the Viennese garrison to his aid.

Close of the First Period of the Revolutionary Movements of 1848; Austrian Revival (August) and the Attack on Hungary

Just at this point the populace of Vienna asserted itself, and initiated the next phase of the revolution, the popular Republican phase. By this time many bourgeois Liberals, having lost business by the turmoil, and many liberal-minded country-gentlemen, having lost their income from manorial dues, and the clergy, longing for peace, had abandoned the revolution to the more radical masses, the emancipated peasants, the Republican clubs, and the discontented workingmen, who had only their lives to lose. The bloody June Days in Paris fitly prefaced the series of tragedies which now ensued.

Second Period of the Revolutionary Movement: the Republican Phase, October, 1848– June, 1849

For three reasons the masses in Vienna opposed the coercion of Hungary. (1) As democrats, they felt a noble sympathy with Kossuth's heroic efforts to democratize Hungary. (2) As German nationalists, they would gladly have allowed the Magyars

to go their way, so that German Austria might be free to join
the new Germany — perhaps the republic of Germany.   (3) As
The Prole- revolutionaries, they made common cause with the
tarian Insur- Magyars as enemies of reaction.   When, therefore,
rection in the Viennese troops were ordered out against Hungary,
Vienna,
October, the Viennese mob hanged the minister of war from
1848 a lantern post, 6 October, 1848.   Next day Vienna
was a city of barricades, manned by desperate proletarians, who
had stormed and despoiled the armory.   The garrison, expelled
from the city, joined Jellachich, who now, in concert with Windischgrätz (from Prague), moved on Vienna.   On 26 October
Windischgrätz began the attack.   In their extremity, the
Viennese looked for help to the Magyar army; but on 30 October from the spire of St. Stephen's they beheld with sinking
hearts the defeat of that army by Jellachich, at Schwechat.
On 31 October Windischgrätz took possession of Vienna.   A
score or so expiated their revolutionary attempt with their lives.

Reaction triumphant now assumed the reins of government
in the person of Prince Felix Schwarzenberg, soldier, diplomat,
Restoration cynic, aristocrat, and brother-in-law of Windisch-
of Law and grätz.   A strong and united monarchy was to him,
Order in as to Prince Metternich before him, the mainstay
Vienna
of the moral order.   In his task of rejuvenating the
monarchy, he had a young sovereign as master; for on 2
Schwarzen- December, 1848, the Emperor Ferdinand had ab-
berg dicated in favor of his eighteen-year-old nephew
Francis Joseph.   That distasteful legacy of revolution, the
Francis *Reichstag*, was transferred to Kremsier, and there
Joseph allowed to elaborate a theoretical constitution, until
on 4 March, 1849, Schwarzenberg suddenly proclaimed an
entirely different constitution, based on the idea of welding all
the Habsburg dominions into a strong and undivided monarchy.

The strong and united monarchy did not yet exist in fact.
Hungary, having declared Francis Joseph's accession illegal,
The was at war with Austria.   At first, the Magyars had
Hungarian been thrown into a panic by Jellachich's rapid advance
Republic into Hungary and by his occupation of Budapest
(5 January, 1849).   Windischgrätz, the conqueror of Prague
and of Vienna, who was likewise now invading Hungary,

inflicted a serious defeat on the revolutionary Magyar army. All western Hungary was at his mercy. With indomitable and reckless courage, Louis Kossuth rallied the lesser nobility, the lower middle classes, and the Magyar peasantry to the national cause, issued banknotes, and searched for competent generals. Encouraged by timely triumphs in Transylvania, Croatia, and Slavonia, and by news that the main Magyar army had out-maneuvered Windischgrätz, Kossuth in an exultant oration proposed a Hungarian Declaration of Independence. On 14 April, 1849, the independence of Hungary was proclaimed.

It was the high tide of Republican Revolution in the spring of 1849, with Republican triumphs in Italy and Germany as well as in Hungary. Mazzini's "Young Italy" party was responsible for outbreaks in Rome and in Leghorn which replaced the pope and the grand-duke of Tuscany by republican forms of government in the Papal States and Tuscany respectively (February, 1849). And the democratic party in Sardinia reopened the war against Austria. In Germany, too, Republican clubs, disgusted with the futile federative efforts of the Frankfort Assembly, fomented revolution early in 1849. The month of May, 1849, witnessed the establishment of provisional republican governments in the Rhenish Palatinate and in the kingdom of Saxony, the erection of barricades at Breslau (Prussia), and the outbreak of a revolution in Baden, where the provisional government, set up in June, was soon able to muster more than 30,000 troops. For a moment it seemed as if this second spring contagion of revolution would plant republics as widely as the first had spread constitutions.

The Republican Revolution had hardly begun before it failed, and the tide of Restoration set in. In March, 1849, the king of Naples suppressed his Parliament, and two months later the ragged revolutionaries of Sicily were crushed by his royal army: absolutism was restored in southern Italy. The republic of Rome was extinguished at the end of June; and Pius IX returned, supported by French arms, converted to Conservatism by the excesses of the anti-clerical Republicans. In Tuscany, as early as 11 April, 1849, upper classes and peasantry had united to restore the grand-duke. In the north, Austrian arms again triumphed. Hopelessly defeated by Radetzky (23 March, 1849), Charles Albert abandoned the throne of Sardinia to his son Victor Emmanuel II, and fled to Portugal, there to die a year later. In May Austrian troops entered Florence; and the Austrian general Haynau so cruelly punished the Lombard city of Brescia for its revolution, that he earned the unenviable nickname of "General Hyena." Finally, the city-republic of Venice, besieged and bombarded, starving and cholera-stricken, surrendered to the Austrians at the end of August, 1849. With the exception of the liberal monarchical constitution which Sardinia retained, Restoration was complete: pope and princes in peaceful possession of their thrones, and Austrian soldiers insolently swaggering in the streets of Venice, Milan, and Florence.

The end of the Hungarian Republic was no less tragic. The climax of Kossuth's career was reached on 6 June, 1849, when he joyously returned to Budapest just after that city had been recaptured from the Austrian invaders. Then quickly the catastrophe came. Jellachich moved north from Croatia with almost 40,000 men; Baron von Haynau approached with the main body of 60,000 Austrian troops; while from across the Carpathians advanced an army of 80,000 Russians, sent by the Tsar Nicholas I, that stern autocrat, to aid his young brother-monarch, Francis Joseph, to reëstablish absolutism in Austria-Hungary. In July, Budapest again surrendered to Austrian captors. By the middle of August one Magyar army had been routed by General Haynau, while the other, facing overwhelming odds, had surrendered to the Russians. Thirteen revolutionary generals and more than one hundred civilians were executed, and two thousand were imprisoned. Louis Kossuth escaped to Turkey, whence, after two years' imprisonment, he journeyed to the United States and Great Britain, finally settling in Turin, ever piteously pleading for a cause that was dead.

2. The End of the Hungarian Republic

To restore order, to consolidate the monarchy, and to fortify the crown against future attacks, the young emperor and his loyal Schwarzenberg now bent all their energies; and their policy received the hearty assent of the revolution-weary church, the outraged court, and the exultant army. The Hungarian Constitution, and the Austrian Constitution of March, 1849, were now abrogated, in the name of "the unity of the empire and monarchical principles." The Transylvanian, Croatian, and Serbian territories which Hungary had annexed were again detached. Hungary lost its last vestiges of independence, and submitted, together with the other provinces of the monarchy, to German officials sent out from Vienna. The revolutionary reforms were all undone, excepting only that the nobles never regained their former power in local politics or their exemption from taxation or their seigniorial rights. Serfdom was a thing of the past in the Habsburg dominions.[1]

3. Restoration in Austria-Hungary

Meanwhile, Republicanism had fared no better in Germany than in Italy or Hungary. The Prussian government, having restored order at Breslau, felt sufficiently secure to send troops to suppress the May Revolution in Saxony, to restore order in the Palatinate, and, with somewhat greater difficulty, to defeat the revolutionaries in Baden (June–July, 1849). Their dreams of a united republican Germany shattered, many of the revolutionaries emigrated to the republic across the Atlantic, — the United States, — a republic which they were soon called upon to defend from disintegration.

4. Suppression of Republicanism in Germany

The Republican outbreaks in Germany had followed upon the failure of the Frankfort Assembly. That body, after deeply offending Austria-Hungary by resolving to exclude all non-German lands from the proposed German Empire, had completed the draft constitution, and early in April had offered the title of hereditary German Emperor to Frederick William IV, the king of Prussia. That weak-minded monarch, undecided as usual, was both reluctant to accept a "crown of shame" from a revolutionary assembly of his social inferiors, and fearful of offending Austria or Russia; nevertheless he evaded a point-blank refusal by asking the acquiescence of the other German governments. Twenty-eight smaller states approved the creation of the empire, but the four kings of Bavaria, Württemberg, Saxony, and Hanover dissented, and Austria vigorously disapproved. Fred-

Failure of the Frankfort Assembly, 1849

---

[1] Except in Galicia.

erick William thereupon refused the imperial crown, 28 April, 1849. Finding its plans obstinately blocked by Austria and Prussia, the discouraged Frankfort Assembly gradually melted away. Its work was a failure.

After the collapse of the National Assembly, and the extinction of the Republican Revolutions, rival plans for the reorganization of Germany were propounded by Prussia and Austria. The Prussian plan was due to Radowitz, the friend and adviser of Frederick William IV. Radowitz, a devout Catholic, believed in a free church in a free state. The latter half of his program, he believed, could be realized by the establishment of a German Union which would exclude Austria-Hungary. To this end, he drafted a constitution, startlingly similar to that of the present German Empire, providing for Prussian hegemony, an administrative council, and a popular assembly. Seventeen states joined the Union, and a Parliament was elected early in 1850. The failure of the plan was due to Frederick William's timid apprehension of Austrian or Russian displeasure, as much as to the determined efforts of the Austrian minister, Schwarzenberg. Prince Schwarzenberg proposed to reorganize the old Germanic Confederation, which should include the entire Austrian monarchy, Hungary and all, and should be provided with a directory of seven members, alternately presided over by Austria and Prussia. After the defeat of the Hungarians, Schwarzenberg was able to press his plans with redoubled vigor, making no secret of his hatred for Prussia. When he called a conference at Frankfort to reorganize the Confederation, Prussia convoked a rival congress at Berlin, and then, menaced by a truculent coalition of Austria, Württemberg, and Bavaria, and fearing that the conservative Nicholas of Russia would again come to Francis Joseph's assistance, Frederick William wavered and weakly gave way. Even Schwarzenberg's plan of reorganization was now discarded, so complete was the reactionary triumph; and the old Germanic Confederation, as organized in 1815, was reëstablished.

The Diet proceeded to undo the work of the revolution, by repealing "the fundamental rights of German citizens," and by appointing a committee, popularly called the

Renewed Preponderance of Austria, and the Humiliation of Prussia, 1850

Restoration of the Germanic Confederation, 1851

"reactionary committee," to eliminate such dangerous principles as universal suffrage from the constitutions of 1848. Under Schwarzenberg's influence, as formerly under Metternich's domination, the German governments after 1850 rigorously repressed Liberalism, and stamped their hatred of progress upon courts, chambers, schools, and clergy.

Reaction in the Germanies

Ardent German patriots were deeply disappointed in King Frederick William IV of Prussia, who had miserably failed to coöperate with the Frankfort Assembly or to withstand Austria or to become a great national leader. Likewise, German Liberals were chagrined at his obstinate opposition to the establishment of real political democracy in Prussia. The supposedly Liberal constitution, which had been granted in December, 1848, was subsequently revised by royal commissions and reactionary statesmen, until, as finally promulgated by the king on 31 January, 1850, it was a thoroughly Conservative document. However, it proved to be the one permanent result of the Revolution of 1848 in Prussia; and, with changes only of detail, it has remained the constitution of Prussia from

Constitutional Government in Prussia: the Conservative Document of 1850

1850 to the present and throughout these years has preserved the form, if not the spirit, of representative, constitutional government. The Prussian Constitution of 1850 was decreed by royal authority, like the French Charter of 1814; it embodied an elaborate declaration of individual rights and liberties, though without adequate provision for rendering them effective; it asserted the " divine right " of the monarch to reign and intrusted wide powers to the king. The king is head of the army, of the church, and of the whole civil service. The upper legislative chamber (*Herrenhaus*) is recruited almost exclusively by royal appointment. And all measures, before they become law, require the king's assent; though, by reason of the monarch's control of the *Herrenhaus*, no measure of which he disapproves is likely to be enacted. Even the lower chamber (*Abgeordnetenhaus*), while nominally chosen by universal manhood suffrage, represents plutocracy rather than democracy, for, by a peculiar three-class system of indirect elections, equal representation is accorded to the few rich men whose fortunes aggregate one-third of the total taxable wealth of the community, to the middle class whose moderate possessions comprise another third, and to the masses whose combined savings constitute the last third of the total wealth.   And finally, in Prussia the ministry is responsible not to the parliament but to the king.

The revolutionary movements which had so shaken the foundations of European politics had seemingly accomplished but little.   Switzerland, Holland, Denmark, Prussia, Sardinia, and a few other states had secured con-stitutional government; servile dues had been abol-ished in Austria; but, for the rest, the democratic innovations of the revolution had vanished before the victorious armies of Conservatism.   In Austria-Hungary, in the Italian and German states, autocracy again wielded the censor-ship; in Great Britain the Chartist fiasco had left democracy dis-graced and disheartened; in France the fierce June Days augured ill for the new republic.   Despite its defeat, the political demo-cratic movement was not destroyed: it lived on in the des-perate dreams of the workingmen who had beheld, even if only for a moment, democracy triumphant in Europe.   For the present, however, nationalism, which, by its conflicting claims, had defeated the revolution, still dwarfed all other considerations, refusing to be downed while Italy remained divided, Germany disunited, and Hungary subject to Austrian rule.

Significance of the Revo-lutionary Movements of 1848–1849

ADDITIONAL READING

Growth of Democracy in Great Britain.   Brief general narratives: Gil-bert Slater, *The Making of Modern England*, new rev. ed. (1915), ch. v–x, xii–xiv; A. L. Cross, *History of England and Greater Britain* (1914), ch. l, li; Justin McCarthy, *The Epoch of Reform, 1830–1850* (1897); J. H. Rose, *The Rise and Growth of Democracy in Great Britain* (1898); A. D. Innes, *History of England and the British Empire*, Vol. IV (1914), ch. iv, v; *Cambridge Modern History*, Vol. X (1907), ch. xviii–xx.   Much general information may be derived from the series of biographical sketches *The Prime Ministers of Queen Victoria*, ed. by S. J. Reid.   On the removal of religious disabilities: W. J. Amherst, *The History of Catholic Emancipation, 1771–1820*, 2 vols. (1886); Bernard Ward, *The Dawn of the Catholic Re-vival, 1781–1803* (1909), *The Eve of Catholic Emancipation, 1803–1829*, 3 vols. (1912), *The Sequel to Catholic Emancipation, 1830–1850*, 2 vols. (1915); G. J. Shaw-Lefevre, *Peel and O'Connell: a Review of the Irish Policy of*

Parliament from the Union to the Death of Sir Robert Peel (1887); Robert Dunlop, *Daniel O'Connell* (1900) in the "Heroes of the Nations" Series; W. E. H. Lecky, *Leaders of Public Opinion in Ireland*, new ed., 2 vols. (1903), especially Vol. II which is a biography of Daniel O'Connell; H. W. Clark, *History of English Nonconformity*, Vol. II (1913), Book IV, ch. ii, iii. On the Réform Bill of 1832 : J. R. M. Butler, *The Passing of the Great Reform Bill* (1914), the most important single work on the subject; G. L. Dickinson, *The Development of Parliament in the Nineteenth Century* (1895); Spencer Walpole, *Life of Lord John Russell*, 2 vols. (1889); S. J. Reid, *Lord John Russell* (1895); W. N. Molesworth, *The History of England, 1830-1874*, 3 vols. (1874), is particularly valuable for the reform of 1832. On humanitarian legislation : Edward Jenks, *A Short History of the English Law* (1912), an able summary; Sir J. F. Stephens, *History of the Criminal Law of England*, 3 vols. (1883), a standard work; L. O. Pike, *A History of Crime in England*, Vol. II (1876); Sidney and Beatrice Webb, *The State and the Doctor* (1910), concerning the campaign for public health, 1832-1854. Of the English Poor Law the classical treatment is Sir George Nicholls, *A History of the English Poor Law in connection with the State of the Country and the Condition of the People*, new ed., 2 vols. (1898), with a third and supplementary volume — 1834 to date — by Thomas Mackay (1899). On the rise of philosophical and political Radicalism in England : Sir Leslie Stephen, *The English Utilitarians* (1900); C. B. R. Kent, *The English Radicals* (1899); William Harris, *History of the Radical Party in Parliament [to 1867]* (1885); W. L. Davidson, *Political Thought in England: the Utilitarians from Bentham to J. S. Mill* (1915), in the "Home University Library"; Elie Halévy, *La formation du radicalisme philosophique*, 3 vols. (1901-1904), exhaustive and scholarly; A. V. Dicey, *Lectures on the Relation between Law and Public Opinion in England during the Nineteenth Century*, 2d ed. (1914), illuminating throughout, especially valuable for the influence of Bentham; C. M. Atkinson, *Life of Jeremy Bentham* (1905); L. S. Benjamin (pseud. Lewis Melville), *The Life and Letters of William Cobbett in England and America* (1913); E. I. Carlyle, *William Cobbett, a Study of his Life as Shown in his Writings* (1904); Graham Wallas, *Life of Francis Place, 1771-1854* (1898). On various social reformers of the time : H. de B. Gibbins, *English Social Reformers* (1902), brief sketches of such men as Wesley, Wilberforce, Kingsley, Carlyle, Ruskin, and the factory reformers; and Edwin Hodder, *Life and Work of the 7th Earl of Shaftesbury*, 3 vols. (1888), an exhaustive study of the career of the greatest of the factory reformers. On the Chartist movement : R. G. Gammage, *History of Chartism*, new ed. (1894), a sympathetic treatment by a leader of the movement, first published in 1854; Thomas Carlyle, *Chartism* (1839), a brilliant pamphlet; Édouard Dolléans, *Le chartisme*, 2 vols. (1912-1913), full but without indication of sources used; P. W. Slosson, *The Decline of the Chartist Movement* (1916), a valuable monograph.

Revolutionary Movements, 1848-1849. Brief General Narratives. C. M. Andrews, *The Historical Development of Modern Europe*, Vol. I

(1896), ch. ix, x; J. H. Robinson and C. A. Beard, *The Development of Modern Europe*, Vol. II (7907), ch. xix, xx; C. D. Hazen, *Europe since 1815* (1910), ch. vi–ix; C. E. M. Hawkesworth, *The Last Century in Europe, 1814–1910* (1913), ch. xiv–xviii; W. A. Phillips, *Modern Europe, 1815–1899* (1901), ch. x–xiii; C. A. Fyffe, *A History of Modern Europe, 1792–1878* (1896), ch. xviii–xx; Oscar Browning, *A History of the Modern World*, Vol. I (1912), Book II, ch. vii–ix; *History of All Nations*, Vol. XVIII, *Restoration and Revolution*, by Theodor Flathe, ch. viii–xvi; H. T. Dyer, *A History of Modern Europe from the Fall of Constantinople*, 3d ed. rev. by Arthur Hassall (1901), ch. lxix, lxx; *Cambridge Modern History*, Vol. XI (1909), ch. ii–viii; *Histoire générale*, Vol. X, ch. x, xvi, Vol. XI, ch. i–iv; H. A. L. Fisher, *The Republican Tradition in Europe* (1911), ch. vii–x.

France under Louis Philippe and the Second Republic, 1830–1850. Paul Thureau-Dangin, *Histoire de la monarchie de juillet*, 2d ed., 7 vols. (1888–1892), the most elaborate French history on the reign of Louis Philippe, Roman Catholic and Conservative in tone; Jean Jaurès (editor), *Histoire socialiste*, Vol. VIII by J. E. Fournière, *Le règne de Louis Philippe* (1906), and Vol. IX by Georges Renard, *La république de 1848* (1848–1852), a social history by prominent French Socialists; Georges Weill, *La France sous la monarchie constitutionelle, 1814–1848*, new rev. ed. (1912), and, by the same author, *Histoire du parti républicain en France de 1814 à 1870* (1900), scholarly and valuable; J. Tchernoff, *Le parti républicain sous la monarchie de juillet: formation et évolution de la doctrine républicaine* (1901), well documented; Eugène Spuller, *Histoire parlementaire de la seconde république* (1891), an important political work; Émile Levasseur, *Histoire des classes ouvrières et de l'industrie en France de 1789 à 1870*, Vol. II (1904), Books IV, V, indispensable for French social history; Louis Blanc, *History of Ten Years, 1830–1840*, Eng. trans., 2 vols. (1844–1845), a famous early attempt to furnish an economic interpretation of the July Monarchy; Lorenz von Stein, *Geschichte der sozialen Bewegung in Frankreich*, 3 vols. (1850), covering in the last two volumes the years 1830–1850, an extremely suggestive contemporary account. Side-lights on important persons of the time are given in the French biographies of *Guizot* by Agénor Bardoux (1894), of *Thiers* by Charles de Mazade (1884) and by Edgar Zevort (1892), and of *Lamartine* by Pierre Quentin-Bauchart (1903).

With Special Reference to the Revolution of 1848 in France. Albert Crémieux, *La révolution de février: étude critique sur les journées des 21, 22, 23 et 24 février, 1848* (1912), the most scholarly and impartial account of the February Revolution; Pierre de La Gorce, *Histoire de la seconde république française*, 7th ed., 2 vols. (1914), anti-Republican and anti-Socialist in tone; Victor Pierre, *Histoire de la république de 1848*, 2d ed., 2 vols. (1878), Conservative and anti-Bonapartist; Louis Blanc, *Historical Revelations*, Eng. trans. (1858), an account of the February Revolution from the point of view of the Socialist leader; Adolphe Blanqui, *Des classes ouvrières en France pendant l'année 1848*, 2 vols. (1849), another contemporary and sympathetic narrative; Ferdinand Dreyfus, *L'assistance sous la seconde république, 1848–1851* (1907), useful for social legislation; J. A. R. Marriott (editor), *The French Revolution in 1848 in its Economic Aspects*, 2 vols. (1913), containing a critical introduction and reprints in French of Louis Blanc's *Organisation du travail* and Émile Thomas's *Histoire des ateliers nationaux*, the latter first published in 1848; N. W. Senior, *Journals kept in France and Italy from 1848 to 1852, with a Sketch of the Revolution of 1848*, the contemporary diary of a celebrated English economist and publicist, ed. by his daughter, M. C. M. Simpson, 2d ed., 2 vols. (1871).

The Revolutions in Central Europe, 1848–1849. General account: C. E. Maurice, *The Revolutionary Movement of 1848–1849 in Italy, Austria-Hungary, and Germany* (1887), full of facts, but dry and poorly organized. Volumes V and VI of Alfred Stern's monumental and authoritative *Geschichte Europas* (1911) treat of the years from 1835 to 1848 in their social and economic aspects as well as the political. On the Austrian Empire: R. P. Mahaffy, *Francis Joseph I, his Life and Times, an Essay in Politics*, new ed. (1915), pp. 1–36, a brief introduction; Louis Leger, *A History of Austro-Hungary from the Earliest Time to the Year 1889*, Eng. trans. by Mrs. B. Hill (1889), ch. xxvii–xxxiii, the most satisfactory account; Heinrich Friedjung, *Oesterreich von 1848 bis 1860*, 2 vols. (1908–1912), an exhaustive study; J. A. von Helfert, *Geschichte Oesterreichs vom Ausgange des Wiener October-Aufstandes, 1848*, 4 vols. in 5 (1869–1886); Anton Springer, *Geschichte Oesterreichs seit dem Wienerfrieden 1809*, Vol. II (1865); Heinrich Reschauer and Moritz Smets, *Das Jahr 1848: Geschichte der Wiener Revolution*, 2 vols. in 1 (1872), and, by the former author, *Geschichte des Kampfes der Handwerkerzünfte und der Kaufmannsgremien mit der oesterreichischen Bureaukratie* (1882); Maximilian Bach, *Geschichte der Wiener Revolution im Jahre 1848* (1898); E. V. Zenker, *Die Wiener Revolution, 1848, in ihren socialen Voraussetzungen und Beziehungen* (1897); Johann Slokar, *Geschichte der oesterreichischen Industrie und ihrer Förderung unter Kaiser Franz I* (1914), for the beginnings of the Industrial Revolution in Austria; C. M. Knatchbull-Hugessen, *The Political Evolution of the Hungarian Nation*, Vol. II (1908), ch. xii–xvi, a readable account of the Magyar insurrection and of its suppression; *Kossuth's Speeches in America*, ed. by F. W. Newman (1854), a defense of the Hungarian insurrection; Louis Eisenmann, *Le compromis austro-hongrois de 1867, étude sur le dualisme* (1904), pp. 1–71, an admirable French account of the " old régime " in Hungary and of the rise of the spirit of Magyar nationalism. On the revolutionary movement of 1848–1849 in the Germanies: G. M. Priest, *Germany since 1740* (1915), ch. viii, ix, very brief but clear; *The Reminiscences of Carl Schurz*, ed. by Frederic Bancroft and W. A. Dunning, Vol. I (1907), a lively account of the revolutionary movement by a famous Liberal sympathizer; Heinrich von Treitschke, *Deutsche Geschichte im neunzehnten Jahrhundert*, Vol. V, *1840–1848* (1896), Eng. trans. in preparation (1916), hostile to the democratic Liberals; Hans Blum, *Die deutsche Revolution, 1848–1849* (1897), the best treatment in German; Karl Marx, *Revolution and Counter Revolution, or, Germany in 1848*, 2d ed. (1904), a collection of papers originally published in the New York *Tribune*, 1851–1852, and setting forth in somewhat disjointed manner a Socialistic interpretation of the revolutionary movement; Theodor von Bernhardi, *Unter Nikolaus und Friedrich Wilhelm IV*, in collected works, ed. by Friedrich von Bernhardi, Vol. II (1894); Gustav Lüders, *Die demokratische Bewegung in Berlin im Oktober 1848* (1909), a painstaking monograph; Paul Matter, *La Prusse et la révolution de 1848* (1903); Franz Wigard (editor), *Stenographischer Bericht über die Verhandlungen der ersten Konstitutionale Nationalversammlung*, 9 vols. (1849), official documents relating to the Frankfort Assembly. On the revolutionary movements of 1848–1849 in the Italian states: W. R. Thayer, *The Dawn of Italian Independence, 1814–1849*, Vol. II (1893), an excellent narrative; Bolton King, *Joseph Mazzini* (1902), an admirable biography; Mrs. Hamilton King, *Letters and Recollections of Mazzini* (1912), containing some very characteristic letters and a description of the last imprisonment and the death of Mazzini; G. M. Trevelyan, *Garibaldi's Defence of the Roman Republic* (1907), useful for the whole Italian situation; R. M. Johnston, *The Roman Theocracy and the Republic, 1846–1849* (1901); Guglielmo Pepe, *Histoire des révolutions et des guerres d'Italie, 1847–49* (1850), and L. C. Farini, *The Roman State, from 1815 to 1850*, Eng. trans. ed. by W. E. Gladstone, 4 vols. (1851–1854), both contemporary accounts by Italian revolutionaries opposed to the Church; H. R. Whitehouse, *Collapse of the Kingdom of Naples* (1899).

CHAPTER XX

THE GROWTH OF NATIONALISM, 1848-1871

BETWEEN 1830 and 1848 the idea of political democracy had made steady progress throughout Europe among both the workingmen and the middle class until in the eventful days of 1848 it had thrown the whole Continent into turmoil.   That it had not produced immediate results commensurate with its aims and purposes was due in part to the fact that certain peoples of Europe divided their allegiance between the idea of political democracy and the notion of patriotic nationalism.   A little reflection upon the national and racial movements in the Habsburg dominions, which have been discussed in the preceding chapter, will furnish concrete examples of the way in which a sense of nationality could fatally choke an aspiration for democratic government.   It appeared as if the patriotic instinct was more primitive and more powerful than the democratic ideal, and that in many instances the forces of reaction might rely upon the former to thwart the latter.   The point was, of course, that in most countries democracy was the program of but particular classes, while patriotism provided a spacious platform on which an entire nation could stand shoulder to shoulder.

Democracy Thwarted in 1848-1849 by Nationalism

Consequently, in the period from 1848 to 1870, the bulk of Europeans seemed to rest from agitation for liberal constitutions and other paraphernalia of democracy, exhausted, as it were, by the chronic factional tumults which, throughout the Era of Metternich, and down to the domestic upheavals of 1848, had stirred every state, and to expend their energies more unitedly upon colossal attempts at nation-building. To be sure, democracy continued to make some headway between 1848 and 1870, but it was

Predominance of Nationalism, 1848-1870

dwarfed in historical significance by such achievements as the national unifications of Italy and Germany.

As the nineteenth-century theory of political democracy was derived mainly from the revolutionary French doctrines of "liberty" and "equality," so contemporaneous na-

"National-ism" a Heritage of the French Revolution

tionalism drew its inspiration from "fraternity." And as "fraternity" under the great Napoleon had meant nations in arms, — the marshaling and fighting of hosts of men, — so now, in the cause of national uni-fications, the international peace which had attended the suprem-acy of Metternich gave place to a new series of wars.

One other mark of the period from 1848 to 1870 was the fitting fact that its most conspicuous personage was another Napoleon

The Bonapartist Heritage

Bonaparte, who, as politician and adventurer, rivaled even the first emperor of the French. The picturesque career of this second Bonaparte merits somewhat detailed consideration on account of the enduring influence which it has exerted upon the fortunes of present-day France, Italy, Germany, and Austria-Hungary.

LOUIS NAPOLEON BONAPARTE AND THE ERECTION OF THE SECOND FRENCH EMPIRE

Louis Napoleon Bonaparte, the son of Louis Bonaparte, erstwhile king of Holland, and of Hortense Beauharnais, was

Louis Napoleon Bonaparte (1808–1873)

born in the palace of the Tuileries at Paris in 1808. His uncle, the Emperor Napoleon, then at the very height of his power, stood sponsor for him at baptism and inscribed his name in the family register with a right of succession.[1] Exiled from France, along with all Bona-partes, by the Ultra-Royalists in 1816, he passed his youth in Switzerland, Savoy, and southern Germany. He attended a *gymnasium* at Augsburg and was put through a thorough course in military science under an able Swiss general, but the credit for his excellent liberal education was due primarily to the

[1] The Bonapartist princes who intervened in the recognized line of succession between Napoleon I and Louis Napoleon Bonaparte were (1) the son of Napoleon I — the king of Rome, titular Napoleon II, who died in 1832; (2) the brother of Napoleon I — Louis, who died in 1846; (3) the older son of Louis and brother of Louis Napoleon — Napoleon Louis, who died in 1831.

devotion of his intellectually gifted mother; and it was from her also that he learned his pet axioms: "With a name like his, he would always be something"; "He ought to know how to amuse the royalist and republican crowds"; "All means of ruling are good, legitimate, and sufficient, provided only that material prosperity is ensured."

Brought up to regard the tradition of his family as identical with that of the Revolution, Prince Louis Napoleon accounted himself from the outset a born leader of Liberalism, a predestined custodian of the principles of liberty, equality, and fraternity. Had not the bourgeois government of Louis Philippe been formed too quickly, he would have gone straight to Paris in 1830 and there claimed the fruits of the overthrow of Charles X and the other reactionaries. As it was, he joined in Italy the revolutionary society of the *Carbonari* and participated in the insurrection of 1831 against the pope, but he soon fell into the hands of the Austrians, and was released only through his mother's tears. Then he intrigued simultaneously with French republicans and with Polish rebels, but the watchfulness of Louis Philippe on one hand, and the firm action of the Russian tsar on the other, reduced the Bonapartist prince to the necessity of wielding the pen rather than the sword.

Louis Napoleon's Liberalism

In a series of writings which culminated in the *Napoleonic Ideas* (1839), he set forth his political theories. The French Empire, he maintained, had been the perfect realization of the principles of 1789. It had rested upon a foundation of national sovereignty; it had recognized universal manhood suffrage in its domestic affairs, and in its foreign relations it had upheld the cause of separate nationalities; it had been solidified, directed, and rendered glorious by its Cæsarism, that is, by intrusting power to an emperor whose absolutism was conditioned only by his ability to promote public prosperity and to retain popular support. Such, according to Louis Napoleon, had been the aims of the first Napoleon and such would be his aims in endeavoring to reëstablish the empire in France.

Louis Napoleon's "Cæsarism"

We know now that these writings of Louis Napoleon presented a very falsely idealized picture of the First Empire, but they fitted in very nicely with the "Napoleonic Legend," [1] which, spun on sea-girt St. Helena by the great Napoleon himself, already had obtained sentimental credence in many a French cottage. And circumstances of the reign of Louis Philippe (1830–1848) tended to exalt the legend and incidentally to feed the ambition of Prince Louis Napoleon. The French monarchy which owed its erection to the July Revolution was, as we have seen, a bourgeois compromise between Bourbon reaction and Republican liberalism, and the very concessions which it was obliged to make to the latter were fuel to the Bonapartist flame. Thus the tricolor again supplanted the white flag as the national ensign, and had not the tricolor been the banner of Napoleon? Thus, too, the detested fleur-de-lis atop the Vendôme column was replaced by an iron statue of the Little Corporal, and had not that column been cast from cannon which Napoleon himself had captured from the Austrians? The completion of the monumental arch of triumph in Paris (1836) in commemoration of the military exploits of Napoleon brought the ignominious foreign policy of the bourgeois king into glaring contrast with the glorious victories of the emperor; and Louis Philippe paid the crowning tribute to Bonapartism when he had the bones of the emperor brought back from St. Helena (1840) to repose under the stately dome of the *Invalides*, just as the exile had willed, "on the banks of the Seine among the people whom he had so dearly loved."

Influence of the "Napoleonic Legend"

Twice during the reign of Louis Philippe, Louis Napoleon made premature attempts to take advantage of the growing Bonapartist sentiment in France and to reëstablish the empire. The first time, in 1836, raising his standard at Strassburg and being speedily arrested, he was released on condition that he emigrate to America. The second time, in 1840, landing at Boulogne with the declaration that the emperor's bones should rest only in a "regenerated France," he was condemned to imprisonment for life, and the next six years he spent in the fortress of Ham. It was during this period of captivity that Louis Napoleon added a mild variety of Socialism to his other political theories. He readily perceived that the government of

Premature Attempts of Louis Napoleon to Seize the French Government

[1] See Vol. I, pp. 572 f.

Louis Philippe existed primarily in the interests of the bourgeoisie and that the body of French workingmen, whose numbers and misery the Industrial Revolution was then rapidly increasing, were its most natural enemies. His humanitarian impulses and his sense of " good politics " led him forthwith to espouse the cause of the workingmen. From prison he corresponded with Louis Blanc, the Socialist, and with Proudhon, the Anarchist, and he wrote another book, the *Extinction of Pauperism*, that promised, as the cornerstone of his projected régime, the material prosperity of all classes. It would be his business, he said, to assist the capitalists by opening up new fields of industry; the peasants, by stimulating the cultivation of the land through the aid of governmental grants; and the industrial proletarians, by providing work in abundance and so increasing their power of purchase. In this way work would be found for the unemployed, a demand would be created for every product, and poverty would eventually disappear. "The triumph of Christianity abolished slavery; the triumph of the French Revolution abolished serfdom; the triumph of democracy will abolish pauperism." And, of course, democracy, so far as France was concerned, was a cryptogram, to which Prince Louis Napoleon alone had the key.

Socialistic Leanings of Louis Napoleon

Louis Napoleon was lucky. In 1846 he managed to escape from the prison of Ham, in the guise of a workingman, curiously enough, and to make his way to England. Two years elapsed and he was recalled with open arms by all France. The year 1848 marked the first success in the Great Adventure.

As soon as news reached him in February, 1848, that a joint uprising of bourgeois Republicans and Socialist workingmen had effected the deposition of Louis Philippe, Louis Napoleon crossed over to Paris. The radicals welcomed him, but the more moderate members of the provisional government were insistent that he should leave the country forthwith. It was wonderfully fortunate for him that he obeyed instructions and again withdrew to England, because in that way he was absent from France when the bourgeois Republicans and the Socialist workingmen fell to fighting, and thus he escaped the opprobrium which the latter heaped upon the former for the horrible bloodshed of the

Louis Napoleon and the February (1848) Revolution

June Days. At the same time, the offer of his services to the aged duke of Wellington, then gallantly overawing the British Chartists, gave guarantees to the middle class of France, the lovers of law and order, that his radicalism was not of the dangerous sort.

It was thus that the name of a Bonaparte presented itself to all Frenchmen as a pledge of peace and security. In the midst of most unseemly quarrels between Socialists, bourgeois Radicals, Moderate Republicans, and Catholics, — each faction interpreting "liberty" and "equality" after the desires of its own heart, — Louis Napoleon stepped in and with the charming word "fraternity" stilled the tumult, — "fraternity," the memory of the proudest achievements of French nationality, the single foundation on which all factions might unite. In June, 1848, Prince Louis Napoleon was elected to the Assembly, and in December he was raised to the presidency of the republic by an overwhelming popular majority.[1] At the close of 1848 he took the oath "to remain faithful to the democratic republic; . . . to regard as enemies of the nation all those who may attempt by illegal means to change the form of the established government." Henceforth, for twenty-two years the history of Louis Napoleon is the history of France.

Champion of Law and Order and of Nationalism

As president of the second republic (1848–1852), Louis Napoleon proved to be one of the greatest as well as first of democratic politicians in Europe. "Politicians," in the more recent American sense of the word — persons who can influence voters and control elections — have been everywhere an essential by-product of democracy; and it was no oddity that the establishment of universal manhood suffrage in France by the revolution of 1848 was attended by the rise of a "politician." From the outset of his administration Louis Napoleon consciously set about enlisting the support of all political and

Prince Louis Napoleon, President of the Second French Republic, 1848–1852

---

[1] That Louis Napoleon received hearty support from all factions is attested by the fact that while he received 5,434,226 votes, General Cavaignac, the candidate of the moderate bourgeois Republicans, received only 1,448,107, while the Socialist workingmen's candidate, Ledru-Rollin, received but 370,000, and the clerical Lamartine a paltry 17,000.

social groups in the state, "making himself," in the American phrase, "solid with the country." While he patted and praised the workingmen and threw them a sop in the form of a voluntary old-age insurance (1850) which should be guaranteed by the state, he was craftily utilizing the bourgeois and Catholic majority in the Assembly to pass such legislation as would win him the favor of these groups. On one hand, business was protected and encouraged, and domestic order was strictly enforced; and, on the other, a French military expedition was dispatched to Rome (1849) to reinstate Pope Pius IX in the temporal sovereignty from which the revolutionary movement of the preceding year had deposed him, and a sweeping measure in 1850 restored the great privileges which the Catholic clergy had exercised in the days of Charles X over the education of French children. Thus, ardent Catholics, whose consciences had been outraged by the irreligious policies of the bourgeois government of Louis Philippe, now found themselves favored by Louis Napoleon; and the bourgeois themselves discovered that their particular economic interests were safeguarded as jealously by the Bonapartist president as by the "king of the green umbrella" (Louis Philippe).

The close alliance between Louis Napoleon and the Clericals, many of whom in politics were outspoken reactionaries, might have cost the president the support of the radical and revolutionary elements on which, during his earlier years, he had chiefly relied, had not a constitutional question arisen between the president and the Assembly which gave the former an opportunity to show his loyalty to democracy. It will be recalled that both the president and the Assembly had been elected in 1848 by universal manhood suffrage. The Assembly, however, composed largely of middle-class persons who were fearful of the results of the exercise of the franchise by the working classes, passed an electoral law in 1850, depriving of the suffrage those who had not lived and paid taxes three years in the commune in which they voted. In effect this statute disfranchised the ever-moving artisans of the large towns and deprived three million adult males, out of a total of nine millions, of the ballot. In this situation, Louis Napoleon perceived his chance

not only to win the workingmen but to ruin the Assembly.   He
at once declared that as the elected representative of the entire
nation he was under obligation to prevent the Assembly from
disfranchising Frenchmen. In November, 1851, he formally
proposed the reëstablishment of universal manhood suffrage,
and upon the refusal of the Assembly, he executed
Louis
Napoleon's   in December a *coup d'état* that in its general purposes
Coup d'état,   and results resembled the celebrated *coup d'état* of the
December,
1851   18th and 19th Brumaire (1799), when the first
Bonapartist adventurer had overthrown the government of the First Republic.

On 2 December, 1851, the anniversary of the battle of Austerlitz, Prince Louis Napoleon issued a manifesto, proclaiming a
temporary dictatorship, the dissolution of the hated Assembly,
the restoration of universal suffrage, and the submission to
popular vote (*plébiscite*) of a proposal to intrust the Prince-
President with the task of revising the constitution.   Louis
Napoleon had counted shrewdly upon the acquiescence of most
Frenchmen; a careful disposition of loyal troops overawed the
minority; a few riots were quelled with some bloodshed; prompt
stifling of the press and activity on the part of the faithful
secret police prevented the spread of counter-agitation; and the
most dangerous leaders of the opposition, such as the Liberal
Monarchist Thiers and the Republicans Cavaignac and Victor
Hugo, were seized and hustled out of the country.   Under these
circumstances, the French people decided, on 21 December,
1851, by 7,500,000 votes against 640,000, to delegate to Louis
Napoleon the right of drawing up a new constitution for the
Second Republic.

In January, 1852, the new constitution was promulgated.
It was a travesty of republicanism.   To be sure, provision
was made for a popularly elected Legislative Body of 250
members, but the president might rearrange electoral districts
at will, and the powers of the Body were carefully restricted:
it might not initiate legislation or amend bills submitted by
the government; it might not control the ministry or question
the policy of the administration; it might not determine the
details of the budget which it voted; it might not publish its
proceedings or even elect its own presiding officer.   The presi-

dent, whose term of office was lengthened to ten years, became a kind of legitimate dictator: the Ministry no longer constituted a parliamentary cabinet, but was appointed by him and removable at his pleasure alone; a Council of State, chosen by him, drafted bills for submission to the Legislative Body; and a Senate, the members of which were named and salaried by the president, might revise the laws, propose new ones, and interpret the constitution. The president himself commanded the army and navy; he could make war and peace; he appointed local officials, judicial and administrative; he possessed the right of pardon; and he subjected the press to rigid surveillance. By means of the *coup d'état* of 1851 and the ensuing promulgation of this remarkable constitution, — always in the name of democracy, — Louis Napoleon, the adventurer, had taken a long step toward the destruction of democracy.

The year 1852 in France was one of transition from republican to imperial institutions. Louis Napoleon, now president nominally for ten years, put his own effigy upon the coins and restored the gilt eagles in the army. He kept up a show of universal suffrage. He made state processions throughout the country, accompanied by a subservient staff of newspaper reporters and by a paid group of shouters, who, stationed at strategic points in the audiences, led the applause and opportunely cried *vive l'empereur*. He spoke honeyed words to peasants, to artisans, to capitalists, to rich and poor, to reactionaries and revolutionaries, to agnostics and those religiously inclined. And his reward was speedy and complete. On 2 December, 1852, he became in name what he was already in fact, and was solemnly proclaimed, with the approval of eight million votes, Napoleon III, emperor of the French.[1] The imperial constitution was simply an adaptation of the "republican" constitution of January, 1852.

The new régime, according to Napoleon's pompous declaration, was to be the final flower of the Revolution, and the emperor

Napoleon III, Emperor of the French, 1852–1870

---

[1] His title of "Napoleon III" implied the right to reign of "Napoleon II," that unfortunate son of Napoleon I, *L'Aiglon* (the Eaglet), who, styled in his cradle king of Rome, had been reared at the Austrian court as a Habsburg prince under the title of duke of Reichstadt, and who had closed a brief feeble life at Vienna in 1832.

himself was to be "the beneficent motive force of the whole social order." For eight years (1852–1860), in truth, Napoleon III preserved his popularity virtually unimpaired and the government of the Second Empire appeared to be the most stable that France had enjoyed since the Revolution.

The reason for the seeming stability of the Second Empire was the support which various classes, formerly hostile to each other, now unitedly accorded it. While Napoleon III carefully maintained the centralized administration and the subordination of the elected Assemblies to his own will,[1] and sternly repressed distinctively Republican or Radical agitation,[2] he retained the loyalty of Liberals by preserving universal manhood suffrage, however illusory it was in practice, as the underlying theory of his governmental system. He was perpetually rolling revolutionary phrases upon his tongue and was proud to confess that his empire rested on the suffrages of all France.

Seeming Stability of the Second Empire

Liberals

At the same time, the brilliance of his imperial court could fascinate many Conservatives. In the drawing-room or over the teacups, Napoleon III was infinitely more at home than his uncle; and his marriage in 1853 with Eugénie, countess of Montijo, a Spanish princess, gave him a helpmate, whose beauty, elegance, and charm of manner were of the utmost service in making the French court once more the center of European styles and fashions. The Empress Eugénie, moreover, by her pious attachment to the Catholic Church and by her famed charities was recognized both as the champion of Clerical policies and as the friend of the poor.

Conservatives

To the workingmen Napoleon III addressed words of cheer and encouragement. He assured them he was one of them. He rode in engine cabs with locomotive engineers; he talked familiarly with artisans upon the boulevards;

Workingmen

[1] The election expenses of "official candidates" — those approved by the emperor — were paid from the state treasury, while other candidates were obliged to defray their own expenses. Moreover the electoral machinery was almost completely in the emperor's hands, and by act of 1858 every candidate had to take an oath of fidelity to Napoleon.

[2] The freedom of the press continued to be greatly abridged, and a law of 1858 allowed the government to intern political offenders in France or in Algeria or to exile them without trial.

he drank healths to masons, carpenters, and plumbers. He subsidized their unions, and he and the empress endowed charitable institutions for their betterment. It was for the working class, he affirmed, that his government of cheap bread, great public works, and holidays primarily existed. He gloried in the appellation, "emperor of the workmen." Nevertheless, when one turns from promises to achievements, from words to deeds, one is astonished to find how little Napoleon III deserved the appellation. Only the mildest beginnings of social legislation were discoverable in the permission extended to laborers to form coöperative societies, as in England, for collective buying and selling (1863); in the legalization of trade unions and the recognition for the first time of the right of strikes and lockouts (1864); and in the extension of state guarantees to workmen's voluntary insurance against death and industrial accidents (1868). Perhaps, however, it was worth while to have inaugurated social politics in France.

It was to the capitalists and business men, however, that Napoleon III made his most constant appeal. While he restricted liberty in political matters, he increased it in economic affairs. Governmental regulation of industry was lessened; the organization of commercial corporations was facilitated; the merchant marine was subsidized; a system of savings banks was established; a policy of free trade, borrowed from England, was gradually introduced; and both industry and trade were stimulated by a series of remarkable public works. Not only were harbors improved, swamps drained, canals dug, and roads repaired, but the Second Empire was the period of railway construction throughout France. It was likewise during this period that Paris was beautified and adorned under the supervision of the emperor's great friend, Baron Haussmann, and became the pleasure city of the world.[1] Many were the fortunes made or swelled during the Second Empire. And the bourgeoisie, who were the chief beneficiaries, were loyal to Napoleon III for many years.

For generations the bourgeoisie had been of all classes in France the one most affected by hostility to the Catholic

Middle-class Capitalists

[1] The international expositions held in Paris in 1855 and in 1867 attested the magnificence of the city and the growth of material comfort throughout the nation.

Church, and bourgeois Radicals had been most zealously combated by Clericals.   It was a tribute to Napoleon's art as a politician that he was able to yoke these two unruly

Simultane-
ous Concili-
ation of
Catholics
and
Bourgeois
Radicals

parties together for his own use.   From one hand he
fed the bourgeoisie with material nutriment; from
the other he fed the churchmen with spiritual and
intellectual pabulum.   While he was showering economic blessings upon the middle class, he was strengthening the hold of the clergy upon the universities and
the public schools, maintaining French troops at Rome for
the protection of the pope, and posing as the international
champion of Roman Catholicism.

In one important respect — in the furtherance of a vigorous
colonial policy — Napoleon found an identity of interests

New French
Imperialism

between Clericals and business men.   The latter
desired new markets for their goods and favorable
places for the investment of surplus capital; the former were
bent on missionary enterprise, the conversion of distant peoples
to Christianity; both asked state protection for their undertakings.   Such a request the emperor was sure to heed.   Under
his direction the conquest of Algeria was speedily completed
(1857); a permanent civil government was established in Algeria in 1858; and the administration of Marshal MacMahon
(1864–1870) consolidated French influence in northern Africa.
Islands were peacefully acquired in the Pacific, notably New
Caledonia (1853).   A brief war wrested favorable commercial
concessions from China (1860); and the murder of missionaries
was avenged by expeditions into Cochin China and Annam
(1858) and by the erection of a French protectorate over Cambodia (1863).   Despite the disastrous termination of the Mexican
enterprise (1863–1866), which had been undertaken alike for
commercial and religious motives, the Second Empire witnessed
the rehabilitation of the French as colonizers and traders on a
scale second only to the British.

It seemed as though the words which Napoleon addressed to
the French people on one of his trips across France, just prior to
his assumption of the imperial dignity, had been prophetic of
his greatest achievements.   "I would conquer," he said, "for
the sake of religion, morality, and material ease, that portion

of the population, still very numerous, which, in the midst of a country of faith and belief, hardly knows the precepts of Christ; which, in the midst of the most fertile country of the world, is hardly able to enjoy the primary necessities of life. We have immense uncultivated districts to bring under cultivation, roads to open, harbors to construct, rivers to render navigable, canals to finish, and our network of railways to bring to completion. . . . This is what I understand by the empire, if the empire is to be reëstablished. These are the conquests which I contemplate, and all of you who surround me, who, like myself, wish the good of our common country, you are my soldiers." [1]

Peaceful Achievements of Napoleon III

In another part of the same speech the prospective emperor had sought to allay a fear which might haunt equally the business man and the pious Christian. "There is, nevertheless, one apprehension, and that I shall set at rest. A spirit of distrust leads certain persons to say that the empire means war. I say the empire means peace. France longs for peace, and if France is satisfied, the world is tranquil. Glory is rightly handed down hereditarily, but not war." If Napoleon III had fulfilled this prophecy as earnestly and truthfully as he fulfilled the other, the subsequent history of France and of the world might have been quite different.

From the outset, the empire did not mean peace; it meant war. It was based — and Napoleon III knew it was based — on nationalism, on patriotism, on the memory of the glory of French military success. The emperor's peaceful protestations were mainly for foreign edification; at home he was prepared to embark the entire nation upon warlike enterprises whenever an outburst of martial enthusiasm might serve to mollify the rivalries of partisan politics or to unite conflicting social classes. It was the inherent weakness of a governmental structure which was founded rather upon the traditions of the First Empire than upon the less spectacular but more imperishable ideals of liberty and equality that inspired the First Republic.

Militarism the Weakness of the Second Empire

The very year of his accession to the throne — the very year of the address quoted above — Napoleon III plunged into

---

[1] The Bordeaux Address, 9 October, 1852.

preparations for a war with Russia.   Quarrels at the holy places
in Palestine between monks of the Roman Catholic communion
and those of the Greek Orthodox faith were seized
upon by the Tsar Nicholas as the pretext for claiming a protectorate over all Christians in the Ottoman
Empire and by the Emperor Napoleon as the occasion for reasserting the ancient protective privileges of France in the Levant.   Napoleon was doubtless piqued
by the grudging recognition which the tsar accorded his title and
aware that the preservation of Turkey against Russian aggression would find favor alike with ecclesiastical and with commercial interests in France; he felt certain, moreover, that a defeat
of Russia would avenge the first Napoleon's Russian campaign
and would redound to the eternal prestige of the Bonaparte
family and of the French nation.

Dispute with Russia Concerning the Holy Places

Fortune kindly supplied Napoleon III with allies.   The
British government feared that a Russian protectorate over all
Eastern Christians would be speedily followed by Russian annexation of European Turkey, and that Russia,
ensconced at Constantinople, would be an infinitely
graver menace than the Turks to British communication with India and to British trade in the eastern
Mediterranean.   Great Britain accordingly backed Napoleon
in the demand for the preservation of the integrity of the sultan's sovereignty.   The little kingdom of Sardinia, for reasons
of its own which will be later indicated, likewise joined the
alliance.   The Austrian government preserved a troubled neutrality, wavering between apprehension of Russian territorial
expansion at Austrian expense and desire to befriend reactionary
Russia, which, as recently as 1849, had assisted it in putting
down the Hungarian revolt.   The king of Prussia alone was
really "benevolent" toward Russia; but he was too timid to
assist the tsar openly.

Foreign Affairs Favorable to Napoleon III

The war began between Turkey and Russia in 1853, and in
the following year France and Great Britain formally joined
Turkey.   With the allies Sardinia joined in 1855.   The struggle,
confined mainly to military operations in the peninsula of the
Crimea, and notably to a protracted siege of Sevastopol, has
been known in history as the Crimean War.   The allies met

with such unexpectedly stubborn resistance that it was not until 1856 that Russia was forced to sue for peace. The losses, too, were enormous: among all the combatants, more than half a million lives were sacrificed and at least two billion dollars were spent. It seemed a very dear price to pay for a treaty which merely bolstered up the Ottoman Empire for a few years longer, abolished the Russian protectorate over Moldavia and Wallachia, established the free navigation of the Danube, and neutralized the Black Sea by forbidding warships to enter it. Great Britain, it is true, had her commercial supremacy guaranteed in the eastern Mediterranean, but what had Napoleon III secured as compensation for his own expenditure of 75,000 French lives and two billion francs? He had the satisfaction of holding the peace congress in his own capital; he heard the plaudits of surviving soldiers; he beheld signs of his increasing popularity among the Clericals and among the sentimentally-minded; but these rewards were temporary. On the other hand, he had won the undying enmity of Russia and had paved the way for a fateful intervention in the Italian peninsula.

The Crimean War, 1854–1856

THE POLITICAL UNIFICATION OF ITALY

At the time of the Congress of Paris (1856), the agitation for the political unification of the various Italian states had already reached an acute stage. Ever since the Congress of Vienna (1815), the sentiment of nationalism had been steadily growing throughout the peninsula. Everywhere patriots protested against Austrian predominance: in the provinces of Lombardy and Venetia, actually owned by Austria; in the three small duchies of Tuscany,[1] Parma, and Modena, ruled by members of the Habsburg family; in the Papal States, governed by the pope with the aid of foreign soldiers; in the kingdom of the Two Sicilies, whose despicable sovereigns one after another were kept at their post by the aid of Austrian bayonets; and in the kingdom of Sardinia,[2] bullied by Austrian diplomacy and beaten by Austrian troops.

Nationalism in the Italian States, 1815–1856

---

[1] Lucca had been incorporated into Tuscany in 1847.
[2] It must be borne in mind throughout this section that the names "Sardinia" and "Piedmont" have been often used interchangeably to designate the state in

For many years the efforts of Italian patriots had been nullified by divergent views as to the best method of realizing their common aspiration. These divergencies represented the political ideals of three different factions. It will be remembered that one faction, headed by Mazzini and composed of extreme Radicals, desired that the new Italy should be a republic with Liberal institutions and laws. A second faction, which was Clerical and Conservative and tended to be reactionary, favored a federal government for Italy preferably under the presidency of the pope. The third faction — moderate and bourgeois — looked to an annexation of the other states by Sardinia and the consequent erection of a constitutional kingdom of Italy under the House of Savoy.

Three Factions in Italy with Divergent Views as to the Method of Unification

By 1856 the third faction was in process of absorbing the other two. Republicanism was too radical to attract at once the mass of Italians, who had long been steeped in monarchical traditions; and Mazzini's efforts in Rome in 1849 had served only to disgust the order-loving middle class and the religiously-inclined peasantry and to transform Pope Pius IX from a Liberal patriot into a reactionary supported by French and Austrian troops. This transformation on the part of a pope who had once aroused the liveliest expectations of the Italian people, cost the federal party in Italy its leader, but it was perfectly natural. What Pius IX saw of Mazzini's republic convinced him that Radicalism was inimical to peace and justice and essentially irreligious. He also began to fear, as his predecessors for centuries had feared, that the political unification of Italy, with the attendant establishment of a strong secular government, would decrease his own spiritual influence, would cause non-Italian nations to look upon him merely as a kind of chaplain for Italy rather than as Christ's vicar for the whole world. From 1849 until his own death in 1878, therefore, Pope Pius IX made every possible effort to combat Italian unity. But in summoning good Catholics to side with him, he found in many instances that he had to

Weakness of Republicans and Clericals; Strength of Liberal Monarchists

northwestern Italy ruled by princes of the House of Savoy. Technically, Sardinia and Piedmont were different parts of one state — the former an island and the latter the mainland about Turin.

FRANCE

GERMAN CONFEDERATION

Danube R.

SWITZERLAND

EMPIRE OF AUSTRIA

48°

46°

KINGDOM OF HUNGARY

SAVOY
Ceded to France 1860

KINGDOM
OF
PIEDMONT
SARDINIA

Chiavenna
Tirano
Vaitellina
Trent
Udine

Como
Bergamo
R. Piave
R. Tagliamento

LOMBARDY-VENETIA

L. Garda
Treviso

Varese
Vercelli
Magenta
Milan
Brescia
Solferino
Verona
Vicenza
Venice
Padua

Turin
Casale
Alessandria
Novi

Pavia
Lodi
Mantua
Villafranca
Legnano
R. Adige

Piacenza
Parma
Reggio
Rovigo
R. Po

DUCHY
OF
PARMA

DUCHY
OF
MODENA
Bologna
Ferrara
Comacchio

Genoa
Pontremoli
Carrara
Massa
Imola
Forli
Ravenna

Monaco
Nice

DUCHY OF LUCCA
Lucca
Pisa
R. Arno
Florence

San Marino
Pesaro
Urbino
Ancona
Castelfidardo
Loreto

Ceded to France 1860

GRAND DUCHY
OF TUSCANY
Arezzo
Siena
Perugia
C. di Castello
Jesi

Umbria

STATES
OF
THE
CHURCH

CORSICA
(To France)

Orvieto
Spoleto
Aquila

Viterbo
Civita Vecchia
Mentana

42°

LA MADDALENA I.
CAPRERA I.

Rome
Velletri
R. Tiber

Gaeta
Capua
R. Volturno

Foggia
Benevento
Barletta
Trani
Bari

SARDINIA

Naples
Salerno

KINGDOM

Taranto

40°

(Part of Kingdom of Sardinia)

Cagliari

Otranto

TYRRHENIAN

SEA

OF
THE

LISSA I.

ADRIATIC SEA

APENNINES

CALABRIA

Aspromonte

38°

Trapani
Marsala
Calatafimi
Palermo

Messina
Milazzo
Scylla
Reggio

TWO SICILIES

Catania

Girgenti
Syracusa

36°

AFRICA

MALTA
(To Great Britain)

THE
ITALIAN STATES
1856
Scale of Miles
0   25   50   75   100

Longitude   12°   East   from   14°   Greenwich   16°

WILLIAMS ENGRAVING CO., N.Y.

deal with patriots as well as with Christians, and as time went on it became increasingly evident that a great number of Italian Catholics who loyally confessed the spiritual supremacy of the bishop of Rome were bent on disregarding the pontiff's incursions into politics and on coöperating, against his instructions, even with his enemies, for the unification of their country. At last the opposition of the head of the Catholic Church to the growth of nationalism was a losing cause.

There were various reasons why Italian nationalists who had formerly pinned their faith to republicanism or to the papacy gradually transferred it to the kingdom of Sardinia. The kingdom of Sardinia included Piedmont, a particularly fertile and progressive district, the industrial development of which was stimulating the growth of a wealthy and educated middle class. Then, too, Sardinia was the only Italian state which since 1815 had not been controlled by Austria; in fact, it was Sardinia which in 1848–1849 had undertaken to achieve single-handed the herculean task of driving the hated Austrians from the peninsula. Despite reverses, the leadership of Sardinia seemed to practical patriots to offer a more promising means of achieving national independence and unity than idealistic republicanism or cosmopolitan religion. Moreover, the grant of a constitution by the Sardinian king, Charles Albert, in 1848, attracted the favorable attention of Italian Liberals. And, finally, it was Sardinia that supplied three most striking personalities to the national movement, — Victor Emmanuel, Garibaldi, and Cavour. *Sardinia the Leading State in Italy*

King Victor Emmanuel II, who succeeded to the throne of Sardinia upon the abdication of his father, Charles Albert, in the disastrous days of 1849, endeared himself to Liberals by retaining, alone of all the Italian princes, the constitution which had been granted in 1848; and in the eyes of all patriots he gained favor by doing so in spite of persistent Austrian protests. Victor Emmanuel, moreover, had several qualities which won him wide popularity: his sobering common sense in great crises, his powers of military organization, his loyal support of his ministers, his straightforward truthfulness that earned him the title of "the honest king," and, last but not least, his simple, bluff manners *Victor Emmanuel II, King of Sardinia, 1849–1878* and his commanding figure which confirmed his reputation as a hero. The recognized piety of the royal family, too, conciliated many Catholics; and Victor Emmanuel was himself the sort of king whom Republicans would respect.

An even greater inspirer of emotional patriotism than the king was Giuseppe Garibaldi (1807–1882), the brave, handsome

Garibaldi soldier whose breast perpetually burned, through exploits that partook of the nature of romance rather than of prosaic fact, with a consuming devotion to liberty and a devouring love of Italy. A native of Nice, he had early entered the Sardinian navy, but participation in a republican plot of Mazzini had obliged him to quit Sardinia. Then for ten years he had fought in South America for the freedom of the Portuguese and Spanish colonies.[1] Returning to Italy, he had been willing to give assistance to any person or faction that might hasten his country's liberation: he had vainly offered his services to Pope Pius IX in 1847; in 1848 he had raised a volunteer army of 3000 men to aid the king of Sardinia against the Austrians; in 1849 he had gallantly but hopelessly defended Mazzini's Roman Republic. Following the dismal failure of this last venture, Garibaldi had fled to New York, where, first as a candle-maker and afterwards as a trading skipper, he had managed to amass a small fortune. In 1854 he had returned once more to Italy and purchased the island of Caprera, on which thenceforth he made his home. By the year 1856 Garibaldi, at heart a radical republican, perceived that the hope of uniting Italy lay in Victor Emmanuel, and, for the sake of his country, he was prepared to sacrifice his personal political preferences and to accept a constitutional monarchy. Like many other Italian republicans, Garibaldi was developing a sincere admiration for the Sardinian king.

Less popular than Garibaldi or Victor Emmanuel, but easily the most potent single factor in the unification of Italy, was

Cavour Count Camillo di Cavour (1810–1861). Born in the very year that Metternich became chancellor of Austria, and belonging to a noble family which conserved the traditions of the old régime, Cavour was destined to become a greater, at least a more permanently successful, diplomat

---

[1] Victories of Garibaldi in 1846 helped to assure the independence of Uruguay.

than Metternich, and to acquire fame as the foremost Liberal nation-builder of the nineteenth century. It was in his teens, while serving in the army, that he imbibed his strongly marked Liberal notions and his uncompromising dislike of absolutism and Clericalism, ideas which an extensive reading of English authors and a subsequent sojourn in Great Britain confirmed. In fact, the Liberalism which Cavour espoused was that of contemporary England : a king who would reign without ruling; and a parliament which would represent primarily the middle class and which would insure to the nation the greatest amount of liberty in political, ecclesiastical, intellectual, and economic affairs.

During the reign of Charles Albert, whose unsteady waverings between Liberalism and Conservatism were the despair of rational beings, Cavour had taken no important part in government. He had helped to manage his family estates; he had traveled and studied; and latterly he had edited, in conjunction with other Italian patriots, a celebrated journal, *Il Risorgimento*, which advocated constitutional reform in Piedmont and the preparation of that country for leadership in the cause of national unification. After the grant of the constitution (*Statuto*) and the accession of Victor Emmanuel, Cavour came rapidly to the fore. Entering the cabinet in 1850, he became prime minister in 1852 and at that post he remained, with but one brief interruption, until his death in 1861.

As premier, Cavour labored diligently for several years to promote the material welfare of his country so that in the forthcoming struggle Sardinia might be better able to cope with Austria. To realize this part of his program he relied upon the parliamentary and popular support of moderate Constitutionalists, as opposed to extremists, whether revolutionary Republicans or reactionary Clericals : and, inasmuch as the moderate Constitutionalists were essentially a bourgeois party, the reforms which they effected were naturally such as the middle class everywhere then favored. Free trade was adopted. Shipping was subsidized. The building of factories was encouraged. Waste land was brought under cultivation. Railway construction was begun. Education was stimulated. The public budget was

Cavour and Liberal Reform in Sardinia, 1850–1859

reorganized, and the taxes, though increased, were more equitably distributed. To lessen the influence of the Clericals who, in conformity to the admonitions of the pope, were now becoming more openly hostile to the unification of Italy under Sardinian auspices, many monasteries were suppressed and the Jesuits were expelled from the country. In this action Cavour professed to inaugurate a new policy of divorcing religion and politics, a "free Church in a free state," as he phrased it, but in fact it was the beginning of a rancorous conflict in Italy between Church and state. For the time being, thanks to the fact that his party was the party of patriotism and nationalism, Cavour commanded the unquestioned support of the bulk of his fellow-citizens.

It must be borne in mind that these reforms were made in Sardinia at the very time when every other Italian state was

Cavour and the Unification of Italy

suffering from the worst oppressions of petty princes backed by powerful Austria: no wonder that the eyes of patriots and of Liberals were turned towards Sardinia as towards a messiah. Yet Sardinia seemed at best but an insignificant state: twice it had dismally failed to emancipate Italy, and its population still aggregated less than five millions. Cavour, however, was not easily disheartened: reforms within Sardinia were but a prelude to a far more ambitious scheme, — the political union of the entire peninsula under the House of Savoy, — and the greater the obstacles, the more dogged was his determination to surmount them. He coöperated with Victor Emmanuel in reorganizing the army and improving its discipline. He had mysterious interviews with the arch-rebel, Garibaldi. He patronized secret societies which had been formed throughout Italy in order to bind together the scattered elements of resistance to Austrian control. But most significant of all was the masterful diplomacy with which Cavour conducted foreign affairs. In fact, just as the successful maintenance of constitutional government was his monumental achievement in Sardinia, so decisive diplomacy was his great contribution to the cause of Italian unification.

Cavour's first diplomatic step of importance was to cause diminutive Sardinia in 1855 to join France and Great Britain in the Crimean War against Russia. His primary purpose in this

seemingly visionary procedure was to take advantage of the expected alliance of Austria with Russia in order to secure the
immediate support of Great Britain and France
against Austria. Although the persistent neutrality   Sardinian
of Austria rendered this part of his scheme abortive,   tion in the
Cavour had the satisfaction of reaping other rewards   Crimean
which he had foreseen. Sardinia gained two power-   War
ful friends in western Europe and was recognized as the leading
state in Italy, and Cavour was afforded an opportunity, in the
presence of the staid diplomats assembled in the Congress of
Paris (1856), to expose, in the angry tones of which he could be
master, the horrors of Austrian rule.

His next step was to draw closer the friendship between
Sardinia and France, for he had made up his mind that French
assistance would be required to expel the Austrians   Napoleon
from Italy. This task was not an easy one. Probably   III and the
Napoleon III was personally sincerely desirous of aid-   Unification
ing the Italians. The Bonaparte family had not yet   of Italy
forgotten its Italian origin. Napoleon I had erected a "kingdom
of Italy." Napoleon III himself had been a *Carbonaro*. At this
very time he was championing the cause of Rumanian nationality
by urging the union of Moldavia and Wallachia; why should
he not champion the cause of Italian nationality? All these
considerations were constantly dinned into the ear of Napoleon
by the calculating Cavour.

But the emperor's personal enthusiasm was somewhat cooled
by the reflection that for centuries it had been the part of French
foreign policy to foster political disunion beyond the northern
and eastern frontiers — in the Germanies and in Italy — with
a view to checking the growth of too powerful neighbors. If,
therefore, he were to decide on intervention, it should be only
partial and productive of French, rather than Sardinian, advantage. One vital consideration, however, made Napoleon wary
about interfering in Italy at all, — that was a consideration of
practical French politics, — the danger that such a move
would split wide apart the important factions of Clericals and
bourgeois Liberals on whose united support his control of France
depended. Were he to intervene sufficiently to be of real service
to Italian nationalism, he would augment the prestige of Sar-

dinia, whose recent anti-Clerical legislation had aroused the
enmity of ardent Catholics in France, and at the same time he
would dangerously weaken the position of the pope : the French
Clericals, in sympathy with Pope Pius IX, therefore, opposed
French intervention in Italy. On the other hand, were Napoleon not actively to countenance Italian aspirations, he would
alienate French Liberals by playing into the hands of reactionary Austria, and he would so anger Sardinia that she might
adopt retaliatory measures against French industry and trade :
the bourgeois Liberals of France, therefore, seconded Cavour
in urging Napoleon to fight Austria.

Napoleon III was indeed between the devil and the deep sea.
Good politician as he was, he temporized and put off the decision
as long as possible.   The situation was an ironical commentary
upon the desperate political game that he was playing in France.
The suspense might have continued indefinitely had not an Italian fanatic, Orsini, by name, made an attempt upon Napoleon's
life in January, 1858, and thereby touched the little chord of
cowardice which was usually concealed beneath the emperor's
sphinx-like features. Napoleon was terrified into action ;
he feared lest longer delay might invite other Italian fanatics
to make more successful attempts upon his life ; and within a
month of the outrage he laid before Cavour a proposal for a
Franco-Sardinian alliance. He would temporarily risk the
reproaches of the Clericals.

At an "accidental" meeting between Napoleon and Cavour
at Plombières in July, 1858, an informal agreement was reached,
whereby France was to assist Sardinia in driving the
Austrians from Lombardy and Venetia and to allow
the formation of a single north Italian state, and, in
return, France was to receive the Alpine duchy of
Savoy and the Mediterranean port of Nice : Prince
Victor Napoleon, the emperor's worthless cousin, was to marry
Victor Emmanuel's daughter. The emperor still hesitated to
assume responsibility for opening the war himself ; and it required a nice exercise of Cavour's diplomatic talents to pick a
quarrel with Austria.

Alliance between Sardinia and France, 1858

At length in April, 1859, the Austrian government was led
to present an ultimatum to Sardinia, demanding immediate

demobilization.   The prompt rejection of the ultimatum was the signal for the outbreak of the war which, with Austria on one side and France and Sardinia on the other, French In-lasted only from April to July, 1859, and constituted tervention the first successful step toward Italian liberation. in Italy: the War of 1859 French troops under the emperor and Marshal MacMahon entered Piedmont, where they were received with enthusiasm and were joined by the Sardinians under King Victor Emmanuel and General La Marmora. The allies then advanced into Lombardy: the victory of Magenta early in June, which opened the gates of Milan to them, was shortly followed by that of Solferino; and the Austrians fell back upon their strong fortresses in Venetia.

Meanwhile the hurried withdrawal of the Austrian garrisons from other parts of the peninsula had enabled the Italian people everywhere to display their real feelings.   From the three duchies of Tuscany, Parma, and Modena, the Popular Revolutions Habsburg princes were unceremoniously expelled; in the and throughout that part of the Papal States known Italian Duchies as the Romagna, including the important city of Bologna, the temporal sovereignty of the pope was formally repudiated; all these regions of north-central Italy clamored for annexation to Sardinia, and Cavour responded by sending special commissioners to take charge of them in the name of Victor Emmanuel.

This was more than Napoleon III had bargained for. In attempting to enable Sardinia to annex Lombardy and Venetia, he seemed unwittingly to have inspired such an out- Hesitation burst of nationalism as could result only in unification of Napoleon of the whole peninsula and in serious danger to France. III Moreover, the uprising in the Papal States was naturally referred by French Clericals to the emperor's sacrilegious intervention, and the eloquent Bishop Dupanloup from his cathedral pulpit branded Napoleon as the "modern Judas Iscariot." Then, too, the threatening attitude of Prussia along the Rhenish frontier heralded a greater danger to France in the Germanies than in Italy. Besides, the Austrian forces were now well intrenched in Venetia, from which it might prove difficult to dislodge them.   And, quite unlike his illustrious uncle, Napoleon

III was troubled by the spectacle of the dead and wounded upon battlefields, and it was an open secret that he did not enjoy the rattle of musketry or the smell of powder.

For these and possibly other reasons the emperor of the French, without previously informing Cavour, hastened to

Villafranca (1859): Cession of Lombardy to Sardinia

conclude an armistice with Emperor Francis Joseph of Austria at Villafranca in July, 1859, whereby Lombardy was to be ceded to Sardinia, Venetia to remain Austrian, the deposed princes to be reinstated, and the pope made president of an Italian confederation. It was now the turn of the Italian patriots and of the French Liberals to assail Napoleon as a traitor. Loud were the protests. King Victor Emmanuel, left in the lurch by his powerful ally, could do nothing but accede to the truce, but Cavour denounced it and resigned his office in disgust. The terms of the truce of Villafranca were ratified by the treaty of Zurich in the following November.

Napoleon, however, had not reckoned with the resolution of the Italians themselves. The inhabitants of the duchies

Incorporation of the Duchies with Sardinia and Cession of Savoy and Nice to France, 1860

and of most of the Papal States would not hear of a papal federation or of the restoration of their several former rulers: they held *plébiscites* and voted well-nigh unanimously for incorporation into the kingdom of Sardinia. Napoleon at first positively refused to allow such incorporation. From the seeming *impasse*, Cavour, who had swallowed his pride and returned to his post, negotiated an escape. By the treaty of Turin, signed in March, 1860, between Napoleon III and Victor Emmanuel II, the latter ceded both Savoy and Nice to France, just as if Napoleon had carried out the original bargain and had freed Italy "from the Alps to the Adriatic"; and, in return, France recognized the annexation to Sardinia not only of Lombardy but of the duchies of Tuscany, Parma, and Modena, and of the former papal possession of the Romagna.

Close upon the heels of this unifying tendency in the North there came in the southern part of the peninsula a similar movement, the credit for whose inception and guidance belongs, however, not to Cavour nor to Victor Emmanuel but to Garibaldi.

The tyranny of the Bourbon kings of the Two Sicilies had already reached a point which was unendurable. Ferdinand II, the infamous "Bomba," had been succeeded in 1859 by Francis II, but the change of sovereign meant no change of system. The very next year the Sicilians, encouraged by the stirring events in the North and incited by Mazzini, rose in revolt. At this juncture Garibaldi assembled at Genoa his compact volunteer army — the thousand famous "Redshirts" — in preparation for a filibustering expedition to support the Sicilian rebels. As the governments of Sardinia and the Two Sicilies were theoretically on amicable terms with each other, it was the duty of Cavour as the responsible minister of the former to prevent the use of the Sardinian port of Genoa as a base of attack against the latter. But Cavour believed that in this case the obligations of international law should be subordinated to the expediencies of Italian nationalism; while openly he threatened the "Redshirts" with arrest, secretly he intimated to Garibaldi that the expedition might depart.

Garibaldi and the Annexation of the Two Sicilies to Sardinia, 1860

Garibaldi left Genoa with his valiant volunteers in May, 1860, and was received by the Sicilians with enthusiasm. Within three months he was master of the island. Thence he crossed over to the mainland and in September took possession of the city of Naples. Such a marvelous feat exalted Garibaldi to the position of a popular idol and he might easily have made himself a sort of Sicilian dictator for the rest of his life. Garibaldi was not merely bold and brave; he was noble and self-sacrificing, and although he would have preferred to see Italy a republic, he felt that for many years to come his country would prosper most under liberal monarchical institutions. He loved his country more than he loved himself. In November, 1860, of his own accord, he turned over the government of the Two Sicilies to King Victor Emmanuel of Sardinia, and king and liberator rode through the streets of Naples side by side, amid the bravos of the populace. A *plébiscite* had already ratified the annexation of the state to Sardinia, and the surrender of Francis II at Gaeta, whither he had taken refuge under protection of French warships, to King Victor Emmanuel in February, 1861, completed the work. In order to insure communication by land between Victor Emmanuel's northern provinces and his new provinces in the South, Cavour had directed in September, 1860, an attack upon the Papal States and had appropriated the town of Ancona and the eastern districts known as Umbria and the Marches.

Thus within the incredibly brief space of two years, 1859–1861, through the determination of the Italian people, the **The Kingdom of Italy, 1861** intervention of Napoleon III, the diplomacy of Cavour, and the campaign of Garibaldi, the greater part of Italy was united. On 18 February, 1861, a parliament met in Turin, representing a newly united nation of more than twenty-two millions; and on 17 March, Victor Emmanuel assumed the title of king of Italy. Less than three months later Cavour died, a victim of his own restless energy, but his great task was done : Italy was united, and Italy was Liberal.

In saying that Italy was united, qualifications must, of course, be made in respect of Venetia, which still remained in Austrian hands, and of the territory of Rome, where the pope was protected by French troops, but before his death Cavour had made clear the diplomatic means by which both regions were to be secured. It was only a question of time, for every patriot was determined that two such glorious Italian cities as Rome and Venice should belong to the new Italy.

The story of the consummation of Italian aspirations is bound up with another momentous movement of nationalism — **Addition of Venetia to the Italian Kingdom, 1866** the unification of Germany, which, as we shall presently see, was achieved between 1866 and 1871. It was in 1866, in the course of the Seven Weeks' War between Austria and Prussia, that Italy allied herself with the latter and endeavored by force of arms to wrest Venetia from the former. Although the Italians suffered defeat on land and water, Prussia was so successful that Austria was obliged to cede Venetia to Italy. At the Venetian *plébiscite* held in October, 1866, there were 647,246 votes recorded in favor of union with Italy, only 69 against it.

Repeated attempts of Garibaldi and other Italian patriots to capture Rome were frustrated by French and papal troops.[1]

---

[1] Thus, Garibaldi's "Redshirts" were defeated with heavy loss at Mentana in the Papal States in November, 1867.

But in 1870 the outbreak of war between Prussia and France and the defeat of Napoleon III led to the withdrawal of the French garrison; and on 20 September, in face of the protests of Pope Pius IX and notwithstanding a show of force on the part of the papal guards, Italian regulars occupied Rome. The city voted overwhelmingly in favor of annexation to the monarchy and, in July, 1871, was proclaimed the capital of Italy. Italy was at last a united and independent nation.

Addition of Rome to the Italian Kingdom, 1870

THE DECLINE OF THE SECOND FRENCH EMPIRE,
1860–1870

The unification of Italy had important consequences for the career of Napoleon III. Until 1859 surprising success had attended his astute appeals to all Frenchmen — rich and poor, liberal and conservative, clerical and irreligious — to unite in "one great national party" to follow his leadership along the glorious paths of a "new nationalism." But his intervention in Italy suddenly dispelled the dream. French Clericals blamed him for going too far; French Liberals abused him for not going far enough. After 1859 the breach between these two influential factions ever widened, and the emperor's efforts to keep his grasp on both, at first grotesque, ended in tragedy.

Influence of Italian Intervention upon the Empire of Napoleon III

In 1860, to appease the Liberals, Napoleon made a pretense of liberalizing his empire: he permitted the Legislative Chamber to discuss his policies and to criticize his ministers; he removed some of the restrictions on the freedom of speech both inside and outside of the parliament; and he permitted the full publication of the parliamentary debates. At the same time, to appease the Clericals, he reaffirmed his determination never to allow the Italian government to deprive the pope of the temporal power. But on both sides these concessions were far from satisfactory: Liberals and Clericals were henceforth united on one ominous point, — opposition to the emperor.

"Liberalizing" the Empire, 1860

For a brief space in 1863, an opportunity seemed to present itself to Napoleon of regaining the support of both Clericals and

Liberals. The period since 1848, so rich in national aspirations throughout Europe, had witnessed a notable revival of national-

The Polish Insurrection of 1863 ism among the Polish people, who, after a secret agitation extending over several years, at length rose in revolt in 1863 against their reactionary Russian masters. France was the traditional ally of Poland, and Poles had fought desperately for the first Napoleon; why should not the third Napoleon, the friend of oppressed nationalities, assist the Poles? French Liberals urged him to do so because the

Attitude of Napoleon III Polish revolt was directed by Liberals. French Clericals besought him to do so because the Poles, ever a most devoted Catholic people, were struggling for independence against schismatics and heretics. The appeal was urgent, but Napoleon turned a deaf ear. He feared that intervention on behalf of the insurgents would bring both Prussia and Austria, because of their own Polish populations, to the support of Russia and thereby precipitate a war which would prove disastrous to France. He was also maturing another, and to him a grander, scheme to recover the political favor of the influential factions in France. Consequently the French government contented itself with filing a feeble protest with the tsar; Great Britain did likewise; and the Poles, unfriended and desperate, were left to carry on the most hopeless and yet most heroic struggle of modern times. The insurrection really never had the remotest chance of success, and in the end it was relentlessly suppressed, and every remnant of Polish autonomy which had survived the revolt of 1831, was obliterated. And as Napoleon III stood calmly by, reproaches were heaped upon him in France by Clericals and Liberals alike.

But the emperor of the French was already disclosing his grander, if somewhat easier, plan to win anew the affections of

Napoleon's Interest in Mexico Clericals and bourgeois Liberals. It was a dream as fantastic as any that had obsessed the mind of Napoleon I. It was none other than to reëstablish a French colonial empire in America. The chance was afforded him by troubled conditions in the republic of Mexico and by the Civil War (1861–1865) which distracted the attention of the United States. In the former country, chronic struggles between the poor half-breed or Indian peasantry on one hand and the wealthy landowning Spanish-Mexicans on the other had become identified with a divergence on political and ecclesiastical questions, the landlords inclining to monarchical and clerical principles, and the peasants to a republican and anti-clerical program. In 1861, after a protracted conflict, the republican leader, Benito Juarez (1806–1872),[1] overthrew a conservative government and applied a series of radical measures against the Catholic Church in Mexico: monastic orders were suppressed, all ecclesiastical property[2] was confiscated, civil marriage was established, cemeteries were transferred to secular control, and, in short, the Church was not only disestablished but persecuted. The Juarez government likewise repudiated the public debts which its predecessor had contracted.

Then it was that Napoleon III turned towards Mexico. At first he merely engineered an agreement with Spain and Great Britain, — countries affected by the Juarist repudiation of debts, — for joint seizure and retention of Mexican customs houses until satisfaction of the debts should have been obtained. Within four months financial adjustments were made satisfactory to Great Britain and Spain, and the forces of these Powers were withdrawn, but the French still tarried. In the autumn of 1862 Napoleon dispatched 30,000 veteran troops to Mexico, who, with the aid of constant reënforcements from France, captured Mexico City in June, 1863, and drove Juarez into the mountain fastnesses of the North. Instead of annexing the country outright to France, Napoleon preferred to control it indirectly. By prevailing upon the Archduke Maximilian, brother of the Emperor Francis Joseph of Austria, to become emperor of Mexico (1864), Napoleon sought to mollify the Austrian Habsburgs for their losses at his hands in Italy; and by supporting Maximilian with French troops, he was assured that the Mexican emperor would not act contrary to French interests. He counted on the well-known loyalty of the Habsburgs to the Catholic Church to undo the anti-clerical work of Juarez and to please the French Clericals; and he believed that a sense of obligation would lead Maximilian to grant many favorable industrial and commercial concessions to French

French Intervention in Mexico, 1862

Maximilian, Emperor of Mexico, 1864–1867

---

[1] Juarez was of unmixed Indian blood. [2] Valued at $45,000,000.

business men, a policy which could not but please the French bourgeoisie, whose devotion to Liberal politics was secondary only to their anxiety for liberal profits.

But "the great idea of his reign," as Napoleon termed it, proved singularly disastrous. From the outset, Maximilian's position in Mexico was precarious; to the formerly partisan force of Juarez was now added the strength of the national patriotism of the great bulk of Mexicans against foreign interference and domination. The French troops had a sorry task in accustoming themselves to the necessary methods of guerrilla warfare. And the close of the Civil War in the United States (1865) enabled the American government to reassert the principle of the Monroe Doctrine in no uncertain tones. Against a million veterans of a great war Napoleon could not hope to pit his slender expedition in the New World. Accordingly he faced about, and in February, 1867, completed the French evacuation of Mexico. Maximilian, who bravely remained at his post, was soon captured and shot, and the victorious Juarez was universally recognized as president.

The Mexican enterprise was not only disastrous in itself; it was a veritable boomerang against Napoleon. The sacrifice of Maximilian embittered the relations between Austria and France. The restoration of Juarez meant at once the enforcement of all the Mexican anti-clerical legislation and the annulment of numerous profitable franchises of French financiers. Thus, instead of improving French foreign relations, the expedition had positively impaired them. Instead of conciliating his Clerical and Liberal subjects, the emperor of the French had significantly wounded them in conscience or in purse. Not even "glory" had been secured.

Henceforth the opposition to the Second Empire was less veiled. Ardent French Catholics among the bishops and priests, in the universities, among the nobility and peasantry, spoke out against the emperor with boldness, and many of them quite openly urged another Bourbon restoration. On the other hand, the defection of many business and professional men — the middle class — tended to give leaders and material strength to the Republican party which had hitherto been struggling along against Napoleon III with the aid only of a few doctrinaire radicals and of groups of ill- **Republican** organized workingmen. From the disintegration of **Opposition** the curious Bonapartist combination, were now emerging once more the parties of Monarchists and Republicans, based, as before the adventurer's appearance, on class distinctions and ecclesiastical predilections.

The insidious danger to the Empire was unmistakably manifested to Napoleon by the parliamentary elections of 1869, which, despite governmental manipulation, returned fifty **Liberal** Liberal Monarchists and forty Republicans. At once **Reforms** the emperor sought to maintain his throne by dint **in France,** of liberal concessions. He submitted to ministerial **1869** responsibility. He authorized the public sale of newspapers. He promised to do away with the custom of arbitrarily reshaping electoral districts and of supporting official candidates. He called Liberal Monarchists to office. He agreed to a revision of the constitution whereby the Senate should become an Upper House sharing legislative power with the elected Chamber, and the constituent authority should henceforth rest with the nation. These reforms might partially conciliate Orleanists [1] and other Liberal Monarchists, who admired the parliamentary system of Great Britain, but they could not prevent the growth of Republicanism nor really consolidate the Empire. Against the Republican and Socialist propaganda, the audacity of which increased day by day, even Ollivier and the other new Liberal ministers of Napoleon found themselves constrained to apply the methods of absolutism. Even they suppressed newspapers and kept their opponents under police surveillance.

Uneasiness still prevailed in imperial circles. The *plébiscite* of May, 1870, on the new constitution, was not thoroughly satisfactory. Although over seven million votes were cast in its favor, not all of them could be reckoned as indorsements of the Empire; besides, a million and a half votes were cast against the constitution, and nearly two million qualified voters absented themselves from the polls.

---

[1] The Liberal Monarchists who supported the claims of the count of Paris, grandson of that duke of Orleans who had been King Louis Philippe.

One means of saving the Empire from destruction was still untried — the familiar one of uniting domestic factions against a
foreign foe, of cloaking interior troubles in the exterior

**Final
Attempt to
Preserve
the Second
Empire:
War with
Germany,
1870**

glamour of successful war. Napoleon himself was
already broken in health, but he cherished the father's
pride in his young son, the Prince Imperial, and the
Napoleonic ambition that his family might retain the
throne of France. The Empress Eugénie, moreover,
strong, loyal, ambitious, turned even more willingly
to the military expedient. In 1870 the imperial family of
France were ready to gamble heavily; in offering armed opposition to the political unification of Germany they were playing
their last trump card, and they were beaten.

THE POLITICAL UNIFICATION OF GERMANY

The period from 1848 to 1871 was quite as significant in the
history of the Germanies as in that of Italy or France, for it
was during these years that the aspirations of the German people
for political unification, long thwarted, at last reached fruition.
It was then that powerful Prussia first vigorously essayed to
play the rôle of leader.

Several factors contributed to the growing faith of patriotic
Germans, whether Conservative or Liberal, in the destiny of

**The German
Problem,
1815–1866**

Prussia, until in time German unification became
synonymous with Prussian success. It was obvious
from history since 1815 that the Germanic Confederation which had been created at the Congress of Vienna and which
at best was but a feeble alliance of princes, could never be transformed into a compact national state. It was likewise obvious
that Austria, with her dependent Hungarians, Croats, Czechs,
Slovaks, Poles, Rumans, and Italians, could never honestly
espouse the cause of any one nationality, certainly not that of
German nationality. It was also obvious that the princes of
the southern and central German states — the states which
in the Confederation held a kind of balance of power between
Austria and Prussia — could not be expected to favor a nationalism which endangered their own positions. And, finally, it was
obvious from the failure of the revolutionary Frankfort Assembly

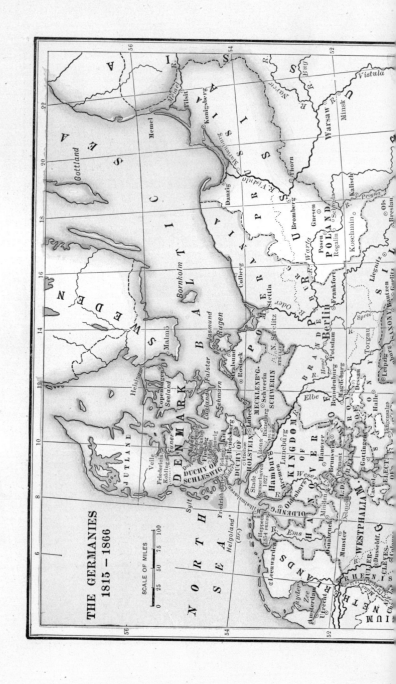

THE GERMANIES
1815–1866

SCALE OF MILES

0 25 50 75 100

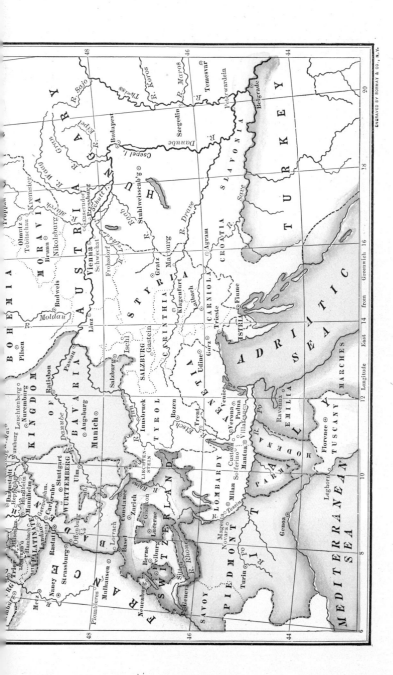

ENGRAVED BY BORMAY & CO., N.Y.

of 1848 that the new Germany was not to be founded on democratic principles or by a popular movement undirected by
princes. To express these lessons of experience in another way,
it may be said that by 1860 the conviction was growing
among German patriots that as preliminary steps to
the political unification of their country, the Germanic
Confederation would have to be dissolved; a stop
would have to be put to the meddling of Austria in German
affairs; and compromises would have to be found, on one hand,
between the princes and the nation, and, on the other, between
reactionary Conservatism and revolutionary Liberalism.

Prerequisites of German Unification

For the achievement of these arduous steps the kingdom of
Prussia alone seemed fitted. Prussia was the home of that
patriotic thought and emotion, which, centered in the
University of Berlin and expressed in the days of the
Regeneration, had stimulated the national resistance
to Napoleon I and had survived the repressive régime of Metternich. Prussia, moreover, was, in contrast with Austria, a real
German state: with the exception of an impotent minority of
Poles, all her subjects spoke the German language and shared
German culture. Prussia, likewise, had already succeeded,
where Austria had failed, in effecting an important measure of
economic unification by means of the *Zollverein*. Prussia, too,
was the only German state which, by reason of its size and resources, could hope to meet Austria on the battlefield on anything like equal terms. Besides, the distrust that German
Liberals entertained of Prussia, whose earlier traditions had
been peculiarly militaristic and reactionary, was partially allayed
by the promulgation in 1850 of a constitution, which, if not
radical, was at least indicative of a desire on the part of the king
to effect a compromise with Liberal principles.

Prussia the Natural Leader

For seventy years since the death of Frederick the Great
(1786) the Hohenzollern kings of Prussia had been poor cringing
creatures, utterly unfit to lead any movement, except
possibly one of pietistic religion. But the insanity
and death of Frederick William IV called to the
helm a different kind of person in his brother William,
who became regent in 1858 and king in 1861. William I, like
his immediate predecessors, was rigidly conservative, deeply

William I, King of Prussia, 1861–1888

religious, and fully convinced of the divine right of kingship, but, unlike them, he had a mind of his own and an almost inordinate pride in military affairs that recalls the Hohenzollerns of the eighteenth century. In intellectual matters he was not brilliant, but he was remarkable enough to know his limitations. Besides, he was conscientious, industrious, benevolent, and absolutely trustworthy in his dealings. And, as he had the faculty of appointing capable men to governmental posts and of reposing the fullest confidence in them, he was enabled by their help to do a greater work than had even Frederick the Great.

At the very beginning of his regency, William appointed as chief of the general staff of the army Hellmuth von Moltke

Moltke and Roon (1800–1891) who was later to achieve fame as the greatest strategist of the second half of the nineteenth century. The next year William named as war minister Albrecht von Roon (1803–1879), a remarkable organizer, without whose help it is probable that the struggle to subdue and unite Germany would have been vain. Both appointees, especially the latter, were extremely conservative in politics, despising popular government, and both gave zealous encouragement to William's natural proclivities in the direction of paternalism and militarism. The new Germany, according to king and ministers alike, was to be builded by a divinely authorized fatherly monarch with the aid of a loyal, disciplined soldiery.

In one domain — that of the military — William was himself an expert. He was a soldier to the core. He knew the faults

Prussian Militarism vs. the Prussian Parliament, 1861–1862 of the Prussian military system, which had not been corrected since 1814, and he was resolved on its radical reorganization so that the Prussian army should become the strongest force in Europe. In improving the equipment and discipline of the army already existing, he relied largely upon the ability of Moltke and Roon, but the king took the initiative himself in urging upon the Prussian parliament the authorization of military increases. He desired compulsory service for all able-bodied males in fact as well as in theory — the enrollment every year of 63,000 instead of 40,000 new recruits; he desired the extension of the term of reservists from two to four years; and he demanded such increased appropriations as would render these military reforms immediate.

On the whole, the parliament was hostile to the new military policy. Many extreme Conservatives, who did not relish additional taxation for the sake of a fight with reactionary Austria, made common cause with the Liberals, who feared lest military exaltation would be detrimental to Liberalism. At first, the parliament consented to lengthen the term of service in the regular army to three years, but in 1861 positively refused to authorize increased financial expenditures or the enrollment of additional regiments without a compensatory diminution of the term of service. New elections in 1862 tightened the deadlock between king and parliament: in the new Lower Chamber there were now 100 Conservatives, 23 Moderate Liberals, and 235 Progressives, — the last a new party which was resolved to compel the king to abandon his military projects and to submit to real parliamentary government.

In this struggle the very character of the future institutions of Germany was at stake. King William knew that his pet scheme for the unification of the country could not be realized without a large and efficient army. On the other hand, the Progressive Opposition perceived that the realization of the king's scheme would fix militarism as a mighty prop of divine-right monarchy and would accordingly imperil individual liberties and the triumph of constitutional government. Should the future united Germany be militaristic? Should it be Liberal?

It was neither the king nor the parliament that gave the decisive answer. It was Bismarck, with the momentous words: "Not by speeches and resolutions of majorities are the great questions of the time decided — that was the mistake of 1848 and 1849 — but by iron and blood." And Bismarck was a Conservative of the Conservatives.

Otto von Bismarck (1815–1898)[1] belonged to the most influential social class in Prussia — the *Junkerthum* or country gentry, who for centuries had divided their attention between the supervision of numerous peasant tenants upon **Bismarck** their large agricultural estates and the public service, military or bureaucratic, of their Hohenzollern sovereigns. Born in

---

[1] Otto Eduard Leopold von Bismarck was created count in 1865, prince in 1870, and duke of Lauenburg in 1890.

the comfortable ancestral manor-house at Schönhausen, some forty miles west of Berlin, in 1815, the year of the Congress of Vienna, he was brought up to combine the traditions of the Prussian squirearchy with the patriotic enthusiasm of the German "Regeneration." As a student at the universities of Göttingen and Berlin he acquired a reputation not as a scholar but as a dashing fraternity-member and a leader in beer-drinking bouts, a reputation which was subsequently enhanced by his dismissal from the public service because of "deficiency in regularity and discipline" and by the stories which came up to Berlin of the furious hunts and nocturnal carousals of the young squire of Schönhausen. His happy marriage in 1847 with the pious daughter of a neighboring landowner worked a great change in Bismarck. He became deeply religious and attached to the Evangelical State Church, and very serious in the expression of political ideas which harmonized nicely with those of his social class. He began to insist that the Christian state is the ideal political organization and that a true Christian state is impossible without monarchical absolutism.

Throughout the revolutionary movements of 1848–1849 Bismarck consistently defended divine-right monarchy against the Liberals. He offered to bring his peasants to Berlin to protect Frederick William, and, when the Prussian king promised to grant a constitution, Bismarck voted in a minority of two against returning thanks. He scoffed at the efforts of the Frankfort Assembly to unify Germany on a platform of constitutional liberties and backed Frederick William in declining to take a crown "from the gutter."

Conservatism of Bismarck

Obliged to accept the constitution of 1850, Bismarck at once sought practical means of preventing its further liberalization. He was one of the founders of the famous newspaper, the *Kreuzzeitung*, which speedily crystallized a definite Conservative party. This Conservative party was recruited almost exclusively from the agricultural classes; it was distinctively Prussian and believed that the unification of Germany, if effected at all, should signify the Prussianization of Germany; it strenuously opposed any extension of the suffrage or legislation inimical to landed interests; it championed the royal prerogative, the army, and the Lutheran Church.

It was in the realm of diplomacy, however, that Bismarck was to win his first great title to fame, and the years from 1851 to 1862 were important in affording him valuable diplomatic experience. As Prussian representative in the revived Diet of the Germanic Confederation from 1851 to 1859, he not only acquired an unrivaled knowledge of German politics but a deep-seated distrust and dislike of Austria. As ambassador at Petrograd for three years, he learned Russian and gained the warm regard of the tsar. A few months' residence as Prussian ambassador at Paris in 1862 gave him a pretty accurate insight into the curious complexities of Napoleon's character.

Diplomatic Experience of Bismarck, 1851-1862

Now, in the autumn of 1862, Bismarck was summoned to Berlin by King William, chiefly on the advice of Roon, in order to "tame" the self-willed parliament. It was a task after Bismarck's own heart. With the king's military policy, he was in hearty sympathy: he felt it was essential to the rôle which he hoped Prussia would play in the unification of Germany. And both his political principles and his class consciousness gave added zest to the prospect of an encounter with the obstructionist Progressives, for the Progressive party (*Fortschrittspartei*) represented many university professors [1] and other members of the middle class who defended individual rights, idealized the limited monarchy of Great Britain, and, in general, stood for all those principles which everywhere throughout western Europe the bulk of the bourgeoisie championed.

Bismarck as " Tamer " of the Prussian Parliament

From the Progressive majority in the Lower Chamber, Bismarck, as president of the ministry, tried to win the desired military increases successively by compromise, by cajolery, by entreaty, and by threats, but always in vain. The Progressives stubbornly insisted that militia was preferable to a professional army, and in 1863 they refused to vote the appropriations necessary for the conduct of government.

Thereupon Bismarck, with the king's consent, proceeded to govern the country without a budget and without a parliament. In flat violation of the constitution of 1850, taxes were arbitrarily levied and collected, the military reforms were fully

---

[1] Their leader was the distinguished scientist Rudolf Virchow (1821-1902).

carried out, and Prussia was duly prepared to wage a decisive war with Austria for the hegemony of the Germanies. For this unprincipled and high-handed procedure, Bismarck was cordially hated by sincere Liberals, but unpopularity and insults did not change his course. For nearly four years he maintained the unconstitutional régime under the questionable maxim that the end justifies the means. He went ahead on the assumption that in the long run the generality of Prussians would not care how German unity was achieved so long as it was achieved. The assumption was correct. To the undoing of his Progressive opponents, patriotism was a more basic attribute of most Germans than Liberalism, and the reformed army — splendid machine as it was — proved a powerful stimulus to Prussian patriotism and a potent preventive of radical or revolutionary novelties. Militarism had already begun in Germany its twofold mission of exalting nationalism and curbing Liberalism.

Bismarck's immediate purpose in perfecting the army was, of course, in order to use it with such deadly effect against Austria that that Power would cease to be a factor in German politics and that a new Germany would be builded about Prussia. To wage war against Austria, an excuse had to be found that would be popularly justifiable. And the possibility of such an excuse Bismarck cleverly detected in the so-called Schleswig-Holstein question.

Bismarck as Promoter of German Nationalism

In the peninsula between Denmark and the Elbe River were three duchies, — Holstein, Schleswig, and Lauenburg, — which, though peopled largely by Germans, were joined in a personal union under the king of Denmark. Since 1815, moreover, Holstein had been a state of the Germanic Confederation, and Schleswig was indissolubly linked to Holstein. Danish sovereigns had long been anxious for the complete incorporation of the duchies into their monarchy, but this was opposed both by the national feeling throughout the Germanies and by the Duke Frederick of Augustenburg who had strong claims upon the duchies though none upon Denmark. A conference of the Great Powers at London in 1852 had attempted to compromise the issues at stake by buying off the claims of the duke of Augustenburg

The Question of Schleswig-Holstein

and by confirming the succession in the duchies to the Danish kings, while providing that the union between Denmark and the duchies should be purely personal.

Now in 1863, upon the death of Frederick VII of Denmark, his successor, Christian IX, stirred by an overwhelming enthusiasm on the part of his Danish subjects, signed a constitution which, contrary to the London agreement, unified the political institutions of Denmark and the duchies. The German response was an opposing wave of national patriotism and combined threats from Austria and Prussia, neither of which would be outdone by the other in this bid for the leadership of a national cause. Christian IX refused to budge. And in 1864 followed a brief war between Denmark on one side and Austria and Prussia on the other. The Danes fought furiously, but, overcome by force of numbers, were obliged to submit in October, 1864, to the treaty of Vienna, whereby their king renounced all his rights in the duchies in favor of the emperor of Austria and the king of Prussia.

Danish Nationalism vs. German Nationalism

The War of 1864: Denmark Defeated by Prussia and Austria

The sequel to the Danish War of 1864 was, as Bismarck anticipated, a bitter quarrel between Austria and Prussia over the disposition of the spoils. Austria at once proposed that the duchies should be handed over to the duke of Augustenburg, and, under her influence, the Diet of the Germanic Confederation by a small majority indorsed the proposal. Bismarck's reply was to deny the right of the Diet to interfere and to press forward ostentatious preparations for the transformation of the port of Kiel into a great Prussian war-harbor. An angry correspondence ensued; but as neither Power was quite ready for war a temporary adjustment was made by the convention of Gastein (August, 1865), whereby, pending a final settlement, Schleswig was to be occupied and administered by Prussia, Holstein by Austria, while Lauenburg was made over absolutely to Prussia in return for a money payment. The convention of Gastein was a diplomatic triumph for Bismarck: it temporarily put the duke of Augustenburg out of the way; and by surrendering to Austria the duchy of Holstein, encircled by Prussian territories, it provided a splendid field

Dispute between Prussia and Austria over Schleswig-Holstein

Convention of Gastein, 1865

in which Bismarck could engineer exasperating plots against Austrian rule.

Before precipitating the inevitable struggle, Bismarck was anxious to insure Prussia against the danger of foreign inter-

International Situation Favorable to Prussia rather than to Austria

vention in behalf of Austria. He knew that defeat of Austria would involve the dissolution of the Germanic Confederation; yet the Germanic Confederation had been created by the Congress of Vienna and existed under guarantee of the Great Powers. Would the Great Powers sit tamely by and allow Prussia to tear up the treaties of Vienna and to revolutionize the political

Diplomacy of Bismarck

organization of the Germanies? The diplomatic craft of Bismarck was equal to the danger. From Great Britain he rightly expected no opposition, for British

Great Britain

sympathy unmistakably was veering toward Prussia, partly by reason of the favorable low-tariff relations between England and the Prussian *Zollverein*, and partly because of the contemporary development of a theory among certain famous English historians and publicists and its diffusion among the English masses to the effect that Englishmen and Germans belonged to a single and noble Teutonic race, whose superiority over all other races would be further attested by the political unification of Germany.

But neither France nor Russia could be expected to view German unification with perfect equanimity. It had been the

Russia

weakness and disunion of the Germanies that had enabled Russia to expand westward and France to seize cities along the Rhine. Yet in disarming the traditional fears of his French and·Russian neighbors, Bismarck was aided by curious domestic situations that then perplexed both states. In the case of Russia, it was the Polish insurrection of 1863: Bismarck had promptly offered Prussian armed assistance to his personal friend, the tsar, and now, without base ingratitude,

France

the tsar could not turn against Prussia. In the case of France, it was the personal character and political exigencies of Napoleon III: Bismarck knew how to work upon Napoleon's vague sentimental attachment to the principle of nationalism, upon his vanity, and upon his desperate readiness to clutch at any chance to secure a little additional territory for

France in order to win national glory among the French for himself and for his dynasty. In October, 1865, Bismarck paid a visit to the French emperor at Biarritz : exactly what occurred there has been a subject of fruitless speculation ever since, but it appears certain that at least Napoleon was induced to give his assent to a joint attack of Prussia and Italy upon Austria on an oral understanding that no objection would be raised to the acquisition of territorial "compensations" by France. Reference may have been made to a possible French annexation of Belgium or of part of the Rhine province of Prussia. Probably Napoleon thought that the parties to the impending struggle would be so evenly balanced as to render subsequent French intervention easy, decisive, and highly gainful.

Bismarck was certain that the smaller German states would side with Austria : the pride of their princes, the fear of militarism on the part of their Liberal citizens, the sympathy of Catholics in Bavaria and Württemberg with Catholic Austria, — all these facts gave strength to the opposition of the governing classes in those states to any close union of Germany under Prussian auspices. *Lesser German States Allied with Austria* To offset this opposition, Bismarck negotiated in April, 1866, a treaty of alliance with Italy, providing that, if war broke out within three months, Prussia and Italy should coöperate against Austria, and the latter should be indemnified by the cession of Venetia. *Italy Allied with Prussia*

By means of diplomacy as astute and unscrupulous as that with which he had isolated Austria from foreign support, he next proceeded to provoke a war with her. He complained that the Austrian government was violating the convention of Gastein by continuing to encourage the claims of Frederick of Augustenburg to the duchies. *Renewal of Dispute between Prussia and Austria* Both powers mobilized their armies. The crisis was reached in June, 1866, when Austria brought the quarrel into the Diet of the Germanic Confederation, and Prussia, declaring that as a result of Austria's action the Convention of Gastein had ceased to exist, sent troops into Holstein, and dispossessed the Austrians. Almost simultaneously, Prussia submitted to the Diet a scheme for the complete reformation of the Confederation, involving the exclusion of Austria. Thus Bismarck made Prussia appear not simply as the aggrieved party in a petty territorial dispute but also as the undaunted champion of national unification. Austria, however, prevailed upon a majority of the Diet to reject Prussia's reform proposal, and at the same time to order a mobilization of the federal forces to punish Prussia for the infraction of Austrian rights in Holstein. This action of the Diet was interpreted by Bismarck as tantamount to an attack upon Prussia, amply justifying that state's indignant secession from the Germanic Confederation. Prussia appeared to be fighting a defensive war.

This war between Prussia and Italy, on one side, and Austria and the lesser German states, on the other, was of such surprisingly brief duration as to earn it the popular designation of the Seven Weeks' War. Within two weeks Prussian expeditions had overcome all resistance in the smaller states, and the detachment of a large Austrian army for the defense of Venetia against the Italians afforded an opportunity for the main Prussian army to fall with superior numbers as well as with superior discipline and equipment upon the remaining Austrian forces in Bohemia. The battle of Sadowa (Königgrätz), on 3 July, 1866, was the decisive engagement of the war: the victory of the Prussians not only fixed their reputation for military preëminence in Europe but it had important effects on the national movements both in Germany and in Italy [1] and on the internal politics of Prussia, of the South German states, of the Austrian Empire, and of France.

The Seven Weeks' War, 1866

By the treaty of Prague (23 August, 1866), which concluded the Seven Weeks' War, Austria lost no territory, except Venetia to Italy and her claims upon Holstein to Prussia, and was obliged to pay only a light war indemnity, but she was forced to consent to the dissolution of the Germanic Confederation after its inglorious existence of half a century, and to acknowledge the right of Prussia to assume the leadership of the Germanies. Thus the first actual steps toward real German unity were achieved: the heterogeneous Habsburg dominions were excluded and the absurd Confederation was dissolved.

Dissolution of the Germanic Confederation, 1866

The next steps toward national union likewise came imme-

---

[1] For its effect on the national movement in Italy, see above, p. 174.

diately out of the Seven Weeks' War. They were, first, the Prussian annexations, and secondly, the formation of the North German Confederation.

For diplomatic reasons Bismarck had deprived Austria of very little territory; he correctly perceived that leniency of treatment would be most liable to secure needed Aus- Prussian trian friendship in the future. At the same time, the Annexations, Prussian premier was anxious to round out his state's 1866 somewhat misshapen territories, to increase its population and economic resources, and to obtain for it a number of strategic points. Accordingly Prussia formally annexed the duchies of Schleswig and Holstein, affording her the site of her subsequent important naval base of Kiel and of her invaluable Kaiser Wilhelm ship canal from the North Sea to the Baltic. She also took advantage of her military triumph over the lesser German states to annex the kingdom of Hanover, the electorate of Hesse-Cassel, the duchy of Nassau, and the free city of Frankfort-on-Main. These annexations were of immense significance. For the first time the Hohenzollerns were lords of continuous lands stretching from Poland and the Baltic to the River Main and the French frontier; they gained more than 27,000 square miles of territory and almost five million subjects. Henceforth, excluding Austria, two-thirds of the area and two-thirds of the population of all the Germanies were comprised within the kingdom of Prussia.

All the lesser German states north of the River Main that were not annexed by Prussia — twenty-one in number — were constrained to join her in the North German Confed- The North eration, whose constitution, adopted in 1867, was German another sample of Bismarck's handiwork. The execu- Confedera-
tion under tive authority was vested in the king of Prussia as Prussia's hereditary president, assisted by a federal chancellor; Presidency, the legislature was to consist of (1) a federal council 1867-1871 (*Bundesrat*) of representatives of the princes of the several states, and (2) a diet (*Reichstag*) elected by universal manhood suffrage. The local princes retained certain sovereign rights: they still might summon local parliaments and levy taxes, but the whole conduct of foreign affairs, the control of the army, and the declaration of defensive war were intrusted to the president.

The North German Confederation differed from the older Germanic Confederation in that it was dominated by Prussia rather than by Austria and the lesser princes, that it was more compact in extent and infinitely more unified and influential, and that it recognized the principle of popular participation in government. Likewise, Prussian militarism was extended throughout the Confederation, for it was provided that every constituent state should maintain compulsory military service on the Prussian model.

The only strictly German states that remained outside the North German Confederation were the four states south of the River Main [1] — the kingdoms of Bavaria and Würtemberg and the grand-duchies of Baden and Hesse-Darmstadt. In these states, with the exception of Baden, where the French were particularly distrusted, both princes and people at first opposed a close political union with Prussia, the princes fearing a diminution of their own powers and prestige, and the people dreading the certain imposition of compulsory military service and the probable enactment of anti-Catholic and anti-Liberal legislation. Toward these south German states Bismarck adopted a most conciliatory attitude. He did not penalize them for assisting Austria in the Seven Weeks' War. He did not force them into his new North German Confederation. He scrupulously respected their independent position. Meanwhile, he missed no chance to fill them with alarm at the possibility of French aggression; he drew closer with them the economic bonds of the *Zollverein;* and he cunningly concluded secret treaties of defensive alliance with them, whereby if Prussia or one of them should be attacked by a foreign Power the others should come to the assistance of the party attacked. Bismarck trusted to the growth of the sentiment of nationalism in south Germany in order to bring the four states naturally into political union with Prussia ; and in order to stimulate that sentiment, he relied chiefly upon provoking an armed conflict with France.

One thing that aided Bismarck in gaining a considerable

Independent Position of the Four South German States, 1866–1871

---

[1] Hesse-Darmstadt, one of the four, was a member of the North German Confederation for its territories north of the Main, while its lands south of that river were accounted outside the Confederation.

amount of popular support in south Germany as well as in the North was the change in his political views which the Seven Weeks' War seemingly produced. The brilliant suc- *Bismarck's* cess of his diplomatic and military policies put him on *Conces-* better terms with the Prussian Liberals: the Liberals *sions to* no longer distrusted Bismarck's patriotism, and, on *Liberalism* the other hand, Bismarck no longer feared Liberal obstruction to his plans; the former arch-Conservative, still retaining ultra-Conservatism as the ideal of his innermost strivings, perceived a practical need of effecting a compromise with the Liberals preliminary to utilizing them in his own future causes. Bismarck was nothing if not practical. Accordingly, he promptly restored the full operation of the Prussian constitution and asked a bill of indemnity from the Diet for the illegalities of which he had been wantonly guilty during the preceding four years, and the bill was passed with unanimity and enthusiasm. Likewise, in the constitution of the new North German Confederation he secured the incorporation of a provision for the election of the *Reichstag* by direct and universal manhood suffrage, assuring, as he did so, certain Conservative critics that the German masses bade fair to be more conservative than the middle class, and to prove more patriotic supporters of a militaristic state. As a result of these Liberal concessions, soon after the Seven Weeks' War a new political party *Rise of the* took shape known as the National Liberal party, re- *National* cruited largely from the industrial classes and in many *Liberal* instances from former Progressives. The main ob- *Party in* ject of the new party was to uphold Bismarck in his *Germany* national endeavors and for this purpose to subordinate, though not to surrender, the struggle after constitutional development. Incidentally, it favored a strongly centralized government, militarism, and free trade, and was inclined to be anti-Clerical as regarded both the Lutheran and the Roman Catholic churches. The National Liberals, essentially a German, not a Prussian party, became valuable missionaries in south Germany in the cause of German nationalism, alike for its own sake and as a bulwark against France.

Before tracing the stormy course of Franco-German relations from 1866 to 1871, which were to culminate in the completion of German unification under Prussian hegemony, it will be

Effects of
the Seven
Weeks' War
on Austria convenient to point out certain momentous consequences of the period to the chief combatant defeated
in the Seven Weeks' War — Austria.

For Austria the war of 1866 was a final blow at all
those fine policies which Metternich had ably maintained through-

Final
Destruction
of the
System of
Metternich out the first half of the nineteenth century, — absolute
authority vested in the Habsburg monarch, centralized
administration of all the varied territories of the
empire, chronic interference in the internal affairs of
all the Germanies and of all the Italian states, complete defiance of the forces of democracy and nationalism.   The
cause of democracy had been continually abetted within Austria-
Hungary by the growing demands for participation in government not only of the old landed nobility but also of the
bourgeoisie and urban proletariat whom the recent Industrial
Revolution had been producing.   At the same time a keen sense
of nationalism had been stimulated by the reviving literatures
and political aspirations of the numerous subject populations,
particularly of the four chief nationalities — Germans, Magyars,
Slavs, and Italians.

What the revolutionary movements of 1848-1849 had failed
to do — utterly to destroy the system of Metternich — was

Exclusion of
the Habs-
burgs from
German and
Italian
Affairs achieved by means of the disastrous foreign wars of
1859 and 1866.   These two wars obliged the Emperor
Francis Joseph to renounce the right of Austrian interference alike in Italy and in Germany, and to center
his attention upon the Germans of Austria proper,
upon the Magyars of the ancient kingdom of Hungary, and
upon the Slavic peoples who were directly dependent upon
the crowns either of Austria or of Hungary.   In other words,
the racial problems confronting the empire were somewhat
simplified by the exclusion of the Habsburgs from German
and Italian affairs; and the center of gravity of the Habsburg
monarchy gradually shifted eastward in the direction of Magyars
and Slavs.

Then, too, the decline of Austrian prestige which marked each
war's reverses was utilized now by Liberals and now by nationalists to wring concessions from the Emperor Francis Joseph.

Thus in 1860, immediately after the loss of Lombardy, additional powers of local self-government were accorded to provincial diets, and Hungarian political institutions were restored as they had existed prior to the revolt of 1849; and in the following year (1861), a formal constitution made provision for a united parliament for the whole empire, to be elected by the provincial diets, to sit at Vienna, and to perform functions of legislation and taxation. Austrian Constitution of 1861

The constitution of 1861, fairly liberal though it was, was far from satisfying the Magyar longing for nationalism. From his exile, Louis Kossuth (1802–1894) still preached rebellion against the Habsburg dynasty, while a more practical Magyar, Francis Deák (1803–1876), worked out a plan by which the Habsburg dominions should be divided into two parts — Austria and Hungary — each managing its own internal affairs by means of separate parliamentary institutions and united only by a common sovereign, a common army, and common foreign relations. Thanks to Deák's efforts the Magyars remained loyal to Francis Joseph during the trying days of 1866, and, as a fitting reward, the political dualism, for which Deák had labored, was formally established in 1867. This settlement, known as the *Ausgleich*, or Compromise, fixed the general character of government in the Habsburg dominions as it has existed ever since. The Seven Weeks' War may be said, therefore, to have won national independence for Hungary as well as for Germany and to have established the present-day government of the Dual Monarchy of Austria-Hungary just as it foreshadowed the erection of the present German Empire. Deák and Hungarian Nationalism The Ausgleich (1867): Establishment of the "Dual Monarchy" of Austria-Hungary

Worse than Austria fared France as a result of the Seven Weeks' War. The lightning rapidity of the campaign upset entirely the calculations of Napoleon III, and the giant stride of Prussia toward the unification of Germany filled him with consternation. His army was in no condition immediately to combat the victorious Prussians and his best troops were still in Mexico, in Algeria, or at Rome. Instead of stepping in as a well-compensated arbiter at the close of a long civil war in the Germanies, he now found himself actually begging from Bismarck some trifling territorial Effects of the Seven Weeks' War on France "compensation" — anything, in fact, that would save his face with the French people.

With appropriate reminders of the interview at Biarritz, Napoleon in 1866 asked that the Rhenish Palatinate be ceded to France. Bismarck shrugged his shoulders and showed the emperor's note to the king of Bavaria, to whom the Palatinate belonged: the result was merely to strengthen the defensive alliance between Prussia and Bavaria. Napoleon next demanded leave to annex Belgium; again he was put off, and later, in 1870, his demand was artfully communicated by Bismarck to the British government, which was anxious to maintain Belgium's integrity. Meanwhile, Napoleon made a strenuous effort to secure Luxemburg.

Failure of Napoleon III to Secure "Compensations"

The grand-duchy of Luxemburg, a small state on the northern frontier of France, adjacent to Belgium, occupied a curious international situation in Europe. Ruled by the king of the Netherlands, it had been a member of the Germanic Confederation, and was garrisoned by Prussia. Early in 1867 Napoleon negotiated with the Dutch king for the purchase of the grand-duchy. The king was willing but Bismarck again interposed, and, as Napoleon was not ready for war, the anomalous question of Luxemburg was submitted to a conference of the Powers in London (May, 1867). By the resultant treaty of London the grand-duchy was neutralized under European guarantee; the king of the Netherlands retained the sovereignty; the fortifications of Luxemburg were demolished, and the Prussian garrison was withdrawn. Bismarck thereby shrewdly exposed to Europe a seemingly conciliatory attitude on the part of Prussia and a land-grabbing ambition on the part of France; and Napoleon had obtained not even Luxemburg.

Thrice thwarted in his efforts to secure "compensation" for France, Napoleon at length perceived what Bismarck had appreciated all the time, that the Seven Weeks' War was but the forerunner of a great war between France and the new Germany. From 1868, preparations were made on both sides. Elaborate plans for an offensive campaign were set on foot by Moltke, the Prussian commander; and some reforms were instituted in the French army. Both Bismarck and Napoleon resorted

Strained Relations between France and Germany

to diplomacy, the former to insure foreign neutrality, the latter to gain allies. In the diplomatic as well as in the military game advantage was on the German side. Thanks to Napoleon's earlier actions and to Bismarck's recent negotiations, France was internationally isolated. Russia had not forgotten Napoleon's part in the Crimean War nor Bismarck's kind offers of assistance against rebellious Poles. Italy could not forget Napoleon's betrayal of her cause in 1859 or the subsequent compensatory aid obtained from Bismarck. Austria contrasted Napoleon's harsh treatment of her in 1859 with Bismarck's lenient conduct in 1866. Great Britain and the south German states alike resented Napoleon's ambition for territoral aggrandizement : the former sympathized with Prussia ; the latter signed military conventions with Prussia. For a while the emperor of the French thought he would be able to form a triple alliance between Austria-Hungary, Italy, and France ; but his unwillingness, in view of Clerical opposition in France, to withdraw the French troops from Rome caused the complete failure of his negotiations with King Victor Emmanuel ; and veiled threats from the tsar were enough to induce Emperor Francis Joseph to await actual French victories before casting in his lot with Napoleon. To the very last, Napoleon deluded himself with the idea that the south German states would join France rather than Prussia.

Inter-national Isolation of France

War fever was the inevitable effect of the rising nationalist temperature in Germany and in France. It was most remarkable how every class in each of the two countries felt that its own interests would best be served by inflicting injury upon the corresponding class in the other country, and how, in each country, over all social classes and all political parties, welding them together and, as it were, hypnotizing them, was the genius of nationalism — the firm, mutual conviction of a superiority of blood and of destiny. Only small groups sought to allay the fever — the advanced Republicans in France who feared lest the results of war should accrue to the advantage of the Second Empire, and in Germany a handful of Socialists who splendidly but vainly preached the brotherhood of all the world's workingmen. The governments of both countries fed the popular fever, for both Bismarck and Napoleon

French Nationalism vs. German Nationalism

had ambitions that could not be readily realized by any other means. Bismarck desired war with France because he would be able in the enthusiasm engendered by military prowess to complete German unification and to place the seal of triumph upon the achievements of the German people. Napoleon was willing to undertake a war with Prussia because a victory for his arms would reunite his subjects and preserve his throne and dynasty.

As both sides expected war, a pretext was not long lacking. It was supplied by the Hohenzollern candidature for the throne of Spain. Having expelled the absolutist Queen Isabella II, the Spanish Liberals in 1869 proclaimed a constitutional monarchy and offered the crown to Prince Leopold of Hohenzollern-Sigmaringen, a Catholic cousin of King William of Prussia. Prince Leopold was not eager for Spanish adventures and at first refused the offer; but Bismarck, who scented the possibilities of the situation, procured a renewal of the request and, 2 July, 1870, its acceptance by the Prussian prince. Napoleon, who at once professed to see an attempt to join the German and Spanish crowns and thereby to revive the sixteenth-century empire of Charles V, to the eternal detriment of France, informed King William that he would regard the accession of a Hohenzollern to the throne of Spain as a sufficient ground for war; and on 12 July it was announced in Madrid that Prince Leopold of his own accord had revoked his acceptance of the crown. Here the business might have ended, had not Napoleon blindly sought an additional rebuff for Prussian diplomacy. Accordingly, acting upon instructions from his emperor, the French ambassador [1] to Prussia approached King William on the promenade at the famous watering-place of Ems and demanded that the king should pledge himself never to permit a Hohenzollern prince to become a candidate for the Spanish throne. This William refused to do, and, when the persistent ambassador requested yet another interview, the king politely informed him that he was leaving Ems that night and could not receive him. The news of this indecisive interview was telegraphed by the king to Bismarck, who, after consulting the military heads and as-

Pretext for War: The Hohenzollern Candidature for the Spanish Throne

[1] Count Vincent Benedetti (1817-1900).

suring himself that Prussia was prepared for war, communicated
the dispatch to the public press; not, however, in the original
form in which he had received it from the king, but
in a form so cleverly and unscrupulously abbreviated
as to convey the impression to Germans that the Prussian king had been insulted by the French ambassador and to Frenchmen that their ambassador had been insulted by the Prussian king. The edited dispatch was rightly
calculated to have the effect, in Bismarck's own cynical words,
"of a red rag upon the Gallic bull."

Bismarck's Utilization of the Pretext

The distorted report of the Ems interview, received in Paris
on 14 July, 1870, the anniversary of the fall of the Bastille and
the French national holiday, threw France into a
ferment. That very night Napoleon III and his
Council decided upon war; the next day the French
Chambers, with but ten dissenting votes, sanctioned
a formal declaration of war, and mobilization began
on either side of the Rhine. To the chagrin of Napoleon and
the delight of Bismarck the south German states, believing that
Prussia was attacked, promptly took her part and that of the
North German Confederation in accordance with the treaties
of defensive alliance.

The Franco-German War, 1870–1871

The Franco-German War of 1870–1871 brought into sharp
contrast the real rottenness of the Napoleonic régime in France
and the efficiency of the German governmental machine under
Bismarck. On the German side, the campaign was conducted
like clock-work, all departments, — finance, commissary, strategy,
supply, movement of troops, conduct of military operations,
offensive and defensive, civil administration, diplomacy, — working together with perfect precision. On the other hand, the
French soldiers, although they displayed wonderful courage and
dash, were badly led and hopelessly outnumbered; they
lacked organization, plans, supplies. Napoleon, who was
suffering from an incurable malady, was himself excessively
timid, and his entire military establishment was overrun by
dishonest officials and corrupt contractors. The outcome could
not long remain in doubt.

Early in August, 1870, Marshal MacMahon, who had been
hurriedly recalled from Algeria to command the French army

near Strassburg, suffered such serious reverses at the hands of
the Crown Prince Frederick of Prussia that he was obliged to
evacuate the greater part of Alsace and to fall back upon
Châlons.   On 18 August, another German army under
Moltke defeated the French army of the Rhine under
Marshal Bazaine in the bloody battle of Gravelotte
in Lorraine and shut it up in the fortress of Metz.   Marshal
MacMahon, whom the Emperor Napoleon now joined, and to
whom the French pinned their faith, counseled a rapid retreat
to Paris in order to afford time to raise new armies and retake
the field with some chance of ultimate success, but the Empress
Eugénie, who knew that such an acknowledgment of defeat
would spell the ruin of the dynasty, wired him to go forward at once
to the relief of Metz.   With heavy hearts Marshal MacMahon
and the Emperor Napoleon moved their inferior forces down
the River Meuse, endeavoring to find a place where they might
cross and thence drive back the Germans.   At Sedan, almost
down to the Belgian border, they made the despairing attempt,
1–2 September, 1870.   Outnumbered and finally surrounded,
they surrendered themselves with 81,000 men, having lost in
killed and wounded about 25,000.   The first phase of the
Franco-German War was over ; it had lasted barely six weeks.

Battle of Sedan, September, 1870

When on 4 September, 1870, it became generally known in
Paris that Napoleon III, together with the last important French
army in the field, was a prisoner of the Germans, what
might easily have been foreseen actually happened.
A group of self-appointed Republicans, among whom
Léon Gambetta was conspicuous, solemnly proclaimed
in the city-hall the deposition of the Bonapartes and
the establishment of the Third Republic.   The Empress Eugénie fled to England, and a "Government
of National Defense" was hastily formed to rule the country
until peace could be restored and the nation consulted on the
nature of the permanent government for France.

Downfall of Napoleon III and Proclamation of the Third French Republic

Now that Napoleon III was deposed and the Republicans in
power, peace might have been promptly concluded had not
Bismarck been bent on "regaining" Alsace and Lorraine for
Germany and reducing France to such a desperate plight that
she could never again seriously interfere with the German na-

tion. In view of this fact, the patriotic assertion of the new revolutionary foreign minister of France that he would not "cede an inch of French soil nor a stone of French fortresses" rendered the prolongation of the war inevitable.

The second part of the Franco-German War — the part with which the government of the Third French Republic was concerned — was longer and more complicated than the first part in which the Emperor Napoleon III had been implicated, but it was less important from a military or political standpoint. The new Government of National Defense, dominated by the inspiring personality of Léon Gambetta, improvised armies out of surviving remnants of regiments, and proclaimed a *levée en masse* of all men from twenty-one to forty years of age. This unforeseen resistance astonished the invading Germans, but the outcome was never in doubt. The struggle reduced itself on one side to a siege of Paris and on the other to repeated but hopeless efforts to raise the siege.

Paris held out against the Germans from the middle of September, 1870, to 28 January, 1871, and then surrendered only because its population were freezing and starving. Surrender of Paris, Already, late in September, Strassburg had capitu-January, lated, and, in October, Marshal Bazaine, with shameful 1871 pusillanimity if not positive treachery, had delivered the great fortress of Metz, together with a well-equipped army of 150,000 men, into the hands of the Germans. Four days after the surrender of Paris, an armistice was arranged in order to admit of the election of a French National Assembly which would have authority to ratify a peace. The preliminaries, concluded at Versailles, between Bismarck and Thiers, were most reluctantly ratified by the Assembly on 1 March; and the final treaty was signed at Frankfort on 10 May, 1871.

By the treaty of Frankfort, France ceded to Germany the whole of Alsace, excepting Belfort, and eastern Lorraine, together with the great fortresses of Metz and Strassburg, and Treaty of agreed to pay an indemnity of five milliards of francs Frankfort, (one billion dollars). German troops were to be left 1871 in occupation of northern France until the indemnity was wholly paid. Of the numerous and far-reaching results of the Franco-German War, perhaps the most striking was the completion of German unification and the establishment of the present-day German Empire. Just as Bismarck had expected, the fact that South Germans had fought shoulder to shoulder with North Germans and that the great triumph of German arms had been achieved by Bavarians and Württembergers as well as by Prussians sent throughout the Germanies a patriotic thrill potent enough to overcome princely ambition or academic distrust of conservatism and militarism, and by November, 1870, treaties of union had been concluded between Bismarck, representing the North German Confederation, and the governments of the four south German states — Bavaria, Württemberg, Baden, and Hesse-Darmstadt. These treaties, as ratified by the several diets and sovereigns, simply extended the North German Confederation so as to include the southern states and changed its name to the "German Empire." The king of Prussia was henceforth to be called German emperor instead of president of the Confederation. By a curious irony of fate, it was in the palace of Louis XIV at Versailles,[1] " in the ancient center of a hostile power which for centuries had striven to divide and humiliate Germany," that the solemn proclamation of the German Empire was made on 18 January, 1871, exactly one hundred and seventy years after the assumption by the Prussian Hohenzollerns of the title of king. There, surrounded by sovereigns, generals, and soldiers, Bismarck read the imperial decree which sealed the first part of his life-work, and the grand-duke of Baden led the cheers for King William of Prussia, now, by the grace of God and the will of his fellow-princes, German emperor.

Union of the Four South German States with the North German Confederation

Proclamation of the German Empire, January, 1871

Not only did the Franco-German War hasten the completion of German unification, but it served to remove every foreign danger of its early undoing. The war confirmed beyond the peradventure of a doubt the preëminence of the German military machine; henceforth, Austria must abandon every thought of avenging Sadowa, and France, for many a year to come, would be unequal to the task of avenging Sedan.

In the internal affairs of France the war had the utmost significance. The gigantic imposture of the Napoleonic Empire

[1] It will be recalled that the Germans were still besieging Paris.

perished in the midst of national disaster, and with the most bitter travail was born the Third Republic.   From 1789 to 1870 the political history of France had been marked by more or less chaotic attempts to realize now one and now another of the great revolutionary principles of liberty, equality, and fraternity; and in particular under Napoleon III the first had been foolishly sacrificed to the third.   Sedan and the cession of Alsace-Lorraine were terrible blows to French national self-esteem, but the Third Republic, as it gradually settled down after 1870, and attained to a permanence not equaled since the pre-revolutionary Bourbon monarchy, taught that democracy has its blessings no less than nationalism.   In a way, it may be said, the Franco-German War recalled France to her European mission of pointing all three paths of liberty, equality, and fraternity.

Effect of the Franco-Prussian War on France

A less certain good derived from the war was the continued bitterness between France and Germany.   In sharp contrast to the lenient treatment which Bismarck had accorded to Austria in 1866 were the harsh and humiliating terms which the German chancellor imposed on France in 1871; and the results displayed a corresponding discrepancy.   In the case of Austria, the soreness of defeat soon disappeared and within a comparatively short time the emperors William and Francis Joseph were sworn friends and allies.   On the other side, the French remained painfully aware of their disgrace and fully resolved as soon as possible to recover Alsace-Lorraine. The war fanned, rather than banked, the fire of mutually vindictive patriotism on either side of the Franco-German frontier. And it was this war, more than any other single event, which throughout the next forty years gave complexion to international politics, saddled Europe with enormous crushing armaments, and constituted the first link in that causal chain of circumstances that led straight on to another and vaster European war. Perhaps in punishing the French, Bismarck allowed himself for the first time in his career to be influenced by emotion and took a false step.

The Franco-Prussian War of 1870 a Prelude to the War of the Nations of 1914

The Franco-German War had important consequences for the temporal power of the papacy and for the new kingdom of

Italy.　Military need obliged Napoleon III to withdraw (19 August, 1870) the last of the French troops who, since 1849, had upheld the temporal sovereignty of Pope Pius IX in Rome.　And when the collapse of the French Empire at Sedan made it clear that Napoleon III would never be able to return the expedition, the government of Victor Emmanuel, with Bismarck's approval, sent a royal army of 60,000 men into the remaining Papal State. Force, however, had to be used against the pontiff; a breach had to be made in the walls of Porta Pia; but at the first tidings of bloodshed, Pope Pius ordered his little papal army to cease firing, and on 20 September, 1870, — less than three weeks after Sedan, — the troops of Victor Emmanuel held Rome.　Thus did the temporal power of the bishops of Rome come to an end after a duration of more than twelve centuries, and thus was the political unification of the Italian people, begun as recently as 1859, successfully consummated.

Effect of the Franco-Prussian War on Italy

End of the Temporal Rule of the Pope, September, 1870

One other result of the Franco-German War merits passing attention.　The fall of Napoleon III permitted the reversal of another part of his work.　In this instance, the Russian government, again with Bismarck's approval, denounced (31 October, 1870) the articles of the treaty of Paris of 1856 which limited Russian naval forces and armaments in the Black Sea, and a conference of the Powers in London in March, 1871, formally ratified the accomplished fact.　It was the sign of the resumption of the Russian policy of vigorous interference in the Ottoman Empire and among the Balkan nationalities.

Effect of the Franco-Prussian War on Russia

The Franco-German War affords a convenient point at which to halt temporarily the story of the growth of nationalism.　The years from 1848 to 1871 witnessed some striking achievements of national patriotism throughout central Europe.　Every popular literature was affected.　Scholars came under the racial spell.　Individuals were acutely conscious of their nationality.　In the name of nationalism, an adventurer ruled France for twenty-two years.　Because of nationalism the Habsburg dominions were tumultuously shaken.　Political independence was assured to the Magyars, and political

Nationalism, 1848–1871

unification, after the aspirations of centuries, was secured to Germans and Italians.

It must not be supposed that throughout this era of nationalism the growth of democracy was suspended. On the contrary, a review of the present chapter will show (1) that in France political Liberalism was steadily gaining strength, despite Napoleon III, until by 1870 it was embodied in the Third Republic; (2) that in Italy Cavour was quite as ambitious to establish constitutional government as to effect political unification; (3) that both in Austria and in Hungary the emperor-king Francis Joseph was constrained to declare his conversion to constitutionalism; and (4) that in Germany even Bismarck at last consented to play with parliaments and with universal manhood suffrage. From following chapters, moreover, it will be possible to learn that it was between 1848 and 1871 (5) that in Great Britain the elective franchise was radically extended; (6) that in Spain another revolution paved the way for the final establishment of parliamentary government; and (7) that even in Russia important steps were taken looking toward the grant of local self-government and toward the complete abolition of serfdom. It was not that these democratic advances were unimportant; it was simply that they were outweighed in contemporary interest by the spirit of nation-making.

Democracy, 1848–1871

Nor must it be supposed that the growth of nationalism stopped or even lagged after 1871. Combined henceforth more inextricably with the growth of democracy, the progress of nationalism, if somewhat more subtle, was nevertheless a continuously moving force in the world's history. For forty-three years of peace throughout western and central Europe it was a potent factor in shaping the internal development of Great Britain, France, Germany, Austria-Hungary, and Italy. During an equal term of unrest in eastern Europe, it affected the relations of the Russian Empire with subject nationalities and it hastened the dismemberment of the Ottoman Empire. In the most remote places and among the most diverse peoples nationalism throve, — in Ireland, in Norway, in Finland, in Poland, in Greece, in Latin America, in India, in Japan. Not only literatures and the other blessings

Continued Growth of Nationalism after 1871

of peaceful patriotic rivalries was nationalism destined to bring forth in future years but many bloody rebellions as well and the calamitous War of the Nations.

ADDITIONAL READING

Brief General Accounts. C. D. Hazen, *Europe since 1815* (1910), ch. ix–xiii; Charles Seignobos, *A Political History of Europe since 1814*, trans. ed. by S. M. Macvane (1900), ch. vi, xi, xv, xvii, xxvii; J. H. Robinson and C. A. Beard, *The Development of Modern Europe*, Vol. II (1907), ch. xxi, xxii; C. E. M. Hawkesworth, *The Last Century in Europe, 1814–1910* (1913), ch. xix–xxiv; C. A. Fyffe, *A History of Modern Europe, 1792–1878* (1896), ch. xxi–xxiv; J. A. R. Marriott, *The Remaking of Modern Europe, 1789–1878* (1910), ch. xiv–xx; W. A. Phillips, *Modern Europe, 1815–1899* (1901), ch. xiv–xviii; Oscar Browning, *A History of the Modern World*, Vol. I (1912), Book II, ch. vi, x, xii–xiv, Vol. II (1912), Book III; *History of All Nations*, Vol. XIX by Theodor Flathe, *The Reconstruction of Europe*, ch. i–ix; Harold Murdock, *The Reconstruction of Europe: a Sketch of the Diplomatic and Political History of Continental Europe from the Rise to the Fall of the Second French Empire* (1898); *Cambridge Modern History*, Vol. XI, *Growth of Nationalities* (1909); *Histoire générale*, Vol. XI, ch. v–viii, xiii, xxi, xxii; Constantin Bulle, *Geschichte des zweiten Kaiserreiches und des Königreiches Italien* (1890); Sir Edward Hertslet, *The Map of Europe by Treaty*, Vol. II, *1828–1863*, and Vol. III, *1864–1875* (1875), the standard collection of the principal treaties and conventions, translated into English. See also J. H. Rose, *Nationality in Modern History* (1916).

Louis Napoleon and the Second French Empire. There is no convenient adequate biography of Napoleon III, but the following may provide material for a good understanding of his character and policies: F. A. Simpson, *The Rise of Louis Napoleon* (1909); H. A. L. Fisher, *Bonapartism* (1908), six brilliant lectures, suggestive rather than informing; F. H. Cheetham, *Louis Napoleon and the Genesis of the Second Republic: being a Life of the Emperor Napoleon III to the Time of his Election to the Presidency of the French Republic* (1908), readable but not profound; Archibald Forbes, *The Life of Napoleon the Third* (1897), very superficial; *Memoirs of Dr. Thomas W. Evans: the Second French Empire*, ed. by E. A. Crane (1905), a warm appreciation of the emperor by his American dentist; Blanchard Jerrold, *The Life of Napoleon III derived from State Records, from Unpublished Family Correspondence, and from Personal Testimony*, 4 vols. (1874–1882), the best and fullest apology in English; Victor Hugo, *The History of a Crime*, and *Napoleon the Little*, English translations in several editions, bitter arraignments of Louis Napoleon; N. W. Senior, *Conversations with Distinguished Persons during the 2nd Empire from 1860 to 1863*, 2 vols. (1880), interesting side-lights afforded by the associations of an eminent English economist; *Life and Works of Louis Napoleon*, 2 vols.

(1852), an Eng. trans. of some of his most important writings; H. Thirria, *Napoléon III avant l'empire*, 2 vols. (1895-1896), apologetic and ill-balanced, but containing numerous extracts from contemporary newspaper comments; A. L. Guérard, *French Prophets of Yesterday: a Study of Religious Thought under the Second Empire* (1913), well-written and scholarly. The most exhaustive histories of the reign of Napoleon III are Pierre de La Gorce, *Histoire du second empire*, 4th ed., 7 vols. (1896-1905), the chief secondary authority, marked by Clerical leanings, and Taxtile Delord, *Histoire du second empire*, 6 vols. (1869-1876), scholarly and strongly opposed to the empire. On social and economic aspects of the Second Empire: Georges Weill, *Histoire du mouvement social en France, 1852-1910*, 2d ed. (1911), ch. i-vi; P. L. Fournier, *Le second empire et la législation ouvrière* (1911); Émile Levasseur, *Histoire des classes ouvrières et de l'industrie en France de 1789 à 1870*, Vol. II (1904), Book VI; Jean Jaurès (editor), *Histoire socialiste*, Vol. X by Albert Thomas, *Le second empire* (1907); and Maurice (Comte) Fleury, *La société du second empire*, 3 vols. (1911). On the *coup d'état* of 1851 and the continuance of Republican opposition: Eugène Ténot, *Paris in December, 1851*, Eng. trans. by S. W. Adams and A. H. Brandon (1870); J. Tchernoff, *Associations et sociétés secrètes sous la deuxième république, 1848-1851* (1905), an important collection of documents, and, by the same author, *Le parti républicain au coup d'état et sous le second empire* (1906); Georges Weill, *Histoire du parti républicain en France de 1814 à 1870* (1900). On Napoleon III's foreign policies, there are the pretentious volumes of A. W. Kinglake, *Invasion of the Crimea*, 9 vols. (1863-1901), highly critical of the French emperor; the diplomatic study of the papal question by Émile Bourgeois and É. Clermont, *Rome et Napoléon III* (1907); the contemporary account of Napoleon's colonial policy in Jules Duval, *Les colonies et la politique coloniale de la France* (1864); and the popular narrative of P. F. Martin, *Maximilian in Mexico: the Story of the French Intervention, 1861-1867* (1914). The most thorough treatment of the constitutional changes in France is that of Henry Berton, *L'évolution constitutionelle du second empire* (1900). The most elaborate account of the last ten years of Napoleon III's régime is the monumental apology of Émile Ollivier, *L'empire libéral*, 17 vols. (1895-1914). An interesting Catholic Liberal-Monarchist narrative of the last days of the Empire and the early days of the Third Republic is Samuel Denis, *Histoire contemporaine: la chute de l'empire, le gouvernement de la défence nationale, l'assemblée nationale*, 4 vols. (1897-1903).

The Political Unification of Italy. Bolton King, *A History of Italian Unity, 1814-1871*, 2 vols. (1899), the best and most readable account in English; Evelyn (Countess) Martinengo-Cesaresco, *The Liberation of Italy, 1815-1870*, sympathetic and charming; R. S. Holland, *Builders of United Italy* (1908), brief essays on Gioberti, Mazzini, Garibaldi, Cavour, and Victor Emmanuel II; J. A. R. Marriott, *Makers of Modern Italy, Mazzini — Cavour — Garibaldi* (1889), popular sketches. On Cavour: W. R. Thayer, *The Life and Times of Cavour*, 2 vols. (1911), the standard biography; Evelyn (Countess) Martinengo-Cesaresco, *Cavour* (1898), brief but so happily written that it might serve as a model biography; Pietro Orsi, *Cavour and the Making of Modern Italy, 1810–1861* (1914) in " Heroes of the Nations " Series; William de La Rive, *Count Cavour: Reminiscences, Life and Character*, Eng. trans. (1862), a character-sketch by an intimate friend; F. X. Kraus, *Cavour, die Erhebung Italiens im neunzehnten Jahrhundert* (1902), the popular account of a scholarly German Catholic; and for letters of Cavour see especially the editions of Nicomede Bianchi, *La politique du comte Camille de Cavour de 1852 à 1861, lettres inédites* (1885), and of Luigi Chiala, *Lettere edite ed inedite di Camillo Cavour*, 2d ed., 10 vols. (1883–1887).   On Garibaldi: *Autobiography of Giuseppe Garibaldi*, Eng. trans. by A. Werner, 3 vols. (1889); and the interesting books of G. M. Trevelyan, *Garibaldi and the Thousand* (1909) and *Garibaldi and the Making of Italy* (1911).   A sympathetic biography of the king is that of G. S. Godkin, *Life of Victor Emmanuel II, First King of Italy*, 2 vols. (1879).   For special phases of unification: H. C. Wylly, *The Campaign of Magenta and Solferino* (1907); H. R. Whitehouse, *Collapse of the Kingdom of Naples* (1899); Raffaele de Cesare, *The Last Days of Papal Rome, 1850–1870*, abridged Eng. trans. by Helen Zimmern (1909), based on important unpublished sources and anti-Clerical in tone; Enrico della Rocca, *The Autobiography of a Veteran, 1807–1893*, Eng. trans. ed. by Janet Ross (1898), interesting reminiscences of an active participant in events from 1848 to 1870; *The Birth of Modern Italy*, ed. by the Duke Litta-Visconti-Arese (1909), memoirs of Jessie White Mario, an enthusiastic friend and admirer of Mazzini and Garibaldi, prejudiced against Cavour.

The Political Unification of Germany.   Brief narratives: G. M. Priest, *Germany since 1740* (1915), ch. ix, x; E. F. Henderson, *A Short History of Germany*, new ed. (1916), Vol. II, ch. ix, x; Ferdinand Schevill, *The Making of Modern Germany* (1916), ch. v; Wilhelm Müller, *Political History of Recent Times, 1816–1875*, Eng. trans. by J. P. Peters (1882), ch. xv–xxvi; *Cambridge Modern History*, Vol. XI (1909), ch. xv, xvi; Henri Lichtenberger, *Germany and its Evolution in Modern Times*, trans. from French by A. M. Ludovici (1913), Book II, pp. 65–137; J. W. Headlam, *Bismarck and the Foundation of the German Empire* (1899), in the " Heroes of the Nations " Series, judicial and well-written; G. B. Malleson, *The Refounding of the German Empire, 1848–1914*, new ed. (1914), chiefly military. Standard works: Heinrich von Sybel, *The Founding of the German Empire by William I*, Eng. trans. by M. L. Perrin and Gamaliel Bradford, 7 vols. (1890–1898), the work of a famous German patriot-historian who had access to the Prussian state archives for the period preceding 1867; Wilhelm Maurenbrecher, *Gründung des deutschen Reiches, 1859–1871*, 4th ed. by W. Busch (1911); Hans von Zwiedineck-Südenhorst, *Deutsche Geschichte von der Auflösung des alten bis zur Errichtung des neuen Kaiserreiches, 1806–1871*, 3 vols. (1897–1905), partisanly patriotic in much the same way as Von Sybel; Wilhelm Oncken, *Das Zeitalter des Kaisers Wilhelm*, 2 vols. (1890–1892); Ottokar Lorenz, *Kaiser Wilhelm und die Be-*

gründung des Reichs, 1866–1871, 2d ed. (1902); P. Kloeppel, *Dreissig Jahre deutscher Verfassungsgeschichte, 1867–1897,* Vol. I, *Die Gründung des Reichs und die Jahre der Arbeit, 1867–1877* (1900); Ernest Denis, *Le fondation de l'empire allemand, 1852–1871* (1906), an excellent treatise by a French scholar. Special contributions: Sir H. M. Hozier, *The Seven Weeks' War: its Antecedents and its Incidents,* 2 vols. (1867), based on letters written during the war from Bohemia to the London *Times;* Heinrich Friedjung, *Der Kampf um die Vorherrschaft in Deutschland, 1859–1866,* 2 vols. (1897–1898); Ludwig Hahn (editor), *Zwei Jahre preussisch-deutscher Politik, 1866–1867* (1868) and *Der Krieg Deutschlands gegen Frankreich . . . die deutsche Politik 1867 bis 1871* (1871), valuable collections of documents relating to the foundation of the German Empire; *Memoirs of Prince Chlodwig Hohenlohe-Schillingsfürst,* Eng. trans. by G. W. Chrystal, 2 vols. (1906), useful for relations between the North German Confederation and the south German states, especially Bavaria. Of almost innumerable lives of Bismarck, the following are the best and most serviceable: Munroe Smith, *Bismarck and German Unity,* 2d rev. ed. (1910), an admirable sketch; Charles Lowe, *Prince Bismarck* (1899), an abridgment of the same author's longer work *Prince Bismarck: an Historical Biography,* 2 vols. (1885); Erich Marcks, *Bismarck, eine Biographie,* now in course of publication, promises to be the most satisfactory account in German — Vol. I is entitled *Bismarcks Jugend, 1815–1848* (1909); Paul Matter, *Bismarck et son temps,* new ed., 3 vols. (1914), the chief French authority, remarkably fair-minded. See also *Prince Bismarck's Letters to his Wife, his Sister, and Others, from 1844 to 1870,* Eng. trans. by Fitzh. Maxse (1878). A very elaborate history of Bismarck — a coöperative enterprise in twelve volumes — is in course of publication as *Geschichte des Fürsten Bismarck in Einzeldarstellungen* (1907 *sqq.*).

For Austria-Hungary, 1848–1871, consult the bibliography appended to Chapter XXIV, below.

The War of 1870–1871. *Cambridge Modern History,* Vol. XI (1909), ch. xxi, a compact account by Sir J. F. Maurice; J. H. Rose, *The Development of the European Nations, 1870–1900,* Vol. I (1905), ch. i–iv, clear and interesting; Lord Acton, *Historical Essays and Studies* (1907), ch. vii, viii; Émile Ollivier, *The Franco-Prussian War and its Hidden Causes,* trans. by G. B. Ives (1912), an apology for and by the French premier at the outbreak of the war; George Hooper, *The Campaign of Sedan, August–September, 1870* (1914); Lonsdale Hale, *People's War in France* (1904), based on Fritz Hönig, *Der Volkskrieg an der Loire im Herbst 1870 . . .,* 8 vols. (1893–1897), and useful for the campaigns after Sedan; Arthur Chuquet, *La guerre de 1870–1871* (1895), a good brief narrative; Jean Jaurès, *La guerre franco-allemande, 1870–1871,* in Vol. XI (1908) of the *Histoire socialiste;* Edmond Palat (pseud. Pierre Lehautcourt), *Les origines de la guerre de 1870: la candidature Hohenzollern, 1868–1870* (1912), a valuable study in diplomacy, and, by the same author, *Histoire de la guerre de 1870,* 7 vols. (1901–1908), very detailed and stopping with the surrender of Metz in October, 1870, and the briefer *Guerre de 1870–1871*, 2 vols. (1910); Hellmuth von Moltke, *Franco-German War of 1870–1871*, Eng. trans. by Clara Bell and H. W. Fischer, 2 vols. (1891), important but technical; the very elaborate documentary histories published under the auspices of the French General Staff and the German General Staff respectively; Albert Sorel, *Histoire diplomatique de la guerre franco-allemande*, 2 vols. (1875); Antonin Debidour, *Histoire diplomatique de l'Europe*, *1814–1878*, Vol. II (1891), ch. vii–x; Moritz Busch, *Bismarck in the Franco-German War, 1870–1871*, Eng. trans., 2 vols. (1879); *Bismarck's Letters to his Wife from the Seat of War, 1870–1871*, Eng. trans. by Armin Harder (1903); *Diaries of Emperor Frederick during the Campaigns of 1866 and 1870–1871*, Eng. trans. by F. A. Welby (1902); E. B. Washburne, *Recollections of a Minister to France, 1869–1877*, 2 vols. (1887), and, by the same author, who was American minister to France, *Franco-German War and Insurrection of the Commune* (1878); E. A. Vizetelly, *My Days of Adventure : the Fall of France, 1870–1871* (1914), memoirs of an eye-witness.

EUROPE
1871

Scale of Miles
0   100   200   300   400   500

ARCTIC CIRCLE

Iceland
(Danish)

FAROE IS.
(Danish)

SHETLAND IS.

ROCKALL

ORKNEY IS.
C. Wrath

HEBRIDES

Wick

Trondhjem

Molde

Bergen

Christiania

Stavanger

Christiansand

The Naze

The Skaw

Göteborg
(Gothenbu

60°

Scotland
Aberdeen
Dundee
Perth
Edinburgh

Malin Head
Londonderry
Belfast
Galway Dublin
Ireland
Limerick

BRITISH
ISLES

Glasgow
Carlisle

Newcastle

NORTH SEA

DENMARK
Copenhagen
Malmö

HELIGOLAND
(Br.)

Kiel
RÜG

50°

VALENTIA I.
C. Clear

Cork

Liverpool
Irish Sea
Manchester

Hull

England

Hamburg

Bremen   Berlin

Hanover

GERMA

Elbe

Cassel
Leipzig
Dresde

Birmingham

Bristol
Plymouth   London
Southampton Dover
Lands End   Strait of Dover

Amsterdam
Rotterdam

HOLLAND

Cologne

Frankfurt   Prague

Nuremberg

Elbe R.

Wales

C. Ortegal
Coruña

Oviedo

C. Finisterre

Vigo

Oporto

Lisbon
C. Roca

C. S. Vincent

PORTUGAL

Santander
S. Sebastian
Bayonne

Bordeaux

Douro R.
Duero R.
Valladolid

SPAIN
Madrid

Tagus R.
Guadiana R.
Cordova
Seville

Toledo

Granada
Guadalquivir R.

Cadiz
Tarifa Pt.

Ebro R.

Saragossa

Valencia

Murcia

Cartagena

Malaga
Gibraltar
(Br.)

MOROCCO

Channel Is.
Brest

Havre

Rouen

Paris
Orleans

Tours

Nantes

Loire R.

FRANCE

Bay of Biscay

St. Etienne

Toulouse

Garonne R.

Cette

ALGERIA

English Channel

Calais

Brussels
BELGI
Antwerp
Luxemburg

Metz

Seine R.

Dijon

Nevers

Lyon

Nice

Marseille

Toulon

BALEARIC IS.
MINORCA
MAJORCA
Palma
IVIZA

Algiers

Strassburg

Basel

Bern
SWITZERLAND
Geneva

Genoa

CORSICA
Ajaccio

Stuttgart

Munich

AUS

Innsbruck

Milan
Turin

Verona

ITA

Leghorn

Florence

Rome

SARDINIA

Sassari

Cagliari

MEDIT

Po R.

Venice

ADRI

Naples

ELBA

Strait of Bonifacio

Rhine R.

Tunis

TUNIS

LIPARI IS.
Palermo

SICILY

Messi

STRO

Longitude West   0°   10°   Longitude East

20°   10°   0°   10°

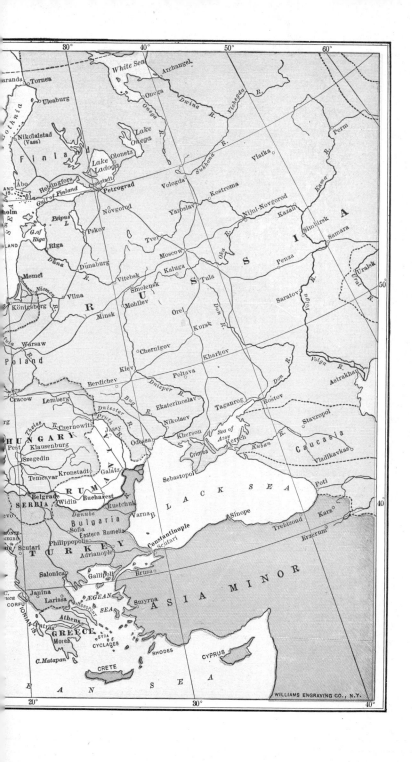

30° 40° 50° 60°

White Sea Archangel

Saranda Tornea
Uleaburg Onega
Onega R. Dwina R. Vichegda R.
Nikolaistad Lake Perm
(Vasa) Onega
F i n l a d Olonetz Vologda R. Viatka
Lake Suchona R. Kama
Ladoga Vologda Kostroma R.
Abo Helsingfors Kronstadt Petrograd Vologda R Nijni-Novgorod Samara
AND IS. Gulf of Finland Yaroslav Kazan
Stholm Novgorod Oka R Simbirsk R U S S I A
Peipus Pskov Tver Kostroma
G. of L Moscow Simbirsk
Riga Riga Kaluga Tula Penza Samara
Dvina Dünaburg Vitebsk
Memel R. Smolensk Orel Volga R Saratov Uralsk
Niemen Mohilev Don R. 50°
Königsberg R. Vilna R U Minsk Orel Kursk
Warsaw Chernigov Kharkov Don R. Volga R Astrakhan
P o l a n d Kiev Poltava
Cracow Lemberg Berdichev Dnieper R. Rostov
Czernowitz Dniester R Ekaterinoslav Taganrog Stavropol
rg Theiss R. Jassy Bug Nikolaev Don R Caucasia 40°
H U N G A R Y Pruth R. Odessa Sea of Kerch Vladikavkaz
Pest Klausenburg Kherson Azov Kuban R.
Szegedin R U M Crimea Poti
Temesvar Kronstadt Galatz Sebastopol B L A C K S E A 40°
Belgrade Bucharest Rustchuk Trebizond Erzerum
SERBIA Widin Danube Varna B Sinope Kars
vo Sofia Eastern Rumelia
MONG B u l g a r i a Constantinople A S I A M I N O R
EGRO Philippopolis Scutari
Scutari T U R K E Y Adrianople
Salonica Gallipoli Brusa
Janina Larissa ÆGEAN
C. HELLESPONT Smyrna
ruca SEA
CORFU Athens
Patras GREECE SYRA RHODES CYPRUS
Morea CYCLADES
C. Matapan CRETE
E A N S E A A
20° 30° 40°
WILLIAMS ENGRAVING CO., N.Y.

CHAPTER XXI

SOCIAL FACTORS IN RECENT EUROPEAN HISTORY, 1871-1914

IT is always dangerous to emphasize the "periodizing" of history, for the pretty obvious reasons (1) that the label applied to a particular period or era, no matter how appro- *Dangers in* priate it may be, can emphasize but one element in the *"Periodiz-* events of the time and may, therefore, blind the eye *ing" His-* *tory* to secondary but none the less significant features, and (2) that the roots of any period often lie far back in other and widely scattered periods, from which they cannot be arbitrarily separated without destroying their vitality. Thus, in the last chapter, the idea of "nationalism" has been stressed, but "nationalism" is by no means a complete explanation of a multitude of historical facts during the years from 1848 to 1871— the growth of democracy, the furtherance of Christian missions, the increased wealth of capitalists, the vogue of marble-topped tables, black-walnut furniture, and hoop-skirts. Nor is "nationalism" a novelty of the period: its foundations, as we know, rest upon a Napoleonic myth, upon a revolutionary sentiment styled "fraternity," and upon a consciousness of kind that can be traced back far beyond the sixteenth century.

Convenience of treatment becomes the real justification for guiding the stream of history into little pools and eddies. Politically speaking, "nationalism" was undeniably the most potent factor in shaping the course of Europe from 1848 to 1871; and if the student remembers constantly that this fact must be conditioned in his own mind by a grasp on contemporary developments in science, art, religion, and society, he will then be in a better position to appreciate the whole flow of human events down through the tortuous and rocky channel of the nineteenth century.

Whatever qualifications must be made in treating the years from 1815 to 1830 as the "Era of Metternich," or those from 1830 to 1848 as marked by "Democratic Reform and Revolution," or those from 1848 to 1871 as distinguished by the "Growth of Nationalism," there can be no doubt that at least in politics and government a new era was inaugurated about 1871, — an era of peace among the Great Powers of Europe, which was to endure some forty-three years, — an era of steady domestic development along lines whose general character it is the purpose of this chapter to set forth.

"THE ERA OF THE BENEVOLENT BOURGEOISIE,"
1871–1914

First and most striking of the political facts of the new era is that its beginning is approximately the beginning of nearly all the present-day governments of Europe. From the war which ended the preceding period date the German Empire and the Third French Republic. The kingdom of Italy, proclaimed in 1861, was not territorially complete until 1870. The dual relationship between the empire of Austria and the kingdom of Hungary, together with the final establishment of constitutional government in each, dates from 1867. In the same year, the grant of the elective franchise to workingmen inaugurated the democratic monarchy in Great Britain. Constitutional revisions in 1866 determined the subsequent representative systems of Denmark and Sweden. To-day the fundamental law of Switzerland is the constitution of 1874, and that of Spain, a document of 1876. Even the present-day constitutional régime in the Ottoman Empire is only an application of a scheme prematurely promulgated in 1876. Greece secured a new dynasty and a new constitution in 1864. And the independence of Rumania, Serbia, and Montenegro, and the autonomy of Bulgaria, were definitely acknowledged in the 'seventies.

It is, therefore, a politically new Europe with which we have to deal after 1871. But it is one in which the great principles of the French Revolution have triumphed or seem about to triumph. Barely six decades had elapsed since Metternich had played host

The Governments throughout Europe, 1871–1914

to the gold-laced Congress of Vienna and had found in every dignitary or potentate there assembled a willing ally [1] in disregarding nationalism, in seeking to repress liberalism, and in scoffing at equality. But from 1815 to 1871, through stress of revolutions and storms of international wars, Metternich and his whole political school had been beaten and buffeted about and relegated, as it were, to ancient history. By 1871 the victory of the French Revolution was at last certain. Henceforth, for an indefinite period, the ideal unit of organized political life would be the nation, a group of people speaking the same language, sharing the same general customs and traditions, and conscious in every case, whether justifiably or not, of its own "racial superiority." This was vital "nationalism," this was the new patriotism, this was the logical outcome of that fraternity which the revolutionaries had preached and the literary people inculcated and which now the whole world cherished.

Definitive Triumph of the Principles of the French Revolution

Nationalism

Henceforth, also, the ideal method of organized political life would be constitutionalism, that is to say, a solemn understanding on the part of the inhabitants of every country that government, whether monarchical or republican, centralized or federal, parliamentary or congressional, should have no power to restrict certain rights and privileges that were held to inhere in the individual citizen, and, at the same time, that what powers it did enjoy should be exercised only by regularly elected representatives of the nation. This was the achievement of "liberty," as the revolutionaries had conceived it and as the Liberals had propagated it.

Constitutionalism

Of "equality" much the same sort prevailed in fact after 1871 as had been maintained in theory by the French bourgeoisie nearly a hundred years earlier. It was the sort which combated special privileges, of whatever character, of the ancient landowning aristocracy and of the Christian clergy, whether Catholic or Protestant; which tended to make business men and professional men the social equals of priests and landlords; and which, for the

Preëminence of the Middle Class

[1] The only exception was the Tsar Alexander of Russia. It is a curious fact that the only European monarch who zealously fought the principles of the Revolution after 1871 was the tsar of Russia.

people at large, was simply a guarantee of equality before the law and of theoretical equality of individual rights. In a word, it was the "equality" which registered everywhere the economic, intellectual, and social preëminence of the middle class — the bourgeoisie. It was not economic equality or necessarily even complete equality of opportunity.

Thus, the period after 1871 was the consummation of the bourgeois Revolution. Its political principles and practices were mainly those of the French bourgeoisie of 1789. Its statesmen belonged in sympathy if not by birth to the middle class. The bulk of its legislation was in the interest of the middle class — the merchants, the traders, the " captains of industry."

Bourgeois Character of the Era 1871–1914

The bourgeois character of the new era is easily explained by reference to the fact that the period was as much the economic result of the Industrial Revolution as the political outcome of the French Revolution. The downfall of Metternich, the theatrical adventures of Napoleon III, the rise of Cavour and Bismarck, must not obscure the development and expansion of the factory system that had been steadily going on ever since the momentous year 1768, when Richard Arkwright had erected in Nottingham his first power factory. From that time down to 1871 and afterwards, water or steam was ever turning busy wheels of industry, spinning at incredible speed millions upon millions of spindles in cotton factories, moving the tireless steel arms of the mechanical loom, lifting and bringing down the ponderous steam-hammer with crushing weight. Not only in England were factories springing up, but since 1815, like mushrooms, in the towns of France and Italy and Germany and the Low Countries and even in the realms of the Habsburg emperor. Blast furnaces belched forth their lurid breath along the Rhine as well as in Wales; and black-faced miners in an endless search for coal were sinking shaft after shaft in Belgium, in France, and in Bavaria. The steam locomotive was ever invading new territories, startling quiet countrysides with its noisy puffings and darkening the blue sky with its trail of smoke; like a vast network, the railways were extending themselves over France and Belgium, through the passes of the Alps, down the valleys of the

The Era Socially the Outcome of the Industrial Revolution

Rhine and the Po, across Prussia and Austria, and on through the bleak plains of Russia and the Siberian wastes to the ancient Oriental marts, — railways, new trade-routes of a great new era !

The social effect of this resistless march of the Industrial Revolution becomes clear only when one remembers that each factory, each mine, each furnace, each railway was owned by some bourgeois capitalist or company of bourgeois capitalists. If Sir Richard Arkwright was the "father of the factory system," as he is so often called, he was likewise the father of the factory-owner, and his was a numerous and powerful progeny. By thousands they now appeared — shrewd, enterprising, intelligent business men, usually self-complacent and always self-reliant. In Russia, in Italy, in Hungary, as well as in France and England and Belgium, the new business man was making his place in society and in politics.

When European states since 1871 are styled "bourgeois," it must not be supposed that nobility, clergy, peasants, and workingmen had ceased to exist or that all of them had been transformed into a perfect middle class. These variations in human society have certainly survived to the present moment, constituting in sum the large majority of the population of every country, but in economic interests they have become increasingly dependent upon the bourgeoisie. The period under review, then, is bourgeois because the bourgeoisie, among all social classes, is the most influential. *Persistence in Recent Times of Classes Other than the Bourgeoisie*

The rise of the bourgeoisie, — a long process, patronized by the Commercial Revolution, enormously quickened alike by the French Revolution and by the Industrial Revolution, seemingly consummated in the second half of the nineteenth century, — had tremendous effects on the fortunes of all the other traditional classes in society. Thus, the ancient landed aristocracy was in time *Altered Relations of Other Classes to the Bourgeoisie* actually revolutionized. The nobleman who formerly had prided himself upon ownership exclusively of land and had despised the bourgeois as a vulgar shopkeeper and tradesman, now perceiving that his own profits from the soil were not *The Nobility* keeping pace with the capitalist's profits from factory, railway, or mine, himself began to invest his surplus wealth in the stocks of

commercial or industrial enterprises, to take up residence in the
city, to become a director of great chartered companies, and to use
his landed estates as secondary assets, in many cases as hunting
preserves for his personal recreation. On the other hand, especially wealthy bourgeois bought large estates from impoverished noblemen and sometimes even purchased titles of nobility for themselves. From both sides a gradual process was
welding together the landowning aristocracy and the industrial
and commercial bourgeoisie. In earlier days the rivalries of
these two classes had characterized much of the social history of
England, France, Spain, the Netherlands, the Germanies, and
Italy; after 1871 their alliance bespeaks a new character of
social evolution. In this respect, as in every other, conditions
varied from one country in Europe to another, from one region to
another, but, in general, it may be accepted as axiomatic that
wherever the Industrial Revolution was most in evidence, there
the solidarity of nobility and middle class was most pronounced.

Peasants and artisans and day-laborers came also, though in
a different way, under the spell of the new bourgeois wealth.
The Peasantry Peasants who were in the category of thrifty independent farmers, as was frequently the case in France,
began discreetly to invest their little hoardings in stocks or
bonds and to become identified in a small way with the capitalist system: in company with nobles and bourgeois they now
opposed any state action that would be likely to endanger their
investments or to reduce their dividends. Peasants who were
less independent, such as the generality of rural laborers in Great
Britain, gradually perceived that their wages bore some relation
to their landlord's gains or losses in business and on the urban
exchange, and accepted the conclusion that, therefore, their
own welfare depended upon others' prosperity. The peasants
who, finding their plight on the farms too miserable, wandered
away to seek relief in factory-employment, learned from the
carpenters, bricklayers, plumbers, and tailors, from day laborers
and factory hands already cluttered together in the towns, that
The Artisans the independence of every wage-earner, urban as well
as rural, was conditional upon the current situation
in the money-market and in the market of supply and
demand, that a slump in stocks might suddenly throw thousands

out of work, and that the livelihood of all was in fact contingent upon the prosperity of the bourgeoisie. Ever since David Ricardo (1772–1823) and J. R. M'Culloch (1789–1864), those intellectual contributors to the cause of the bourgeoisie, had insisted in their learned works on political economy that wages are derived from capital, professors and parliamentarians had vied with one another in pointing out to the masses that their very sustenance is from the bounty of one class. Backed by such authority the notion made rapid conquests. It naturally possessed the minds of all the middle class, including the professional men who were more or less subordinate to the great capitalists, and by the preachments of newspapers and more impressively by the hard experiences of daily life, it was in turn gradually communicated to the lower classes. Eventually, therefore, it seemed as if the first duty incumbent upon all citizens, regardless of class, was to promote industry and trade and to enable the bourgeois capitalist to add wealth to riches. So far was the argument pushed that business prosperity was accepted in many quarters as the end and aim of national patriotism. The acceptance of this prosaic doctrine was made easier for the lower classes in Europe by the knowledge that now and then an individual from their midst rose to be an industrial magnate and by the widespread belief that all of them might rise in the social scale, were they but thrifty and honest and sober. It was what those who had already risen — the bourgeoisie — termed "equality of opportunity."

Bourgeois Materialism

Under the circumstances of their economic supremacy it was possible and even advantageous for the bourgeoisie to be sincere supporters of the democratic governmental doctrines of the French Revolution. "Liberty" would guarantee them important individual rights, not least among which was the fundamental right of private property. "Liberty" would also, through its emphasis on representative government, entitle them to a decisive share in making and executing the laws; and even the grant of universal manhood suffrage, while flattering to the lower classes, could do the bourgeois no serious harm, so long as the wage theories of the classical economists were generally

Bourgeois Devotion to the Principles of the French Revolution

taught and respected. "Equality" was a little dimmer and vaguer : for the present it was still a theoretical equality before the law and an assumed equality of opportunity; for the future, it was hoped, the ideal of equality might be rendered more practicable by the diffusion of popular education and the increase of wealth and human efficiency. But "fraternity" could be immediately vital; vigorous national patriotism was in itself desirable and incidentally distracted attention from economic inequalities; it could unite a whole nation in common allegiance to a glorious emotion; it could conveniently serve the middle class of one country in competing industrially or commercially with the middle class of another country. Small wonder that the triumph of the principles of the French Revolution was assured by the triumph of the bourgeoisie !

We are now in a position to summarize three great characteristics of the period of European history from 1871 to 1914.

Summary of the Chief Characteristics of the Era 1871–1914 (1) Politically speaking, the beginning of the period was marked by the beginning in nearly every country of a new form of government, which has lasted to the present. (2) Socially, the period was marked by the preëminence of the middle class — a preëminence which rested directly upon the economic foundations of the Industrial Revolution and which profoundly modified the activities and ambitions of other classes. (3) Politically again, the period was marked by the exaltation, under middle-class auspices, of three of the major principles of the French Revolution : (a) individual liberty; (b) constitutionalism, including representative government, and, in most countries, universal manhood suffrage; and (c) nationalism.

Within the confines of a single chapter it is impossible to tell the story of this period in any such detail as that with which the history of earlier eras has been narrated. The reasons are simple. In the first place, it was an unusually long period — forty-three years. Secondly, as a period of unbroken peace in the relations of the Great Powers of Europe with one another, it was devoid of such great military deeds as served to provide a unifying theme for reviewing the career of Napoleon or the growth of nationalism just prior to 1871. Thirdly, it was dominated by no single domestic development common to all Europe

— by no such unique figure as Count Metternich, by no such universally unsettling occurrence as the Industrial Revolution, by no such instantly ubiquitous movements as the political upheavals of 1848. Lastly, the internal development which forty-three years of peace allowed to most countries of Europe was very far-reaching and is deserving of detailed study.

Accordingly, the main facts of the period, in so far as they relate to the domestic politics of Europe, will be treated, country by country, in the following five chapters. In view of the significance of these facts not only to the period itself but to the future as well, it is believed that five chapters will not prove too many — one on Great Britain and Ireland, one on Latin Europe, one on Teutonic Europe, one on Russia, and one on the dismemberment of the Ottoman Empire. The five, taken together, will undertake to do for the years from 1871 to 1914 what the single chapter on Metternich did for the years from 1815 to 1830.

In the present chapter the aim is simply to indicate a few striking points of resemblance in the histories of all the European countries during the period and to offer a somewhat more detailed explanation than has yet been found necessary of certain problems which were destined in novel ways to agitate and trouble almost every government, — the relations between the state and religion, and the rise of Socialism.

In the next five chapters the details of the story will vary greatly as we pass from one country to another. But certain general facts will appear again and again with almost tiresome iteration. Under the newly constituted government of almost every European state will be revealed the primary characteristics of the period which have already been mentioned, — the economic, social, intellectual, and political supremacy of the bourgeoisie, and the rapid furtherance of the principles of political democracy and patriotic nationalism. For a thorough understanding of the period, however, it will not be enough to remember these primary factors, derived respectively from the Industrial Revolution and from the French Revolution: in addition, it will be necessary to watch for their common concrete manifestations, which, perhaps, may be called secondary characteristics.

Among the secondary characteristics of the period from 1871 to 1914 which may be readily detected and summarized, the following seem particularly significant:

(1) Legislation directly favorable to private industry and commerce, such as the maintenance of order and security, advan-

Summary of Practical Achievements of the Era 1871–1914

tageous corporation laws, protection of private property against arbitrary confiscations, and legislative aids and public subsidies to private business. State action only slightly less direct in its favors to private industry and commerce is evidenced under the next headings (2)–(5).

(2) Readjustment of taxation-systems, so as to inflict as little injury as possible upon business interests. This implied the imposition of a slowly but steadily augmenting customs tariff upon goods imported into almost every Continental country, for the avowed purposes of providing revenue and protecting native industries against foreign competition. Great Britain alone of all the more important states retained the free-trade system prevalent in the preceding period; she did so because of her relatively greater need of raw materials for her factories and because of the lead in industry which she still enjoyed over the rest of the world, though she did so against the loud protests of a determined minority. In either case — protective tariff or free trade — the policy was pursued which best served the prosperity of the industrial class.

(3) Unparalleled growth of merchant marines. Not only ships of Great Britain, but those of France, Germany, Italy, Greece, the Netherlands, and Norway became conspicuous sea-carriers. In many countries commercial expansion was fostered by a system of governmental bounties.

(4) A new era of imperialism, in which the business man's desire for new fields for the investment of surplus capital and for new markets for the sale of surplus products was identified with a very real national longing to have a particular flag wave over as wide and varied an expanse of the earth's surface as possible. This is national imperialism, a process in which the several European governments, backed by their peoples, engaged in a mad scramble for the partition of the globe. Under the impetus of this national imperialism, greater progress was made

in Europeanizing the world in the years from 1871 to 1914 than in all the preceding centuries since the discovery of America.[1]

(5) Militarism, the maintenance on the part of European states, large and small, of heavier armaments on land and sea than the world had ever before witnessed, despite the fact that the whole period of forty-three years was essentially peaceful. It was at once the outcome of the international struggles of the preceding era and a pledge of the contemporary spirit of national patriotism, and it was actively advocated by a great number of the middle class who perceived in it a guarantee of the maintenance of the capitalistic system, a kind of public insurance against the attacks of other nationalities upon their colonies, their commerce, and their industry. In this connection it is significant to add that the chief efforts of diplomacy were directed during the period, not as once to dynastic aggrandizement, but to the advancement of business enterprises.[2]

(6) Gradual evolution of governmental institutions in the direction of political democracy. Here belong the succession of written constitutions that now encircle the globe; the diminution of royal power and the increase of parliamentary functions; the almost universal extension of the suffrage to adult males, and the beginnings of serious agitation for female suffrage; the trial of such expedients as the initiative and referendum in Switzerland and proportional representation in Belgium. It will be noticed that these political concessions were never strenuously resisted by the middle class; on the contrary, they were often instigated by them. It sufficed the middle class to maintain their economic mastery: in every other field they were self-effacing and magnanimous. It must be remembered that the bourgeoisie preserved, as a class, their old tradition of being educated, enlightened, and benevolent. The next headings (7)–(10) bespeak this fact: together with (6), they embrace the benevolent endeavors of an enlightened bourgeoisie.

(7) Free, public, secular education, — the attempt, begun and carried forward under bourgeois auspices, to establish an

---

[1] "National Imperialism," on account of its far-reaching importance, is reserved for fuller treatment to Part V of this volume, particularly to Chapters XXVII–XXIX.

[2] The international relations of the period are briefly treated in Chapter XXX.

intellectual democracy.   Institutions of learning and research
were munificently endowed.   Never before had European countries devoted so much thought and money to the erection of
public schools.   By the close of the period the highest percentage
of literacy in relation to illiteracy had become an added general
object of international rivalry.

(8) Growing appreciation on the part of the middle class of
the necessity of safeguarding the physical well-being of the
lower classes.   All along the line, signs were multiplying of an
effort to do away with the earlier enmity between factory-
owners and factory-workers and to substitute in its place a
sense of social solidarity.   Thoughtful business men perceived
that social efficiency might be increased, rather than decreased,
by the industry of a well-fed, healthy, contented working class.
Statesmen, too, perceived that the strength and loyalty of the
numerous working class were essential to the military power
of their nations.   Beginning with Bismarck's notable measures
in Germany, one European state after another took steps,
usually with the support of at least a large element of the middle
class, to insure a minimum degree of material comfort to the
lower classes.   Such were factory- and mines-legislation; full
legalization of trade unions; national insurance against illness,
death, accident, and unemployment; minimum wage-rates in
particular industries; town-planning; tenement-house inspection; and free medical service.

(9) Steady advance in science, especially in biology and
geology and in applied science, — an advance zealously fostered
by the wealthy capitalists and redounding to the practical benefit
of the whole world.   A few of the main facts in this advance,
which were of considerable indirect importance in politics, will
be indicated presently in this chapter.

(10) Neglect of religion and tendency toward the separation
of church and state.   This tendency was likewise championed
everywhere by a large element of the middle class, whose opposition to "Clericalism" was as traditional as their patronage of
science.

These ten characteristics will be found in the history of nearly
every European country from 1871 to 1914, betokening in all
cases the juncture of forces of the Industrial Revolution with

those of the French Revolution. But it will also be found that a good deal of resistance was offered during the very same period to the supremacy of the bourgeoisie and to several of the tendencies and characteristics with which they were now impressing the era.

Elements of Dissent from the Spirit of the Era 1871–1914

The resistance came chiefly from two groups, who, from the outset, were naturally prone to quarrel with each other: (1) ardent Christians, particularly Roman Catholics, regardless of social class; and (2) Socialists, recruited chiefly from among the working classes, though sometimes led by persons whose birth and environment placed them in the middle class. After 1871 much of the history of the several European states, with the possible exception of Great Britain, will be found to turn upon the efforts of the bulk of the bourgeoisie and its allies to beat down now the opposition of Catholics, now that of Socialists, now that of both. In order to appreciate the reasons for the resistance and the relative strength of the combatants, it will be convenient at this point to present certain recent developments in the history, first, of Catholic Christianity, and secondly, of Socialism. Incidentally, it will be possible and desirable to refer to the scientific and other intellectual developments of the era.[1]

1. " Clericals ";
2. Socialists

CHRISTIANITY AND POLITICS

In the second half of the nineteenth century, as in earlier times, all Europe could practically be called Christian.[2] It

[1] Let it here be observed, once for all, that the following sections in this chapter are not intended to serve as well-rounded outlines of the nineteenth-century development either of Christianity or of natural science; they are designed merely to provide a background for some understanding of the recent acute struggles waged in many European countries between "Clericals" and "Anti-Clericals." Though these struggles will perhaps seem strange and alien to the average American collegian, some understanding of them is absolutely prerequisite to a real understanding of the domestic history of contemporary Europe. At the same time, because of certain social differences between the United States and Europe, the American collegian should be on his guard against reading too diligently into the recent history of his own country such distinctively European terms as "Clerical" and "Anti-Clerical," and likewise "bourgeois" and "proletarian."

[2] Excepting, of course, Mohammedan districts in southeastern Europe, and groups of Jews widely scattered over the Continent.

was Christian in that the vast majority of its population drew most of their moral ideals and many of their common customs from historic Christianity and that they utilized the services of Christian clergy at least in such crises of life as death and marriage. But in the degree in which the Christian religion was believed and practiced, the widest diversity existed. At one extreme were thoughtful persons who assailed all revealed religion — Christianity, of course, included — as an absurd and superstitious survival of a primitive and ignorant state of human society, as an anachronism in an age of enlightenment and progress. At the other extreme were thoughtful persons who defended the dogmas of the Church and insisted that a repudiation of Christianity would be attended by the worst immoralities and crimes. Between these extremes were the masses, who, while preserving a good deal of indifference as to whether Christianity was an anachronism or a moral necessity, could be depended upon to take sides on concrete questions in accordance with a great variety of religious, and even political, preconceptions and predilections. In general this was the situation in Protestant Scandinavia, Germany, and England, as well as in Roman Catholic Spain, France, Italy, and Austria.

Europe Still Nominally " Christian" but Practically and Fundamentally Divided on Religion

In two particulars, however, the conflict between the extreme religionists — the so-called Clericals — and the extreme anti-religionists — the so-called anti-Clericals — was bound to be sharper in Roman Catholic than in Protestant Europe. In the first place, there was the matter of dogma: the essence of the Catholic faith was still the persistent belief that it was a body of unalterable truths once delivered by Christ to the apostles, which could not be added to, nor subtracted from, even in order to bring it "into harmony with the times," and which could properly be explained only by clergymen; on the other hand, the disintegration of Protestantism, which had been steadily progressing ever since the days of Luther and Calvin and Cranmer, was now in a fair way to effect in practice what Luther had championed in theory, — the right of private judgment, the subordination of dogma to a purely

Conflict More Acute in Roman Catholic than in Protestant Countries

1. Because of Dogma

subjective act of the individual, — with the result that every
Protestant layman and ecclesiastic was free to harmonize his
profession of Christianity with the latest hypothesis in science
or with the most recent experiment in politics. In a word, dogmatically speaking, Roman Catholicism was uncompromising
and clerical; Protestantism was conciliatory and strictly individualistic.

In the second place, there was a vital difference of organization between Catholicism and Protestantism. Protestantism,
being essentially individualistic, had, from the very   2. Because
nature of things, never developed any strong ecclesi-   of Organi-
astical organization, and whatever organization it   zation
did possess was in the form of churches that tended to be pretty
rigidly national in scope, and in action thoroughly subservient
to the secular governments. Roman Catholicism, on the contrary, with its insistently international character, an anti-
national pope, a disciplined hierarchy, and an authoritative
manner of speaking its mind, was ever a possible check upon
the supremacy of the lay state. Thus, irreligious statesmen
who could afford to ignore organized Protestantism usually
found it necessary to guard against anathemas from the bishop
of Rome.

Just prior to 1871, two forces were operating throughout
Catholic Europe to widen the breach between
Clericals and Anti-Clericals and to provide the latter   Religious
with a considerable leverage with which to pry the   Division in
mass of the population of Catholic countries into a   Europe both
position of latent hostility towards the Catholic   Political and
Church. One was political and the other was intellectual. Intellectual
Each requires special consideration.

The first difficulty was the pronounced unwillingness of the
Catholic Church, at least officially, to indorse the new political
tendencies of the nineteenth century. When one
recalls what the French Revolution meant to the   Catholic
Catholic clergy, — the loss of many of their privileges,   Opposition
the confiscation of much of their property, the whole-   to the
sale diminution of the number of their monasteries,   French
of their schools, and of their charitable institutions, — one   Revolution
ceases to wonder at their stubborn universal fight against the

principles of the Revolution. It becomes thoroughly comprehensible, moreover, why, for many decades, the hierarchy, from
the pope down, inveighed against a "liberty" of individual
belief, an "equality" of all religions, and a "fraternity" which
endangered the international character of the Church. The
result, already apparent from the review of the history of the
first half of the nineteenth century, was that in the politics of
every European state the Catholic clergy were Conservatives
and, as such, found allies and friends from among the old landowning nobility and the peasantry and such exceptional bourgeois and workingmen as were more religious than Liberal. On
the whole, it seemed obvious that, because of political reasons,
a sharp social cleavage was appearing in the Catholic Church,
for the bourgeoisie, as a whole, were fully committed to the principles of the French Revolution and many workingmen expected from the realization of those principles an amelioration
of their own lot.

For a time a "Liberal Catholic" movement had given some
promise of staying the cleavage. It had been pointed out that
the first and foremost aim of the Church was the sal-
vation of souls for the life of the world to come and
that the form of government in the present world was
not a matter of serious concern to the Church; that,
in fact, the institutions of democracy might serve her
mission better than the institutions of absolute monarchy; and this line of reasoning had been fortified
by the accurate assertion that popular sovereignty,
in so far as it was recognized as resting on divine sanction, had never been explicitly condemned by the pope. "Liberal
Catholicism" had been furthered by such practical work as that
of Daniel O'Connell in Great Britain and that of Lamartine and
his friends in the French revolutionary movement of 1848.
And its triumph had temporarily seemed imminent when Pius
IX [1] mounted the papal throne in 1846, for not only was he
known to be pious and kindly, but he was suspected of a favorable disposition toward Liberalism.

But the excesses which accompanied the revolutionary outbreaks of 1848, and especially his own experience in that year

Marginal note: Attempt of the "Liberal Catholics" to Compromise between Catholicism and the French Revolution

---

[1] Giovanni Maria Mastai-Ferretti (1792–1878).

with Mazzini's brand of Republicanism, had changed the politics of the pontiff and brought Liberal Catholicism into disrepute. From that year until his death in 1878 Pius IX was the zealous and aggressive opponent of the new régime — of liberty and equality and likewise of nationalism, as then understood and translated into action throughout Europe. With the aid of the whole Catholic clergy he waged implacable warfare against practices which everywhere the bourgeoisie and many workingmen now championed. He espoused the reactionary cause with such success that the Conservative governments of Spain and Austria signed concordats with him (1851 and 1855, respectively), restoring to the Church many of its ancient privileges. He strengthened the machinery of the Church by reëstablishing Roman Catholic hierarchies in England (1850) and Holland (1853). And all this while he denounced the new social and political order in repeated and ringing invectives, culminating in the famous encyclical *Quanta cura* and the accompanying *Syllabus of Errors* (1864).

Reactionary Character of the Pontificate of Pius IX, 1846–1878

Papal Condemnation of the New Social and Political Order

In the encyclical, the pope not merely condemned the widely accepted notions that a secular state had supreme power and authority over all affairs within its territories and that every state had a moral obligation to accord religious liberty, but he vehemently upheld the older ideal of the Catholic state based on the complete independence of the ecclesiastical power and on the compulsory unity of faith. The Syllabus "of the principal errors of our times" reproduced in a very abbreviated form all the doctrines condemned by him, political as well as strictly religious. Its condemnations covered many groups: freethinkers and agnostics, who would destroy the Church; indifferent people, who would take away its official privileges and reduce it to the condition of a private, voluntary association; supporters of religious neutrality or equality, who would establish lay marriage and lay schools; advocates of secular sovereignty, who would abolish ecclesiastical courts and obligatory vows and nationalize the clergy by restricting their communication with Rome; opponents of the temporal power

The Encyclical Quanta Cura and the "Syllabus of Errors," 1864

of the papacy; even the Liberal Catholics, who would admit of religious liberty.

Although Dupanloup, a famous French bishop and one of the leaders of the Liberal Catholic party, wrote a book to show that the *Syllabus of Errors* was not half so bad as it sounded, — that it had been issued as a weapon of defense against the persecutions of the Church on the part of the new Italian kingdom, and that it was intended simply to condemn general revolution and the abuses of modern liberty, — and although his book received the approval of Pius IX and of more than six hundred other Roman Catholic bishops, nevertheless the champions of the principles of the French Revolution and the patriots of the new nationalism utilized the Syllabus and the encyclical of 1864 as occasions for attacking "Clericalism." In "Clericalism" the statesmen and the powerful bourgeoisie, who were shaping the unifications of Italy and Germany or agitating for political democracy in France and in Spain, perceived an enemy of the new order, and, by calling the Catholic Church unpatriotic and undemocratic, they secured allies for themselves from among the numerous working class.

Another occasion for attacking "Clericalism" was soon afforded by the Vatican Council (1869–1870), the first general council the Catholic Church had held since that of Trent, three centuries earlier. The Vatican Council was convened by Pius IX, attended by nearly eight hundred prelates, and made famous by its solemn ratification, despite earnest opposition from a minority of its members, of the dogma of papal infallibility. The actual definition of papal infallibility laid it down as "a dogma divinely revealed, that the Roman pontiff, when he speaks *ex cathedra*, — that is, when in discharge of the office of pastor and doctor of all Christians, by virtue of his supreme apostolic authority, he defines a doctrine regarding faith or morals to be held by the universal Church, — by the divine assistance promised him in Blessed Peter, is possessed of that infallibility with which the divine Redeemer willed that His Church should be endowed for defining faith or morals; and that therefore such definitions of the Roman pontiff are *per se*

Political Opposition to the Catholic Church

The Vatican Council (1869–1870) and the Dogma of Papal Infallibility immutable and independent of the consent of the Church. But if any one — which God avert! — presume to contradict this our definition: let him be anathema." The fathers who subscribed to this doctrine of papal infallibility in 1870 did not think that they were devising a "new" dogma; they believed that they were merely interpreting and defining what had been in the mind of the Church ever since the days of St. Peter and of Christ Himself; and certainly not many of them could have thought that they were departing from what had been a well-recognized practice for many centuries.

Nevertheless, the definition of papal infallibility elicited immediate opposition. It was to be expected that agnostics would scoff at it and that Protestants would denounce it as an unwarranted or even blasphemous assumption. But, while no Catholic bishop left the Church and while it was only a few thousand laymen in southern Germany and in Switzerland who, following the lead of a group of university professors, actually seceded and formed the "Old Catholic" sect, it was difficult for many nominal Catholics not to be adversely influenced by the critics of the dogma. Several historians wrote learned works in an endeavor to prove that various popes in the past had been "fallible." Controversialists maintained that the doctrine was essentially new and that it was in flat contradiction to the Council of Constance and to the long-supported "liberties of the Gallican Church." But the most telling blows were in the field of politics. Statesmen represented the Vatican Council as an astute scheme on the part of Pius IX to secure a ratification from the whole hierarchy of his policies against liberty and nationalism, and in the decree of papal infallibility they pictured a monstrous attempt to exalt the papacy above all secular states and to extend "faith and morals" to the political domain. The fear became general. The Austrian government promptly denounced the decree and took occasion to annul the Concordat of 1855.[1] Bismarck soon inaugurated a campaign against the Catholic Church in Prussia. Even Gladstone thought it worth

---

[1] The Spanish Concordat already (1869) had been annulled by the new Republican government.

his while to indite a pamphlet to his fellow-Britishers on the need of combating papal intolerance and papal interference with the civil power.

Following closely upon the heels of the Vatican Council came the seizure of Rome by the troops of the Italian kingdom (1870) and the destruction of the temporal sovereignty of the papacy. Henceforth, Pius IX, as the voluntary "prisoner of the Vatican," poured forth fresh vials of wrath upon that Liberalism and nationalism which, exemplified in the new kingdom of Italy, had despoiled God's earthly vicar of his rights, his liberties, and his goods. Henceforth, his greatest efforts were exerted toward the formation of Conservative-Clerical groups in the several Catholic countries which would urge their governments to intervene in Italy in order to reëstablish his temporal rule. Naturally into such Clerical groups neither rational Liberals nor emotional nationalists could be drawn.

Destruction of the Pope's Temporal Sovereignty, 1870

The upshot, then, of the whole pontificate of Pius IX, politically speaking, was a widespread conviction that ardent belief in Roman Catholicism made a person a Clerical and that Clericalism was synonymous with opposition to nationalism and Liberalism, and a consequent political denunciation of Clericalism by most of the bourgeoisie and by many of the working class.

Democracy and Nationalism Seemingly Arrayed against Clericalism

It was not merely politics that increased the numbers and clamors of the Anti-Clericals. There was a growing intellectual difficulty as well, and it is to this intellectual difficulty that we must now turn our attention.

Intellectual Complications

THE NEW SCIENCE

During the very years that embraced the pontificate of Pius IX and that witnessed the growing disaffection on the part of many nominal Catholics toward the political tendencies of the clergy, developments occurred in the realm of natural science which, in the minds of many prominent persons, seemed to strike at the roots of revealed religion and to render the basic dogmas of Christianity no longer tenable.

"Science" was certainly, along with the Industrial Revolution and with Liberalism and nationalism, a great distinguishing characteristic of the whole nineteenth century. From certain standpoints, scientific progress in the nineteenth century cannot be deemed so epochal as that in the eighteenth century, which has been described in an earlier chapter,[1] yet in three ways it proved more thorough and more widely influential. In the first place, the path of experimental science, plainly indicated in the eighteenth century, was persistently pursued throughout the nineteenth century by an ever-increasing number of acute observers and patient experimenters, who continually, if slowly, enlarged the bounds of human knowledge of the material universe: a galaxy of chemists and physicists, who explained the transmission of heat and light by minute waves in the ether, discovered properties and uses of electricity, detailed the atomic theory of the constitution of matter, and laid down the principles of thermodynamics; a group of astronomers and mathematicians, who dilated upon the nature and history of the sun and stars, developing and perfecting the mechanical theory of the planetary system which Sir Isaac Newton had first formulated, or adding such a theory as the nebular hypothesis to account for the mode of origin of that system; biologists, who evolved the theories of the cell and of the protoplasm as explanations of the organization of living creatures, and worked out the theory of bacteriology that germs are the cause of disease. All these devotees of experimental science and likewise the devotees of geology, botany, zoölogy, and paleontology, as well as of newer social sciences such as philology, archæology, ethnology, anthropology, and comparative religion, were perpetually observing and classifying, naming and theorizing, — they were literally detailing the work seriously begun in the eighteenth century. And like their predecessors, their absorption in scientific study usually left little time or inclination for any absorption in positive religion.

In the second place, and unlike most of the scientific advance in the eighteenth century, a good deal of that of the nineteenth century was in the direction of applied science, that is to say,

Importance of Science in the Nineteenth Century

Far-reaching Development of Experimental Science

[1] Volume I, Chapter XIII.

it was the application of scientific discoveries and inventions to practical uses in ministering to the health and comfort of mankind. Merely to catalogue the successive detailed contributions of the scientists of the century to the daily life of the present would fill a good-sized chapter.

Extensive Utility of Applied Science

To mention but a very few would involve reference to electric lighting and electric motive force; automobiles and aëroplanes; telegraph, telephone, and wireless; photographing and electrotyping; phonographs, stereopticons, and cinematographs; concrete-construction in building; anæsthetics, aseptic surgery, and sanitation; aniline dyes, and many products of coal tar and of rubber; purification of water and improvement of crops.[1] Enthusiasm for scientific and mechanical triumphs of this kind soon obsessed the minds of the great mass of people everywhere and gave plausibility to the idea that the practical application of scientific knowledge would extend indefinitely, and that future ages would see no limit to the growth of man's control of his physical environment and of his intelligent use of it for the betterment of his race. Material comfort was exalted, with a result that the ancient Christian ideas of sacrifice and suffering and pain and death seemed alien and downright perverse to this "age of progress." Health of body appeared a more needful, if not a nobler, goal for which to strive than cure of souls. The practical scientists were frankly materialistic in their aims: their kingdom was of this world, not of a world beyond the grave. Some of them even went so far as to maintain that crime and wrongdoing could be extirpated by means of surgery or of scientific breeding. It was not so much that such scientists were anti-Christian as that the general atmosphere of belief and of opinion created by their achievements was increasingly non-Christian. In fact, it was from their materialistic achievements and purposes that proceeded the new and popular philosophy of pragmatism, the notion that the value of moral and religious ideals is to be judged solely by their practical effects — by the way they "work."

But Christianity suffered in the nineteenth century from the indifference of painstaking experimenters or even from the

[1] Applied science, moreover, was closely related to the Industrial Revolution. See Chapter XVIII, pp. 69–75, above.

contempt of practical inventors to no such extent as from a third class of scientists — the evolutionists and their philosophical interpreters and popularizers. These were the group who directly or indirectly brought the Biblical narrative into question, who cast doubt upon the historicity of the sacred Scriptures on which all historical Christianity — Catholic and Protestant — ultimately rested. The group was too numerous to be treated of in detail but clearly too famous to be passed over in one sentence. The mention of a few of the most illustrious names in the group may serve our purpose of explaining the general character of their contribution. It will be noticed that, by a curious coincidence, the significant achievements of all these men belonged almost uniformly in point of time to the pontificate of Pope Pius IX.

The Vogue of Evolution and Philosophical Science

First was Alexander von Humboldt (1769–1859),[1] naturalist and traveler, whose memorable expedition to the Americas with its bearings upon the sciences of physical geography and meteorology made him, next to Napoleon Bonaparte, the most famous European of his day. It was he who, at the age of seventy-six, brought out in 1845 the first volume of the *Cosmos*, a work completed in the next thirteen years, which undertook to gather together and to harmonize all the scientific accomplishments of the eighteenth century and of the first half of the nineteenth and to demonstrate the existence of a supreme unity amid the complex details of nature. The *Cosmos* was at once a useful scientific encyclopedia and a highly imaginative conception of the universe; and its picturesque, almost poetical, style, as well as its stores of information, commended it to a wide circle of intelligent readers. Half scientific and half philosophical, it ignored, if it did not deny, the existence of any power outside and beyond nature, and thereby contributed potently to the propagation of materialistic conceptions among the educated middle class.[2]

Alexander von Humboldt

Secondly was Sir Charles Lyell (1797–1875), the revolutionizer

[1] Friedrich Heinrich Alexander, Baron von Humboldt, a brother of Wilhelm von Humboldt, who was the educational collaborator with Stein in the regeneration of Prussia. See Vol. I, p. 557.

[2] A somewhat similar work in our own day is Carl Snider's masterpiece in materialistic pessimism, *The World Machine*. Humboldt's work inspired Edgar Allan Poe's "prose poem," *Eureka*.

of geology.   By close observation of geological processes at
work in his own time, — volcanoes pouring out vast masses of
Sir Charles   molten rock, rivers wearing away their banks and de-
Lyell   positing strata which could naturally be transformed
into sandstone, earthquake shocks producing faults in the rocks,
vegetation preparing future coal-beds, land almost everywhere
either rising or sinking, — he reached the conclusion that the
The New   continuous operation of the same processes over an
Geology   almost incalculable period of time would be sufficient
to explain how the earth had assumed its present physical appearance.   This conclusion — the so-called uniformitarian theory
— was the thesis of his *Principles of Geology, an attempt to explain
the former changes of the Earth's surface by reference to causes
now in operation*, a work appearing in three volumes in 1830–
1833.   Received at first with some opposition, so far as its leading
theory was concerned, the work had eventually so great a success
that, between 1830 and 1872, eleven different editions were
published, each enriched with new material and with the results
of riper thought.   In 1863 Lyell published another famous
work — *The Geological Evidences of the Antiquity of Man* — in
The   which he gave a general and readable summary of the
Antiquity   arguments for man's very early appearance on the
of Man   earth, derived from the discoveries of human implements and other remains in lower strata, which, according to
the calculations of the new geology, could have been deposited
not less than fifty thousand years before, and possibly much
earlier.   Alongside of Sir Charles Lyell's ideas, which speedily
secured acceptance on the part of all contemporary geologists [1]
of repute, that man had lived possibly a hundred thousand years
on the globe and that the globe itself had taken shape slowly
and naturally throughout the course of untold æons, were now
set in sharp contrast the long-accepted Biblical account of the
miraculous creation of the universe in six days and the Anglican
bishop's seventeenth-century exposition [2] from Biblical chro-

[1] The subsequent tendency of a majority of geologists was to lengthen, rather
than to shorten, the history of the earth and of man.   Important contributions
to the study of glaciers as well as to zoölogy were made during the time of Lyell by
the famous Swiss-American, Jean Louis Rodolphe Agassiz (1807–1873).

[2] James Usher (1581–1656), Protestant bishop of Meath in Ireland, and subse-

nology that the first man — Adam by name — had been created on a Friday in the month of October in the year 4004 B.C.

In *The Antiquity of Man* (1863) Lyell expressed not merely his belief in the slow, evolutionary fashioning of the earth but also his conversion to a theory of the evolution of all   The Theory forms of life, a theory which had just been advanced   of Evolution through the independent labors of two of the most eminent scientists of all time — Alfred Russel Wallace (1823–1913) [1] and Charles Darwin (1809–1882).

Darwin, sent to Edinburgh to study medicine and transferred to Cambridge in order to fit himself for the Anglican priesthood, displayed in his youth but one ambition —   Charles to become a great naturalist.   In his twenty-third   Darwin year, with the reluctant permission of his family, he abandoned the clerical calling and embarked as a naturalist on a surveying vessel, the *Beagle;* he was gone for five years on a voyage through the South Sea islands and to Brazil, which proved to be an excellent preparation for his life-work.   His observations on the relationship between animals in islands and similar animals in the nearest continental regions, near akin and yet not exactly the same, and between living animals and those most recently extinct and fossilized in the same country, here again related but not the same, led him to reflect deeply upon the possible variations of species due to differences of environment and of natural needs.   For a number of years after his return to England, Darwin was engaged in detailed study along the numerous lines of inquiry suggested by the expedition of the *Beagle.*   He was particularly struck by Lyell's *Principles of Geology*, which was already accustoming men's minds to the vast changes which could be brought about by natural processes and which paved the way for the statement of a complete evolutionary hypothesis. He was also struck by Malthus's *Essay on Population*,[2] which had emphasized the idea that the increase of population is dependent upon a struggle for existence among mankind.   Why,

---

quently archbishop of Armagh, whose *Annales veteris et novi testamenti* were published in 1650–1654.

[1] Alfred Russel Wallace was also famous as an ardent advocate of land nationalization in England and as a sympathetic ally of Henry George in that field. See below, p. 304.

[2] See above, p. 83.

thought Darwin, could not the principle of Malthus be extended to the whole organic creation and utilized to explain the variation of species? In June, 1842, he wrote out a sketch of his new theory of biological evolution, which two years later he expanded into a pretentious essay, but it was not until fourteen years thereafter that he made public his theory, and then only when Wallace had independently arrived at the same hypothesis.

Wallace, a younger British naturalist, who had already spent several years in exploration on the Amazon and in the East Indies, was lying ill with fever at Ternate, in the Moluccas, in February, 1858, when he too began to think of Malthus's *Essay on Population*, read several years before: suddenly the idea of the survival of the fittest flashed over him. In two hours he had "thought out almost the whole of the theory," and in three evenings had finished his essay, which he promptly mailed to Darwin.

Alfred Wallace

Darwin in England at once recognized his own theory in the manuscript which in June, 1858, he received from the young and almost unknown naturalist in the tropics. "I never saw a more striking coincidence," he wrote to Lyell: "if Wallace had my Ms. sketch written out in 1842, he could not have made a better short abstract! Even his terms now stand as heads of my chapters." Darwin then no longer hesitated; he read his own manuscript essay and that of Wallace before a learned society in London, and the so-called Darwinian theory of evolution was launched. The flash of intuition which distinguished Wallace was fortified in the case of Darwin by the results of many years of patient and laborious observations and experiments; and the rivalry between the two men in the discovery of the principle of natural selection proved the beginning of a lifelong friendship.

Darwin's ideas of evolution were explained at length in his great work, published in 1859, *On the Origin of Species by Means of Natural Selection, or the preservation of favored races in the struggle for life,* and were subsequently elaborated in certain particulars in the *Descent of Man and Selection in Relation to Sex* (1871), and in numerous other publications. These ideas are too technical and too involved, and have been too much modified in certain details since their first

"Darwinism"

expression, to be fully described in the present volume, but the great central idea — the quintessence of Darwinism — is comparatively simple. It is the idea that life — animal and vegetable — in its present very diverse forms and aspects has all come from a common, though very distant, source, in a very natural evolutionary way. The manner of evolution, according to Darwin, is slightly more complex, but may be summed up as follows : The pressure of the struggle for life favors those individuals in each species which possess particular variations from the normal type that are of direct advantage to them in their surroundings ; such individuals tend to survive at the expense of their fellows, and to produce offspring ; the new generation shows variation also, and, once more, those individuals which depart from the ordinary in the most useful way have a better chance of survival than the others ; and, thus, gradually, after the lapse of enormous periods of time, differences so far accumulate in the descendants of each one of the original type that really new types, or species, may be formed, — the inevitable result of minute and almost imperceptibly accumulated variations.

That there were resemblances among all forms of life, no one could fail to perceive ; that these resemblances might be traceable to some form of evolutionary development had been suggested by several scientists before Darwin or Wallace ; but it was the achievement of Darwinism to offer a working hypothesis of the manner in which such development actually took place. By making out a good case for natural selection, Darwin really made evolution a fundamental scientific hypothesis.

From the outset, Darwin's ideas had a redoubtable champion in Wallace, whose volume, *Contributions to the Theory of Natural Selection*, published in 1871, did more than any other single work, except the *Origin of Species*, to promote among scientists a clear understanding of natural selection and confidence in its truth.[1] But the extensive vogue which Darwinism has enjoyed and the deep

Popularization and Application of Darwinism

impress which it has left on all sorts of human activities, — political, social, religious, and artistic, — is to be explained by

---

[1] Next to Wallace in importance as scientific champions of Darwinism were the celebrated American botanist, Asa Gray (1810–1888), and the English botanist, Sir Joseph Dalton Hooker (1817–1911).

reference not so much to technical discussions by extremely
critical scientists as to more general expositions by enthusiastic popularizers. Of the latter kind, Darwinism found its
most militant champions in Huxley and Spencer.

It was in 1860 — the year following the publication of the
Origin of Species — that Herbert Spencer (1820-1903) set
forth the prospectus of his *Synthetic Philosophy*, an

**Herbert
Spencer
and his
Synthetic
Philosophy**
enormous work in ten volumes, upon which he was
engaged for the next thirty-six years, and which
undertook to carry the principle of evolution into
the realms of philosophy, psychology, sociology, and
ethics. Whatever may be the ultimate estimate of the value of
Spencer's philosophy, there is no doubt that it did noteworthy
service in the cause of evolutionary conceptions. "Development," "growth," "progress," — these and similar terms were
stamped by Spencer as the common coin of future study and of
future literature. It was Spencer who first used the phrase,
"survival of the fittest."

According to Spencer, everything organic and inorganic — the
earth, the heavens above and the waters beneath, and all flying,
crawling, and walking creatures that be on the face of the earth,—
everything has been quite naturally evolved out of a more simple
and primitive state, the law of existence in all cases being
development "from the homogeneous to the heterogeneous." [1]
Back of this universal and eternal law of evolution, Spencer
reasoned there must be an inscrutable Power, which, however,
could not be better defined than as the Unknowable. So this was
the point whither the Spencerian philosophy of evolution tended :
straight toward materialism and agnosticism. It is small wonder that many advocates of revealed religion took fright.

Even more explosive were the bombs which Thomas Huxley
(1825-1895) hurled into the theological camp. Huxley combined
a good deal of sound knowledge about biology with

**Thomas
Huxley and
his Attacks
on Revealed
Religion**
distinct literary gifts ; he was, moreover, a "square-
jawed person greedy of controversy." And in *Man's
Place in Nature* (1863) he sought, with the aid of
epigrams as well as with that of scientific facts, to
show that man himself was but a transitional stage in the natural

[1] Spencer's *The Development Hypothesis* (1852).

evolution from lower to higher types. Huxley's work in this book and likewise in a host of other writings in vulgarizing the new ideas can hardly be overestimated. But it was in perpetual attacks upon the foundation of revealed religion that Huxley acquired his greatest significance. Starting with the assumption that "doubt is a beneficent demon," he declared that "there is no evidence of the existence of such a being as the God of the theologians." Christianity he rejected bodily and with no appreciation of its possible historic effect as a civilizing agency: he claimed that what "since the second century has assumed to itself the title of orthodox Christianity" has been a "varying compound of some of the best and some of the worst elements of Paganism and Judaism, molded in practice by the innate character of certain peoples of the Western world."

In rejecting Christian theology, Huxley consistently rejected the theoretical bases of Christian morality — the divine Lawgiver and the freedom of will in the human being. And his substitution was fatalism in conduct, based on natural evolution, — "scientific Calvinism," it has been termed. "The actions we call sinful," averred Huxley, "are part and parcel of the struggle for existence." "The moral sense is a very complex affair — dependent in part upon associations of pleasure and pain, approbation and disapprobation, formed by education in early youth, but in part also on an innate sense of moral beauty and ugliness (how originated need not be discussed), which is possessed by some people in great strength, while some are totally devoid of it."

The last name to be mentioned in connection with the new generalizations of science which characterized the middle of the nineteenth century, is that of Ernest Renan (1823– 1892), the offspring of pious fisher-folk of Catholic Brittany, who left his Roman Catholic seminary in 1845 not to offer priestly ministrations to Christian believers but to wage implacable lifelong warfare against historic Christianity. An early convert to the scientific ideal — to the certitudes of physical and natural science, — he performed his greatest services as an Orientalist and an exponent of the study of comparative religion. While he was still a seminarian, he made up his mind that the second part of the canonical book of Isaias

Ernest Renan and "Higher Criticism"

differs from the first not only in style but in date; that the grammar and the history of the Pentateuch are posterior to the accepted dates of Moses; and that the book of Daniel is quite apocryphal.   Henceforth, he gave himself to researches in the Levant, to study of the ancient languages, and to acute criticism of the whole Bible, gradually reaching the conclusion that the Scriptures and Christian theology were but a development — an evolution — of primitive fable and myth.   Appointed professor of Hebrew in the Collège de France (1862), he referred to Christ in his inaugural lecture as "an incomparable *man*," and the following year [1] he published his best-known work, the *Life of Jesus*. This was an attempt to treat Christ as a perfectly natural human being, but it was a treatment so lucid in expression and so felicitous in phrase — Renan was a littérateur quite as much as a scientist — that it gave an actual heart-warmth to agnosticism.   After Renan [2] skepticism was no longer a merely negative position with reference to Christianity: it was henceforth itself a glowing cult which could enthrall the emotions as well as command the intellect.

CHRISTIANITY AND SCIENCE

It is to be remembered that all these eminent scientists whose names have just been reviewed belonged by birth or training to the middle class,[3] and, what is far more important, that the bulk of the people who read their books or heard their lectures or followed their investigations belonged to the middle class.   It was the middle class, therefore, — university students, physicians, lawyers, and, to a certain extent, business men, — who were first infected with the

Influence of Science upon the Bourgeoisie

[1] 1863.   The next year the French government of Napoleon III, anxious not to antagonize the Catholics further, deprived Renan of his professorship.   The Anti-Clericals at once hailed Renan as a martyr to free thought.

[2] Even before Renan, David Friedrich Strauss (1808–1874), a German, had published (1835) a *Life of Jesus*, assailing the inspiration of the New Testament and denying the miracles and other supernatural attributes of Christ.   Strauss subsequently accepted Darwinism, and a group of his associates and disciples in the Protestant Faculty of Theology in the university of Tübingen (Württemberg) secured fame as the Tübingen School of "higher critics" of the Bible and of all so-called revealed religion.

[3] The one exception was Baron von Humboldt.

new evolutionary conceptions and with the accompanying virulence against dogmatic religion. In Catholic countries the infection came at the very time when Pope Pius IX was not only identifying Clericalism with reactionary Con- *Seemingly* servatism in politics, but insisting vehemently that *Basic Conflict* Catholic Christianity is a thoroughly dogmatic *between* religion, a truly revealed religion, and a religion that *Science and* in the intellectual sphere satisfactorily explains the *Catholicism* chief phenomena of existence. It was the time when the encyclical *Quanta Cura* and the *Syllabus of Errors* were issued at Rome (1864); when the dogma of the Immaculate Conception of the Blessed Virgin Mary was promulgated by the sovereign pontiff (1854); and when the Vatican Council solemnly decreed the infallibility of the pope (1869).

The upshot of the pontificate of Pius IX, intellectually speaking, was a widespread conviction among many educated and influential persons, mainly of the middle class, that an ardent belief in Roman Catholicism made a person a Clerical, and that Clericalism was synonymous with opposition to science and free thought. Consequently the Anti-Clericals added to their political arguments against Catholic Christianity the intellectual ones that the Clericals were unprogressive, inimical to reason, and bent on keeping the people in ignorance. And such arguments were not without weight among the workingmen.

Much the same situation prevailed in Protestant countries. Strict Protestants as well as faithful Catholics greeted Darwin's *Origin of Species* and similar works with storms of *Protestant* opposition and in large numbers expressed their un- *Opposition* willingness to accept evolution at all. Like the *to Darwinism* Copernican system of astronomy, which had once threatened to depose the earth from its divinely ordained central position in the Universe, the Darwinian hypothesis was thought to dethrone man, who had been "made in the image and likeness of God," and to be inconsistent with the accepted dogma of the special creation of each distinct species and the separate creation of the human race as a final personal act of the divine Creator. Lutheran clergymen were one with those of Calvinistic sects and with those of the Established Church in England in denouncing the new science which, as many of them maintained, would trace man's descent from monkeys rather than from God and would remove the sanction and obligation of Christian morality.

In one respect Protestantism was threatened by Darwinism more than Roman Catholicism. While the Catholic faith was

Effect of Science upon Protestantism

based on the writings of the Christian Fathers and on "tradition," as well as on the Old and New Testaments, Protestants ever since John Calvin had insisted that the Scriptures were for them the sole rule of faith and the sole guide of conduct. Now, when scientific theories which appeared capable of demonstration indicated that the Bible in places was downright erroneous and throughout was hardly more than a "unique record of the evolution of a nation's moral consciousness," the Protestant notion of authority was rudely shaken, and the thoughtful Protestant felt himself constrained to modify his theological opinions. But in so doing, he had a certain advantage over his Catholic neighbor, because, while the sincere Catholic was bound in belief by the dogmatic utterances of the officials of the Catholic Church, he himself, by reason of the absence of an efficient, authoritative Protestant organization, and likewise by reason of the traditional encouragement of the "right of private judgment," was enabled profoundly to revise his opinion of the Bible and still to call himself a Protestant Christian.

Of Darwinism, therefore, the immediate effects on religion were somewhat divergent in Catholic and Protestant countries. In

Immediate Religious Effects of Darwinism divergent in Catholic and Protestant Countries

the former a sharp line was drawn between (1) those who continued to believe in revealed religion and to accept the dogmas of the Roman Church, — they were Roman Catholics who in faith might be equally at home in the nineteenth and in the sixteenth century, — and (2) those who unconditionally received the new generalizations of science : they were out-and-out skeptics and agnostics, — heretics and infidels, from the standpoint of the Church ; champions of enlightenment and progress, from their own standpoint. In Protestant countries, on the other hand, the people divided into three general groups on the religious question : first, real agnostics, a conspicuous minority, who felt that science and any form of Christianity were mutually incompatible, and that sound reason compelled the rejection of Protestantism no less than of Catholicism; secondly, "old-fashioned Protestants," another minority, at the outset larger but in the course of time possibly diminishing, who stoutly maintained, like the first group, that science and Christianity were mutually incompatible, but that simple faith compelled the unquestioning rejection of un-Christian scientific hypotheses; and thirdly, a slowly growing majority, who sought to effect a reconciliation between religion and science. In Protestant countries it was this third group who eventually appeared to have carried the day. They tended more and more to accept, though often with many qualifications, the theories of evolution and of the antiquity of man and the universe, and all manner of profane studies of the Scriptures. They tended more and more to emphasize morals and conduct at the expense of faith and dogma, to such an extent, in fact, that to many minds the very word "dogmatic" became unbearable, connoting repulsive ideas, akin to the word "superstitious." Gradually they stripped the Old Testament and even the Gospel story of most of the miraculous, refashioned Christ as a simple moral teacher and social worker,[1] and frankly admitted that Christianity was but one — though the best — of evolving, uplifting world religions. Almost uniformly they continued to call themselves Protestants, but Protestantism at the close of the nineteenth century was, in general, a fundamentally different set of religious ideas from the Protestantism of the sixteenth and seventeenth centuries. Darwinism worked a greater change dogmatically in Protestantism than the whole Protestant revolt had effected in the Catholic Church. One universal Protestant doctrine, however, still remained as the link with the past, — the right of private judgment; and it was a real tribute to the potency of that doctrine that historic Protestantism had so readily absorbed Darwinism.

To these rather sweeping generalizations, exceptions must be remembered not only in the case of groups of Lutherans,

Protestant Compromise between Science and Religion

---

[1] One of the most noteworthy products of this kind of Protestantism was the social activity and the social "reform" championed by the churches and represented, especially in large cities, by the "institutionalizing" of Christianity.

Presbyterians, Methodists, Baptists, Quakers, and other like bodies, who, in different degree in different localities, clung with

Exceptions to the Protestant Compromise

greater tenacity to the literal teachings of Martin Luther or John Calvin, but also, and more particularly, in the case of an important section of the Anglican Church — the so-called "high church" party. Just on the eve of the work of Darwin, Spencer, Huxley, and Renan, a few young clergymen of the Anglican communion,

"The Oxford Movement" in the Anglican Church

including John Keble (1792–1866), John Henry Newman (1801–1890),[1] and Edward Pusey (1800–1882), had set themselves to revive what they thought to be true religion, and their agitation, because it centered in the university of Oxford, became known as the Oxford Movement.[2] Its way had been prepared by the publication of Keble's *Christian Year* (1827), and his sermon at Oxford on *National Apostasy* (1833) had indicated its aims. Its cardinal teaching was that the Anglican Church was not Protestant, but was a very real part of the Holy Catholic Church and had unbroken episcopal connection with the primitive Christian Church; and its disciples accordingly inculcated the medieval doctrine of the seven sacraments, including what was very close to, if not identical with, the dogma of transubstantiation, and tended to emphasize points of agreement in forms and ceremonies, as well as in doctrine, with those branches of the Catholic Church, notably the Roman Catholic and the Greek Orthodox, which could claim apostolic succession. The Oxford Movement grew in spite of the opposition of extreme Protestants, who declared that it was essentially "Romanizing," until 1845, when it was disrupted by the secession of Newman and several others from the Anglican Church to the Roman Catholic Church. Nevertheless, largely under Pusey's leadership, the dogmatic principles of Catholicism were kept alive within the Anglican communion and were henceforth shared by an apparently increasing number of clergy and laymen. In this way the Anglican Church developed by the latter half of the nineteenth century three main

[1] Newman was received into the Roman Catholic Church in 1845 and created a cardinal by Pope Leo XIII in 1879.

[2] Its promoters urged their views in *Tracts for the Times* and were therefore nicknamed Tractarians. They were also referred to, especially later, as Puseyites.

schools of thought among its members: (1) "high church," which, intellectually and dogmatically, approached nearest to the official Roman Catholic position; (2) "low church," which adhered to the more strictly Protestant and evangelical character that had marked Anglicanism in the eighteenth century; and (3) "broad church," which represented rather advanced rationalism, and which, in line with the newer tendencies of the time in Lutheran and Calvinistic bodies, sought to reconcile religion with science by accepting the findings of the latter and by retaining of the former the name, the forms, and many of the deeper emotions. By the close of the nineteenth century, it was obvious to many observers that both the "high church" and the "broad church" parties were growing at the expense of the "low church," and that the conflict for predominance within the Anglican Church in the immediate future was likely to be between these two factions — between those inclined to reaffirm revealed religion according to traditional Catholic standards and those inclined to find in natural science a broad basis for a new and comprehensive religion.

Divisions in the Anglican Church

But in England, as well as in the other lands that have commonly been called Protestant, the religious organizations have never effectually questioned the practical supremacy of secular government. Consequently, whatever might have been the intellectual and dogmatic differences between Protestant Christians and their non-Christian fellow-citizens, Darwinism brought in its train no great political conflict between them.

Conflict Acute only in Catholic Countries

It was otherwise in Roman Catholic countries. By 1871 "Clericals" and "Anti-Clericals" were arrayed against each other, both on political and on intellectual grounds, in Germany, Austria-Hungary, Italy, France, Spain, Portugal, Belgium, and Latin America. And the combat was destined to fill a conspicuous place in the internal history of each of these states from 1871 to 1914, a place which is all too briefly indicated in the following chapters.[1]

In studying Anti-Clericalism the student will notice that its warmest advocates will be intellectual and political radicals,

[1] Chapters XXIII and XXIV. See below, pp. 351 ff., 407 ff.

drawn ordinarily from the middle class, and that its greatest successes will be gained by statesmen who are jealous of the en-

The " Anti- croachments, real or fancied, of an ecclesiastical organi-
Clericals " zation upon national sovereignty. He will observe that Anti-Clericalism will appeal constantly and everywhere to sentiments of Liberalism and nationalism and will profit by the unrest of workingmen and by the apathy and indifference of many professing Catholics in country and in town.

That Roman Catholicism — or Clericalism (call it as one may) — will not be utterly routed in any country will also become obvious to the student who follows closely the succes-

Continued sion of events from 1871 to 1914. Not only will he find
Aggressive- that many peasants and artisans and unprogressive
ness of the scions of the ancient nobility continue to conform to
Catholic
Church Catholicism, but a goodly number of thoughtful persons from the well-educated classes will renew their faith in, or be converted to, the dogmas of the Roman Church. This phenomenon — the continued aggressiveness of the Roman Catholic Church in the face of its seeming political and intellectual unpopularity — demands a few words of explanation.

It was due to an apparent alteration in the policy of the Roman Catholic Church. The causes of the Church's unpopu-

Pontificate larity were most active, as we have seen, during the
of Leo XIII, reign of Pius IX, with the result that when that pope
1878-1903 died in 1878, after the longest and one of the most remarkable pontificates in history, he left the Church shaken to its very foundations and in feud with almost every secular government. But the succeeding pontificate of Leo XIII (1878–1903)[1] served to change matters. In contrast to his predecessor, Leo was a man of slow and calm deliberation, and a gifted diplomat. Moreover he was endowed with a good deal of erudition, and possessed a nice appreciation of good literature, being a distinguished Latinist himself. As nuncio in Brussels before his election he had become sympathetically acquainted with the machinery of democratic politics and of parliamentary government.

Under Leo XIII it gradually became apparent to many persons that a working compromise was possible, whether in the

[1] Gioacchino Pecci (1810–1903).

field of politics or in that of intellect, between the Roman Catholic Church and modern society. The intellectual gulf was narrowed by several happenings. In the first place, there was the study, revived and intensified under papal auspices, throughout all Catholic seminaries and colleges, of the writings of Thomas Aquinas, the greatest theologian and philosopher of the middle ages, who had taught that natural law and supernatural religion could not be in ultimate conflict because both were from one and the same God, and who had actually forearmed Catholic theology against the Darwinian attack by declaring that it mattered not at all whether natural creation had been effected by one original divine act or by an infinite succession of divine acts. Following out the suggestion of Thomas Aquinas, Catholic philosophers and Catholic theologians began to take a position something like this: that Darwinism was only a hypothesis, which was being confessedly weakened in certain details;[1] that the Darwinian theory, if true, could explain only the evolution of man's material body, not the creation and life of immortal spirits; that the spiritual side of humanity still belonged to the realm of faith and religion as unquestionably as its material side belonged to the province of natural science; that the possibility of an allegorical interpretation of the account of Creation in the book of Genesis as well as a literal interpretation had always been recognized by foremost fathers of Christianity; and that a subsequent confirmation of Darwinism might even serve to enlarge man's comprehension of the wonder-working ways of God.

Revived Study of Thomas Aquinas

Catholic Attitude toward Darwinism

Secondly, under Leo XIII, there was the encouragement of the study of church history. To this end the pope placed the valuable archives and library of the Vatican at the disposal of historians, his belief being that the publication of historical documents, far from injuring the Church, would actually enhance its prestige by showing its past contributions to the development of human civilization.

Study of Church History

Thirdly, there was the papal patronage or, at least, friendly toleration of experimental science among eminent Roman Catho-

---

[1] Notably in respect of Darwin's theory of "sex selection," and in the face of the newer Mendelism. See below, p. 249.

lics, both priests and laymen.   Thus, Leo XIII at his own expense placed costly astronomical instruments in the Vatican ob-
servatory, providing accommodation and endowment
for a whole staff of officials.   Thus, too, he congratu-
lated many Catholic scientists upon their achievements.   It was during his pontificate, moreover, that
the fame of two of the greatest scientists of modern times —
both of them Roman Catholics — seemed to refute the charge
that no person could be at once a sincere Catholic Christian and
an eminent scientist.   These two scientists were Louis Pasteur
and Gregor Mendel.

Catholicism and Experimental Science

Pasteur (1822–1895), a devout Catholic layman, revolutionized organic chemistry.   He it was who first clearly explained the nature of, and gave the name to, bacteria,
the minute animal organisms that are everywhere, in
air, water, or earth, and that are the cause of infectious diseases.
His painstaking observations and experiments enabled him to
secure results which not merely rendered his name immortal, but
benefited humanity in a manner and to a degree for which no
one could have ventured to hope.   His work was the starting-
point of all present-day achievements in aseptic surgery and in
the prevention of disease.   His discoveries on fermentation
inaugurated a new era in the brewing and wine-making industries.
His practical researches enabled growers of silkworms to stamp
out a dreadful plague that threatened the destruction of the whole
silk industry in France.[1]   And throughout the world, the success
of his endeavors to reduce the mortality of infants and to find a
cure for the dread disease of hydrophobia are witnessed respectively in the "pasteurization" of milk and in the treatment of
rabies by "Pasteur Institutes."

Louis Pasteur

Gregor Mendel (1822–1884) — peasant-boy, priest, and finally
abbot of an Augustinian monastery at Brünn in Germany
— devised and carried out in the garden of his
cloister the experiments which are to-day the foundation of that knowledge of the physiological process of heredity
which, known as Mendelism, biologists are rapidly extending
in various directions.   Though Mendel published an account of

Gregor Mendel

---

[1] Huxley estimated the money value of these discoveries as sufficient to cover
the whole cost of the war indemnity paid by France to Germany in 1871.

his experiments in a Catholic periodical as early as 1866, it was not until 1900, in the last years of Leo's pontificate, that men of science generally came to appreciate the import of his discoveries. In recent years the application of Mendel's principles on a wide scale has served not only to throw much light upon the important and complex problem of heredity, but also to raise objections to some of the theories of the evolutionists.

Of the political principles of Pius IX, Leo XIII professed not to change a jot or a tittle. He expressed in his encyclicals the same ideal of Christian society and reproduced the *Political* same condemnations of many phases of nationalism *Views of Leo* and Liberalism. Again and again he insisted that the *XIII* Christian Church should superintend and direct every form of civil life. But unlike his predecessor, Leo never appeared as a furious partisan of any particular form of government — absolutist or constitutional, monarchical or republican. He was never a reactionary in the earlier political sense; and as his pontificate wore on he perceived that democracy might prove fully as serviceable as monarchy for the preservation and strengthening of Catholic principles. This is probably the *Liberal* true interpretation of his emphatic encouragement *Catholic* of Catholic political parties, with distinctly Liberal *Political* tendencies, in Germany and in Belgium; his zeal in *Parties* urging the establishment of Catholic publications and Catholic parochial schools everywhere and for all classes; his friendly attitude toward the rapidly growing and prospering Church in the United States, and eventually toward the government of the Third French Republic; and, last but not least, his interest in the social questions which the Industrial Revolution had injected into contemporary democracy.

A famous encyclical, called *Rerum novarum*, which Leo XIII issued in 1891, aimed to apply Christian principles to the relations between capital and labor. Against Socialism, it affirmed the holding of private property to be an individual right based on abstract justice and older than any state; it insisted that a certain amount of suffering and toil is the lot of fallen humanity; and it combated the idea "that class is naturally hostile to class and that the wealthy and the workingmen are intended by nature to live in mutual conflict." On the contrary, the en-

cyclical maintained the efficacy of Catholic Christianity, "in
drawing the rich and the poor bread-winners together by re-
minding each class of its duties to the other, and es-

Leo XIII
and the
Working-
men: the
Encyclical
*Rerum
Novarum*,
1891
pecially of the obligations of justice. Thus religion
teaches the laboring man and the artisan to carry
out honestly and fairly all equitable agreements
freely entered into; never to injure the property
nor to outrage the person of an employer; never to
resort to violence in defending their own cause, nor to
engage in riot or disorder; and to have nothing to do with men
of evil principles, who work upon the people with artful promises,
and excite foolish hopes which usually end in disaster and in re-
pentance when too late. Religion, moreover, teaches the wealthy
owner and the employer that their work-people are not to be
accounted their bondsmen; that in every man they must respect
his dignity and worth as a man and as a Christian; that labor
is nothing to be ashamed of, if we listen to right reason and to
Christian philosophy, but is an honorable calling, enabling a
man to sustain his life in an upright and creditable way; and
that it is shameful and inhuman to treat men like chattels to
make money by, or to look upon them merely as so much muscle
or physical power." As immediate remedial measures, the
encyclical approved factory legislation, the regulation of the
hours of employment, especially of women and children, the
creation of labor unions of Catholic workingmen, and an increase
of small landowners. Employment is a right, Leo held: "each
one has a right to procure what is required in order to live;
and the poor can procure it in no other way than through work
and wages." This encyclical of *Rerum novarum* was translated
into the chief modern languages, and many thousands of copies
were circulated among the working classes in Catholic countries.
It not only won for Leo XIII the title of "the workingman's
pope," but it gained important followings for the Roman Catholic
Church among the poorer classes of southern Germany, Belgium,
Austria-Hungary, Italy, Spain, and France, as well as confirming
the faith of Irish and Polish industrial emigrants scattered over
the world.

Encouraged possibly by the reflection that in comparison
with the pontificate of Pius IX that of Leo XIII was distinctly

"liberal" and "progressive," a goodly number of Roman
Catholic apologists began early in the twentieth century to agitate openly in favor of a basic revision of the dogmas Modernism
and policies of their Church. Influenced certainly by in the Cath-
the vogue of Darwinism and by the development of olic Church
Biblical criticism, these apologists sought to stop the leakage of
intellectual bourgeois from the Catholic Church by urging the
frank recognition on the part of Catholics that their religion
must be "modernized." Although these so-called "Modernists" differed considerably among themselves, they generally
held that dogma is not immutable but evolutionary, that the
Catholic Church must be maintained not because of any divine
origin but because of its human utility, that ecclesiastical authority must be weakened, that science must traverse every
field of investigation without fear of conflict with the Church,
that the State must not be hampered by religious authority,
and that the inspirations of private conscience must not be
overridden by papal definitions or anathemas. Starting in
Italy, the movement soon won supporters in France, England,
Germany, and other countries. For a brief period it appeared
as though Darwinism might be destined to work as great a
dogmatic change in Catholicism as in Protestantism. Pius X
However, during the pontificate of Pius X (1903– (1903–1914)
1914),[1] several influential Modernists were excom- and his Con-
municated; the whole movement was denounced in a of Modern-
Syllabus of the Holy Office and in the papal encycli- ism
cal *Pascendi* (1907); and Roman Catholic priests were obliged
to take an oath against Modernist teachings. By 1914 Modernism seemed to have been extirpated from the Catholic Church.
Although Pius X preserved intact the general policies of Leo
XIII, there could be no doubt that the Modernist movement
was in part responsible for a recrudescence during his pontificate
of the bitter conflict between "Clericals" and "Anti-Clericals."

Enough has now been said to afford some notion of the conflicts waged in Catholic countries during the period from 1871
to 1914 between Clericals and Anti-Clericals. The latter, despite the conciliatory attitude of Leo XIII and the intellectual
and political developments within Catholicism, continued to

[1] Giuseppe Sarto (1835–1914).

comprise the majority of the bourgeoisie, many intellectual radicals in the universities and among artists and scientists, scattered supporters among the nobility and peasantry, and numerous vigorous allies in Socialistic working-men. The Clericals, on the other hand, embraced conspicuous individuals alike from the intellectual and from the industrial middle class, the majority of the peasantry and of the old nobility, and well-organized minorities of the working class. Among the Clericals, too, were small groups of persons, regardless of class, who had been drawn to Catholic Christianity because they longed for an authoritative voice that would give rest to them from the tumults and uncertainties of contemporary philosophy and science, or because they found in the Church's championship of order and private property the most promising safeguards against social revolution, or because they believed that religion and morality as taught by the Catholic Church were indispensable conditions of future human progress.

Relative Position of "Clericals" and "Anti-Clericals" in the Twentieth Century

THE SOCIAL PROBLEM AND THE DECLINE OF *LAISSER-FAIRE*

A characteristic of the period from 1871 to 1914, more portentous in many ways than conflicts between Clericals and Anti-Clericals, was the steady growth in numbers and influence of the urban working classes — skilled laborers, factory operatives, miners, and cheap day-laborers. In an earlier chapter — that on the Industrial Revolution — some indication has already been given of the process by which, in every civilized country, a large class of wage-earners came into existence; and the wretchedness and misery therein described as their common lot continued to attend them until well after 1871. In general it may be said that the workingmen gave invaluable support in the middle of the nineteenth century both to Liberalism and to nationalism, but neither principle effected any striking improvement in their economic condition. After 1871, however, the benevolence and self-interest of the industrial bourgeoisie combined, as has been intimated earlier in this chapter,[1] to inaugu-

[1] See above, p. 222.

rate a new policy in respect of the lower classes. Instead of vigorously and logically holding fast to the doctrine of *laisser-faire* and thwarting every attempt on the part of the State to interfere in private business, as they consistently had done during the first two-thirds of the nineteenth century, many manufacturers were converted in the last third of the century to the idea of the advisability of partial governmental regulation of industry.

Accordingly, the reader will discover that in the history of every important industrial country since 1871 a section is allotted to "social legislation" — legalization of trade-unions, factory laws, wage-boards, old-age pensions, national insurance, etc. It is indicative of the constantly broadening functions of the modern state.

That this tendency toward "social legislation" was a very general one is witnessed by the fact that it was not only Anti-Clericals like Bismarck and Briand who fostered it, but that it was encouraged by Pope Leo XIII and by prominent Anglican clergymen, and advocated by the newer Clerical parties on the Continent. It seemed as if middle-class Clericals and Anti-Clericals were bidding against each other for the support of the working class. And there was no doubt that by 1914 both groups of bidders had been in part successful. The Roman Catholic Church and, to a lesser extent, the Anglican Church and the Protestant sects, counted among workingmen numerous followers and political allies; and, on the other hand, had it not been for the approval or consent of numerous other workingmen the many Anti-Clerical measures which appeared on European statute-books could not have been enacted.

KARL MARX AND MODERN SOCIALISM

While a large group of workingmen was drawn toward Clericalism and another large group toward Anti-Clericalism — both groups being fairly well attached to bourgeois Liberalism and to most of the principles and policies of the modern state, — a third group of workingmen was waxing more and more vehement in denunciation of those very principles and policies and was proving more and more vexatious to the middle class, — this was the group which was being drawn toward Socialism. Modern Socialism, though combated alike by Church and State, grew steadily in Europe throughout the period from 1871 to 1914, making important strides toward the realization of its aim to bring all workingmen within its economic and political organization. To the bourgeois state, it caused even greater uneasiness than did Clericalism; in fact, had Socialism and Clericalism been thoroughly compatible, they might in union have dealt a mortal blow at the supremacy of the middle class.

The real roots of modern Socialism lie back of 1871 in the Industrial Revolution itself. As long ago as 1794 the French-

Early Socialism: Babeuf

man Babeuf had declared that it was idle to talk about political or social equality so long as equality of wealth or of economic opportunity was lacking. "When I see the poor without the clothing and shoes which they themselves are engaged in making," said he, "and contemplate the small minority who do not work and yet want for nothing, I am convinced that government is still the old conspiracy of the few against the many, only it has taken a new form." But nothing came of Babeuf's activities except in 1797 his own death warrant.[1]

In the comparatively early stages of the Industrial Revolution the cause of the workingmen was espoused by such men

"Utopian" Socialism: Robert Owen

as Fourier, Saint-Simon, and Owen,[2] who were called "Socialists,"[3] but whose doctrines and purposes were so different from those of present-day Socialists as to justify the application of the qualifying adjective "Utopian" to their brand of Socialism. The Utopian Socialists were what to-day we would prefer to style philanthropists — individuals of a higher social position who sought to do good to the men under them. And Utopian Socialism usually took the form of ideal communities whose members would live in common and share on equal terms the labor and the profits. To the present it has left the legacies of profit-sharing in certain indus-

[1] See Vol. I, p. 513.
[2] See above, pp. 86 f.
[3] The word "Socialist" appears to have been first used in a letter written to an English newspaper in August, 1835, by an anonymous disciple of Robert Owen. The Utopians have often been styled "Owenites."

trial establishments, and in some countries important systems of coöperative stores with collective buying and selling. But in its dream of an immediate reorganization of society Utopian Socialism proved a failure, and to later Socialists it hardly appeared as Socialism at all.

A little later came the Socialism of Louis Blanc,[1] with its national workshops, a kind of Socialism that might have been styled government-ownership. It did conspicuous service in France in the 'forties in organizing working- *Govern-ment-Own-ership So-cialism: Louis Blanc* men against the bourgeois government of Louis Philippe and in precipitating the revolutionary movement of 1848, and it reaped some reward in the subsequent almost universal tendency toward national ownership of telegraphs, telephones, railways, and forests, and municipal ownership of public utilities, such as water-supply, gas- and electric-lighting, tramways, libraries, markets, docks, baths, etc. But as Socialism it was so completely swallowed up by yet another variety — the Marxian — that Louis Blanc himself, appearing in the French Chamber of Deputies as an old man in the 'seventies, declared that he was no longer a "Socialist," only a "Radical."

Marxian or "Scientific" Socialism, which supplanted both the Utopian and the Blanc kinds, and from which all present-day forms of Socialism are directly derived, takes *Recent Socialism Marxian* its designation from the name of its classical formulator — Karl Marx.

Karl Marx was born at Trier in Rhenish Prussia in 1818. His father, a Jewish lawyer, in his love of learning, in his devotion to Voltaire and other eighteenth-century phi- *Karl Marx* losophers and scientists, in his swelling patriotism for Prussia, in his outward conformity to Lutheran Christianity,[2] and in his sycophantic office-holding, was a typical bourgeois product of the times. In middle-class society, therefore, young Karl was reared, showing early aptitude for study, especially of Greek, Latin, and literature, and graduating from the *gymnasium* of his native town when he was sixteen years old. After a year

[1] See above, pp. 87 f.

[2] The elder Marx with his whole family, Karl included, was baptized in 1824, taking that occasion to change the family name from Mordechai to Marx.

spent in the University of Bonn, he was transferred to the University of Berlin in the hope that a larger institution with a smaller amount of "college life" would tend to mold the youth more after his father's heart. The father was bent on making his son a conventionally respectable lawyer like himself, but the son already displayed a passion for unusual speculation and stayed away from lectures on law in order to attend those on philosophy and history. From the father's point of view, therefore, Karl's university career was a dismal failure, and henceforth the relations of father and son were strained. Nevertheless, well steeped in history and philosophy, Karl obtained the degree of Ph.D. from the University of Jena in 1841.

At Berlin, Karl Marx had come under the then all-powerful influence of Hegel [1] and had joined the informal group of "Young Hegelians," who enthusiastically accepted the master's philosophy of history — the idea that the history of the world is a development of political institutions from the era (the "Oriental") in which the single despot possessed freedom, to the era (the "Germanic") in which man as man enjoys freedom of thought and action. With this developmental theory of politics in mind, Marx became a pronounced Liberal and criticized the existing Conservative government of Prussia so frankly that the public authorities prevented him from realizing his desire to be a university professor and in 1843 suppressed the newspaper — the *Rheinische Zeitung* — through whose columns, as editor, he was waging a vigorous fight for the freedom of the press.

Influence of Hegel

To Paris Marx then went and there gradually shifted his opinions from bourgeois Liberalism to working-class Socialism. He began to study factory conditions. He became interested in the writings of the Utopian Socialists, especially of Robert Owen. He made the acquaintance of Louis Blanc, then at the height of his influence, and of Proudhon and Bakunin, who later secured fame as founders of rival schools of Anarchism. He found a sympathetic soul in the poet Heine and particularly in Friedrich Engels,[2] the man who was destined

Friedrich Engels

[1] Georg Wilhelm Friedrich Hegel (1770–1831), the philosopher, who was professor at the University of Berlin from 1818 until his death.

[2] Friedrich Engels (1820–1895), like Marx, a German Jew, born at Barmen in

to be his lifelong friend and co-laborer — his veritable *alter ego*. In order to eke out a living, he did a good deal of hackwriting at Paris and edited the Radical publication *Vorwärts* for his fellow-exiles from Germany. In 1845, however, *Vorwärts* was suppressed by Louis Philippe's prime minister, Guizot, on the urgent representation of the Prussian government, and Marx moved on to Brussels.

At Brussels, where he resided for the next three years, Marx did a number of notable things. He repudiated middle-class Hegelianism. He conducted wordy polemics with Proudhon, which served to bring into bold relief the fundamental differences between Socialism and Anarchism, differences that will be noticed later. He agitated for political democracy. He organized workingmen's clubs.

It was as a statement of principles for these workingmen's clubs [1] that Marx, in conjunction with Engels, prepared and published early in 1848 the celebrated *Communist Manifesto*, the "birthcry of modern Socialism." The little pamphlet passed practically unnoticed at the time, — the great political revolutions of 1848 monopolized public attention, — but much later it was recognized as containing in concise and vivid form the doctrines of the founders of "scientific" Socialism — Marx and Engels.

"The Communist Manifesto," 1848

Deferring for the moment an analysis of the *Communist Manifesto*, it may be said that the remonstrances of the Prussian government having induced the Belgian authorities to "invite" him to leave Brussels, Marx was again in Paris during the February days which witnessed the downfall of Guizot and

---

the Rhine province, educated in the *gymnasium* of Elberfeldt, served in the army from 1837 to 1841, sent in 1842 to Manchester, England, to look after a cotton-spinning business of which his father was principal owner. His investigation of factory conditions made him a Socialist and the publication of his work, *The Condition of the Working Class in England in 1844*, earned him the friendship of Karl Marx.

[1] A "Communist League" had been formed in Paris as early as 1836 by German refugees and traveling workmen, and was apparently related to Mazzini's revolutionary societies in Italy. After 1840 it became an "International Alliance" with loosely attached and struggling branches in several important industrial centers, and in November, 1847, Marx and Engels attended its first international congress at London. It was out of the discussions there that the *Manifesto* seems to have been developed.

Louis Philippe and the proclamation of the Second French Republic. Then when news reached him of the spread of the revolutionary wave to his native land, he hurried to Cologne and began the publication of the radical Socialistic *Neue Rheinische Zeitung*. But the reactionary developments of the following year disillusioned and embittered Marx: everywhere he saw Conservatives again in the political saddle and middle-class capitalists in the economic saddle. Though acquitted in a Prussian court of the charge preferred against him of inciting to armed resistance, he was obliged again to leave his country.

This time Marx sought refuge in England, and there he lived from 1849 to the day of his death in 1883, disturbed only by financial difficulties. Generous and hospitable to a fault, and a fond husband and father, he experienced incessant hardship in "making both ends meet." He continued to earn a precarious living by hack-writing. He translated books. He dabbled in journalism, contributing a series of interesting articles to the *New York Tribune*. But during the thirty-four years of arduous exile, Marx found time to perform two great works, which, in connection with his contribution to the *Communist Manifesto*, constitute his chief titles to fame. In the first place he prepared a great study of political economy, *Das Kapital*,[1] that was regarded by his followers as doing for its author what the *Wealth of Nations* did for Adam Smith. In the second place, he organized in 1864 an international society among workingmen for the propagation of his ideas.

Karl Marx in England, 1849–1883

It may now be profitable to sketch briefly the distinguishing features of this new Marxian Socialism which, backed by the erudition of *Das Kapital*, was outlined in the *Communist Manifesto* and embodied for action in the International Workingmen's Association.

According to the *Communist* [2] *Manifesto*, the contemporary economic conflict between capitalists and wage-earners is but a

---

[1] The first volume appeared in 1867; the second, third, and fourth, revised and edited by Engels, were not published until after the death of Marx.

[2] The word "Communist" was employed by Marx and Engels to distinguish their program from that of the Utopians, who were then regularly styled "Socialists." Subsequently, when Utopianism had virtually expired, the word Socialism was accepted by Marx and Engels as equivalent to their "Communism," and has since supplanted it.

phase of the age-long economic struggle between social classes. History is simply the record of how one class has gained wealth and then secured political power only to be overthrown and succeeded in wealth and political power by an- other class. At the present time the factory system has magnified the wealth and political influence of the bour- geoisie — has, in fact, created the "capitalist class," — but it has also produced men who are destined to deal capitalism its death blow, the workingmen, the "proletarians," herded into towns and exploited on a large scale. These proletarians "are increasing in power and are becoming conscious of their power," reënforced by the lower middle class, the artisans, and the peasants who are falling into the proletariat. As time goes on, the *Manifesto* prophesies, capital will be controlled by a few, and the many will be proletarians; at that time the many will be able by political means to dispossess the few and to inaugurate the Communist state.

Tenets of Marxian Socialism

The aims of "Communism," as set forth in the *Manifesto*, are to organize the proletarians in a class party, to have the prole- tariat gain political power, and to abolish middle-class property ownership, "created by the labor of wage-earners for the profit of capitalists." The realization of these aims will mean the transformation of private-owned capital into rightful common property, and the abolition of middle-class free trade, of the "middle-class family," of traditional middle-class religion and morality, and of hostility between nations; and the realization will be wrought by political processes. As transitional measures toward the ultimate goal, the *Manifesto* urges the proletarians to demand the following: (1) confiscation of land rent; (2) high direct taxes; (3) abolition of inheritance; (4) confiscation of the property of emigrants; (5) centralization of credit by a national bank with public capital and exclusive monopoly; (6) public ownership of all means of transportation; (7) national factories and national cultivation of land; (8) compulsory labor for all; (9) gradual abolition of the distinction between town and country by a more equable distribution of the population over the country; and (10) free public education for all chil- dren. The famous conclusion of the *Manifesto* is at once inter- national and revolutionary: " The proletarians have nothing to lose but their chains. They have a world to win. Workingmen of all countries, unite !"

In estimating the significance of Karl Marx, four facts stand out clearly and prominently. In the first place, he systematized existing socialistic theories. Secondly, he emphasized the political, as well as the economic, character of Socialism, insisting that political democracy would be an indispensable antecedent to the collective ownership of all the means of production and distribution of economic goods. Thirdly, he conferred upon Socialism a philosophy and a claim to be considered a "science." His philosophy, which has been frequently styled "economic determinism," or, far more commonly, the economic or materialistic interpretation of history, may be embraced in three comprehensive formulas : (1) that the course of history has always been determined by economic factors ; (2) that present society has been evolved gradually out of many class struggles of the past; (3) that the present capitalistic society will inevitably be transformed into another type of social organization. These three formulas, taken together, constituted a philosophical synthesis to which the name "Marxism" was applied just as the name "Darwinism" was contemporaneously applied to the body of Darwin's teaching. In fact, it was pointed out that Marx did for social science what Darwin did for natural science. And there is certainly little doubt that Marx's emphasis upon the economic interpretation of history has tremendously influenced a growing number of historians since his time, regardless of whether they have called themselves Socialists, Conservatives, or Clericals. To such an extent, certainly, the methods of Karl Marx could be deemed scientific as well as philosophical.

Finally, Karl Marx made his appeal not so much to theorists or philanthropists or altruistic bourgeois, like the Utopians, as directly to the workingmen themselves. Although he was by birth and early training a bourgeois himself, — and so was Engels, and so were many other leaders of modern Socialism, — nevertheless he insisted that by the law of historical evolution nothing could be really achieved for the workingmen except by the workingmen ; the only function of middle-class agitators like himself would be to make the workingmen class-

(Signifi- cance of Karl Marx)

conscious and to assist them in organizing. And it was not to the workingmen of any one country that Marx appealed : "workingmen have no country," he declared; and it was internationalism rather than nationalism that Marxism espoused.

In order to realize the aims of the new Socialism, Karl Marx took a leading part in organizing and directing the "International Working Men's Association" — usually described simply as "The International." Originating in an informal gathering of English, French, and Belgian laborers at the London Exposition of 1862, the society assumed permanent form in 1864 and adopted the Marxian teachings essentially *in toto*. The International was a federation of self-governing "sections" on national lines : for several years it held annual congresses, and at one time it included "sections" in England, Germany, France, Italy, Belgium, Holland, Switzerland, and the United States. Despite the strenuous efforts of Marx, several events conspired in the 'seventies to bring about the failure of the International as an organization. Its members were always few and, without exception, poor, which meant the lack of financial support. Then, too, the renewed impetus given to nationalism by the Franco-German War of 1870–1871 was temporarily destructive of all international movements. Again, the failure of the Communist uprising at Paris in 1871, with which Marx heartily sympathized and which will subsequently be described, brought the International into wide disrepute with friends of law and order. Finally, the small society was torn by internal dissensions between the Socialist followers of Marx and the disciples of the Anarchist Bakunin. The last real congress of the International was held at Geneva in 1873; and the formal dissolution of the organization was decreed by a few of the faithful assembled at Philadelphia in 1876.

Organization of Socialism: "The International"

But the failure of the International meant by no means the failure of Marxian Socialism, the principles of which were already producing fruit in national movements independent of the "sections" of the International. The successful organization of the movement, in fact, was not to be ascribed to Karl Marx, but rather to another German Jew, the brilliant and somewhat erratic

Ferdinand Lassalle and the Social Democratic Party in Germany

Ferdinand Lassalle (1825-1864), a well-educated, well-to-do bourgeois, famed both as a man of decidedly fashionable and luxurious habits and as a veritable "messiah of the poor." Lassalle's *Open Letter* of March, 1863, which revived Louis Blanc's ideas of universal suffrage and national workshops, was the beginning of a political party in Germany which could rightfully lay claim to the old name of "Social Democrat." Side by side with the Social Democracy came into existence the German "sections" of Karl Marx's International, including such famous leaders as the scholarly bourgeois Wilhelm Liebknecht (1826-1900), and the eloquent Saxon woodturner, August Bebel (1840-1913). And the fusion of the two rival groups in 1875 formed a single Social Democratic party, essentially Marxian in theory, which made an ever-widening appeal to German workingmen. From 1875 to 1914 Marxian Socialism grew in Germany by leaps and bounds.

The Social Democratic party of Germany became the type after which the national organizations of Marxian Socialism

National Socialist Parties were modeled in other countries, and with such rapidity that by 1914 every civilized nation had a Socialist party whose gospel, at least in theory, was the teaching of Karl Marx. And in order to unite the national parties in a bond of mutual sympathy and encouragement, there had been a recrudescence of annual international congresses, whose functions, however, were advisory and consultative rather than governmental. Although in some countries only a relatively small minority of workingmen could be called Socialists, nevertheless it was clear that everywhere wage-earners were being attracted to Socialism in increasing numbers.

The growth of Marxian Socialism was combated throughout the period from 1871 to 1914 alike by Clericals and by ordinary

Opposition of Many " Clericals " and " Anti-Clericals " to Socialism supporters of the bourgeois régime. To the Clericals, as has already been intimated, Socialism seemed too radical and too revolutionary: its attacks on private property were unjust and unnatural; its maintenance of the doctrine of the class-struggle was un-Christian; and the extreme views of some of its advocates on the subject of marriage gave color to the widely entertained belief that it was anti-religious and immoral. To the average respectable and comfortable middle-class person, regardless of ecclesiastical affiliations, Socialism appeared downright dangerous: its diatribes against private property were held to be destructive of individual initiative; its appeals to a single class in the community were likely to array that class against all others, to ruin business, and to lead to civil war; and its insistence upon international solidarity was positively unpatriotic. Against ever so many dominant political tendencies of the period, Socialism sternly set its face: it generally opposed militarism and imperialism and protective tariffs and all forms of indirect taxation and commercial or industrial concessions to private individuals or corporations. With Socialism nearly every statesman of the period had to contend.

In conducting their political campaigns during the period, the Socialists came to differ among themselves, not on the question of violence, for violence was universally condemned by official Socialism, and not on any question of abandoning basic Marxian principles, but rather on the question of the political tactics which they should pursue in order to gain as quickly as possible their common economic ends. On this question of tactics, the differences which appeared more or less prominently in almost every national Socialist party gave rise to two groups more or less distinct: the "strict" Marxians, usually called "Marxists," and the "loose" Marxians, variously styled "Reformists," "Revisionists," "Possibilists," etc. The differences related chiefly to imperialism, Clericalism, agriculture, and trade-unionism.

Division of the Socialists into "Strict Marxists" and "Reformists" on Questions of Political Tactics

On the question of imperialism, the Marxists, true to the letter of their master's instructions, unequivocally championed international peace and protested against every seizure of colonies and every increase of armaments. On the other hand, the Reformists heeded the instructions with less assurance: they were prone to talk about national peculiarities, the promotion of civilization, "Slav perils," or "Yellow perils"— the very language of anti-Socialist imperialists. The Reformists certainly held pretty generally that it was the duty of every nation to defend itself by force of arms against the attacks

1. Imperialism

of less socialistically inclined nations, and that national patriotism was not in every instance an evil thing.

On the question of clericalism, the Marxian theory that religion was a private concern was badly strained by the anti-Socialist **2. Religion** activity of Christian clergymen in many countries, especially Roman Catholic. The result was that the Reformists tended to lay stress upon the demand for secularizing education and for stopping the payment of ecclesiastical salaries by the state and that in Catholic countries they were frankly Anti-Clerical.

Similarly on the question of the peasantry, the original Marxist contention that the agricultural classes should be left un- **3. Agriculture** heeded to succumb to capitalism was sorely weakened in practical politics by the increasingly obvious fact that on the Continent the resistance to Socialism, electorally speaking, depended upon the peasantry, who were not succumbing to capitalism at all rapidly and who naturally feared Socialism as the despoiler of their little farms and holdings. This discrepancy between theory and practice induced many Reformists to undertake a propaganda of "enlightenment" among the peasantry and to bid for their political support.

Originally the Marxists, thoroughly recognizing the value of the achievements of the trade unions, were jealous of them, **4. Trade-Unionism** fearing that they would conflict with the organizations of simon-pure Socialism. But the wonderful growth of trade-unionism during the period — a growth even more remarkable than that of Socialism — soon convinced the Reformists that well-organized trade unions afforded the best kind of stepping-stones to Socialism. Consequently, the Reformists championed trade-unionism, and wherever they could, they either, as in Germany, annexed unions to the Socialist party or, as in Great Britain, entered into alliances with independent trade-unionists under the joint designation of Labor parties.

For most practical purposes the national Socialist parties were able to carry on their work with the united support of Marxists and Reformists. As time went on, there was no doubt, however, that the latter group were in the ascendant and that their tactics were becoming the tactics of Marxian Socialism. Only in one particular — the refusal of the leaders of the Socialist party to become members of coalition cabinets with non-Socialist leaders — did strict Marxism appear triumphant, and even in this particular the tremendous military crisis of 1914 was destined to effect a moderating change.

ANARCHISM AND SYNDICALISM

Not all the workingmen of the period from 1871 to 1914 can be distributed among Socialism, Clericalism, and non-political trade-unionism, though a large majority of the whole class and the mass of skilled laborers fit into one or another of these three categories. Yet one more group remains to be mentioned — the disciples of Anarchism.

Modern Anarchism like modern Socialism was a product of the Industrial Revolution: both started as more or less systematized theories on the part of reforming middle-class philanthropists of the best way in which to get rid of poverty and other ills that followed in the wake of poverty; both tended to become panaceas for the workingman and to promise much the same ultimate goal; but from each other the two differed fundamentally in their means of attaining that goal. Socialism would employ a democratic government. Anarchism would employ no compulsory government of any sort.

Modern Anarchism a Product of the Industrial Revolution

William Godwin (1756–1836), a shy and retiring ex-parson, who lived in England during the period of the French Revolution, has always been acclaimed as the father of philosophical Anarchism, but his learned work, *The Inquiry concerning Political Justice, and its Influence on General Virtue and Happiness* (1793), was hardly simple enough in argument or style to make a popular appeal to day-laborers. A far more influential person — the one who coined the word "Anarchist" — was Pierre Joseph Proudhon (1809–1865), a French contemporary of Karl Marx.

William Godwin

Proudhon, poor but bright and ambitious, went up from a printer's shop in the provinces to Paris in 1839 at the age of thirty to pursue an ascetic and studious life. It was just the time when the Industrial Revolution

Pierre Joseph Proudhon

was coming into France from England; when machinery and factories were being rapidly put up at Paris; when the lines were growing sharper between new classes — the wealthy factory owners and the impoverished factory workers. It was also the time when many sorts of political opposition were appearing against the compromising middle-class monarchy of Louis Philippe; when the factory owners were beginning to demand a larger share in government.

In this environment Proudhon went to work and in 1840 published his first important book, *What is Property?* The audacity of his answer, "Property is Theft," proved to be a spectacular commencement of his revolutionary career. With the proceeds of journalistic hack-writing he managed to keep body and soul together, and all of his spare time he gave to the "cause." In 1846 he published his greatest work, the *System of economic contradictions or the Philosophy of Poverty*, a thoroughly Anarchistic work, to which Karl Marx promptly replied with a thoroughly Socialistic criticism, gayly entitled the *Poverty of Philosophy*. Proudhon took some part in the revolutionary movement of 1848 and served as a member of the Constituent Assembly. Between 1848 and 1850 he started four different newspapers, all of which were in turn suppressed as anarchistic and obnoxious. An attempt to found a voluntary bank which should operate without charging interest led to his imprisonment for two years. Four years after his release he published his third important work, *Of Justice in the Revolution and in the Church*, in which he attacked existing political and ecclesiastical institutions with such unusual fury that he was obliged to flee to Brussels to escape a second incarceration. After the amnesty which Napoleon III granted to political offenders in 1860, Proudhon returned to France and died quietly at Passy in 1865.

Proudhon left no clear, concise statement of his opinions, but from his various writings the following have been gathered as indicative of the Anarchism which he preached. In the first place, he was one with Marx in his definition of private property and capital as the power of exploiting the labor of other men, of claiming the results of labor without giving an equivalent. "As slavery," said he, "is assassination inasmuch as it destroys all that is valuable and desirable

Proudhon's Attack on Property

in human personality, so property is theft inasmuch as it appropriates the value produced by the labor of others without rendering an equivalent." For private property, however, he would substitute, not public property as the Marxian Socialists would do, but simply individual possession, every man having an equal right to use property and to enjoy the full product of his own labor.

Secondly — and herein lies the basic difference between Anarchism and Socialism — Proudhon rejected all forms of authoritative government, social democratic as well as monarchical or oligarchical. He held that "all parties, without exception, in so far as they seek for power, are varieties of absolutism, and that there would be no liberty for citizens, no order for societies, no union among workingmen, until in the political catechism the renunciation of authority should have replaced faith in authority." He summed up his political creed in the phrases, "No more parties, no more authority, absolute liberty of man and citizen."

Proudhon's Attack on Government

Thirdly, Proudhon was at once a moralist and an optimist in rearing his constructive schemes. He believed that a sense of justice is inherent in every man, that the Golden Rule is the immutable law of the individual conscience. Justice demands, according to him, a social human life on the basis of a single law that contracts must be lived up to. This was what Proudhon meant by Anarchism. After the abrogation of the present-day state and of man-made laws, men are still to live together in society, not by any supreme authority, but only by the voluntary, yet legally binding, force of contract. "Thus a régime of voluntary contracts, substituted for a régime of obligatory laws, would constitute the true government of man, the true sovereignty of the people, the true Republic." Proudhon dwelt at length upon the naturalness of his proposed society and cited various voluntary fraternal orders and the Christian Church, when separated from the state, as examples of the very thing which he advocated universally. And he optimistically held that human nature is of such a high order that, emancipated from the bondage of the State and the tyranny of laws, it would spontaneously react in Anarchistic society against all wrongdoing.

Proudhon's Optimism

Finally, Proudhon was a perfectibilist, that is to say, he believed that man is capable of an infinite amount of self-better-
Proudhon's Faith in Human Progress ment. This belief led him to decry violence as a means of overthrowing existing political, economic, social, and ecclesiastical institutions and of ushering in the ideal Anarchism. He always insisted that man could be gradually educated up to an understanding of abuses in the present system and of the advantages of the anarchistic régime. When that day should come, society would be intelligently transformed of its own volition. In Proudhon's system there was no place for violence.

It will be observed that the essence of the Anarchism of Proudhon was a tremendous reliance on individualism. To
Nature and Tenets of Philosophical Anarchism escape the economic and social conditions of the time — whose evils both bitterly arraigned — Proudhon departed in a diametrically opposite direction from Marx. While Marx would vastly increase the powers and functions of the democratic state, Proudhon would diminish them to the vanishing point and would carry the then much-vaunted principle of *laisser-faire* to its logical conclusion. From this very individualism — so inherent in Anarchism — it followed that no central organization, with a common platform of policies, could be devised to carry forward Proudhon's movement. By leaving everything to the individual, it followed that almost as many interpretations were placed on Anarchism as there were individual disciples.[1]

In general it may be said that all Anarchists since the time of Proudhon have clung to the first three of the four funda-
Anarchism and Terrorism mental characteristics mentioned above, and that on the fourth tenet — the employment of violence to work the transformation from capitalistic to anarchistic society — professed Anarchists have tended to separate into two hostile factions. One faction — a small faction, composed mainly of middle-class Radicals, intellectual and philosophical — has adhered to Proudhon's preachments of peaceful propaganda.

---

[1] Among famous Anarchists, Nietzsche has been reckoned a close disciple of Proudhon; Prince Kropatkin and Enrico Malatesta as "anarchist-communists"; Count Tolstoy as a "Christian Anarchist." Anarchistic doctrines also appear in the literary work of Ibsen, Zola, and Walt Whitman.

The other — a growing faction — has encouraged the use of terror and violence : a method whose earliest and most militant champion was a Russian revolutionary, Mikhail Bakunin (1814–1876).

Bakunin came of an aristocratic family in Russia, served in the tsar's army, and studied in Germany, where he accepted the philosophy of Hegel and got into touch with young Radicals in Berlin. Journeying to Paris, he made the acquaintance of Proudhon and the chief Polish exiles, and began his career as a revolutionary agitator. For his participation in an insurrection at Dresden in 1849 he was arrested and handed over to the Russian authorities, who sent him off to a penal colony in Siberia. Managing to escape in 1861, he spent the remainder of his life in western Europe, principally in Switzerland. In 1869 he founded the Social Democratic Alliance, a society of workingmen, whose members were recruited largely from the countries of southern Europe, and in the same year affiliated it with Karl Marx's International Working Men's Association. It was not long before the irreconcilable differences of Marx and Bakunin became manifest : the former would secure economic reforms through political action and peacefully ; the latter would improve the lot of the workingmen through general strikes — "direct action"— without reference to government and with the help of terrorism. In 1872 Bakunin was outvoted and expelled by the Marxian Socialists, and the attendant secessions from the International were not only a contributing cause of the failure of that general movement of workingmen but also a recognition of the formal schism between Socialism and Anarchism which has survived to the present day.

Mikhail Bakunin

Break between Anarchism and Socialism

After Bakunin's death in 1876 workingmen everywhere were far more inclined to join the Socialist parties than to become Anarchists, and for a score of years Anarchism of the Bakunin type was largely limited to secret conspiracy, terrorism against illiberal government, such as that of Russia, isolated bomb outrages, and murderous attacks on representatives of royalty or on particularly objectionable capitalists. The spirit underlying the numerous instances of Anarchistic violence occurring between 1871

The Spirit of Revolutionary Anarchism

and 1914 is clearly indicated in the following passage of the famous *Revolutionary Catechism*, written by an associate of Bakunin: "The [revolutionary Anarchist] will use every means and every effort to increase and intensify the evils and sorrows, which must at last exhaust the patience of the people and excite them to insurrection *en masse*. By a popular revolution the [individual Anarchist] does not mean a movement regulated according to the classic patterns of the West, which, always restrained in the face of property and of the traditional social order of so-called civilization and morality, has hitherto been limited merely to exchanging one form of political organization for another, and to the creating of a so-called revolutionary state. The only revolution that can do any good to the people is that which utterly annihilates every idea of the State and over-throws all traditions, orders, and classes, as in Russia. With this end in view, the [revolutionary Anarchist] has no intention of imposing upon the people any organization whatever coming from above. The future organization will, without doubt, proceed from the movement and life of the people; but that is the business of future generations. Our task is destruction, terrible, total, inexorable, and universal."

Although anarchistic workingmen were to be found among the Paris communists of 1871 and among the abettors of political

Syndical-
ism, a Re-
cent Form
of Revolu-
tionary
Anarchism

disorder in Spain during the 'seventies, it was not until the 'nineties that Anarchism could be said to have made any considerable headway with the working class, and then not under the formal name of Anarchism, but rather under the more ambiguous designation of Syndicalism. Starting in France, where Anarchist agitators got control of several trade unions (*syndicats*, as the French style them), Syndicalism rapidly spread among the laborers, particularly in the unskilled trades, in southern and central Europe, in Great Britain, in Australia, and, as the "Industrial Workers of the World," in the United States.

From usual trade-unionism, Syndicalism differed in that it would organize the workers by whole industries rather than by trades or crafts: thus, all men engaged in railroading, or even in transport work of any sort, would be brought into one mammoth body which could thereby achieve control over the entire industry. From Socialism, Syndicalism differed in the emphasis that it would place upon direct action, that is to say, upon the action which would bring immediate pressure upon the employer and which is opposed to political action or the betterment of conditions through legislative and other governmental intervention. As "direct action" the Syndicalists would count the general strike and "sabotage," the latter being the destruction or spoiling of materials, the choking of machinery, and other crippling of the industrial processes so as to reduce or destroy the profits of the employer. In aims and tactics the Syndicalists were part and parcel of revolutionary Anarchism.

Though in 1914 the number of Syndicalists throughout the world was distinctly inferior to the number of Socialists, they were making serious inroads upon Socialism and were beginning to appear to statesmen, ecclesiastics, and capitalists as enemies infinitely more dangerous than the Socialists.

We have now completed the task which we set before ourselves for this chapter. Our attention has been directed to several striking characteristics of the whole period from 1871 to 1914, and we have acquired some familiarity with certain forces in economics, science, and religion, which were destined in novel ways to affect the era. We are thus in a more advantageous position to follow, in the ensuing five chapters, the separate sketches of the recent history of the various European states.

ADDITIONAL READING

Textbooks and Manuals on Recent European History. In addition to the texts cited in the bibliography appended to Chapter XVII, above, the following are useful as indicating broad lines of European development in the period since 1870: G. P. Gooch, *History of Our Time, 1885–1911* (1911), in "Home University Library," brief but suggestive; J. H. Rose, *The Development of the European Nations, 1870–1900*, 4th ed., 2 vols. (1914); *History of All Nations*, Vol. XX, *Contemporary Europe, Asia, and Africa, 1871–1901*, by C. M. Andrews (1902); Gottlob Egelhaaf, *Geschichte der neuesten Zeit von Frankfurter Frieden bis zur Gegenwart*, 4th ed. (1913), recent general history from the standpoint of a patriotic German; Édouard Driault, *Les problèmes politiques et sociaux à la fin du XIXe siècle* (1900), and, by the same author, *Le monde actuel* (1909), interesting and informing essays by an acute French observer of public affairs; A. W. Andrews, *A Text-Book of Geography* (1913), up-to-date descriptions of principal countries with greater emphasis on the physical and social than on the political; and the series of popular descriptions of present-day government and recent history of the chief national states edited by P. L. Haworth (" Problems of the Nations," 1915 *sqq.*), and likewise the series edited by D. P. Barrows and T. H. Reed (" Government Handbooks," 1915 *sqq.*). For Annuals and general publications dealing with the most recent history, see the bibliography appended to Chapter XXX, below.

Political Developments and Problems, 1871–1914. Brief surveys: *Cambridge Modern History*, Vol. XII (1910), ch. i; J. H. Robinson and C. A. Beard, *The Development of Modern Europe*, Vol. II (1907), ch. xxxi. Special treatises: M. I. Ostrogorski, *Democracy and the Organization of Political Parties*, Eng. trans. by Frederick Clarke, 2 vols (1902); F. A. Ogg, *The Governments of Europe* (1913), an indispensable guide-book, with extended bibliographies; W. F. Dodd, *Modern Constitutions*, 2 vols. (1909), English translations of the chief constitutions of the world, arranged country by country in alphabetical order; *Handbuch des öffentlichen Rechts der Gegenwart in Monographien*, ed. by Heinrich Marquardsen and others in many volumes (1883 *sqq.*), authoritative studies of various governments throughout the world; J. W. Burgess, *Political Science and Comparative Constitutional Law*, 2 vols. (1902), and, by the same author, *The Reconciliation of Government with Liberty* (1915); Jesse Macy and J. W. Gannaway, *Comparative Free Government* (1915); F. J. Goodnow, *Comparative Administrative Law*, 2 vols. in 1 (1903); Percy Ashley, *Local and Central Government : a Comparative Study of England, France, Prussia, and the United States* (1906); W. B. Munro, *The Government of European Cities* (1909); F. C. Howe, *The Modern City and its Problems* (1915); Käthe Schirmacher, *The Modern Woman's Rights Movement: a Historical Study*, Eng. trans. by C. C. Eckhardt (1912); B. L. Hutchins, *Conflicting Ideals : Two Sides of the Woman's Question* (1913); J. S. Mill, *The Subjection of Women*, new ed. (1906), a famous article particularly valuable for the description of woman's position at the time it was first published, in 1869.

Social Developments and Problems, 1871–1914. *Cambridge Modern History*, Vol. XII (1910), ch. xxiii, a brief summary of social movements, by Sidney Webb; Charles Seignobos, *A Political History of Europe since 1814*, Eng. trans. ed. by S. M. Macvane (1900), ch. xxii–xxiv; James Samuelson (editor), *The Civilization of Our Day* (1896); A. R. Wallace, *The Wonderful Century: its Successes and its Failures* (1898); *Un siècle : mouvement du monde de 1800 à 1900* (1900), a valuable and comprehensive survey of the social, political, and intellectual developments of the nineteenth century, published in 3 vols. with profuse illustrations and in one volume without illustrations, prepared by a group of scholarly French Catholics under the patronage of Pope Leo XIII; F. A. Ogg, *Social Progress in Contemporary Europe* (1912), a popular account, clear and suggestive; W. D. P. Bliss (editor), *The New Encyclopædia of Social Reform* (1908), a large work of reference, claiming to include " all social reform movements and activities, and the economic, industrial, and sociological facts and statistics of all countries and all social subjects "; Alfred Marshall, *Principles of Economics*, 6th ed. (1910), a convenient manual on an all-important topic; Arthur Shadwell, *Industrial Efficiency: a Comparative Study of Industrial Life in England, Germany, and America*, 2d ed., 2 vols. (1909); F. L. McVey, *Modern Industrialism* (1904), of much the same scope as Shadwell's work; D. A. Wells, *Recent Economic Changes and their Effect on the Production and Distribution of Wealth and the Well-Being of Society*, 2d ed. (1898); Sidney and Beatrice Webb, *Problems of Modern Industry* (1898); Percy Ashley, *Modern Tariff History: Germany — United States — France*, 2d ed. (1910); E. R. A. Seligman, *Essays in Taxation*, 8th ed. (1913); H. L. Moore, *Economic Cycles, their Law and Cause* (1914); F. W. Lewis, *State Insurance, a Social and Industrial Need* (1909); H. R. Seager, *Social Insurance, a Program of Social Reform* (1910); Gabriel Hanotaux, *La démocratie et le travail* (1910); Josef Stammhammer (editor), *Bibliographie der Sozialpolitik*, 2 vols. (1896–1912); Hermann Beck (editor), *Bibliographie der Sozialwissenschaften*, monthly since 1905; R. E. Hughes, *The Making of Citizens: a Study in Comparative Education* (1902), dealing with the educational systems of Great Britain, France, Germany, and the United States; H. B. Binns, *A Century of Education, 1808–1908* (1908); G. P. Gooch, *History and Historians in the Nineteenth Century* (1913); George Saintsbury, *A History of Nineteenth Century Literature, 1780–1895* (1912).

Science and Thought in the Nineteenth Century. *Cambridge Modern History*, Vol. XII (1910), ch. xxiv, a brief survey of the " Scientific Age " by W. C. D. Whetham; A. R. Wallace and others, *Progress of the Century*, a collection of interesting essays by distinguished men, summing up the main scientific achievements of the nineteenth century; *Histoire générale*, Vol. X, ch. xx, Vol. XI, ch. xxv, Vol. XII, ch. xvii, clear and admirable summaries by Paul Tannery; J. T. Merz, *A History of European Thought in the Nineteenth Century*, 4 vols. (1896–1914), a thorough and highly prized work; A. W. Benn, *The History of English Rationalism in the Nineteenth Century*, 2 vols. (1906), and, by the same author, *Modern England: a Record of Opinion and Action from the Time of the French Revolution to the Present Day*, 2 vols. (1908); Sir Oliver Lodge, *Pioneers of Science* (1893); J. M. Robertson, *A Short History of Free Thought*, 3d ed., 2 vols. (1915); Karl Snider, *The World Machine* (1907), a highly colored and none too accurate history of modern science from the standpoint of an enthusiastic believer in the mechanistic theory of the universe; G. T. Bettany, *Life of Charles Darwin* (1887), a convenient biography in the " Great Writers " Series; *Life and Letters of Charles Darwin*, ed. by Francis Darwin, 2 vols. (1887); H. F. Osborn, *From the Greeks to Darwin* (1894), a brief history of the theory of evolution; G. J. Romanes, *Darwin and After Darwin: an Exposition of the Darwinian Theory and a Discussion of Post-Darwinian Questions*, 3 vols. (1906–1910); William Bateson, *Mendel's Principles of*

Heredity (1909), containing an English translation of Mendel's papers and a biography as well as an account of more recent scientific work on Mendelian lines; R. C. Punnett, *Mendelism*, 3d ed. (1911), a good brief account of the subject. The *Encyclopædia Britannica*, 11th ed., includes uniformly excellent articles on the lives and achievements of famous scientists in the nineteenth century.

Christianity in the Nineteenth Century. On the Roman Catholic Church: Joseph MacCaffrey, *History of the Catholic Church in the Nineteenth Century*, 2 vols. (1910), the most extended and best treatment of the subject from the Roman Catholic point of view; William Barry, *The Papacy and Modern Times* (1911), ch. vi, vii; Fredrik Nielsen, *History of the Papacy in the Nineteenth Century*, Eng. trans. by A. J. Mason, 2 vols. (1906), an unsympathetic treatment from the pen of a Danish Lutheran bishop; J. A. G. (Cardinal) Hergenröther, *Catholic Church and Christian State*, Eng. trans. by C. S. Devas, documentary and polemical, valuable for its interpretation of the Syllabus of 1864; *Cambridge Modern History*, Vol. XI (1909), ch. xxv, an unfavorable view of papal policies from 1846 to 1870; Justin McCarthy, *Pope Leo XIII* (1896), a convenient popular biography; *Great Encyclical Letters of Leo XIII*, Eng. trans. ed. by J. J. Wynne (1903), useful; Georges Weill, *Histoire du catholicisme libéral en France*, 1828–1908 (1909), clear and scholarly; J. J. Walsh, *Catholic Churchmen in Science* (1906); Georges Goyau and others, *Le Vatican, les papes et la civilization, le gouvernement central de l'église* (1895), elaborate essays by distinguished French Catholics on the relation of the papacy to the newer political and intellectual tendencies. On the newer social program of Roman Catholicism: George Metlake, *Christian Social Reform: Program Outlined by its Pioneer Bishop von Ketteler* (1912); Joseph Husslein, *The Church and Social Problems* (1914); F. S. Nitti, *Catholic Socialism*, trans. from 2d Ital. ed. by Mary Mackintosh (1908); Anatole Leroy-Beaulieu, *Papacy, Socialism and Democracy*, Eng. trans. by B. L. O'Donnell (1892), suggestive and controversial rather than informing; Edwardo (Count) Soderini, *Socialism and Catholicism*, Eng. trans. (1896); C. S. Devas, *Political Economy*, 2d ed. (1901), an attempt to provide a basis in economics for Catholic social reform; *The Catholic Social Year Book*, an annual publication of the Catholic Social Guild in England (1910 sqq.). *La Civiltà Cattolica* (1850 sqq.) publishes regularly current papal decrees, bulls, encyclicals, etc., both in the original Latin and in Italian; English translations of the more important papal documents appear in *Rome*, a weekly journal established in 1906. On the Anglican Church and the Oxford Movement: F. W. Cornish, *A History of the Church of England in the Nineteenth Century*, 2 Parts (1910), the chief work; R. W. Church, *Oxford Movement: Twelve Years, 1833–1845* (1900); John Stoughton, *Religion in England from 1800 to 1850*, 2 vols. (1884); Wilfrid Ward, *William George Ward and the Catholic Revival* (1893), and, by the same author, *The Life of John Henry, Cardinal Newman, based on his private journals and correspondence*, 2 vols. (1912); J. H. (Cardinal) Newman,

Apologia pro Vita Sua (1864, frequently reprinted). See, also, for the general effects of Darwinism on Protestantism, A. C. McGiffert, *The Rise of Modern Religious Ideas* (1915), and, for the political and social setting of modern Protestantism, the two books of William Cunningham, *Christianity and Social Questions* (1910) and *Christianity and Politics* (1915).

Marxian Socialism. An excellent introduction is J. G. Brooks, *The Social Unrest: Studies in Labor and Socialist Movements* (1913); another admirable survey of the rise and evolution of Socialism, with special reference to its political aspects, is S. P. Orth, *Socialism and Democracy in Europe* (1913). Expositions by Socialists: John Spargo, *Socialism: a Summary and Interpretation of Socialist Principles*, new rev. ed. (1909); J. R. Macdonald, *The Socialist Movement* (1911) in the " Home University Library "; W. E. Walling, *Socialism as it is: a Survey of the World-Wide Revolutionary Movement* (1912); Friedrich Engels, *Socialism: Utopian and Scientific*, Eng. trans. by Edward Aveling, 3d ed. (1911); John Spargo, *Karl Marx, his Life and Work* (1910), the best biography of Marx; Karl Kautsky, *Social Democracy and the Catholic Church*, Eng. trans. (1906); Robert Hunter, *Socialists at Work* (1908). Documents and source material relating to Socialism: the *Communist Manifesto* of Marx and Engels, procurable in many cheap editions; Karl Marx, *Capital: a Critique of Political Economy*, Eng. trans., 3 vols. (1906–1909), an elaborate attempt to provide a basis in economics for Marxian Socialism; Gabriel Deville, *The People's Marx, a Popular Epitome of Karl Marx's Capital*, Eng. trans. by R. R. La Monte (1900); R. C. K. Ensor, *Modern Socialism, as set forth by Socialists in their Speeches, Writings, and Programmes*, 3d ed. (1910), an indispensable source-book; Jane T. Stoddart, *The New Socialism, an Impartial Inquiry* (1909), largely a source-book; *Fabian Tracts*, published by the English Fabian Society (1884 *sqq.*); *The Socialist Year Book and Labour Annual: a Guide Book to the Socialist and Labour Movement at Home and Abroad*, pub. by the National Labour League in Manchester (1913 *sqq.*). Expositions of Socialism by opponents: Albert Schäffle, *The Quintessence of Socialism*, trans. from 8th German ed. by Bernard Bosanquet (1880); Paul Leroy-Beaulieu, *Collectivism*, abridged trans. by Sir Arthur Clay (1908); W. H. Mallock, *A Critical Examination of Socialism* (1907); John Rae, *Contemporary Socialism*, 4th ed. (1908); V. G. Simkhovitch, *Marxism versus Socialism* (1913); Yves Guyot, *Where and Why Public Ownership Has Failed* (1914); R. T. Ely, *Socialism: an Examination of its Nature, its Strength and its Weakness, with Suggestions for Social Reform* (1894); Victor Cathrein, *Socialism, its Theoretical Basis and Practical Application*, trans. ed. by V. F. Gettelmann (1904), a scholarly criticism from the Roman Catholic standpoint; Benedetto Croce, *Historical Materialism and the Economics of Karl Marx*, Eng. trans. by C. M. Meredith (1914); H. O. Arnold-Forster, *English Socialism of Today*, 2d ed. (1908); T. G. Masaryk, *Die philosophischen und sociologischen Grundlagen des Marxismus: Studien zur socialen Frage* (1899); Alfred Fouillée, *Le socialisme et la sociologie réformiste* (1909). There is an important biography of *Lassalle*, the father of the Social Democratic party in Germany, by Hermann Oncken, 2d ed. (1912). For additional titles consult Josef Stammhammer, *Bibliographie des Socialismus und Communismus*, 3 vols. (1893–1909).

Trade-Unionism and the Coöperative Movement. Sidney and Beatrice Webb, *The History of Trade Unionism*, new ed. (1911), a full and scholarly treatment of the movement in England, and, by the same authors, *Industrial Democracy*, 2 vols. in 1 (1902), a detailed analysis of aims and methods; Catherine Webb, *Industrial Coöperation*, 3d ed. (1907), an elementary account of the coöperative movement in the United Kingdom; L. T. Hobhouse, *The Labour Movement*, 3d ed. (1912); G. J. Holyoake, *The History of Coöperation in England: its Literature and its Advocates*, rev. ed., 2 vols. (1906); C. R. Fay, *Coöperation at Home and Abroad: a Description and Analysis* (1908); Aneurin Williams, *Co-Partnership and Profit-Sharing* (1913) in "Home University Library"; Henry George, *Progress and Poverty*, new ed. (1912), Introduction and Books I and II, a famous attack on the doctrines of the classical economists.

Anarchism and Syndicalism. E. V. Zenker, *Anarchism: a Criticism and History of the Anarchist Theory*, Eng. trans. (1898); Paul Eltzbacher, *Anarchism*, Eng. trans. by S. T. Byington (1908), illuminating extracts from the writings of seven prominent Anarchists; J. H. Harley, *Syndicalism* (1912), a clear, brief statement; Philip Snowden, *Socialism and Syndicalism* (1913); Robert Hunter, *Violence and the Labor Movement* (1914); Louis Levine, *The Labor Movement in France* (1912); Paul Louis, *Histoire du mouvement syndical en France, 1789–1910*, 2d ed. (1911), and, by the same author, *Le syndicalisme européen* (1914); Dufour, *Le syndicalisme et la prochaine révolution* (1913).

ENGLAND AND WALES
IN THE NINETEENTH CENTURY

ENGLISH MILES

0   50   100

CHAPTER XXII

THE UNITED KINGDOM OF GREAT BRITAIN AND IRELAND, 1867-1914

THE gradual completion of political democracy, its application to meet social needs, and its entanglement with nationalist and imperialist sentiments,— this is in brief the history of the United Kingdom since 1867. Less courageous than France in experimenting with democratic institutions, less precipitate than Germany in venturing social legislation, but more successful in colonial expansion, the United Kingdom exemplifies more perfectly than either France or Germany the influence of the Industrial Revolution upon politics; for of that revolution England was the birthplace and is the result. The more advanced development of British industries gave to the British bourgeoisie greater wealth, power, and independence than was enjoyed by their Continental compeers. To that superiority the British middle classes owed their ability on the one hand to gain political power for themselves by the "bloodless revolution" of 1832, and on the other hand to resist the demand of the masses for complete democracy. Throughout the first thirty years of the long reign of Queen Victoria (1837–1901), the middle classes maintained their ungenerous opposition to thorough democratic reform and at the same time gave tacit support to the retention of the obsolete feudal nobility and House of Peers — into which many of them had purchased their way. This denial of democracy they had the effrontery to excuse and even to glorify, saying that "British Common Sense" wisely preferred peaceful political evolution to the terrors and turmoil of revolution. Content with their compromise between radicalism and conservatism, the middle classes of mid-century England gave every intimation of their belief that with their own exaltation the evolutionary process had reached its climax.

The "Victorian Compromise"

All the while, the lower classes, forced down by the factory system into a mire of misery, vice, poverty, and despair, were crying
aloud for justice.   And little by little, morsel by morsel, justice
they have obtained, first in political, then in economic, affairs.
This story of the political and social reforms in England now
engages our attention.

POLITICAL REFORM

The beginning of political democracy in Great Britain is usually
dated from the early part of the nineteenth century, when, as we
The Legacy have noticed in an earlier chapter,[1] Dissenters and
of Chartism Roman Catholics were accorded political rights
(1828–1829), and the middle classes gained representation in
Parliament (1832).   Between the Parliamentary Reform of
1832 and the second Reform Act, thirty-five weary years elapsed.
Midway between the two reforms occurred the tragedy of 1848,
when that popular petition which anticipated many political
achievements of the next half century — the "People's Charter"
— was rejected, and Chartism disgraced.   Nevertheless, there
persisted among the masses, even after the passionate faith in
Chartism had disappeared, a profound discontent.

To trade-unionism the more intelligent members of the discontented working class looked for the relief which Chartism
Trade   had failed to bring.   Believing that by united action
Unions and   they could force employers to concede them fair wages,
Democracy   workingmen everywhere organized themselves into
trade unions.   When it came to enforcing their demands, however, the unionists could only go on strike, or resort to violence.
Either course was practically prohibited by law.   Obviously the
law must be changed.   If the Parliament of shopkeepers and
squires would not make this alteration in the law, the workingmen must needs themselves obtain control of Parliament.   In this
fashion the trade-union movement, after ignoring political
methods for a time, returned again to the old plea of the People's
Charter for more democracy.   And the democratic demand, now
backed by a powerful and extended trade-union organization,
was not lightly to be dismissed.

[1] See above, pp. 102–116.

During the three decades which had elapsed since the Reform of 1832, the Liberals had been in power most of the time and had shown no disposition to make any changes in an electoral system which preserved their predominance; while the Conservatives still retained that distaste for democratic innovation which had moved the old Tories to oppose the Reform of 1832. Two great statesmen, however, — one a Liberal and the other a Conservative, — saw clearly that without some voice in the government, the working classes would never be content, and that to the party which could put itself at the head of the reform movement, the people would give grateful support. Upon this point, if upon no other, Gladstone and Disraeli were agreed, and each endeavored to make his own faction the party of Reform, — moderate Reform, — thus earning for the present the support of the popular democratic movement, and for the future, undying glory.

Attitude of Major Political Parties toward Parliamentary Reform, 1832–1867

William Ewart Gladstone had long delayed to espouse the cause of democracy. As a youth he had been well educated at Eton and at Oxford, and even been allowed a trip to Italy by his father, a Liverpool merchant-prince, who, having himself acquired sufficient wealth, wished his son to win distinction and social position as a statesman. For such a career the youth was eminently fitted : his diligence, his sterling uprightness of character, and his remarkable oratorical powers were popularly commended. Best of all, he showed no tendency toward radical political doctrines; in a college oration he so eloquently condemned the Reform Bill of 1832 that the Tory duke of Newcastle had him elected to Parliament from the "pocket borough" of Newark. In Parliament Gladstone speedily attracted attention as a young Conservative of great promise, but, by supporting Sir Robert Peel in the repeal of the Corn Laws (1846), he estranged himself from the main body of his party. Fortunately for his future political career, Gladstone chanced in 1850 to visit the Italian kingdom of the Two Sicilies, just then in the throes of reaction, and was so shocked by that example of royal absolutism that he was at least partially converted to moderate democratic principles, and inclined toward Liberalism. His change of heart did not immediately become

Gladstone, 1809–1898

evident, however, for upon his return to England he still allowed himself to be counted one of the Peelites, as the free-trade faction of the Conservative party was called. When in 1852 the Peelites united with the Liberals to form a coalition ministry, it was still as a Peelite that Gladstone accepted the office of Chancellor of the Exchequer. Only in 1859 did he finally affiliate with the Liberals, accepting from the Liberal premier, Lord Palmerston, the office of Chancellor of the Exchequer, which he held for the ensuing seven years.

During these years Gladstone made himself famous, not indeed as a Parliamentary Reformer, but as a financier. The free-trade movement, it will be remembered, had swept away the protective duty on grain and had opened other breaches in the tariff wall; in 1860 a further step was taken when France and Great Britain made reciprocal reductions; but all these changes cut down the revenue from customs duties and made imperative a readjustment of governmental finance. To Gladstone fell the task of reorganizing the national budget on a basis of free trade. He approached the problem with rare enthusiasm. The Commons sat enthralled as he expounded his schemes, infusing a passionate eloquence into the very figures he quoted. In a series of remarkable budgets he shifted the burden of taxation to income-, inheritance-, and liquor-taxes, and swept away the import duties on hundreds of articles. Before his first budget (1853) there had been 466 dutiable articles; after his budget of 1860 there were only 48. He did away with duties on soap, paper, and other manufactures; the tariff on foodstuffs completely disappeared. Business throve under the free-trade régime, prosperity increased by leaps and bounds; and every man who bought a cheaper newspaper, or ate cheaper food, or drank cheaper tea had William Ewart Gladstone to thank. His free-trade budgets were Gladstone's greatest work; they secured him an enduring reputation for statesmanship; and they won him the friendship of the middle and even of the lower classes.

Gladstone's Free Trade Budgets

All this time Gladstone had controlled the zeal he presumably felt for Parliamentary Reform, out of deference to the premier, Lord Palmerston, who was notoriously opposed to any extension of the electorate. But Lord Palmerston died in 1865, and the

Liberal party, having for over thirty years repelled the idea of further Reform, came under the control of Gladstone *Death of* and Lord John Russell, now Earl Russell.   At last *Lord* *Palmerston,* Gladstone stepped forward as the champion of Re- *1865* form, and urged working-class Radicals to support the Liberal party.

Already a rival bid for popularity had been offered by Benjamin Disraeli,[1] acting on the part of the Conservatives.   Benjamin Disraeli was as much the antithesis of Glad- *Benjamin* stone in character, as the antagonist of Gladstone in *Disraeli,* politics.   Against the somber background of Glad- *1804–1881* stone's middle-class conventionality, Disraeli's bizarre personality stands out in bright relief.   As the son of an apostate Jew, he was regarded askance by British society; as the cleverest man in England, he delighted to make sport of society's stupid conventions.   London hardly knew what to think of a young man who appeared at dinner parties arrayed in green velvet trousers, a canary-colored waistcoat, low shoes, silver buckles, lace dangling at his wrists, and his hair falling in ringlets.   While in conversation he was undeniably brilliant, sober-minded matrons were bewildered by his scintillating wit and baffled by his exasperating paradoxes.   When first he addressed the House of Commons, his outlandish appearance and affected language provoked derision, but unabashed he promised that one day his words would command attention.   Novels he wrote, courageous as they were clever: in *Coningsby* he outraged the fashionable complacency with which the upper classes regarded the reform of 1832, by asserting that the liberties of the crown and of the people had been stolen by an oligarchy; in *Sybil* he confronted the smug self-satisfaction of the Victorian age with the assertion that a greedy landed aristocracy was neglecting a miserable peasantry, while the industrial bourgeoisie was using the fallacious *laisser-faire* theory to excuse its heartless exploitation of factory labor.

Upon the policy of his party, Disraeli's ideas made a deep and lasting impression.   Of late the Tories, or, as they were now called, the Conservatives, had gained an unenviable reputation for resisting all progress.   Mere opposition to change was not Disraeli's conception of Conservatism.   He would, it is true,

---

[1] He was created earl of Beaconsfield in 1876.

loyally conserve the venerable institutions of royalty, Established Church, and aristocracy. At the same time he would have the Conservatives offer a positive program. (1) Following the tradition of Tory Radicals, such as Shaftesbury, they could pass laws to improve factory conditions and adopt a benevolent attitude toward the lower classes. From such a course the Conservatives would not be restrained by *laisser-faire* theories, as were the Liberals; nor would they suffer personal loss from it, as would the Liberal factory-owners. (2) Secondly, the Liberals, ever fearful lest business should be interrupted by war, and compelled to be cautious about incurring military expenditure while they were reducing the tariff, had pursued so inglorious a foreign policy, that the county would rally with patriotic enthusiasm to Conservatism, if certain that Conservatives would make Great Britain both respected and feared by other nations. (3) Finally, Disraeli proposed that instead of weakly consenting to parliamentary reforms after they had been made, the Conservative party should boldly declare itself in favor of a reasonable extension of the franchise, thus taking the wind out of the Liberal sails, and at the same time giving proof that Conservatism was the true champion of the people. Disraeli had actually proposed a moderate Reform Bill in 1859; its failure was a matter of course, but its purpose was to familiarize his followers with the idea that Reform and Conservatism were not contradictory terms.

Disraeli and Constructive Conservatism

It was now a question which of the two great parties would take under its protection the popular movement for a democratic franchise. Just as the question was becoming acute, the American Civil War (1861–1865) occurred, and the interruption of the cotton supply from the Southern States threatened to throw thousands of English cotton operatives out of work. Working-class agitation increased, and the workingmen, who openly sympathized with the struggle of the democratic North against the landed and slaveholding aristocracy of the South, were not likely to support the party of the landed aristocracy in England — the Conservative party. Nor were they, on the other hand, wholly pleased with the Liberal party, for Gladstone and other members of the government seemed to favor the South.

Influence of the American Civil War

In this juncture the man who best expressed the sentiments of the industrial classes was John Bright, a warm partisan of the Northern States, and an active advocate of Parlia- John mentary Reform. John Bright was not himself a Bright, workingman, but a member of the middle class, whose 1811-1889 father owned a cotton mill in Lancashire. From the time when he first learned to speak in public — at a meeting of the local Juvenile Temperance Society — to his death, John Bright never allowed his talent for public-speaking to grow rusty; he employed his eloquence in the service of whatever seemed to him a worthy cause, whether it was the abolition of capital punishment, of church rates (Bright was a Quaker), of flogging in the army, or the disestablishment of the Anglican Church in Ireland, or the admission of Jews to Parliament, or preventing the restriction of the hours of labor in factories. His passionate oratory had resounded all over the island during the Anti-Corn-Law agitation of the 'forties and made him one of the most popular men in England. So it was that when John Bright threw himself heart and soul into the campaign for Parliamentary Reform, addressing monster mass-meetings in the great cities, his name and his eloquence took the popular democratic party by storm. It so happened that as a Non-Conformist John Bright was opposed to Disraeli's defense of the Established Church; as a factory-owner he resented Disraeli's criticism of the industrial system; as a Quaker he abhorred Disraeli's "jingoism." To Gladstone, on the other hand, John Bright was drawn by the fact that both were middle-class Free Traders. With Gladstone, then, John Bright and his popular following affiliated.

Upon the death of Lord Palmerston in 1865, Gladstone became the leading spirit in the Liberal party, although the aged Earl Russell, father of the first Reform Bill, headed the Failure of ministry. Reform was made the issue of the hour, the Liberal and Gladstone brought in a bill extending the franchise Reform Bill, to £14 householders in counties and £7 householders 1866 in boroughs. The measure was hardly radical enough to please John Bright's artisan supporters; and it was too democratic for the taste of a group of old-fashioned Liberals in Parliament, who promptly combined with the Conservatives to overthrow the ministry (1866). Shortly afterwards Earl Russell retired from political life and Gladstone became the acknowledged leader of the Liberal party (1867).

Little excitement had been aroused by the introduction of Gladstone's very moderate Reform Bill; when that measure was **Popular** rejected, however, and a Conservative cabinet formed, **Demonstra-** a wave of indignation swept over the country at this **tions and** seeming defeat of Reform. John Bright, with cus- **the Conser-** **vative Re-** tomary heat, persuaded the populace of the great **form Bill** cities that the installation of a Conservative ministry was a declaration of war against the working classes. The trade unions resolved to compel the government to yield, and trade-union officials openly took part in organizing a National Reform League. When the cabinet locked the gates of Hyde Park (London) to prevent the League from holding a mass-meeting there, an immense mob defiantly threw down the railings. Demonstrations in favor of universal manhood suffrage stirred the working classes in all the important industrial centers. Whether they would or no, the Conservative ministers must deal with Parliamentary Reform. In this crisis the premier, Lord Derby, allowed Disraeli, who was the real leader of the party, to present a Reform Bill, even though some of the less progressive ministers angrily withdrew from the cabinet. For the bill as first presented Disraeli could not obtain a majority in the House of Commons. Then he executed an astonishing political maneuver. Rather than allow Gladstone to gain the credit of accomplishing what the people demanded, Disraeli calmly permitted his bill to be amended until it became more democratic than even Gladstone's Bill of 1866. It was, as the premier said, "taking a leap in the dark"; faint-hearted Conservatives grew pale at its sweeping provisions; but it was Disraeli's supreme effort to win the masses to Conservatism.

As enacted into law, the measure contained the following provisions: (1) Fifty-eight seats in the House of Commons were **Provisions** transferred from smaller boroughs to more populous **of the Re-** districts. (2) The franchise in the counties was con- **form Act of** ferred on tenants-at-will of property worth £12 a year **1867** (formerly £50), and to lease- or copy-holders of land worth £5 a year (formerly £10). (3) In the boroughs, whereas before 1867 a man could vote if his residence was worth £10 annual rent, henceforth the franchise was extended to all men who occupied separate dwellings, of no matter what value; and even to those lodgers in tenement-houses, who had rented for one year rooms worth £10 annually, unfurnished. Suffrage was still regarded as the privilege of a minority rather than the right of all; there were still only two and one half million voters out of a population of almost thirty-two millions; and great inequality still disfigured the representative system. The Reform of 1867 was, nevertheless, the turning-point in British constitutional history. It almost doubled the electorate by creating a million new voters,[1] mostly drawn from the working classes in the cities. How these new electors would use their power no one could tell; but every one knew that the middle-class compromise of 1832 had at last been abandoned, and that Great Britain was definitely committed to a policy of "More Democracy."

If Disraeli expected that his Reform of 1867 would win the popular party away from Gladstone and Bright, he sadly miscalculated. In the very next election (1868) these two orators contrived to defeat Disraeli by making the contest turn upon the Irish question, which was just then particularly pressing. After that election the middle-class Liberals continued to coöperate with

Further Reform by the Liberals: the Ballot Act, 1872

their more radical working-class allies, and further democratic reforms were accomplished under Liberal auspices. In 1872 Gladstone was responsible for the Ballot Act, a measure long demanded by working-class Radicals. Heretofore electors had signified orally which candidate they preferred, so that a landlord might easily, and often did, discover and punish those of his tenants who voted contrary to his wishes; or a political "boss," having bribed an elector, could see that the vote was actually cast as stipulated. With the Australian[2] ballot, which was introduced into all British municipal and Parliamentary elections in 1872, the elector marked the name of his candidate secretly on a slip of paper, and, theoretically at least, no other person could discover which name he marked. The voter was henceforth far

---

[1] These figures are for the entire United Kingdom. The Act of 1867 applied only to England and Wales; but in 1868 almost identical measures were enacted for Scotland and Ireland.

[2] So called because it had previously been invented and adopted by the British colonists in Australia.

less likely to be bribed and far more independent in casting his ballot for whomsoever he chose.

After the Reform of 1867, the agricultural laborers loudly complained that in the counties electoral qualifications were more exclusive than in the boroughs. To remove this injustice, Gladstone in 1884 put through a Representa-
tion of the People Act, which, by making the county franchise identical with that of the boroughs, enfran-
chised two millions of rural workers and increased the electorate by 40 per cent. The great majority of men over 21 years of age were henceforth qualified to vote, either (1) as owners or tenants of land or rooms worth £10 a year, or (2) as owners or tenants of a dwelling house, or part of a house used as a separate dwelling, no matter of what value, or (3) in counties, as owners of land worth forty shillings a year, or (4) as graduates of a university, for three universities send two members each to Parliament, or (5) under some other of the many qualifications surviving from earlier times. In 1913 there were some eight million electors out of about ten million adult males, and out of a total population of more than forty-five millions. The franchise is still far from democratic. The ballot is not yet every man's right, or any woman's right, and about half a million men, possessing qualifications in several constituencies, are entitled to cast two, three, or even as many as twenty, votes apiece. Moreover, the laws regarding the franchise are so complicated that endless confusion and litigation are inevitable.

What the law of 1884 did for the franchise was done for the representation by the Redistribution of Seats Bill passed in 1885. The existing system, with its obvious inequalities of representation, had grown up by a haphazard process of giving to this or that borough and to every county, irrespective of its population, two seats in the House of Commons. The law of 1885 attempted to introduce a little rational order into the represen-
tation by dividing the country into constituencies so that, roughly speaking, each member of the Commons would represent 50,000 people. The county of Lancashire, for instance, which had been divided into four two-member districts, was subdivided to form twenty-three constituencies of one member each. The principle was by no means thoroughly applied, however,

Gladstone and the Reforms of 1884 and 1885

and, as no redistribution has been made since 1885, Ireland in 1914 had thirty-eight seats which should belong to England, and other glaring inequalities were demanding attention.

Political democracy, then, is not yet completely realized in the United Kingdom; but so far as it has gone the progress of democratic reform has in a striking manner conformed to the Six Points of the Chartists. (1) Universal (adult male) suffrage was substantially, although not perfectly, achieved in 1884. (2) The principle of equal electoral districts was recognized, if not completely carried out, in 1885. (3) The secret ballot was obtained in 1872. (4) Parliaments are not yet elected annually, as the Chartists demanded, but, by a law of 1911, the maximum life of a single Parliament has been shortened from seven to five years. (5) The abolition of the property qualification for members of the House of Commons was accomplished in 1858. (6) Finally, salaries (of £400 a year) for members of Parliament have been appropriated since 1911. However incompletely realized, these reforms, as the Chartists anticipated, have enabled the working-men to enter politics, to elect working-class representatives, and to insist that the government shall attempt to cope with the problems of modern industrialism.

Partial Fulfillment of the " Six Points " of the Chartists

While successive reform measures were converting the House of Commons into a more or less democratic body, the other half of Parliament remained thoroughly aristocratic, quite impervious to popular influences. From the passing of the first Reform Bill on through the nineteenth century, as time and again the will of the House of Commons was checkmated, it became increasingly clear that the House of Lords must be "mended or ended."

Aristocratic Nature of the House of Lords

What most offended believers in democracy was the fact that the upper chamber was frankly and avowedly the organ of the titled aristocracy. The great majority of its members [1] were noblemen, — dukes, marquesses, earls, viscounts, and barons, —

[1] The membership of the House of Lords in 1914 totaled more than 600, and comprised (1) hereditary peers, (2) 16 elective Scottish peers, (3) 28 elective Irish peers, (4) 26 Anglican prelates, (5) princes of the blood, (6) 4 "law lords," ranking as barons, appointed for life by reason of their special juristic qualifications to exercise the judicial functions which the House of Lords possesses as supreme Court of Appeal.

most of whom sat in Parliament not because they were eminently
qualified, but because they had inherited the privilege as hereditary peers.   Too often the hereditary peers preferred the pleas-
ures of their country estates to the dull routine of Parliamentary
business, and left the burdens of legislation to a handful of the
more conscientious.   Then when they did appear to vote on some
measure in which they felt a personal interest, their unfamiliarity
with Parliamentary procedure and their unfitness as legislators was
often patent.   A few of the peers — 16 elected by the Scottish
nobility and 28 by the Irish nobility — might be expected to show
more political ability than the hereditary peers, but they were no
less opposed to democratic interests.   This, then, was the great
objection to the House of Lords, that it was composed of titled
aristocrats, many of whom were unfit for their duty, and dominated by their class interests as members of the landed aristocracy.

A second objection to the House of Lords was felt most keenly
by Non-Conformists.   It was held to be manifestly unfair that
The Anglican Bishops
the Anglican Church should be represented by the
archbishop of Canterbury and 25 other bishops,
whereas the other religious denominations possessed
no official representation.   This injustice became especially
grievous when the Anglican bishops habitually used their position
in Parliament to maintain the privileges, church-rates, and educational institutions of the Established Church to the disadvantage
of the Non-Conformists.

To these two grievances was added a third and more powerful
consideration.   The House of Lords was distinctly a partisan
Partisan Character of the House of Lords
assembly opposed to Liberalism.   While the Conservatives were in power, harmony existed between the two
chambers, but when the Liberals controlled the House
of Commons, the House of Lords simply afforded the
Conservatives a veto on Liberal legislation.   The
House of Lords had opposed the Reform Bill of 1832 and the
Municipal Corporation Reform of 1835; it had thrown itself
in the way when the Liberals had sought to grant Home Rule to
Ireland, to disestablish the Anglican Church in Ireland, or to
regulate the liquor traffic.[1]   The situation became intolerable

---

[1] All this was the Liberal contention.   On the other hand, the Conservatives
insisted that the House of Lords performed a highly valuable service in blocking

when the Lords, after obstructing important measures of the Liberal ministry, had the temerity in 1909 to throw out the Finance Bill passed by the House of Commons and popularly known as the Lloyd George Budget, thus contravening a long established usage which bound the Upper House to give perfunctory assent to finance bills as prepared by the Commons. The Liberal premier, Mr. Asquith, backed by an angry Liberal majority in the House of Commons, declared the action of the Lords to be "a breach of the Constitution," appealed to the electorate, and, being returned to office, proceeded to frame a bill to restrict the veto power of the House of Lords.

Realizing that something must be done to satisfy democratic demands, the Conservatives (or Unionists, as they now were called) proposed an alternative measure which would leave finance bills to the Commons and would settle other disputed questions by joint sessions of the two Houses or by referendum to the country. Another election was held in order that the electorate might choose between the two plans. The Liberals again being returned with a working majority pressed forward their bill, and the Lords were forced to assent, as in 1832, by Mr. Asquith's threat to have the king create, if necessary, enough Liberal peers to pass the Bill. On 18 August, 1911, the famous Parliament Act became law. By that Act,[1] (1) Money bills passed by the Commons automatically would become law one month after being submitted to the House of Lords; (2) Other public bills might become law, despite repeated rejection by the Lords, if passed by the House of Commons in three successive sessions,[2] provided,

Curbing the Lords: the Parliament Act, 1911

proposed Liberal legislation and thereby obliging a Liberal ministry to appeal to the country; the House of Lords, they asserted, had never blocked measures which the voters of the country had unmistakably indorsed, and as special proof of their assertion they cited the instance in 1893 when the House of Lords had blocked Gladstone's second Home Rule Bill and in the ensuing general elections had been upheld by the country. It is certainly a tribute to the growth of the democratic spirit in the United Kingdom that the Liberal party should be attacking the House of Lords in the name of democracy and that at the same time the Conservative party should be defending the House of Lords as a bulwark of real democracy.

[1] The Parliament Act also limited the maximum duration of a Parliament to five years.

[2] If a bill is amended during this time, it is considered a new bill for the purpose of the Act.

however, that at least two years must elapse between the first consideration of such a Bill and its final enactment. The first provision of the Parliament Act confirmed the complete authority of the House of Commons in financial measures. The second provision left the Lords with only a suspensive veto in other matters. Even this suspensive veto may prove a serious obstruction to Liberal legislation, however, as the Asquith ministry discovered when it attempted under the provisions of the Parliament Act to pass a bill to abolish plural voting,[1] a bill to disestablish the Anglican Church in Wales, and a bill to confer Home Rule on Ireland. The last two measures were passed three times by the Commons, and thus enacted into law, but only after a long and embarrassing struggle. And the execution of both was delayed by the outbreak of the War of the Nations (August, 1914).

To the Unionists (Conservatives), the Parliament Act was extremely distasteful. Insisting that the House of Lords is a venerable part of the British Constitution, and is a

Future Reform of the House of Lords

wholesome check upon the impulses of an imprudent or an unrepresentative House of Commons, the Unionists still demand that the Upper Chamber shall retain its legislative powers. They are willing, however, that the House of Lords shall be made more efficient by reducing the number of hereditary peerages and by allowing the crown (the ministry, in effect) to bestow life peerages upon men distinguished in various walks of life. The Liberals, on the other hand, contemplate establishing the Upper Chamber "on a popular instead of an hereditary basis." [2] Many of the more radical politicians would go still further, and abolish the House of Lords altogether, as an unnecessary impediment to the fulfillment of the popular will, undemocratic in principle and unwarranted in practice.

THE GOVERNMENT OF THE UNITED KINGDOM

Here at the end of our story of political reforms in Great Britain, and before taking up the social reforms, we shall do well to pause

---

[1] The Plural Voting Bill was passed by the Commons in 1913 and again in 1914, but on both occasions was rejected by the Lords.

[2] Preamble to the Parliament Act, 1911.

a moment in contemplation of the British political system, as it exists to-day. To a citizen of the United States, the government of the United Kingdom is remarkable in three respects: (1) it is based on an ever evolving rather than a fixed and written constitution; (2) it is parliamentary rather than congressional; (3) it is central rather than federal. *Three Characteristics of the British Government*

The British Constitution is not a document but a miscellany. International treaties, Magna Carta (1215), the Petition of Right (1628), the Bill of Rights (1689), the Habeas Corpus Act (1679), the Municipal Corporations Act (1835), the various Reform Acts (1832, 1867, 1884), the Parliament Act (1911), and countless other statutes, *1. Evolutionary Character of the Constitution* together with the intangible body of legal precedents known as the Common Law, are no more important parts of the British Constitution than the set of traditional usages which are so many unwritten laws governing the conduct of king, ministry, and Parliament. New laws are never declared unconstitutional by the courts, for every bill dealing with Constitutional subjects — no matter how trifling or how momentous — becomes a part of the Constitution directly it is enacted into law, previous laws to the contrary notwithstanding. Because it is so easy to amend, the British Constitution is extremely flexible; it is never fixed, but ever-evolving.

As a result of this easy process of constitutional evolution, British institutions are historical rather than rational. Divine-right monarchy still survives in the title of the present monarch, "George V, by the Grace of God of the United Kingdom of Great Britain and Ireland and of *The Crown: a Relic of Absolutism* the British Dominions beyond the Seas King, Defender of the Faith, Emperor of India." [1] Theoretically the king still has most of the powers of an Henry VIII. Practically, however, the sovereign is only a polite gentleman, who graces public functions with his benign presence, entertains royal visitors, reads speeches (prepared by his ministers) at the opening and closing of Parliament, and occasionally even exerts some slight influence upon public

---

[1] George V, the eighth of the House of Hanover, succeeded Edward VII, his father, in 1910. George V is the grandson of Victoria, who reigned from 1837 to 1901. See below, p. 729.

affairs by talking with prominent politicians. But if in some mad moment George V should act like an absolute monarch, every one knows he would be deposed by Parliament, as was James II.

No less an anachronism is the House of Lords. France has deprived her feudal nobles of superior political privileges; but

The House of Lords: a Relic of Feudalism

Great Britain still allows her dukes and barons by hereditary right to sit in the Upper Chamber of Parliament as in the days of King Edward III. Here again, while the form has remained, the fact has changed. The peers are no longer warlike barons, each surrounded by his men-at-arms; they are gentlemen landlords, bankers, merchants, ex-brewers, captains of industry, who have been elevated to the peerage in return for services to the nation or monetary contributions to the party in power. Only a few, like the duke of Norfolk, trace their descent back of 1500.

While the king still remains the chief dignitary of the state, and the House of Lords still wields a two-year suspensive veto in legis-

Democracy: the House of Commons

lation in addition to exercising judicial functions as supreme court of appeal, the dominant force in the British polity is democracy, represented by the House of Commons. Even this body possesses an ancient pedigree,[1] descending without break from Simon de Montfort's assembly of knights and burgesses (1265). It has become, however, an essentially modern institution. The House of Commons consists of 670 representatives, elected by almost universal manhood suffrage — 495 from England and Wales, 72 from Scotland, 103 from Ireland, — sitting in Westminster Palace regularly from February to August each year to make the nation's laws. Clergymen,[2] government contractors, sheriffs, English and Scottish peers, and youths under 21 years of age are debarred from membership. Otherwise any registered elector is eligible for Parliament; and the salary of £400 a year enables poor men as well as rich to devote themselves to legislative labors.

With the number and qualifications of the voters who elect the House of Commons, we are already familiar. The manner of election, however, deserves our attention. When a general elec-

[1] See Vol. I, pp. 265 ff.
[2] Except of Protestant Non-Conformist Churches.

tion[1] is to be held, writs of election are sent out to the sheriffs of all Irish and Scotch constituencies, to the sheriffs of English counties, and to the mayors of English boroughs, **Electoral** who act as returning officers.   The returning officer in **Procedure** each constituency immediately designates an election day, which must not be more than nine days after the receipt of the writ, in the case of counties, or four days in the case of boroughs.   On election day there is no balloting, but nominations are then received for the first time, in writing, and each must be supported by nine registered electors.   Frequently, as for instance in the overwhelmingly Nationalist districts of Ireland, only one candidate is nominated for a seat, and he is at once declared to be elected without the expensive formality of polling.

Where an election is contested by rival candidates, however, the returning officer fixes a polling day in the boroughs not more than six and in the counties from two to six days after election day.   On polling day the real election takes place, when each elector presents himself at the polls, receives a ballot-paper on which the names of the candidates are printed, and enters a small booth, where unobserved he may mark a cross opposite the name of his choice.   The papers are deposited in a locked ballot-box, and counted at the end of the day in the presence of the returning officer,[2] who declares the election of the candidate with the largest number of votes.   It is important to notice that under this system election and polling take place on different days in different constituencies, so that for the entire country a general election may last two weeks, and a plural voter may, for example, vote in London on Monday, in Liverpool on Tuesday, and in Bristol on Thursday.[3]   Naturally, as the elections proceed, excitement increases until it is finally known whether or not the Opposition has overthrown the Ministry.   This brings us to the second remarkable feature of the British political system.

[1] Between general elections there are frequent "by-elections" in single constituencies to fill places vacated by death or retirement.   A member appointed to office in the ministry, moreover, usually resigns his seat and offers himself for reëlection.

[2] In university constituencies voting by word of mouth and by proxy still prevails.

[3] To prevent this was the design of the Plural Voting Bill passed by the Commons and rejected by the Lords in 1913 and in 1914.

In the United Kingdom, the ministry, or rather the cabinet, is dependent upon a majority in the House of Commons. This

2. The Parliamentary System: the Cabinet is the essence of parliamentary government, as contrasted with congressional government, where the administrative officials are appointed independently by the president, or the monarch, as the case may be. The term "ministry," be it understood, technically denotes the numerous hierarchy of administrative officials, of whom the "cabinet" includes only the more important heads of departments; in common speech, however, ministry and cabinet are interchangeable, since the cabinet both controls the policy and determines the personnel of the entire ministry. The cabinet system again illustrates the English habit of fitting new practices into the shells of decayed institutions. Before the law, cabinet officers are members of the large and now purely honorary Privy Council, whose function is "to advise the king"; in fact, the cabinet is a Parliamentary committee, selected from the party uppermost in the House of Commons, to direct legislation, determine policy, and administer the laws. Although the number of men in the cabinet is not rigidly fixed, it usually includes about a score of the most important officials of the realm : the first lord of the treasury, who is usually prime minister ; the lord president of the council ; the lord high chancellor ; the secretaries of state for foreign affairs, for India, for the home department, for the colonies, and for war ; the chancellor of the exchequer ; the first lord of the admiralty ; the chief secretary to the lord-lieutenant of Ireland ; the presidents of the board of trade, local government board, the board of education, and of the board of agriculture ; the secretary for Scotland ; the postmaster-general ; the first commissioner of works ; the attorney-general ; and the chancellor of the duchy of Lancaster. In practice every department of the administration is thus subjected to the cabinet.

The cabinet system combines efficiency with representative government. The former quality is assured by the fact that the cabinet controls both legislation and administration. It drafts most of the important measures — including the budget — which Parliament passes, and then superintends their execution. Harmony is maintained by frequent secret sessions, and by the leadership of the prime minister. The prime minister is, in-

deed, the ruler of the nation.   Powerful as it is, the ministry is
an instrument of democracy rather than of autocracy, because it
is responsible to the elective chamber of Parliament.
In the first place, the king, in appointing a prime   **Efficiency
and Re-**
minister, is bound by custom to select the recognized   **sponsibility
of the**
leader of the most numerous party; the prime minis-   **Cabinet**
ter, in turn, is expected to choose as subordinates the
prominent politicians in his own party.[1]   The cabinet, therefore,
represents the majority in the House of Commons.   Should the
ministry for any reason lose the support of the majority, an unwritten law compels the premier immediately to resign, and the
other ministers with him.   Thereupon the king seeks out a new
premier capable of commanding a Parliamentary majority.   Or,
if the defeated premier believes Parliament to be out of harmony
with the electorate, instead of resigning he may dissolve Parliament and call a general election.   In case the new House of
Commons is unfriendly, he inevitably resigns.   This power of the
ministry to call new elections at any time has occasionally been
used in order to make sure that the House of Commons represented the wishes of the people, before proceeding with some
weighty matter — as, for instance, just before the enactment of
the Parliament Act.   In 1913, again, the Unionists demanded a
general election before the Home Rule Bill should be passed,
claiming that the question of Irish Home Rule had not been the
dominant issue in the last election (December, 1910); the Liberal
Government, on the other hand, asserting that its victory in the
elections of 1910 at least implied popular approval of Home
Rule, refused the demand for a special election and allowed the
Parliament to live out its full legal term of five years.[2]

Before we leave the subject of Parliament, it may be well to
insert a word about the way in which bills [3] are actually handled.

[1] Under the abnormal conditions prevailing after the outbreak of the War of
the Nations, party lines were partly obliterated, and in May, 1915, several
Unionist leaders were brought into Mr. Asquith's cabinet. In this "coalition
cabinet" places were created for a "minister of munitions" and a "minister
without portfolio."

[2] In fact, on account of the exigencies of war, the provision of the Parliament
Act respecting the five-year elections of members of the House of Commons was
suspended, and the duration of the Parliament elected in 1910 was prolonged.

[3] These very general remarks are subject to exceptions in the case of finance
bills and private bills.

Bills go through three readings in each House. The first reading is merely introductory. At the second reading general principles are debated. Next the bill is handed over to a committee for detailed consideration and possible amendment. After the committee has reported it back to the House, a vote is taken upon the third and final reading, which means the acceptance or rejection of the bill as a whole. Then the measure is considered by the other House of Parliament, and if both houses agree, it receives the perfunctory assent of the crown and thus passes into law.

The third respect in which the government of the United Kingdom [1] merits attention is its realization of the idea of central

3. Central and Local Government rather than of federal government. One might expect Scotland, Ireland, Wales, and England each to have its own Parliament, as each state in the United States has its own legislature. This, in fact, is what some politicians are demanding. But at present the Parliament at Westminster makes laws for the whole United Kingdom, as it has done ever since the unions with Scotland (1707) and Ireland (1801). In administration the divisions are somewhat separate, Ireland having its lord-lieutenant and local government board and both Ireland and Scotland having separate secretaries in the common cabinet. With this exception, the local government is substantially similar throughout Great Britain and Ireland, and is supervised by the five central authorities : [2] the home office (regulating factory-inspection and police), the board of trade (regulating commercial enterprises), the local government board (superintending charities, sanitation, finance), the board of education, and the board of agriculture. The old counties, with their military lord-lieutenants, their sheriffs, and their justices of the peace — all crown officers — have been largely superseded by new administrative units. The most important units are now (1) the administrative counties [3] and (2) county boroughs.[4] (1) The administrative counties have each their popularly elected county councils, supervising finance, bridges, roads, public

---

[1] We are here leaving the colonies out of consideration. See below, ch. xxix.

[2] Some of these boards are separate for Ireland and Scotland but under general cabinet control.

[3] There are 62 of these in England (and Wales).

[4] There are 74 county boroughs in England (and Wales).

buildings, asylums, industrial schools, education, and, to a limited degree, police. Each county has also its clerk, treasurer, chief constable, coroners, and educational officials. The county is subdivided into rural districts (each of which usually comprises several parishes), and urban districts or towns; both urban and rural districts have their subordinate elective councils to care for highways and sanitation. There are also chartered municipal boroughs within the counties, with governments similar to those of the larger county boroughs, but less autonomous. (2) The county boroughs are cities large enough (at least 50,000 inhabitants) in effect to become counties by themselves. Each such borough is a chartered municipal corporation, governed by an elective borough council. The borough council, comprising councilors, aldermen, and mayor, is one of the most significant features of British government, for it not only exercises the familiar sanitary, police, and educational functions, but frequently ventures on socialistic experiments, such as municipal ownership of tramways, gas-works, and electric-plants. (3) Finally, the position of London has always been unique. London is now an administrative county made up of twenty-eight metropolitan boroughs, besides a district which still calls itself the City — as indeed it was in the sixteenth century — and takes pride in its pompous lord mayor.

BRITISH POLITICAL PARTIES

While dwelling on the evolution of democratic political machinery in the United Kingdom, we have almost lost sight of the fact that each epochal alteration in the British constitution has been attended by significant transformation in the composition and ideals of the political parties. A brief review of the transmutation of British political parties in the nineteenth century may throw new light upon already familiar events, as well as upon the domestic situation in 1914.

Political Reform and Party Transformation

In the rivalries of Whigs and Tories, prior to the Reform of 1832, the masses had no part. Government was notoriously corrupt, absurdly unrepresentative, and hopelessly reactionary. The faction in power — the Tories — still reiterating their horror of revolution, censored the press, dispersed mass-meetings, and hanged popular agitators, — all in the name of the ancient

Whigs and Tories, and the Middle Classes

Crown, the Established Church, and the glorious Constitution.　While the miserable lower classes were helpless under the yoke, the prosperous middle classes asserted their rights and gained representation in Parliament.　The former Whig Opposition, — which had consisted of a few aristocratic families with a following of Non-Conformist tradesmen, — having identified itself with the Reform, received into its bosom the grateful factory-owners and shop-keepers who had benefited by the Reform; from the new recruits the old Whigs learned to call themselves Liberals, and to advocate bourgeois reforms.　A considerable number of the new electors, however, either from fear of further reform or from loyalty to the Established Church, were attracted to the Tory party, which had heretofore relied mainly upon the landed gentry, the clergy, and some of the old mercantile families.　These factory-owners were ill at ease, however, among the old Tories : under Sir Robert Peel they repudiated the Tory protective tariff, and subsequently, for the sake of free trade, many of them followed William Ewart Gladstone into the Liberal party.

From 1832 to 1867 was the era of the bourgeois compromise — the "Victorian Compromise" between democracy and oligarchy, whereby the bourgeois enjoyed political rights and left the lower classes to shift for themselves.　It was tacitly assumed that if a man was poor, it was due either to his own fault or to inexorable economic laws, — and in either case he was unfit to vote.　Against the compromise a few philosophical Radicals feebly protested, then lapsed into silence.

The second upheaval in the party system was caused by the rise of the working classes.　The Chartist agitation gave proof

Liberals and Conservatives, and the Working Classes

that the leaven of democratic doctrine was powerfully at work among the discontented masses.　The trade-union movement disclosed an astonishing spirit of self-help, independence, and class-conscious organization on the part of the workingmen.　Slowly the older parties realized that the workingmen were becoming a factor in politics.　Disraeli would have bound the lower classes to the ancient institutions of crown, church, and nobility by golden chains of patriotism, veneration, and gratitude: he would have had the Conservative party feel, as he himself did, quick sympathy with Chartism, and a desire to take immediate and practical steps for the benefit of the unhappy millions. When the sweeping electoral reform of 1867 was sponsored by a Conservative cabinet, it seemed as if the Conservatives were becoming the democratic party.

Disraeli's move was counteracted by Gladstone, the Liberal free trader, and Bright, the Radical orator, who persuaded democratic audiences that the Conservatives were landed aristocrats and Disraeli an insincere charlatan. The election of 1868 established Gladstone and Bright in power for the six years 1868–1874. It also swamped the older aristocratic Whiggish element of the Liberal party in a sea of working-class votes. Gladstone, as a Liverpool merchant's son, and Bright, as a Lancashire factory-owner, naturally avoided factory legislation, and by attacking privilege — the privilege of the landed aristocracy and of the Anglican clergy in Ireland, — by introducing the ballot, by extending the franchise, by promoting popular elementary education, by shouting "peace, retrenchment, and reform," made the workingmen forget low wages and long hours.

In 1874, however, Disraeli came into power as the champion of vigorous foreign policy and of social reform. He gave the city artisans better dwellings; he safeguarded the savings of the poor against wild-cat insurance companies; he enabled tenant-farmers to claim compensation for improvements when resigning their holdings. Unfortunately Disraeli's attention was devoted more to securing glory abroad than to insuring contentment at home. His acquisition of a controlling financial interest in the Suez Canal (1875) was an unmixed advantage; but his intervention in the Balkan peninsula and support of the Ottoman Empire against Russian aggrandizement (1877–1878) [1] were censured by Gladstonian Liberals. At the same time the appearance of an Irish Home Rule party still further embarrassed the Conservative ministry.

The election of 1880 returned Gladstone to power. Gladstone's administration, however, proved to be more peaceful than Disraeli's, and certainly was less glorious. The Irish Home

[1] See below, pp. 505 f.

Rule party, far from being mollified by Gladstone's incomplete concessions, combined with the Conservative Opposition. Then it was that Gladstone, in order to win the support of the Home Rule faction, which he needed in order to obtain a majority, reversed his former Irish policy and consented to support Irish Home Rule (1886).

Gladstone's sudden change of front on the Irish question threw the Liberals into dire confusion. For twenty years he had dominated the party, but his convincing eloquence was failing, and his followers discontented. The Whiggish Liberals resented his democratic reforms. The Radical Liberals, too, were unsatisfied, although for the opposite reason. The tendency to a split was only too obvious: only the energy of a forceful personality was needed to effect the complete disruption of the Liberal party.

Such a personality was that of Joseph Chamberlain (1836–1914). As Gladstone represented the old-fashioned *laisser-faire* bourgeoisie, so Joseph Chamberlain stood for the younger generation, the most progressive element of the capitalist class. While yet a young man, he became well known as one of the most energetic and successful manufacturers in Birmingham, distinguished for political views more radical than those of the ordinary Liberal. Restless energy carried young Chamberlain from business into local politics, and won him immediate recognition. In 1874 he was elected mayor of Birmingham. After cleaning up the city slums, and establishing municipal ownership of gas and water supply, Chamberlain entered national politics and secured a seat in Parliament (1876). The more radical Liberals speedily acknowledged him as their chief, and subscribed to his doctrines of free education, small holdings, graduated taxes, and the development of local government. For a time Chamberlain submitted to Gladstone's leadership, but his patience must have been sorely tried by Gladstone's old-fashioned oratory, antiquated politics, and neglect of social reform.

When Gladstone took up Irish Home Rule, to which Chamberlain was unalterably opposed, Chamberlain openly rebelled, and John Bright with the rest of the radical Liberals followed him. The seceding Liberals, with Chamberlain as their leader, for a time constituted an independent group, adopting the name

Joseph Chamberlain and the Liberal Unionists

Liberal Unionists, to advertise their refusal to dissolve the legislative Union of Ireland and Great Britain. As Gladstone, now more dependent than ever upon Irish votes, continued to make Irish Home Rule the main feature of Gladstonian Liberalism, the Liberal Unionists began to discover that in loyalty to the Union, in patriotism, and occasionally even in social reform, they could coöperate with the Conservatives. In 1895 Chamberlain finally allied himself with the Conservative leader, the marquess of Salisbury, and the coalition thus formed was able to control the government for the next ten years. By virtue of its predominant purpose — the preservation of the Union — the coalition was usually called the Unionist party. Despite the fact that Chamberlain was a Unitarian Non-Conformist, the Unionists in general preserved the traditional Conservative respect for the Established Church and the House of Lords. On the other hand, Chamberlain and his followers contributed an enthusiasm for progressive social reform. In this respect the influence of Joseph Chamberlain in the 'nineties strikingly resembled the influence of Benjamin Disraeli in the 'sixties.

Coalition of the Liberal Unionists and Conservatives (1895): the Unionist Party

In respect of its membership, the Unionist party was now more comprehensive than the old Conservative party. In addition to the nobility, clergy, and gentry, the Unionists controlled the bulk of the lawyers and of the university graduates, and the majority of prominent merchants, manufacturers, and financiers in the great cities, — for it must be remembered that Joseph Chamberlain was himself a university man and a manufacturer. Many clerks, tradesmen, and shopkeepers, and even a considerable section of the lower classes followed their employers in adopting Unionist principles.

The great appeal of Unionism to the patriotic ardor of the masses no doubt won the party many adherents, but at the same time weakened it internally. Joseph Chamberlain, while colonial secretary (1895–1903), became intensely interested in building up the strength and unity of the British Empire. As he studied the problem, he became convinced that the Liberal policy of peace, small armaments, and loose relations between the colonies and mother-

Joseph Chamberlain and the Tariff

country was all wrong. The colonies should be closely federated to the United Kingdom, he believed, and should not only be induced to coöperate in the work of defending the empire, but should be bound to England by commercial ties. This he proposed to accomplish by establishing a system of imperial preference, whereby the United Kingdom would impose a customs tariff on imports — a low duty on foodstuffs, 10 per cent on manufactures, no duty on raw materials — except from her colonies, and the colonies would reciprocate by giving British manufactures a preference. Three purposes thereby would be served : (1) the preferential agreement would cement the empire ; (2) the tariff protection would stimulate British industry and allow British employers to pay higher wages and still compete with foreign manufacturers; (3) the customs receipts would bring in revenue sufficient to enlarge the navy and to accomplish expensive social reforms such as old-age pensions. The propaganda was launched in 1903, when a Tariff Reform League was formed, and a lively campaign ensued. The Liberal-Unionist wing of the party acquiesced; but the Conservative wing, now almost as fondly attached to free trade as once it had been to protection, conceived a violent dislike for "taxes on food." The resulting lack of harmony between the two sections of the Unionist party enabled the Liberals to carry the election of 1906, and continued to embarrass the present Unionist leader, Mr. Andrew Bonar Law.

When it is remembered that in 1886 Joseph Chamberlain represented the radical wing of Gladstone's party, his alliance **The Labor Party** with the Conservatives — still regarded as aristocrats — and his gradual subordination of social reform to imperialism, become all the more significant. Ever since the Reform of 1867 the organized labor vote had been a political factor of increasing importance, and had generally supported the progressive Liberals. By Joseph Chamberlain's defection, this labor vote was left completely stranded. Clearly there was opportunity for the trade unions to enter politics independently of the Liberal and Unionist parties. The first general trade-union Congress, held at London in 1899, convoked an assemblage of representatives of all working-class organizations which would be willing to coöperate in securing an adequate representation of labor interests in Parliament. This body met in the following year and formed a "Labor Representation Committee." The need for such action was felt all the more keenly by trade-unionists in 1901, when strikes were practically prohibited by a judicial decision of the House of Lords (The Taff Vale Railway Company *v.* the Amalgamated Society of Railway Servants), which rendered trade unions liable to suits for damages whenever their action (as in a strike) caused loss to other persons. Hot with wrath, the trade unions pressed forward with renewed vigor the plans of the Labor Representation Committee to establish a regular Labor party in Parliament, which would secure the enactment of laws favorable to trade unions, and to labor interests in general. The Fabian Society (an association pledged to educate the public in Socialism), the Social Democratic Federation (a small Socialist organization with strict Marxist principles), and the Independent Labor Party (a rival Socialist organization of workingmen, founded as early as 1893 by Mr. Keir Hardie, and already represented in Parliament) gave the Labor Representation Committee their whole-hearted support. At the election of 1906, the committee secured twenty-nine representatives in the House of Commons, who, together with eleven representatives of miners' associations, and fourteen other workmen (Liberal Laborites and Independent Laborites), gave the working classes 54 members of Parliament. The Labor party, as the organization is now called, represented in 1914 some 1,500,000 constituents, and controlled 40 seats in the House of Commons, under the leadership [1] of Mr. Ramsay Macdonald.

Meanwhile a remarkable change had come over the Liberal party. Dismayed by the Unionist secession (1886), discouraged by their inability to overcome the Lords' resistance to Gladstone's Irish Home Rule Bill (1893), and disheartened by the death of their veteran leader (1898), Gladstonian Liberals were forced for ten years (1895–1905) to sit on the opposition benches in gloomy meditation. While the Liberals were thus despondent, three influences were at work re-vitalizing their creed. In the first place, since the agricultural laborers had been enfranchised (1884), the land problem had begun to loom larger on the political horizon.

The Regeneration of the Liberal Party

---

[1] Mr. Keir Hardie, an ex-miner, led the Independent Labor Party (Socialist).

Great Britain, it will be remembered, had not swept away the
lingering power of feudal landlordism, as had the Revolutionary
1. Influence   France; and consequently instead of being, like the
of Henry   French, a nation of contented peasant-proprietors
George   (or small land-owners), rural England was still a
nation of grasping landlords and discontented laborers. Discussion of this agrarian problem had recently been stimulated by
the proposal of Henry George, an American reformer, that the
nation should impose a "single tax" on land-owners, with the
purpose of taxing the landlords out of existence and ultimately
establishing national ownership of the land. This nationalization of the land, explained Henry George in *Progress and Poverty*
(1879), would not only abolish the idle landlord, but would
powerfully work to increase the wages and independence of urban
workingmen. The theory, ably expounded, was eagerly taken
up by associations in Great Britain as well as in America. It
appealed with particular force to the middle-class Gladstonian
Liberals, who had always looked with disfavor upon the landed
aristocracy, and were now sorely tempted to try an experiment
which could in any case injure only the landlords and which promised to exterminate all poverty. The Liberals did not unreservedly adopt Henry George's theories, but a number of them,
and notably Mr. David Lloyd George, were incited to formulate
a less revolutionary program of land reform.

A second circumstance by which the Liberals profited was
Joseph Chamberlain's advocacy of a return to a protective tariff.
2. Opposi-   The free-trade plank of the Liberal platform, which
tion to the   had become a commonplace since Gladstone's free-
Tariff Pro-   trade budgets, suddenly assumed fundamental im-
posals   portance. Endless statistical speeches were again in
vogue, as Liberal orators endeavored to prove that to free trade
alone Great Britain owed her wealth; that a tariff would increase
the price of the workingman's loaf of bread. To the revival of
the tariff issue, and to the general aversion of the country from
tariff experiments, the Liberals chiefly owed their increased
popularity.

A third factor in the regeneration of Liberalism was the influence of the Boer War (1899–1902). The war grew out of a
conflict between the aggressive British colonists and the older

Dutch population (Boers) in the Transvaal region of South Africa.[1]
The Unionist government, under whose régime the war occurred, aroused in the United Kingdom the most bit- 3. The Boer
ter criticism. The Opposition alleged that the war War
was an unjustifiable aggression, that the management of military
operations was disfigured by shameful corruption and inefficiency.
The Liberals, as the advocates of peace and army reform, were
thus able to deliver telling blows at the ministry.

In another way the Boer War was of vital importance. In
enlisting army recruits for the war, the military authorities made
the appalling discovery that many factory-workers were such
poor, stoop-shouldered, anemic, ill-nourished, deformed, con-
sumptive creatures as to be physically unfit for service in the
army. Further investigation only confirmed the fact that the
working population was deteriorating physically, as well as
mentally and morally, under the debasing influence of long hours
and starvation wages. It meant that something must be done
immediately to lift the lower classes out of the quagmire of
poverty, vice, and disease into which they had been thrust.
The old *laisser-faire* Liberalism, which declared the state must
not interfere with the free economic relations of employer and
employed, was now contemptuously cast aside as a The New
disgraceful failure, and in its place a new Liberalism Liberalism
arose with ardent enthusiasm, determined "to wage implacable
warfare against poverty and squalidness." The new ideal of
government for the people fired the ardent spirits of many
younger men, among them David Lloyd George and Winston
Churchill, who infused the old party with fresh life. The new
Liberals reminded the workingmen that Joseph Chamberlain,
since his alliance with the Conservatives, had become absorbed
in imperialistic schemes and had forgotten his former zeal for
social reform. The new Liberals were becoming the party of
social reform.

This new-born determination of the Liberals to improve the
economic condition of the lower classes made possible Alliances
an alliance with the Labor party. As the Liberals and Victory
were already allied with the Irish Nationalist faction, of the New
they now commanded a large majority of the electo- Liberalism

[1] For a treatment of the Boer War, see below, pp. 651 f.

rate, and in the elections of 1906 succeeded in marshaling against
the Unionists 4,026,704 out of 6,555,301 voters.   From this
Liberal
Achieve-
ments,
1906-1914   overwhelming victory to the outbreak of the War of
the Nations, the Liberal coalition was continuously
in office, first with Sir Henry Campbell-Bannerman,
then with Mr. Herbert Asquith (1908), as premier.
The activities of these nine years (1906–1914) may be summed
up under five heads.

(1) *Fiscal.*   The Liberals maintained free trade, repealed
some of the taxes left over from the Boer War, and effected some
economies.   But for naval increases and for social reforms, larger
revenues were needed.   These David Lloyd George, chancellor
of the exchequer, proposed in his famous budget of 1909 to find
by a graduated income tax;[1] an inheritance tax; taxes on the
unearned increment of land-values, on undeveloped land, on
motor cars, motor cycles, and gasoline; stamp-taxes, licenses,
and excise taxes on beer, spirits, and tobacco.   This budget
had the threefold effect of providing ample revenues, of attacking landlordism, and of shifting part of the tax-burden to the
shoulders of those best able to bear it — the rich.

(2) *Non-Conformist.*   Inasmuch as no small portion of the
Liberal party is made up of the Non-Conformists of England,
and especially of Scotland and Wales, it is not surprising that
the Liberal program should have given evidence of Non-Conformist interests.   As the Non-Conformist sects had found it
difficult to establish denominational schools of their own, the
Liberals advocated the establishment of state lay schools, in
which no religion should be taught.   The Non-Conformist conscience also demanded regulation of the liquor traffic.   These
two measures were vetoed by the Lords.   A third bill to disestablish the Anglican Church in Wales, where most of the
population is Non-Conformist, was carried over the Lords' veto
(1914) by means of the Parliament Act.

(3) *Democratic.*   In the interests of political democracy, the
Liberals passed (1911) the Parliament Act, of which we have
already made sufficient mention.   Their bill to abolish plural
voting, twice carried through the House of Commons (1913, 1914),
was both times rejected by the Lords.   For a sorely needed

---

[1] *I.e.*, large incomes were taxed at a higher rate per cent than small incomes.

redistribution of Parliamentary representation, the Liberals showed no enthusiasm. On the question of extending the suffrage to women, the Liberals were divided, and since the Asquith cabinet refused to make woman suffrage a government measure, the "suffragettes" manifested their furious displeasure by repeated remonstrances, by breaking windows, by dropping acid in mail boxes, and by placing bombs in churches.

(4) *Irish.* To satisfy their Irish Nationalist allies, the Liberals passed a Home Rule Bill, with which we shall deal in a following section.

(5) *Social.* Finally, the Liberal government enacted a number of benevolent and far-sighted laws in an attempt to bring about "that good time when poverty and wretchedness and human degradation which always follows in its camp will be as remote to the people of this country as the wolves which once infested its forests."

It is worth while noting that the dependence of the Liberals upon their Laborite allies tended to accelerate the work of social reform just as the Liberal dependence upon the Nationalist group redoubled the government's efforts to enact the Home Rule Bill. Although theoretically the two-party system still prevailed in British politics, in fact there were in 1913 at least four important parties : the Unionists with 281 members, the Liberals with 265, the Laborites with 40, and the Irish Nationalists with 84. Manifestly, the Liberal government was supported not by the largest party, but by a coalition of three more or less harmonious parties. This multiplication of parties, the essence of the so-called "group" system, although usually regarded as characteristic of Continental rather than Anglo-Saxon governments, has in practice become a feature of British politics.

Political Fact and the Two-party Theory

BRITISH SOCIAL LEGISLATION

The fifth category of Liberal activities — social legislation — is worthy of closer examination; for it exemplified in striking manner how political democracy might serve social needs. By successive political reforms, the British government had come more and more to represent the interests

The Social Problem

of the common people, and the democratic state was bound sooner or later to attack the problems which weighed most heavily upon the common people. These problems might be summed up under two heads. In the first place, the factories, mines, railways, and shops were owned by private capitalists who enjoyed superabundant wealth and leisure; while their employees — including most of the men in the realm, many of the women, and some of the young boys and girls — had neither hours enough for rest, wages enough to buy satisfying food, security of employment, nor decent homes in which to bring up their children. The life of the workingman was one constant battle with starvation, vice, and disease. Secondly, the land was owned mostly by a few thousand great landlords,[1] as in feudal days, who without toil or merit of their own were entitled to collect millions of dollars annually in rent. In the cities this meant that grasping landlords were exacting heavy toll on the wages of the workingman and the profits of the shopkeeper. In the country it meant that the majority of agricultural workers, instead of being prosperous yeomen, were miserable hirelings laboring for pittances on rich men's farms.

A drastic remedy for these maladies of society was prescribed by Mr. Keir Hardie and other Socialists. They maintained that land, factories, mines, and railways were of vital importance to the whole people; that such public utilities should not be exploited for profit by private capitalists; that the common people would continue to suffer from injustice, greed, dishonesty, and inefficiency, so long as factories, mines, land, and railways continued to be controlled and owned by selfish individuals instead of by the state. The Liberals, and even some of the Laborites, were unwilling to go to the full length of public ownership of public utilities; but in devising less radical remedies to meet immediate needs, the Liberal-Labor coalition was quite willing to adopt many of the reforms which the Socialists had long advocated. These reforms attacked the industrial and agrarian problems from three angles: (1) they would shield the poor from disease, overwork, poverty, and accident; (2) they would encourage education and trade-unionism as means whereby the

General Nature of Suggested Solutions of the Problem

---

[1] Fewer than 5000 persons owned half of Great Britain.

workingman might help himself ; (3) they would tend to equalize wealth by imposing heavier burdens upon "swollen" and unearned fortunes.

In the first department of social reform, the protection of the poorer classes, the most obvious and worst-needed measures had been enacted before the accession of Mr. Asquith, **Factory and** — measures insuring sanitary conditions in factories, **Mines Acts** preventing the labor of young children, and limiting the labor of women in factory, mine, and shop.   There had been much opposition to overcome, however.   At the beginning of the nineteenth century the owners of factories, mines, and shops were firmly convinced that the government had no right to interfere with a man's private business, and they strenuously resisted governmental regulation of industrial conditions.   Because the business men insisted upon "industrial liberty," little could be done to relieve the cruel conditions in mine and in factory.   The first attempts to cope with the situation were inadequate.   We read with amazement, for example, that it was necessary to pass a special act (the Act of 1819) just to declare that children under nine years of age should not be compelled to work more than twelve hours a day in cotton mills.   Even by the Factory Act of 1844, grown women were allowed to work twelve hours every day, and children twelve hours on alternate days or six hours every day, and this act made no attempt to deal with any but textile factories.   In 1847 the working day in textile mills was cut down from twelve to ten hours.   During the 'sixties the workers in other industries than textile were given the benefit of similar regulations.   In 1874 children under ten years of age were legally prohibited from working in textile factories.   These and other haphazard regulations, together with provisions for the inspection and sanitation of factories, were codified by the great Consolidating Act of 1878.   A second revision and codification took place in 1901, when the minimum age of child-workers was raised to twelve years, elaborate provisions were designed to secure sanitary working-conditions, and careful inspection was organized.

In the coal-mines, conditions were at the outset even worse than in factories and relief equally slow.   Not until 1842 were women, girls, and boys under ten years of age excluded from the mines, where they had hitherto worked with the men, half-naked, struggling along in the dark damp underground passages, dragging bags of coal or pulling carts of ore. The great event in the history of mining was the preparation of a code of mines regulations in 1872, by which women, girls, and boys under 12 years were excluded from underground labor. Mine-owners were compelled to take reasonable precautions for the safety of their employees.

The purpose of factory and mine acts passed between 1819 and 1901 had been to insure safe and healthful conditions in mines and **Sweated** mills, also to prevent the employment of women and **Labor** children, which was breaking up the home and ruining the health of the following generation. In 1909, however, the Liberal government struck out in a new direction by asserting the right of the state to regulate wages, in addition to supervising the conditions and hours of labor. The new principle was incorporated in the Trade Boards Act of 1909, which established wages boards — composed of representatives of employers and employed in equal numbers — to fix the minimum wage which should be paid to workers in the so-called "sweated trades," *viz.* tailoring, cardboard box-making, machine-made lace-making and finishing, and ready-made blouse-making. This was confessedly an exceptional measure to cope with the evils of sweated labor. For in the sweated trades, the workers were particularly defenseless, being compelled to work irregularly, at home or else in overcrowded, foul-smelling rooms ("sweat-shops"), at extremely low wages.

The principle of governmental regulation of wages, as introduced for the benefit of sweated laborers, was destined three **The Mini-** years later to receive an important and somewhat **mum Wage** unexpected application. In 1912 the coal-miners went **for Miners,** out on strike as a result of a dispute about wages. **1912** More than a million miners ceased work, and by stopping the supply of coal they threatened to paralyze the business world. In order to avert such a disaster, Mr. Asquith hurriedly induced Parliament to enact a Minimum Wage Bill which would concede the main principle, if not the exact details, of the miners' demands. The miners contended that every adult miner should **receive a minimum wage of at least 5s. a day ($1.25) for his**

labor and each boy of 14 years 2*s*. a day.   Instead of establishing
the fixed rate of 5*s*. a day for the entire kingdom, the government's bill provided that the exact figure of the minimum wage
should be determined separately in each district by a local
board.   But the principle that the government may establish a
minimum wage by law was firmly established.

The Minimum Wage Act was hailed by Socialists as a joyous
harbinger of future triumph, foreshadowing the happy day when
the government would insure to every citizen a full   Justice and
and fair return for his labor.   But the Act of 1912   the Mini-
contemplated no such revolutionary purpose : it pro-   mum Wage
posed to establish not a fair wage, but simply a minimum wage.
The distinction is important.   It is the same distinction which
ran through all the social legislation of the Liberal government.
It is the distinction between abstract justice and practical
benevolence.   The Liberals were not so much concerned about
apportioning to every man what is justly his, as they were intent
upon guaranteeing to every man at least a certain minimum of
health, wealth, and happiness.   Even the poorest and most
unfortunate pauper must not be allowed to sink below a certain
level of comfort and civilization.   To bring up the straggling
rear-guard of civilization is the ideal of the new Liberals, and of
their laws.

The statesmanlike altruism of Liberals like Lloyd George
and Winston Churchill may sometimes work in harmony with
the less lofty motives of calculating business men.   Altruism
Many employers of labor have recently come to the   and
conclusion that in the long run it pays to have work-   Efficiency
ingmen clean, intelligent, well-fed, well-housed, comfortably
clad, and self-respecting.   What is lost in higher wages and additional expenses may be gained in the increased efficiency, energy,
and honesty of the workers.   This at least is the argument which
has persuaded many capitalists to abandon their former opposition and actually to encourage the enactment of social legislation.
Thus altruism and efficiency go hand in hand.

Altruistic reformers had much to do besides regulating the
conditions, hours, and wages of labor.   None of the above-
mentioned measures relieved what was probably the most acute
suffering of all — the suffering of the poor who were unable to

work, the sick and disabled, the children, the old people, and
those who could not find employment. For the benefit of these
the Liberal government devised a series of benevolent
laws. First of all was considered the case of those unfortunate workmen who, being accidentally injured,
were disabled from earning a living. Every month 400
workpeople were being killed, so it was asserted, and 7000 injured
in one way or another: sometimes through their own fault,
sometimes through the neglect of the employer to establish
proper safeguards, sometimes through inevitable accidents, as
in mining. In any case the result was grief and destitution
for the family of the unhappy workman. And in any case the
government resolved that the workman, or his bereaved family,
should receive compensation sufficient to prevent starvation.
The principle of workmen's compensation for accident had
already been applied to a few trades by an Act of 1897, and to
agricultural laborers in 1900; in 1906 the Liberal Parliament
extended compensation to almost all industries. By the Act
of 1906 the workman received from his employer a sum not
exceeding $5.00 a week in case he was disabled by accident;
in case of mortal injury the family of the workman received a
lump sum of from $750 to $1500. It is an interesting fact that
in the 23 years from 1884 to 1907, twenty other countries adopted
similar measures for the compensation of workmen.

Working-
men's Com-
pensation,
1897–1906

The protection of those who were either too young or too
aged to help themselves was also attempted by the Asquith
ministry. School-teachers had reported that many
poor children came to school without sufficient food;
the Education Act of 1906 made it possible to provide
such children with free meals. Subsequent acts provided play
centers and free medical inspection for the children, and attempted to provide proper medical care for infants. The
Children Act of 1908 contained a host of provisions, dealing with
every phase of child life, from the protection of infant children,
the prevention of burns, the correction of juvenile criminals,
and the treatment of children in industrial schools, to the prohibition of juvenile smoking.

Child
Welfare,
1908

The problem of the aged and infirm was next attacked. Under
the Poor Law of 1834, poor people too old or too feeble to sup-

port themselves had usually been taken away from home and friends and sent to one of those grim workhouses — the last resort of the poor — more like prisons than houses of **Old Age** charity. Various alterations of the workhouse system **Pensions,** were made from time to time as the century wore **1908** on, but the question was not settled. In 1906, however, the Labor members in Parliament asked that the state should provide pensions for all old people whose incomes were insufficient for their support, just as it provided pensions for soldiers. The Ministry, approving the idea, in 1908 introduced a bill which guaranteed to every person over seventy years of age, whose annual income failed to exceed $105, a weekly pension of $1.25. In 1913 almost a million old people were receiving pensions.

In the following year, Parliament took up the question of the unemployed. Always there were in London, and in every large city, thousands of able-bodied men, starving and without work, many of them through no fault of their own. **The Un-** A panic in some distant stock market, the failure of the **employed:** American cotton crop, or a falling-off in the demand **Exchange** for calicoes, might be the ultimate cause for the closing **Act, 1909** down of an English factory and so throw a thousand English laborers out of work; other thousands were left stranded by the fluctuations of the ice-business, or the coal traffic, or the building trades. Whatever the cause, it was a great pity that the workman should be left destitute, simply because he could find no work to do. By an act of 1909, accordingly, the government created a system of government employment-bureaus, or labor exchanges, to inform unemployed workmen where there was work to be had, and, if necessary, to pay the workman's carfare to the place where work was offered. It did not guarantee employment to every workman, but it enormously assisted the idle to find work.

The labor exchanges by no means ended all unemployment, and the problem of providing for unemployed workmen remained to be solved. In 1911 David Lloyd George proposed **National** the government's partial solution: the National Insur- **Insurance** ance Bill. The Bill, enacted as the National Insur- **Act, 1911** ance Act, had two main provisions. One was that workmen should pay $2\frac{1}{2}d$. per week, to which the employers and state

would add, as insurance against unemployment. The workman
would then be entitled, if thrown out of work, to receive 6s. or
7s. a week. This applied only to the engineering and building
trades, including some 2,300,000 men. The other and more
important section of the bill aimed "to provide for Insurance
against loss of Health and for the Prevention and Cure of Sickness." It affected almost fifteen millions of workers directly,
and indirectly millions more. By this law, the wage-earner was
compelled to insure himself against sickness, by paying from
1d. to 4d. a week, to which the employer added 3d., and the state
2d. In return the workman would receive free medical attendance, free treatment at hospitals, and weekly allowances while
sick. Approved insurance companies and benefit societies already
in existence were allowed and encouraged to act as the machinery
for the National Insurance scheme, although the state itself
would provide for those who preferred to insure themselves
through the post office rather than through a society. The
results of National Insurance are not yet fully apparent, but it
appears not unlikely that the provision for medical attendance
will materially diminish the prevalence of sickness and disease
and enormously relieve suffering.

All the measures thus far described represent in one way or
another the Liberal government's benevolent desire to protect
the poor from overwork, disease, poverty, and accident.
Education
The second phase of social reform is that of encouraging the poor to help themselves, and it is done chiefly in two ways,
— by the provision of education and by the encouragement of
trade-unionism. As late as 1870 almost half the children had no
regular schooling; there was no system of free, compulsory
education; and the establishment of schools was left by the
government to the Church of England or to voluntary societies.
The progress of education was hindered then, as now, by the
fact that there were in England a multiplicity of religious sects,
some of which demanded that religion should be taught in the
schools, some that education should be non-sectarian. To meet
this embarrassing situation, the Education Act of 1870 provided
that, while "voluntary" or church schools giving religious instruction should receive financial aid from the government,
there were also to be established — wherever the need was clear

non-sectarian "Board Schools," in which no denominational religious teaching should be allowed. These Board Schools would be supported partly by parents' fees, partly by local rates (taxes), and partly by government subsidies. Since 1870 the extent and cost of education has been enormously expanded, so that in 1913 the amount expended on education from local taxes and government funds exceeded £30,000,000 ($150,000,000), and there were in 1913 more than 6,500,000 children attending school. A large number of schools still remained under the control of religious denominations, while receiving generous monetary grants from the government. Inasmuch as the great majority of these were schools of the Anglican Church, the Dissenters continued to protest; and the Liberal party, representing the Dissenters, attempted to remove public education from denominational control by a bill of 1906. The bill was thrown out by the Lords, however, and the intention of the Liberals to create a system of universal, public, non-sectarian, elementary education remained unfulfilled. Although it failed in this respect, the Liberal government did make a real contribution to education by providing meals for poor students, by establishing industrial schools, and by enforcing medical and sanitary regulations to improve the health of school children.

We can hardly exaggerate the importance of this expansion of education in enabling the lower classes to play a more important and intelligent rôle in society. For the laboring man who can read in the newspapers what Parliament is doing to help or injure him, and can read in pamphlets new doctrines of social and economic democracy, is more and more inclined to demand larger consideration in politics.

Even more important in training the workingmen to look out for their own interests has been the development of trade-unionism. The movement, as we have stated in another Trade-connection, had gathered headway in the first two- Unionism thirds of the nineteenth century despite serious legal hindrances. To remove these checks, the trade-unionists had inaugurated a political movement, had obtained the vote (1867), and by Acts of 1871–1876 had obtained recognition as legal associations. The trade unions, annually assembling in Trade Union Congresses to discuss the problems of laboring men, and since 1899 united in a General Federation of Trade Unions, rapidly became a powerful factor in industrial and political life. Alarmed by their activity, the House of Lords in 1901 handed down the famous Taff Vale decision, whereby employers were able to exact damage-compensation from trade unions in consequence of strikes. That year the number of industrial disputes (strikes and lockouts) fell off from 642 to 442. It was for this reason that the resentful trade unions so strongly supported the Labor party, and it was to pacify them that the Liberal government in 1906 passed its Trade Disputes Act, which safeguarded the funds of trade unions from suits for damages, and permitted trade-union "pickets" to use "peaceful persuasion" in endeavors to induce their fellow-workmen to strike with them. Again in 1909 the House of Lords attempted to circumscribe trade-union activities by making it illegal for trade unions to collect compulsory contributions for the support of the labor members in Parliament. And again the trade unions triumphed, in 1911 securing the payment of all members of the House of Commons and in 1913 the right to use trade-union funds for political purposes, although the members of the union might not be compelled to contribute to the "political fund" of the trade union.

The Liberal government has thus removed the most serious obstructions to trade-union activity, political and industrial. Moreover, since the government has entered the field to assist in bearing what once were the heaviest burdens of the trade union, — the support of the sick, aged, and unemployed, — the trade unions have been able to devote their resources more effectively than ever before to the struggle for the rights of labor, for higher wages, for shorter hours. The struggle has been waged unceasingly in the industrial world by means of the strike, and in the Parliamentary world by means of the ballot. To the trade-union movement above all things else the workingman owes his increased comfort and independence, his influence upon politics, and his training in democratic self-government.

Finally, we come to the third department of social reform, Taxation of the attack on arbitrary privilege and unearned wealth. the Rich In order to defray the enormous expense of old-age pensions, of national insurance, of public education, of naval armament, the government had to find new sources of revenue. How

Lloyd George's budgets have imposed increasing burdens upon large incomes, inheritances, and luxuries, we have already set forth; it is here necessary only to recall the fact. But his attack on the unearned revenues and privileges of the landlord class deserve more than passing attention.

To the minds of David Lloyd George and his colleagues it seemed absurd and iniquitous that ten men should own a quarter of the city of London, that landlord peers should pos- **The Land** sess whole villages; that the landlords should have **Problem** the legal power at will to tear down cottages or dispossess industrious tenant-farmers or turn farm land into wilderness; that in the last half-century the rural population should have fallen off by 600,000 while in the last sixty years the gamekeepers increased from 9000 to 23,000; that over 60 per cent of the adult agricultural laborers should be receiving less than 18s. ($4.50) a week while rents still soared; that wealthy landlords should be allowed to exact rent for thousands upon thousands of miserable cottages and tenements unfit for human habitation. The Liberals, therefore, set themselves to remedy these evils.

Faint-hearted beginnings had already been made, even before Mr. David Lloyd George, the most eloquent advocate of land reform, set his hand to the task. In Ireland the government had stepped in to cut down exorbitant rents, to protect the tenants, to lend peasants money from the public treasury to purchase their holdings outright. Land legislation in England, however, had lagged behind. The first important step was the appointment of a commission (1884) to investigate the problem. In reporting to Parliament, the commission made it clear that pauperism, drunkenness, disease, physical degeneration, excessive death-rates, and crime were in no small part traceable to the insanitary and overcrowded tenements in which the poor in town and country were forced to live. Consequently an act was passed in 1890 for the housing of the working classes. This, with the more important Housing and Town Planning Act (1909), passed nineteen years later by the Asquith ministry, enabled local authorities (county councils) to close up the damp cellars and tear down the airless tenements in which miserable families were living, and, if necessary, to purchase from landlords land on which to erect light, clean, and airy tenements for the poor. As a result, —

prior to 1914, — 56,318 dwelling houses were condemned as unfit for human habitation; county and borough councils purchased possibly 200,000 acres of land; in London, for example, a hundred thousand tenants were living in sanitary dwellings erected and owned by public authorities; and scores of towns adopted definite plans for the future beautification and deliberate development of playgrounds and parks. In the Small Holdings and Allotments Act (1907) the Liberals made a beginning in the direction of "giving every laborer a garden patch." In his famous budget of 1909, David Lloyd George gave notice that henceforth the burden of taxation would fall ever more heavily upon the land-lords. The same year witnessed an act for the development of rural roads and forests, and the beginning of a five-year census or survey of everything concerning land-ownership — a modern parallel of William the Conqueror's eleventh-century *Domesday Book*. These were but the opening skirmishes in the battle which Lloyd George began in the winter of 1913–1914.

In a series of stirring speeches that winter, the chancellor of the exchequer expounded the government's program of land

Lloyd George's Program of Land Reform, 1913–1914

reform. For the supervision of land reforms, a new administrative department, the ministry of lands, was to be created. Commissioners acting under the minister of lands would be endowed with large powers: (1) They would protect the tenant against arbitrary eviction and unfair rent. (2) They would regulate the hours of farm-labor, and work towards the establishment of a minimum wage for agricultural laborers. (3) The "game nuisance," the ruining of crops by deer and the inclusion of agricultural land in the useless deer parks of the nobility, was to be restricted. (4) The millions of acres of land now lying waste would be reclaimed and afforested, — at least in part. (5) The provision of healthful houses and garden patches for the working classes would be pushed forward under national, rather than local, auspices. (6) Finally, the value of land would be accurately and equitably estimated, both for the purpose of regulating the selling price of real estate, and as a basis of future taxes and land reforms.

When in August, 1914, Great Britain was drawn into the great European war, forgetting all else in the mad conflict of arms, Lloyd George's promise of land reform was as yet unful-filled.   Possibly future historians will write that the first period of Liberal land reform, as well as Liberal social and industrial legislation, was abruptly terminated by the disastrous War of the Nations.   It is, of course, impossible to foresee what the future holds in store, but it is difficult to believe that the ringing words of David Lloyd George will be entirely forgotten :

" You have hundreds of thousands of men — working unceasingly for wages that barely bring them enough bread to keep themselves and their families above privation.   Generation after generation they see their chil-dren wither before their eyes for lack of air, light, and space, which is denied them by men who have square miles of it for their own use.   Take our cities, the great cities of a great Empire.   Right in the heart of them everywhere you have ugly quagmires of human misery, seething, rotting, at last fermenting.   We pass them by every day on our way to our com-fortable homes.   We forget that divine justice never passed by a great wrong.   You can hear, carried by the breezes from the north, the south, the east, and the west, ominous rumbling.   The chariots of retribution are drawing nigh.   How long will all these injustices last for myriads of men, women, and children created in the image of God — how long?   I believe it is coming to an end."

THE IRISH QUESTION

As the preceding section explained the coöperation of the Liberals with the smaller Laborite party to effect social reforms, so the present section is devoted to the alliance of the Liberals with the other minor Parliamentary group, — the Irish Nationalists, — for the purpose of righting the wrongs of Ireland.   The Liberal-Irish coalition first came to the fore in the election of 1868, when Gladstone seized upon the need of reform in Ireland as a most effective campaign issue upon which to overthrow Disraeli's Conservative government.   From that day to this, Irish reform has figured prominently in the platform of the Liberal party.   At the time of Gladstone's first ministry (1868–1874), three Irish grievances — religious, agrarian, and nationalist — demanded attention. How each of these grievances arose, what Gladstone did to redress it, and what further redress has since been obtained, we shall consider separately.

Gladstone's Advocacy of Irish Reforms

The persecution of the Roman Catholic faith in Ireland goes
back to the sixteenth century, when Henry VIII, unable to make
the Irish accept Anglicanism, suppressed the Irish
monasteries, appropriated the churches, established an
Anglican hierarchy in Ireland, and assumed the title
"king of Ireland." Despite bloody strife under
Queen Elizabeth, despite Oliver Cromwell's deporta-
tion of Catholics to the West Indies in the seventeenth century,
despite cruel coercive laws in the eighteenth century, three-
quarters of the Irish population remain to this day steadfastly
Roman Catholic; and Protestantism is represented only by the
half million Protestant Episcopalians (of the so-called Church
of Ireland), and a somewhat smaller number of Presbyterians,
who are descendants respectively of English and Scotch settlers.
The Protestants are congregated chiefly in the industrial city of
Belfast, and the surrounding nine counties — grouped in the
province of Ulster. Even in Ulster, however, there are almost as
many Roman Catholics as Protestants. For three centuries the
Protestant minority, supported by British arms, imposed upon
the Catholic majority the most crushing legal burdens; only in
the nineteenth century has anything like religious equality been
obtained.

*1. Ecclesi-
astical:
Grievances
of the
Irish
Catholics*

With the first steps towards religious liberty, we are already
familiar.[1] The Catholic Emancipation of 1829 removed the
political disabilities of Roman Catholics, and practical
freedom of worship had already been gained. But the
Catholics were still compelled to pay tithes[2] to the
Protestant "Church of Ireland" for the support of
Protestant clergymen, many of whom lived in England.
Against the tithes Daniel O'Connell, the Irish leader, had vainly
directed his eloquence. But when Gladstone came into power in
1868, after an especially violent outbreak of Irish unrest, he proposed to pacify Ireland by removing some of the worst grievances.
The fulfillment of his promise was the disendowment and disestablishment of the "Church of Ireland." Disestablishment
meant that the Protestant Episcopal Church was no longer the
state church of Ireland, and could no longer collect tithes. It

*Disestab-
lishment of
the Irish
Church,
1869*

[1] See above, pp. 103 f.   [2] Commuted, 1838.

retained, nevertheless, the use of its churches and cathedrals, and the clergymen affected received personal compensation.

The ecclesiastical question was thus practically settled, and Gladstone was free to attack the even more pressing agrarian problem. Ireland's once promising woolen industry, **2. Agrarian** we should remember, had been destroyed by English **Evils and** legislation, and Ireland's native population reduced to **Reforms** squalor and misery by the English landlords who owned most of the island. This poverty-stricken peasantry, subsisting mainly on a meager but cheap diet of potatoes,[1] suffered periodically from famine — as in 1739 when one out of every five persons is supposed to have perished, or in 1846, when thousands of starving peasants fell dead on the roads, and other thousands fled to America, so that the population fell from more than eight millions in 1845 to six and a half millions in 1851. The landlords, cheated of their rent by the famine of 1846, then evicted their poorer tenants who, in case of another famine, would be unable to pay their rents. The resentment of the peasantry fired up in revolt in 1848, but without effect. In 1850 a Tenant-Right League was formed to demand the "three F's" — fair rent, fixity of tenure (which meant that a peasant could hold his land as long as he paid rent), and free sale (*i.e.*, the right of a peasant to sell his tenancy). These rights, thought the Leaguers, would insure the tenant against arbitrary eviction. Nothing was acccomplished, however, until the enactment of Gladstone's Land Act of 1870, which forbade the landlord to raise rents at will, or arbitrarily to evict a peasant without paying for whatever improvements the peasant had made. The Act of 1870 was ineffectual, however, and the agitation for the "three F's" was renewed in the next decade by the Land League. The Irish peasants were rapidly coming to the conviction that the agrarian system would never be reformed unless Ireland could gain the right to govern itself, and they, therefore, gave hearty support to a political movement for Home Rule. In vain the government attempted to suppress the movement. The situation became so threatening that Gladstone attempted to pacify the peasantry by granting their demands. His Second Irish Land Act (1881) practically conceded the "three F's," establishing a Land Court to fix fair

[1] The potato was introduced into Ireland from America.

rents, protecting peasants against unjust eviction, and allowing them to sell their holdings. The Land Court succeeded in reducing rents by a quarter but did not give permanent satisfaction.

The great Irish agrarian reform was not the work of Gladstone, but of the Conservatives. After tentative efforts the second **The Land Purchase Act, 1891** Salisbury ministry in 1891 carried a general Land Purchase Act, under which a tenant was enabled, if willing, to purchase his holding outright from the landlord by borrowing from the government a sum equal to the full purchase price. For five years the peasant would pay four and three-quarters per cent on the loan, and for forty-four years four per cent; but this payment amounted to much less than his rent had been, and after 49 annual payments he would be an independent landowner. Thousands of tenants rushed to avail themselves of the scheme, and the foundations of a more prosperous Ireland were firmly laid. Another Land Act of 1896 still further facilitated the creation of a free Irish peasantry, and the Local Government Act of 1898 gave Ireland autonomous county government, which still further improved agrarian conditions. Famines and evictions were not yet ended, but rural Ireland was immeasurably happier than ever before.

Before the close of the nineteenth century, then, Ireland's religious and agrarian complaints had been at least partially **3. Irish Nationalism** heeded, but there remained political discontent, and it was due to nationalism. Let us now go back and trace the development of nationalism in Ireland. Before the twelfth century Ireland, independent though disunited, had possessed her **Prior to the Act of Union, 1800** own kings, her own culture, her own speech. In the fateful twelfth century, however, English invaders had conquered at least part of Ireland for King Henry II. Under Henry VII, "Poyning's Law" had been passed, subjecting all the acts of the Irish Parliament to the approval of the English government. Henry VIII had assumed the title "king of Ireland." Meanwhile great Irish estates had been granted to English nobles, but English authority was not much respected outside of the small district in the east, known as the Irish Pale. Under James I, English and Scotch colonists were extensively settled in Ulster. In 1641 the native Irish rebelled against the foreigners, but were cruelly subdued (1649–1652) by Oliver

Cromwell. Again, at the time of the Revolution of 1689, Ireland rose in rebellion only to be defeated in the battle of the Boyne, 1 July, 1690. Thousands of the defeated rebels emigrated and their descendants made Irish names famous in French history.[1] A century later, a new revolt occurred in Ireland, engineered this time, however, by the Protestant settlers who resented English restrictions on Irish trade. The insurrection was successful, and, as a result, Ireland gained Home Rule or legislative autonomy for eighteen years (1782–1800) — that is, Protestant Ireland gained Home Rule, for until 1793 the Catholics had no voice in the Irish Parliament. During the period of Home Rule, a society of United Irishmen was organized under the influence of the French Revolution, and instigated the unsuccessful insurrection of 1798. This gave the British government an excuse for terminating the Home Rule régime. The Irish Parliament was bribed to abolish itself, and Ireland was joined with England and Scotland in the United Kingdom of Great Britain and Ireland (1801). Laws were henceforth made for Ireland by the Westminster Parliament, in which sat twenty-eight Irish peers and a hundred Irish Commoners.

Subordination to a British Parliament was in itself irritating to Irish patriots, and, when that British Parliament showed itself consistently hostile to Irish interests, the yoke became intolerable. Yet the first great agitation for repeal of the Act of Union was orderly and peaceful under the leadership of the famous Daniel O'Connell. When O'Connell's peaceful Repeal movement was suppressed in 1843, more violent spirits took up the cause, formed a "Young Ireland" party, and unsuccessfully imitated the Continental revolutions of 1848. In the next generation Ireland's cause was again revived when thousands of Irish-Americans who had fought in the American Civil War (1861–1865) organized the "Fenian Brotherhood" to emancipate Ireland, and in 1867 attacked Canada while simultaneously raising the standard of revolt in Ireland. As always, revolt failed; but not entirely, for the Fenian disorders convinced Gladstone that Irish reform was sadly needed. Gladstone, as we have seen, then secured the Disestablishment (1869), and passed a Land Act (1870); but under a new leader — Charles

Irish Agitation against the Union

---

[1] Marshal MacMahon, for instance.

Stewart Parnell, able, enthusiastic, and a Protestant withal —
Irish nationalism persisted. The Nationalists persuaded the discontented peasantry that in Home Rule was the only sure cure
for Ireland's ills, and organized a political Home Rule party,
which appeared with nearly eighty representatives in the Parliament of 1880. Gladstone again sought to buy off the Home
Rulers by passing a Land Act (1881). When the agitation only
redoubled in vigor, the government for a time imprisoned Parnell
and forty other Irish leaders.

All this time Gladstone had championed Irish reform while he
opposed Home Rule and antagonized Home Rulers. In 1886,

Gladstone's First Home Rule Bill, 1886   however, a Conservative ministry was in office, and
Gladstone, leading the Liberal Opposition, needed the
86 votes of Parnell's Home Rule faction. Then was
concluded the alliance between Liberalism and Home
Rule: the Irish members helped Gladstone into office, and Gladstone prepared a bill to establish a quasi-independent Dublin
parliament. Many of the Liberals revolted against Gladstone's
bargain, however, and united with the Conservatives to defeat

Gladstone's Second Home Rule Bill, 1893   the Home Rule Bill of 1886 and to oust Gladstone.
Seven years later Gladstone's coalition, again control-
ling a majority in the Commons, passed the Second
Home Rule Bill (1893). The bill was defeated by
the House of Lords, however, and Gladstone, now over eighty
years of age, soon withdrew from public life.[1] In the years from
1895 to 1905 the disorganized Liberal party remained in opposition, and Home Rule in the background, the Unionist ministry
endeavoring to ignore nationalism while instituting agrarian reforms, hoping thus to "kill Home Rule by kindness."

Home Rule would not be killed. The Irish Nationalist party,
now led by John Redmond, with eighty-odd members in the

The Home Rule Bill of 1912   House of Commons, persisted in its demand for Home
Rule. However, the general election of 1906, which
returned the Liberals to power, did not lead immediately to the realization of Nationalist aspirations. The Liberals
in the House of Commons now outnumbered all the other parties
combined, and accordingly were not dependent upon the votes
of the Irish Nationalists as Gladstone had been in 1886; besides,

[1] Gladstone died 19 May, 1898, at the advanced age of eighty-eight years.

the Liberals were so absorbed in schemes of British social reform that they gave little attention to Irish demands, and even had they carried a Home Rule bill through the Commons, they would have been certain to find it blocked by the overwhelming Unionist majority in the Lords. The situation was changed in 1910–1911, when, as the results of new elections and the passage of the Parliament Act, the House of Lords was shorn of its constitutional right to exercise more than a suspensory veto over legislation and the Liberal ministry found itself reduced to dependence upon a coalition of Liberal-Laborite-Nationalist votes in the House of Commons. Then it was that the Liberal ministry definitely returned to Gladstone's policy of urging the immediate establishment of Home Rule. On 11 April, 1912, Mr. Asquith, the prime minister, introduced a Government of Ireland Bill, whereby Ireland, while retaining 42 representatives in the British House of Commons at Westminster, would receive limited rights of self-government, with a bicameral Irish parliament at Dublin. The lord lieutenant, as the king's personal representative, would govern Ireland through ministers responsible to the Dublin parliament.

The Home Rule Bill encountered furious opposition at the hands of the Scotch-Irish and English-Irish inhabitants of Ulster, whose sentiments and traditions were naturally incompatible with the nationalism of the native Irish. The Ulster opposition was stimulated by the fact that the prosperous business men of Belfast would probably be heavily taxed Ulster and by an Irish parliament representing the peasant Unionist majority. This strong economic motive for resisting Opposition Home Rule was reënforced by an appeal to religious bigotry, and the Protestant minority, having long oppressed the Catholic majority, now became fearful lest the situation should be reversed, and Home Rule mean "Rome Rule." The provision in the bill making it impossible for the Irish parliament to endow any religion, or to impose any religious disabilities whatsoever, was of no avail to reassure Protestant Ulster. The Unionists, therefore, led on by the fiery eloquence of Sir Edward Carson and with the acquiescence of the Unionists in England, held imposing mass-meetings, bound themselves by a "solemn covenant" never to submit to an Irish parliament, and actually proceeded to drill and equip volunteer armies with the avowed intent of resorting to civil war. Curiously enough, they insisted that all these acts were inspired by undying devotion to the crown. Perhaps at first Sir Edward Carson intended the Ulster volunteer movement merely to intimidate the Liberal government and thus to stave off Home Rule. Perhaps, also, many English Unionists abetted the movement as a convenient means of discrediting and overturning the Asquith ministry and thereby preventing further Liberal attacks on the House of Lords, the landed aristocracy, and the Anglican Church. Nevertheless, the Asquith government proceeded resolutely with its Home Rule Bill, and, after the seeming failure of efforts at compromise, was preparing in the summer of 1914 to place it upon the statute book despite the real menace of civil war in Ireland. Blood was shed in Dublin on 26 July.

At this juncture came suddenly the outbreak of the Great War and the temporary obscuring of all domestic differences by the heat and haze of the vast international struggle. In zeal to repel the German invasion of Belgium, Unionists and Liberals could now present a united front; and Mr. John Redmond, the Nationalist leader, evoked a round of applause from the House of Commons by stating "that the coast of Ireland will be defended from foreign invasion by her armed sons, and for this purpose armed Nationalist Catholics in the South will be only too glad to join arms with the armed Protestant Ulstermen in the North." Under these circumstances a truce was quickly arranged for the hostile factions in Ireland. The Home Rule Bill, which had already twice passed the House of Commons, was now passed a third time; and, though still not sanctioned by the House of Lords, it received the formal assent of the king on 18 September, 1914, and thus, despite the bitter protest of the Unionists, became law in accordance with the provisions of the Parliament Act of 1911. At the same time a bill was passed temporarily suspending the Government of Ireland Act.[1]

The Home Rule Act, 1914

---

[1] The official title of the Home Rule Act. The operation of the Welsh Disestablishment Act, passed also in 1914, was postponed until the conclusion of the war.

ADDITIONAL READING

General. Brief summaries: A. L. Cross, *History of England and Greater Britain* (1914), ch. lii–lvii; J. H. Robinson and C. A. Beard, *The Development of Modern Europe*, Vol. II (1907), ch. xxv, xxvi; C. D. Hazen, *Europe since 1815* (1910), ch. xx, xxi; Gilbert Slater, *The Making of Modern England*, new ed. (1915), ch. xv–xxiii, essentially social; C. W. Oman, *England in the Nineteenth Century* (1900), ch. vii–ix; J. A. R. Marriott, *England since Waterloo* (1913), Book III, ch. xviii–xxvi; *Cambridge Modern History*, Vol. XI (1909), ch. xii, *1856–1868*, by Sir Spencer Walpole, and Vol. XII (1910), ch. iii, *1868–1910*, by Stanley Leathes; A. D. Innes, *History of England and the British Empire*, Vol. IV (1914), ch. vi–xi; Sidney Low and L. C. Sanders, *Political History of England, 1837–1901* (1907), ch. x–xix. More detailed works: Sir Spencer Walpole, *History of England since 1815*, new ed., 6 vols. (1902–1905), reaching down to 1858, and, by the same author, an eminent scholar and in politics a moderate Liberal, *History of Twenty-Five Years, 1856–1880*, 4 vols. (1904–1908); J. F. Bright, *History of England*, 5 vols. (1884–1904) — Vol. IV, *Growth of Democracy, 1837–1880*, and Vol. V, *Imperial Reaction, 1880–1901*, fair-minded and excellent; R. H. Gretton, *A Modern History of the English People, 1880–1910*, 2d ed., 2 vols. (1913), popular and pronouncedly Liberal, but clear and emphasizes economic and social history; Sir Herbert Maxwell, *A Century of Empire*, Vol. III, *1867–1900* (1911), Conservative in point of view and rather narrowly political; H. W. Paul, *A History of Modern England*, 5 vols. (1904–1906), covering the years 1845–1895, vivid, political, and Liberal; Justin McCarthy, *A History of Our Own Times, 1837–1901*, 7 vols. (1879–1905), journalistic, anecdotal, and at times diffuse. Special treatments: G. K. Chesterton, *The Victorian Age in Literature* (1913) in the " Home University Library," suggestive synthesis of broad outlines in history, economics, and literature; Ernest Barker, *Political Thought in England from Herbert Spencer to the Present Day* (1915), another handy volume in the " Home University Library "; C. A. Whitmore, *Six Years of Unionist Government, 1886–1892* (1892); H. R. Whates, *Third Salisbury Administration, 1895–1900* (1900); Paul Mantoux, *À travers l'Angleterre contemporaine* (1909).

Biographies. Sir Sidney Lee, *Queen Victoria: a Biography* (1903); A. C. Benson and Viscount Esher (editors), *The Letters of Queen Victoria, a Selection from Her Majesty's Correspondence between the years 1837 and 1861*, 3 vols. (1907); W. F. Monypenny, *The Life of Benjamin Disraeli, Earl of Beaconsfield*, 2 vols., *1804–1846* (1910–1912), continued by G. E. Buckle, Vol. III, *1846–1855* (1914), and Vol. IV, *1855–1868* (1916), a monumental work for which the authors had access to Disraeli's papers; Georg Brandes, *Lord Beaconsfield, a Study*, Eng. trans. by Mrs. George Sturge (1880), an appreciation of Disraeli primarily as a man of letters; T. P. O'Connor, *Lord Beaconsfield: a Biography*, 7th ed. (1896), a hostile estimate; T. E. Kebbel (editor), *Selected Speeches of Benjamin Disraeli*, 2 vols. (1882), and *Lord Beaconsfield* *and other Tory Memoirs* (1907); John (Viscount) Morley, *The Life of William Ewart Gladstone*, new ed., 3 vols. in 2 (1911), containing copious extracts and quotations from Gladstone's letters and speeches; G. M. Trevelyan, *The Life of John Bright* (1913), scholarly, sympathetic, and brilliantly written; William Robertson, *Life and Times of John Bright*, new ed. by A. M. Perkins (1912); Thorold Rogers (editor), *Speeches of John Bright* (1869) and *Public Addresses of John Bright* (1879); Alexander Mackintosh, *Joseph Chamberlain, an Honest Biography*, new ed. (1914); C. W. Boyd (editor), *Speeches of Joseph Chamberlain*, 2 vols. (1914); Lytton Bulwer, *Life of Sir H. J. Temple, Viscount Palmerston*, 2 vols. (1871), continued by Evelyn Ashley, Vol. III (1874); George Saintsbury, *Earl of Derby* (1892); W. S. Churchill, *Lord Randolph Churchill*, 2 vols. (1906); H. D. Traill, *Marquis of Salisbury* (1891); Sir G. O. Trevelyan, *The Life and Letters of Lord Macaulay*, 2 vols. (1876).

The British Constitution. Standard treatises: A. L. Lowell, *The Government of England*, new ed., 2 vols. (1912); Sidney Low, *The Governance of England*, new ed. (1914); Sir William Anson, *The Law and Custom of the Constitution*, 3d ed., 3 vols. (1907-1909); A. V. Dicey, *Introduction to the Study of the Law of the Constitution*, 8th ed. (1915); Sir Thomas E. May (Lord Farnborough), *Constitutional History of England since the Accession of George the Third*, ed. and cont. by Francis Holland, 3 vols. (1912); Walter Bagehot, *The English Constitution*, new ed. (1911), a brilliant but older interpretation; D. J. Medley, *A Students' Manual of English Constitutional History*, 5th ed. (1913), a topical treatment, useful for reference. Excellent brief compendiums of the whole subject are F. A. Ogg, *The Governments of Europe* (1913), ch. i-viii, and T. F. Moran, *The Theory and Practice of the English Government* (1903). Important monographs: Sir Courtney Ilbert, *Legislative Methods and Forms* (1901), and, by the same author, in the "Home University Library," *Parliament, its History, Constitution and Practice* (1911); Charles Seymour, *Electoral Reform in England and Wales* (1915), a historical survey of the extension of the franchise from 1832 to 1885; Josef Redlich, *The Procedure of the House of Commons: a Study of its History and Present Form*, Eng. trans. by A. E. Steinthal, 3 vols. (1908); Josef Redlich and F. W. Hirst, *Local Government in England*, 2 vols. (1903); F. C. Howe, *The British City, the Beginnings of Democracy* (1907).

Political Parties in Great Britain. A. V. Dicey, *Lectures on the Relation between Law and Public Opinion in England during the Nineteenth Century*, 2d ed. (1914), an illuminating study; Lord Hugh Cecil, *Conservatism* (1912), a popular sketch of the principles of the Conservative party, to which the author belongs; L. T. Hobhouse, *Liberalism* (1911), a similar sketch of the principles of the Liberal party, likewise in the "Home University Library"; W. L. Blease, *A Short History of English Liberalism* (1913); W. S. Churchill, *Liberalism and the Social Problem* (1909), a collection of speeches comprising an excellent statement of the position of the new generation of Radical Liberals; L. T. Hobhouse, *The Labour Movement*, 3d ed.

(1906); A. W. Humphrey, *A History of Labour Representation* (1912); S. P. Orth, *Socialism and Democracy in Europe* (1913), ch. ix, a clear statement of the rise and organization of the Labor party; F. J. Shaw (pseud. Brougham Villiers), *The Socialist Movement in England* (1908); M. Beer, *Geschichte des Sozialismus in England* (1913); W. L. Blease, *The Emancipation of English Women*, new ed. (1913), an admirable historical survey; Emmeline Pankhurst, *My Own Story* (1914), interesting statement by the leading militant suffragist; Hilaire Belloc and Cecil Chesterton, *The Party System* (1911), a severe indictment.

Social Politics in the United Kingdom. Carlton Hayes, *British Social Politics* (1913), a collection of documents illustrating action of the British government from 1906 to 1913 for the partial solution of grave social problems; George Howell, *Labour Legislation, Labour Movements, and Labour Leaders*, 2d ed. (1905); C. G. F. Masterman, *The Condition of England*, 4th ed. (1910); Charles Booth (editor), *Life and Labour of the People in London*, 17 vols. (1892–1903), the result of a detailed investigation of the wages, homes, and general living conditions of the working classes of London, a mine of social information; B. S. Rowntree, *Poverty: a Study of Town Life*, 2d ed. (1902), a painstaking study of the condition of the working class in the city of York, comparable in importance to the work of Charles Booth though much slighter in bulk; Édouard Guyot, *Le socialisme et l'évolution de l'Angleterre contemporaine, 1880–1911* (1913), a French interpretation of the factors making for the increased public interest in British social problems; B. S. Rowntree, *How the Labourer Lives, a Study of the Rural Labour Problem* (1913); Sidney and Beatrice Webb, *English Poor Law Policy* (1910), dealing with developments from 1834 to 1908; B. S. Rowntree and Bruno Lasker, *Unemployment: a Social Study* (1911); W. H. Beveridge, *Unemployment*, 2d ed. (1912); M. F. Robinson, *The Spirit of Association, being some account of the Gilds, Friendly Societies, Coöperative Movement, and Trade Unions of Great Britain* (1913); Beatrice Potter (Mrs. Sidney Webb), *The Co-operative Movement in Great Britain* (1899); Sidney and Beatrice Webb, *The History of Trade Unionism*, new ed. (1911); H. H. Schloesser and W. S. Clark, *The Legal Position of Trade Unions*, 2d ed. (1913); H. L. Smith and Vaughan Nash, *Story of the Dockers' Strike* (1889); B. L. Hutchins and A. Harrison, *A History of Factory Legislation*, 2d ed. (1911); Olive J. Dunlop, *English Apprenticeship and Child Labor: a History* (1912); Frederic Keeling, *Child Labour in the United Kingdom : a Study of the Development and Administration of the Law Relating to the Employment of Children* (1914); A. S. C. Carr, W. H. Garnett, and J. H. Taylor, *National Insurance*, 4th ed. (1913); E. R. Dewsnup, *The Housing Problem in England, its Statistics, Legislation, and Policy* (1907); A. R. Wallace, *Land Nationalisation, its Necessity and its Aims* (1882); A. H. Dyke Acland (chairman), *The Report of the Land Enquiry Committee*, 2 vols. (1914); Gilbert Slater, *The English Peasantry and the Enclosure of the Common Fields* (1907); F. G. Heath, *British Rural Life and Labour* (1911); R. E. Prothero, *English Farming Past and Present*

(1912); W. J. Ashley, *British Industries*, 2d ed. (1907), and, by the same author, *The Tariff Problem* (1903); William Cunningham, *Rise and Decline of the Free Trade Movement*, 2d ed. (1905), like Ashley's work, a plea for the acceptance of Joseph Chamberlain's tariff proposals; George Armitage-Smith, *The Free Trade Movement and its Results* (1898); William Smart, *Return to Protection* (1904); Graham Balfour, *The Educational Systems of Great Britain and Ireland*, 2d ed. (1903).

The Irish Question. Sketches of Irish history: W. O'C. Morris, *Ireland, 1798–1898* (1898); Charles Johnston and Carita Spencer, *Ireland's Story* (1905); Goldwin Smith, *Irish History and the Irish Question* (1905); Alice S. Green, *Irish Nationality* (1911), in "Home University Library." Somewhat more detailed or specialized works: Louis Paul-Dubois, *Contemporary Ireland*, Eng. trans. (1908), containing an excellent account of the land question and of educational and religious problems, with much historical background; Alice E. Murray, *A History of the Commercial and Financial Relations between England and Ireland from the Period of the Restoration* (1903); W. P. O'Brien, *Great Famine in Ireland and a Retrospect of the Fifty Years 1845–1895* (1896); T. P. O'Connor, *Parnell Movement, with a Sketch of Irish Parties from 1843*, 2d ed. (1886); R. B. O'Brien, *Life of Charles Stewart Parnell*, 2 vols. in 1 (1898); J. H. Parnell, *Charles Stewart Parnell* (1914), a brother's intimate study; G. J. Shaw-Lefevre (Baron Eversley), *Gladstone and Ireland, the Irish Policy of Parliament from 1850–1894* (1912); Michael Davitt, *The Fall of Feudalism in Ireland, or the Story of the Land League Revolution* (1904); Sir Horace Plunkett, *Ireland in the New Century* (1904); T. D. Ingram, *A History of the Legislative Union of Great Britain and Ireland* (1887), an attempt to justify English policies toward Ireland; S. Rosenbaum (editor), *Against Home Rule : the Case for the Union* (1912), a collection of partisan articles by A. J. Balfour, J. A. Chamberlain, Sir Edward Carson, and other conspicuous Unionists.

THE "NATIONS" OF EUROPE
IN THE NINETEENTH CENTURY

Scale of Miles
0   50   100   200   300

SHETLAND IS.

ORKNEY IS.

HEBRIDES

Scotland

Edinburgh

Dublin
Pwllheli

London

Calais

CHANNEL IS.

Brest

Rouen

Paris

Orleans

Bordeaux

Tolosa
Bilbao   BASQUES

Madrid

Valencia

BALEARIC IS.

Amsterdam

West
Friesland
Low
Flemings
Brussels
Walloons
Aix
la Chapelle
Luxemburg
Strassburg
Basel
Lyons
Marseilles
Barcelona

Hamburg
Hanover
Cassel
Cologne
Frankfurt
Mayence
Stuttgart
Munich
Milan
Genoa
Florence
CORSICA
Ajaccio
Catalans
SARDINIA

Chri

Longitude   West   0°   5°   Longitu

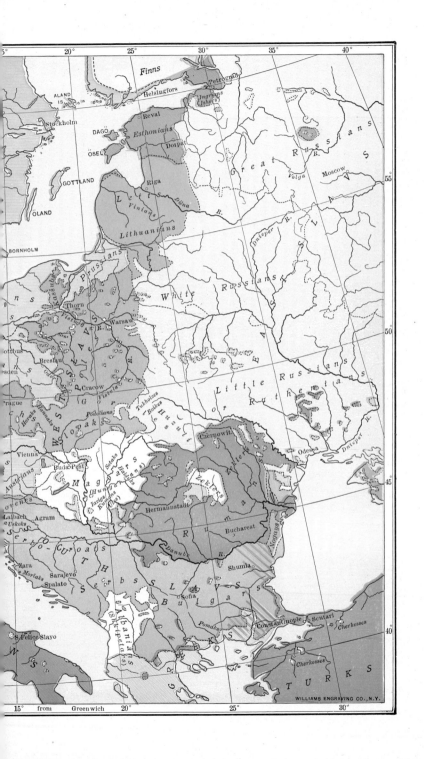

CHAPTER XXIII

LATIN EUROPE, 1870–1914

1. THE THIRD FRENCH REPUBLIC

THE MAKING OF THE REPUBLIC

THE French political groups that during the last years of Napoleon III had supplied the chief criticisms of his imperial régime, were the Republicans, the Liberal Monarchists, and the Socialists. It was only natural, then, that when disaster overtook the imperial arms at Sedan, these same factions at Paris should hasten to declare (4 September, 1870) the deposition of Napoleon III and his dynasty. They proclaimed a "republic" to take the place of the discredited empire, because that was the only name which seemed sufficiently comprehensive and elastic to hold together their discordant elements. By "republic" each of these three groups meant a different thing: most Republicans thought of it as a restoration of the bourgeois Jacobinism of 1792 and 1848; Liberal Monarchists perceived in it a temporary scaffolding for the erection by a democratically inclined Bourbon prince of a government in France modeled after that of England; and the Socialists dreamed of the speedy fulfillment of Karl Marx's communist schemes and economic, as well as political, democracy.

Revolutionary Proclamation of the Third Republic, 4 September, 1870

So long as Paris was besieged by Germans, the three groups held together fairly well. Socialists participated actively in the national defense. Gambetta, the Republican leader, and Thiers, the Liberal Monarchist, were the two most conspicuous supporters of the provisional government: Gambetta, escaping from Paris in a balloon, became the heart and soul of that stubborn patriotic resistance which protracted the hopeless struggle for several

The National Assembly, 1871–1875

331

months, while Thiers undertook a diplomatic mission to every important European capital in a vain endeavor to obtain foreign assistance for France.   But when at length in January, 1871, Paris surrendered to the Germans and a truce was agreed to in order that the French people might elect a National Assembly to treat for peace with the victors, then a cleavage appeared between Republicans and Monarchists.   The latter were willing for the sake of peace to make even unfavorable terms with the Germans; the former, anxious not to handicap the republic at the outset with a disastrous foreign treaty, were bent on continuing the war.

On this issue the first electoral campaign under the Third Republic was waged in February, 1871, with the result that of the seven-hundred-odd representatives who were elected by universal manhood suffrage of the French nation, five hundred were reckoned as Monarchists and only two hundred as Republicans.   The apparent triumph of the Monarchists did not prove that the nation preferred a monarchical form of government but simply showed that the overwhelming majority of the French people were sick and tired of the German War.

Its Monarchist Complexion

The National Assembly, meeting at Bordeaux, naturally refused formally to sanction the Republic, contenting itself with choosing Thiers as "head of the executive power" and with deciding that he should exercise his power under the supervision of the Assembly and with the aid of ministers chosen and directed by himself. Having thus by the so-called Compact of Bordeaux (17 February, 1871) arranged temporarily for the internal government of France, the National Assembly, with its Monarchist majority moved to Versailles, and in due time ratified the humiliating treaty of Frankfort (May, 1871), according to which, as we have learned,[1] Alsace and the greater part of Lorraine were ceded to the newly created German Empire, and France promised to pay a war indemnity of five billion francs.   Thus the first work of the National Assembly — the work for which it had been specifically convoked — was accomplished and peace was restored.

Its Conclusion of Peace with Germany

[1] See above, p. 201.

But before the ratification of the treaty with the Germans, another cleavage appeared in the groups that had acclaimed the "republic," a cleavage between the Parisian work- ingmen and the bourgeois Assembly, a cleavage that led to the brief but terrible civil war known as the Commune. "Commune" in France is the ordi- nary word signifying the local government of what in the United States would be termed a township or a municipality. *Its Difficulties with the Revolutionary Commune of Paris, 1871* Now it so happened that, in the troubled con- ditions within Paris consequent upon the rigorous five-month siege of the city by the Germans, an unofficial "central com- mittee," which had been elected by the workingmen to look after their interests, and had been installed in the headquarters of the Socialistic "International," fused with another "central committee" of Republican guardsmen to form a Joint Com- mittee which established itself in the city-hall and took over the actual government of the Commune of Paris. This revolu- tionary Commune, reënforced by a municipal election conducted under its auspices, constituted the real government of Paris from March to May, 1871.

This Commune was at no time a homogeneous body. Of its members, nearly half were bourgeois Radicals of the type of 1793, while the other half, composed of workingmen, were divided about equally between Socialist members of the Inter- national — followers of Karl Marx — and Anarchist disciples of Proudhon. Yet common grievances held it together. Paris, especially its workingmen, had suffered from the recent war more severely than any other part of France. Paris, being pre- dominantly Republican, distrusted the Monarchist Assembly and disliked the transfer of the national capital from Paris to Versailles. Worst of all was the economic distress in the city. Not only were the factories shut down and the labor-market glutted by the sudden disbanding of a host of regular troops, but the Versailles government ordered the resumption of the payment of rents and notes, which had been suspended during the war, and at the same time suppressed the payment of the franc-and- a-half daily wage to the national guardsmen, which had been the sole means of subsistence to a large majority of workingmen in the city. No doubt these last measures were urgently demanded in view of the exhausted condition of the national treasury, but they were quite naturally deemed by the workingmen to have been dictated not so much in their interest as in that of the upper and middle classes.

So the Commune of Paris revolted against the National Assembly, declaring that the city was free and sovereign and that the French state should consist simply of a loose federation of self-governing Communes. Most of France, outside of Paris, angered by this outrage on national patriotism, flocked to the support of Thiers and of the Versailles Assembly, and fighting began. The actual military operations, which lasted from 1 April to 28 May, 1871, were the usual story of the siege and sacking of a city: the slow advance of the besiegers, who were better disciplined, armed, and generaled, the taking of outpost after outpost, the attack on a weak position of the rampart near the St. Cloud gate, the entrance of the Versailles troops, the desperate defense behind the barricades, the capture of one section after another, the firing of public buildings, the assassination of the archbishop, the frantic efforts of the conquerors to stay the flames and to exterminate the rebels, the frenzy of the vanquished and the ferocity of the victors, the piles of dead, the ruined buildings and squares, the wholesale massacre of prisoners, the deportations and imprisonments. The number of Parisians killed by French soldiers in the last week of May, 1871, was at least 15,000, and possibly double that number. It was a terrible fate that such a cruel siege and capture of Paris should follow so closely upon the siege and capture of the city by the Germans, but it was an inevitable aftermath of the trickery and ambition which had precipitated the Franco-German War. The real authors of the Paris Commune of 1871 were not the workingmen, but Bismarck and Napoleon III.

Its Suppression of the Parisian Rebellion

The suppression of the Commune made it certain that for many years to come the Third French Republic would preserve its moderate and bourgeois character. The numbers both of Socialists and of Anarchists were greatly diminished, and their principles were discredited in the eyes of the nation. At the same time, the extreme bitterness which rankled in the minds of Communists who

Significance of the "Commune of 1871"

survived, served in the long run to commit a group of French workingmen to ultra-Radicalism.

By the end of May, 1871, Thiers and the National Assembly had made peace with the Germans and had restored order in France. The Assembly, however, despite Republican protests, gave no indication of a purpose to termi- nate its career. In fact, the Monarchist majority proceeded on 31 August, 1871, to enact the Rivet Law, whereby the Assembly arrogated to itself full power not only to make laws for France but also to draw up a constitution for the country and conferred upon Thiers the new title of "president of the French Republic," stipulating that he should thereafter be responsible to the Assembly and implying that he would be removable by majority vote. From August, 1871, more than four years were to elapse before the National Assembly would dissolve, and they were to be four years of supreme importance in laying the foundations for a new era. Throughout two of the four years Thiers himself was the guiding spirit.

The Rivet Law (1871): Thiers "President"

In the first place, the government reorganized the national finances and floated additional loans with such amazing success that in 1873 the final installment of the war indemnity of five billion francs was paid to Germany and the last German troops were withdrawn from French soil. The fact that the great bulk of the prodigious loans were subscribed to by Frenchmen, and a goodly part of them by peasants, was at once a proof of the wealth of the country and a guarantee of the stability of the new régime.

The National Assembly's Financial Achievements

Secondly, elaborate military reforms were inaugurated. Following the example of victorious Prussia, universal compulsory service was decreed, the term being fixed as five years in the active army and eleven years in the reserve, and the only exemptions allowed being in the cases of clergymen, teachers, and sons of widows. Moreover, strong fortresses were erected along the new German frontier and the defenses of Paris were strengthened; the provision of arms, ammunition, and other supplies was perfected; and naval construction was quickened. It was apparent that France, though lately defeated, was resolved to retain her position and prestige as a

Its Military Reforms

Great Power, and that many influential Frenchmen were already thinking of a "War of Revenge" for the recovery of Alsace-Lorraine. Militarism became an early attribute of the Third Republic.

Thirdly, it was this same National Assembly that reformed the local government of the country and devised the form of the central government, which, with slight modifications, has endured in France for a longer period than any governmental system since the days of the old régime and of Bourbon absolutism.

In reforming the local government the members of the National Assembly, whether Monarchist or Republican, were in

Its Conservation of Earlier System of Local Government

practical agreement. The system of local administration, planned during the Revolution and developed under Napoleon I, had since been preserved by Louis XVIII, Charles X, Louis Philippe, the Second Republic, and Napoleon III; and now that the Paris Commune had been suppressed, there was no serious demand from any quarter for an essential change. For administrative purposes, therefore, France continued to be divided into 86 Departments, or 87 if the "territory of Belfort" — a remnant of Alsace — be considered as a separate Department, with the addition, for most purposes, of the three Departments of Algeria. Each Department remained under a Prefect, named by the central government, and assisted by a General Council elected for six years by universal manhood suffrage. Under the Third Republic the powers of this General Council were extended so as to include the apportionment of taxes, relief of the poor, and care of the highways and public schools.[1] Each Department continued to be divided into several Arrondissements, or Districts, which were under Sub-Prefects, likewise appointed by the central government and advised by popularly elected Councils of the Arrondissement. Each Arrondissement continued to be divided into Communes, the lowest units of local government. By 1911 there were 36,241 Communes in France, of which more than half had fewer than 500 inhabitants each and only a few had a population in excess of 20,000. The local administration of each Commune was vested in a Municipal Council elected for four years by universal man-

---

[1] In accordance with a law of August, 1871.

hood suffrage, and in a Mayor chosen by the Municipal Council.[1]
In an intermediate position between the divisions of the Arrondissements and the Communes survived the Cantons, not as
administrative districts, but as seats of justices of the peace.

Such is the framework of local government that has existed
in France throughout the period of the Third Republic.   To its
absolute uniformity, the only exception is in the ad-   Local
ministration of Paris,[2] where the duties of government   Government
are distributed among a special Prefect of Police and   of Paris
the regular Prefect of the Department of the Seine — both
appointed by the central government — and a peculiar Municipal
Council, composed of four elected representatives from each of
the twenty Arrondissements (Wards) into which the city is
divided, each Arrondissement possessing a Mayor of its own.

Of this whole framework, centralization is still the distinguishing characteristic.   The central government has the right
to nominate all Prefects and Sub-Prefects, as well as   Chief
the right to veto any act of a General Council, a Coun-   Character-
cil of an Arrondissement, or a Municipal Council.   The   istics of the
French
ninety Prefects, moreover, are the very eyes and the   System of
right arms of the central government; they make fre-   Local
Government
quent reports to it of what goes on in their Departments; they appoint numerous subordinate officials; they supervise the execution of national laws, control the local police, and
themselves enjoy the power of veto over the acts of any representative body within their respective Departments.   The Prefects
are the real successors of the Intendants of the days of Cardinal
Richelieu.   The centralization of administration, which has
proceeded further in France than in any other country of the
world, operates in practice to insure the faithful, uniform execution of national laws throughout the entire country and to
enable one readily to fix the responsibility for any non-enforce-
ment of law.   Moreover, involving, as it does, the popular
election of but three or four officials, it tends to produce the
advantages of the "short ballot," particularly simplicity and the
centering of public attention upon the qualifications of the few
who are elected.   But, on the other hand, despite the elaborate
system of administrative courts, which are supposed to safeguard

[1] Only since 1884.   [2] And in the administration of Lyons.

civil servants against arbitrary dismissal from office, the centralized government has often been accused of using its
control of local government to promote personal and partisan ends, to influence national elections and to reward
friends with offices.

While the members of the National Assembly proved to be
unanimous in 1871 in their desire to maintain and fortify
the relatively venerable institutions of French local
government, they fell to quarreling bitterly about
the future form of the central government. Should
it be a republic or a monarchy? When it is recalled
that five hundred out of the seven hundred deputies
were avowed Monarchists, it may seem surprising
that the question was not promptly and vociferously
answered with the word "monarchy." But a grave
difficulty lurked in the fact that the Monarchist majority was split into three seemingly irreconcilable factions, none
of which alone possessed a controlling vote. Of the three factions,
the Imperialists, as the followers of Napoleon III were henceforth
styled, were naturally, in view of the recent disastrous war, an
almost negligible quantity, but the other two — Legitimists
and Orleanists — were numerous and very quarrelsome. The
Legitimists supported the claims of the count of Chambord
(1820–1883), the grandson of Charles X, and worked for the
restoration of a government as far as possible in harmony with
the ancient traditions of French royalty. On the other hand,
the Orleanists upheld the cause of Liberal Monarchy as exemplified in the governmental system of Great Britain and as
feasible in the person of the count of Paris (1838–1894), the
grandson of that bourgeois duke of Orleans, Louis Philippe.
Between the count of Chambord and the count of Paris no love
was lost, for the grandfather of one had not so long ago been
chased out of France by the grandfather of the other; and
among their respective partisans their divergent principles were
still kept alive. Under these curious circumstances the National Assembly for a long time made little progress in framing
a constitution for the Third Republic. The Republicans were
hopelessly outnumbered and the Monarchists were disputing
among themselves.

Strife in Na-
tional
Assembly
concerning
Form of
Permanent
Central
Govern-
ment: Re-
public or
Monarchy?

In 1872, however, the Monarchists were temporarily brought together by the confession of Thiers that their bickerings had converted him from Liberal Monarchy to Republicanism and that in his opinion the majority of the French people desired a Republican form of government. In the following May they united in forcing his resignation and in electing as president the unwavering Monarchist and Clerical, Marshal MacMahon (1808–1893). And by August it seemed as if their differences were quite composed and as if they could proceed forthwith to proclaim the Bourbon Monarchy, for in that month the count of Paris traveled to Austria, threw himself at the feet of his cousin, the count of Chambord, begging pardon and friendship, and consented to an arrangement whereby the latter should succeed to the French throne as " Henry V," while he himself should be recognized as heir-apparent.

Temporary Advantage of Monarchists

But the agreement of the Monarchists was short-lived. The announcement in October, 1873, by the prospective "Henry V" of his unalterable determination not to abandon the principles of divine-right monarchy nor the white flag of the Bourbons sealed his fate, and incidentally that of the monarchy. The Orleanists drew back and reaffirmed their devotion' to Liberalism. Marshal Mac-Mahon, sturdy soldier and zealous Monarchist, acutely observed that at the very sight of the white flag of absolutism "the rifles in the army would go off by themselves." And the revulsion of feeling displayed itself throughout the country in the victory of the Republicans at the by-elections which were held to fill vacancies in the Assembly. The French people were obviously too steeped in the constitutional doctrines of the Revolution to accept a very obstinate prince, just as he was, with his old-fashioned principles and his moth-eaten flag.

The Chambord Incident, 1873

Henceforth but one practicable course presented itself to the Orleanists and other Liberal Monarchists, and that was to organize, in conjunction with the Republicans, a government which could serve as a makeshift till the count of Chambord had taken the white flag to the grave and had left the way to the throne open to the count of Paris. The first step in such a course was taken in

Halting Acceptance of the Republic by the National Assembly

November, 1873, when a bill was passed bestowing upon Marshal MacMahon the title and office of President of the Republic for a definite term of seven years. So great, however, were the natural antipathies between the two factions, on whose joint action the adoption of even a makeshift now depended, that it was not until January, 1875, that the National Assembly took the next step. At that time it adopted by the slender margin of one vote an amendment which provided for the election of future presidents of the Republic, thereby practically recognizing the Republic. Then followed more rapidly two constitutional laws in February and a third in July. These "constitutional laws," thus loosely drafted and voted piecemeal by a National Assembly which had been elected four years earlier to make peace with the Germans, and in which Monarchists still predominated, proved to be, with very few subsequent amendments, the permanent constitution of the Third French Republic.

The " Constitutional Laws of 1875 "

Unlike earlier instruments of government in France, the constitutional laws of 1875 were of an essentially practical nature: they laid down no theoretical principles, and their provisions were confined to what was necessary to insure the proper operation of governmental machinery. In many respects they showed clear borrowing from the British system of parliamentary government, and in other respects compromises between the Republican and Monarchist framers. The system which they established may be sketched as follows:

Government of the Third Republic

The legislative power was given to a parliament, consisting of two elective Chambers, a majority vote of both of which is necessary to enact laws. The two Chambers, when they meet jointly as a National Assembly, have the right to amend the constitutional laws and the duty of electing the President of the Republic. One Chamber, the Chamber of Deputies, which in 1914 comprised 602 members, is elected by direct universal manhood suffrage,[1] and is renewed every four years; the other, the Senate,

[1] The manner of election of Deputies has been modified several times since 1871. The *scrutin de liste*, under which each elector votes for as many Deputies as the entire Department has to elect, was introduced in 1871. In 1876 it was replaced by the *scrutin d'arrondissement*, under which each Department is divided into a number of Arrondissements, each elector voting for one Deputy only; in 1885 there was a return to the *scrutin de liste;* in 1889 resort was again had to the

consists of three hundred members, chosen by indirect election [1] for nine years, a third of the house being renewed every three years. The executive power was intrusted to a President, elected by the National Assembly for seven years and eligible for reëlection. His powers are theoretically extremely broad, including the initiative in legislation jointly with the Chambers, the appointment of all civil and military officers, the right of individual pardon, the conduct of foreign relations and the conclusion of treaties (which, however, in some cases must be ratified by the Chambers), the mobilization of the army (although a formal declaration of war may be made only with the approval of the Chambers), and, with the consent of the Senate, the dissolution at any time of the Chamber of Deputies and the direction of new elections thereto. But in practice, not a single one of these wide powers may be exercised by the President without the written countersignature of a member of the Ministry, who are severally and jointly responsible to the Chambers.

In this way the French parliament is supreme in the execution of laws as well as in the making of laws and in the amending of the constitution. The Ministry, who discharge the functions of the President and who likewise control the whole machinery of local government throughout France, must maintain a majority in the Chambers; if they fail to carry the measures they propose or if the Chambers pass a vote of "lack of confidence," they must resign and leave to the President the task of forming a new cabinet which can command

Supremacy of the Parliament

---

scrutin d'arrondissement; and since then the same system has remained. In 1889 it was enacted that each candidate is bound to make, within the fortnight which precedes the elections, a declaration as to his being a candidate for a given constituency, and for one constituency only — all votes which may eventually be given him in other constituencies being reckoned as void. Elections are conducted under the auspices of a commission of Councilors-General appointed by the Prefect of the Department. As in most Continental countries, elections are held on Sunday, and a Deputy-elect must have received an absolute majority, rather than a mere plurality of all votes cast; if a clear majority is not forthcoming in a given constituency, a second ballot must be taken two weeks later.

[1] The Senators are chosen in each Department by special electoral colleges that include the Deputies and the Councilors-General of the Department, and the members of the Councils of the Arrondissements and delegates elected by the Councils of the Communes into which the Department is divided. Until 1884 provision was made for the election of 75 Senators for life.

the Chambers' confidence. Thus, unlike the American Republic, the French Republic does not recognize the principle of a division of political powers but subordinates all of them to an elected parliament. In this respect it approaches the parliamentary system of Great Britain. In fact the French President is reduced to the position of a fine figure-head, a kind of elected British king, whose chief obligations are of a social and ceremonial character.

Having drafted the constitutional laws, whose main provisions have just been indicated, the National Assembly closed its manifold labors late in 1875; and the first regular elections under the Third Republic were held. The result was the return of a Republican Chamber of Deputies and of a Monarchist Senate, and a renewal of fierce partisan strife between the two factions for the control of the whole machinery of government.

Close of the National Assembly, 1875

In these trying days, while it was still a doubtful question of republic or monarchy, the real Monarchist leader was President MacMahon himself. He did all he could to extend that party's propaganda. He appealed with much success to the old nobility, to the peasantry, and to the soldiers. To the same end, he utilized his secular patronage and his right, in accordance with the Concordat of 1801, to name the French bishops. In order to identify French Clericalism fully with the political cause of monarchy, he gave moral support to the agitation for French intervention in Italy in behalf of the pope's temporal power and he gave liberally toward defraying the expense of building, "as an expiation for the sins of revolution," the great Church of the Sacred Heart on the heights of Montmartre, where crowds of Communists had been shot down in 1871. And in the duke of Broglie (1821–1901), MacMahon had for some time a prime minister who actively sought to further all these policies.

Marshal Mac-Mahon, President and Monarchist

On the Republican side, the foremost leader was Léon Gambetta. Born in southeastern France in 1838, the son of a grocer of Genoese descent, Gambetta had become a lawyer in Paris and was already a hostile critic of Napoleon III when in 1868 he acquired national notoriety as the brilliant successful attorney for a certain Delescluze, a journalist

Gambetta, Republican Leader

who was on trial [1] charged with collecting subscriptions for a monument to a man who had resisted the *coup d'état* of 1851. Gambetta was speedily elected in 1869 to the Chamber of Deputies, where he joined the small Republican minority and in the following year voted with them against the German War. But once the war was well under way and the French were suffering severe reverses, the patriotism of Gambetta became the central point of national resistance. He it was who helped to proclaim the republic on 4 September, 1870; he it was who for the next five months, as a member of the Committee of National Defense and virtual dictator of the country, displayed immense energy and skill in bringing army after army of raw recruits against the unconquerable Germans; and he it was whose unquenchable spirit, never admitting defeat, fought vainly in February, 1871, both in the electoral campaign and in the National Assembly against yielding Alsace-Lorraine and making peace with the national foe.

Although Gambetta distrusted Thiers and detested the Monarchist majority in the National Assembly, he entertained little sympathy for such extreme Radicalism as was exemplified in the Paris Commune, and he was doubt- less glad to retire to Spain during the spring of 1871 while the Versailles government was suppressing civil war. Gambetta was an early type of a host of politicians who have figured in the annals of the Third Republic — a middle-class Radical, extremely patriotic, very much devoted to the assurance of business prosperity, a true friend of internal security, whose Radicalism was primarily of a political and religious character not much given to special theorizing about the welfare of the working classes. In other words, Gambetta and most of the Republican leaders after him supported Capitalism with one arm and with the other dealt staggering blows at Clericalism. This is really what is meant when the opinions of Gambetta are referred to as "Moderate."

It was the moderation of Gambetta as well as his remarkable gifts of oratory that enabled him after June, 1871, when he took

Gambetta a "Moderate" Republican

---

[1] Delescluze (1809–1871) was a member of the Socialist "International," and subsequently a member of the Paris Commune, and died fighting on the barricades in May, 1871.

a seat in the National Assembly, to hold the Republican minority together and gradually in the course of the ensuing four years to effect compromise after compromise with the faction of Liberal Monarchists. Next to the exigencies of the Orleanists, the political ideas and maneuvers of Gambetta were the most potent factor in actually shaping the constitution of the Third French Republic.

Now that the new form of government was in operation, it devolved upon Gambetta to lead the political struggle against

Gambetta and the Rise of Anti-Clericalism

President MacMahon's subversive tendencies and to enlist wider popular support for the Republican régime. Shrewdly taking advantage of the objections to the intellectual and political position of the Catholic Church, objections which were undoubtedly growing in the last years of the pontificate of Pope Pius IX, he raised the question of Clericalism. In the Chamber and in the country he poured out floods of oratory now against the Monarchists because they aided the Church and now against the Church because it was run by Monarchists and for Monarchists. As he expected, his attacks upon the Clericals became increasingly popular and gradually swelled the number of Republicans. And an especially bitter diatribe which he delivered in the Chamber on 4 May, 1877, in the course of which he uttered the memorable phrase — "Clericalism, there is the enemy" — was the immediate occasion for the real test of strength between Gambetta and MacMahon.

Tiring of the chronic disputes between himself and the Republican Chamber and believing that the Republican leader's

Issue of the Struggle between MacMahon and Gambetta

rampant Anti-Clericalism would be properly rebuked by the country at large, the Monarchist President on 16 May, 1877, appointed a Clerical ministry under the duke of Broglie and adjourned the Chamber of Deputies for a month, and then formally dissolved it, with the constitutional consent of the Senate, and directed that new elections should be held throughout France. The ensuing electoral campaign was one of the most spectacular and stubbornly contested in history. Both Gambetta and the President made speech-making tours. None could deny that both had loved their country and deserved well of the nation; none could doubt MacMahon's sincerity; but few could withstand Gambetta's eloquence. The campaign proved to be one of the most decisive in history, for the Republicans won, securing almost as large a majority in the new Chamber as they had possessed in the old, and a Republican ministry replaced that of the duke of Broglie. For another year the Monarchist and Clerical Marshal-President doggedly struggled on against powerful odds, but when, early in 1879, partial elections to the Senate insured Republican control of that house as well as of the Chamber of Deputies, he finally perceived the hopelessness of his situation. He resigned the presidency in January, 1879, and was succeeded by Jules Grévy (1813–1891), a thorough-going Republican. In the following year (1880), the seat of government was transferred from Versailles to Paris, and the fourteenth of July — the anniversary of the fall of the Bastille and the day dear to French Revolutionaries — was formally proclaimed the national holiday. France was Republican.

Thus the Third French Republic, proclaimed in 1870, came fully into Republican hands first in 1879. Gambetta, to whom must be awarded chief credit for the outcome of the nine years' political struggle, did not long survive; after a brief term as prime minister, he was accidentally killed (1882) under tragic circumstances. But the Republicans, though they were thereby deprived of their ablest leader and henceforth tended to break up into petty factions, never lost control of the state. On the contrary, from 1879 to 1914, the Republicans were always growing in number and strength and the Monarchists were steadily declining to the position of an inconsequential faction.

Republicans in Control of the Republic, 1879

The Bourgeois Character of the Republic and the Repression of Clerical and Military Opposition

As general features in the history of the Third Republic under Republicans and down to the year 1914 may be remarked first the bourgeois character and policies of the dominant statesmen and politicians, witnessed alike in internal affairs and in external relations; secondly, the conflict with Clericalism; and thirdly, the problems of militarism.

The Republic under Republicans

In following the history of the Third Republic one is struck by the almost complete absence of the names of noblemen and

The Governing Class in France, 1879-1914 clergymen from the list of prominent statesmen and publicists; one is also struck by the utter lack of any person who during the period stood politically head and shoulders above other persons; in a word, one is struck by the simple fact that the working majority in the parliament, the chief local officials, the cabinet-members, and the presidents were, almost without exception, lawyers, or teachers, or business men, — members of the middle class, intelligent, well-educated, and competent, but on a uniform level of society and of achievement.

That such a company of public men should devote their best efforts to promoting material prosperity was to be expected;

Promotion of Material Prosperity and it is a fact that under the Third Republic France made greater economic advance than in any earlier period of like duration. In line with policies of Louis Philippe and of Napoleon III, agriculture, industry, and commerce were encouraged in every conceivable way. Between 1879 and 1904 public moneys equal in amount to the huge war indemnity paid to Germany were expended on works of peace within France: approximately 200,000 kilometers of splendid new highways were built; 200 kilometers of canals were added to the existing 1000, and all were freed from public dues (1880) and from private tolls (1889); 30,000 kilometers of new railway were laid; harbors were deepened at Dunkirk, Dieppe, Rouen, Nantes, and Bordeaux, and spacious new ones were constructed

Agriculture at Le Havre and St. Nazaire. Upon the agricultural classes, still relatively very important in France because of the fertility of the country and the traditional thrift of the numerous peasant proprietors, many favors were conferred: a special ministry of agriculture was created (1881); large financial grants were made in aid of the vine-growers (1879); bounties were repeatedly voted to foster the culture of silk, flax, and hemp, and for the breeding of horses; farmers were authorized (1884) to form coöperative societies for collective buying and selling; mutual loan banks and insurance companies were established (1894) under state guarantees to assist the peasants; agricultural schools were opened and endowed; and a system of tariff protection in favor of agricultural produce, especially of wheat and beet-root sugar, partially secured by a law of 1885, was completed by the great tariff act of 1892. The efficacy of these measures is partly registered in the fact that the annual value of the agricultural output of France, which between 1800 and 1860 only rose from four to six billions of francs, reached in 1913 a total in excess of eleven billions.

But the growth of French industry during the period was even more remarkable than the agricultural advance. The machines in the factories increased in number from 30,000 to 90,000, multiplying themselves tenfold in power, from 870,000 horse-power to 8,600,000. The output of the coal mines was doubled, and that of the blast-furnaces was multiplied sixfold. Though the chief market for French industries was at home, there was none the less an increase of 25 per cent in exported goods. It was to protect industry as well as agriculture that the Republic adopted in 1892 the policy of a high customs tariff.

Industry

It was likewise to the advantage of French business that under the Third Republic a particularly vigorous colonial policy was pursued. Deferring until Part V of this volume a detailed treatment of the manner and extent of French colonial expansion, it will suffice in this place to state three facts: first, that by 1914 France possessed a new colonial empire in Africa, in Indo-China, and in island archipelagoes of the Pacific, to say nothing of the scattered remnants of the old-time empire in America and in India, which in total area and population ranked second only to the British Empire; secondly, that of these holdings, considerably more than three-fourths of the area and of the population were added under Republican auspices between 1879 and 1913; and thirdly, that the annual trade of France with her colonies steadily increased during the period from 350 million francs to nearly two billions. To French capitalists, the new colonies afforded not only good markets for the sale of the surplus products of their factories and farms but excellent fields for the investment of surplus capital in such lucrative enterprises as the development of natural resources and the introduction of internal improvements. By means of constant military expeditions and the maintenance of

Vigorous Colonial Policy

a powerful navy for many years surpassed in tonnage and armor only by that of Great Britain, the French Republic preserved order throughout her colonial empire and incidentally guaranteed to her capitalists safe financial returns on their investments.

Of course business was not the sole motive that actuated this distant empire-building of the Third Republic. Religion played its part, too. The devout Catholic priest who found in the French flag and arms a valuable protection for his missionary zeal among infidels and heathen, was able, at least on one question, to agree with the worldly business man; and on the other hand, the business man, often strenuously Anti-Clerical at home, discovered the missionaries to be so useful in preparing the natives for the commodities of Western civilization that on colonial matters he could afford to be tolerably Clerical. But even more controlling than religion — because it was more universally entertained by Frenchmen — was the potent motive of nationalism in colonial expansion. For a nation which since the sixteenth century had had a glorious, if somewhat unfortunate, history of exploration and colonization and which recently had suffered at German hands a sharp diminution of international prestige and the loss of two rich provinces in Europe, it was perfectly natural to transfer ambitions and energies beyond the seas to other continents. Humiliated at home, France sought consolation abroad; and imperialism was the one thing which could unite the nation. Capitalists and Clericals led the way, and all patriotic people followed. A boasted pilot of political democracy in Europe, the Third Republic definitely embarked upon a wholesale policy of proudly and arbitrarily ruling "inferior" races in other parts of the globe.

Thus, by means of colonialism, of tariff protectionism, and of the matchless domestic developments in industry, commerce, and agriculture, — all attended and supported by a great show of militarism, — the wealth of France enormously increased under the Third Republic. Not only did Frenchmen continually add to their investments of capital in their own country and in their colonies, but they became the foremost money-lenders of the Continent, as regards both the bond-issues of foreign governments and the stock-sales of foreign development-companies.

Clerical Support of Colonialism

Increase of Wealth

In France, as in other countries affected by the Industrial Revolution, the increase of wealth was not evenly distributed. There still remained the proletariat, working long Social hours for small wages, huddled in the cities or in the Legislation mines, and deprived of most comforts of life. To reduce the number of this class the Third Republic did little, but to ameliorate their lot it enacted several measures. In thus entering the sphere of social politics and impressing a new character upon the whole period, Republican statesmen were undoubtedly moved by three motives : first, a sense of fair-play in the minds of many respectable middle-class citizens, mingled in some cases with an idea that a contented healthy working class would be a most valuable national asset; secondly, a certain fear of Socialism and a willingness to grant some concessions to workingmen in order to avoid what might otherwise be a dire necessity of conceding all the Socialist demands; and thirdly, a political bid for the support of the working classes against Monarchy and Clericalism. Sometimes it was one of these motives behind a bit of social legislation, sometimes another, sometimes all three.

Of the social legislation which belonged to the Third Republic during the era from 1871 to 1914, the following significant measures may be cited. (1) The great Act of 1892,[1] as subsequently amended in certain particulars, regulated the employment of women; forbade the employment of children under thirteen years of age; provided a maximum working day of ten hours for all workingmen; prohibited all manual work on Sunday, except in certain industries, in which, however, another day of the week must be substituted for Sunday as a day of rest; and placed elaborate restrictions on labor in the mines. (2) An act of 1893, amended in 1903, made adequate provision for the hygiene and safety of workers in industrial establishments, and another act of the year 1893 insured free medical attendance for workingmen and their families. (3) An act of 1900 required shopkeepers to provide seats for all the women and children employed by them, and extended many of the factory laws to cover retail shops. (4) An act of 1905 provided for miners a maximum working-day of nine hours, which was reduced to eight hours by an act of 1907. (5) A very important act of 1884 followed

[1] This act was a development of measures passed in 1848, 1874, and 1885.

up the Napoleonic act of 1864, which had partially recognized trade unions, by according full protection and encouragement to the numerous activities of combinations of workingmen, with a result that by 1913 French trade unions (*syndicats*) numbered more than 12,000 with at least two million members, many of them possessing employment bureaus, libraries, insurance funds, and even professional and technical schools. (6) An act of 1892 created machinery for official but voluntary conciliation and arbitration in the case of collective disputes between employers and workmen. (7) An important act of 1898 obliged employers to compensate workmen for injuries received in the course of their employment. (8) In 1911 a system of old-age pensions came into force in France, embracing all wage-earners with the exception of railway servants, miners, and sailors, for whom special provision already had been made, and including domestic servants and farm laborers; the system is compulsory and contributory, the premiums being paid partly by the workers, partly by the employers, and partly by the state.

The Third Republic acquired a merited reputation not only for an attempt to confer some measure of "social justice" upon **Guarantees of Individual Liberties** the workingmen, but likewise, and in line with its heritage from the French Revolution, for repeated statutory guarantees of the rights and liberties of the individual. "Liberty" was stressed. A law of 1881, as amended twenty years later, established the right of holding meetings without any preliminary authorization on the part of the government and full freedom of speech. Another act of 1881, which assured the freedom of publication, is one of the most liberal press laws in the world: by it all offenses committed by any kind of publication are submitted to a jury; and the punishment for mere expression of obnoxious opinions is abolished, the only penalties being for slander, libel, inciting to crime, and in certain instances the publication of false news. A third act, the famous Associations Act of 1901, decreed the freedom of association, by recognizing, on condition of a simple declaration to the administrative authorities, the legal status of all voluntary societies, the objects of which are not contrary to law or to public order or morality, the monastic congregations of the Catholic Church alone being excepted.

In this connection it may be noted that the Third Republic in harmony with a general tendency of the era adopted a good deal of humanitarian legislation. Between 1871 and 1914 there were more than fifty enactments involving important modifications of the criminal law, due to more scientific ideas of punishment and to a tenderer regard for offenders. Moreover, an important act of 1899 not only gave much better protection to children who are ill-treated or morally neglected, but also modified the Code Napoléon so as to reduce the power of the father over the family. On the other hand, divorce, which had been permitted by the Code but abolished under Clerical influence in 1816, was restored by an act of 1884.

Humanitarian Legislation

More spectacular and perhaps more distinctive of the Republican régime in France than economic progress has been the growth of Anti-Clericalism. Clearly indicated by Gambetta in 1877 as the chief issue, it came promptly to the fore as soon as the Republicans secured control of the machinery of government. At that time, politically speaking, Monarchist and Clerical were practically synonymous terms. Consequently the wholesale dismissal of Monarchist office-holders throughout the country deprived the Clericals of the influence in local government which they had notoriously been utilizing to serve the interests of the clergy and the hoped-for Monarchy; and the new Republican prefects and sub-prefects became so many centers of energetic Anti-Clerical agitation.

Steady Growth of Anti-Clericalism

The first and perhaps most basic source of conflict between Republicans and Clericals was the question of education. The preëminence in the instruction of the youth which the Catholic Church had continued to enjoy in France throughout the greater part of the nineteenth century, and which had been magnified under Napoleon III, was now assailed by Republicans on the ground that the church-schools were hot-beds of Monarchist propaganda and that it was the duty of a democracy to provide education for all children without displaying any favoritism in behalf of any particular religion. In other words, the Republicans championed "neutral" schools, which the Clericals denounced as

Source of Conflict with Clericalism

Education

atheistical and immoral. Largely through the efforts of Ferdinand Buisson (1841–   ), who was director of primary education from 1879 to 1896, a new system of public instruction was gradually evolved and applied, the first important legislative authori-

The Ferry Laws zation being a series of enactments introduced in the early 'eighties by the Republican minister of education, Jules Ferry (1832–1893). These so-called Ferry Laws established primary education in France on much the same basis as that which obtained in the United States: compulsory attendance at some school was prescribed for all children, but it was left to parents to decide whether their children should attend a public school or a private (church) school; [1] only the public schools should receive financial support from the state, and in the public schools none but laymen should teach and no religious instruction should be given.

This educational program of the Republicans, together with their revival of obsolescent eighteenth-century statutes against "unauthorized" communities of monks and nuns, and their legalization of civil marriage and divorce — all effected in the early 'eighties — naturally aroused the most bitter opposition of the Clericals, who now, almost to a man, worked directly as Monarchists for the subversion of the Republic.

For a while in the late 'eighties the Monarchist-Clericals almost succeeded in embarrassing the Republic. It was in connection with the curious Boulanger episode. In

Clerical Opposition and the Boulanger Episode view of the obvious need of assuring the utmost efficiency to the national defense, the Republicans had not removed Monarchists from military command at the time when they were getting rid of Monarchists in the civil employments, with the result that the army was the one public service still filled with Monarchists and, from its very nature and discipline, peculiarly dangerous to the Republic. Boulanger (1837–1891) himself, though a general in the army, posed at first as an ardent Radical Republican, becoming minister of war in 1886. But when his jingoistic utterances about a "war of revenge" against Germany had rendered him the most

[1] In France the private schools are customarily called "free," referring to the freedom of religious instruction in them; while in the United States the word "free" is applied to the public schools.

popular man in France — a really national figure — he began to show signs of an ambition to play a role not unlike that of General Bonaparte. Distrusted now by his former colleagues and forced out of the cabinet (1887), General Boulanger secured a large Monarchist following in the army and in the nation alike from Orleanists and from Imperialists, while retaining the noisy allegiance of many other particularly patriotic people. At the same time the publication of positive proof that President Grévy's son-in-law had been guilty of trafficking in the decorations of the Legion of Honor gave color to the Boulangist party's allegations that the whole Republican regime was hopelessly corrupt and unpatriotic. Though the Republican majority in the parliament prevailed upon Grévy, whom they had just re-elected as president for a second term, to resign (1887), and although they chose as his successor Sadi Carnot (1837–1894), the grandson of the very famous Carnot who had organized the armies of national defense in the days of the Great Revolution, the Boulangist movement was not thereby stayed. All elements opposed to the parliamentary Republic seemed to unite to espouse a military dictatorship under General Boulanger and a thorough revision of the constitution. Dismissed from the army, the redoubtable adventurer was elected a deputy from several Departments, capping the climax by being returned from Paris by an overwhelming majority (January, 1889).

If General Boulanger's ambition was as far-reaching as General Bonaparte's, his ability was infinitely less than the Corsican's. It is probable that had he acted promptly upon his electoral victory in Paris, he might have overthrown the Republic by a *coup d'état*. But he was merely a talker and a swaggerer; he possessed no constructive plans whatsoever. He let the chance slip. Too timid to appeal to armed violence, when the Republican ministry prepared to bring charges of conspiracy against him, Boulanger preferred personal safety to precarious power, ignominiously fled across the border into Belgium, thence to England, and was convicted in his absence. In the general elections of 1889, Boulanger's supporters were able to win only 38 seats, whereas the various Republican factions, uniting in the face of danger, elected 366 deputies (out of a total of 576) — an overwhelming majority. Disillusioned and discredited, the groups which had supported Boulanger had already fallen to quarreling among themselves, when the adventurer with his own hand dealt the last blow to the movement by committing suicide at Brussels in 1891.

Several results of the Boulanger episode deserve mention. In the first place the Republic was unquestionably strengthened in public opinion, both in France and abroad: the haunting fear of a military *coup d'état*, such as had overthrown the First and Second Republics, was largely banished from the Third Republic. Secondly, there was a marked tendency at once to lessen jingoism and to republicanize the army: a new law of 1889 reduced the term of active service in the army from five to three years, and required those formerly exempt to serve one year with the colors; and many Monarchist officers were retired and succeeded by Republicans. Thirdly, the cause of the Monarchists was seriously compromised by the open support which both the Bourbon and Bonapartist pretenders had given to an adventurer who had proved himself utterly incompetent and worthless. Finally, Clericalism suffered sorely — so much so, in fact, that in 1892 Pope Leo XIII issued a famous encyclical letter to French Catholics, urging them to desist from further attacks upon the Republic, to accept the new form of government cheerfully and definitively, and to utilize it for the furtherance of legislation favorable to the Church. A small number of Roman Catholics in France — the so-called *Ralliés* — promptly heeded the papal admonition and became Republicans, but the majority, more zealous than prudent, more unbending than the pope, clung tenaciously to Monarchism and fought the Republic at every turn. This open breach in the ranks of the Clericals on a question of political tactics proved to be a potent factor in the subsequent triumphs of Anti-Clericalism.

Not long after the collapse of the Boulanger movement, the Monarchist-Clericals were able to make another effort to discredit the Republic. A certain Édouard Drumont, already famous as the author of a widely-read book, *Jewish France*, a violent Anti-Semitic work written to denounce the influence exercised by Jewish financiers on the politics of the Third Republic, founded at Paris in 1892 a scandalous newspaper, *La Libre Parole*, which made strong appeals in many directions for a "national" union against the Jews.[1] It appeared as a friend of the workingmen, telling them that their real oppressors were the Jewish capitalists who dominated Republican politics. It enlisted the support of many Catholics by blaming the irreligious and Anti-Clerical legislation of the Republic upon the Jews. It adroitly appealed to national patriotism to rid the army of Jewish influence, insisting that the Jews **Anti-** had designs upon the French military establishment **Semitism** and that they were in practice the secret agents of their German kinsmen. Thus Anti-Semitism became in France a rallying-cry whereby the Monarchists could draw to themselves numerous diverse elements and gather them into a single Nationalist party, bent upon the overthrow of the "bourgeois and Jewish" republic. This process was hastened by two notable events in 1894 : first, the exposure of grave financial scandals in connection with the construction of the Panama Canal, in which several Jewish bankers and Republican deputies were implicated ; and secondly, by the news that a certain Alfred Dreyfus, a Jewish captain of artillery attached to the general staff of the French army and in politics a Republican, had been convicted by court-martial of selling military secrets to the Germans and had consequently been sentenced to degradation and to penal servitude for life on Devil's Island off the coast of French Guiana. Here, apparently, were convincing proofs of the truth of Drumont's assertions ; and Anti-Semitism naturally grew by leaps and bounds.

Of the Panama scandals no exculpation was possible, but they were soon dwarfed by the political importance which, by virtue of new developments, the "Dreyfus **"Dreyfus-** affair" assumed. In 1897 Colonel Picquart, a new **ards" vs.** head of the spying system of the French army and a **"Anti-** **Dreyfus-** Republican withal, came to the conclusion that Drey- **ards"** fus had been convicted unjustly and that the real offender was

[1] This so-called Anti-Semitism characterized the politics in the last quarter of the nineteenth century not only of France, but of Germany and Austria-Hungary, and produced most deplorable results in Russia and Rumania. For details of the entire movement see the clear and interesting statement by Lucien Wolf in the *Encyclopædia Britannica*, eleventh edition, Vol. II, pp. 134–146.

a certain Major Esterhazy, a soldier of fortune and an avowed Monarchist. But the "honor" of the French army was regarded by its chiefs as bound up in the original verdict, and thus the strength of organized militarism was thrown on the side of Anti-Semitism, with the result that Esterhazy was acquitted and Picquart was disgraced (1898). Then Émile Zola, the novelist, entered the lists in behalf of Dreyfus, publishing a scathing accusation of all who had taken a decisive part in the case — the Anti-Semitic press and party, the alleged forgers of the incriminating documents, and the army generals who had countenanced the conviction of an innocent man. Though Zola was promptly convicted of libel, his open letter was a most effective means of crystallizing French opinion on the Dreyfus case. On one side were arrayed the "Anti-Dreyfusards" — Monarchists, Clericals, army officers, Jew-baiters, and considerable numbers of workingmen; on the other side, the "Dreyfusards" — Republicans of every stamp, including even the Socialists, drawn together by the common danger to democratic institutions.

The victory of the "Dreyfusards," foreshadowed by the zeal of Zola, was little in doubt after the confession and suicide of

Victory of the "Dreyfusards" one of the Monarchist forgers and after Esterhazy's flight from France late in 1898. The following year Dreyfus was retried on the order of the supreme French court by a new court-martial at Rennes, which, though still so much under Anti-Dreyfusard influence that it again found him guilty, nevertheless in view of "extenuating circumstances" recommended him to presidential clemency. Anti-Semitism speedily collapsed. Dreyfus was pardoned by President Loubet; and in 1906 the Supreme Court annulled the Rennes verdict unconditionally, and restored him to the army. Dreyfus was promoted to the rank of major, and made a chevalier of the Legion of Honor. Picquart also was vindicated and restored, and in 1908 served as minister of war. Zola, who died in 1902, was rewarded with a state burial within the Pantheon.

The outcome of the "Dreyfus affair" was much the same as that of the Boulanger episode, except that it was more decisive. First, Monarchism was thoroughly crushed and discredited.

Secondly, all Republican factions, the Socialists included, were welded together in a compact *bloc*, which for many years commanded a large majority in the parliament and directed the policies of the Republic. Thirdly, by means of new appointments Republicans gained control of the army, and by means of an act of 1905 the term of active military service was reduced to two years, no exemptions, not even of prospective priests, being allowed. Finally, legislation assumed a distinctly Anti-Clerical tone. Doubtless many Clericals had been Anti-Dreyfusards only because they had believed sincerely in the guilt of Dreyfus, and certainly not all French Catholics had sympathized with the Anti-Semitic agitation, but now the whole Catholic Church was assailed as the one remaining menace to the Republic. And it is not without interest that many nominal and professed Catholics upheld this Anti-Clerical legislation, obviously out of disgust or disappointment with the fatal thirty years' alliance of Clericalism and Monarchism against Republican institutions; it was unmistakable evidence of the increasing stability and popularity of the Third Republic.

Outcome of the Dreyfus Affair : Anti-Militarism and Anti-Clericalism

Chief among the Clericals who were accused of systematic plotting against the Republic were the "regular clergy" — monks and religious of various orders, Jesuits, Assumptionists, Christian Brothers, Eudists, Franciscans, Dominicans, etc., — many of whom conducted educational and charitable establishments, and some of whom, — like the famous Carthusian monks, — were engaged in commercial and industrial undertakings. Against them the first blow was struck. By the Associations Act of 1901 it was provided that no religious order should exist in France unless it had received governmental authorization and that no member of an unauthorized order should be permitted to teach in any school in France. The law was rigidly applied, the government refusing to grant most of the applications made by the numerous unauthorized associations, with the result that within two years hundreds of religious were driven out of France and obliged to seek refuge in Spain, Belgium, Great Britain, or the United States, and that ten thousand church schools were closed. It was a proud boast of the stern Anti-Clerical prime

The Associations Act, 1901

minister, Émile Combes,[1] under whose auspices the measure was so severely enforced, that the Associations Act not only exiled and silenced the Republic's most active foes but greatly weakened the religious schools by depriving them of their teachers. It was in line with the latter policy that Combes secured the enactment (1904) of another bill on the congregations, whereby all members of religious associations, whether authorized or unauthorized, would be deprived within ten years of the right to teach in private as well as public schools.

From that time forward it became increasingly difficult for the Catholic Church to maintain its schools. There was an alarming shortage of lay teachers who would or could take the place of the clergymen; time was required to train the new ones; and more money than the Church possessed was needed to support them. A sudden growth of the public non-religious schools at the expense of the private religious schools followed, as was expected and planned: in the year 1912–1913 there were more than four and a half millions of French children in the former and only about one million in the latter.

But before the effects of the Associations Act were fully apparent, Combes was inducing the Anti-Clerical *bloc* in the

Separation of Church and State, 1905 parliament to give serious attention to an even more radical proposal — the abrogation of the concordat which had regulated the relations of church and state in France for more than a century. The pretext for this epochal proposal was the protest of the recently elected Pope Pius X against President Loubet's official visit to the king of Italy in Rome (April, 1904). In May the parliamentary leader of the Socialist party, Jean Jaurès (1859–1914), demanded reprisals for what he deemed foreign interference in the political affairs of France, and Théophile Delcassé (1852–), the minister of foreign affairs in the cabinet of Combes, recalled the French ambassador from the Vatican. Already a gifted and rising young Socialist, Aristide Briand (1862–), had been at work with a parliamentary commission drafting a bill for the separation of church and state, and now that diplomatic relations with the Vatican were ruptured, his proposals were em-

---

[1] Émile Combes (1835–), premier from 1903 to 1905. The Associations Act was passed during the ministry of Waldeck-Rousseau.

bodied in law at the close of 1905 after a long and exciting debate.

Under the Separation Law of 1905, the Concordat of 1801 was formally denounced, the adherents.of all creeds were placed on an equal footing and were authorized to form associations of laymen (*associations cultuelles*) for public worship, and the state was relieved from payment of salaries. As transitory measures, ecclesiastics over 45 years of age and of over 25 years of service were entitled to pensions and all other ecclesiastics were to receive a grant during a period of from four to eight years. All buildings actually used for public worship and as dwellings in that connection were to be made over, after an inventory was taken, to the associations for public worship; the places of worship for the total period of the existence of these associations, the ecclesiastical dwellings for a time. On the other hand, the Church was henceforth to be free to manage its own internal affairs without state intervention.

To the pope and to many prominent Catholics the Separation Act seemed very objectionable. In its preparation the ecclesiastical authorities had not been consulted. It was contrary to the principles of international usage because it involved the denunciation of the concordat by one party without the agreement of the other. It was opposed to canon law because it authorized laymen to participate by means of the associations for public worship in the management of ecclesiastical affairs. It was repugnant to fundamental laws of nature and justice in that it confiscated a good deal of ecclesiastical property, and by ceasing to pay salaries to churchmen, repudiated a debt which the state owed the Church ever since the wholesale secularization of church property in the days of the French Revolution. For these reasons, Pope Pius X condemned the law and forbade its observance; and French Catholics formed no associations for public worship.

Reasons for Continued Clerical Opposition

After two years of chaos in the affairs of the Catholic Church in France, during which time extreme Anti-Clericals declared that they would close all the church edifices and put an end to Catholic worship, while faithful Clericals insisted that they would die on the thresholds of the churches as martyrs in de-

fense of the Christian religion, a practical compromise was at
length reached through the tactful efforts of Briand in enacting
the law of 1907, by which, failing the formation of associations for public worship, the churches with their
ornaments and furniture were left to the disposition of
the faithful and clergy for the purpose of exercising the
cult, and, on certain conditions, the long use of them
might be granted as a free gift to the clergy.   In other words,
the Catholics, though obliged to submit to the separation of
church and state and to the cessation of public payment of
ecclesiastical salaries, were suffered to manage their affairs as
they would and in harmony with the pope and to continue to
use their churches as places of worship.

Working Compromise between Church and State

Thus between 1871 and 1907 the Catholic Church completely
lost in France the financial and moral assistance of the state, the
right to form any religious associations except for the
purposes of charity, the preponderance of religious
schools, and even the privileges of exemption from
military service and from taxation which from time
immemorial had been accorded to the Christian clergy.
This noteworthy decline of the public prestige of Roman Catholicism was undoubtedly due not only to a general increase of
skepticism and agnosticism in France but to the quite
mistaken politics of the Clericals.   Nevertheless, from a long-
maintained position of aggression against the Republic, the
Clericals were now gradually being forced into a new position
of defense of such democratic principles as freedom of religion,
freedom of worship, freedom of association, freedom of speech
and publication.   Perhaps it was an indication of the revolution that was going on within the Church and a portent of the
democratic and more fortunate rôle that Clericalism would
play in future France.   At any rate, there was little doubt that
despite the Education and Associations Acts and the Separation
Act, the Roman Catholic Church in France showed in 1914
increasing, rather than decreasing, vigor and determination.

Summary of Anti-Clerical Legislation under the Republic

Before 1914 evidences were not lacking that the parliamentary
bloc, or coalition of all Republican factions, which the "Dreyfus
affair" had called into existence and from which had issued all
the Anti-Clerical legislation of the first decade of the twentieth

century, was in process of dissolution, and now, with the Republic undoubtedly strengthened, the various groups which had constituted the *bloc* could fittingly and naturally renew hostilities with each other on questions other than ecclesiastical.

THE POLITICAL GROUPS IN FRANCE

At this point it behooves us to have in mind a peculiarity of the political life of France distinguishing it since 1871 very markedly from that of Great Britain or of the United States. In the latter countries there are well-organized national political parties, usually two in number, that alternate in the conduct of public business. In France, on the other hand, there are very many political groups, usually local and temporary and often composed of a purely personal following, which in opinion shade into one another from one extreme to the other and in practical politics sometimes work together and sometimes fly apart. Now while constitutionally and formally the parliamentary systems of France and Great Britain are much the same, the so-called "group system" of political parties that obtains in the former gives to their actual operation an appearance of wide divergence. Thus many writers have contrasted the "instability" of the French government with the "stability" of the British, to the obvious detriment of the group system and to the corresponding advantage of the two-party system. The chief argument which they can advance to substantiate their contention is the unquestionable, and at first thought convincing, statement that from the close of the Franco-German War in 1871 to the outbreak of the War of the Nations in 1914, Great Britain has had nine different ministries while France has had not fewer than fifty!

But the fallacy of this reasoning lies in the fact that changes of French ministries are not attended by such consequences as normally result from changes of ministry in Great Britain. In Great Britain the members of any given cabinet are members of a single political party and are expected to forward all the projects of that particular party; when they lose their majority in the House of Commons, they are succeeded by a ministry all of

The "Group System" of France Distinguished from the Two-party System of Great Britain and the United States

whose members are drawn exclusively from the rival party and
are bent on the furtherance of the principles of their party.

Instability of French Ministries with Relative Stability of Policy Were this to happen with every change of ministry
in France — fifty times in forty-three years — it is
obvious that there could be no stability in public
policies, domestic or foreign. But with the one exception in the late 'seventies of the change from a
ministry of Monarchists to one of Republicans, a
change of ministry in France means simply that a given cabinet
has lost the support of one group out of three, four, or more
groups upon whose temporary coalition its parliamentary majority depended (for no one group of itself has ever been sufficiently
numerous and well organized to command a clear majority),
and that a new cabinet has been formed which has merely added
representatives of some hitherto unrepresented group to representatives of groups who were included in the previous cabinet.
Expressed a little differently, a change of ministry in France
usually operates only to stress or weaken the emphasis upon
one part of the general policy pursued by the government and
actually leaves most under-officials of the various great state
departments unchanged. In fact, it is surprising how in the
changes of French ministries the same names of individual
members will perpetually bob up, as in a kaleidoscope, remind-
ing one that though the positions are somewhat shifted the component parts are strangely familiar. And it is obvious from a
survey of French history under the Third Republic that fifty
changes of ministry have not prevented a steady, consistent development of public policies. In every important particular, —
Anti-Clericalism, democratizing the army, promotion of colonialism and of protectionism, internal betterment of agriculture,
industry, and commerce, pursuit of a foreign policy [1] of cement-
ing an alliance with Russia and gradually isolating Germany, and
development of republican institutions and usages, — ministerial
changes have meant changes of persons and not of policies. In
summary it may be truthfully affirmed that the French "group
system" has carried in its wake both an alarming instability of
ministries and a conservative stability of policies.

[1] For a treatment of the foreign policy of the Third French Republic, see Chapter
XXX.

To write a brief history of the manifold political groups which appeared in France under the Third Republic is an impossible task, but some idea of recent tendencies in political groupings may be gathered from a hurried sketch of the parliamentary situation during the first decade of the twentieth century. *The French Groups*

It should be borne in mind that in the French parliament, as in the parliaments of most Continental states, the members sit according to their general political notions, the extreme conservatives on the extreme right of the presiding officer, and the extreme liberals on the extreme left, so that Right and Left are frequently used to denote the opposites of political opinion. In France the extreme Right and the extreme Left are respectively the Monarchists and the Socialists, relatively small groups, squarely opposed to each other, and in the main opposed alike to the larger intervening groups of the Center. *"Right" and "Left"*

On the extreme Right the Monarchists at the opening of the twentieth century were greatly reduced from their former estate. Only a handful of deputies [1] without able leaders, the group continued to draw electoral support from the few aristocratic sections in Paris, where Monarchism was still a badge of social distinction, or from certain isolated communities like Brittany, where with peasants and fisher-folk it was a habit. Impotent to carry out any constructive plans the group still continued to preach militarism and Clericalism and to make clamorous complaints against the Republic as a corrupt and cowardly government. *The Monarchists*

Quite different was the attitude on the extreme Left, where the Socialists were steadily growing in numbers and in influence. Prior to 1900 the growth of Socialism had been slower in France than in Germany, due to the relatively greater strength of the agricultural population, to the discredit which the failure of the Paris Commune had cast upon French Socialism, and to the more pronounced tendency to split up into little warring factions. But after 1900, despite the fact that many workingmen were lost to Syndicalism, Socialism *The Unified Socialists*

[1] In 1914 there were 26 deputies of the Right, still divided between support of the Bourbon pretender and of the Bonapartist pretender.

advanced rapidly.   Thanks to the united efforts of the Marxist
leader, Jules Guesde, and of the Reformist leader, Jean Jaurès,
the Unified Socialist party was formed in 1905.   This group is
the nearest French approach to a political party in the British
or American sense.   It is national in extent, having annual
congresses, an executive committee, and a definite platform
of principles.   In 1914 it polled 1,250,000 votes and won
102 seats in the Chamber of Deputies, to say nothing of the
votes polled by 30 "Independent Socialists" who occupied
adjacent seats in the Chamber but acted independently of the
Unified party.

Another political group in France, somewhat resembling in
organization a British or American political party, is the *Action*
The Action   *Libérale* (Liberal Action), a group organized in 1901
Libérale   under the able leadership of the Count de Mun (1841–
1914) for the purpose of reconciling Catholicism with Republicanism.   It is fairly well organized with local and national committees and has an enrolled and paying membership of a quarter
of a million.   While it stands strongly for the repeal of Anti-
Clerical legislation and for this purpose is willing to coöperate
with the Clerical Monarchists, it frankly supports the Republic.
Moreover it accepts the social program of Pope Leo XIII and
appeals for the aid of the working class by championing factory
legislation, old-age pensions, workingmen's insurance, and trade-
unionism.   Its immediate political demands are embraced
in the so-called "three r's": *représentation proportionelle*, or
parliamentary representation of minorities; *représentation pro-
fessionelle*, the organization of a special parliament composed
of representatives of economic groups, such as day-laborers,
lawyers, farmers, factory-owners, etc., apportioned according to
numerical strength, in order to advise the existing Chamber of
Deputies in law-making; and *répartition proportionelle*, public
financial support for Catholic and other private schools as well
as for the public schools.   In spite of the fact that the *Action
Libérale* polled a hundred thousand more votes in 1914 than the
Unified Socialists, it secured but 34 seats in the Chamber of
Deputies to the latter's 102.[1]

[1] This surprising discrepancy is due to the greater concentration of the Socialists
in certain industrial constituencies, and to the French practice of second ballotings

Between the Socialists on the Left and the Monarchists and *Action Libérale* on the Right sat from 1900 to 1910 the famous *bloc* of Republican groups, which, brought into harmo- The Bloc nious relations with one another by the exigencies of the Boulanger episode and the Dreyfus affair, continued to coöperate throughout these years in naming the ministries and in controlling the policies of the Republic. Reckoning from Right to Left, the *bloc* included (1) Progressist Republicans, headed Progress- by Paul Deschanel (1856– , for many years presi- ists dent of the Chamber), recruited from the upper middle class and from the small propertied class, devoted to the individual rights and liberties proclaimed by the Revolution, especially to the basic right of private property; (2) Radicals of varying Radicals titles, the core, and by far the most numerous, of the *bloc*, true disciples of Gambetta, shapers of bourgeois policies, intellectual radicals, most stalwart Anti-Clericals, including in 1910 such influential politicians as Senators Clémenceau (1841–) and Combes and Deputy Caillaux; and (3) Radical Socialists, or, as would be more accurately descriptive, the "social- Radical istically inclined Radicals," a remarkable group, who Socialists with pronounced Anti-Clericalism combined a determination to drag their more or less unwilling allies along the path of social reform and to do for the working classes what the French Revolution did for the bourgeoisie, a "bourgeois party with a popular soul," championing not only strict governmental regulation of industry but government ownership of all means of communication and transportation, likewise of national resources like mines, forests, oil-fields, etc. Among the Radical Socialist group were to be counted several brilliant men, such as Briand, Millerand, and Viviani, who called themselves plain Socialists but who were read out of the regular Socialist camp because of their willingness to enter coalition ministries with representatives of non-Socialist groups.

Anti-Clericalism was the issue which held the *bloc* together from 1900 to 1910 and enabled it to expel the religious orders from France, to separate church and state, and to strengthen

upon which Radical Republicans often unite with the Socialists to insure the defeat of Clerical candidates. It accounts for the fact that in France the Socialists are opposed to "electoral reform" while the *Action Libérale* espouses it.

non-religious education. But by 1913 other questions had
arisen which tended to produce a different alignment of political
Political   groups. There was first the question of an income
Issues in   tax and further social reform, which was urged by
1913   the Socialists, Radical Socialists, and *Action Libérale*,
and resisted by many Radicals and Moderates. There was
secondly the question of militarism, for many Radicals joined
with the Socialists in offering a wordy, though vain, opposition
to the enactment and enforcement of a new army bill (1913),
which this time, in view of particularly troubled international
relations, lengthened the term of active service in the French
army from two to three years. Thirdly, there was still the
question of Anti-Clericalism in its various phases : many Radical
Socialists felt that the dangers of Clericalism were now sufficiently remote to allow the Republic to turn its attention and
energy elsewhere ; many Radicals thought otherwise and were
resolved to maintain against the Catholic Church a fight which
was already proving advantageous to them in distracting public
attention from grave economic ills ; while the *Action Libérale*
was growing more vehement in its demand for the repeal of past
Anti-Clerical legislation. Finally, there was the newly raised
political question of electoral reform : proposals for the revival
of the *scrutin de liste*, with provisions for proportional representation of minorities, received powerful support from the *Action
Libérale*, the Moderates, and the Radical Socialists, who believed them more fundamentally democratic than the existing
system of elections to the Chamber of Deputies ; on the other
hand, many Radicals and most Socialists denounced them as
tending to increase the strength of the Right and to imperil the
Anti-Clerical legislation of the preceding decade.

Of these four questions, only the second — that of militarism
— was immediately settled. The army bill was voted in 1913
Renewed   in a burst of patriotism which overspread all groups
Militarism   except the Unified Socialist. It was probably due at
least in part to the campaign which in press and speech the
Unified Socialists waged against the three-year army bill that
Jean Jaurès, the able Socialist leader and editor, was assassinated
by a fanatical patriot on the eve of the outbreak of the War of
the Nations (1914). But it was a significant fact that once war

was declared the Unified Socialists shared the common national emotions and that within a month Jules Guesde, the strait-laced Marxist, accepted a post in the cabinet with Viviani, Millerand, and Briand.

Differences of opinion among members of the *bloc* upon the three other questions were quite apparent in the elections of April–May, 1914. Of the bourgeois groups formerly included in the *bloc*, the Progressists (Federated Republicans) adhered to their earlier principles and maintained their strength practically unimpaired. But the Radicals and Radical Socialists were split up *Newer Political Groups: the Unified Radicals* into a number of groups, which tended, both in the parliament and in the country at large, to gravitate toward one or other of two new and rival combinations. The first was the Unified Radicals, including such men as Caillaux, Combes, and Clémenceau, bent upon the vigorous prosecution of more extreme Anti-Clerical legislation, especially legislation against private church schools, generally hostile to electoral reform, and lukewarm in the cause of labor legislation. The second new coalition was the Federation of the Left, whose principles were championed by Briand and by Poincaré, who had been elected to the presidency in January, 1913: it urged both labor legislation and parliamentary reform, and while *The Federation of the Left* not favoring any repeal of Anti-Clerical legislation, it was unwilling further to open the breach between Catholics and non-Catholics.

Such was the general political situation when the War of the Nations broke out in August, 1914, sweeping France into a maelstrom of blood and suddenly engulfing all domestic differences in a wave of national enthusiasm. The certain fact that it was a politically stronger and more *Outbreak of the Great War, 1914* united France which went into the war of 1914 than the France which plunged into the war of 1870, is of itself an eloquent tribute to the achievements of the Third French Republic.

2. THE KINGDOM OF ITALY

The chief social and political events in the history of Italy from 1870 to 1914 were connected either with problems which grew out of the Industrial Revolution and therefore were common to all countries in a like stage of industrial development, or with problems which were incidental to the manner in which the peninsula was politically unified and were accordingly more or less peculiar to Italy. To the latter category belonged various administrative and governmental problems and likewise those involved in the curious new relations between the national Italian kingdom and the papacy.

In dealing with Italian governmental problems, it should be borne in mind at the outset that the kingdom had been very suddenly created by the consolidation within eleven years (1859–1870) of eight formerly distinct states, and that, thanks largely to the intense nationalism of the Italian people and to the patriotic policy of Cavour, the resulting kingdom in 1871 was not a federation but a single state. Italy thus furnished a unique instance of a union of different states without a federal government. In its centralization Italy approximated to France and Great Britain rather than to Germany or the United States.

Italy a Centralized State

Now while this centralization of political institutions was a laudable achievement of national patriotism, it made it incumbent upon the central government to equalize taxation and expenditure throughout the entire peninsula and at the same time to bring the different regions to the same level of education and economic well being. Here was a most serious difficulty. Between northern Italy — the fertile valley of the Po and the prosperous district of Piedmont — and that part of southern Italy which had suffered for centuries under the paralyzing despotism of the Sicilian Bourbons, the most startling discrepancies were at once evident. In the North, there were railways and all manner of internal improvements, a wealthy bourgeoisie, cities with large industrial populations, and a relatively high percentage of literacy. In the South, on the other hand, there were few modern public works, comparatively little industry, prevalence of brigandage, and an ignorant peasantry of whose adult males not one in ten could read or write. The economic unification of Italy thus presented an even more perplexing problem than had the political unification of the peninsula and

Problem of Social and Economic Unification

Contrast between North and South

one to which Italian statesmen devoted a good deal of attention between 1870 and 1914. Much certainly was accomplished. The state built and operated thousands of miles of new railways which served not only as arteries of internal trade and travel but as valuable means of unifying the culture of the country. Good highways were constructed, harbors were improved, and land surveys undertaken. Encouragement was given to the spread of the factory system to Naples, Palermo, and Messina, as well as throughout the flourishing cities of Lombardy and Tuscany. A law of 1877, which decreed compulsory education for children between six and nine years of age, though imperfectly applied for financial reasons, proved a potent factor in gradually lowering the percentage of illiteracy throughout the whole kingdom.

Economic unification, however, was expensive. To a national treasury already burdened by heavy financial outlays in the cause of political unification were now added the enor- **Burdens of** mous expenditures in behalf of public works and in- **Taxation** ternal improvements. Taxes steadily rose to a height greater per capita than in any other country of contemporary Europe. Not only did the taxes increase the misery and poverty of the working classes but they called forth repeated complaints from more well-to-do taxpayers of the North that the sums collected were being expended disproportionately and too lavishly upon the South. On the other hand, Sicilian politicians protested that the public offices were being monopolized by Northerners who too often diverted the public funds into their own private pockets, with the result that the South was not particularly better off under the House of Savoy than it had been under the Bourbons. Although this internal friction long remained an element in the domestic politics of Italy, it did not seriously menace national unity. With the exception of an unimportant separatist movement in Sicily led by a certain Signor Nasi, a politician and self-seeker, there was no expressed desire to break up the nation as constituted by the spectacular exploits of 1859–1860. It was too apparent that actual improvements were being made and that the national finances were surely, if very slowly, becoming solvent.

Centralization of government was but one of Cavour's ideals

which the new Italian kingdom had realized.   A second was that
of a parliamentary government modeled after Great Britain's.
Parliamen-   Quite as significant as the political unification was
tary Govern- the extension of the Sardinian *Statuto* of 1848 to the
ment   entire peninsula, for in accordance with its liberal
and constitutional provisions the whole kingdom has been governed since 1870.   By virtue of this document and of the usages
that have grown up about it, supreme authority is vested in a
parliament of two houses — an elective Chamber of Deputies
and an appointive and aristocratic Senate [1] — and in a ministry
responsible to the parliament, the position of the king of Italy
being not unlike that of the British sovereign.   Inasmuch as the
"group system" of political parties prevails in Italy, the actual
operation of the parliamentary system resembles more nearly
that of France than that of Great Britain.   For many years
property and educational qualifications for the exercise of the
franchise assured a completely bourgeois character to the Chamber of Deputies, but finally both the Socialist and the Catholic
pressure for political democracy became so great that in 1912 [2]
an important electoral law was passed, making the suffrage
almost universal for men and denying the franchise only to
those under thirty years of age who had neither performed their
military service nor learned to read and write.[3]

Growing out of the problems of national unification and
political democracy was the particularly perplexing problem of
              the relation of church and state.   Here again Cavour
Problems of   had indicated the ideal which the statesmen of the
the Rela-
tion of   Italian kingdom sought to realize — "a free church
Church and   in a free state."   It was an ideal derived from Liberal-
State   ism but difficult of attainment because of the development of the Anti-Clericalism common to all Continental

---

[1] The Senate is composed of a few princes of the royal family and of an unlimited
number of members above forty years of age who are nominated by the king for
life; a condition of the nomination being that the person shall either have filled a
high office, or have acquired fame in science, literature, or any other pursuit tending to the benefit of the nation, or, finally, shall pay taxes to the annual amount
of $600.

[2] An important extension of the suffrage had been made in 1882, increasing the
electorate from 600,000 to 2,000,000.

[3] The electoral reform of 1912 increased the number of voters to more than
6,000,000.

countries, and because of the peculiar position which the papacy occupied in Italy. Church and state were not separated: the Italian government continued to pay the salaries of the clergy and to pass upon the appointment of bishops; religious instruction was still given normally in the public schools; divorce was not sanctioned by the state. But following Cavour's example in Piedmont the number of monastic establishments throughout the whole kingdom was gradually reduced and the property of the Church was repeatedly subjected to complete or partial confiscation. In respect of the papacy, Position of whose temporal possessions had been appropriated by the Papacy the Italian government in 1870, the greatest difficulty was encountered. In 1871, shortly after the occupation of Rome by Italian troops, the Italian parliament enacted a "law of papal guarantees," whereby the new monarchy under- The Law of took to allow the pope a considerable latitude of free- Papal Guarantees, 1871 dom. The pope was to be accorded sovereign rights on a par with those of the king of Italy — inviolability of his own person, the right to receive and send ambassadors, and the honor due a reigning sovereign, — and over the Vatican and Lateran buildings and gardens and the villa of Castel Gandolfo he was to enjoy full sovereignty. Moreover the papal government was to have free use of the Italian telegraph, railway, and postal systems, and, as compensation for the loss of the temporal possessions, to receive an annual subsidy from the royal treasury of 3,225,000 *lire*. This law Pius IX promptly condemned on the ground that it was in the nature of a simple law of the Italian kingdom rather than an international agreement and that its acceptance would involve papal recognition of a government which had despoiled " God's vicar " of his lands and Papal of his real freedom. The pope feared lest by becom- Opposition ing a pensioner of the Italian kingdom he should lose much of his influence and prestige in foreign countries.

Not only did Pius IX condemn the law of papal guarantees. He obstinately refused to accept any part of the financial grants; he shut himself up as a "prisoner" in the Vatican; he summoned Catholic princes to coöperate in restoring the temporal power; and he positively forbade any Italian Catholic to vote or to hold office under the royal government (the so-called *non expedit*).

This papal attitude seriously embarrassed both the foreign and the domestic relations of the kingdom. In Italy a sharp line was drawn between loyal patriots and faithful Catholics, with unfortunate results both for state and for church. On the one side, while the bulk of Italians continued to describe themselves as Catholics, the church by combating nationalism weakened its hold upon them. On the other side, the conscientious abstention of many good and honest people from politics left the Italian government in the hands of men indifferent, if not opposed, to religion, and weakened the state. Only slight improvement was registered by special permissions accorded from time to time by Pius IX and Leo XIII (1878–1903) to Catholics to participate in local elections, and it was not until the practical abolition of the *non expedit* for parliamentary elections by Pius X in 1905 that an effective compromise seemed possible. All three popes persisted in styling themselves "prisoners," and one of the first pronouncements of Benedict XV, who mounted the papal throne in 1914, was a plea for the restoration of the temporal power.

From 1870 to 1876 the destinies of the Italian kingdom were presided over by a group of statesmen from the "Right" —
Italian Politics, 1870–1914 a group whose chief electoral strength lay in Piedmont, Lombardy, and Tuscany, and whose main achievement had been the completion of national unification during the stormy days from 1859 to 1870. It was this group which dictated the Italian constitution, enacted the law of papal guarantees, centralized the local administration after the French model, ruthlessly imposed and collected taxes, nationalized the railways, reorganized the army and navy (1875) on a basis of compulsory military service, and betrayed again and again a latent hostility to democracy.

The Régime of the Right, 1870–1876

For a whole decade after 1876, with two short interruptions, the premiership was controlled by Agostino Depretis (1813–1887),
The Régime of the Left the leader of the Left. Under him the Sicilians and Neapolitans were favored at the expense of the Northern Italians, and the suffrage was radically extended (1882). Nevertheless Depretis proved himself as ardent a nationalist and as warm a friend of the industrial class as Cavour.

He maintained the large army and strengthened the navy; he completed the railway system and leased it out to private operating companies;[1] he formed the Triple Alliance of Italy with Germany and Austria-Hungary (1882); and he initiated a colonial policy by the occupation of Massawa in Africa. His predecessors had made Italy a nation; he would make it a Great Power. To reach this goal he vastly increased indirect taxation, seriously impaired the stability of Italian finance, and caused much distress among his poorer countrymen; at the same time he practiced political corruption unparalleled in the history of the monarchy and inaugurated a system of government by factions and sectional interests which long disgraced Italy.

Depretis, 1876–1887

The policies of Depretis were carried forward after his death (1887) by Francesco Crispi (1819–1901), a proud self-centered Sicilian who had once been a companion-in-arms of Garibaldi. Militarism was confirmed. The Triple Alliance was renewed. Imperialism was vigorously prosecuted in Eritrea and Somaliland. Dictatorial methods were employed to make public revenue and expenditures balance and to crush opposition whether from Clericals or from Socialists and Republicans. It was an ironical and tragic commentary on Crispi's policies that his downfall was occasioned by the decisive defeat which the Italian colonial troops suffered at the hands of the Abyssinians at Adowa (1896), and that King Humbert, who had succeeded his remarkable father, Victor Emmanuel II, in 1878 and who had loyally supported both Depretis and Crispi, was assassinated (1900) by an Anarchist.

Crispi, 1887–1896

The passing of Crispi and King Humbert marked almost a new era in Italian politics. The new king, Victor Emmanuel III (1900–   ), was enlightened, amiable, and democratically-minded; and the statesmen who served under him frankly accepted the more liberal policy that the country demanded. It is true that any reduction in armaments was steadfastly opposed[2] and that

Newer Developments in Italy, 1896–1914

---

[1] In 1885. The state resumed operation of the railways in 1905.

[2] The expenditures for the army amounted in 1871 to $30,000,000, and in 1913 to $85,000,000. Naval expenditures amounted in 1871 to $4,500,000, and in 1913 to $51,300,000.

colonial failure in Abyssinia was more than compensated for by
success in a war against Turkey and in the accompanying occupa-

*Militarism
and Imperi-
alism*   tion of Tripoli and Cyrenaica (1911–1912). It is also
true that the interests of the industrial class were
zealously safeguarded by means of protective tariffs
and governmental bounties, with such results as the following
figures indicate. From 1871 to 1897 the annual amount of
exports and imports (excluding the precious metals) did not
vary much from 440 million dollars, but after 1897 it rose
steadily until in 1913 it reached the figure of 1200 million
dollars. The increase in exports of manufactured goods between
1897 and 1913 was almost threefold. The exports of raw and
manufactured silk rose from 66 million dollars in 1897 to 90

*Industrial
and Com-
mercial De-
velopment*   millions in 1913, Milan surpassing Lyons as the
greatest silk market in the world; and during the same
period Italian cotton goods not only captured the
home market but also increased as exports from
5 millions to nearly 50 millions. The Italian merchant marine
in 1914 numbered 1060 ships of over a hundred tons each and
possessed a total tonnage of 1,668,296, — ranking close to the
Japanese, which then was exceeded only by the British, German,
American, Norwegian, and French.

Parallel with the growth of Italian commerce and industry
from the close of the nineteenth century went new and increas-

*Social
Legislation*   ing efforts on the part of the government to guarantee
a minimum of comfort to the growing industrial proletariat. Factory acts of 1886 regulating child labor were now
strengthened and applied to women, who, together with children
under thirteen, were excluded from underground and night work.
An employers' liability act of 1898 required employers to insure
their workingmen against accidents, and another act of that
year established contributory systems of sickness insurance and
old-age pensions. An act of 1908 made provision for a weekly
day of rest for laborers. An act of 1912 nationalized life insurance. Municipalities were authorized to own and operate
public utilities. Trade unions were legalized and their funds
and activities protected. Some progress was made in the arbitration of chronic labor disputes and of the strikes with which
the first decade of the twentieth century teemed. Coöperative

societies for banking and for wholesake buying and selling
were encouraged, especially in the rural districts. And the
electoral reform of 1912, which instituted almost universal
manhood suffrage, augured still further experiments in social
legislation.

It was the cities that most benefited by these reforms, although
it was the country districts that most needed them. Despite
her relatively great advance in commerce and indus- Italian
try, Italy could not hope permanently to rival Great Agriculture
Britain, France, Germany, or the United States, which were far
more liberally supplied by nature with iron and coal and other
mineral resources. Italy was still chiefly an agricultural nation.
In 1913 over a third of her population were agricultural laborers.
Yet in agriculture Italy was remarkably backward. In Naples
and Sicily, whither the land reforms of the French Revolution had
never thoroughly penetrated, the soil was still held largely by
great landowners, whose miserable peasantry, hopeless and
helpless, toiled in diminishing numbers on soil scourged by the
mysterious *pellagra* and malarial fever, ravaged by untamed
watercourses, or periodically desolated by earthquakes and vol-
canic eruptions. In northern Italy the large estates had been
broken up into small holdings, on which thrifty and hard-work-
ing farmers, with the aid of the coöperative societies, rural
credit banks, and improved methods of tillage, were gradually
but perceptibly bettering their lot. Yet over all the agricultural
classes of Italy fell the shadow of taxation — taxation for militarism, for imperialism, for education, for public improvements,
— taxation far heavier than was to be found in any other
country of Europe.

With these facts in mind, together with the additional fact
that for several years the increase in Italian population surpassed
the average annual increase of the other European Emigration
states, it is easy for us to understand why Italian emigration was particularly heavy at the close of the nineteenth century and in the first decade of the twentieth. In 1900 the
number of emigrants was 353,000 and in 1911 it was 533,000.
This exodus did not represent a total loss of population, for nearly
half returned after earning money abroad. Thus, in 1911 some
219,000 returned, of whom 140,000 were from the United

States. Nevertheless, it was officially stated in 1910 that Italy had lost to date about 5,558,000 citizens, who had permanently settled in foreign countries, mainly in the United States, Argentina, Uruguay, and Brazil, and that peasants, chiefly from southern Italy, constituted 80 per cent of this loss.

In dealing with social and economic problems the Italian government was handicapped by the mutual rivalries and conflicts of four distinct political groups, each one of which was more or less hostile to the existing political régime. (1) The Clericals displayed increasing strength after the removal of the *non expedit* in 1905. They were perfecting their organization, founding newspapers, and developing political platforms, which, on the one side, denounced Socialism and state infringements on the rights and liberties of the papacy and the Church, and, on the other side, urged social reform — factory legislation, extension of workingmen's insurance, the breaking up of large landed estates into small holdings, and coöperative movements for the rural classes. In the general election of 1913 — the first under universal manhood suffrage — professed Clericals won 35 seats in the Chamber of Deputies, a gain of 14, besides securing from some 200 Moderate Monarchist members promises to oppose Anti-Clerical legislation. (2) Middle-class Anti-Clerical Republicanism of the type championed in the first half of the nineteenth century by Mazzini and Garibaldi, despite its temporary eclipse by the success of the Monarchists in unifying the nation, had subsequently remained a political tradition with many Freemasons and other intellectual radicals. These Republicans sought any opportunity to embarrass the monarchy and to pave the way for the establishment of an Italian Republic. In the elections of 1913 they lost six seats but still retained seventeen. (3) Socialism made little headway in Italy till early in the 'nineties, when its social gospel attracted several ardent young intellectuals and a considerable number of workingmen in industrial Milan and in the North generally. In spite of chronic factional disputes and a virtual split of the Socialist party into the two groups of Marxists and Reformists, Socialism grew steadily in Italy. The election of 1913 returned 78 Socialists to the Chamber, — a noteworthy gain for

Opposition to the Government

1. The Clericals

2. The Republicans

3. The Socialists

them, under universal manhood suffrage, of 37 seats. (4) Dangerous to the government, disquieting to the Clericals, and a source of dissension to the Socialists was the comparatively rapid development among the industrial proletarians of revolutionary Syndicalism, with its strikes and violence and repugnance to governmental authority. 4. The Syndicalists

In studying the history of the Italian kingdom from 1870 to 1914 we must not be so blinded by the violence of Syndicalists or by the partisan appeals of Socialists, Republicans, and Clericals, or even by the grave facts of emigration, industrial distress, poverty, illiteracy, and burdensome taxation, as to lose sight of a most basic factor in Italian political and social life — the factor of nationalism, of patriotism, of a yearning in the breast of every loyal modern Italian to emulate the ancient Romans in culture and in prowess. It was this factor which made possible the political unification of the peninsula in the middle of the nineteenth century. It was this factor which rendered inevitable the ambitious efforts of the statesmen of the new kingdom to make Italy a Great Power, which caused them to develop militarism at home and imperialism in Africa. It was this factor likewise which made every Italian a latent "Irredentist." *Irredentism* was the ideal of annexing those Italian regions, — Trent, Triest, and the eastern coast of the Adriatic, — which still belonged to Austria. Such an ideal the Italian government could not hope to realize so long as commercial and colonial rivalry with France forced Italy to maintain an alliance with Austria-Hungary and Germany (1882–1915), and the government long frowned officially, therefore, upon Irredentist agitation. But improved relations with France in the first decade of the twentieth century, and the precipitation of the vast War of the Nations by an Austro-Hungarian attack on Serbia (July, 1914), gave Italy her chance. Forgetting the grievous burdens of militarism and taxation, the Italian people were now swept off their feet by a wave of Irredentist enthusiasm. In May, 1915, Italy denounced her treaty of alliance with Austria-Hungary and plunged into the war as an ally of Russia, France, Great Britain, Japan, Serbia, and Montenegro. *Italia irredenta* ("Italy unredeemed") must now be redeemed. National Patriotism in Italy

Irredentism and the Participation of Italy in the War of the Nations

For Italians the Great War was but another attack on Austria — a continuation and hoped-for consummation of the wars of 1859 and 1866 for national unity and independence.

3. SPAIN

With an area almost as great as France and considerably larger than Italy, Spain played a distinctly inferior rôle in the history of the nineteenth century and one rather in accordance with her population, which in 1910 was only about half that of Italy or France.[1] Nature handicapped Spain, since the poverty of much of the Spanish soil was a barrier to any phenomenal development of agriculture, and the high mountain ranges which traversed the peninsula militated against commercial progress and the growth of industry. Such drawbacks help to explain the constantly large emigration of energetic Spaniards to Latin America, especially to Argentina, and the relatively small population in Spain itself. And this fact, together with the tragic efforts of Spanish kings and statesmen throughout the sixteenth, seventeenth, and eighteenth centuries to exercise a great world dominion, out of all relation to the resources and population of their country, rendered inevitable the lapse of Spain into the class of second-rate Powers.

Spain Contrasted with Italy and France

For the first seventy-five years of the nineteenth century, moreover, Spain suffered from abominable governments and a series of civil wars. French intervention during the era of Napoleon not only led to the protracted and costly war of independence but also served to crystallize in Spain bitterly hostile factions of Revolutionaries and Reactionaries. Then, it will be recalled,[2] came the reign (1814–1833) of the despicable Ferdinand VII, remembered for his absolutism, for his cruelty and cunning, and for his loss of the bulk of the Spanish Empire in the New World. In setting aside the

Seventy-five Years' Political Disasters in Spain, 1800–1875

Ferdinand VII, 1814–1833

---

[1] In 1910 France had an area of 207,129 sq. mi. and a population of 39,601,509; Italy had an area of 110,688 sq. mi. and a population of 34,671,377; and Spain had an area of 194,794 sq. mi., and a population of 19,611,334.

[2] See above, pp. 20–26.

Bourbon law of inheritance, which fixed the royal succession only in the male line, and in bequeathing the crown of Spain to his youthful daughter, Isabella II, Ferdinand left his country another unfortunate legacy, for Don Carlos, Ferdinand's brother, contested the succession; and from 1833 to 1840 a destructive civil war was waged between *Carlists* and *Christinos* — as the followers of Don Carlos and of Donna Chris- tina, mother of Queen Isabella and regent, were re- spectively called. Don Carlos attracted to his standard the reactionaries, Clericals, and most of the combative elements from the mountainous districts of the north. Christina, on the other hand, won the Liberals by the grant of a parliamentary constitution (1837). *The Carlist War, 1833–1840*

The upshot of the Carlist War was the flight of Don Carlos in 1840 and the general recognition of Queen Isabella. Unfor- tunately, throughout her long personal reign (1843– 1868), Isabella II displayed neither good sense nor the spirit of conciliation. She alienated the Liberals by revising the constitution in a conservative direction (1845) and by her constant attempt to rule despotically with the mere pretense of a parliament, and at the same time she failed to win the loyal support of the Carlist faction. The queen's gross immorality shocked and scandalized the sincere Catholics, and her extrava- gance and addiction to favorites embarrassed the finances. Re- publican doctrines spread among the middle class and in the army. There were repeated revolts and insurrections of grow- ing intensity. *Isabella II, 1843–1868*

A successful revolution in 1868 sent Queen Isabella fleeing as an exile to France, but ushered in a seven-year period of anarchy in Spanish government. A new constitution was adopted in 1869, guaranteeing individual liberties and religious toleration and providing for a monarchical parliamentary régime; but considerable difficulty was encoun- tered in securing a king. After the final declination of Prince Leopold of Hohenzollern-Sigmaringen,[1] Prince Amadeo of Savoy, the second son of King Victor Emmanuel II of Italy, accepted the Spanish crown in 1870. It was a shaky throne which King *The Revo- lution of 1868*

[1] It was the candidature of Prince Leopold which occasioned the Franco-German War of 1870–1871. See above, pp. 198 f.

Amadeo mounted, for neither Carlists nor Republicans would
support him, and the Liberal Monarchists were divided into so
King   many warring groups that no settled policy could
Amadeo,   be consistently pursued. While both Amadeo and
1870-1873   his queen were respected for their personal qualities
by those who knew them intimately, the majority of Spaniards,
intensely patriotic, regarded them as foreigners and intruders.
In disgust Amadeo abdicated in February, 1873, and returned
to Italy; and a republic was proclaimed in Spain.

The Republicans were even less successful than the Liberal
Monarchists. They were at best only a minority, and they
The Spanish   speedily split into two factions: (1) those who favored
Republic,   a centralized state, and (2) those who, under the in-
1873-1875   fluence of contemporary Communism in France,[1]
favored a federal republic. At first the Federalists controlled
the government from February, 1873, to January, 1874, but
their president, Emilio Castelar (1832-1899), an able and conciliatory statesman, was obliged for the sake of public order to
resort to a dictatorship. Then the Republican army chiefs
executed a *coup d'état* and put Marshal Serrano in the presidential chair. This was but a prelude to the destruction of
the unpopular Spanish Republic and the restoration of the Bour-
Restoration   bons. In January, 1875, the son of Isabella II, a young
of the Bour-   man in his eighteenth year, entered Madrid as King
bons, 1875   Alphonso XII amid the plaudits of a wearied nation,
and the work of national consolidation and reform was begun.

The accession of Alphonso XII opened a new and happier
era in Spanish history. The young king himself was benevo-
Alphonso   lent and sympathetic in disposition and a good judge
XII (1875-   of men. And from the two most distinguished
1885): the   Spanish statesmen of the nineteenth century — Mar-
Beginning
of a New   shal Campos (1831-1900), the soldier, and Canovas
Era   del Castillo (1828-1897), the conservative civilian —
he received invaluable encouragement and advice. Under the
generalship of Marshal Campos the last serious Carlist insurrection was suppressed (1876) and law and order were restored
throughout the kingdom; under him, likewise, an insurrection
which had been raging in Cuba since 1868 was ended (1878).

[1] See above, pp. 333 f.

On the advice of Canovas del Castillo a new constitution was drawn up and promulgated in 1876, a moderately liberal document which conciliated most of the nation and which has remained in force to the present time.

The constitution of 1876 contains moderate guarantees of individual liberties and vests supreme political authority in the Cortes — a parliament of two houses: a Senate of not more than 360 members, part of whom are nominated by the crown for life and the rest serve by virtue of the occupancy of some specified office or dignity; and a Congress of Deputies, of 406 members, elected by popular vote. The executive power resides in a ministry responsible to the Cortes; and the king, whose every act must be countersigned by a minister, enjoys an authority hardly superior to that of the British king or the French president. In local government less centralization and a greater degree of autonomy prevail in Spain than in France. *Spanish Government: The Constitution of 1876*

In religious matters the government of Alphonso XII repressed Anti-Clericalism, which had been much in evidence during the revolutionary period from 1868 to 1875, and protected Roman Catholicism, the faith of the vast majority of Spaniards. Not only were the provisions of the papal Concordat of 1851 rigorously enforced, but the Jesuits and religious orders of both sexes were allowed to spread to an extent without precedent in the century and to take hold of the education of more than half of the youth of both sexes in all classes of society. *Relations of Church and State under the Restoration*

During the greater part of the reign of Alphonso XII (1875–1885) Canovas del Castillo was prime minister. Out of the least reactionary groups of the days of Queen Isabella II and out of the more moderate elements of the revolution he constructed a Conservative party, which loyally supported the Constitution of 1876 and the religious settlement favorable to the Church. He insisted upon the retention of a heavy property qualification for the exercise of the suffrage, managed Carlist or Republican opposition with a firm hand, improved the national finances, reorganized the army, sent military expeditions into northern Morocco, showed leanings toward a protective tariff for the advancement of *Conservative Régime of Canovas del Castillo*

Spanish agriculture and industry, and courted abroad the friendship of Germany and Austria-Hungary after contributing to the
marriage of his king to an Austrian archduchess, Maria Christina.
At the same time he cheerfully acquiesced in the formation of a
Liberal party under the leadership of Sagasta (1827–1903),
believing that in the orderly rotation in office of two great political parties the permanence of the new monarchical régime
would be assured.

The first real test of the stability of the Spanish government
came with the premature demise of the gifted Alphonso XII
(1885) and the accession of his posthumous son, Alphonso XIII (1886), under the regency of the Queen-
Mother Maria Christina. Maria Christina was an
intelligent woman who knew how to enforce obedience
and respect. While she never swerved from the
utmost loyalty to the Church and always sought the advice of
the Conservative leaders Campos and Canovas del Castillo,
she gained the admiration of the Liberals at the beginning of
her regency by summoning Sagasta to be her prime minister.
Under Sagasta's Liberal régime a uniform civil code was prepared
and adopted; reciprocity treaties were negotiated with
several foreign countries; liberal press and association laws were enacted; trial by jury was introduced;
and in 1890 universal manhood suffrage was instituted for
elections to the Congress of Deputies. The return to office of
Canovas del Castillo in 1890 led to the reversal of the tariff
policy of the Liberals, the denunciation of the commercial
treaties, and the enactment in 1892 of a highly protectionist
tariff. It led likewise to renewed interference in Moroccan affairs
and to an unyielding attitude toward the demands of the Cubans
for local self-government. At home, however, public business
was fairly well conducted, and it was a source of deep regret to
most patriotic Spaniards that Canovas was assassinated by an
anarchist (1897).

The second real test of the monarchy's stability was the
stubborn Cuban revolt (1895–1898) and the resulting disastrous
war with the United States (1898). By the treaty of Paris
(1898) Spain renounced unconditionally all rights of sovereignty
over Cuba and Puerto Rico and ceded the Philippines and Guam

in consideration of a payment of twenty million dollars. Thus ended a struggle which left to Spain, out of her former huge colonial empire, only the Carolines and a few other islands, which she sold to Germany in 1899 for four million dollars. The war was a serious blow to Spanish prestige and pride and enormously complicated the financial problems of the kingdom. But the queen-regent, with the coöperation of both Liberal and Conservative leaders, weathered the storm and peacefully transmitted her powers to her son, Alphonso XIII, when in 1902 he came of age. The young king endeared himself to the nation by his adventurous and buoyant spirits, by his amiability and upright life, and by his loyalty to the constitutional régime. His marriage in 1906 with the British Princess Victoria insured him direct heirs, and, despite several attempts on the part of fanatical anarchists to assassinate him, the throne of Alphonso XIII seemed in 1915 comparatively safe. Not even Republican influence from France or the revolutionary establishment of a republic in adjacent Portugal (1910) appeared to have shaken it.

War with the United States (1898) and Final Extinction of the Spanish Empire in America and the Pacific

Alphonso XIII, 1902–

Several facts in the history of the reign of Alphonso XIII from 1902 to 1915 deserve mention. In the first place there was a slow but steady improvement in public finances and in the economic condition of the whole kingdom. On one hand, though maintaining a fairly large army and attempting to rebuild a small but effective navy, Spain was not burdened with such crushing militarism as afflicted the Great Powers of Europe. On the other hand, natural resources were developed. During the last decade of the nineteenth century more than 200 miles of railway were opened to traffic every year, and by 1910 some 9020 miles had been completed and the entire country was covered with a network of privately owned railways which linked together all the principal towns. Spain's merchant marine, far from decaying through the loss of her colonies in 1898, seemed to have been given fresh impetus; and the value of Spanish commerce increased from 375 million dollars in 1890 to 450 millions in 1913. Agriculture remained easily the most important Spanish occupation, the eastern provinces of Valencia and Catalonia being particularly well

Economic Development

tilled and producing a considerable quantity of grain, wine, fruit, and sugar; but an industrial revolution was already much in evidence in Barcelona and in the towns of the North, developing a very important cotton business and other manufacturing enterprises, and creating in its wake, as elsewhere, the two new social classes of industrial capitalists and industrial proletarians.

Secondly, despite the seeming stability of the monarchy, there was a growing acrimony among the political groups. The dynastic parties of Conservatives and Liberals tended to break up into factions after the deaths of Canovas del Castillo (1897) and Sagasta (1903). There was a marked recrudescence of Carlism and Federalism. Republicanism gained in the cities, especially in Madrid. Socialism made some appeal to the industrial proletariat. And intellectual anarchism, championed by Francisco Ferrer (1859–1909), who rose from the position of a railway employee to become the head of an anti-clerical "Modern School," and who was put to death in 1909 for alleged complicity in an insurrection at Barcelona, found allies among Syndicalist trade unions. In view of this situation Spanish legislation assumed a more liberal tone. An act of 1907 strengthened universal manhood suffrage by making the exercise of the voting privilege compulsory, as in Belgium and Austria. An act of 1909 granted a greater measure of control to local elected bodies and did away with official interference at the polls. In order to reduce the startlingly high percentage of illiteracy (which was returned officially in 1910 as 63 per cent), the government undertook in 1902 to support public and primary schools, and in 1909 made elementary education obligatory. At the same time efforts were made to utilize arbitration in the settlement of strikes, which in Spain often had a political, as well as an economic, aspect, and to improve the lot of the industrial classes by means of social legislation, such as employers' liability, factory laws, coöperative shops, and state-guaranteed insurance. For a time in 1909–1910 the government seemed bent on an anti-clerical program: Protestant worship was formally legalized; a so-called "Padlock Act" prohibited the establishment of any more Catholic religious houses without governmental sanction; and the Spanish ambassador at the Vatican was recalled. But

Political Factions in Spain

Legislation, 1902–1914

so great was the opposition from Conservatives and Moderate Liberals that diplomatic relations with the pope were restored in 1912 and further anti-clerical projects were abandoned.

Thirdly, there was a revival of imperialism, partially to benefit the influential capitalists, partially for patriotic motives, and partially perhaps to distract attention from grave Spain in domestic ills. To the African possessions which Spain Morocco already had, — the Balearic and Canary Islands, Rio de Oro, the Muni River settlements, and Ceuta, — were added in 1912 by agreement with France the northern coast of Morocco, the enclave of Ifni, and a considerable extension of Rio de Oro. Even this imperialism evoked criticisms and protests from many Spaniards : there were serious mutinies in the army, and repeated anti-militaristic demonstrations; and much difficulty was encountered in subjugating that part of Morocco allotted to Spain. Anti-militarism and anti-imperialism certainly were factors in keeping Spain out of the Great War of 1914 and in enabling her people to husband their strength and resources for the solution of domestic problems.

4. PORTUGAL

Portugal, with a population in 1911 less than one-third that of Spain and with an area only about one-sixth as large,[1] had continued throughout the nineteenth century to Comparison present an historical development, as it had in earlier with Spain centuries, strikingly similar to its neighbor's in the Iberian peninsula. Like Spain, Portugal had suffered from foreign intervention during the era of Napoleon and had subsequently been torn by strife between revolutionaries and reactionaries. Like Spain, Portugal had lost her colonial empire on the American continent in the early 'twenties. Like Spain, Portugal in the 'thirties had been the victim of a dynastic feud, the position and pretensions of Dom Miguel in the smaller country being much the same as Don Carlos's in the larger nation. In Portugal the reign of Queen Maria II (1834–1853) corresponded in kind and approximately in time to that of Queen Isabella II in Spain: Maria was a better woman than Isabella, but she

---

[1] The area of Portugal is 34,254 sq. mi., and its population (1911) 5,545,595.

was no more successful in putting an end to court intrigues, military *coups*, and general lawlessness.

Nominally the government of Portugal had been parliamentary since the grant by Pedro IV of the charter of 1826, but it was not until the last year of Maria's reign that constitutional provision (1852) was made for direct election of deputies and for popular participation in local government. Under Maria's two sons and successors — Pedro V (1853–1861) and Luiz I (1861–1889) — there was a respite from civil war and an orderly operation of constitutional government. Gradually political groups crystallized in Portugal much the same as in Spain : there were the two dynastic parties of Regenerators and Progressives, corresponding to the Spanish Conservatives and Liberals respectively ; there was a growing number of anti-clerical Republicans, formally organized in 1881 ; there were Miguelites, corresponding to Carlists ; there were small followings of Socialism and Anarchism. Despite the seeming popular majority that either Regenerators or Progressives could always command, the period was remarkably sterile of legislative activity. It is true that slavery was abolished in the Portuguese colonies (1869) and that democracy was emphasized by the provision for the gradual extinction of the right of hereditary peers to sit in the Upper House of the Cortes (1885), but the prevalence of political corruption and the exigencies of maintaining a colonial system far beyond the practical power and resources of the kingdom [1] created financial difficulties from which the state seemed unable to extricate itself. And in the meanwhile taxes were most burdensome, education was woefully neglected, needed reforms were postponed, and tens of thousands of the most industrious and enlightened Portuguese were emigrating to the happier and better Portuguese-speaking country of Brazil.

Marginal note: Politics under the Portuguese Monarchy, 1852–1889

[1] Portugal possessed in 1914 a colonial empire surpassed in extent only by those of three Great Powers — Great Britain, France, and Germany. Its total area was about 803,000 sq. mi. — almost twenty-five times the size of the mother country. The empire comprised, in Africa, the Cape Verde Islands, Portuguese Guinea, Angola, and Portuguese East Africa or Mozambique; in India, Goa, Damaun, and Diu; in China, Macao; and in the Malay Archipelago, part of Timor. For a treatment of the Portuguese empire in Africa, see below, pp. 615 f., 625. Between 1870 and 1900, Portugal expended some 75 million dollars from the national treasury for colonial maintenance.

At the very time when Alphonso XII, Maria Christina, and Alphonso XIII, with the aid of distinguished and patriotic statesmen, were putting the Spanish house in order, affairs in Portugal went from bad to worse. Under Carlos I (1889–1908) financial crises recurred with alarming frequency and growing intensity. The two dynastic parties of Regenerators and Progressives *The Disastrous Reign of Carlos I, 1889–1908* passed under the sway of professional politicians whose votes were determined almost wholly by their private interests, and skillful manipulation of the electoral returns enabled these two parties to hold office in fairly regular rotation and to obstruct the election of Republicans and Independents. The king himself was licentious and extravagant, and interfered excessively in politics, oftentimes in a quite undignified manner, to secure public loans and financial privileges for his personal use. On several occasions the king utilized a right accorded him by the constitution to prorogue the parliament and govern the country by means of ministerial decrees — a breach of constitutional practice if not of law. The last occasion — and the most notorious — was in May, 1907, when, following fierce factional strife among the monarchical groups and rebellious outbreaks on the part of Republicans, João Franco, the prime minister, assumed, with royal approval, a practical dictatorship. Franco was honest and patriotic and *The Dictatorship of Franco and Its Inglorious End* determined to introduce sweeping reforms. But his opponents were numerous and active; they included the Republicans, the professional politicians and those officials who feared investigation, the judiciary, the local government boards, and a large body of citizens who still believed in parliamentary government. Newspapers and politicians openly advocated rebellion; Franco replied by suppressing seditious newspapers and by filling jails and fortresses with political prisoners. On 1 February, 1908, King Carlos and the crown prince were assassinated while driving through the streets of Lisbon; and Franco's dictatorship came to an inglorious end.

Manoel II (1908–1910), the inexperienced youth who succeeded his father on the damaged Portuguese throne, was frankly unfit to cope with the situation. Franco, the one strong Monarchist, was now in exile, and the Progressive and Regenerator

chieftains were unable to agree upon any common policy. The
murder of a prominent Republican physician in October, 1910,
was the signal for a revolution. Republican soldiers
in Lisbon, aided by armed civilians and by the warships in the Tagus, overthrew the monarchical régime
after some severe street fighting and proclaimed the
Portuguese Republic. King Manoel fled from the country,
eventually settling in England, and a provisional government
was erected at Lisbon under the presidency of Theophilo Braga,
a distinguished scholar and poet.

*The Repub-
lican Revo-
lution of
1910*

A constitution for the new republic was adopted in August,
1911, modeled rather closely after that of the Third French
Republic. It provided for a legislature (Cortes) of
two Chambers, — a National Council elected by direct
manhood suffrage for three years, and a Second Chamber chosen by local councils and renewable half every
three years, — for a president elected by the combined
Chambers for four years, and for a ministry responsible to the
Cortes. The document went into immediate effect, Dr. Manoel
Arriaga being chosen the first constitutional president (1911–
1915) of the Portuguese Republic.

*Constitution
of the
Portuguese
Republic,
1911*

During the first five years of the republic, Portugal remained
in an acutely troubled condition. The new régime was not
only republican but severely anti-clerical. In 1911
the religious orders were expelled and their property
confiscated for the benefit of the state treasury. In
the same year the separation of church and state was
decreed : the public payment of salaries to the clergy was to cease,
and, under the guise of safeguarding the republic, serious restrictions were imposed upon the freedom of the Roman Catholic
Church in Portugal. And in 1913 the Portuguese legation
at the Vatican was abolished. It was quite natural, therefore,
that the Clericals should oppose the government and should
give at least moral support to the chronic counter-plots of the
Royalists. Then, too, the Republican leaders were mainly
bourgeois who had none too much sympathy for the poorer
working classes and who displayed no undue haste in instituting
economic reforms. The working classes, therefore, led by
extremists of various sorts, embarrassed the new régime by

*Portugal
under the
Republic,
1910–1915*

strikes, mutinies, and political demonstrations. To maintain themselves in power the Republicans resorted to many of the tactics which had brought reproach upon the monarchy : they manipulated electoral returns; they crowded the prisons with political offenders; they restricted freedom of speech; they practiced bribery and corruption. Only the support of the soldiery and the dissensions among its foes enabled the republic to survive.

5. THE KINGDOM OF BELGIUM

How Belgium secured its independence from Holland (1830–1839) and obtained an international guarantee of neutrality from the Great Powers (1839) has been related in an earlier chapter.[1] The constitution of the new state, which was published in 1831 and which underwent very few later modifications, proclaimed Belgium "a constitutional, representative, and hereditary monarchy." The legislative power was vested in a king, a Senate, and a Chamber of Representatives. The king, contrary to the practice in most democratic monarchies, might initiate legislation, but no other act of the king could have effect unless countersigned by a minister responsible to the parliament. The Senate was to consist of 120 members elected for eight years, partly directly and partly indirectly. Elections to the Chamber of Representatives were to be for four years and down to 1893 were based on a fairly heavy property qualification so that in that year there were only 137,000 votes out of a population of six and a half millions.

The Constitution of 1831

Under the enlightened and tactful Leopold I (1831–1865) and the shrewd and enterprising Leopold II (1865–1909), Belgium developed in an almost phenomenal manner. Of two or three phases of this development it is well to make mention.

In the first place there was an almost unparalleled economic growth. Though possessing an area barely one-third the extent of little Portugal, Belgium had in 1910 a population larger by two millions.[2] Unlike the Portuguese or Italians, very few Belgians left their native land; in fact, immigration exceeded emigration. The comparative con-

Economic Development

[1] See above, pp. 53 ff.

[2] The area of Belgium was 11,373 sq. mi. with a population in 1910 of 7,423,784, the density of population being greater than in any other European country.

HISTORY OF MODERN EUROPE

tentment of the Belgians was due to the economic prosperity
of the farmers, who, though in diminishing numbers, had learned
the art and science of intensive cultivation of their small holdings; and, to an even greater extent, it was due to a remarkable
expansion of industry and trade. Valuable mines and other
natural resources, the geographical position of the country, the
splendid harbor of Antwerp, and the network of canals and
railways conspired to promote the Industrial Revolution in
Belgium. Manufacturing and mining were done on an ever-
enlarging scale, and commerce increased by leaps and bounds.
By 1911 some 28,000 steam-engines were operating in Belgium
with a horse-power of 2,750,000; the kingdom possessed a
greater railway mileage in proportion to its area than any other
country in the world; and imports and exports (exclusive of
precious metals) totaled annually more than one and a half
billion dollars — a third more than Italy's and more than five
times the amount of Spain's. Of the vast Belgian shipping over
one-half was carried (1912) in British ships, over a third in German vessels, and over a seventh in Belgium's merchant marine.

A second significant factor in Belgian development was the
relation of the state to the Roman Catholic Church, whose faith
was professed by the great bulk of the nation. The
Constitution of 1831, while requiring the king to be a
communicant of that Church, guaranteed general
religious liberty. The Church was assured full freedom from lay interference, and the state continued
to contribute to the financial support of the clergy of all denominations — Catholic, Protestant, and Jewish. Over the question of public education pronounced differences of opinion
arose. As early as 1847 two political parties had
formed on this question — the Catholic party, which
sought to make moral and religious instruction compulsory in the schools and to intrust it to the Catholic clergy,
and the Liberal party, which espoused the idea of neutral schools
and a mild form of anti-clericalism. From 1847 to
1884 the Liberals managed to maintain ministries for
terms aggregating twenty-eight years, and during
the period of their supremacy they abolished religious instruction in the public schools and for a time actually broke

The Catho-
lic Church
and Politi-
cal Parties
in Belgium

1. The
Catholic
Party

2. The
Liberal
Party

off diplomatic relations with the pope. But towards the close of the nineteenth century the Liberal party dwindled in size and influence, and the Catholics would have had almost no opposition had it not been for the organization (1885) **3. The Socialist Party** of many of the urban workingmen into a Socialist party which not only was bent on radical social legislation but also was inclined to anti-clericalism.

From 1884 to the outbreak of the War of the Nations in 1914 — thirty years — the Catholic party governed Belgium. Partly on their own initiative and partly from Socialist and **Catholic Supremacy,** Liberal pressure they instituted a large number of re- **premacy,** forms. Religious instruction was restored in most of **1884–1914** the public schools; and education was fostered with such noteworthy success as greatly to reduce the percentage of Belgian illiteracy.[1] Political democracy was furthered. In 1894 the property qualification was removed and every Bel- **Education** gian was given one vote on attaining the age of 25 and **and Political Democracy** after one year's residence in his commune; at the **cal Democracy** same time the principle of plural voting was introduced by the grant of one or two additional votes to an elector in possession of certain financial or educational qualifications. In 1899 proportional representation was established for the protection of political minorities, whereby the parliamentary seats to be filled by a given district would be distributed among the parties or candidates in proportion to the number of followers or voters of each. In their opposition to the Catholic party, which had fathered these reforms, both Socialists and Liberals attacked especially the Clerical control of the schools and the institution of plural voting. In 1913 the Socialists were particularly vehement with their slogan of "one man, one vote" and even attempted a general strike in behalf of electoral reform, but the elections of 1914 preserved a comfortable Catholic majority in the Chamber.

The Catholic party during the long period of its ascendancy did not neglect social legislation. An enlightened factory code was prepared; trade unions were protected (1898); **Social** a system of old-age pensions was organized (1900); **Legislation**

---

[1] According to census returns the proportion of the population above eight years of age who could neither read nor write was 30.26 per cent in 1880; 25.0 in 1890; 19.1 in 1900; and 13.1 in 1910.

and considerable progress was made in decently housing the working classes and in otherwise providing for their material well-being.

In 1908 the Belgian government, against the will of a determined minority, took over as a colony the huge African territory of the Congo, which the business acumen of King Leopold II had done much to develop.[1] This step marked the entry of little Belgium into world politics, and was a natural antecedent to the military law of 1909, which substituted compulsory personal service for the formerly lax system of conscription and greatly reduced the number of exemptions. Extensive fortifications were erected at Antwerp and Liège. It was the national wealth, the strategic position of Antwerp, and the new colonial importance of Belgium probably quite as much as the geographical position of the little state between Germany, France, and Great Britain, which invited the Germans in August, 1914, to violate the soil of Belgium, which they had promised to respect, and to launch their attack against France *via* Liège and Brussels, — an action which occasioned the entrance of Great Britain into the War of the Nations.[2] Despite the patriotic and united resistance of the Belgians under their plucky King Albert (1909–   ), the country was speedily overrun by German troops; and the loss of life, the destruction of towns, the devastation of the country, and the general paralysis of productive industry all helped to plunge the Belgian nation into the deepest misery. Whoever was directly responsible for the Great War, it was not Belgium; yet it was Belgium that in 1914–1915 suffered most grievously.

World Politics and the War of the Nations

ADDITIONAL READING

France. General. Brief treatments: C. D. Hazen, *Europe since 1815* (1910), ch. xv; J. H. Robinson and C. A. Beard, *The Development of Modern Europe*, Vol. II (1907), ch. xxiv; J. H. Rose, *The Development of the European Nations, 1870–1900*, Vol. I (1905), ch. iv, v; *Cambridge Modern History*, Vol. XII (1910), ch. v; *Histoire générale*, Vol. XII, ch. i; W. G. Berry, *France since Waterloo* (1909). Important general descriptions of France under the Third Republic: A. L. Guérard, *French Civilization in the Nineteenth Century* (1914), an excellent introduction; E. A. Vizetelly, *Repub-*

---

[1] On the Congo, see below, pp. 619 f.   [2] On the war, see below, pp. 714 ff.

lican France, 1870–1912: her Presidents, Statesmen, Policy, Vicissitudes, and Social Life (1913), good especially for personal portraits; J. C. Bracq, *France under the Republic* (1910), an appreciation by a zealous patriot and Republican; W. L. George, *France in the Twentieth Century* (1909), a collection of interesting essays; Barrett Wendell, *The France of To-day* (1907), a discussion of French culture, " temperament," and ideals; J. E. C. Bodley, *France*, new ed. (1899), written by a patriotic Englishman at a time when relations between France and his own country were strained, a discursive book filled with many prejudices against the French system of government and mode of life; Ernest Dimnet, *France Herself Again* (1914), though primarily a war-book, valuable for its account of the newer tendencies since 1900; Pierre de Coubertin, *The Evolution of France under the Third Republic*, Eng. trans. by Isabel F. Hapgood (1897), pretentious and somewhat philosophical; Frederick Lawton, *The Third French Republic* (1909), a readable sketch; C. H. C. Wright, *The History of the Third French Republic* (1916). More detailed histories of the Third Republic: Gabriel Hanotaux, *Contemporary France*, Eng. trans. by J. C. Tarver, 4 vols. (1903–1909), covering the years 1870–1882, the authoritative work of a distinguished French statesman and historian; Edgar Zevort, *Histoire de la troisième république*, 2d rev. ed., 4 vols. (1898–1901), covering the years 1870–1894, useful and well-written; Émile Simond, *Histoire de la troisième république de 1887 à 1894* (1913); John Labusquière, *La troisième république, 1871–1900* (1909), being Vol. XII of the *Histoire socialiste*, ed. by Jean Jaurès; Louis Hosotte, *Histoire de la troisième république, 1870–1910* (1910); Georges Weill, *Histoire du mouvement social en France, 1852–1910*, 2d ed. (1911), scholarly and indispensable for a thorough study of social problems in France; Léon Jacques, *Les partis politiques sous la troisième république: doctrine et programme, organisation et tactique d'après les derniers congrès* (1913), an attempt to give young voters an impartial account of existing political parties.

France. Relations of Church and State. A valuable account from the standpoint of a moderate non-Catholic is that of Paul Sabatier, *Disestablishment in France* (1906). The Roman Catholic view is ably presented in the *Catholic Encyclopædia* under the article *Concordat*. For special study, consult: Antonin Debidour, *L'église catholique et l'état sous la troisième république, 1870–1906*, 2 vols. (1906–1909), exhaustive and critical; Eugène Spuller, *L'évolution politique et sociale de l'église* (1893), an excellent brief statement; Aristide Briand, *La séparation des églises et de l'état* (1905), the official report presented by the commission to the Chamber of Deputies; Gaspard Odin and Eugène Remaud, *La loi du 9 décembre 1905 concernant la séparation des églises et de l'état* (1906), a carefully annotated study of the Separation Law; E. Lecanuet, *L'église de France sous la troisième république*, 2 vols. (1907–1910), coming down to 1894, the contribution of a Catholic priest; Alfred Baudrillart, *Quatre cent ans de concordat* (1905), an admirable review from the pen of a Catholic scholar; Emmanuel Barbier, *Le progrès du libéralisme catholique en France sous le pape Léon XIII*, 2 vols. (1907).

France. Colonies. Alfred Rambaud and others, *La France coloniale*, 6th ed. (1893), descriptive and historical; Marcel Dubois and Auguste Terrier, *Un siècle d'expansion coloniale, 1800–1900*, new ed. (1902); Paul Gaffarel, *Les colonies françaises*, 6th ed. (1899); Émile Levasseur, *La France et ses colonies, géographie et statistique*, 3 vols. (1890–1893); Louis Vignon, *Les colonies françaises: leur commerce, leur situation économique, leur utilité pour la métropole, leur avenir* (1886), and, by the same author, *L'expansion de la France* (1891); C. B. Norman, *Colonial France* (1886). See, also, the bibliographies attached to chapters in Part V, below.

France. Other Special Topics. On the form of government: F. A. Ogg, *The Governments of Europe* (1913), ch. xv–xviii, the best brief account of governmental machinery and its evolution since 1789; A. L. Lowell, *The Governments of France, Italy, and Germany* (1915), an abridgment of the author's *Governments and Parties in Continental Europe*, 2 vols. (1897), of which Vol. I, ch. i, ii, treats of French politics, good on the law of the constitution but too prejudiced in favor of a two-party system to make clear its actual operation; Raymond Poincaré, *How France Is Governed*, Eng. trans. (1914), a simple narrative told originally by the president of the republic for French school-children, useful in view of the lack of more advanced and sympathetic treatises in English; a partial antidote for the preconceptions of Lowell and of Bodley, cited above, is the illuminating little article by J. T. Shotwell on *The Political Capacity of the French* in the "Political Science Quarterly," Vol. XXIV (March, 1909). On the struggle between Republicans and Monarchists in the 'seventies: Sir F. T. Marzials, *Life of Léon Gambetta* (1890) in the "Statesmen" Series; P. B. Gheusi, *Gambetta: Life and Letters*, Eng. trans. by Violette M. Montague (1910); *Lettres de Jules Ferry, 1846–1893*, ed. by Eugène Jules-Ferry (1914); *Memoirs of M. Thiers, 1870–1873*, Eng. trans. by F. M. Atkinson (1915); Jules Simon, *The Government of M. Thiers from 8 February, 1871, to 24 May, 1873*, Eng. trans., 2 vols. (1879); Samuel Denis, *Histoire contemporaine: la chute de l'empire: le gouvernement de la défense nationale: l'assemblée nationale*, 4 vols. (1897–1903), Liberal Monarchist in sympathy; Marquis de Dreux-Brézé, *Notes et souvenirs pour servir à l'histoire du parti royaliste, 1872–1883*, 4th ed. (1899). On the Commune of 1871: P. O. Lissagaray, *History of the commune of 1871*, Eng. trans. by Eleanor M. Aveling, 2d ed. (1898), interesting memoirs of an ardent sympathizer; Edmond Lepelletier, *Histoire de la commune de 1871*, 2 vols. (1911–1912), the most recent and best account; Maxime Du Camp, *Les convulsions de Paris*, 5th ed., 4 vols. (1881), detailed and Conservative in tone; Louis Dubreuilh, *La commune, 1871*, in Vol. XI (1908) of the *Histoire socialiste*, ed. by Jean Jaurès; Jules Claretie, *Histoire de la révolution de 1870–1871* (1872). On the Dreyfus case: Narcisse Leven, *Cinquante ans d'histoire: l'alliance israélite universelle, 1860–1910*, Vol. I (1911), for the general growth of anti-Semitism; Joseph Reinach, *Histoire de l'affaire Dreyfus*, 7 vols. (1898–1911), the standard work, very sympathetic toward Dreyfus; Alfred Dreyfus, *Lettres d'un innocent* (1898), and *Cinq années de ma vie*

(1901), both in English translation; Paul Desachy, *Bibliographie de l'affaire Dreyfus* (1905); and Paul Fesch, *Bibliographie de la franc-maçonnerie et des sociétés secrètes*, 2 parts (1912–1913). On social problems and social policies under the Third Republic: H. O. Meredith, *Protection in France* (1904), a summary of the fiscal policy; Émile Levasseur, *Histoire du commerce de la France*, Vol. II (1912), and, by the same author, *Questions ouvrières et industrielles en France sous la troisième république* (1907), important works by an eminent authority; S. P. Orth, *Socialism and Democracy in Europe* (1913), ch. v, a brief outline of the rise of Socialism in France; Alexandre Bourson (pseud. Zévaès), *Le socialisme en France depuis 1871* (1908), *Le syndicalisme contemporain* (1911), and (editor), *Histoire des partis socialistes en France*, 11 vols. (1911–1912); Eugen Jäger, *Die sociale Bewegung in Frankreich*, 2 vols. in 1 (1900); Roger Fighiéra, *La protection légale des travailleurs en France* (1913), a valuable commentary, the best on the subject; Paul Pic, *Traité élémentaire de législation industrielle: les lois ouvrières*, 4th ed. (1912), a convenient summary of labor legislation; Henry Ferrette, *Manuel de législation industrielle, . . . avec le texte des lois ouvrières et des tableaux analytiques* (1909), a collection of labor laws.

Italy. C. D. Hazen, *Europe since 1815* (1910), ch. xvi, and J. H. Robinson and C. A. Beard, *The Development of Modern Europe*, Vol. II (1907), ch. xxi, parallel brief summaries; *Cambridge Modern History*, Vol. XII (1910), ch. viii, by Thomas Okey, the best historical outline in English; *Histoire générale*, Vol. XII, ch. viii, a good French outline; Bolton King and Thomas Okey, *Italy To-Day*, 2d ed. (1909), an excellent and detailed study of Italian public problems; W. R. Thayer, *Italica* (1908), containing suggestive essays on " Thirty Years of Italian Progress " and " Italy in 1907 "; F. M. Underwood, *United Italy* (1912), deals with Italy since 1870 in a way calculated to give the reader a satisfactory understanding of present-day conditions; W. J. Stillman, *Francesco Crispi* (1899), a useful biography of a prominent statesman; *Memoirs of Francesco Crispi*, Eng. trans. of documents collected by Crispi's nephew, 3 vols. (1912–1914), valuable for both domestic and foreign policies; *Italy's Foreign and Colonial Policy: a Selection from the Speeches Delivered in the Italian Parliament by the Foreign Affairs Minister, Senator Tommaso Tittoni, 1903–1909*, Eng. trans. by Bernardo Quaranta di San Severino (1915); Ernest Lémonon, *L'Italie économique et sociale, 1861–1912* (1913), a valuable monograph on the more recent social history of Italy; A. L. Lowell, *Governments and Parties in Continental Europe*, Vol. I (1897), ch. iii, iv, and the subsequent abridgment of the work under the title, *The Governments of France, Italy, and Germany* (1915); F. A. Ogg, *The Governments of Europe* (1913), ch. xix–xxi.

Spain and Portugal. Brief general accounts: C. D. Hazen, *Europe since 1815* (1910), ch. xxiv; Charles Seignobos, *Political History of Europe since 1814*, Eng. trans. ed. by S. M. Macvane (1907), ch. x; F. A. Ogg, *The Governments of Europe* (1913), ch. xxxiii, xxxiv; *Cambridge Modern*

History, Vol. XI (1909), ch. xix, and Vol. XII (1910), ch. x; *Histoire générale*, Vol. XI, ch. ix, and Vol. XII, ch. ix.   The fullest English narrative of Spanish history in the nineteenth century is that of Butler Clarke, *Modern Spain, 1815–1898* (1906), which, however, is ill-balanced and ineffectively presented; a better general account is that of M. A. S. Hume, *Modern Spain, 1788–1898* (1900) in the " Story of the Nations " Series. On the reign of Isabella II in Spain: Francis Gribble, *The Tragedy of Isabella II* (1913); Gustave Hubbard, *Histoire contemporaine de l'Espagne*, 6 vols. (1869–1883), a standard work covering the years 1814–1868; Hermann Baumgarten, *Geschichte Spaniens vom Ausbruch der französischen Revolution bis auf unsere Tage*, Vol. III (1871), dealing with Isabella and the Carlist Wars.   On the revolutionary period, 1868–1875: H. A. L. Fisher, *The Republican Tradition in Europe* (1911), ch. xii, suggestive; E. H. Strobel, *The Spanish Revolution, 1868–1875* (1898), clear and scholarly; H. R. Whitehouse, *The Sacrifice of a Throne* (1897), the history of the short reign of Amadeo of Savoy; David Hannay, *Don Emilio Castelar* (1896), a biography of the Republican leader.   On Spain since 1870: J. L. M. Curry, *Constitutional Government in Spain* (1889), memoirs of an American minister at Madrid; Yves Guyot, *L'évolution politique et sociale de l'Espagne* (1899), a description of public life in Spain at the close of the nineteenth century; Angel Marvaud, *La question sociale en Espagne* (1910) and *L'Espagne au XXᵉ siècle* (1913), useful recent studies; J. W. Root, *Spain and its Colonies* (1898); J. D. Fitz-Gerald, *Rambles in Spain* (1910), a popular work of travel.   On Portugal: Francis Gribble, *The Royal House of Portugal* (1915); Angel Marvaud, *Le Portugal et ses colonies* (1912), including a discussion of social conditions and of the causes of the overthrow of the monarchy; Gustav Diercks, *Das moderne Portugal* (1913), a similar work in German; and the popular treatment of W. H. Koebel, *Portugal, its Land and People* (1909).

Belgium.   R. C. K. Ensor, *Belgium* (1915), a brief study of present-day Belgium in the " Home University Library "; J. de C. MacDonnell, *Belgium, her Kings, Kingdom, and People* (1914), another brief and useful study, sympathetic with the Clericals as Ensor with the Liberals and Socialists; B. S. Rowntree, *Land and Labour: Lessons from Belgium* (1910), the most painstaking work on social problems in Belgium; D. C. Boulger, *Belgian Life in Town and Country* (1904), a general survey of social conditions, and, by the same author, *The History of Belgium*, Vol. II, *1815–1865* (1909); *Cambridge Modern History*, Vol. XI (1909), ch. xxiii, and Vol. XII (1910), ch. ix, a sketch of Belgian history since 1839; S. P. Orth, *Socialism and Democracy in Europe* (1913), ch. vi, a good account of the Belgian Labor party; F. A. Ogg, *The Governments of Europe* (1913), ch. xxix, an excellent account of political institutions; Louis Bertrand, *Histoire de la démocratie et du socialisme en Belgique depuis 1830*, 2 vols. (1906–1907), written from the Socialist position; Charles Woeste, *Échos des luttes contemporaines*, 2 vols. (1906), Belgian politics treated by a distinguished Catholic; Léon Dupriez, *L'organisation du suffrage universel en Belgique, vote plural, vote obligatoire, représentation proportionelle* (1901).

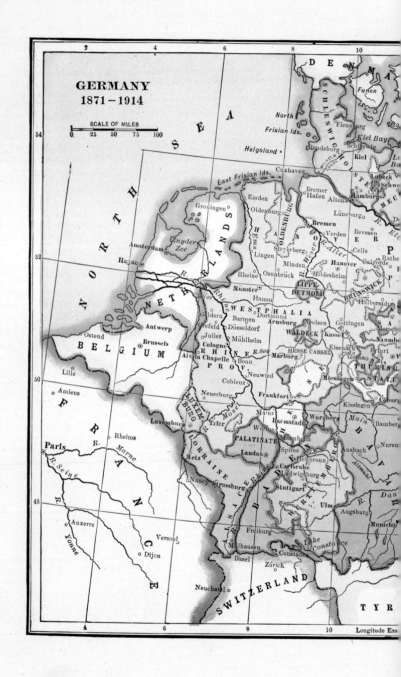

GERMANY
1871–1914

SCALE OF MILES
0   25   50   75   100

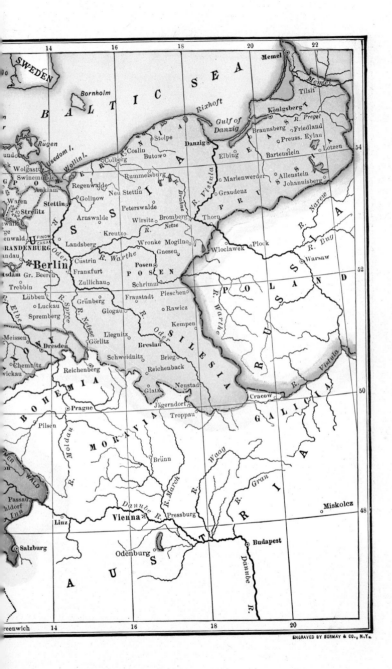

CHAPTER XXIV

TEUTONIC EUROPE, 1871–1914

1. THE GERMAN EMPIRE

THE CONSTITUTION AND GOVERNMENT OF GERMANY

IT has been pointed out in an earlier chapter [1] how the German Empire was created under the leadership of Prussia as the result of three wars during the seven years from 1864 to 1871.

The constitution of the new empire, bearing date of 16 April, 1871, was in the nature of permanent treaties between the North German Confederation and the four south German states, and consecrated a federal "union for the protection of the realm and the care of the welfare of the German people." Supreme direction of the military and political affairs of the empire was vested in the king of Prussia, who, in this capacity, was accorded the title of *Deutscher Kaiser* (German Emperor). To the emperor was intrusted command of the army and navy, appointment of the imperial chancellor, and power to declare war if defensive, as well as to enter into treaties with other nations and to appoint and receive ambassadors. But in case of treaties relating to matters regulated by imperial legislation, and in case of declaration of offensive war, the emperor must have the consent of the *Bundesrat* (Federal Council), in which body, together with the *Reichstag* (Imperial Diet), were vested the legislative functions of the empire. Over the laws passed by these bodies the emperor was accorded no direct veto.

Just as in the federal government of the United States the Senate represented the states and the House represented the

The German Constitution, 1871

The Emperor

---

[1] See above, pp. 180–203.

people, so in Germany the people were represented in the *Reichstag* and the states in the *Bundesrat*. But whereas the German
The Federal *Reichstag*, being elected by adult males over 25 years
Govern- of age, resembled rather closely the American House
ment:
Reichstag of Representatives, the *Bundesrat* presented a marked
and contrast to the American Senate. While the Senate
Bundesrat
  contained equal representations from all the American states, the votes in the *Bundesrat* were distributed in some relation to the size and influence of the twenty-six component states of the empire; and whereas in the United States a Senator was free to vote in accordance with his own will or with that of his political party, in Germany the representatives of the states in the *Bundesrat* were bound to vote as units in accordance with instructions received on every question from their respective state governments. In these respects the *Bundesrat* more nearly resembled a permanent congress of diplomats than a legislative and deliberative body. Representing the state governments (in many cases, the princes), the *Bundesrat* also was aristocratic rather than popular.

The table on the opposite page gives the names of the various states of the German Empire, their area and population (1910), their number of votes in the *Bundesrat*, and the number of deputies elected from each to the *Reichstag*.

A primary problem that confronts every federal state is the distribution of powers between the central government and the
Relations local governments. The German constitution, like
between the that of the United States, specified certain legislative
Federal powers which the central government — that is, the
Government
and the *Bundesrat* and the *Reichstag* — might exercise, and
State Gov- affirmed that all powers not specifically delegated to
ernments
  the central government should be reserved to the various federated states. The scope of such delegated powers, however, was broader in the German Empire than in the American Republic, for they included not only the regulation of foreign and interstate commerce, the coining of money, and the determination of weights and measures, but also the control of intra-state commerce, of banking, of telegraphs and telephones, and the establishment of uniform criminal and civil law [1] through-

---

[1] By amendment to the German constitution.

States of the Empire	Area (Sq. Mi.)	Population (1910)	Number of Votes in Bundesrat	Number of Deputies in Reichstag
1. Kingdom of Prussia	134,616	40,165,219	17	236
2. Kingdom of Bavaria	29,292	6,887,291	6	48
3. Kingdom of Saxony	5,789	4,806,661	4	23
4. Kingdom of Württemberg	7,534	2,437,574	4	17
5. Grand-duchy of Baden	5,823	2,142,833	3	14
6. Grand-duchy of Hesse	2,966	1,282,051	3	9
7. Grand-duchy of Mecklenburg-Schwerin	5,068	639,958	2	6
8. Grand-duchy of Saxony (Saxe-Weimar)	1,397	417,149	1	3
9. Grand-duchy of Mecklenburg-Strelitz	1,131	106,442	1	1
10. Grand-duchy of Oldenburg	2,482	483,042	1	3
11. Duchy of Brunswick	1,418	494,339	2	3
12. Duchy of Saxe-Meiningen	953	278,762	1	2
13. Duchy of Saxe-Altenburg	511	216,128	1	1
14. Duchy of Saxe-Coburg-Gotha . . .	764	257,177	1	2
15. Duchy of Anhalt	888	331,128	1	2
16. Principality of Schwarzburg-Sondershausen	333	89,917	1	1
17. Principality of Schwarzburg-Rudolstadt[1]	363	100,702	1	1
18. Principality of Waldeck	433	61,707	1	1
19. Principality of Reuss (Elder Line) .	122	72,769	1	1
20. Principality of Reuss (Younger Line)	319	152,752	1	1
21. Principality of Schaumburg-Lippe .	131	46,652	1	1
22. Principality of Lippe	469	150,937	1	1
23. Free Town of Lübeck	115	116,599	1	1
24. Free Town of Bremen	99	299,526	1	1
25. Free Town of Hamburg	160	1,014,664	1	3
26. Imperial territory (Reichsland) of Alsace-Lorraine [2]	5,604	1,874,014	3	15
Total	208,780	64,925,993	61	397

[1] Schwarzburg-Rudolstadt was joined with Schwarzburg-Sondershausen in 1916, thereby reducing the number of states in the German Empire to twenty-five.

[2] Alsace-Lorraine, which was acquired from France by the treaty of Frankfort (May, 1871), was without local self-government and without any voice in the *Bundesrat* until 1911. The *Bundesrat*, therefore, contained but 58 votes from 1871 to 1911.

out the entire empire.[1] At the same time the execution of imperial laws was placed, not as in the United States in the hands of a hierarchy of federal officials distinct from the state administration, but directly in charge of the states themselves. This meant in practice that some differences prevailed in various parts of Germany as to the rigor with which imperial legislation was enforced; nevertheless, in extremities it was always possible for Prussia, with her paramount army, to coerce the other states to execute laws of which her government approved, while all the other states unitedly could hardly hope to force Prussia to execute a law of which the Prussian government seriously disapproved. To several states, other than Prussia, the German constitution accorded special privileges. For example, Bavaria was to manage her own railways, post-offices, and army (in time of peace); in Saxony was to be held the supreme court of the empire; and of the five members of the *Bundesrat's* committee on foreign affairs one each was to be from Bavaria, Saxony, and Württemberg.

The constitution of the German Empire has been extolled as a mark of the utmost genius in adjusting the political difficulties which had long militated against national unification, — in effecting a nice compromise between powerful militaristic Prussia and the proud princes of the lesser states, and in yoking up the newer influences of liberalism and democracy with the older forces of aristocracy and divine-right monarchy. But when one examines closely the practical operation of the German constitution, one begins to perceive that something is to be said also for the recurring denunciations of an arrangement which favored the aristocratic classes and rendered Germany the least democratic country of western Europe.

Conflicting Estimates of the German Government

It was quite natural that Prussia should exercise the predominant influence in the new Germany, for Prussia embraced approximately two-thirds the area and two-thirds the population of

[1] Reserved entirely to the several German states are, however, such important powers as the determination of their own form of government, of relations between church and state, of questions pertaining to their internal administration, the framing of their own budgets, police regulations, land laws, and the control of public instruction.

the whole empire. Prussia, it must be remembered, continued to be governed in accordance with the constitution promulgated by King Frederick William IV in 1850 — a severely conservative constitution, with its three-class sys- **Privileged** tem of voting, which gave political preponderance **Position of** to the landed aristocracy, and with its provision **the German** for a ministry largely independent of the parliament, **Empire** which enabled the king to exercise very wide financial and military powers.[1] This king of Prussia was now *ipso facto* German Emperor. In his latter capacity he appointed the imperial chancellor. And the chancellor, according to the constitution of the empire, enjoyed a commanding position so long as he retained the confidence of the emperor. He was **The** the active agent of the emperor, the link between the **Imperial** Prussian Kingdom and the German Empire.[2] He pre- **Chancellor** sided over the *Bundesrat;* he cast the seventeen votes of Prussia in that body; he might address the *Reichstag* whenever he desired; he proposed most of the legislation both in Prussia and in the empire; he customarily named the heads of departments of imperial administration and supervised their work; he was charged with the promulgation and execution of all imperial laws.

Not only did the constitution confer these extensive powers upon the chancellor, who was usually a Prussian and who in practice was responsible only to the king of Prussia, but it made the oligarchical *Bundesrat* distinctly superior **Undemo-** in law-making to the democratic *Reichstag*. Thus, it **cratic Char-** was for the *Bundesrat* to pass upon the constitu- **acter of the** tionality of proposed laws and normally to initiate **Government** legislation. Thus, too, it was provided that the constitution could not be amended, taxes could not be decreased, and the military establishment could not be reduced, if on any of these proposals fourteen adverse votes were cast in the *Bundesrat* — and the chancellor alone had seventeen votes at his disposal. Again, through the indirect influence which the Prussian gov-

[1] For the constitution of Prussia, as distinct from that of Germany, see above, pp. 143 f.

[2] Customarily, the imperial chancellor was also the head of the Prussian ministry.

ernment could exert upon the governments of a number of the smaller states, several of which were completely surrounded by Prussian territory, it was nearly always possible for the chancellor to control a clear majority of the votes in the *Bundesrat* — and a clear majority of the *Bundesrat* could constitutionally veto any proposal originating in the *Reichstag*, no matter how large the majority which it commanded in the popularly elected House. The *Reichstag* was a debating society for the nation; on occasion it might even embarrass the chancellor and the emperor by refusing, or threatening to refuse, to approve new taxes or increased armaments or changes of public policy indorsed by the *Bundesrat;* but its real powers were slight compared with those of the British House of Commons or the French Chamber of Deputies or even the American House of Representatives. Moreover, inasmuch as there was no reapportionment of its seats throughout the period from 1871 to 1914, even the *Reichstag* was not thoroughly representative of the democratic electorate : the relatively rapid growth of German cities during the period was paralleled by no shift of representation in the *Reichstag*, with the result that in 1912 the average number of voters in a district in Conservative and agricultural East Prussia was 121,000, while in Socialist and industrial Berlin it was 345,000; in 1912 twelve of the most populous electoral districts of the whole empire contained 1,950,000 voters and twelve of the least populous had 170,000.

It may seem surprising that the German people, living in an age and on a continent pretty thoroughly permeated by democratic ideals, should have suffered the establishment

Reasons for the Stability of the German Government

and maintenance of an essentially undemocratic national government. Certainly in the revolutionary movements of 1848–1849 the German people had displayed markedly democratic proclivities. In explanation of the phenomenon, three facts must be borne in mind. First, the Prussian political tradition since the days of the Great

1. The Prussian Tradition

Elector in the seventeenth century had been a tradition of militarism, bureaucracy, and divine-right monarchy, and it was under this triune ægis that Bismarck, the Prussian statesman, had accomplished in the second half of the nineteenth century what democratically

minded poets and philosophers had failed to achieve in the first
half — the national unification of the country; and, as has
been previously remarked, nationalism was a more potent factor
than democracy in fashioning nineteenth-century Europe.
Secondly, the new German government was undoubtedly strong
and efficient, if not democratic, and under its effi-
ciency the nation made such notable progress in indus- **2. Efficiency and Material Prosperity**
trial development and in foreign prestige as to neu-
tralize and even to disarm the Particularist[1] critics
who would strengthen democracy in the various states by weakening the central government, and the Radicals who would
at once nationalize and democratize all the political machinery
in Germany. Thirdly, the ideal of democracy still remained
in the German heart and mind: if only slightly realized in the
organization and operation of the new federal government, it
actuated a number of achievements in local government. It
was efficiency, leavened by democracy, that revo- **3. Local Political Reforms**
lutionized the administration of German cities and
caused them to become exemplars to the world of the
advantages of urban ownership and control of all manner of
public utilities. It was the same elements which prompted
the state-purchase of most of the railways. It was a more
or less conscious imitation of British democracy that led the
Prussian government to establish (1872–1889) a new form of
local government, by a redivision of the kingdom into provinces, districts, and circles, whose officials were to be in part
appointed by the king and in part elected by the people. And
it was democracy which inspired the gradual constitutional
changes in the lesser German states. In 1909 Saxony substituted for her former three-class suffrage a new system of plural
voting based on that of Belgium. Bavaria obtained parliamentary government with ministerial responsibility, and in 1906
adopted the direct secret ballot. Universal manhood suffrage
for state elections was introduced in Baden in 1904 and with
provision for proportional representation in Württemberg in
1906. Of the twenty-six German states, only the Mecklenburgs
remained in 1914 without written constitutions and without
some form of popular participation in government.

[1] "Particularism" is the word commonly applied in Germany to what in the
United States passes under the name of "States' Rights."

The German Empire under Bismarck, 1871–1890

Prince Otto von Bismarck's political career may be separated into two important parts by the year 1871.   In the nine years
preceding that date he had made King William I of

Bismarck,
Maker of
United
Germany
and First
Chancellor
of the
Empire

Prussia, whom he found on the point of resigning, the most powerful ruler in Europe and had given to Germany national unity and constitutional government. For almost twenty years after 1871 Bismarck as first chancellor of the German Empire remained the chief figure in the domestic politics of his own country and in the international politics of Europe.   Reserving to a final chapter [1] the account of how he preserved friendly relations with the British Empire, promoted friendship with the Russian tsars, and created the Triple Alliance with Austria-Hungary and Italy, thereby isolating France, preventing a French war of revenge, and securing the peaceful integrity of the recently founded German Empire, we shall here confine ourselves to a review of political developments within Germany from 1871 to the downfall of Bismarck in 1890.

At the outset a good deal of legislation was enacted to meet the changed political conditions.   (1) Far-reaching legal reforms
were effected.   The common code for trade, commerce,

Consolida-
tion of the
Empire,
1871–1877

and banking, and the uniform code of criminal law, both of which had been adopted by the North German Confederation in 1869, were now extended to the whole empire.   An imperial commission of distinguished jurists,

Legal

working steadily from 1871 to 1877, compiled similar codes for civil and criminal procedure and for the organization of law courts, which were then promulgated throughout the empire.   Greater difficulties were encountered in preparing a uniform civil code which would harmonize the widely divergent property laws of the several states, and it was not until 1896 that an agreement was reached and not until 1900

Financial

that the imperial civil code became fully operative. (2) Financial uniformity was effected.   The imperial government speedily made use of its constitutional right to regulate coinage: the new coins, bearing likenesses of the

[1] See below, pp. 691–697.

emperor's head and of the arms of the empire, were so many gospelers of the new régime far and wide throughout Germany. The Bank Act of 1875 transferred the control of banking from the state governments to the *Bundesrat*. The establishment in 1876 of the famous Imperial Bank (*Reichsbank*), under the superintendence and management of the empire, enabled the central government to conduct its financial operations more expeditiously and guaranteed the economic stability of the German Empire. (3) An act of 1873 created an imperial railway bureau, which did much in the matter of unifying the various systems of state railways and of regulating **Railway** their relations to the military, postal, and telegraphic organizations of the empire. (4) There was further military development. From the large war indemnity extorted from France, large sums were expended on coast defense, on fortifications, on replacing the equipment and stores destroyed during the war of 1870–1871, and on pensions. **Military** Though technically the various German states retained their own armies, the imperial constitution provided that the whole of the Prussian military system, including not only the obligation to military service, but the rules for recruiting, organization, drill, and uniforms, must be followed in all the states. To give full force to this provision, a common system of military jurisprudence was introduced in 1872 for the whole empire except Bavaria. Over the size and financial support of the military establishment much haggling occurred. Bismarck, and the ardent Conservative nationalists who supported him, felt that wholesale militarism was destined to be the one safe bulwark for the preservation of the German Empire as it had been the one trustworthy weapon in creating the empire. He demanded, therefore, that the provisional arrangement made in 1867, whereby the authorized standing army in time of peace was reckoned at 1 per cent of the population and the annual financial appropriation at $165 for each soldier, should be extended throughout the empire and rendered permanent. In the face of determined opposition, Bismarck carried the main part of his military program, fixing the peace strength of the German army at about 400,000 men, but he was obliged (1874) to accept financial grants for it from the *Reichstag*, not in perpetuity as

he desired, but for a limited period of seven years [1] — the so-
called "septennate." The principle of compulsory military
"The Sep-   service was subsequently maintained and strength-
tennate"   ened, but the periodical votes on appropriations
for the army became crucial occasions for formally testing
the strength of the chancellor's government.

Of the three German political parties mentioned in an earlier
chapter, [2] — the Conservatives, the Progressives, and the Na-
Political   tional Liberals,— it was the last named which elec-
Parties   torally benefited most by the establishment of the
under   German Empire and upon which Bismarck chiefly
Bismarck   relied in inducing the *Reichstag* to nationalize legal
procedure, banking, railways, and the army. The National
1. The Na-   Liberals were of two sorts: the bourgeoisie, partic-
tional   ularly the business men, who had economic motives
Liberals   for strengthening the national government at the
expense of the state governments; and the patriots, regardless of social class, whose opposition to states' rights flowed
naturally from their exaltation of united Germany. In the
National Liberals, therefore, Bismarck found stanch champions
of most of his imperial policies. The Conservatives were al-
2. The Con-   most wholly a Prussian agricultural party, who could
servatives   hardly be expected to offer serious resistance to Bismarck so long as Prussia preserved its hegemony in Germany
and Bismarck did not disturb their economic mastery in Prussia.
3. The Pro-   Only the Progressives — those intellectual liberals and
gressives   radicals — continued to assert an undying faith in
democracy and an unswerving hostility to Bismarck's political
ideals; but the success of Bismarck's policies in unifying the
nation had greatly weakened the hold of the party on the people,
and their objections to his later practical proposals were more
often platonic than really vigorous.

In the early 'seventies, however, arose a fourth political party —
the Catholic, or, as designated from the seats which its repre-
4. The   sentatives occupied in the *Reichstag*, the Center.
Catholics,   Recruited almost exclusively from the liberally in-
or Center   clined Rhenish province of Prussia, which distrusted
the ruling Conservative majority in that kingdom, and from the

---

[1] Reduced to five years, in 1893.   [2] See above, pp. 184 f., 193.

south German states of Bavaria, Württemberg, Baden, and Hesse, which were traditionally jealous of their own privileges, the Center party was essentially a states' rights' party and inimical to the nationalizing tendencies of the federal government. For this reason, if for no other, Bismarck and the National Liberals would have combated the Catholics. But there were other reasons for the sharp conflict between Bismarck and the Catholic Church, which characterized German politics throughout the decade of the 'seventies. One of these reasons was that many Catholics were embittered against Bismarck by his refusal to intervene in Italy in order to reëstablish the temporal rule of the papacy, and that the chancellor, on his side, accused the Catholics of seeking to embarrass the foreign relations of the newly founded empire by stirring up trouble between Germany and Italy. Another was the fear in the minds of Bismarck and other German nationalists that the doctrine of papal infallibility decreed by the Vatican Council (1869–1870), together with the *Syllabus of Errors* of Pius IX (1864), was intended to register a divine sanction for attempts on the part of the pope to interfere in the domestic politics of Germany. Still another reason was the growing breach, in Germany as elsewhere, between the intellectual position of the Catholic Church and that of popular scientists and philosophers. In domestic politics most of the latter were Progressives, and it was a curious irony of fate that for his anti-clerical policies Bismarck could count upon the support of the Progressives and some of the Lutheran Conservatives as well as upon that of the National Liberals.

Reasons for the Conflict between Bismarck and the Catholics

The occasion for the opening of hostilities between church and state,— the combat which was dignified in popular parlance by the name *Kulturkampf* ("struggle for civilization"),— was Roman Catholic opposition to the support rendered by the state governments even of south Germany to the faction of "Old Catholics" who had rejected the decree of papal infallibility. Though the Roman Catholics rallied to the aid of their bishops and formed a compact Center party in south Germany, it was not until 1890 that they secured definite control of the Bavarian government and finally revoked the concessions which had been granted

Outbreak of the Conflict — Kulturkampf — in South Germany

earlier to the "Old Catholics." With the eventual collapse of "Old Catholicism" the Roman Catholics regained all that they had lost in south Germany.

Meanwhile, in 1872, Bismarck had inaugurated the *Kulturkampf* in Prussia and throughout the whole empire. In that year the Jesuits were expelled from Germany and diplomatic relations between Prussia and the Vatican were broken off. Within the next two years several drastic laws were enacted in Prussia, sometimes called the "May Laws," and sometimes cited, from the name of the Prussian minister of education, as the "Falk Laws." The most important of these acts provided that no one should be appointed to any office in the Catholic Church except a German, who must have received his education in a German *Gymnasium* (high school), have studied for three years in a German university, and have passed a state examination in philosophy, history, German literature, and the classics; all ecclesiastical seminaries were placed under the control of the state, and all seminaries for boys were forbidden. The Roman Catholic bishops in Prussia appreciated at once the fact that this law represented a complete reversal of the policy pursued by the Prussian government since 1850 of not interfering in the appointment of bishops and priests and of leaving the education of prospective priests entirely in the hands of the hierarchy; these bishops, therefore, with the moral encouragement and active support of their fellow-bishops in the other German states and of the pope, condemned the "May Laws" and refused to obey them. Then an open conflict ensued, fought not by powder and ball but by clerical manifestoes and decrees and by repressive measures on the part of Bismarck and the Prussian government.

On the governmental side, further laws were passed, forbidding the exercise of ecclesiastical functions by unauthorized persons, providing that any one who had been convicted of disobedience to the state could be deprived of his rights of citizenship, ordered to live in a particular district, or even expelled from the country, and authorizing the suspension, in every diocese where the bishop proved recalcitrant, of the payment of that financial contribution to the Roman Catholic Church which had been given by Prussia in accordance with the concordat of 1817.

The margin note: The Kulturkampf in Prussia and the Empire, 1872–1879

So great was the severity with which these measures were enforced that within a single year six Prussian bishops were imprisoned and in over 1300 parishes Catholic worship ceased.

On the side of the Church, the Catholic laity flocked to the support of their persecuted clergy. The Center party, hitherto weak in numbers and devoid of concrete political issues on which to stand, now came forward as the champion of religious liberty and by adroit promises of laboring for radical social legislation enlisted the votes of the Catholic workingmen, with the result that in the imperial elections of 1874, despite governmental counter efforts, the Center polled 1,443,000 votes and increased its representation in the *Reichstag* from 63 to 91.

Bismarck did not triumph in the *Kulturkampf;* he merely raised up a compact party which, with the aid of disgruntled Poles, Danes, Hanoverians, and representatives from Alsace-Lorraine, and of a section of sympathetic Con- servatives, threatened to block his nationalistic and militaristic schemes. Worse still for the imperial chancellor was the appearance in the *Reichstag* of a small but growing group of talkative and troublesome Socialists; and Socialism, in Bismarck's mind, was a more serious menace to the new empire than Catholicism. To break the unholy alliance between Socialists and Centrists in the *Reichstag*, Bismarck gradually abandoned the *Kulturkampf* in Prussia. In 1880 the king was empowered to use his own discretion in administering the "May Laws"; diplomatic relations were restored with the Vatican; and in 1886 most of the anti-clerical legislation was formally repealed. The termination of the *Kulturkampf* did not signify the dissolution of the Center party. On the contrary, the Catholic Party was permanently solidified; and, with its pretty constant vote in the *Reichstag* — slightly under a hundred — it maintained throughout the period from 1874 to 1914 a very independent position, sometimes supporting and sometimes opposing the government. Under the able leadership of Windhorst, an ex-minister of the defunct kingdom of Hanover, the Center party adopted a platform of principles favoring the claims of the Catholic Church, social legislation, indirect taxation, and states' rights, and resisting excessive militarism and imperialism.

Reasons for Bismarck's Failure in the Kulturkampf

Permanence of the Center Party

On the heels of the *Kulturkampf* came Bismarck's war on
Socialism.   In 1875 the fusion of the followers of Karl Marx
5. The   with those of Ferdinand Lassalle created a united na-
Social   tional "Social Democratic party," whose principles
Democrats   of absolute political democracy, drastic direct taxation, revolutionary social legislation, and anti-militarism were
the very antitheses of Bismarck's and were calculated, according to the chancellor's opinion, to destroy the family, the state,
and civilization.   Yet the new party was obviously making an
ever-widening appeal to German workingmen.   In the imperial elections of 1874 the Socialists had secured nine seats in
the *Reichstag;* in 1877 they polled half a million votes and increased their representation in the Imperial Diet to twelve.
Bismarck was alarmed and at once resolved to institute repressive measures against the Socialists.

Making use in 1878 of the public excitement aroused by two
unsuccessful attempts on the part of alleged Socialists to assas-
Bismarck's   sinate Emperor William I, Bismarck prevailed upon
War on   the imperial parliament, despite the protests of the
Socialism,   Progressives and Centrists, to enact a law for the sup-
1878–1890   pression of Socialism.   This law, originally enacted for
a term of four years, was subsequently reënacted and remained
on the German statute-books until Bismarck's retirement in
1890.   Its sweeping provisions prohibited the spread of Socialist opinions by means of books, newspapers, or public meetings, empowered the police to break up meetings and to
suppress publications, and legalized the arbitrary arrest and
punishment of Socialist offenders.   It smacked of the Carlsbad
Decrees and other enactments of the reactionary governments
of sixty years earlier, and placed Bismarck in a class with Metter-
Growth of   nich.   In spite of the rigorous enforcement of the legis-
Socialism   lation against Socialism, the Socialists preserved their
organization, conducted an energetic propaganda from neighboring countries, and steadily increased their influence in the
Reichstag.[1]

[1] In the elections of 1881 they secured 12 seats; 24 in 1884; 11 in 1887; and
35 in 1890.   Their progress was naturally more marked after the lapse of the
repressive legislation : they obtained 44 seats in 1893; 56 in 1898; 81 in 1903;
43 in 1907; and 110 in 1912.

The decade of the 'eighties was characterized in German history not only by Bismarck's repressive legislation against Socialism but also by a very real and fairly fruitful effort on the part of the chancellor to promote the material and economic welfare of the whole German nation. Ever since the formation of the *Zollverein* in the 'thirties, German agriculture had been holding its own and German manufactures and commerce had been enjoying a period of rapid growth and expansion, with the result that between 1830 and 1870 the territory which subsequently comprised the German Empire advanced in the value of its annual foreign commerce from $185,000,000 to $1,060,000,000. For a time in the 'seventies the payment of the huge French war indemnity tended to make money too plentiful in Germany, to cause over-speculation, to raise unduly the cost of living, and to create financial panics and great economic distress among employers and workingmen alike. The resulting unrest Bismarck believed to be the chief cause of the rise of Socialism, and to remove this cause the chancellor inaugurated quite a new economic policy.

[margin: Bismarck's Interest in Economic Development]

The National Liberals, upon whom Bismarck had relied throughout the 'seventies to effect his nationalistic schemes, were committed in fiscal affairs to the principles of *laisser-faire*, which distinguished contemporary Liberalism in Great Britain and in Italy and which had become traditional in the tariff arrangements of the German *Zollverein*. Bismarck was the first important statesman of the nineteenth century to react against the doctrines of *laisser-faire*: he gradually accepted the theories of a group of German economists that trade and industry must be regulated by the state, and in prosecuting his new economic policy he naturally abandoned his alliance with the National Liberals and formed a somewhat fantastic one with the recently despised and hated Centrists.

[margin: Bismarck's Break with the National Liberals and his Abandonment of Laisser-faire, 1879–1890]

The new policy was threefold — a protective tariff, imperialism, and social legislation. In 1879, with the coöperation of the Catholic Center and the Prussian Conservatives,[1] Bismarck

---

[1] Likewise with the coöperation of a small but active group of Anti-Semites. See below, p. 417, footnote.

secured tariff protection for German farm products and domestic manufactures together with excise taxes and a high duty
on tobacco and sugar. The chancellor's purpose in
this reform was not only to protect "infant industries"
and to steady German economic life, but also to provide adequate income for the imperial government and thereby
to relieve the empire of the necessity of making unwelcome as-
sessments (*matricula*) upon the federated states, as it
had been forced to do since 1871. The tariff invested
the central government with new strength and further unified
the empire. The tariff likewise gave a marked impetus to
industrial development.

The New Economic Policy

1. Protective Tariff, 1879

Before the adoption of a protective tariff Bismarck had
opposed colonialism; in 1871 he dismissed with a sneer the French
offer to cede colonies in lieu of Alsace-Lorraine;
throughout the 'seventies he professed to believe that
Germany should devote all her energies to maintaining
her position on the continent of Europe and should
avoid colonial enterprises as likely to embarrass the
empire's foreign relations. But the merchant's desire to sell
his surplus products and the capitalist's desire to invest his surplus profits and the missionary's desire to convert the heathen
to Christianity and the patriot's desire to see Germany not only
a Great Power in Europe but also a real World Power, all
worked to develop· an irresistible national desire for German
colonies beyond the seas. Merchants and missionaries led the
way. In 1879 a German Mercantile Marine Company acquired
privileges in the Samoan Islands. In 1882 a German Colonial
Union was formed. Business men of Hamburg, Lübeck, and
Bremen obtained concessions in Africa, — German Southwest
Africa, Togoland, Kamerun, German East Africa, — and in the
South Seas — the Marshall Islands, a part of New Guinea,
Kaiser Wilhelms Land, and a group of islands in the New Britain
archipelago, later rechristened the Bismarck archipelago. Bismarck, in his new rôle as champion of German merchants, swallowed his earlier prejudices and followed the merchants and
missionaries. In 1884–1885 he prevailed upon the *Reichstag* to
establish protectorates over the distant commercial posts in
Africa and in the Pacific. In 1886 he secured governmental

2. Acquisi-
tion of
Colonies in
Africa and
in Oceanica,
1884–1885

subsidies for steamers which plied regularly between Germany and the protectorates. And before his retirement in 1890 the process was already far advanced of transforming the mercantile protectorates into crown colonies, administered by imperial officials and policed by German troops.[1]

Protectionism and imperialism were but one side of Bismarck's new economic policy, — the side favorable primarily to employers, — though both were supposed secondarily to assist employees by raising wages and opening new forms of employment. On the other side, — direct state action 3. Social Legislation, 1881–1890 in behalf of workingmen, — Bismarck was a pioneer among European statesmen and Germany set the example which sooner or later every industrial country was moved to follow. Bismarck was led to espouse social legislation not only in order to remove the chief economic grievances on which Socialism throve but also to guarantee the efficiency of German militarism by providing that the recruits from industrial establishments and from the cities should be physically fit and fairly contented. In advocating social legislation Bismarck was supported by the new school of political economists, by the old Prussian tradition of benevolent paternalism, and by the party pledges and deciding votes of the Catholic Center. The novel experiment was foreshadowed in the speech from the throne of 17 November, 1881, in which Emperor William I asked the help of the *Reichstag* for "healing social ills by means of legislation . . . based on the moral foundations of Christianity." In 1883 a bill was passed insuring workingmen against sickness and in 1884 employers were obliged to insure their laborers against accidents. In 1887 laws were adopted limit- Workingmen's Insurance ing child and female labor, establishing a maximum number of working hours, and setting Sunday apart as a day of rest. In 1889 a law was passed, by a very close vote, providing for a compulsory insurance of workingmen against old age and incapacity, which became effective on 1 January, 1891. It was arranged that all the various insurance-funds should be administered by joint boards of employers and employees, under general governmental supervision; of the premiums for old-age and incapacity insurance, the employer should contribute one-

[1] On the German colonies, see below, pp. 594, 621 ff., 633 ff.

half and the employee one-half, while of those for sickness insurance the employer should contribute one-third, the employee two-thirds, and the central government should pay $12.50 for each pension.

This scheme of workingmen's insurance, which was somewhat extended and strengthened by divers amendments between 1890 and 1914, produced inestimable benefits. In 1907, according to an official report, "the number of those insured against illness in the German Empire amounted to thirteen millions, those insured against accident to twenty millions, those insured against incapacity to fifteen millions. The amount of compensation paid in 1907 in all three branches of insurance was 626 million marks ($156,500,000), the total sum for the years 1885–1907 being 6310 million marks ($1,577,500,000)." National insurance, together with enlightened factory regulations, an admirable system of labor exchanges, and the remarkable growth of trade-unionism, prepared the German people from below, as protectionism and imperialism aided them from above, to become one of the most efficient industrial nations in the world.

Before his new economic policies were entirely worked out and applied, the long period of Bismarck's domination was

Emperor Frederick III, 1888 — coming to a close. The death of the aged Emperor William I (9 March, 1888), his sturdy ally and loyal friend, called to the throne of Prussia and of the empire Frederick III,[1] whose well-known attachment to Liberalism boded no good to Bismarck. Frederick III, however, was fatally ill at the time of his accession and died after a reign of only ninety-nine days (15 June, 1888). William II,[2] the young man who thereupon ascended the Hohenzollern thrones, entertained ideas of divine-right monarchy and of militarism more

Accession of William II, 1888 — characteristic of his grandfather William than of his father Frederick, but his impulsiveness and egotism were very irritating to Bismarck, who had long been in the habit of handling the reins of government himself and who was now an old man. From the new emperor's standpoint it soon became a question, as he subsequently expressed it,

[1] Frederick III, the son of William I, was born in 1831.
[2] William II was born in 1859, the son of Frederick III and of the Princess Victoria, daughter of Queen Victoria of Great Britain.

"whether the Hohenzollern dynasty or the Bismarck dynasty should reign." In March, 1890, differences between the young emperor and the old chancellor reached a climax. William II refused to sanction Bismarck's proposals to renew the repressive legislation against the Socialists and to cow people and parliament into submission, if necessary, by armed force. Bismarck declined to accept a cabinet order whereby as chancellor he would no longer be the intermediary between the other ministers of state and the emperor. The emperor demanded Bismarck's resignation and the Iron Chancellor withdrew to his large private estates in Lauenburg. There the man who had done more than any one else to unite the Germanies and for twenty years to shape the foreign and domestic policies of the empire lived in more or less open criticism of the emperor and the new ministers until his death at the advanced age of eighty-three, on 31 July, 1898.

Dismissal of Bismarck, 1890

The German Empire under William II, 1890–1914

From 1890 to 1914 Emperor William II occupied the chief position in Germany and preserved Germany's leadership in Europe. One of the best brief summaries of the character and aims of William II, written by a distinguished German historian on the occasion of the twenty-fifth anniversary (1913) of the emperor's accession, is here inserted.

Emperor William II

"William II has desired to be something more than the heir of a great name, the mere representative of an institution. He has striven for no lower an object than to be the real leader of the nation. And yet his personality does not seem to embody that resolute simplicity characteristic of the born leader of men, but, in its singular mixture of traditional and modern traits, embraces a whole world of contradictions. . . . On one side there is a conception of his duties as a monarch directed by a religious and extremely personal sense of responsibility . . ., a strongly marked taste for all that has become historic, all that is anchored fast to authority, tradition, and discipline of life, and a predilection for the Prussian words of military command, definite and incisive as they are, even in contests for which they were not suited. On the other side is the thoroughly modern man, sanguine in temperament and speech, singularly receptive and impressionistic, struggling to understand every problem of business, of commerce, of science or art, which the many-sided and congested life of the present day thrusts upon us — a monarch, in short, the tenor of whose life and leanings has carried immeasurably far from the simpler type of his forefathers."

The bulk of the domestic policies inaugurated by Bismarck were preserved and developed by William II. The historic Hohenzollern ideal of divine-right monarchy was affirmed in no uncertain terms. The conservative character of the central federal government was maintained. Militarism was extolled, and the emperor, whose fondness for military reviews became proverbial, asserted in true Bismarckian style that "the soldier and the army, not parliamentary majorities, have welded together the German Empire — my confidence is placed in the army." At the same time the Christian character of the imperial régime was emphasized: the emperor declared in his first proclamation to the German people that he had assumed the government "in presence of the King of kings and had promised God to be a just and clement prince, to cultivate piety and the fear of God." While social legislation was furthered and education promoted and the laws against Socialism allowed to lapse, William II remained, like Bismarck, a pronounced enemy of the Socialists and free-thinkers, a natural ally of fire-eating militarists, of landowning aristocrats, of conservative university professors, and of the newer industrial magnates.

Under William II German industry and trade continued to expand by leaps and bounds. Protectionism and imperialism now combined with national thrift and scientific progress to produce amazing economic results. In 1882 the number of German citizens employed in manufacture and commerce was about twenty millions; in 1910 it was thirty-five millions. In 1885 less than 4 million tons of pig iron were smelted in Germany; in 1913 some 15 million tons were smelted. In 1891 the German coal mines yielded 73 million tons and in 1913 more than 185 million tons. The number of spindles in the cotton mills doubled between 1897 and 1912. Germany's share in the world's mer-

Retention of Most of Bismarck's Policies

Economic Development of Germany under William II

chant shipping increased from 6 per cent in 1890 to 11 per cent in 1913. The phenomenal increase of the value of the export trade of the German Empire from three and one-half milliards of marks in 1890 to ten milliards (two and one-half billion dollars) in 1913 bears eloquent testimony to the industrial progress of Germany which on the eve of the War of the Nations made that country second only to Great Britain as a manufacturing state.

Parallel with the development of economic prosperity was the growth of population. Germany, which was not much more populous than France in 1871, was over one and one-half times as populous in 1910: the population of the empire was forty-one millions in 1871 and close to sixty-five millions in 1910. Of the total increase, the chief part was urban rather than rural: in 1910 there were forty-eight German cities each containing more than 100,000 inhabitants. Moreover, emigration, very heavy in the middle of the nineteenth century and amounting annually even in the 'eighties to nearly a quarter of a million, was gradually checked, so that in 1913 only 25,843 German citizens left their country as emigrants and those chiefly for America. *Growth of Population*

Political life in Germany remained much the same under William II as under Bismarck. Of the five major political parties [1] in the *Reichstag*, the Centrists, Conservatives, and National Liberals almost, if not quite, held their own; the Progressives dwindled; and the Socialists increased. In the general elections of 1912 the Socialists polled four and a quarter million votes to two millions polled by the Catholic Center, 1,720,000 by the National Liberals, 1,500,000 by the Progressives, and 1,500,000 by the Conservatives.[2] The apparent growth of Socialism was *The Five Major Political Parties under William II*

---

[1] A sixth political party in Germany was that of the Anti-Semites, a group of extreme nationalists, definitely organized in 1879, who sought to lessen Jewish influence in politics and finance, and whose representation in the *Reichstag* fluctuated from one to twenty in the years between 1887 and 1907. In 1907 this party polled about a quarter of a million votes throughout the empire.

[2] Some indication of the need of a redistribution of seats in the *Reichstag* is afforded by the fact that these political parties secured from the elections of 1912 seats in the *Reichstag* as follows: Socialists, 110; Centrists, 90; National Liberals, 45; Progressives, 42; Conservatives, 57.

explicable in large part in three ways : (1) the Social Democratic party, unlike most of the others, put up candidates in
constituencies in which they had little or no chance of winning,
and the scattered votes for such candidates were reckoned in the total poll of the party; (2) the Social Democratic party possessed numerous allies and supporters
from among workingmen, especially trade-unionists,
who hoped to obtain economic amelioration through the political triumph of Socialism; and (3) the Social Democratic party
attracted votes from many middle-class radicals, who, though
not enthusiastic about the economic doctrines of Socialism, felt
that its growth was the most promising means of liberalizing
imperial institutions and establishing real political democracy
in Germany. However, the extensive enrollment of steady-
going trade-unionists and of bourgeois radicals as Social Democrats tended to render Socialism not only more popular but less
extreme and less anti-nationalistic in Germany than in any
other European country and paved the way for the almost
universal support accorded to the government by the German
people on the outbreak of the War of the Nations.

Reasons for the Growth of German Socialism

To the political opposition offered the imperial and Prussian
governments almost constantly by the Socialists and spasmodically by Centrists and Progressives, was added during the reign of William II as well as throughout the
chancellorship of Bismarck a pretty constant resistance
by a number of small national groups represented
in the *Reichstag* or in the Prussian parliament. There were
always a few "Guelfs" from the province of Hanover
who never missed an opportunity to protest against
the forcible annexation of their kingdom to Prussia in 1866.[1]
There was always a Dane or two in the *Reichstag*
who demanded the retrocession of Danish-speaking
Schleswig to the king of Denmark. There were always the
members of the *Reichstag* from Alsace-Lorraine, who
almost to a man resisted the steady "Germanization"

Minor Political Groups in Opposition

1. Guelfs

2. The Danes

3. Alsace-Lorrainers

[1] The renunciation of his claims to the throne of Hanover by the pretender
Ernest Augustus, his marriage with the daughter of Emperor William II, and his
accession to the throne of Brunswick, promised in 1913 to end the long feud between
Guelfs and Hohenzollerns and to remove the *raison d'être* of the Guelf party.

of the two provinces which against their will had been torn from France in 1871, and who, in some cases, earned the epithet of "traitors" by agitating openly for reannexation to France. Not even the grant in 1911 of a considerable measure of local autonomy served immediately to reconcile a majority of the inhabitants of Alsace-Lorraine to the German Empire.   Finally, there were compact groups of Poles from the districts centering in Posen, anti-German in speech, in customs, **4. Poles** and in national consciousness, who were always allying themselves with Centrists or Socialists or any other party which at any given time threatened to embarrass the government.   Against Prussia the Poles felt their chief bitterness. Following the failure of Bismarck to prevent the use of the Polish language in the public schools of Posen and West Prussia and to colonize Polish estates with German peasants, the Prussian government in the early 'nineties adopted a conciliatory attitude toward its three and a quarter million Polish-speaking subjects.   But even conciliation would not wake the Poles from their dream of national independence, and repressive measures were renewed. In 1901 the use of the Polish language was again limited by requiring that religious instruction be given henceforth **Prussian** only in German.   In 1906, when many thousand **Measures** Polish school children went on strike, their parents **against the** were fined and imprisoned; newspapers were sup- **Poles** pressed; public speeches in Polish were prohibited; and Polish peasants were forbidden to build houses on their own land. In 1907 the Prussian government was authorized to compel the sale of many Polish estates to prospective German buyers and thereby to drive the dispossessed Poles off the land.   Although the Prussian government encountered many difficulties in enforcing these measures, up to the outbreak of the War of the Nations the Poles obtained no respite from official per- **German** secution. **Politics**

One other political factor of the reign of William II **(1890–** — and that a novel one — merits attention. It is the **1914):** fact that, after the retirement of Bismarck in 1890, the **"William II** emperor personally exercised a controlling influence **His Own** **Chancellor"** over the domestic and foreign policies of Germany.   In the words of Bismarck, "William II became his own chancellor."

Of course, the succession of designated chancellors continued constitutionally, — Caprivi (1890–1894), Hohenlohe (1894–1900), Bülow (1900–1909), and Bethmann-Hollweg (1909–   ), — but none exercised such independence of initiative or judgment as Bismarck, and all took their cues from the emperor. Some idea of the more recent political developments in the German Empire may be derived from a brief summary of the principal events in each chancellorship.

Count von Caprivi (1831–1899),[1] who succeeded Bismarck in 1890, was rigidly militaristic and religious, and, not being a
Caprivi, 1890–1894 great landowner like his predecessor, relied for political support in the *Reichstag* more upon the National Liberals than upon the Conservatives. By treaty with Great Britain (1890) Germany secured the cession of the valuable strategic island of Heligoland in the North Sea and the settlement of outstanding colonial disputes in Africa. Likewise, the German protective tariff was partially modified by the recognition of the principle of reciprocity and by the conclusion of commercial treaties with Austria-Hungary, Russia, Rumania,
Reciprocity and Agrarian Opposition and Italy, whereby the import duties on grain were lowered in return for favorable foreign treatment of German exports. This arrangement was as distasteful to German farmers as it was advantageous to German manufacturers; and the extreme Prussian Conservatives — the Agrarians — were moved mightily against Caprivi. In vain the chancellor sought to humor them by strengthening the influence of the Lutheran Church in Prussian education and by reducing the term of active military service to two years.[2] They demanded his dismissal by the emperor, and the emperor complied in 1894.

Caprivi's successor as chancellor was Prince Hohenlohe (1819–1901),[3] who in his younger years had been the stoutest

---

[1] Georg Leo von Caprivi, descended from an Italian family of Carniola which had settled in Prussia in the eighteenth century, was a life member of the Prussian House of Lords, and had served as an army officer in the wars of 1866 and 1870–1871.

[2] Though the term of active service was reduced, the number of exemptions was greatly reduced, so that the peace footing of the German army was actually strengthened by Caprivi's reform.

[3] Prince Chlodwig Hohenlohe-Schillingsfürst, a Catholic and a Liberal, sat in the Bavarian parliament from 1846 to 1866, was prime minister of Bavaria from 1866 to 1870, pursuing a nationalist and anti-clerical policy, was German ambassador in Paris from 1873 to 1885, governor of Alsace-Lorraine from 1885 to 1894, and chancellor from 1894 to 1900.

champion in his native Bavaria of national unification, who had
served in the Franco-German War, then in the diplomatic service, and then as imperial governor of Alsace-Lorraine. Hohenlohe,
On account of the new chancellor's advanced age — 1894–1900
he was seventy-five — the actual conduct of imperial affairs
was less in his hands than in those of the emperor and of Prince
von Bülow, the secretary of state for foreign affairs. In domestic
matters the government persevered in its resolute independence
of the Agrarian group in Prussia and leaned heavily for political
support upon the National Liberals. This fact gave to German
history during Hohenlohe's administration an im- Germany a
perialist complexion. It caused Germany to become " World
definitely a World Power. Power "

In a way the transition of Germany from the rôle of the chief
Power in continental Europe to that of a prominent World
Power was not sudden. It had certainly begun in the Inevitable
days of Bismarck. Although that astute chancellor Result of
was ever preaching the necessity and desirability of Bismarck's
Germany's devoting all her energies to the consolida- Policies
tion of her power and influence in Europe and warning his fellow-
countrymen of the dangers of distant entanglements, it was
under his auspices that Germany imposed her protective tariff
and established her first and most important colonies in Africa
and in Oceanica and expanded her industry and merchant marine and increased her wealth and accumulated vast masses
of private capital. And these things were the raw stuff out of
which a great world policy was to be fashioned. The fashioning was hurried forward in the 'nineties by the formation of the
Dual Alliance between France and Russia, which Process
changed fundamentally the European relations of Rapid in
Germany, and by the deliberate efforts of William II, Late
Hohenlohe, and Bülow, which were directed toward 'Nineties
obtaining compensation outside of Europe.

Three great kinds of German achievement in world politics
marked the years from 1894 to 1900. First was a renewed
activity in the acquisition of colonies. The emperor himself declared in 1895 that "the German Empire has become a world
empire." In 1897 the murder of two German missionaries in
China was made the pretext for landing troops in the bay of

Kiao-chau and for securing the lease of some 200 square miles of Chinese territory on the peninsula of Shan-tung. In 1899, fol-

Renewed Activity in Acquisition of Colonies, 1897–1900

lowing the Spanish-American War, Germany purchased from Spain the Caroline, Pelew, and Marianne islands in the Pacific. In 1899–1900 by agreement with Great Britain and the United States she acquired the two largest of the Samoan Islands. In 1900 German troops coöperated with those of other European Powers and of Japan and the United States in suppressing the Boxer uprising in China.

Secondly, there was imperial encouragement and protection of German investments in comparatively undeveloped foreign

Multiplication of German Investments Abroad

countries. In the Ottoman Empire, the German government, assisted by the personal efforts of William II, who theatrically visited the sultan at Constantinople, gained important concessions for German commerce and German investment. The Turkish army was drilled and commanded by German officers, and in 1899 a group of German financiers secured a valuable concession for building a railway from Bagdad to Constantinople: German influence began to supplant both British and Russian in Turkey. Similarly, in obtaining the lease of the Chinese port of Kiao-chau, the German government also secured for German capitalists important concessions for railway construction in China. In Brazil, organized private enterprise, backed by the moral support of the imperial government, established a considerable settlement of German immigrants, and, though there was no prospect of acquiring political power, German investment and German trade increased greatly throughout South America.

Thirdly, during Hohenlohe's administration there was a pronounced stimulus to navalism, and the beginnings of the power-

Beginnings of Extensive German Navalism, 1898–1900

ful German fleet. For many years Germany had been the foremost military state in the world; now she aspired to rival even Great Britain in the size and strength of armaments on sea. Several reasons may be assigned for the rise of German navalism: the steady growth of nationalism and the resultant popular desire, since the German army was organized on a state basis, to possess in a navy a system of armaments organized on a national basis and controlled directly by the imperial government; the preachments of many German economists, merchants, and professional militarists that a powerful navy constituted the surest protection of large foreign commerce and investment; the lesson of the importance of sea power learned from the American victory over the Spaniards and from the British conquest of the Boer republics in South Africa; the widespread propaganda of the German Navy League, which in the late 'nineties aroused national patriotism and enlisted electoral and financial support for the building of a navy; the personal enthusiasm of the emperor, whose natural art of phrase-making did excellent service to the cause in such pithy sayings as "Germany's future lies upon the water," or "the ocean is essential to Germany's greatness"; and last but not least the organizing and persuasive ability of Admiral von Tirpitz, who was appointed secretary of state for the imperial navy in 1898 and who was still acting in that capacity in 1914. Whatever the reasons may be, German navalism speedily became an important factor in international politics. The acquisition of Heligoland (1890) enabled Germany to establish a new naval base off the mouth of the Elbe. The completion in 1896 of the Kaiser Wilhelm Canal afforded a valuable strategic connection between the Baltic and North seas. And two great Navy Acts, passed by the German parliament in 1898 and 1900 respectively, inaugurated that prodigious program of naval construction, which, pursued consistently up to the outbreak of the War of the Nations, gave Germany a wonderful array of dreadnoughts, super-dreadnoughts, battle cruisers, and submarines, — representing a total tonnage second only to that of Great Britain, — and cost the German people an ever-enlarging national appropriation, rising from 30 million dollars in 1898 to 120 millions in 1913.

The retirement of the aged Prince Hohenlohe in 1900 and the promotion to the chancellorship of Prince von Bülow (1849–   ),[1] a great Prussian landowner, served to promote more cordial relations between the imperial government and the Prussian Conservatives. In harmony with the

Bülow,
1900–1909

---

[1] Bernhard von Bülow served in the Franco-German War of 1870–1871, in the imperial diplomatic service from 1876 to 1897, as foreign secretary under Hohenlohe from 1897 to 1900, and as chancellor of the empire from 1900 to 1909.

well-known wishes of the Agrarians, the policy of commercial
reciprocity, which had been followed since the advent of Caprivi,
was gradually abandoned; and a new tariff law of 1902 re-
imposed heavy protective duties on the import of
The Tariff
of 1902 and   foreign grain and other foodstuffs. At the same time
the Bloc   Bülow did not repudiate the manufacturing and trading classes: for several years he relied for legislative assistance
in the *Reichstag* upon a curious coalition — the famous *Bloc*
— of Conservatives and National Liberals, and primarily for
the benefit of the latter he strove ever more zealously to realize
the growing German ambition for world power. Germany
strengthened her economic grip on Turkey and endeavored
to block French advance in Morocco. She supplied munitions
of war to Russia in the Russo-Japanese War (1904–1905), and
then forced Russia to accept Austro-Hungarian aggres-
Vigor in
Foreign   sion in the Balkans (1908–1909). These actions, ac-
Policy   companied by the emperor's striking references to
Germany's "mailed fist" and by the growth of Pan-Germanist
sentiment in the public press and popular mind, evoked lively
feelings of apprehension in Russia and France and particularly
in Great Britain. Italy, too, showed symptoms of weakening
in her attachment to Germany. That a vigorous world policy
was creating dangerously jealous foreign enemies for Germany,
few impartial observers could now deny. And even in Germany
were to be found numerous protestants against the newer policies of emperor and chancellor. Neither Socialists nor Centrists
had ever taken kindly to the enormous financial outlays for
army and navy; and the difficulties which the government
experienced in putting down a native rebellion in German Southwest Africa were seized upon by these parties and their allies
in the *Reichstag* as an occasion for withholding additional colonial
appropriations (1906). In the ensuing electoral campaign,
imperialism and world power were the vital issues, and so influential were the patriotic appeals made to the German people
by the emperor himself and so unscrupulous was the
The Deci-
sive Elec-   chancellor's interference in the campaign that the
tions in 1907 elections of 1907 served as a decisive indorsement of
militarism, navalism, and imperialism, and the Socialists, though
increasing their popular vote, found their representation in the

Reichstag reduced from 79 to 43. Henceforth both Centrists and Socialists were chastened in their opposition to the world policies of the emperor and the patriots. And it was a curious fact that the resignation of Bülow in 1909 was caused not by the Socialists or Center but by the hostility of Conservatives to his taxation proposals and by the demonstration of the military party, led by the crown prince, against what they considered the chancellor's lack of forcefulness in checking the French in Morocco.

Bethmann-Hollweg (1856–   ),[1] who succeeded Bülow as chancellor, maintained his predecessor's foreign and domestic policies essentially intact, though relying for legis- Bethmann-Hollweg, lative assistance chiefly upon a coalition of Conserva- Hollweg, tives and Centrists. He displayed no lack of force- 1909– fulness in asserting Germany's right to be considered a World Power, and, despite the fact that the Socialists more than doubled their representation in the *Reichstag* by the general elections of 1912, he succeeded in obtaining the support of all the political parties, the Social Democrats alone excepted, for his great Army Bill of 1913, which raised the peace footing of The Army the empire from 656,000 men to 870,000 and involved Bill of 1913 the extraordinary expenditure of almost a billion marks. Even the Socialists voted in favor of the required new taxes when the government consented to make the special war levy Seeming in the form of direct taxation on incomes and estates. Solidarity It was obvious that at last nationalism was weld- of Political ing the whole German people together. Parties

Reserving for another place an attempt to assemble the causes of the Great War, with which Germany was most conspicuously concerned, it may properly be remarked here that, once the herculean struggle was begun, the whole Ger- The War of man nation almost to a man appeared to give enthusi- and the astic support to the emperor and his government. To German the thoughtful student of German history from 1871 to 1914 the willing sacrifice of life and money on the part of

[1] Theobald von Bethmann-Hollweg, the son of a wealthy Rhenish landowner, studied law, entered the Prussian civil service in 1882, became governor of the province of Brandenburg in 1899, Prussian minister of the interior in 1905, and in 1907 imperial secretary of state for the interior under Bülow.

millions of Germans should occasion no surprise. Rightly or wrongly the German people believed that they were maliciously attacked by a circle of jealous and greedy foreign states and that their empire, created by their fathers' life-blood in the anxious days of 1866–1871, was now in jeopardy. Their brave loyalty was certainly a tribute to the growing respect which from 1871 to 1914 they had learned to entertain for that empire. In their opinion it was an empire that had grown great, an empire that had striven to harmonize conflicting interests of farmers and business men, of capitalists and workingmen, an empire that had cherished literature, the arts, and the sciences, an empire that personified efficiency and culture — *Kultur*, — an empire that by reason of these and other achievements had justly earned its right to survive not merely as a European nation but as a World Power of the first magnitude. Patriots knew that a defeat for German arms would mean certainly the loss of Alsace-Lorraine to France and possibly the cession of the Polish provinces to Russia and of Schleswig to Denmark, perhaps the dismemberment of Prussia and the undoing of national unification. Merchants and manufacturers and capitalists knew that a defeat would entail not only the loss of invaluable industrial and mining districts in Europe and of the colonies in Africa and Oceanica but also the lessening of that prestige which enabled them to sell their wares or make investments in far-off regions of the world. Catholics felt that a defeat would spell ruin for Austria-Hungary as well as for Germany and would thereby remove the last obstacle to the victorious onward march of the Orthodox Church of the eastern Slavs. Progressives and Socialists professed to believe that German defeat would signify Russian triumph — the triumph of autocracy and barbarism at the expense of efficiency and social democracy. Germany, quite disunited in 1815, seemed quite united in 1915. But possibly the Great War showed that unity had its curses no less than disunion.

2. THE DUAL MONARCHY OF AUSTRIA–HUNGARY, 1867–1914

In spite of the disastrous Seven Weeks' War of 1866, which excluded Austria from membership in the German Empire and

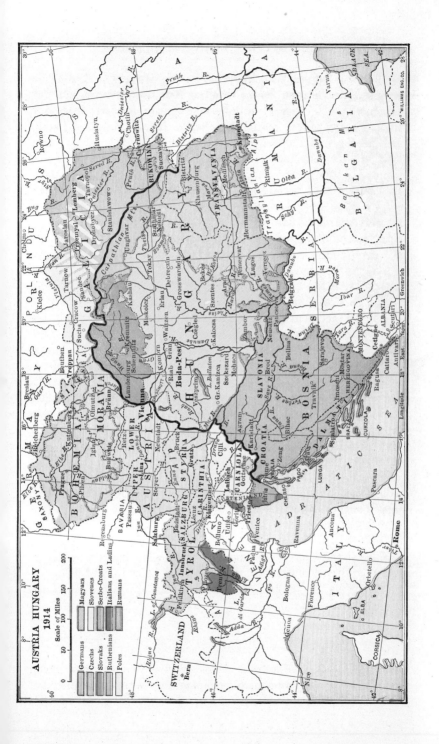

AUSTRIA HUNGARY
1914

Scale of Miles

Germans	Magyars
Czechs	Slovenes
Slovaks	Serbo-Croats
Ruthenians	Italians and Ladins
Poles	Rumans

deprived her of the rich Italian province of Venetia, Francis
Joseph, the German Habsburg, in his historic castle in Vienna,
was still lord of dominions the area, population, and   The Habs-
natural resources of which entitled him to rank as a   burg Mon-
sovereign of a Great Power. In one important re-   archy and
spect—vitally important in the nineteenth century—   Nation-
the Habsburg dominion was unlike any other Great   alities
Power: it was based upon personal loyalty to the reigning family
and upon an ancient tradition of cosmopolitanism, not upon
the nationalism which now distinguished France, Great Britain,
Italy, Spain, Germany, and even Russia. Although the dynasty
was Teutonic, and likewise much of the civilization and the most
generally used official language, nevertheless out of a total population of 51,300,000 in Austria-Hungary in 1910, there were
only twelve million Germans, while the non-Teutons numbered
over thirty-nine millions. What enabled the Teutonic minority
to exercise a predominant influence in the monarchy was not so
much the proximity of the powerful allied German Empire as
the divisions among the non-Teutonic majority. In 1910, of
the 39,000,000 non-Germans, 10,000,000 were Magyars, 4,000,000
were Latins (3,250,000 Rumans in Transylvania and Bukowina
and 750,000 Italians in Triest, Istria, and Trent), and 24,250,000
were Slavs. But the Slavs, who appeared to be the most numerous, were in fact widely diverse in language and customs
and the most separated geographically. There were 17,500,000
northern Slavs and 6,750,000 southern Slavs. Among the former
were reckoned 8,500,000 Czechs and Slovaks in Bohemia, Moravia, Austrian Silesia, and northern Hungary; 5,000,000 Poles
in Cracow and western Galicia; and 4,000,000 Ruthenians in
eastern Galicia. As southern Slavs were accounted 5,500,000
Serbo-Croats in Croatia-Slavonia, Bosnia, and Dalmatia; and
1,250,000 Slovenes in Styria and Carniola.

The *Ausgleich* (Compromise) of 1867 [1] determined the general
character of the Habsburg government of these mani-   Its Govern-
fold peoples during the period under review. By this   ment: the
arrangement the whole dominion was split into two   Ausgleich
autonomous parts: (1) the empire of Austria, includ-   of 1867

[1] For an account of the preliminaries to the *Ausgleich*, see above, pp. 126–131,
137–141, and especially 194 f.

ing the archduchies of Upper and Lower Austria, the kingdoms
of Bohemia, Galicia, and Dalmatia, the margravates of Moravia
and Istria, the duchies of Salzburg, Styria, Carinthia, Carniola, and Bukowina, the county of Tyrol, and the city of
Triest; (2) the kingdom of Hungary, including Hungary
proper, the kingdom of Croatia-Slavonia, and the principality
The King-   of Transylvania.   In accordance with the agreement,
dom of   Francis Joseph assumed the joint title of emperor of
Hungary   Austria and king of Hungary; each of the two major
divisions was to manage all of its local affairs; and for purposes
Political   of common action provision was made for the appoint-
Connec-   ment by the emperor-king of a joint ministry of foreign
tions
between   affairs, army, and finance, for ten-year treaties on
Austria and   trade, tariff, public debt, and railways, and for the
Hungary   creation of a curious joint parliament, known as the
Delegations, to supervise the work of the joint ministry and to
promulgate laws affecting the common concerns of the two
The " Dele-   states.   In order to emphasize the parity of Austria
gations "   and Hungary, it was arranged that the members of
the Delegations — 120 in all — should be elected annually,
half by the Austrian parliament and half by the Hungarian parliament, that their meetings should be held alternately in Vienna
and in Budapest, that they should assemble in separate chambers, the Austrian delegates using the German language and
those from Hungary speaking Magyar, the two groups communi-
cating with each other in writing — both in Magyar and in
German, — and that only in the event of a failure to agree after
a third exchange of written communications might all the Delegates meet in joint session, and then simply to vote, not to
debate.

Contemporary with the adoption of the *Ausgleich*, parlia-
mentary government was firmly established in Austria.   Already
The   in 1861 imperial decrees had granted a large measure
Government   of home-rule to popularly elected Diets in the seven-
of Austria   teen provinces of Austria, and now the constitutional
laws of December, 1867, created a supreme parliament — the
Reichsrat — for the entire Austrian half of the Dual Monarchy.
The *Reichsrat* was composed of two chambers: a House of
Lords, containing hereditary nobles, ecclesiastical dignitaries,

and a majority of peers named for life by the emperor; and a House of Representatives, elected at first by a restricted class-suffrage.[1] Thenceforth laws could be made only by consent of a majority of each of the two Houses of the *Reichsrat*, and their execution was solely in the hands of an Austrian ministry, responsible to the *Reichsrat*.

At the same time the Hungarian Constitution of 1848, which had been in abeyance since the suppression of the Magyar insurrection in 1849, was restored in its essentials The (1867) for the regulation of the central govern- Government ment in the Hungarian half of the Dual Monarchy. of Hungary By this constitution the law-making power was vested in a parliament of the familiar type,— a Table of Magnates, embracing several clergymen, a few appointed members, and a relatively large body of hereditary noblemen, and a Chamber of Deputies of 453 members, elected by means of a highly illiberal franchise, — while the execution of laws and oversight of administration were intrusted to a ministry responsible to the parliament. In grants of home-rule to subject peoples the Hungarian government was less liberal than the Austrian. Transylvania was deprived of its local Diet in 1868; and even the home-rule accorded to Croatia-Slavonia in 1868 was qualified by conferring extensive powers upon the local *ban*, or Croatia-governor, who in practice was named by the Hun- Slavonia garian government, by restricting the suffrage in Croatia-Slavonia largely to the "Magyarized" section of society, and by carefully circumscribing the privileges of Croatian representatives in the Hungarian parliament.

Since the adoption of the *Ausgleich* in 1867 and the definite establishment of parliamentary government in Austria and in Hungary, the Dual Monarchy, like the countries of western Europe, has been greatly affected by the Industrial Revolution and by the growth of democracy; but, far more than any other European state, it has been peculiarly troubled by the jealousies and conflicts of its numerous races and nationalities.

Between Austria and Hungary the most cordial relations have not always prevailed since 1867. Every tenth-year renewal of

[1] The size of the Austrian House of Representatives was gradually increased from 203 members in 1867 to 516 in 1907.

the treaties on commerce, taxes, and railways became an occasion for the display of rabid nationalism on the part of Magyars

Relations between Austria and Hungary under the Ausgleich and Germans. By the first set of treaties Austria promised to contribute 70 per cent of the total funds required for joint expenditure, and Hungary 30 per cent; but the relative advantage which Hungary enjoyed under this arrangement was somewhat lessened by the treaty of 1907, which reduced Austria's share to 63.6 per cent and increased Hungary's to 36.4 per cent. Then, too, the fact that Austria became an important industrial state while Hungary remained preponderantly agricultural, led to tariff reform during the years from 1881 to 1887, whereby protective duties were levied not only upon foreign manufactures but also upon the importation of grain from Rumania and Russia. The establishment in 1868 of compulsory military service both in Austria and in Hungary assured the Dual Monarchy's position as a Great Power, but produced many bickerings between the two governments as to the recruiting and officering of the joint forces. It was arranged ultimately that these matters should be left to the respective governments of Austria and Hungary and that the joint minister of war should not assume charge of the whole army until the two contingents were duly recruited and officered. Hungarian insistence that the commands addressed to their contingent should be in the Magyar language was a primary cause of the failure to renew the treaties at the appointed time in 1897; the general use of German was enforced, however, through annual decrees of the emperor-king; and the treaties were again formally renewed in 1907 without express settlement of the question of language. Similarly, the Hungarians protested against the Austro-Hungarian Bank, which had been incorporated at Vienna in 1878, and demanded in its stead the establishment of separate banks for Austria and Hungary with, at most, common superintendence. Although in this respect, as in that of the army, the Magyars secured no concession, they obtained a promise that after 1917 commercial treaties with foreign nations should be signed, not merely by the common minister of foreign affairs, but by a special Austrian and a special Hungarian representative.

Despite the friction between the two members of the Dual

Monarchy, they found it possible and desirable to present a united front to the world on the major questions of foreign affairs. Hungary, quite as much as Austria, was hostile to the national aspirations of Rumania and Serbia and to the aggrandizement of Russia. It was of economic advantage to Hungary, no less than to Austria, to carve a sphere of influence out of the western part of European Turkey. In the pursuit of a vigorous foreign policy in the Balkans, therefore, the statesmen of the Dual Monarchy, whether Germans or Magyars, came to espouse militarism and a strong navy in the Adriatic, to lean heavily upon the alliance with the German Empire, and to support the Triple Alliance with Germany and Italy, which endured from 1882 to 1915. In 1878 the military occupation of the two Turkish provinces of Bosnia and Herzegovina was intrusted to Austria-Hungary, and in 1908 they were formally annexed to the Dual Monarchy. In 1910 civil government was set up in the two provinces by means of a constitution, which provided for a local Diet whose acts, however, must receive the assent of both the Austrian and the Hungarian ministry. In back of the annexation of Bosnia-Herzegovina was a desire of Austro-Hungarian capitalists to build railways and otherwise to exploit the economic possibilities not only of the two provinces but also of Albania, western Macedonia, and Salonica. It was a desire which ran counter to the achievements of the Balkan Wars (1912–1913),[1] especially to the territorial gains of Serbia, and was the direct cause of the War of the Nations (1914).

Meanwhile there was marked progress in each of the halves of the Dual Monarchy. In the empire of Austria the rapid march of the industrial revolution was registered in the increasing numbers and wealth of the middle class and likewise in the growth of political democracy. Elementary public instruction was made compulsory in 1869. Electoral reform in 1896 more than tripled the number of voters; and an important act of 1907 established universal manhood suffrage for members of the House of Representatives and rendered the exercise of the franchise obligatory. Political parties in the *Reichsrat* were formed

Marginal notes: United Foreign Policy in the Balkans — Bosnia and Herzegovina — Austrian Progress, 1867–1914 — Political Democracy

[1] See below, pp. 538 f.

mainly along national lines, — Germans, Czechs, Poles, Ruthenians, etc., — but three groups had more than a racial appeal:
(1) the Liberals, a bourgeois group tinged with anti-clericalism,
Political   who dominated the state in the 'seventies; (2) the
Parties   Christian Socialists, a Catholic group, who in their
defense of the privileges of the Church and in their espousal of
social legislation resembled the Center party in Germany and
the *Action Libérale* in France; and (3) the Social Democratic
party, a Marxian group, definitely organized in 1888 and greatly
strengthened in political influence by the grant of universal
manhood suffrage in 1907.

Under the influence of the Christian Socialists, ably led by
the redoubtable Karl Lueger (1844–1910),[1] and of their Polish
Social   and Czech allies, not only was religious instruction
Legislation   securely established in the public schools but a good
deal of social legislation was enacted. In 1884 and 1885 measures were passed regulating the work in the mines and factories
and introducing a maximum working day of eleven hours in
factories and ten hours in mines. Sunday labor was forbidden,
and the employment of women and children was limited. The
wide powers which at first were given to the government to re-
lax the application of these laws in special cases and special
trades were closely restricted by a supplementary law of 1893.
In 1887–1888 Austrian statutes, modeled on the new German
legislation, established compulsory insurance of workingmen
against accidents and sickness. Trade unions were legalized,
and the public ownership of railways — a policy already inaugurated in the 'seventies by the Liberals — was expedited.
And the growth of Socialist strength with the advent of universal suffrage — the Social Democrats increased their representation in the *Reichsrat* from 11 in 1901 to 87 in 1907[2] —

[1] Lueger was a bitter and outspoken opponent of the Jewish capitalists who
constituted an important factor in the Liberal party and who were accused of gross
political corruption, especially in the municipality of Vienna. Under Lueger's
administration of Vienna, that city was certainly transformed. Nearly trebled
in size, it became a model to the world in perfection of municipal organization and
in success of municipal ownership.

[2] In the elections of 1907 — the first under universal manhood suffrage — the
Social Democrats won 87 seats; the Christian Socialists, 67; Clericals of various
national affiliations, 86; Liberals of various national affiliations, 122; while the
remainder were distributed among small national groups.

seemed to betoken an ever-widening popular sympathy with social reform.

That more social legislation was not enacted was due in large part to the overshadowing importance which nationalism assumed in the Austrian *Reichsrat*. Poles, Czechs, Ruthenians, Slovenes, and Italians became equally clamorous with Austrian Germans in demanding special privileges and almost equally liable to embarrass the operation of parliamentary government. The Czechs, infuriated that the Austrian government had not granted the same rights to Bohemia as it had accorded to Hungary, absented themselves for several years from the House of Representatives, and when they did appear they displayed much skill in throwing ink-bottles at the presiding officer and otherwise in provoking the wildest tumult. The Poles, toward whom the Austrian government, unlike the Prussian or the Russian, adopted a conciliatory attitude, were not so obstreperous; but Ruthenians, Slovenes, and Italians required no instruction from the Czechs to learn the lesson of parliamentary disorder. On their part the officials of the central Austrian government learned that concessions to any one nationality served only to arouse bitter resentment among the others and to inspire demands for imperial recognition of the local language and for the erection of national institutions of learning. Systematic nationalist obstruction repeatedly brought parliamentary government at Vienna to a standstill; and the half-hearted loyalty of the minor nationalities augured ill for the military triumph of Austria in the War of the Nations. Only a fear of what might become of them, were the Habsburg Empire to be partitioned, and a sense of personal affection for the Emperor Francis Joseph, induced these nationalities to support the Dual Monarchy in its hour of need.

Conflict of Nationalities in Austria

In Hungary the racial animosities were even more bitter than in Austria. The Magyars, though constituting but a meager half of the total population of the kingdom, were particularly illiberal in their treatment of the large minorities of Rumans and Serbo-Croats. They preserved their economic hold on large landed estates. They forced their language upon the public schools. They abolished all traces of local autonomy in Transylvania

Reactionary Politics and Racial Conflicts in Hungary

and seriously abridged the rights of self-government in Croatia-Slavonia. They steadily refused to extend the franchise to servants, apprenticed workingmen, or agricultural laborers; and so high were the property qualifications which they retained and so intricate the electoral laws that in 1910, out of a total population of 20,886,000 in the Hungarian kingdom, there were not more than 1,000,000 voters, and in the same year, out of 413 members of the Chamber of Deputies privileged to vote on all questions, there were only seven non-Magyars. Among the disgruntled minorities the resulting bitterness gave rise to nationalist movements looking toward the incorporation of Transylvania into the kingdom of Rumania and the inclusion of the Serbo-Croats in the kingdom of Serbia. On the other hand, the Magyars undertook to justify their policy on the ground that they were the cultural element in the kingdom of Hungary and that concessions to Rumans or Serbo-Croats would undermine the state and put an end to its civilizing mission in south-eastern Europe.

It was the poorer classes of Magyars as well as Serbo-Croats and Rumans who suffered from the undemocratic régime in Hungary. Though popular education was zealously promoted and though some of the worst grievances of the peasants against their landlords were removed, the great landowners and the governmental oligarchy were the chief beneficiaries of the wonderful agricultural development of Hungary between 1867 and 1914. This fact was evidenced by the alarmingly heavy emigration from the country, — amounting to over a million for the years from 1896 to 1910, — and by a widespread popular agitation for electoral reform, which in the first decade of the twentieth century brought the kingdom to the verge of civil war. These domestic problems were still unsolved when the outbreak of foreign war in 1914 threatened Hungary's very existence.

Demand for Political and Social Reform in Hungary

In Hungary as well as in Austria existed a deep-rooted respect for the Emperor-King Francis Joseph, whose long reign since 1848 had been full of stirring scenes, — the wars of 1849, 1859, and 1866; the establishment of the *Ausgleich;* the economic and political transformation of the Dual Monarchy. It was Francis Joseph who bridged the gap between Metternich and the War of the Nations; he had witnessed the rise and fall of Napoleon III, the achievements of Gladstone, Disraeli, and Lloyd George, the rise and retirement of Bismarck.

It was Francis Joseph whose counsels in Austria-Hungary since 1867 had almost invariably been on the side of concessions to democracy and nationalism. And with popular respect was mingled human sympathy for a series of domestic tragedies, — the execution of his brother Maximilian, emperor of Mexico, in 1867; the mysterious suicide of his only son Rudolph in 1889; the assassination of his wife by an anarchist at Geneva in 1897; and the murder of his nephew and heir, the Archduke Francis Ferdinand, by Serb conspirators at Sarajevo, the capital of Bosnia, in 1914. Following closely upon this last domestic tragedy came to the old emperor-king, now in his eighty-fifth year, the Great War, the greatest catastrophe of his long and eventful career.

The Emperor-King Francis Joseph, 1848–1916

3. THE SWISS CONFEDERATION

Mountain-girt little Switzerland, like the broad Danubian plains of Austria-Hungary, presents a spectacle of divergent races and languages rather arbitrarily brought together, through the historical development of centuries, to form a political union and something resembling a national culture. Within a territory, perched high upon the common Alpine watersheds of the Rhine, Danube, and Rhone, hardly larger than Holland and smaller than the combined areas of Vermont and New Hampshire, were included in the second half of the nineteenth century some twenty-two diminutive communities, or cantons, differing among themselves in language, religion, and customs, according to their geographical proximity to Germany, France, or Italy. In fifteen cantons — two-thirds of the entire population of the Confederation — the German language prevailed; of the remainder, five were predominantly French-speaking and two were Italian. Protestants were in a majority in twelve of the cantons and Roman Catholics in ten.

A Country of Diverse Languages and Religions

That racial antipathies did not produce results as unfortunate in Switzerland as in Austria-Hungary was due in large part to the fact that the Swiss nationalities were generally separated by cantonal boundaries and that each of the twenty-two cantons was treated as a sovereign state and its citizens were allowed to exercise wide powers of self-government. In fact, with the exception of a brief period of enforced centralization during the era of Napoleon I, the Swiss Confederation from its earliest beginnings in the middle ages down to the year 1848 was merely a defensive alliance between practically independent communities, involving more or less regular meetings of cantonal ambassadors, but leaving the domestic affairs of the several states quite untouched.

Early Emphasis upon Local Self-Government

In 1848, however, following a brief civil war, in which a party of Liberals, or Centralists, coerced the freedom-loving Catholic mountaineers of central Switzerland, the Swiss people voted by an overwhelming majority to adopt a written constitution, which made provision for a fairly strong federal government. The Swiss Constitution of 1848, modeled after that of the United States, really inaugurated the Swiss Confederation as we know it to-day. It established a central legislature of two chambers, — a Council of States, consisting of two representatives from each canton, chosen in such manner as the canton might direct, and a National Council, elected by universal manhood suffrage in proportion to population, — and a central executive in the form of a Federal Council of seven members designated for three-year terms by the legislature. The Federal Council was to act as a kind of cabinet under the chairmanship of a President of the Confederation, elected annually by the legislature. The Constitution of 1848 conferred on the new federal government power to conduct the foreign relations of Switzerland, to levy customs duties and other taxes, to raise a national army, and to regulate interstate commerce. A common Swiss citizenship was created and elaborate guarantees of individual liberties were proclaimed. All Christians were accorded the free exercise of their religion, but, conformably to the anti-clerical tendencies of the constitution-framers of 1848, the Jesuits and similar religious orders of the Roman Catholic Church were not to be received in any canton. German, French, and Italian were recognized as national languages.

The Constitution of 1848 and the Real Formation of the Swiss Confederation

The history of Switzerland from 1848 to 1914 was marked by three general characteristics: (1) the gradual paring down of the many rights still reserved to the cantons by the Constitution of 1848; (2) the economic development of the country; and (3) the radical extension of political democracy and the trial of novel governmental experiments both in federal and in cantonal affairs.

General Characteristics of Swiss History, 1848–1914

In respect of the first of these three general characteristics, it may be pointed out that soon after 1848 a beginning was made of organizing the different public services which had been brought within the scope of the federal authority. Thus, a uniform postal service was established; a single coinage replaced the confusing cantonal currencies; all customs duties between cantons were abolished; and the metric system of weights and measures was made obligatory. A complete revision of the Swiss Constitution in 1874, though making no important change in the organization of government, further enlarged the federal powers by authorizing the establishment

Increase of Federal Power at the Expense of the Various Cantons

The Constitution of 1874

of a system of free elementary schools under the superintendence of the Confederation but managed by the several cantons, and by introducing the principle of the referendum in national law-making. As a corollary to the referendum, the initiative (*i.e.*, the right of any 50,000 Swiss citizens to demand the submission of any measure to popular vote, or referendum) was introduced in federal legislation in 1891. Thenceforth, by means of the initiative and referendum, as well as through indirect action on the part of the central legislature, federal authority was extended to many domains. In 1891 the principle of a national bank was indorsed, though such a bank was not opened until 1907. In 1891 the Swiss departed from their traditional free-trade policy and established a protective tariff, which was considerably increased in 1903. In 1898 the federal government was authorized to prepare and enforce uniform codes of civil and criminal law and to purchase and operate the privately owned railways. In 1908 the immense water power supplied by the many rivers and mountain torrents became a monopoly of the federal government. Though the principle of compulsory insurance of workingmen against

Federal Referendum and Initiative

sickness and accidents was approved by popular vote in 1890, a definite plan was not found acceptable until 1913. In the matter of militarism, the Swiss people, in view of the growing armaments of all the surrounding Great Powers and the fear that their own neutrality, despite the solemn guarantees of the Congress of Vienna (1815), might not be respected in case of a

The Militia great international war, thought it necessary to sanction the compulsory enrollment of all able-bodied young men and military training for a certain number of days every year. Such a national militia, approved in 1874 and later strengthened, especially by a law of 1907, earned the reputation of being a most efficient force for national defense, but cost the Swiss people almost a third of their total federal income.

To the economic prosperity of Switzerland three factors contributed. First was the thrift of the hardy natives who still

Economic Prosperity in considerable numbers herded flocks upon the mountain-sides or practiced the science of intensive cultivation in the narrow but fertile valleys. Secondly was the influx, steadily augmenting, of wealthy foreign tourists who interspersed their mountain-climbing and sight-seeing with liberal expenditure to innkeepers and to purveyors of Swiss souvenirs. Thirdly was a noticeable growth of manufacturing, stimulated by the imposition of the protective tariff, and represented in 1905 by nearly 250,000 industrial and commercial establishments, embracing factories for textiles, gloves, pottery, watches and clocks, and milk chocolate.

With the increasing wealth and prosperity of the country and the enlarging scope of the federal government, the growth

Political Democracy in the Cantons and in the Confederation of political democracy kept pace. In four of the smallest cantons the people continued to exercise their local powers direct, without the intervention of any parliamentary machinery, all male citizens of full age assembling together in the open air, at stated intervals, making laws and appointing their administrators. In the other cantons, whose size naturally militated against such "town meetings" (*Landsgemeinden*), local government was carried on by means of representative institutions, but in all of them the suffrage was extended to every adult male, regardless of wealth or education, and in nearly all of them the referendum obtained constitutional recognition. The principle of the referendum was most fully developed in the canton of Zurich, where all laws and the chief matters of finance, as well as proposed constitutional amendments, must be submitted to popular vote. In many cantons the popular initiative was likewise introduced. In federal affairs, the successful operation of the referendum and initiative served not only, as we have seen, to strengthen the central government but also to develop the democratic spirit throughout Switzerland and to apply it to social reform.

4. THE KINGDOM OF THE NETHERLANDS (HOLLAND)

Shorn of its Belgian provinces by the revolution of 1830, the kingdom of the Netherlands retained in Europe a territory [1] less than half the size of little Portugal, though beyond the seas it continued to possess a large part of the proud imperial domain which had been a source of great wealth to Dutch burghers in the seventeenth century. Dutch government was still maintained in Java, Sumatra, the Spice Islands, Borneo, and New Guinea, — an East Indian empire fifty-eight times as large as the mother-country and six times as populous; while 46,500 square miles of land and a population of 140,000 constituted the Dutch possessions of Guiana (Surinam) in South America and Curaçao in the West Indies.

The Kingdom and Its Colonial Empire

For twenty-five years after the Congress of Vienna (1815) the government of the Netherlands was conducted by King William I, a prince of the famous Orange family, whose stubborn refusal to make concessions to Belgium cost him disastrous foreign war and whose incessant opposition to any liberalizing of the conservative constitution of 1815 earned him grave unpopularity at home so that in 1840 he saw fit to abdicate. From his son and successor, King William II, the Dutch Liberals, excited by the general revolutionary movement that pervaded Europe, wrung in 1848 a new constitution, which established the form of Dutch government that obtained, with slight change, from then until 1914. By this constitution the royal ministers were

William I, 1815–1840

The Constitution of 1848

---

[1] Its European territory embraced 12,648 sq. mi. with a population in 1910 of 5,858,175.

made responsible to the States-General, a central parliament consisting of a First Chamber, chosen by the provincial states, and a Second Chamber, elected by a closely restricted popular suffrage. At the same time a large measure of autonomy in local affairs was guaranteed to the elective "states" of the eleven provinces into which the kingdom was divided.

During the long reign of the enlightened and benevolent King William III (1849–1890), the chief struggle of the political

King William III, 1849–1890

parties in the States-General centered in religious education. On one side were the Liberals, drawn largely from the commercial classes in the towns, who demanded the establishment of a system of free, public, secular schools. On the other side were the Protestant Conservatives, supported by the Calvinistic peasantry, and the Roman Catholics, who, growing in numbers in the nineteenth century, came to represent about one-third of the total population. The outcome of the struggle was in the nature of a compromise: elementary schools in which no religious instruction was given, were opened in large numbers and were maintained at public expense; but in 1889 the Conservatives and Catholics obtained governmental financial assistance for their private parochial schools; compulsory attendance either at public or at private school was enacted in 1900. At the same time the property qualifications for exercise of the franchise were gradually lowered, so that the number of voters in the elections to the Second Chamber was doubled in 1887 and again in 1896. Despite these concessions, political democracy made slower headway in the Netherlands than in any other country of western Europe; in 1914 only about five-eighths of the Dutchmen over 25 years of age possessed the suffrage.

William III was succeeded on the Dutch throne in 1890 by his daughter Wilhelmina, who came of age in 1898. The young

Queen Wilhelmina, 1890–

queen was personally very popular, but her marriage in 1901 to Prince Henry of Mecklenburg-Schwerin was distasteful to many Dutch patriots, who feared German political influence in their country. The birth of an heiress to the throne, the Princess Juliana, in 1909 seemed to render more remote the danger of German intervention in the Netherlands, but the chief efforts of Dutch statesmen from 1890 to

1914 were directed toward perfecting the national defense. A law of 1898 reorganized the militia, on the Swiss basis, with provision for compulsory personal service. The army was further strengthened in 1912; and in 1913 an extensive program of naval construction was approved, and elaborate fortifications were begun at Amsterdam and at Flushing. The Dutch people appeared ready and determined in 1914 to offer serious resistance to any combatant in the War of the Nations who should attempt to violate their neutrality.

Throughout the period under review, the economic prosperity of the Netherlands continued to depend upon agriculture — especially dairying and gardening — and upon colonial Economic commerce and shipbuilding. In an increasing degree Prosperity it depended likewise upon trade in the industrial products of the surrounding countries of Germany, Great Britain, and Belgium.[1] Because of the country's lack of mineral resources, Holland did not become an important manufacturing state; and because of its economic dependence upon its neighbors, the Netherlands remained, almost alone of all Continental states, a free-trade country.

In conclusion a word should be said about the diminutive grand-duchy of Luxemburg, which, lying on the borders of France, Belgium, and Germany, was a member of the The Grand-Germanic Confederation from 1815 to 1866, was Duchy of recognized as neutral territory in 1867, and was Luxemburg united in a personal union with the Netherlands until the death of King William III in 1890. Then, when Queen Wilhelmina ascended the throne of Holland, the grand-duchy of Luxemburg passed to her male kinsman, Adolphus, duke of Nassau, who, with a local parliament, governed the grand-duchy until his death in 1905. Curiously enough, upon the death of the succeeding Grand Duke William in 1912, the sovereignty of Luxemburg devolved upon another female member of the Orange family, the Grand-Duchess Marie Adelaide. Despite the international assurance of its territorial integrity and neutrality, Luxemburg was occupied by German troops at the very opening of hostilities in the War of the Nations (August, 1914)

[1] The total commerce of the Netherlands in 1912 reached a value of more than two and a half billion dollars.

and used by them as a strategic point of departure for their invasion of France.

5. THE SCANDINAVIAN STATES: DENMARK, SWEDEN, AND NORWAY

The three peoples of northwestern Europe, — Danes, Swedes, and Norwegians, — very much alike in origin, language, religion, and conditions of life, continued in the nineteenth and twentieth centuries to pass through similar social and political evolutions. All three countries became limited monarchies; in all three, the bulk of the population lived by agriculture, commerce, and fishing, rather than by manufactures; all three nations retained almost unanimous allegiance to the Lutheran Church, though they gradually granted religious toleration; popular education was fostered under ecclesiastical supervision; all three peoples developed native literatures and a lively sense of nationalism; and in all three, social and political democracy made steady progress.

Developments Common to the Scandinavian Nations

Denmark, by ceding Norway to Sweden in 1814 and by surrendering the duchies of Schleswig-Holstein to Germany in 1864, was restricted in Scandinavia to the peninsula of Jutland and its adjacent islands, and became the smallest of the three Scandinavian countries.[1] Alone of these countries, however, Denmark possessed a colonial empire in Iceland, Greenland, and the West Indian islands of St. Croix, St. Thomas, and St. John. By a Constitution of 1849, revised in 1866, the king of Denmark shared his power with a parliament (*Rigsdag*), which consisted of two Houses — a conservative *Landsthing*, composed of members partly appointed by the crown and partly chosen by indirect election, and a democratic *Folkething*, elected by the majority of males over thirty years of age. Throughout the greater part of the long reign of Christian IX (1863–1906) a bitter political struggle was waged between the king and his ministers and the *Lands-*

The Kingdom of Denmark

Its Government

---

[1] The area of Denmark in 1911 was 15,582 sq. mi., including the Faroë Islands but excluding an area of 86,634 sq. mi. in the colonies of Iceland, Greenland, and the West Indies. Denmark's population in 1911 was 2,775,076. At the same time, Sweden had an area of 172,876 sq. mi. and a population of 5,522,403, while Norway had an area of 124,643 sq. mi. and a population of 2,391,782.

thing, on one side, and the *Folkething* and the majority of peasants, on the other side. The latter demanded the complete establishment of parliamentary government by making the ministry responsible to the *Folkething;* the former, bent upon the strengthening of Danish armaments, persistently refused to make concessions to a House which declined to increase appropriations for military purposes. From 1872 to 1901 the constitution was reduced almost to waste paper; during the period huge budgets were repeatedly put into effect by simple decree of the king and ministers. Meanwhile, however, the Danish peasantry were steadily improving their economic condition by means of intensive cultivation of their small holdings and by a remarkable development of dairy-farming and of coöperative enterprise, and thereby they were enabled to bring such political pressure to bear on the government that in 1901 the aged king yielded to the well-known wishes of his people and installed a cabinet representing the majority party in the *Folkething*.

Under the new Danish régime (1901–1914) the chief political interest shifted from the army, which was left on a basis of national militia, as in Switzerland, to electoral reform. The death of Christian IX in 1906 and the accession of his democratically minded son, Frederick VIII (1906–1912), gave an impetus to the democratic agitation, championed by Danish Liberals and by a small but rapidly growing group of Danish Socialists. After protracted debates and several exciting elections, after the death of Frederick VIII, and the accession of Christian X (1912–   ), constitutional amendments were adopted, 1914–1915, which reduced the age limit of electors from 30 to 25, extended the suffrage for the *Folkething* to all males and also to most females, and abolished the appointive seats in the *Landsthing*. Home rule was conferred upon Iceland in 1903.

Political Democracy in Denmark, 1901–1914

As results of the Napoleonic Wars at the beginning of the nineteenth century Sweden had lost the grand-duchy of Finland to Russia, had gained Norway from Denmark, and had secured the founder of a new royal dynasty in the person of King Charles XIV (1818–1844), erstwhile Marshal Bernadotte of France.[1] All of these results

Sweden in the Nineteenth Century

---

[1] See Vol. I, pp. 541, 575.

had marked significance for Swedish history throughout the nineteenth century.   The Bernadotte dynasty, despite its French origin, proved to be more loyally attached to royal prerogatives than the Danish monarchs.   The loss of Finland stimulated popular ill-feeling toward Russia and led to a more pronounced militarism in Sweden than in Denmark.   And the artificial union of Sweden and Norway produced a long-standing feud between these two Scandinavian peoples.

Sweden and Norway were not compatible in political union. Sweden was a country of large landed estates, with a powerful nobility and a poverty-stricken peasantry.   Norway was divided into small holdings with a farmer class accustomed to economic independence and to a feeling of contempt for titles of nobility.   As the nineteenth century advanced, manufacturing and iron-mining tended to develop numerous capitalistic and proletarian urban classes in Sweden, while Norway remained predominantly agricultural and commercial.[1]   In political institutions, too, there was wide divergence.   Just before the conclusion of the agreement for the union of Sweden and Norway, the Norwegians had prepared and adopted (1814) a very democratic constitution, which vested supreme authority in a parliament, or *Storthing*, elected indirectly by male tax-payers.   On the other hand, in Sweden the only check upon the royal authority was until 1863 the clumsy old device of the Four Estates of nobles, clergy, burghers, and peasants.   The Swedish Constitution of 1863, it is true, substituted for this four-chamber representation a bicameral parliament (*Riksdag*), but the wealthy classes were strongly intrenched in the Upper House and the king retained an absolute veto over all proposed legislation.

Differences between Sweden and Norway

Norwegian Government

Swedish Government

By the agreement of 1815, Norway was recognized as "a free, independent, and indivisible kingdom, united with Sweden under one king."   Accordingly, under the union Norway and

---

[1] It is an interesting fact that Norway, with an insignificant navy, possessed a merchant marine in 1913 totaling more than two and one-half million tons and ranking in size next to those of Great Britain, Germany, and the United States. Even the Swedish merchant marine was larger than the Russian or the Austro-Hungarian.

Sweden each preserved its own constitution and exercised autonomy in all domestic affairs: only foreign relations and military matters were managed in common under the supervision of the joint king. Nevertheless, the king always considered himself first a Swede and secondly a Norwegian; he appointed Swedes rather than Norwegians to the most responsible and most lucrative posts in the joint service and, backed by Swedish popular sentiment, he urged again and again a closer union between the two states. The union was already too close to suit the Norwegians: inspired by a noteworthy literary and nationalist revival, they began to clamor for the recognition of their national flag and for the establishment of a Norwegian consular service distinct from that of Sweden. It was this last demand which finally ruptured the union. Following the determined refusal of Oscar II (1872–1907) to sanction the appointment of Norwegian consuls for foreign cities, the Norwegian *Storthing* on 7 June, 1905, by unanimous vote decreed the dethronement of their Swedish king and the complete independence of Norway. The decree was indorsed by a *plébiscite* of the Norwegian people, and was grudgingly accepted by the Swedish government in the same year. Thereupon the *Storthing*, in spite of considerable republican sentiment in their country, invited the second son of the Danish monarch to become king of the newly independent Norway: this prince, whose election was ratified by a large popular majority, assumed the title of Haakon VII (1905–   ). In 1907 a treaty guaranteeing the integrity and neutrality of Norwegian territory was signed at Christiania by representatives of Norway, Great Britain, France, Germany, and Russia.

Personal Union of Sweden and Norway, 1815–1905

Independence of Norway, 1905

The dissolution of the union between Sweden and Norway undoubtedly furthered democratic tendencies in both countries. In Norway universal manhood suffrage had already been introduced (1898); now direct elections were substituted for indirect (1906); the franchise was extended to women, at first (1907) with property qualifications, and ultimately (1913) on the same broad basis as to men. In fact Norway was the first sovereign state in Europe to permit women to vote at general elections

Growth of Political Democracy in Norway, 1905–1914

and to sit in parliament. In 1913 the royal veto was entirely
abolished in Norway. In Sweden, also, political democracy
became a potent factor. Constitutional amendments, adopted
in 1909, established proportional representation for both Cham-

In Sweden, bers of the *Riksdag*, introduced universal manhood
1905–1914 suffrage in the elections to the Lower Chamber, and
lowered the property qualifications for members of the Upper
Chamber. A government bill of 1912, which proposed to confer the franchise on all persons over 24 years of age without
distinction of sex, temporarily failed of passage because of an
acute conflict between King Gustavus V (1907–   ) and his
Liberal ministry concerning the royal advocacy of a thorough
military reorganization involving large expenditures for universal training and for an elaborate system of fortifications.
The elections of 1914, influenced by the outbreak of the Great
War in Europe, were favorable to the king and militarism, although the opposing Socialists obtained 87 seats out of the total
230 in the Lower Chamber.

The remarkable growth of Socialism attested the existence
of a large body of urban workingmen in Sweden as certainly as

Emigration the imposition of a protective tariff in 1888 witnessed
to the growing influence of landlords and business men.
Sweden, more than any other Scandinavian country, was entering into competition with great industrial nations. In
Sweden, as in other European countries, the government did
a good deal to promote social legislation. In 1901 the *Riksdag*
accepted a bill for state insurance of workingmen against accidents and for the limitation of working hours of women and
children. Both Norway and Denmark secured similar legislation, but with them, as with Sweden, the social reforms only
increased the numbers and radical demands of the Socialists.
Some index to the need of economic betterment was afforded
by the large emigration of Scandinavians to the United States:
Sweden, the worst sufferer in this respect, lost in the second half
of the nineteenth century a million citizens, nearly all of whom
settled permanently in America.

ADDITIONAL READING

Germany. General. Brief historical narratives: G. M. Priest, *Germany since 1740* (1915), ch. xi, xii; J. H. Robinson and C. A. Beard, *The Development of Modern Europe*, Vol. II (1907), ch. xxiii; C. D. Hazen, *Europe since 1815* (1910), ch. xiv; Ferdinand Schevill, *The Making of Modern Germany* (1916), ch. vi, appendices d–f, h; E. F. Henderson, *A Short History of Germany*, new ed., Vol. II (1916), ch. xi–xiii; *Cambridge Modern History*, Vol. XII (1910), ch. vi; *Histoire générale*, Vol. XII, ch. x. Detailed descriptions of contemporary Germany: W. H. Dawson, *The Evolution of Modern Germany* (1908), perhaps the best; T. B. Veblen, *Imperial Germany and the Industrial Revolution* (1915); F. C. Howe, *Socialized Germany* (1915); J. E. Bárker, *Modern Germany, her Political and Economic Problems, her Foreign and Domestic Policy, her Ambitions, and the Causes of her Success*, 5th rev. ed. (1915); Henri Lichtenberger, *Germany and its Evolution in Modern Times*, Eng. trans. by A. M. Ludovici (1913); W. P. Paterson (editor), *German Culture: the Contribution of the Germans to Knowledge, Literature, Art, and Life* (1915), nine essays by British specialists; Antoine Guilland, *Modern Germany and her Historians*, Eng. trans. (1915); John Dewey, *German Philosophy and Politics* (1915). Among the mass of German histories of the empire reference may be made to Gottlob Egelhaaf, *Geschichte der neuesten Zeit*, 4th ed. (1913), a brief work, and Karl Lamprecht, *Deutsche Geschichte der jüngsten Vergangenheit und Gegenwart*, 2 vols. (1912–1913); and for a curious exposition of the " racial superiority " of the Germans consult the elaborate work of the ex-Englishman, H. S. Chamberlain, *The Foundations of the Nineteenth Century*, trans. from the German by John Lees, 2 vols. (1911). On the political institutions of Germany: F. A. Ogg, *The Governments of Europe* (1913), ch. ix–xiv, a satisfactory résumé; B. E. Howard, *The German Empire* (1906), an exhaustive analysis of the structure of the imperial government; Fritz-Konrad Krüger, *Government and Politics of the German Empire* (1915), a clear account, with critical bibliographies, in the " Government Handbooks " Series; A. L. Lowell, *Governments and Parties in Continental Europe*, 2 vols. (1897), ch. v–vii, an excellent study, and likewise its more recent abridgment and revision in *The Governments of France, Italy, and Germany* (1915); H. G. James, *Principles of Prussian Administration* (1913), a valuable monograph; W. H. Dawson, *Municipal Life and Government in Germany* (1914); Paul Laband, *Das Staatsrecht des deutschen Reiches*, 4th ed., 4 vols. (1901), the standard German work on the subject, and, by the same author, *Deutsches Reichsstaatsrecht*, 6th ed. (1912); Gaëtan (Vicomte) Combes de Lestrade, *Les monarchies de l'empire allemand, organisation constitutionelle et administrative* (1904), an admirable French study of German government — imperial and state; Felix Salomon, *Die deutschen Parteiprogramme*, 2d ed., 2 vols. (1912), containing the texts of party platforms or similar documents from 1845 to 1912; Oskar Stillich, *Die politischen Parteien in Deutschland:*

eine wissenschaftliche Darlegung ihrer Grundsätze und ihrer geschichtlichen Entwickelung, a monumental history of German political parties projected in five volumes, of which two have appeared — Vol. I, *Die Konservativen* (1908), and Vol. II, *Der Liberalismus* (1911) ; and, for an even more detailed history of German Liberalism, Oskar Klein-Hattingen, *Geschichte des deutschen Liberalismus,* Vol. I, to 1871 (1911). For an important phase of the work of the Center party, consult C. D. Plater, *Catholic Social Work in Germany* (1909).

Germany under Bismarck, 1871–1890. In addition to the biographies of Bismarck mentioned in the bibliography to Chapter XX, above, the famous chancellor left his own account, *Reflections and Reminiscences,* Eng. trans. ed. by A. J. Butler, 2 vols. (1899), which, however, should be used with caution and in the light of criticism supplied by such eminent scholars of Bismarck historiography as Gustav Schmoller, Max Lenz, Erich Marcks, and Hans Delbrück (1899) ; also of interest are *Bismarck's Speeches and Letters,* selections ed. by Herrmann Schoenfeld (1905) ; *Die politischen Reden des Fürsten Bismarck,* ed. by Horst Kohl, 12 vols. (1892–1894) ; Moritz Busch, *Bismarck — Some Secret Pages of his History,* Eng. trans., 2 vols. (1898), a diary kept by the writer during 25 years' official and private intercourse with the chancellor ; Hermann Hofmann, *Fürst Bismarck, 1890–1898, nach persönlichen Mitteilungen des Fürsten und eigenen Aufzeichnungen des Verfassers, nebst einer authentischen Ausgabe aller vom Fürsten Bismarck herruhrenden Artikel in den " Hamburger Nachrichten,"* 2 vols. (1913), very important for Bismarck's criticisms of the imperial government after his own retirement from the chancellorship. Standard German histories of the period : Erich Marcks, *Kaiser Wilhelm I,* 5th ed. (1905), admirable ; Wilhelm Oncken, *Das Zeitalter des Kaisers Wilhelm,* Vol. II (1892) ; Hans Blum, *Das deutsche Reich zur Zeit Bismarcks : politische Geschichte von 1871 bis 1890* (1893), a work mainly inspired by Bismarck ; P. Kloeppel, *Dreissig Jahre deutscher Verfassungsgeschichte, 1867–1897,* Vol. I, *1867–1877* (1900). On the *Kulturkampf :* J. W. Kissling, *Geschichte des Kulturkampfes im deutschen Reiche,* projected in 3 vols., of which Vol. I (1911) comes down to 1871, promises to present the Clerical side of the controversy ; Georges Goyau, *L'Allemagne religieuse, 1800–1870 : le catholicisme,* 4 vols. (1905–1909), and, by the same author, the leading authority, *Bismarck et l'église : le Culturkampf, 1870–1887,* 4 vols. (1911–1913) ; Ludwig Hahn, *Geschichte des Kulturkampfes in Preussen* (1881), important documents. The best account of the tariff changes in the empire is W. H. Dawson, *Protection in Germany, a History of German Fiscal Policy during the Nineteenth Century* (1904). On social legislation in Germany there are three authoritative volumes of W. H. Dawson, *Bismarck and State Socialism* (1891), *The German Workman : a Study in National Efficiency* (1906), and *Social Insurance in Germany, 1883–1911 : its History, Operation, Results, and a Comparison with the [British] National Insurance Act, 1911* (1912). On German Socialism : S. P. Orth, *Socialism and Democracy in Europe* (1913), ch. vii, viii, an excellent introduction ; Edgard

Milhaud, *La démocratie socialiste allemande* (1903); August Bebel, *Aus meinem Leben*, 3 vols. (1910–1914), an interesting autobiography of the great Socialist leader, trans. in an abridged English edition as *My Life* (1912); and see also the general bibliography on Socialism appended to Chapter XXI, above.

Germany under William II. In addition to the works of general description cited in the first paragraph of the present bibliography, the student would do well to consult E. D. Howard, *The Cause and Extent of the Recent Industrial Progress of Germany* (1907); Charles Tower, *Germany of To-day* (1913), a handy volume in the " Home University Library "; and Bernhard von Bülow, *Imperial Germany*, Eng. trans. by Marie A. Lewenz (1914), an illuminating apology for newer tendencies in foreign and domestic politics, written by a distinguished chancellor under William II. Glimpses of the character and policies of Wiliam II: Herbert Perris, *Germany and the German Emperor* (1912), popular and impressionistic; Hermann Oncken, *Germany under William II, 1888–1913*, an interesting résumé on the occasion of 25th anniversary of the emperor's accession, in the " Quarterly Review," Vol. CCXIX (October, 1913); *The Kaiser's Speeches, Forming a Character Portrait of Emperor William II*, Eng. trans. ed. by Wolf von Schierbrand (1903); Christian Gauss, *The German Emperor as Shown in his Public Utterances* (1915); A. H. Fried, *The German Emperor and the Peace of the World* (1912), a Nobel Prize Essay, setting forth the German emperor as the well-convinced friend of peace; K. F. L. von Behr-Pinnow, Eduard Dietrich, and Dr. Kayserling, *Soziale Kultur und Volkswohlfahrt während der ersten 25 Regierungsjahre Kaiser Wilhelms II* (1913), an elaborate appreciation of social development in Germany under William II; F. W. Wile, *Men around the Kaiser: the Makers of Modern Germany* (1913), thirty-one biographical sketches by the Berlin correspondent of the London *Daily Mail* and the New York *Times*. On German colonies and world politics: Archibald Hurd and Henry Castle, *German Sea-Power, its Rise, Progress, and Economic Basis* (1913); Alfred Zimmermann, *Geschichte der deutschen Kolonialpolitik* (1914); Kurt Hassert, *Deutschlands Kolonien: Erwebungs- und Entwickelungsgeschichte, landes und wirtschaftliche Bedeutung unserer Schutzgebiete*, 2d ed. rev. (1910); Kurt Herrfurth, *Fürst Bismarck und die Kolonialpolitik* (1909) being Vol. VIII of the *Geschichte des Fürsten Bismarck in Einzeldarstellungen;* Theodor Schiemann (editor), *Deutschland und die grosse Politik*, a German annual since 1901, mainly a reissue in book form of the weekly reviews appearing in the celebrated Conservative *Kreuzzeitung;* R. G. Usher, *Pan-Germanism* (1913), an exposition of the views of some of the extreme German advocates of world-empire; Herman Frobenius, *The German Empire's Hour of Destiny*, Eng. trans. (1914), an apology for Germany's part in the War of 1914. See also the titles listed in the bibliography to Chapter XXX, below.

Austria-Hungary, 1866–1914. *Cambridge Modern History*, Vol. XII (1910), ch. vii, an excellent general narrative by Louis Eisenmann; Geoffrey Drage, *Austria-Hungary* (1909), valuable descriptions with an appendix containing important laws and treaties and statistical tables; H. W. Steed, *The Hapsburg Monarchy*, 2d ed. (1914), an interesting study by an Englishman who served ten years in Vienna as correspondent of the London *Times;* Bertrand Auerbach, *Les races et les nationalités en Autriche-Hongrie* (1898), a painstaking investigation of racial problems in the Dual Monarchy; Sidney Whitman, *The Realm of the Hapsburgs* (1893), readable but somewhat out-of-date; F. A. Ogg, *The Governments of Europe* (1913), ch. xxiv–xxvii, indispensable for political institutions and parties; A. L. Lowell, *Governments and Parties of Continental Europe*, Vol. II (1897), ch. viii–x; Louis Eisenmann, *Le compromis austro-hongrois de 1867, étude sur le dualisme* (1904), an important monograph; Josef Ulbrich, *Das oesterreichische Staatsrecht*, 3d ed. (1904), the standard work on Austrian public law; Alexandre de Bertha, *La constitution hongroise* (1898), a good outline of constitutional development in Hungary from 1848 to 1897; J. A. von Helfert, *Geschichte Oesterreichs vom Ausgange des Wiener October-Ausstandes 1848*, 4 vols. in 5 (1869–1886), the standard Austrian history; R. W. Seton-Watson (pseud. Scotus-Viator), *Corruption and Reform in Hungary: a Study of Electoral Practice* (1911), provided with numerous documents, and, by the same author, *Racial Problems in Hungary* (1908) and *The Southern Slav Question and the Habsburg Monarchy* (1911); C. M. Knatchbull-Hugessen, *The Political Evolution of the Hungarian Nation*, Vol. II (1908), ch. xvii–xx, an historical summary since 1860; Alexandre de Bertha, *La Hongrie moderne, 1849–1901* (1901), another sympathetic treatment of Magyar history; Rudolf Sieghart, *Zolltrennung und Zolleinheit: die Geschichte der oesterreichisch-ungarischen Zwischenzoll-Linie* (1915), an exhaustive study of the vexed questions of the economic relations between Austria and Hungary; R. P. Mahaffy, *Francis Joseph I, his Life and Times an Essay in Politics*, new ed. (1915); Sir Horace Rumbold, *Francis Joseph and his Times* (1909); F. F. von Beust, *Aus drei Viertel-Jahrhunderten: Erinnerungen und Aufzeichnungen*, trans. into English as *Memoirs*, 2 vols. (1887); Florence A. Forster, *Francis Deák, Hungarian Statesman, a Memoir* (1880); Alexandre de Bertha, *Magyars et Roumains devant l'histoire* (1899), an Hungarian statement of the issues in the racial rivalries of Magyars and Rumans; André Chéradame, *L'Europe et la question d'Autriche au seuil du XXᵉ siècle* (1901); Ferdinand Schmid, *Bosnien und die Herzegovina unter der Verwaltung Oesterreich-Ungarns* (1914); Theodor von Sosnosky, *Die Balkanpolitik Oesterreich-Ungarns seit 1866*, 2 vols. (1913–1914).

Switzerland. W. D. McCrackan, *Rise of the Swiss Republic*, 2d ed. (1901), a brief historical sketch; Karl Dändliker, *A Short History of Switzerland*, Eng. trans. (1899), a hasty summary; F. G. Baker, *The Model Republic, a History of the Rise and Progress of the Swiss People* (1895), an outline; *Histoire générale*, Vol. XII, ch. v, a good account of the period from 1848 to 1900; H. D. Lloyd, *A Sovereign People: a Study of Swiss Democracy*, ed. by J. A. Hobson (1907); J. M. Vincent, *Government in Switzerland* (1900); F. A. Ogg, *The Governments of Europe* (1913), ch. xxii, xxiii; A. L. Lowell, *Governments and Parties in Continental Europe*, Vol. II (1897), ch. xi–xiii; W. H. Dawson, *Social Switzerland, Studies of Present-Day Social Movements and Legislation in the Swiss Republic* (1897); Paul Seippel (editor), *La Suisse au dix-neuvième siècle*, 3 vols. (1899–1901), a coöperative work by a group of Swiss writers, full and authoritative; Wilhelm Oechsli, *Geschichte der Schweiz im neunzehnten Jahrhundert*, a monumental undertaking of which two volumes have appeared (1903–1913), covering the years 1798–1830; I. B. Richman, *Appenzell, Pure Democracy and Pastoral Life in Inner Rhoden* (1895).

Holland. *Cambridge Modern History*, Vol. XI (1909), ch. xxiii, and Vol. XII (1910), ch. ix; P. J. Blok, *History of the People of the Netherlands*, Vol. V, *Eighteenth and Nineteenth Centuries*, Eng. trans. by Ruth Putnam (1912), the work of the foremost Dutch historian; Clive Day, *The Policy and Administration of the Dutch in Java* (1904), a valuable monograph; George Renwick, *Luxembourg: the Grand Duchy and its People* (1913).

The Scandinavian Countries. R. N. Bain, *Scandinavia, a Political History of Denmark, Norway, and Sweden, from 1513 to 1900* (1905), ch. xvi, xvii; *Cambridge Modern History*, Vol. XI (1909), ch. xxiv, and Vol. XII (1910), ch. xi; Povl Drachmann, *The Industrial Development and Commercial Policies of the Three Scandinavian Countries* (1915); Knut Gjerset, *History of the Norwegian People*, Vol. II (1915); J. Carlsen, H. Olrik, and C. N. Starcke, *Le Danemark, état actuel de sa civilisation et de son organisation sociale* (1900); Gustav Sundbärg (editor), *Sweden, its People and Industries* (1904), historical and statistical, published by order of the Swedish government; Fridtjof Nansen, *Norway and the Union with Sweden* (1905), presents the Norwegian side of the controversy; Karl Nordlund, *The Swedish-Norwegian Union Crisis, a History with Documents* (1905), a Swedish rejoinder to Nansen; H. A. L. Fisher, *The Republican Tradition in Europe* (1911), ch. xiii, an illuminating essay on republicanism in Norway.

CHAPTER XXV

THE RUSSIAN EMPIRE, 1855–1914

THE REIGN OF ALEXANDER II (1855–1881): REFORMS, REACTION, AND THE RISE OF TERRORISM

IN 1855 the scepter of "all the Russias" passed naturally from the Tsar and Autocrat Nicholas I to his son, the Tsar and Autocrat Alexander II, and the event gave promise of a new era in Russian history. Nicholas I (1825–1855), unlike contemporary European sovereigns, had never been obliged to make terms with revolutionaries: fully convinced of the divine mission of Russia in a naughty world and of his own sacred right to rule the elect, he had supported the Holy Orthodox Church and had clung tenaciously to the principles and practices of autocracy; and, blunt soldier as he was, he not only had crushed mercilessly the Decembrist Revolt of 1825 and the Polish Insurrection of 1831 but also had searched out and severely punished any and every Russian abettor of that Liberalism, which, in his opinion, was disgracing western Europe. Only once in his long reign of thirty years had Nicholas I appeared to be on the side of revolution — and that was in the case of the Greek War of Independence, — but even in this case it was not democracy which the autocrat was championing — it was the might and prestige of Russia and of Russia's holy religion.[1]

Yet Nicholas I had not been completely successful. The most repressive legislation that he could devise was not sufficient to keep the cultured educated classes in Russia from gaining some knowledge of, and sympathy with, the democratic developments in western Europe, and as soon as the strong hand of the uncompromising autocrat was withdrawn these classes were sure to clamor loudly for radical

Autocratic Heritage from Nicholas I, 1825–1855

The Demand for Reform

---

[1] For further details of the reign of Nicholas I, see above, pp. 40 f., 49 f., 56 f.

changes in the aims and methods of their rulers. Then, too, the military machine upon the perfection of which Nicholas had set his heart, though of service to the cause of divine-right monarchy in suppressing the Polish Insurrection of 1831 and in affording decisive aid to the Austrian Habsburgs in their attempt to destroy the Hungarian Republic (1849), was not proof against the combined armies and fleets of Great Britain, France, Turkey, and Sardinia, in the Crimean War (1854–1856).[1] In fact, it was in the midst of the diplomatic humiliations and military disasters of the Crimean War that Nicholas I died.

Alexander II (1855–1881) at the time of his accession was thirty-six years of age, untried and inexperienced in affairs of state. He had been brought up in his father's dis- *Alexander* trust of democracy, but, unlike Nicholas, he was *II, 1855–* kindly and tender-hearted, and showed no love of *1881* militarism. Both his natural disposition and his lack of experience made it impossible for him to maintain his father's policies in undiminished vigor. And the importunities of Russian Liberals so changed the stage-setting of Russian history that Alexander II essayed to play the rôle of a great reforming tsar.

Bringing the distasteful Crimean War to a close in 1856, the new tsar devoted the first ten years of his reign to the institution of internal reforms which deservedly estab- *Reforms of* lished an enduring reputation for his able performance *Alexander* of the difficult rôle that had been thrust upon him. *II, 1855–* The major reforms of Alexander II were: (1) the *1865* emancipation of the serfs; (2) the erection of elective provincial assemblies — the *zemstvos* — for participation in local administration; and (3) the radical remodeling of the legal and judicial systems. Each one of these reforms merits some explanation.

Russia was largely an agricultural country, and when Alexander II came to the throne the bulk of his subjects were serfs like the people of western Europe in the middle ages. It is *Serfdom in* true that northern Russia was inhabited by landown- *Russia* ing peasants, that the extreme South was studded with economically independent colonies of Cossacks, and that serfdom had already been abolished in the Baltic provinces and in Poland; but nine-tenths of the whole arable land of the empire was still

---

[1] On the Crimean War, see above, pp. 162 f., and below, pp. 501 f.

held in large estates, part belonging to the tsar and the royal
princes, the rest to about 100,000 noble families. Each such
estate was divided into two parts, the produce of the one going
directly to the noble owner, that of the other being for the sup-

The Mir   port of a village (*mir*) of peasants. Under the Russian
system of serfdom, the lot of the peasants was deplorable. They were attached to the soil, that is, without their
lord's consent they could not leave the estate on which they
were born, and a transfer of an estate from one nobleman to another automatically transferred the peasants' allegiance. To
their lord the peasants paid dues, for him they performed compulsory manual labor, to him they rendered obedience as to a
personal master. Sometimes the noblemen detached their
peasants from the land and sent them to work in the cities,
requiring them to pay a fixed due from their earnings and reserving the right to call them home at will. Sometimes the noblemen employed the peasants in household service virtually as
slaves: of these there were about two millions in 1855. Doubtless in many parts of Russia there were lenient and kind-hearted
noblemen and considerate taskmasters, but too often the nobles
and their overseers were cruel and capricious: they could make
the most exorbitant demands upon their peasants' strength
and funds and visit disobedience with corporal punishment;
they could, and often did, interfere outrageously in the strictly
domestic and family concerns of their peasants.

To reform the Russian land system was an herculean task, and
it is greatly to the credit of Alexander II that any improvement
was effected. Setting an example by freeing first the

Emancipa-
tion of the
Serfs: the
Tsar's De-
cree of 1861

serfs on the lands belonging to members of the imperial
family, and then with dogged pertinacity and cautious
compromise overcoming the opposition of interested
and selfish landlords, the tsar at length revolutionized
the whole agrarian system by decree (*ukase*) of 3 March, 1861,
the sixth anniversary of his accession to the throne. The decree
abolished all legal rights of noblemen over peasants: the serfs
who were living detached from the soil, whether domestic servants or laborers in towns, obtained their personal freedom but
no right to property; the serfs who were working on the large
estates secured not only their liberty but an interest in a portion

of the land which was bought from the nobles with money advanced by the government and which was now turned over to the village communities (*mirs*) to be parceled out for individual use among the resident peasants. Many years elapsed before the decree was fully executed, but the benefits of even partial emancipation of the serfs gradually appeared in an enlarged area of cultivation, increased value of land, greater yield of taxes, growth of export trade, and improved general condition of the peasantry.

There were also less happy results of the abolition of serfdom in Russia. The peasants formerly attached to the soil now found themselves in occupation of farms that in many cases were altogether too small to support themselves and their families. Such peasants, moreover, were obliged for a long term of years to repay to the state installments of the money advanced as compensation to the nobles; and, though released from the jurisdiction of noblemen's courts, they were brought under subjection to the rules and regulations of the *mir* and to the tax-gatherers and police officials of the central government. And the treatment of the emancipated peasants by the state officials was often harsh and corrupt. It has been remarked wisely, though possibly a little strongly, that the decree of Alexander II freed the peasants from the nobles only to make them "serfs of the state." One result of this unfortunate situation was a considerable emigration of ex-serfs from the country to the city. The growth of the urban population of Russia in the second half of the nineteenth century was certainly due to the abolition of serfdom as well as to the introduction of machinery and factories; and ex-serfs became the chief victims of overwork in the dismal factories and of unhealthful life in the congested towns.

The Plight of the Emancipated Serfs

The second great reform of Alexander II was the creation of provincial assemblies. According to a decree of 1864, each district and each province of the thirty-four "governments," into which eighteenth-century Russia was divided, was to have an assembly, or *zemstvo*, composed of large landed proprietors and of delegates indirectly elected by the townsfolk and peasants; and each *zemstvo* was to exercise the right of imposing local taxes

Establishment of the Zemstvos for Local Self-Government: the Tsar's Decree of 1864

and to legislate on such local matters as roads, bridges, public buildings, churches and schools, relief of the poor, prisons, and public health.[1] The execution of local ordinances was intrusted to standing committees chosen by the *zemstvos*.

Prior to the accession of Alexander II, justice had been dispensed by state officials secretly and arbitrarily. In 1862 the tsar decreed that henceforth the judicial power in civil and criminal cases should be independent of the regular administration and reserved to a hierarchy of courts on the Western model, — justices of the peace, elected by municipal councils or by the *zemstvos;* district and circuit courts; and a senate, acting as a court of final appeal. As in the countries of western Europe, laws were codified, prosecuting attorneys were appointed, trial by jury instituted for criminal cases, the judges given secure tenure, and court proceedings made public. In one important respect, however, — trials of political offenders, — the old secret and arbitrary administrative procedure was retained and strengthened.

Judicial Reforms: the Tsar's Decree of 1862

Such were the major reforms of Alexander II : emancipation of the serfs in 1861, reorganization of the courts in 1862, and creation of the *zemstvos* in 1864. In addition to these epochal changes, the tsar encouraged the organization of elementary and technical schools, accorded a considerable degree of liberty to the press, and proposed several schemes for railway construction and for developing more rapidly the vast natural resources of the country.

Other Reforms of Alexander II

By 1865, however, — ten years after his accession, — the reforming spirit of Alexander II was spent. The tsar had never been at heart a democrat or even a liberal; what reforms he had instituted had been in large part a response to popular protest against a reactionary government which had suffered foreign reverses in 1854–1856, but by 1865 the Crimean War was a subject of history. Without doubt the decisive factor in altering the tsar's policy was the Polish Insurrection of 1863. In that

Abandonment of Liberalism by Alexander II

[1] In 1870 Alexander II established municipal councils (*dumas*) for the exercise of such functions in the cities of European Russia as the *zemstvos* discharged in the provinces. The *dumas* were to be elected by the citizens in proportion to their wealth on a three-class basis much the same as prevailed in Prussia.

year the secret agitation and intrigue which Polish patriots for some time had been engineering from Warsaw burst forth into open rebellion against the Russian authorities. It was not nearly as formidable as the revolt of 1831 : it was merely a struggle of ill-armed partisans, never numerous, against regular troops, and was marked by no real battle. The Polish leaders aroused the bitterest hatred of Russian nationalists, Liberals as well as Reactionaries, by their expressed intention of reuniting Lithuania to Poland. And Bismarck, for the sake of his domestic and foreign policies, offered Prussian aid, if needed, to the Russian government. The tsar had no need of Prussian assistance : his own loyal troops readily put an end to the disorders in Poland, and the suppression of the rising was followed by a return to the harsh methods of the Tsar Nicholas I. The Polish nobles, gentry, and ecclesiastics, — the educated classes generally, — were crushed.

The Polish Insurrection of 1863

Statesmen of the old régime in Russia, by whom Alexander II was surrounded, were not slow in pointing out to the humane tsar that the troubles in Poland had been caused by his leniency, and that further introduction of Western novelties into holy Russia would lead just as inevitably to dreadful commotions and bloodshed throughout the empire. Alexander turned back on the political path that he had been following. Henceforth reaction was again in full swing in Russia. The provincial *zemstvos* and municipal *dumas* were forbidden to express political views and their acts were made subject to veto by the imperial governors. Rigorous press censorship was restored. The government assumed the right to distinguish by administrative decree between political offenders and ordinary criminals : the former could be arbitrarily seized by the police and kept indefinitely in prison on mere suspicion or bundled off to some secret place in Siberia without any judicial formalities. The infamous secret police or detective force — the "third section of the imperial chancery," — instituted by Nicholas I in 1826 for the searching out and summary punishment of political offenders, was now reinvigorated and, formally transferred to the imperial department of the interior in 1880, it counted its victims by thousands. Even the educational system

Reactionary Policies of Alexander II, 1865–1881

The Secret Police or " Third Section "

felt the force of reaction : the newer developments in natural and experimental science were carefully expurgated from the curricula as being inimical to the Orthodox religion and conducive to social and political unrest, and in their place was substituted the safer and more sedative study of the ancient languages.   The only reform of Alexander's later years — and that hardly a liberal reform — was the reorganization of the army and the introduction, following the example of Germany, of the principle of compulsory universal military service (1874).

In the younger ranks of the educated classes the gradual conversion of Alexander II to unqualified support of traditional Russian absolutism produced keen dissatisfaction, which soon found vent in three varieties of revolutionary agitation, all closely related.   First of all were the "Nihilists," a group of intellectual radicals, recruited from the universities and professional classes, who admired and lauded science and reason and higher education and the material progress of the countries of western Europe, and who in corresponding degree despised and denounced the Orthodox Faith, the political autocracy, the social institutions, and the general backwardness of Russia.[1] Like the French philosophers of the eighteenth century they would scoff at existing irrational institutions and would educate the people to a proper appreciation of "enlightenment" and "progress"; influenced by nineteenth-century Darwinism, they believed in the infallible evolution of humanity from autocracy to democracy, from barbarism to culture.   The Nihilists at first limited their agitation to academic discussion and clandestine publication, but as the university and press censorship tightened they had recourse to secret associations which undertook to spread their doctrines by word of mouth among the masses and in the army.

Secondly came the influence of Socialism, not the mild mannered Socialism of the workingmen's political parties of western

Rise of Revolutionary Parties under Alexander II

1. The Nihilists

---

[1] The name "Nihilists" was first applied to these Russian devotees of natural science and positivist philosophy, who would leave nothing of the old régime untouched, by the novelist Ivan Turgeniev (1818–1883) in his *Father and Sons* (1862). The name became famous all over Europe and America and was subsequently applied most loosely to every sort of revolutionary or terrorist.

Europe, but the anarchistic Socialism of the followers of the
Russian Mikhail Bakunin.[1] These Russian Socialists of the
'sixties and 'seventies appealed not only to the arti-   2. The
sans of the towns but also to the peasants, whom they   Anarchistic
urged to seize all the land of the noblemen; they ad-   Socialists
vocated the destruction of the state, the church, and the traditional family; and, being unable to conduct their propaganda by
means of parliamentary or other peaceful agencies, they resorted
to the employment of violence.

The more reactionary Alexander II became, and the more repressive his governmental measures against Socialists and Nihilists, the more bitter and violent grew the revolution-   3. The
aries.   Gradually there developed among a small num-   Terrorists
ber of the most extreme radicals the conviction that the tsar and
the governing classes of Russia — officials, nobles, and clergy —
must be terrorized into reforms, that terrorism would be the only
sure way of opening the eyes of the Russian people to the grave
abuses in their social and political life.   The Terrorists thus
constituted the third group of revolutionaries.   Some of them
were Nihilists, some were Socialists or Anarchists, some were
individuals without principles or philosophies, who bore personal
grudges against a judge or a tax-collector.   The center of the
revolutionary Terrorism was a secret committee, organized at
Petrograd in 1878, which ordered and directed attempts against
the authorities.   It operated secret printing shops, laboratories
in which highly explosive bombs were manufactured, and a
system of espionage.   Its members bound themselves to execute
its decrees; and within three years the Terrorists assassinated
six high officials, including the chief of police, and nine governmental spies.   For its part, the government relentlessly pursued
the Terrorists: 31 were put to death, 8 died in prison, and 3
committed suicide.   But the Terrorists did not hesitate.   They
tried on several occasions to take the life of the tsar himself.

The tsar was alarmed.   In vain he intrusted almost   Assassina-
dictatorial powers to one of his faithful ministers.   At   tion of Alex-
length on 13 March, 1881 he signed a decree authoriz-   ander II,
ing the creation of special commissions, composed of   1881
high officials and distinguished private personages, who should

[1] See above, pp. 269 f.

prepare reforms in various branches of the administration. But the seeming reversion of the tsar to his earlier Liberal policies came too late. On the very day that he signed the hopeful decree Alexander II was killed by the explosion of bombs hurled by Terrorists.

THE MAINTENANCE OF AUTOCRACY AND THE PROSECUTION OF "RUSSIFICATION" UNDER ALEXANDER III AND NICHOLAS II, 1881–1905

The tragic death of Alexander II — the "reforming" tsar — brought to the Russian throne his son, Alexander III (1881–

Alexander III, 1881–1894

1894), whose blunt soldierly qualities resembled those of his grandfather, Nicholas I. Alexander III was not well educated, and entertained no sympathy with the culture of western Europe. In his narrow but pertinacious way he sought throughout his reign to correct what he considered the too liberal tendencies of his father. In his opinion, Russia was to be saved from revolution and anarchy, not by parliamentary institutions, such as obtained in Great Britain and France, but by great principles indigenous to Russia and the natural pride of every Russian patriot: autocracy, Slavic nationalism, and Eastern Orthodoxy. Strenuously the new tsar maintained autocracy. Vigorously he pushed the process of "Russification" — exalting the influence of the Slavic race and of the Orthodox religion. Devoted to these policies, he was hardly aware of yet another and an unofficial force that was transforming his country

General Characteristics of his Reign

during his reign, — the introduction into Russia, on a large scale, of the Industrial Revolution,— the erection of factories, the building of railways, the saving of capital, the shift of population from country to town, and the growth of a middle class and of a working class that jointly would do in time for Russia what earlier Nihilists and Socialists and Terrorists had aspired most vainly to do — temper Russian autocracy with Western Liberalism. These three things, then, — maintenance of autocracy, "Russification," and the Industrial Revolution in Russia, — are the great landmarks of the reign of Alexander III, and to each one of the three in turn we must now give attention.

The first acts of Alexander III were to revoke his father's last liberal decree, to inflict summary vengeance upon the assassins, and to proclaim to the world that "the Voice of God orders Us to stand firm at the helm of government . . . with faith in the strength and truth of the autocratic power, which We are called to consolidate and preserve, for the good of the people, from every kind of encroachment." In carrying out his program of thoroughgoing autocracy the new tsar was ably assisted by two men of like mind with himself — Plehve and Pobêdonostsev.

Devotion of Alexander III to the Principle of Autocracy

Konstantine Pobêdonostsev (1827–1907) [1] had studied law at Petrograd, had risen slowly from one rung to another on the ladder of public service, had been professor of civil law in the university of Moscow, had tutored the sons of Alexander II in the theory of jurisprudence and administration, and had been rewarded in 1880 by appointment to the responsible and lucrative post of secular chairman of the governing body of the Russian Orthodox Church ("Procurator of the Holy Synod"). This man, who had tremendous influence on Alexander III, developed a veritable philosophy of reaction. In speech and publication he was always insisting that the newer political and social institutions of western Europe were radically bad in themselves and totally inapplicable to Russia. To him parliaments were nothing but breeding-places of the most selfish and sordid ambitions; newspapers existed primarily to disseminate falsehood; secular education was both dangerous and immoral; limited monarchy was a "vain fancy," and trial by jury was simply a means of practicing the "arts of casuistry." "If all representatives of the people were saints," wrote the reactionary philosopher, "a parliamentary régime would be the very best kind of all; but as popular representatives are usually of a more than doubtful morality, a parliamentary régime is the worst." To the Western novelties which he condemned, Pobêdonostsev found a counterpoise in the respect of the masses for institutions developed slowly and automatically during the past centuries of national life. For Russia, therefore, he believed that the chief function of government was to preserve

Pobêdonostsev, the Philosopher of Reaction

---

[1] Pobêdonostsev's opinions are clearly set forth in his *Reflections of a Russian Statesman*, published in English translation by R. C. Long, in 1898.

the autocracy and to foster among the people traditional veneration for the offices of the national Orthodox Church.

To the support which was accorded Alexander III by the
philosophy of Pobêdonostsev, and by his rigid administration of
ecclesiastical affairs, was added the concrete and direct
political service of Plehve (1846–1904).[1] Appointed
director of the state police in 1881, Plehve not only
ferreted out and punished the assassins of Alexander
II, but likewise pursued all Nihilists and Socialists and Terrorists
with a vigor so great and a success so terrible that the reign of
Alexander III was marked by a seeming lull in revolutionary
propaganda.

*Plehve, the
Practical
Agent of
Reaction*

With the aid of such men as Plehve and Pobêdonostsev,
Alexander III sought to strengthen and centralize the whole
imperial administration and to bring it more completely
under his personal control. He placed the formerly
autonomous government of the peasant communes
(*mirs*) under the supervision of wealthy landed proprietors appointed by the imperial ministry. He
abridged the powers conferred by his father upon the provincial
zemstvos and municipal *dumas;* he revised the constitution of all
these local assemblies by increasing the representation of the
nobles and officials and decreasing that of the peasants and by
excluding the professional classes altogether; and over the acts
of the emasculated assemblies he strengthened the veto power
of the imperial governors. He frowned upon secular education
and confirmed the control of the state church over elementary
instruction. He strove to remove all vestiges of special liberties
or privileges that had formerly been enjoyed by non-Russian
peoples in the empire. At the same time he was ever enlarging
Russian territory in central Asia ; and in foreign policy the apparent decline of Russian influence in southeastern Europe, ascrib-
able, in Alexander's opinion, to Germany's increasing support of
Austro-Hungarian pretensions, caused him to waver in the
hearty friendship which his father had entertained for Bismarck
and the German Empire, and gradually brought this most auto-

*Mainte-
nance of
Autocracy
by Alex-
ander III*

[1] Viatscheslaf von Plehve was of Lithuanian stock, was educated at Warsaw and
at Petrograd, and as a lawyer began his public career in the department of justice
under Alexander II.

cratic of all the Russian Autocrats into particularly friendly relations, curiously enough, with the extremely democratic government of Republican France.

In Russia the autocracy of Alexander III was maintained at a fearful sacrifice of national well-being. No matter how upright and benevolent the autocrat personally might be, he himself could not know first-hand all the needs of his hundred million subjects, nor could he alone execute his manifold decrees throughout the length and breadth of his enormous domain. In all these matters he had to trust to the honor and honesty of his chief ministers and of a vast hierarchy of lesser officials, military, financial, judicial, and administrative. Even a tsar of genius could not be proof against the incompetence or the corruption of a tax-collector, a judge, a police agent, or a distant governor. And Alexander III was not a genius. Then, too, in a country where wealthy nobles were accustomed to exercise political control over large numbers of poor and ignorant peasants, where a powerful military clique were in the habit of dominating the rank and file of a numerous army, where the ordinary officials both in church and in state were traditionally arrogant and thoroughly imbued with a notion of their irresponsibility save to a far-above and far-away master whom they seldom or never beheld, in such a country negligence in administration and dishonesty in financial transactions were bound to flourish. Alexander III's policy of repression only exaggerated the evils of Russian autocracy. The officials became more and more sycophantic; the wider their fields of activity, the narrower grew their vision. As in France before the Great Revolution, incompetence promoted corruption, and corruption fostered incompetence. And the bulk of the Russian people, though dumb under oppression, suffered miserably.

Defects of the Autocratic Régime in Russia

The question has often been raised why autocracy survived in Russia several generations after it had disappeared in western Europe and whether it was not due to peculiar racial traits of the Russian people. Of course, in last analysis, autocracy rested in Russia, as in any other country, on the expressed or tacit consent of the bulk of the population, for had a majority of the people been violently opposed to the existing régime they could certainly have

Reasons for the Maintenance of Autocracy in Russia

dispatched it as did the French in their Great Revolution of 1789. But without reference to any peculiarities of race, which at best are pretty hazy and vague, it may still be possible to account for the maintenance of autocracy as the chief political institution of nineteenth-century Russia by pointing out the following facts. In the first place, the governing classes were

1. Loyalty of the Governing Classes

numerous, powerful, and naturally loyal to the autocrat on whose bounty they fed : the grand-dukes and other members of the imperial Romanov family; the ministers of state; the governors; the army officers; the local administrators; the judges; the thousands of clerks; and the officials of police. Secondly, the Orthodox Church, to

2. Support of the Orthodox Church

which most Russians adhered, had become for political purposes a regular branch of the imperial government : since the days of Peter the Great, its clergy had been appointed and controlled by an imperial board — the Holy Synod — which taught the religiously inclined peasants to exalt the Church as the custodian of national welfare and to

3. Lack of Popular Education

exalt the autocracy as the preserver and defender of the Church. Thirdly, popular education was especially backward in Russia; what there was of elementary instruction was a monopoly of the Church, loyally attached to autocracy; the extent of the empire, the sparsity of inhabitants in many of its districts, and the relative poverty of its national finances, were natural obstacles to any rapid extension of a public-school system; at times the authorities actually discouraged education; and the result was that at the death of Alexander III (1894) the number of illiterates varied from 50 to 90 per cent of the total population in the rural communities, and from 40 to 65 per cent in the urban, — a higher average of illiteracy in Russia than in any other country of Europe. Fourthly, mention should again be made of the rigorous repressive measures employed by the governing classes, particularly under Alexander III, — the

4. Repressive Measures of the Government

arbitrary arrests and imprisonments, the banishments to Siberia, and the executions, — which struck terror into the hearts of many middle-class people who otherwise might have directed a strong Liberal movement against the autocracy. Fifthly, and in noteworthy contrast to this terroristic policy of the government, was the idea sedulously implanted in the minds of the ignorant peasantry by officials of church and state that the Russian nation was a big happy family, that the tsar was the "little father" of his subjects, governing well in consequence of his affection for them and towering above all the rest in consequence of a consciousness of his duty as an autocratic *paterfamilias*.

5. Filial Devotion of the Peasantry to the Tsar, the "Little Father"

Sixthly, Russia remained throughout the nineteenth century largely an agricultural country, and the bulk of the population were serfs but recently and partially emancipated from economic dependence upon great noblemen: such a population was hardly prepared for radical political changes; conservative by instinct and environment, like all agricultural communities,

6. Russia Predominantly Agricultural and therefore Conservative

it clung tenaciously to the principle of autocracy which had done inestimable service to Russia by freeing the country from Mongol, Turkish, Swedish, and Polish interference and by raising up such heroic figures

7. Tradition of Autocracy in Russia

as Peter the Great, Catherine the Great, and Alexander I. No wonder that the glories of Russian history redounded to the glory of Russian autocracy!

But even more important than any one of the explanations already offered for the maintenance of autocracy in Russia was the partially patriotic and partially intellectual motive which actuated such intelligent Russians as Pobêdonostsev and Plehve to give cordial and most active support to the cause of autocracy. This was the idea in their minds and in the minds of many thoughtful Russians that democracy could never be a real success in such an extended empire as Russia and among such diverse peoples as were contained within its borders,

8. Intimate Association of Russian Autocracy with Patriotic "Pan-Slavism" and "Russification"

and that the autocracy was not only a divinely inspired instrument but also a practical necessity for holding the Russian Empire together and for furthering its religious and cultural mission in the world. This was the ideal of Pan-Slavism and the justification of the process, deliberately developed by Alexander III, of "Russification." Foremost Pan-Slavists in Russia were devotees of autocracy; and, conversely, devotees of autocracy were almost to a man ardent patriots of Pan-Slavic stamp.

In order to understand Russian Pan-Slavism and to follow
The Russian intelligently the steps taken by Alexander III and
Empire at Nicholas II to "Russify" their dominions, it is neces-
the Close of
the Nine- sary at this point to present a brief survey of the ex-
teenth Cen- tent and varied populations of the Russian Empire
tury toward the close of the nineteenth century.

(1) The core of the Russian Empire was the region known as
Great Russia (the former grand-duchy of Muscovy with its imme-
Great diate dependencies), with a compact and homogene-
Russia ous population, numbering in 1897 some fifty millions,
speaking the Great Russian dialect of the Slav tongue, — the
literary and official language of the empire, — and belonging
mainly to the Orthodox Church. The only serious source of
dissension in Great Russia was the existence of considerable
numbers of religious dissenters ("Old Believers"), who had
seceded from the state church at the time of the reform of the
liturgy in the seventeenth century, and who now formed numerous small sects, though forbidden by law.

(2) *Little Russia* (Kiev, Ukraine) embraced the steppes of
southwestern Russia and part of the valley of the Dnieper and
Little of the easterly watershed of the Carpathian Moun-
Russia tains. It had a population of some twenty millions
speaking a Russian language and adhering to the Orthodox
Church. But the Little Russian dialect was sufficiently different
from literary Great Russian to have a distinct popular literature,
and the Orthodox Faith was not the only one professed, for, without speaking of scattered colonies of Protestant Germans, many
Polish Jews had settled in the cities (Kiev, etc.), and a number
of Orthodox Christians had joined the Roman Catholic Church
as "Uniates," retaining their married clergy and Slavic liturgy.

(3) The grand-duchy of *Lithuania*, annexed by Catherine II
in the eighteenth century, was peopled in part by some five
White million Russians, speaking yet another dialect — the
Russia *White Russian* — and belonging to the Orthodox
and Church; in part by some two and a half million Lithu-
Lithuania anians — a Slavic people, still preserving their old
national speech, dress, and attachment to the Roman Catholic
religion; and finally by a liberal sprinkling of Jewish townsfolk and of Catholic Polish landlords.

(4) *Southern Russia*, composed of territory taken from the Ottoman Empire, was inhabited by Great Russian colonists — the Cossacks — and by Mongol and other Asiatic Southern tribes, now largely intermarried and united in alle- Russia and giance to the Orthodox Church. *Bessarabia*, which Bessarabia had finally been detached from the kingdom of Rumania in 1878,[1] had a population Orthodox in religion but Ruman in speech and nationality, plentifully interspersed with Jews, especially in the cities.[2]

(5) The *Baltic provinces* (Esthonia, Livonia, Courland), acquired from Sweden and Poland during the eighteenth century, retained a population of two kinds : the peasants The Baltic were mainly Finns or Letts, the latter akin to the Provinces Lithuanians; the upper classes and townspeople, descended from German colonists, still spoke the German language and adhered to Lutheran Protestantism. The district of Petrograd (formerly Ingria), cut off from the Baltic provinces, had lost its original character and, as the residence of the imperial government, had become a melting pot of all the languages and all the religions in the empire, the Great Russian dialect and the Orthodox Faith gradually becoming predominant.

(6) *Caucasia*, added to the empire in the course of the nineteenth century, was an interesting Babel of little peoples, some schismatic Christian (like the Armenians), and others Caucasia Mohammedan (such as the Circassians), but all warlike and all bent on preserving their separate national life — the only exception being the mingling of several princely native families with the Russian aristocracy.

(7) The Russian dominion gradually but mightily extending from the Volga River and the Ural Mountains across northern *Asia* to the Pacific Ocean and well into the central Russia in regions of the Asiatic continent [3] was inhabited by Asia some six million hardy and industrious Russian colonists and by some eight millions of native tribesmen, exhibiting the widest diversity of language and race, and in religion offering ex-

---

[1] As a result of the Russo-Turkish War of 1877–1878. See below, pp. 505 f.

[2] Kishinev, the capital of Bessarabia, was 43 per cent Jewish in 1897.

[3] For a special treatment of the Russian Empire in Asia — Siberia, Turkestan, etc. — see below, pp. 586–592.

amples of Mohammedanism, Buddhism, animal worship, and polytheism.

In addition to these integral parts of the Russian Empire were (8) the kingdom of *Poland* and (9) the grand-duchy of *Finland*.

The Kingdom of Poland Warsaw and surrounding Polish territory had been erected into the kingdom of Poland and intrusted to the sovereignty of the tsar by the Congress of Vienna (1815). The written constitution which King Alexander I then granted had been annulled by Nicholas I, following the Polish Rebellion of 1831; and as a result of the insurrection of 1863 Alexander II, as we have seen, incorporated for administrative purposes his kingdom of Poland into his empire of Russia. The Polish subjects of the tsar constituted a compact and fairly homogeneous population of seven and a half millions, proud of their separate language and literature, enthusiastically loyal to the Roman Catholic Church, and ambitious to reëstablish the political independence of their entire nation. They detested the Russians and despised and often persecuted the million and a quarter Jews who lived among them and who complicated their national problems.

For ninety years after its union with Russia (1809), Finland was practically a distinct state, the tsar as grand-duke governing **The Grand-Duchy of Finland** by means of a nominated senate and a Diet organized on the Swedish model with separate representative bodies of nobles, clergymen, burghers, and peasants. Of the total population of two and one half millions in 1897, the bulk were peasants, descended from the ancient Asiatic race of Finns, preserving their Finnish language and costume; but the upper classes were mainly Swedish, and Swedish was long the official language of the local government. All the inhabitants were Lutheran in religion and jealous of Russian encroachments on their traditional liberties.

In this hodge-podge of territories and populations subject to the Autocrat of All the Russias, Pan-Slavism became a driving **Pan-Slavism in the Russian Empire** unifying force in the latter part of the nineteenth century. Stimulated by the contemporary growth of nationalism in Germany and Italy, a host of Russian politicians, scholars, journalists, and *littérateurs* arose, especially in Great Russia, pointing out the glory and grandeur of the Slav race. They demonstrated that from a common parent-stock had come not only the Great Russians, Little Russians, White Russians, the Lithuanians, Letts, and Poles, — the overwhelming majority of the population of the Russian Empire, — but also the Poles of Prussia, and the Poles, Czechs, Ruthenians, Slovenes, and Serbo-Croats of the Habsburg Empire, and the Serbs and Bulgars in the Balkan peninsula. They showed that of all these Slavic peoples, the Great Russians were by far the most numerous and the most powerful. Their Pan-Slavic program, therefore, assumed a twofold aspect. In the first place, they would force, as far as possible, the language and the institutions of Great Russia upon the heterogeneous peoples within the Russian Empire, — in a word, they would "Russify" the empire. And in the second place they would extend Russian influence abroad — eastward into Asia, westward against Teutonic Habsburg and Hohenzollern, southward into the Balkans. In the latter case Russian Pan-Slavists were ardent sympathizers with the struggles of Bulgaria, Serbia, and Montenegro to increase their territories at the expense of Turkey or of Austria-Hungary, provided of course that these Balkan states remembered their debt of gratitude to their elder brother Russia; and at the same time the alliance between Russia and France, cemented in 1895, was commended by Russian Pan-Slavists as promising to curb the anti-Slav policies of the great Teutonic states of central Europe. Within Russia itself, the Pan-Slavists discovered that the distinctive monuments of the national genius were the Russian language, the Orthodox Church, the village community engaged in agriculture, and the political autocracy. To impress these institutions upon the entire empire, the Pan-Slavists disbelieved in the efficacy of democracy and held that one-man power was much more beneficial for carrying out their program. Just as British patriots and nationalists extolled the slowly evolving form of parliamentary government which had enriched and glorified Great Britain, so the Pan-Slavists in Russia exalted and magnified the autocracy under which their country had gradually grown great and respected. Russian patriotism made for autocracy. Without autocracy Russian Pan-Slavists could hardly hope to realize for the entire empire their ideal of "one law, one language, one religion."

"Russification" was simply the process of attempting to realize the Pan-Slavic ideal throughout the Russian Empire, of endeavoring to stamp out lesser languages and dissident faiths. Efforts at "Russification" in the reigns of Nicholas I and Alexander II, except in the instance of Poland, had been merely occasional and intermittent, but under Alexander III (1881–1894) they became systematic and showed very little consideration for the feelings, wishes, and interests of the people concerned. Both Pobêdonostsev and Plehve were earnest champions of "Russification": the latter, as head of the state police, undertook to suppress public meetings and publications which voiced national aspirations of minority peoples in the empire; the former, as Procurator of the Holy Synod, punished with great severity not only the members of the religious sects separated from the Orthodox Church but also the missionaries of Roman Catholic or Protestant Christianity who occasionally proselyted among the Orthodox; the former likewise compelled the unwilling "reconversion" of thousands of "Uniates" to Orthodoxy and oppressively interfered with the Catholic Church in Poland and with the Lutheran in the Baltic provinces. The tsar himself issued decree after decree, upholding the work of his zealous ministers and prosecuting "Russification" in a hundred different ways. In Poland the harsh laws of Alexander II were confirmed and rendered more harsh: the secondary schools were entirely Russianized; Polish literature and even the Polish language were taught to Poles in Russian; Poles were excluded from government posts in Poland; and from 1885 to 1897 no Pole was permitted to sell land to a non-Russian. In White Russia and Lithuania "Russification" assumed a religious guise: the Catholic Uniates were vigorously persecuted, and their marriages and children the Russian government refused to recognize as legitimate. The tsar, moreover, forbade the printing of any original work in Little Russian, as well as acting, reciting, or singing in that dialect. In the Baltic provinces Russian was introduced as the official tongue in 1885, and at the same time Lutheran churches were not to be constructed without the sanction of the Procurator of the Holy Synod; subsequently the use of German was forbidden in univer-

marginal notes:

" Russification " under Alexander III

In Poland

In the Baltic Provinces

sity lectures and even in private schools, local law courts were suppressed, the press was put under Russian censorship, and German place names were changed to Russian.[1]   In the Caucasus and in Siberia, special favor was shown to Russian colonists who would establish and maintain the supremacy of the Russian language and the Orthodox Church.

Persecution of the Jews was a phase of Pan-Slavism and "Russification." The Russian Empire embraced some five million Jews, settled mainly in Poland, Lithuania, Little Russia (Kiev), and Bessarabia (Kishinev), who preserved not only their religion and national tradi- tions, but also the Yiddish language, a German jargon intermixed with Hebrew words and written with Hebrew characters.   The Jews were particularly disliked because of their propensity to clannishness, to close financial dealings, and to revolutionary propaganda; and Alexander III, backed undoubtedly by popu- lar support, instituted a series of repressive measures against them.   In 1882 he forbade Jews to acquire land or to enter the liquor trade.   To keep them out of the liberal profes- sions he set a limit to the number of Jews that should be admitted to any secondary school or university: at first the number of Jews was not allowed to exceed 10 per cent of the whole student body; later, the percentage was cut down to 3 per cent.   In 1890 he issued a sweeping decree against the Jews: all who had remained in the interior of Russia were now to emigrate to the western provinces, unless they could secure individual authorization to tarry; and in the districts where they were henceforth concentrated — the so-called Jewish Pale — they were forbidden to own or lease lands and were obliged to live in cities where most liberal pro- fessions were closed to them.   Taking their cue from the attitude of the central government, many Russian administrators gave free rein to the anti-Jewish prejudices of an ignorant and bigoted peasantry and townsfolk, and tolerated, if they did not incite, more or less organized popular outbreaks against the Jews — the so-called *pogroms* — attended by plundering and burning and

Measures against the Jews

---

[1] It was in accordance with this spirit that in 1914, just after the outbreak of the War of the Nations, the name of the capital city of Russia was officially changed from the Teutonic form "St. Petersburg" to the Slavic form "Petrograd."

in some cases by massacre. From *pogroms* and repressive legislation the Russian and Polish Jews suffered greatly; and, de-

Pogroms

spite the efforts of the government to make them
stay within the empire, some 300,000 Jews left
Russia in a single year (1891). It was the beginning of the
wholesale immigration of Polish and Russian Jews into the
United States.

The death of Alexander III in 1894 did not serve immediately
to shake autocracy or to lessen the ardor of Pan-Slavists and

Mainte-
nance of the
Principles of
Alexander
III by
Nicholas II,
1894–

"Russifiers." His son and successor, Nicholas II
(1894–　　), though more amiable and less strong-
willed, let it be known from the outset that he considered the weakening of his sovereign authority a
"senseless dream." He reposed the utmost confidence in Pobêdonostsev, who had been his chief tutor
and whom he retained as Procurator of the Holy Synod until
1905; he kept Plehve in office and promoted him in 1902 to the
post of minister of the interior with almost dictatorial powers.
If the new tsar showed himself less inclined than his father to
persecute religious dissenters, he proved himself as docile an
agent of the Pan-Slavists in promoting all the other forms of
"Russification."

Under Nicholas II the Russian government continued to earn
bitter hatred in Poland, in Lithuania, and in the Baltic prov-

Continued
"Russifica-
tion" under
Nicholas II

inces. The Armenian Church in the Caucasus was despoiled. The legislation against the Jews was enforced
and the number of *pogroms* increased, culminating in
the massacre of Kishinev (1903), in which several
thousand Jews lost their lives and to which Plehve himself was
credited with being accessory. At the same time, and always
in the interest of Pan-Slavism abroad, the French Alliance
was upheld; Russian influence in the Balkans was steadily extended; and in the Far East Russian colonists and Russian
diplomacy were stealthily appropriating northern China and
marking out Korea as a suitable conquest for Russian autocracy.
The Russo-Japanese War of 1904–1905 was the result of the
attempt of the Pan-Slavists to extend Russian domination to
the Japanese and Yellow seas — a result singularly disappoint-
ing to Pan-Slavic ambition.

To the grand-duchy of Finland, whose constitution and separate nationalism even Alexander III had respected, a process of "Russification" was applied by Nicholas II. In 1899 the tsar made a wholesale substitution of Russians for Finns in the civil administration of the grand-duchy; he introduced a Russian police; he conformed the Finnish military establishment to the Russian; he decreed that all Finnish legislation must be drafted by Russian ministers in conjunction with the secretary of state for Finland, and only such matters need be submitted to the Finnish Diet as concerned Finland alone; and he capped the climax by appointing (August, 1899) the stern and faithful Pan-Slavist Plehve as secretary of state for Finland.

Nicholas II and Finland

THE INDUSTRIAL REVOLUTION IN RUSSIA AND REVIVAL OF OPPOSITION TO THE AUTOCRACY

Parallel with the rise of Pan-Slavism and the extension of "Russification" was the progress of the Russian Industrial Revolution, which, beginning seriously in the reign of Alexander III, reached large proportions under Nicholas II. Commercial activity showed a marked gain in the 'eighties; after 1895 it developed with prodigious rapidity. The construction of railways in southern Russia (1895–1897) served to tap important coal-fields and iron-mines and thereby to change the face of the whole country. Factories began to spring up like mushrooms. Between 1886 and 1899 the annual output of iron was more than quadrupled, until it exceeded that of France. Other trades developed hardly less rapidly. Textile workers increased from 400,000 in 1887 to 643,000 in 1897; pottery workers from 67,000 to 143,000. The total number of factory operatives in the larger industries increased from 1,318,000 in 1887 to 2,100,000 in 1897, and later exceeded three millions, while the value of manufactured articles more than tripled within ten years. This phenomenal growth of Russian industry was due in part to an increasing supply of cheap labor in the cities, resulting from the influx of poverty-stricken peasants from the country districts, and in part to extensive investments of foreign capital, particularly of French

Growth of Russian Commerce and Industry at the Close of the Nineteenth Century

capital after the consummation of the Franco-Russian alliance. With the aid of French capital and cheap native labor, railway building was everywhere prosecuted. In 1885 the railway mileage within the Russian Empire totaled 16,155; in 1895 it was 22,600; in 1905 it was 40,500; and in 1913 there were built or building some 51,000 miles. The important Siberian Railway, begun in 1891 and completed in 1905, with its branch connections, not only increased the migration of Russian peasants to Siberia and strengthened commercial relations with China and Japan, but also brought to Russian industry and trade the petroleum of the Caucasus, the cotton of central Asia, and the grain, timber, and minerals of Siberia.

Although the Industrial Revolution in Russia did not destroy the predominance of agriculture,[1] nevertheless it created peculiar problems sufficiently grave to tax the resources of the autocracy. Capitalists and urban proletarians arose, clamoring for governmental protection and support. Plehve did all that he could to oppose the industrial and commercial development of Russia on the now familiar lines of western Europe, on the ground that such development involved the existence of a dangerous proletariat and of a prosperous middle class equally inimical to the autocracy and to the agricultural society upon which political autocracy ultimately rested. But Plehve and his many Pan-Slavist partisans were quite unable to resist the operation of the newer economic tendencies. And in Serge de Witte the industrial classes, as well as the autocracy and the Russian patriots, found a valiant friend and champion.

Difference of Opinion as to the Proper Attitude of the Government toward the New Industrial Classes

Serge de Witte (1849–1915)[2] had been born at Tiflis in the Caucasus, where his father (of Dutch extraction) was an imperial administrator, had been educated at the state university of Odessa, had been identified for a time with reactionary journal-

---

[1] In 1860 less than 10 per cent of the entire population of the Russian Empire was urban; in 1897 the urban population constituted 13 per cent of the whole and in 1912 14 per cent. In Poland, whither the Industrial Revolution first penetrated, the urban population in 1912 constituted 30 per cent of the whole.

[2] Witte secured American fame by serving as the Russian agent in the negotiations at Portsmouth, New Hampshire, which ended the Russo-Japanese War (1905). He also worked zealously for a diminution of the prevalent Russian vice of drunkenness.

ism, and had acquired a technical knowledge of railway construction and railway finance by reason of a long official connection with the railway system of southern Russia. This early environment and experience rendered Witte at once an enthusiastic apostle of "Russification" and the maintenance of the principles of autocracy in Russia, and a determined advocate of commercial and industrial development. Appointed head of the department of railways in the imperial ministry of finance by Alexander III, he was promoted to be minister of communications in 1892 and minister of finance in 1893. Thenceforth for ten years he served as finance minister to Nicholas II, introducing foreign capital, rapidly extending the state system of railways throughout the empire, and nearly doubling the public revenues. Like Bismarck in Germany and Joseph Chamberlain in Great Britain, he sought to develop home industries by means of colonial expansion and the imposition of a protective tariff. Thus, he steadily heightened Russian influence in northern China and Persia,—a policy quite in keeping with that of the Pan-Slavists, — and, in order to benefit the capitalists, — though here opposed by most Pan-Slavists,—he established the gold standard for Russian currency, bought up the non-paying privately owned railways, subsidized many industrial enterprises, strengthened the state banks, and in 1891 imposed very large customs duties on coal and iron. By 1894, under Witte's guidance, Russia had become a thoroughly protectionist country, relying for its public revenues upon indirect taxes rather than upon direct levies on land or income. Protection of manufacturers and great landlords, however, cost the poor peasant and workingman very dearly: it was demonstrated in 1905 that the retail price of cotton and sugar was two and one-half times as great in Russia as in Germany, that of iron four and one-half times as great, and that of coal six times as great.

At the same time, Witte, again in common with Bismarck and Joseph Chamberlain, believed that industrial efficiency and national well-being would be promoted by the enactment of social legislation for the benefit of the working classes. And in this belief he was encouraged by the repeated expressions of

Witte, Champion of Industrial Development and Influential Minister, 1892–1903

Colonial Expansion and Imposition of a Protective Tariff

fear on the part of reactionaries lest the ever-recurring strikes
of a miserable proletariat might gradually acquire political sig-
Advocacy of
Social
Legislation nificance and threaten the stability of the autocracy.
Accordingly, the elaborate factory law of 1886 was
extended and enforced. Government officials were to
mediate in all labor disputes. Mines regulations were instituted,
and plans for insurance of all workmen against accidents were
prepared. The chief concern of Witte in social legislation was to
reduce the glaring evils of intemperance : with this end in view he
obtained in 1894 an imperial decree establishing a state monopoly of the sale of spirituous liquors and abolishing all private
retail liquor shops without adequate compensation to their
owners except in Poland and the Baltic provinces.

Witte's policies aroused a host of influential critics and enemies,
including such dominant figures as Plehve and Pobêdonostsev,
Dismissal
of Witte,
1903 with the result that in 1903 the tsar sent his distinguished finance minister into retirement. In the
opinion of all confirmed reactionaries it was high time,
for already the worst fears of Plehve gave promise of realization.
The newer industrial classes were proving themselves a real
menace to the maintenance of Russian autocracy.

At the beginning of the twentieth century, the opposition to
the autocracy which, under the watchful eye and vigorous action
New Forms
of Opposi-
tion to the
Autocracy of Plehve and the secret police, had lain dormant since
the later days of Alexander II, began to reassert itself
more or less openly and in many different ways.
Most important of all, so far as numbers were concerned, was the opposition of many large landowners and peasants to what they deemed the disproportionate emphasis
1. Landed
Classes
Envious of
Favors
Shown to
Industrial
Classes that the tsar had allowed Witte to put upon industrial and commercial development. These landed in-
terests, powerfully intrenched in the local *zemstvos*,
brought such pressure to bear upon the government
that Witte had finally invited committees of the
zemstvos in 1902–1903 to make recommendations to
the ministry as to what reforms — particularly agricultural
reforms — should be undertaken by the tsar. Though the
various *zemstvo* committees were hampered by the government
in every conceivable manner, more than four hundred out of a

total of seven hundred prepared reports pronouncedly hostile to
existing institutions: many asked for a national repre- The
Zemstvo
Reports,
1902–1903
sentation, freedom of the press, and guarantees of individual liberties. It was the blame heaped by Plehve
and Pobêdonostsev upon Witte for the hostile tone of
these reports that directly caused the latter's withdrawal from
the ministry in 1903.

A second source of opposition to the autocracy was the diffusion in the 'nineties of Karl Marx's Socialist teachings among the
new industrial proletariat by such radicals as the novel- 2. Wage-
Earners
Influenced
by Marxian
Socialism
list Maxim Gorky. The strength of the Socialist
propaganda was in the great factories and in the
constant migrations of workmen from one factory to
another. A "Workmen's Social Democratic party" was definitely organized in 1898 with a program similar to that of foreign Socialist parties; and, though persecuted by the "Social
Democrats"
in the Cities
government and torn by internal dissensions, the
Russian party inspired a succession of dangerous
strikes and imparted to thousands of wage-earners a lively desire
for political democracy. Marxian Socialism appealed in Russia
not only to day laborers in the cities but also to many poverty-
stricken or landless peasants, who organized a "Socialist Revolutionary party," with a platform that included the "Socialist
Revolution-
aries" in
the Country
confiscation of all large landed estates and their division into small individual holdings, and with a policy that bordered on violence and terrorism. After
1900 the Socialist Revolutionaries grew faster than the Social
Democrats.

A third source of opposition to Russian autocracy was the
growth of a new liberalism, championed on the one hand by
merchants, factory-owners, and other business men, 3. Middle
Classes
Stirred by
Political
Liberalism
who believed that their economic condition would be
bettered by setting limits to the arbitrariness of autocratic ministers and by establishing some system of
representative government, and, on the other hand, by
enlightened nobles and radical *littérateurs* and intellectual
liberals, such as Professor Milyukóv, who through study, reading,
or travel had been brought into sympathetic touch with the
political institutions of western Europe. These men styled

themselves "Liberators," and their movement centered in the
The "Lib-   universities.   In 1902 they began the publication of a
erators"   paper called "Liberation" at Stuttgart in Germany;
and in 1904 they organized the "Union of Liberators" as a
political party.

A fourth source of opposition to the existing régime in Russia, —
a reflex of Pan-Slavism, — was the intense ill-feeling and determined national protests of Poles, Jews, Finns, Lithu-
4. Opposi-   anians, and Germans of the Baltic provinces, against
tion of
the Lesser   the principles and practices of "Russification."   Each
Nationalities   one of these subject peoples would make alliances with
to "Russifi-
cation"   any faction of Russians who might assail and destroy
             the autocracy.   Many Jews drifted into Socialism.
Most Poles sympathized with the endeavors of the "Liberators."
And in the case of Finland, native Finns and Swedes made
common cause in the struggle which they maintained from
1899 to 1905 for the restoration of the Finnish Constitution
and for the cessation of Russian interference in the internal
affairs of the grand-duchy.

Against all these forces of opposition, Plehve and other loyal
ministers of the autocracy kept up a tireless and seemingly effective fight.   Plehve's system was now (1903–1904) in full swing
throughout the length and breadth of the entire empire; domi-
ciliary visits, illegal arrests and banishments, and the suppression
of newspapers were the order of the day.   Any person was liable
to be apprehended by the police and imprisoned by governmental
order who was merely suspected of harboring anti-Russian,
Liberal, or Socialist opinions.

THE REVOLUTIONARY MOVEMENT OF 1905 AND THE RUSSIAN DUMA, 1906–1914

To the system of Plehve, the Russo-Japanese War (1904–1905)
was a rude and sudden shock.   As telegram followed telegram
from the distant fighting front in Manchuria, admit-
The Effect
of the   ting a succession of Russian defeats, it was borne in
Russo-   upon the Russian people, as never before, that under
Japanese
War   the harsh irresponsible system of Plehve incompetent
             generals and administrators had been promoted, and
corruption and peculation had flourished.   The parties of opposi-

tion seized quickly upon this fact and utilized it to precipitate a revolutionary movement in Russia and thereby to wring some noteworthy political concessions from the Tsar and Autocrat Nicholas II. The feeling of national humiliation changed into a vague uneasiness, which gradually gave way to mutterings and then to disorder. On 28 July, 1904, Plehve, the symbol and incarnation of reactionary autocracy, was blown to pieces by a bomb. In November an informal assembly of eminent members of local *zemstvos* and municipal *dumas* petitioned the tsar to reform the political system by guaranteeing individual liberties, extending local self-government, and establishing a national representative assembly.

As the only reply of the tsar to these forebodings of domestic tumult was the promise (December, 1904) of a few vague reforms and the appointment of General Trepoff, a particularly objectionable reactionary, as head of the police, the opposition assumed a more threatening attitude. Members of the professional classes held political banquets and delivered inflammatory speeches. Workingmen struck in Moscow, Kovno, Riga, Vilna, and other cities of European Russia. At Petrograd a procession of striking laborers, headed by a certain priest, Gapón by name, was fired upon by troops while on its way to present a petition to the tsar, the "little father"; and the resulting bloodshed earned for the day (22 January, 1905) the appellation of "Red Sunday." In the rural districts bands of peasants wandered about under the influence of Socialist Revolutionary leaders, pillaging and burning the mansions of noble landlords and country gentlemen. The reactionary Grand-Duke Serge, the tsar's uncle, was assassinated at Moscow on 17 February; and thenceforth murders of prominent officials became common. Armed outbreaks in Poland and in the Caucasus were put down only by the vigorous action of Russian soldiery. The state railways could be operated only under martial law. The universities were closed.

The Revolutionary Movement in Russia, 1905

Unable to suppress the growing disorders, the tsar painfully and falteringly gave heed to the popular clamors. He decreed religious toleration and licensed the use of the Polish and Lithuanian languages in private schools. He relaxed the enforcement of anti-Jewish legislation. He remitted the arrears of the sums

due from the peasants for their shares in the communal lands.
He agreed to put the trial of political offenders on a more regu-
Concessions   lar basis.   In June, 1905, in reply to a deputation of
of Nicholas   a congress of *zemstvos*, he promised the speedy con-
II   vocation of a national assembly.   In August he promulgated a constitutional law, providing for the creation of such
an assembly, to be known as the Imperial Duma and to counsel
with the tsar in the making of laws.   Then he dismissed Pobêdonostsev, Trepoff, and other ultra-reactionary ministers, summoned Witte to be the first premier of a Russian cabinet under the
The   new régime, and on 30 October, 1905, issued his most
Manifesto   famous manifesto.   The October Manifesto con-
of October,   tained guarantees of the individual liberties of con-
1905: Es-   science, speech, and association; established a
tablishment   moderately popular franchise for the election of the
of the Duma
Duma; and clearly stated that henceforth no law should be
valid without the Duma's consent.   Subsequently, a decree of
December, 1905, virtually granted universal manhood suffrage,
and another of March, 1906, made provision for a bicameral
The Council   national legislature by designating the Duma as the
of the   Lower House and by transforming the old Council of
Empire   State into an Upper House, under the new title of
Council of the Empire, half of whose members should be
appointed by the tsar and half elected indirectly by certain
privileged classes.

· By 1906, however, the revolutionary wave in Russia had spent
its main force, and thenceforth it began slowly but certainly to re-
Decline of   cede.   The conclusion of peace with Japan (Septem-
the Revolu-   ber, 1905) put an end to the series of disgraceful de-
tionary   feats abroad and enabled the government to utilize
Movement,   the army to restore order at home.   Then, too, after
1906
nearly two years' efforts in foreign war and domestic
upheaval, many Russians began to long for peace and quiet and
for the economic advantages which public order would bring.
Moreover, the revolutionary elements commenced to disintegrate
Factions   and to waste their energies in factional quarrels.   Not
among the   only did the Social Democrats and Socialist Revolu-
Revolution-   tionaries maintain separate organizations and distinct
aries   class interests, but the Liberals — professional men

and *zemstvo* members — divided on the constitutional question : a radical group, organized as the "Constitutional Democrats" under the leadership of Professor Milyukóv and popularly known as the "Cadets," refused to recognize the finality of the **The** tsar's decrees and demanded that the first Duma **"Cadets"** should draw up a constitution that would give Russia a thoroughly democratic parliament with supreme legislative powers and with perfect control of the sovereign and his ministers ; another group, styled the "Octobrists" and representing the **The "Octo-** more conservative Liberals, especially the *zemstvo* men, **brists"** were content to accept the famous October decree of the tsar, with its provision for a Duma as a check upon, but not as a complete substitute for, the autocracy. The Cadets stood for constitutional government based on the doctrine of popular sovereignty ; the Octobrists stood for constitutional government based on the voluntary consent of the divinely ordained tsar. Generally, too, the Cadets championed the autonomy of Poland and a federal form of government for the empire, while the Octobrists were influenced by Pan-Slavic ideals and devoted to the patriotic policy of "Russification." Finally, the great landlords, alarmed by the prevalence of disorder in the rural districts and fearful lest a Liberal Duma should confiscate their estates, **Organiza-** began to coöperate with the reactionary court faction, **tion of the** with the army officers, and with old-fashioned Pan-Slav- **Reaction-** ists, to resist the execution of the recent reforming **aries: the** decrees and to maintain the autocracy in its former **"Union of** power and vigor. These reactionaries organized the **the Russian People"** "Union of the Russian People," which early in 1906 inaugurated an active campaign in behalf of the traditional régime. And to the revolutionary terrorism which had characterized Russia in 1904–1905 succeeded now a reactionary terrorism. The "black band" or "black hundreds," as the ruffian agents of the "Union" were branded in popular speech, seemed bent on the exter- **Reactionary** mination of the radical elements : they terrorized the **Terrorism** countryside and particularly against the Jews committed wholesale robbery and murder.

Under the circumstances, the tsar's government could afford to draw back somewhat from the advanced constitutional position which it had taken in 1905. In the decree of March, 1906,

which established the Council of the Empire as the upper house
of the proposed parliament, Nicholas II formally excluded from

The Mani-
festo of
March,
1906:
Limits to
the Powers
of the Duma

parliamentary discussion the fundamental laws of the
empire and the constitution of the legislative bodies;
declared that the control of army, navy, and foreign
policy was an exclusive prerogative of the tsar; gave
power to the imperial ministers to issue temporary
laws when the Duma was not sitting; reserved the
right of negotiating loans to the minister of finance; and
provided that if the parliament should not pass the annual
budget the government might substitute the estimates of the
preceding year. Then in April, 1906, the tsar, yielding to the
terrorism of the Black Hundreds and to the entreaties of the
reactionaries, dismissed Witte from the premiership and appointed as his successor the conservative Goremýkin, with Peter
Stolýpin as minister of the interior. Stolýpin (1862–1911) [1] was

Stolýpin,
Prime
Minister,
1906–1911

the ablest man in the new ministry and the most
prominent official from 1906 to 1911. Becoming
prime minister in July, 1906, he labored to maintain
both the autocracy and the Duma: on the one hand,
he resisted the pressure from the extreme reactionaries to abolish
the Duma altogether; on the other hand, he punished revolutionary crimes with a severity that resembled Plehve's.

Meanwhile the first Russian parliament had been chosen and
had assembled in Petrograd on 10 May, 1906. A fateful question

The First
Duma
(1906) and
its Failure
to Establish
Parliamen-
tary Gov-
ernment

at once confronted the national representatives: who
would be master of the country — the Duma or the
tsar's ministers? The Cadets, who commanded a
majority in the Duma, answered the former. Goremýkin, Stolýpin, and the tsar answered the latter. The
Duma prepared to enact measures looking toward the
establishment of pure parliamentary government and
the expropriation of the landlords. The ministry blocked the
measures and at length on 21 July, 1906, dissolved the Duma by
imperial decree and ordered new elections. This action the

---

[1] Peter Stolýpin, the son of a country gentleman, was born near Moscow,
served in various grades of the civil administration, and as governor of Saratov
early in 1906 attracted the favorable attention of the tsar by his effective repression of terrorism and disorder.

Cadets refused to accept, and, in imitation of the celebrated meeting in the tennis-court at Versailles in 1789, some two hundred
members of the first Duma adjourned to Viborg in   Dissolution
Finland, where they drew up and issued a manifesto   of the First
calling on the Russian people to refuse taxes and mili-   the Ineffec-
tary service.   The Viborg Manifesto produced but   tual Viborg
feeble response: its authors were disfranchised, the   Protest, 1906
Cadet Clubs were closed, the few attempts at armed insurrection
were easily suppressed, and special courts martial, endowed by
the government with summary powers, put many revolutionaries
to death and banished some 35,000 persons in 1906.

   The opponents of autocracy, despite governmental interference
at the polls, secured a majority in the second Duma, which met
on 5 March, 1907.   Again there was the same *impasse*   The Second
between the ministry and the Duma.   Stolýpin's pro-   Duma
posal to effect land reform by emancipating the   (1907) and
peasants from the control of the village communities   Preserve its
(*mirs*) and handing over to them the crown lands and   Independ-
imperial estates, was considered too mild: the Duma   ence
demanded the complete expropriation of all great landowners,
the abolition of the field courts martial, and guarantees of
ministerial responsibility to the parliament.   The Social Democrats were particularly obstreperous in their opposition to the
government; the prime minister accused their leaders of complicity in a treasonable plot to suborn the army and peremptorily
requested the Duma to deliver them over to arrest and punishment.   The Duma, pleading parliamentary privilege, refused the
request; and the tsar dissolved the second Duma by decree of
16 June, 1907.

   This time the tsar, in flat contradiction to his former decree
of October, 1905, fundamentally altered the electoral   Dissolution
law.   Most elaborate and complicated machinery   of the Sec-
was now set up for elections to the Duma, to the   and Altera-
end that the Lower House of the parliament, as well   tion of the
as the Upper, would be assured a clear majority   Electoral
of wealthy Conservative and Pan-Slavist members.   perial De-
The provinces of central Asia were disfranchised al-   cree, June,
together; the representation of Poland, Caucasia, and   1907
Siberia was greatly reduced; the electoral districts were so " gerry-

mandered" as to incorporate radically inclined cities with more populous areas of conservative agriculturists; and by a class-system of voting great landlords were given a controlling influence.

The new electoral law worked as the tsar and Stolýpin had intended. The third Duma, chosen in accordance with its pro-
visions in October, 1907, was composed largely of country gentlemen with a sprinkling of merchants. The majority, made up of Octobrists and Moderate Conservatives, were resigned to the maintenance of the Duma as a consultative body and were quite willing to recognize that the final establishment of real parliamentary government in Russia would be the result only of a slow evolution under the benevolent patronage of the tsar and his ministers. The Cadets, greatly reduced in numbers, though still under the leadership of Professor Milyukóv, consented to drop their obstructionist tactics and to play the rôle of constitutional opposition. Only a few Social Democrats and small irreconcilable national groups, on the one side, and a larger faction of Extreme Conservatives, on the other, preserved an open and uncompromising hostility to the existing régime.

The Third Duma and Its Support of Stolýpin

Until 1909 Stolýpin's government devoted major attention to the restoration of internal order, to the punishment of political crimes, and to the strengthening of the autocratic power which had been so seriously threatened by the revolutionary movement of 1904–1905. Revolutionary violence continued, but with decreasing effect: in 1906–1907 the number of officials killed or wounded by Terrorists, according to public reports, was 4131; in 1908 it dropped to 1009. Sternly Stolýpin coped with the situation. The signers of the Viborg Manifesto were arrested, condemned to three months' imprisonment, and permanently deprived of the franchise. The Social Democratic members of the second Duma, who had been accused of treason, were tried behind closed doors and thirty-one were sent to Siberia. The police were empowered to impose fines or to imprison up to three months any person who published or circulated any article "arousing a hostile attitude to the government." In the three years from 1906 to 1908 at least 2300 political offenders were put to death and many thousands were banished.

Suppression of the Revolutionary Movement, 1906–1909

After February, 1909, there was a steady and rapid fall in the number of executions. Martial law was gradually replaced by milder measures. Greater freedom was allowed to the press than had obtained under Plehve. And the Duma, if shorn of effective control over the ministry and over public finances, still remained a national assembly, counseling the tsar and from time to time inducing the ministers to accept amendments to their legislative proposals. In the Duma the Russian people possessed a body that at least could speak for the nation and that contained the germ of political democracy. That was the fruit of the Russian Revolution of 1905.

Maintenance of the Duma as a National Consultative Chamber

Stolýpin did not live to see the completion of the labors of the third Duma. As one of the isolated outrages in the last expiring gasps of revolutionary terrorism he was killed in September, 1911, in the imperial theater at Kiev, by the dagger-thrust of a Jewish lawyer. Kokovtsev, his successor in the premiership, was an economist of European reputation, who continued his policies, and, in addition, introduced salutary reforms in the national finances. In June, 1912, the third Duma came to an end. Since 1907 it had passed several noteworthy bills. One (passed in 1909) ratified a temporary decree of November, 1906, empowering the peasants to become owners of their allotments, remitting their redemption dues, and practically abolishing the system of ownership by the village community (*mir*) — a measure, if strictly carried out, quite as epochal as Alexander II's original edict of emancipation (1861). Another bill dealt with a general scheme of workingmen's insurance; another, with the reform of the local administration of justice; another, with the extension of elementary education under the auspices of the Orthodox Church. In fact, the third Duma showed unmistakable zeal in supporting patriotic Pan-Slavist proposals whether of Stolýpin or of Kokovtsev. Not only were the laws against the Jews maintained and additional legislation devised to crush the Polish national movement, but the Duma approved in 1912 an extraordinary expenditure of half a billion roubles[1] for the building of a new navy.

Assassination of Stolýpin and Succession of Kokovtsev, 1911

Work of the Third Duma, 1907–1912

[1] A Russian rouble is worth $0.515.

The fourth Duma, quietly elected in 1912, had much the same political complexion as its predecessor, and played much the same rôle. It quarreled with the Council of the Empire about a ministerial proposal for the further "Russification" of Poland, but it indorsed governmental recommendations for strict regulation of the liquor traffic and for lengthening the legal term of active service in the infantry from three to three and one-fourth years (1913). When, in February, 1914, Nicholas II replaced Kokovtsev by the septuagenarian Goremýkin as prime minister, it seemed as if the political organization of Russia had reached a normal equilibrium that could paradoxically but properly be described in the official almanac as "a constitutional monarchy under an autocratic tsar."

The Fourth Duma and the Orderly Operation of the Compromise between Autocracy and National Representation

In one part of the tsar's dominions — the grand-duchy of Finland — the revolution of 1905 had produced results less advantageous to the principle of autocracy. The dogged and determined resistance of the whole Finnish people to the tsar's virtual abrogation of their ancient constitution in 1899 had culminated in November, 1905, in a "national strike." The railway, steamship, telephone, and postal services were suspended. Helsingfors, the capital of the grand-duchy, was without street-cars, cabs, and lights, and no shops except provision stores were open. Nicholas II, shaken by the disastrous outcome of the Japanese War and by the revolutionary movement in Russia, capitulated to the Finns and by decree of 17 November, 1905, restored the Finnish Constitution. The strike ceased at once. A Diet was promptly elected — the first since 1899 — and met in December : it sat for three months and drafted a new constitution for Finland, substituting a single Chamber for the former legislature of four Estates, and establishing proportional representation and universal suffrage alike for men and for women. This reform of the Finnish government was ratified by the tsar in 1906. Subsequently, under the influence of Stolýpin and the Pan-Slavists, Nicholas II insisted that the decision in all Finnish questions affecting the empire must rest with the Russian ministry ; and new efforts to curtail the power of the Finnish Diet

The Finnish Question, 1905–1914

The New Finnish Constitution of 1906

just before the outbreak of the War of the Nations aroused the liveliest apprehension in Finland.

The outbreak of the Great War in August, 1914, witnessed a mighty demonstration of Russian Pan-Slavism. The tsar, addressing his parliament, testified to "the tremen- Russia and dous outburst of patriotic sentiment, of love and the War of loyalty to the throne, which, like a tempest, traversed the Nations our entire land," and went on to say, "We are not only defending the dignity and honor of our country, but we are also fighting for our Slavic brothers, the Serbs, our co-religionists and kinsmen, and at this moment I behold with joy how the union of all the Slavs with Russia is being strongly and unremittingly carried to completion." While the predominant sentiment in Russia was a militant combination of personal fealty to the tsar, zeal for the national Orthodox Church, and pride in the possession of Slavic as opposed to Teutonic culture, at the same time the Russian government made some attempt to conciliate discontented minorities. The struggle with the Finnish Diet was interrupted. The Poles were solemnly promised a restoration of their kingdom and the grant of political autonomy. The execution of the laws against Catholics and Lutherans was eased. Even the Jews were told that the tsar loved them, and were allowed to become officers in the army.

ADDITIONAL READING

General. Elementary narratives: C. D. Hazen, *Europe since 1815* (1910), ch. xxix, xxxi; J. H. Robinson and C. A. Beard, *The Development of Modern Europe*, Vol. II (1907), ch. xxviii; J. H. Rose, *The Development of the European Nations, 1870-1900*, Vol. I (1905), ch. xi. Broader political surveys: *Cambridge Modern History*, Vol. XI (1909), ch. xxii, and Vol. XII (1910), ch. xii, xiii; *Histoire générale*, Vol. XI, ch. xiv, and Vol. XII, ch. xi; Alfred Rambaud, *Histoire de la Russie depuis les origines jusqu'à nos jours*, 6th ed. rev. and completed to 1913 by Émile Haumant (1914), ch. xxxvi–xli, a scholarly work with excellent bibliographies — the original edition of which was published in English translation in three volumes (1881). Valuable descriptions of present-day Russia: Anatole Leroy-Beaulieu, *The Empire of the Tsars and the Russians*, trans. from 3d French edition by Z. A. Ragozin, 3 vols. (1893–1896), admirable particularly in dealing with religious affairs and the position of the Russian Church; Sir D. M. Wallace, *Russia*, new ed. (1908), perhaps the best general treatment of Russian civilization; Maurice Baring, *The Russian People*, 2d ed. (1911), clear, unbiased, and comprehensive; Leo Wiener, *An Interpretation of the Russian People* (1915), brief but illuminating; J. Novicow, *The Russian People, a Psychological Study*, a suggestive essay in Alfred Rambaud, *The Expansion of Russia*, 2d ed. (1904); H. W. Williams, *Russia of the Russians* (1914), a popular account by a former Petrograd correspondent of the *Manchester Guardian;* Gregor Alexinsky, *Modern Russia*, Eng. trans. by Bernard Miall (1913), a comprehensive but partisan survey by a Russian Socialist who sat in the second Duma; Wolf von Schierbrand, *Russia, her Strength and her Weakness* (1904); Alan Lethbridge, *The New Russia: From the White Sea to the Siberian Steppe* (1915), an interesting book of travel; Maxime Kovalevsky, *Russian Political Institutions*, Eng. trans. (1902), historical as well as descriptive, a brief résumé by an eminent Russian scholar; Wiatscheslaw Gribowski, *Das Staatsrecht des russischen Reiches* (1912), a brief but sound exposition of the public law of the empire; U. S. Bureau of Foreign and Domestic Commerce, *Russia, a Handbook on Commercial and Industrial Conditions*, prepared by J. H. Snodgrass, U. S. consul-general at Moscow, and other consular officers, and published by the American government at Washington (1913); W. de Kovalevsky, *La Russie à la fin du XIXe siècle* (1900), prepared in connection with the Paris Exposition of 1900; Maxime Kovalevsky, *Le régime économique de la Russie* (1898); Gaëtan (Vicomte) Combes de Lestrade, *La Russie économique et sociale à l'avènement de S. M. Nicholas II* (1896); August von Haxthausen, *Russian Empire, its People, Institutions, and Resources*, Eng. trans., 2 vols. (1856), valuable for description of social conditions at the time when the work was written. Much useful information concerning conditions in the twentieth century is supplied by *The Russian Year Book*, ed. by H. P. Kennard (1911 *sqq.*), and by *The Russian Review*, a journal published in England since 1912.

The Expansion of Russia and " Russification."   The standard treatise on the territorial growth of Russia since 1815 is F. H. Skrine, *The Expansion of Russia*, 3d ed. (1915); and additional information on this subject is furnished by Geoffrey Drage, *Russian Affairs* (1904), by A. J. Beveridge, *The Russian Advance* (1903), by M. M. Shoemaker, *The Great Siberian Railway from St. Petersburg to Pekin* (1903), and by the books cited in the bibliography appended to Chapter XXVII, below. Important for the development of Pan-Slavism is a careful study of the reign of Alexander III, of whom the best biographies are: Charles Lowe, *Alexander III* (1895); H. G. Samson von Himmelstjerna, *Russia under Alexander III and in the Preceding Period*, trans. from German by J. Morrison (1893). K. P. Pobêdonostsev, the famous Procurator of the Holy Synod under Alexander III and Nicholas II and the stanch champion of autocracy and " Russification," has attempted to defend the régime, of which he was so conspicuously a part, in his interesting *Reflections of a Russian Statesman*, trans. from French by R. C. Long (1898). On the " Russification " of particular peoples, consult: Victor Bérard, *The Russian Empire and*

Czarism, Eng. trans. by G. Fox-Davies and G. O. Pope (1905); Israel Friedlaender, *The Jews of Russia and Poland* (1915); Georg Brandes, *Poland, a Study of the Land, People, and Literature* (1903); J. R. Fisher, *Finland and the Tsars, 1809–1899* (1899); Henry Norman, *All the Russias* (1902), presenting, among many other matters, the Russian side of the Finnish question; W. A. Phillips, *Poland* (1915), ch. ix–xiii, a brief account of Polish history since 1862, in the " Home University Library."

Revolutionary Movements. James Mavor, *An Economic History of Russia*, Vol. II (1914), Books IV–VII, the best general account of the revolutionary movements, with special reference to their economic aspects, particularly good on the agrarian question and on the Industrial Revolution in Russia; Ludwik Kulczycki, *Geschichte der russischen Revolution*, trans. from Polish into German, 3 vols. (1910–1914), covering the years 1825–1900, exhaustive, sympathetic with the revolutionaries, and, when completed, promising to become a standard work; Alphons Thun, *Geschichte der revolutionären Bewegungen in Russland* (1883), useful for the movements during the reign of Alexander II; George Kennan, *Siberia and the Exile System*, 4th ed., 2 vols. (1897), the celebrated work of an American traveler and journalist, highly colored but probably just in its broad outlines; Peter (Prince) Kropotkin, *Memoirs of a Revolutionist*, fascinating impressions of an aristocrat who spent his youth on a great landed estate in Russia and who subsequently became a prominent Anarchist and revolutionary; N. V. Gogol, *Dead Souls*, the famous novel, valuable for its pictures of social unrest in Russia under Alexander II, Eng. trans. by D. J. Hogarth, conveniently published in " Everyman's Library "; the writings of S. M. Kravchinski, an active revolutionist, who employed the pseudonym of Sergius Stepniak, especially *Underground Russia* (1883), *Russian Peasantry, their Agrarian Condition, Social Life, and Religion* (1905), *Career of a Nihilist* (1901), and *At Dawn of a New Reign: Study of Modern Russia: King Stork and King Log* (1895); Maxime Kovalevsky, *La crise russe: notes et impressions d'un témoin* (1906), observations on the revolutionary movement of 1905 by an eminent Russian scholar; Paul Milyoukov, *Russia and its Crisis* (1905), based on lectures delivered in the United States, pronouncedly Liberal in tone; Konni Zilliacus, *The Russian Revolutionary Movement*, Eng. trans. (1905), the work of a well-informed Finn; Bernard Pares, *Russia and Reform* (1907), an important work; G. H. Perris, *Russia in Revolution* (1905), interesting but journalistic; W. E. Walling, *Russia's Message* (1908), a Socialist's view; S. N. Harper, *The New Electoral Law for the Russian Duma* (1908), a valuable study; Paul Vinogradoff, *The Russian Problem* (1914), a brief but suggestive lecture.

For the Russo-Japanese War see the bibliography appended to Chapter XXVII, below. For the foreign policy of Russia from 1871 to 1914 and the outbreak of the War of the Nations consult Chapter XXX, below, and the bibliography appended thereto.

CHAPTER XXVI

THE DISMEMBERMENT OF THE OTTOMAN EMPIRE, 1683–1914

THE OTTOMAN EMPIRE AND ITS DECLINE, 1683–1815

PRIOR to 1683 the advance of the Ottoman Turks had been pretty uniformly successful. In Asia they had established themselves as masters of Asia Minor, Armenia, Syria, Caucasia, the Euphrates valley, and the shore of the Red Sea. In Africa their conquering armies had appropriated Egypt, Tripoli, Tunis, and Algeria. In Europe they had subjugated the Tatars and Cossacks immediately north of the Black Sea; they had conquered the entire Balkan peninsula, including present-day Greece, Bulgaria, Rumania, Bessarabia, Bukowina, Transylvania, Hungary, Bosnia, Herzegovina, Serbia, Montenegro, and Albania; they had even exacted tribute from the Austrian Habsburgs; they had made the Black Sea, the Ægean, and the eastern Mediterranean their own, and occupied the islands of Cyprus, Crete, and Rhodes, as well as the smaller islands of the Ægean.

Extent of the Ottoman Empire, 1683

The immediate occasion of the reversal of Turkish fortunes was the counter success of the expedition led by John Sobieski, the patriot Polish king, which in 1683 relieved the beleaguered city of Vienna and turned back the tide of Turkish conquest. But the real cause of subsequent Ottoman disasters was the decay of political institutions within the huge empire and the growing weakness of the army — a cause which has been explained in an earlier chapter.[1] After 1683, as the Turkish tide gradually receded, there slowly reappeared in the Balkans independent Christian nations that had long lain submerged under Mohammedan dominion. There also appeared the rising ambitions and waxing empires

Failure of the Turks to Capture Vienna, 1683

[1] See Vol. I, pp. 383 ff.

of the Austrian Habsburgs and the Russian tsars.   More and
more wistfully both Austria and Russia looked southward, intent upon profiting by the decline of Turkish power. Austrian
And thus the decline of Turkish power created an in- and Russian
tense rivalry between two great Christian empires Aggrandize-
and complicated the international politics of Europe ment at
for many generations. Turkish
Expense

By the treaty of Karlowitz (1699) the Austrian Habsburgs
permanently secured the greater part of Hungary, including
Transylvania, and thenceforth looked with longing
eye upon the other Ottoman provinces in the Balkan Austrian
peninsula.   The Russians, no less eager to expand at Gains:
the expense of the Turks, by the treaty of Kuchuk Treaty of
Kainarji (1774) obtained Azov at the mouth of the Karlowitz,
1699
Don.   By the latter treaty the Tatars who inhabited the coast-
lands north of the Black Sea — from the Caspian to the Dniester
— were made practically independent of Turkey, and Russian
the Sublime Porte (as the foreign office of the Otto- Gains:
man Empire is magniloquently styled) recognized Treaty of
Kuchuk
Russia as the protector of certain Orthodox churches Kainarji,
in Constantinople.   Before the close of the eighteenth 1774
century Catherine II of Russia had seized the Crimea (1783),
extended her sway over the "independent" Tatars, and pushed
the Russian frontier westward to the Dniester (1792).

During the period of the French Revolution and Napoleonic
Wars, Turkey was repeatedly threatened, — when Napoleon
suddenly invaded Egypt (1798), when Russia and Turkey dur-
Great Britain opened hostilities (1807), when rebel- ing the Era
lion lifted its head in Serbia, in Adrianople, and in of Napoleon
other parts of the empire.   But Europe was then more concerned
with her own intestine wars than with the Eastern Question, and
in the confusion Turkey regained Egypt, although compelled to
cede Bessarabia (1812) to the ever-advancing Russians, thus
moving the Russian frontier from the river Dniester southward
to the river Pruth.

In spite of these losses the dominions of the sultan still formed
a noble empire, with its heart in Asia Minor and its head at Constantinople, and with arms stretching westward through Egypt,
Tripoli, Tunis, and Algeria to touch Morocco, southward to em-

brace the Gulf of Aden and the Persian Gulf, eastward to reach
Persia and the Caspian, and northward to resist the Russians at
The Otto- the river Pruth and the Austrians at the Save. Over
man Empire this vast realm ruled the *padishah*, "King of Kings,"
in 1815 "Shadow of God," or, as the Europeans called him,
the sultan—claiming to be the oldest male of the royal house
of Othman,[1] and the *khalif* or supreme ecclesiastical lord of all
Islam. Notwithstanding his resounding titles the sultan was
so notoriously victimized by his numerous wives, so dependent upon his grand vizier (prime minister) and divan (council
of ministers), so completely at the mercy of his professional
army — the Janissaries, — that his arbitrary authority was as
often disregarded as enforced. This was especially true of the
outlying provinces, like Egypt, where the governors (*pashas*)
resembled tributary princes more than administrative officials. Everywhere the administration was paralyzed by in-
subordination and corruption. Officials purchased their appointment and used their powers shamelessly to enrich
themselves by illegal extortions.

The worst effects of the sultan's misgovernment were felt by
his Christian subjects. It must be remembered that when the
The Chris- Turks first invaded the Near East, they had found
tian "Cat- numerous Christians and Jews living in Egypt, in Syria
tle " of the and in Armenia, and a solid Christian population in the
Sultan Balkan peninsula. With all the ardor of a zealous Mohammedan the Turk believed that he should valiantly fight for
his religion, should put to the sword all heathen idolators, and
should strive to subjugate all Christian and Jewish peoples.
Consequently the victorious Turkish armies of the fifteenth century had spared the lives of conquered Christians but had
exacted heavy tribute. A few of the Christians embraced the
Mohammedan faith, and thereby gained admission to the ruling
class. But the vast majority remained Christians, and the
Turks made slight attempt to convert them. Rather, the sultan
recognized the Christian bishops, — above all, the (Greek Orthodox) patriarch of Constantinople, — as the spokesmen and representatives of the Christian population. The conquered Christian races thus became a submerged people, separated from the

[1] See Vol. I, p. 23.

Turks by religion, by language, by costume, by manners, and, most of all, by hatred. For the Turks prided themselves on being valiant warriors and Mohammedans; they looked down with infinite scorn upon Christian peasants and tradesmen: the Christians were cattle — *rayahs* — fit for nothing better than to obey and to enrich the Turk. It was little wonder that the Christians regarded their arrogant conquerors with hatred. The ill-feeling was aggravated by the fact that under the corrupt misgovernment of the Turks, rapacious tax-collectors were allowed to demand what they would from the peasantry, and heartlessly to enforce their unreasonable demands, if necessary by seizing the peasant's crops, or by forcing the peasant to watch his harvest rot on the ground. Moreover, unruly bands of brigands and irregular bodies of soldiery terrorized the country and repeatedly robbed the peasants. Worst of all were the occasional outbursts of religious fanaticism. Sometimes with provocation, and sometimes without, the Turks would fall upon Christian villagers, slaughter men, women, and children, and enrich themselves with plunder.

The situation was most acute in the Balkan peninsula, where the Turks, even including converts from Christianity, were overwhelmingly outnumbered by the *rayahs*, except in the northeastern part of Bulgaria, in Albania, and in the vicinity of Constantinople and Adrianople. The bulk of the population in what are now Greece, Serbia, Bulgaria, and Rumania belonged to the Greek Orthodox Church, the church which had definitely broken with the Roman Catholic pope in 1054. At the head of the Greek Orthodox Church was the patriarch of Constantinople, appointed by the sultan. The Russian Church, it is worth noting, while governed by its own synod, formed another branch of the Orthodox Church; and the Russian emperors consistently regarded themselves as co-religionists and natural protectors of all the Greek Orthodox Christians. *The Religious Situation in the Balkan Peninsula*

It would, therefore, have been easy, religion alone considered, for the Greek Orthodox majority in what are now Greece, Serbia, Bosnia, Macedonia, Bulgaria, and Rumania, to have revolted unitedly and with the friendly support of the Russians against the Mohammedan Turks.

The Near Eastern Question, however, was not to be answered so easily. As an indirect effect of the French Revolution, the

Balkan Races and Nationalities

sentiment of national and racial patriotism entered particularly into the situation in the nineteenth century and transferred the emphasis from religion to nationality. Consequently the struggles of the nineteenth century were to be essentially wars for national independence and aggrandizement, rather than crusades against the "infidel." What had long been considered by the Turks as the herd of Christian "cattle" began to split into four or five major groups. Those who were once all Christian *rayahs* oppressed by their common enemy, the Turk, now insisted that they were Serbs, or Bulgars, or Rumans, or Greeks, or Albanians. The new enthusiasm for nationality was an echo of what was going on among Italians, Germans, Poles, and Czechs. But in the Balkan peninsula races were so endlessly intermingled that the principle of nationalism, instead of simplifying matters, prepared the way for bitter jealousies and fratricidal wars.

Since the very dawn of history the Balkan peninsula had been a dumping-ground for diverse races. Again and again barbarian hordes from the north and east had invaded the peninsula, and each succeeding invasion had left the blood of the Balkan peoples more mongrel, their languages more confused, and their gaudy costumes more diversified. Nevertheless, intermixed as the races were, at least four considerable "nations" rose in European Turkey during the nineteenth century and asserted their right to independent national existence.

The stalwart Serbs or Servians traced their descent from the Serbo-Croat invaders who swarmed into the peninsula about

1. The Serbs

the seventh century A.D. These Serbo-Croat immigrants left colonies in Macedonia, in Bulgaria, and even in Greece, but settled more thickly in the northwestern part of the peninsula, just south of the Danube. A few embraced the Mohammedan religion and became aristocratic landowners. The Serbo-Croats in Dalmatia, northwestern Bosnia, and Croatia-Slavonia were converted to the Roman Catholic faith. The majority of the Serbo-Croats in Serbia, Montenegro, Herzegovina, and southern Bosnia, however, remained Greek Orthodox Christians. These are the Serbs of to-day. They belong to the

Slavic group of peoples, and are, therefore, kinsfolk of the Russians, Poles, Czechs, Ruthenians, and Slovenes.

The Bulgars or Bulgarians speak a Slavic language somewhat similar to that of the Serbs. Slavic blood — if there be such a thing — flows in their veins, too, but with many ad- **2. The** mixtures. About the fourth century A.D., Slavic **Bulgars** farmers had settled among the ancient Thracian inhabitants of the land. Then had come the fierce Bulgars, Asiatic tribesmen like the Turks, conquering the Slavs, then adopting the Slavic customs and language. Finally had come the Turks. The mixture of these many elements produced the Bulgarian "nation," which now inhabits the kingdom of Bulgaria, Eastern Rumelia, parts of the Dobrudja, and most of the interior of Macedonia.

The Rumans, Vlachs, or Wallachs, are likewise a mixed race, having absorbed Gothic, Tatar, and Slavic invaders; they claim, however, to be descended from the ancient **3. The Ru-** Roman inhabitants of Dacia; they call themselves **mans or** Romans or Rumans, and their language is based upon **Vlachs** Latin in somewhat the same way as are French, Italian, and Spanish. The present kingdom of Rumania (Moldavia and Wallachia) includes less than seven million Rumans, but were all the Rumans to be united in one state, Austria-Hungary would have to give up Transylvania, Bukowina, and part of Hungary; Russia would have to cede Bessarabia; and the Rumans would then form a national state with a population of twelve million.

In the southern reaches of the peninsula, on the islands of the Ægean, and on the Ægean coasts of Macedonia, Thrace, and Asia Minor, dwells a fourth nation, no less mixed in **4. The** origin and even more boastful of its traditions. The **Greeks or** modern Greeks may have in their veins very little of **Hellenes** the blood of the historic Spartans and Athenians; they may in great part be descended from Slavic immigrants of the eighth century, or even from the slaves of the ancient Greeks; their national costume, with its red cap, flowing white sleeves, white kilt, velvet jacket, white hose, and pointed red shoes, was unquestionably borrowed from Albanian tribesmen rather than from Periclean Athens. And there are considerable settlements of Albanians and Rumans in the heart of the Greek peninsula itself. Nevertheless, the Greeks consider themselves the heirs of ancient Hellas; they call themselves Hellenes; and a more passionate national patriotism than theirs does not exist. Nine millions of these new Hellenes, many of them wealthy merchants, learned scholars, and able statesmen, cherish the dream of a new and greater Hellas, including the Asiatic coasts of the Ægean, and the islands, as well as the Greek peninsula. This is what Hellenic patriots have called their "Great Idea."

Besides these four major nationalities and the Ottoman Turks, there are scattered throughout the Balkan peninsula three other **5. The Albanians** peculiar peoples. There are first of all the Albanian mountaineers, already referred to in connection with the Greeks. The origin of this proud and warlike race is a matter of conjecture; their language is a composite of Rumanian, Turkish, Greek, Slavic, and, possibly, ancient Illyrian. They believe themselves to be one nation — the *Skipitari* ("eagle's brood"). Several facts militate against the success of an independent Albanian state, however. The dialect of the northern or *Gheg* tribes is all but unintelligible to the southern Albanian or *Tosc*. The majority are Mohammedans in religion, but the strong Greek Orthodox and Roman Catholic minorities cannot be disregarded. Moreover, there are Greeks, Serbs, and Bulgars in the district known as Albania; and there are many thousands of Albanians in Greece and in Serbia and scattered settlements even in Italy.

The Gypsy tinkers who wander about the peninsula, and the **Gypsies and Jews** numerous Jewish money-lenders and shop-keepers complicate the situation but have no great ambition to become independent Balkan nations.

Among the Serbs, Hellenes, Bulgars, and Rumans, the senti- **Nationalist Propaganda** ment of national patriotism exerted a most powerful influence in the nineteenth century. In every case the nationalist propaganda worked along three channels.

First of all, each nation must have its own language and litera- ture. To this end Greek scholars revived the study of classical **1. Literary** Greek, and, as a result of their labors, the modern literary language of Greece resembles more or less closely the language of Demosthenes. Similarly, patriotic Serbs in the early part of the nineteenth century began to write in the Serb language, to prepare the first Serb grammar and dictionary. With equal pride, Rumanian authors began to eliminate Slavic words from their vocabulary, and, by conforming their language more closely to Latin, sought to emphasize their supposed Roman ancestry. Finally, there was a Bulgarian literary revival, which in 1835 produced the first Bulgarian grammar. Each literary revival implied also the establishment of schools for cultivation of the national language and for the inculcation of patriotism.

Hardly less important was the ecclesiastical aspect of nationalism. So long as all the Balkan peoples were simply downtrodden Christian *rayahs*, they might properly be rep- **2. Ecclesiastical** resented at Constantinople by the Greek Orthodox patriarch. When the Serbs, Rumans, and Bulgars awoke to national consciousness, however, they could no longer bear to be called Greek Christians, or tolerate the authority of the Greek patriarch, — especially since the Greeks utilized this ecclesiastical advantage as a means of disseminating Hellenic speech and ideals. Consequently each nation insisted that its church should be autocephalous, — that is, while remaining Orthodox in doctrine and ritual, each national church should administer its affairs and appoint its clergy independently. During the course of the nineteenth century the Serb and Rumanian churches achieved autonomy and were recognized as autocephalous branches of the Orthodox Church in 1878. Even the Greeks nationalized their church, as a result of the patriarch's unsympathetic attitude toward the Greek revolt of 1821–1829. Among the Bulgars the results of the movement were unique: by decree of the sultan (1870) the Bulgarian church was placed under an exarch, whom the indignant patriarch of Constantinople for more than forty years has refused to recognize. Thus the Orthodox Church in the Balkan countries, just as in Russia, was subordinated to the national state.

The most intense activity of nationalist agitators was, however, neither educational nor ecclesiastical, but political. In their political propaganda, the nationalists found in **3. Political** history a veritable arsenal of potent arguments. Nothing would so fire the patriotism of the Greeks as an appeal to the glorious past: remembering how a handful of Athenians had once repelled the Persian hordes, or how Hellenism had

reigned triumphant in the never-to-be-forgotten splendor of the
Byzantine Empire, — remembering this, how could modern
Hellenes remain under the ignominious yoke of Turkish
despotism?

Likewise the Serbs fed their patriotism on glorious traditions.
Back in the fourteenth century a great Serb monarch, Stephen
Dushan by name, had ruled a mighty empire, including Albania,
Macedonia, Epirus, and Herzegovina, as well as Serbia proper.
Why should not the nineteenth century witness a reawakening
of the Serbs, a restoration of Stephen Dushan's Serbian empire?
Not a whit less proud were the Bulgars, who boastingly referred
to the prowess of the Bulgar Tsar Simeon (893–927) and the
puissance of Ivan Asên II (1218–1241). Nor were the Ruman
inhabitants of Moldavia and Wallachia to be outdone. They,
too, had once been a powerful nation, and under Stephen the
Great of Moldavia (1457–1504) had warred mightily against the
Turks.

Firm in the belief that what their ancestors had done, they
too could accomplish, the patriots of each nationality clamored
first of all for emancipation from the Turk, and secondarily for
the aggrandizement of the nation. Some less enthusiastic
peasants and business men might not always thrill with the same
lofty ambition; nevertheless, the peasant was only too ready to
fight against the hated Turkish oppressors who imposed heavy
taxes; and the business man was persuaded that industry would
flourish better under an enlightened national government than
under the unprogressive rule of the half-civilized Turk. The
new nations would imitate their fellow-Europeans, building railways, safeguarding commerce from brigandage, and protecting
rather than scorning the enterprising industrial capitalist.

THE GREAT POWERS AND THE DISMEMBERMENT OF TURKEY IN EUROPE, 1815–1886

The nationalist agitation among the Balkan peoples could
have but one issue, — the dismemberment of Turkey in Europe.
It was a painful process, the amputation of member after member of the feeble Ottoman Empire, and more than a century was
required for its completion.

We may begin with the revolt of the Serbs.   A small section
of the Serb nation, the indomitable mountaineers of Montenegro,
had been at war with the Turks for over four centuries; their bishop-princes at Cetigne had long been   1. Inde-
practically independent, when in 1799 a grudging   pendence of
recognition of Montenegrin independence was wrung   gro, 1799
from the Turks.   Five years later their brother-Serbs in Serbia rose
in rebellion, with Karageorge ("Black George") as their leader,
expelled the Turks, and defied the sultan.   After a brief period
of triumph, "Black George" himself suffered defeat at   2. Autonomy
the hands of the Turks, and Serbia was reconquered   of Serbia,
for the sultan.   Again the Serbs rebelled in 1815, this   1830
time with Milosh Obrenovich at their head.   Although the sultan was allowed to keep Turkish garrisons in the Serbian fortresses, Serbia obtained the formal grant of self-government with
Milosh as hereditary prince (1830).

Close upon the heels of Milosh's insurrection followed the
Greek Revolt (1821–1829).   How the Greeks gallantly fought
for their independence; how their revolt was regarded
by Christians as a crusade, by Liberals as a war for   3. The
liberty, by patriots as a war for nationalism, by   Greek Re-
poets as the rejuvenescence of Athens; how Russia,   the Inde-
France, and Great Britain joined in the war against   Hellenic
Turkey,—all this we have told in another place.[1]   Kingdom,
Turkey was, of course, defeated and the victorious   1832
Greeks established a republican form of government.   The
Great Powers, however, could hardly sanction republicanism and
nationalism in the case of the Greeks, while at the same time
liberalism and nationalism were under the ban in Europe.   So
the disappointed Greeks had to give up their republic and reluctantly consent to be governed by a Bavarian prince, who was
crowned as King Otto I of Greece in 1833.   The German advisers
and German soldiers whom King Otto imported to carry out
his thoroughly German and despotic ideas of government were
only a shade less unpopular with the Greek people than the
Turks had been.   Worse still, the Hellenes of Crete, of Chios,
Lemnos, and Lesbos, of Asia Minor, of the Ionian Islands, of the
northern Ægean, of Epirus, and of Thessaly were left entirely

[1] See above, pp. 47 ff.

outside of the new kingdom. The Greek peninsula south of a line drawn from the gulf of Arta to the gulf of Lamia, and the Cyclades, — this was but the mutilated torso of Hellas. Only one thing had been gained — the emancipation of a small part of Greece from the Turks.

The war (1821–1829) which produced the Greek kingdom had another important result. It strengthened the influence of

4. Autonomy of the Rumanian Provinces under Russian Protection, 1829

Russia in the Near East. The treaty which Russian armies forced the Porte to sign at Adrianople (1829) not only recognized Greek independence but confirmed the already existing autonomy of the Moldavian and Wallachian principalities (the provinces which were one day to be united as Rumania) under a thinly veiled Russian protectorate. In addition, Georgia and other provinces of the Caucasus were surrendered to Russia, and the exclusive jurisdiction of Russian consuls over Russian traders in Turkey was recognized. The treaty of Adrianople was a triumph for Russia.

The steady advance of Russian influence in the Balkan peninsula, of which the treaty of Adrianople was but one instance,

The Relentless Advance of Russia in the Near East

was the result of persistent and patient efforts on the part of the Russian tsars. Ever since the days of Peter the Great (1689–1725), the rulers of Russia had striven to obtain a "window on the Mediterranean." First they had won a foothold at Azov; then little by little the northern coast of the Black Sea had fallen into their power; and by 1829 the relentless Russian advance was threatening Armenia at the eastern extremity of the Black Sea, and Moldavia at the western end. Moldavia and Wallachia had become practically Russian protectorates, and might at any moment be annexed to the ever-growing empire. Throughout the entire Balkan peninsula Russian agents were at work inculcating the idea that in the tsar of Russia the struggling Balkan nationalities possessed a powerful friend, an ally against the Turk. The Slavic Serbs and Bulgars were taught to regard Russia as the great Slavic nation, the "big brother" of the Slavic nations in the Balkans. To Greeks, Serbs, Bulgars, and Rumans alike, the tsar was represented as the protector of the Orthodox Church, and the Russian Christians as co-religionists of the Balkan Christians. The tendency was not difficult to perceive : the Russian tsars aimed to take the sultan's place in the Balkan peninsula. Whether the Balkan nations should be formally incorporated into the Russian Empire, or whether they should be bound to Russia only by gratitude, by community of religion, of race, and of interests, — in either case Russia would dominate the Near East.

Until 1829 the Russian policy had been to dismember the Ottoman Empire and to dominate those provinces which could not immediately be annexed by the tsar. In the pursuit of this ambition, the Russian government had cleverly obtained the support first of one Power, then of another. Back in the eighteenth century the Austrian Habsburgs had repeatedly made common cause with Russia, believing Turkey to be the enemy of both; and Catherine II had actually proposed to Joseph II that Russia and Austria should divide Turkey in Europe between them, as they had partitioned Poland. The wars of the French Revolution prevented the fruition of this bold plot. Then, in the Napoleonic Era, the tsar had interviewed the Corsican at Tilsit (1807), and the two emperors had agreed to divide the world between them, Napoleon taking the West, and Alexander taking most of Turkey and India. Instead of sharing the world, however, the two sovereigns speedily came to blows; and when in 1812 Russia was able to annex Bessarabia, Great Britain rather than Napoleon was to be thanked. Still later, when the Greek Revolt broke out, France and Great Britain joined with Russia to crush Turkey, although Russia, rather than either France or Great Britain, was the chief gainer by the war.

Shortly after the Greek Revolt, Tsar Nicholas I adopted an entirely new policy. Instead of the arch-enemy, he became the friend of the sultan. This change of front did not mean that Nicholas I had abandoned his ambition. He had simply decided that more was to be gained by dominating than by destroying the Ottoman Empire; he would support the Turkish sultan, and the sultan would become the protégé of Russia. The idea was a shrewd one, but in some way or other it failed to work out to the tsar's satisfaction, and in disgust he reverted to the older plan of dismembering the Ottoman Empire. In 1844, therefore, Nicholas went to London hoping to persuade the

British government that Turkey, "the sick man of Europe," could not live much longer; hence Great Britain should seize Crete and Egypt while Russia wrested the Balkan provinces from the feeble grasp of the dying Ottoman Empire. To be sure, the Balkan provinces would not be annexed by Russia: they would become autonomous under Russian "protection," so the tsar ingenuously promised; but the British ministry remained unconvinced and would have nothing to do with the scheme.

Despite this rebuff, Tsar Nicholas held fast to his determination and awaited a favorable opportunity to fall upon Turkey and drive the Ottomans out of Europe. He did not **The Crimean War (1854–1856) a Temporary Check to Russian Advance** have long to wait. In 1850 a quarrel between Roman Catholic and Orthodox monks about the Holy Places in Palestine afforded an excuse for asserting that all Orthodox Christians in the Ottoman Empire had been placed under Russian protection by the treaty of Kuchuk Kainarji (1774). How France and Great Britain, alarmed by Russia's aggressiveness, came to the support of the sultan and crushed Russia in the Crimean War (1854–1856), we have already made clear in a previous chapter.[1] As a result of the war, the treaty of Paris (1856) denied the right of Russia to protect Christians in Turkey, freed Moldavia and Wallachia from Russian interference, restored a strip of Bessarabia from Russia to Moldavia, established free navigation of the Danube, and neutralized the Black Sea.

By freeing them from Russian domination, the treaty of Paris enabled the Rumans in the two quasi-independent principalities of Moldavia and Wallachia to realize their **5. The Union of Moldavia and Wallachia as Rumania, 1862** long-cherished dream of a united national existence. At first the Powers of Europe sought to thwart the ambition of the Ruman nation, as they had disappointed the Greeks in 1832. A European diplomatic congress in 1858 resolved to prevent the unification of the two Ruman states, although no one could doubt that the Rumans themselves desired to form a united nation. Nothing daunted, the separate representative assemblies of both principalities proceeded to choose Alexander John Cuza simultane-

[1] See above, pp. 162 f.

ously to be prince of Moldavia and of Wallachia. The grudging consent of the Powers to this step was gained two years later, and in 1862 the union of the two states was completed by the establishment of a united ministry and a united assembly. Rumania was united and all but completely independent of Turkey.

For ten years after the Crimean War, Great Britain essayed to perform the rôle formerly played by Russia, the rôle of presiding over the destinies of the Balkan Christians. Great Britain, rather than Russia, induced the sultan to withdraw his garrisons from the Serbian fortresses (1867). It was to Great Britain that the Greeks turned in 1862, after deposing their unpopular King Otto; the British government practically chose King Otto's successor, Prince William George of Schleswig-Holstein-Sonderburg-Glücksburg, who became George I, "King of the Hellenes" (1863). The popularity of Great Britain in Greece was still further enhanced when the British government handed over the Ionian Islands [1] to the Greek kingdom.

Paramount Influence of Great Britain in the Balkans, 1855–1865

In spite of the seeming dominance of Great Britain in the Balkans, the Russian Tsar Alexander II (1855–1881) had no intention of remaining permanently in the background. As soon as Russia had recovered from the Crimean War, Alexander began once more to interfere in the affairs of the Ottoman Empire, with a view to regaining what his country had lost in that war — prestige, a commanding influence in the Balkans, and a slice of Bessarabia. In 1865 the tsar gave encouragement to rebellion in Crete. In 1870 he helped the Bulgars to obtain ecclesiastical independence. In 1871 — in the midst of the Franco-German War — he secured, with the aid of Bismarck, the right to refortify Sebastopol and to maintain a Russian fleet on the Black Sea. Finally, he decided to make war on Turkey.

Renewal of Russian Interference in the Balkans, 1865–1878

It was easy for the tsar to find justification for war. In 1875–1876 popular uprisings in Bosnia, Herzegovina, and Bulgaria had been cruelly suppressed by the Turks, and many native Christians had been butchered by fanatical Moslems. These "Bulgarian atrocities" excited tremendous foreign indignation against Turkey not only

Disorders in the Ottoman Empire, 1875–1876

[1] The Ionian Islands had been a republic under British protection since 1815.

in Russia but also in western Europe. Little Montenegro and Serbia actually took up arms in support of their suffering fellow-Christians. The Ottoman government at Constantinople seemed to be drifting rapidly toward dissolution. Its treasury was bankrupt, its administration paralyzed. Within a single year two sultans were deposed, and a usurper mounted the throne in the person of Abdul Hamid II (1876-1909).

In the desperate crisis of his country's affairs, Abdul Hamid promulgated a liberal constitution (1876) for the whole Ottoman Empire, vainly imagining that a brave pretense of liberalism on his part, however insincere, would satisfy Europe and prevent the Powers from intervening to protect the Balkan Christians. The tsar, however, as the special protector of Orthodox Christians, would not be so easily outwitted, and on 24 April, 1877, Russia declared war on the sultan.

Russo-Turkish War, 1877-1878

Immediately a Russian army invaded Turkey from the north, crossing the Danube in June, 1877. To its surprise, the invading army encountered fierce and effective resistance at the hands of the Turks, ensconced in the stronghold of Plevna, in Bulgaria, just south of the Danube. Twice in July, and again in September, the Russian infantry was hurled back by Plevna's Turkish defenders. Finally, however, after the Russians had settled down to besiege the place, the brave Turkish commander, Osman Pasha, seeing his men slowly starving to death, attempted a desperate sortie. The attempt failed and Osman surrendered with 40,000 men. In January, 1878, a second overwhelming defeat befell the Turks, and another Turkish army of some 36,000 men was forced to surrender. Serbian and Montenegrin troops now boldly advanced into Turkish territory; Bulgars enlisted in the Russian army; Rumanian troops had already given invaluable aid to the Russians. The Turkish soldiers had fought gallantly, their Krupp cannon had performed good service, but faulty generalship had done its fatal work and nothing could now check the triumphant Russian advance. Adrianople fell on 16 January; and the Russian army marched on towards Constantinople. In a panic of fear the Turks sued for peace.

The treaty of San Stefano, concluded 3 March, 1878, was a sad confession of Turkey's humiliation and at the same time a triumph for the Slavs. The sultan was to recognize the complete independence of Serbia, Montenegro, and Rumania, with increased territories; an autonomous tributary principality of Bulgaria was to be created, bounded by the Danube, the Black Sea, the Ægean, and Albania; sweeping reforms were to be carried out in Bosnia and Herzegovina; the straits (Dardanelles and Bosphorus) were to be open at all times to peaceful commerce; and the Turkish forts along the Danube were to be destroyed. These provisions, so favorable to the Balkan Slavs — Bulgars and Serbs, — would make Bulgaria and Serbia forever the grateful debtors of their "big brother" Russia. For his own share in the spoils, the tsar was to receive part of Armenia, a large war indemnity, and a strip of the Dobrudja (which he planned to exchange with Rumania for the valuable territory of Bessarabia).

Turkish Defeat and Russian Success: the Treaty of San Stefano, 1878

The satisfaction with which the Tsar Alexander II regarded the terms of San Stefano was equaled only by the wrath of the Austro-Hungarian and British governments. Lord Beaconsfield (Benjamin Disraeli), as the head of the British cabinet and an advocate of a vigorous foreign policy, was not at all inclined to sit tamely by while Russia made herself supreme in the Near East. Even more emphatic was the Habsburg emperor, Francis Joseph, whose dreams of Austro-Hungarian expansion in the Balkans would not allow either the creation of strong Balkan states or the extension of Russian influence in the Balkan peninsula. The war indemnity, moreover, could not be paid by the bankrupt sultan for years to come, and would give Russian officials a standing excuse for interfering with the Ottoman government. Determined to prevent such a catastrophe, the Austro-Hungarian ministry asserted that if any alteration were to be made in the Balkan situation, it would involve a revision of the terms of the treaty of Paris (1856), and could only be accomplished by the consent of those Powers — Great Britain, Germany, Austria-Hungary, France, Italy, Russia, and Turkey — which had sworn to uphold the treaty of Paris. Foreseeing that this contention would allow him to take a hand in the Balkan question, Lord Beaconsfield heartily indorsed it. Bis-

Opposition of Great Britain and Austria-Hungary to the Terms of San Stefano

marck, conscious that Germany could lose nothing and might at
least gain prestige, gave Austria-Hungary and Great Britain his
support in demanding that the treaty of San Stefano should be

The Congress of
Berlin, 1878

submitted for ratification to the Powers which had
signed the treaty of Paris.   The tsar, of course, feared
that a congress of jealous diplomats would revise the
treaty of San Stefano in such manner as to rob him of the fruits
of victory.   Lord Beaconsfield, however, by threatening Russia
with war, induced the unwilling tsar to submit the whole question
to the congress, which was held in Berlin during the summer of
1878.

The diplomats who assembled at Berlin did not attempt to
bring about a just, reasonable, and permanent settle-

Revision of
the Treaty
of San Ste-
fano in the
Interests
of Austria-
Hungary
and Great
Britain

ment of the Near Eastern Question.   They were too
patriotic for that.   Each was too intensely concerned
in the advantage which his own country might derive
from the situation.   They revised the treaty of San
Stefano, not in the interests of justice and equity,
but in the interests of Austria-Hungary and Great
Britain.   Therefore, the treaty of Berlin, upon which
the congress agreed, 13 July, 1878, was little more than an arbi-

The Treaty
of Berlin,
1878

trary and elaborate compromise between the conflicting interests of Russia, Austria-Hungary, and
Great Britain.

Russia was permitted to regain the Rumanian strip of Bessarabia
north of the Danube delta and east of the Pruth, which she

1. Russian
Gains

had lost by the Crimean War, Rumania being forced
to console herself for the loss of Bessarabia by annexing most of the Dobrudja, a barren region south of the Danube
delta.   Russia also retained Ardahan, Kars, and Batoum, the
Armenian districts at the eastern extremity of the Black Sea
allotted to the tsar by the treaty of San Stefano.

In order to offset Russia's gains, Austria-Hungary was given
the right to occupy and administer the Turkish provinces of

2. Austro-
Hungarian
Occupation
of Bosnia-
Herzego-
vina, 1878

Bosnia and Herzegovina, and to keep garrisons and
maintain military and commercial roads in the adjacent Turkish sanjak of Novi-Bazar.   Montenegro,
moreover, was compelled to concede extensive commercial privileges to Austria-Hungary.

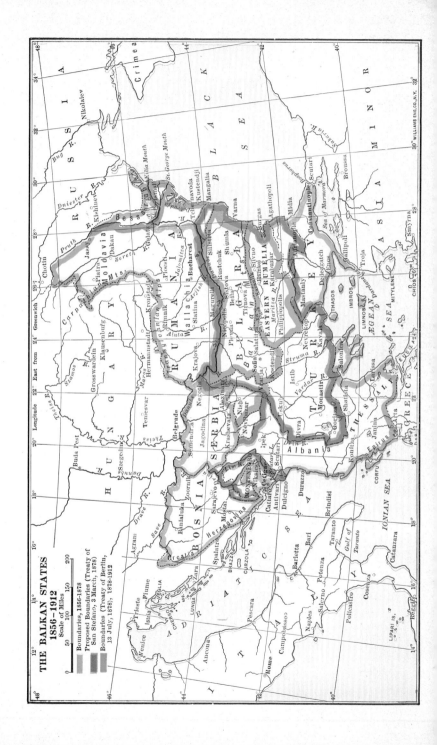

Great Britain's share in the spoils was allotted by a separate Anglo-Turkish Convention (4 June, 1878), which practically formed a part of the Berlin agreement. Russia was not to be allowed further aggrandizement in Asia Minor : to this Great Britain pledged herself. On the other hand, the sultan solemnly promised to introduce radical reforms in the government of his Christian subjects ; and as a pledge of his good intentions he permitted Great Britain to hold and administer the island of Cyprus.

3. British Occupation of Cyprus, 1878

In their treatment of the Balkan nationalities, the Berlin diplomats were neither generous nor far-sighted. The "Big Bulgaria" for which the tsar had stipulated in the negotiations at San Stefano, was divided by the Berlin treaty into three separate parts. The northern portion became the autonomous Christian principality of Bulgaria paying tribute to the sultan. The middle portion — the province of Eastern Rumelia — was left "under the direct military and political control of His Imperial Majesty the Sultan, under conditions of administrative autonomy," with special provision for the appointment of a Christian governor. The third part, comprising Macedonia and the vilayet of Adrianople, was again put fully under Turkish rule. This cruel blow to the national ambition of the Bulgars was delivered because Austria-Hungary feared that a strong Bulgarian state, friendly to Russia, might block the path of future Habsburg expansion toward the Ægean.

4. Autonomy of Bulgaria (1878) : Separation of Bulgaria, Eastern Rumelia, and Macedonia

As in the treaty of San Stefano, Rumania, Serbia, and Montenegro were recognized as completely independent states, with increased territories. But by the treaty of Berlin these states were burdened with a portion of the sultan's debts. Rumania was offended by the Russian annexation of Bessarabia ; Serbia was alarmed at the extension of the Austro-Hungarian protectorate over the Serbs of Bosnia and Herzegovina ; Montenegro, although happy to gain the port of Antivari on the Adriatic, was irritated by the provisions which made Antivari, so far as all naval purposes were concerned, practically an Austrian port.

5. Independence of Rumania, Serbia, and Montenegro, 1878

Greece alone of the Balkan nations profited by the revision of the treaty of San Stefano. By that treaty Greece had been prom-

ised nothing, but as a result of the Congress of Berlin she obtained a considerable extension of territory. The new
boundary was not definitely fixed, however, until 1881,
when Thessaly was formally annexed to the Hellenic
kingdom.

6. Cession of Thessaly to Greece, 1881

The treaty of Berlin left Turkey still in Europe, with a strip
of territory including Constantinople, Adrianople, Rumelia
(Macedonia), Eastern Rumelia, Albania, Epirus, and
Novi-Bazar. The tottering empire of the Turk was
to be propped up a little longer by British diplomacy,
or, if need be, by British arms. The Christians in
Macedonia were to be left in the hands of the sultan, even after
the Bulgarian atrocities of 1876 had shown what kind of treatment the Christian subjects of the sultan might expect. To save
themselves from reproach on this score, the diplomats at Berlin
inserted in the treaty of 1878 various clauses which would appear
to reform the Turkish administration and to safeguard the Christian *rayahs* against Mohammedan oppression. But reforms on
paper were not reforms in practice, and the subsequent history
of Turkey in Europe was no credit to the statesmanship of the
men who designed the treaty of Berlin.

7. Paper Reforms for Turkey, 1878

Hardly seven years elapsed from the signing of the treaty of
Berlin until the treaty was flagrantly violated. The Bulgars in
Eastern Rumelia, who had never acquiesced in the
arbitrary separation of Eastern Rumelia from the
principality of Bulgaria, effected the bloodless revolution of Philippopolis (18 September, 1885), by which
the two Bulgar states were united. Prince Alexander of
Bulgaria was joyously hailed in Philippopolis as the
sovereign of united Bulgaria. None of the Powers
lifted a finger to punish the bold Bulgarian maneuver.
Only little Serbia, jealous of her sister state, declared
war; but the Bulgars proved themselves better fighters,
and peace was restored the following year.

Subsequent Modification of the Berlin Settlement

1. Incorporation of Eastern Rumelia into the Principality of Bulgaria, 1885

Some twenty-three years later, in 1908, the treaty of Berlin
was still further disregarded, when the Bulgarian
prince, repudiating the sultan's suzerainty, declared
himself an independent king (*tsar*). At the same
time (1908) Austria-Hungary formally annexed the

2. Creation of the Kingdom of Bulgaria, 1908

Turkish provinces of Bosnia and Herzegovina, in which by the treaty of Berlin the Dual Monarchy had been authorized merely to carry out certain "reforms." Finally, in 1912–1913, the Balkan nations, defying European diplomacy, divided up Macedonia, the sanjak of Novi-Bazar, and Epirus; an autonomous principality of Albania was created; and Turkey in Europe was restricted to a narrow zone about Constantinople and Adrianople. These later steps in the dismemberment of European Turkey will shortly receive closer attention; but for the present let us turn aside for a moment to see how the sultan lost control of Crete and of his provinces in Africa.

3. Annexation of Bosnia and Herzegovina to Austria-Hungary, 1908

4. Almost Complete Disappearance of European Turkey, 1913

THE AUTONOMY OF CRETE AND LOSS OF THE TURKISH POSSESSIONS IN AFRICA

At the opening of the nineteenth century the island of Crete was a Turkish vilayet or province. Two circumstances then embittered the lot of the island. First of all, the Orthodox Christians who constituted a majority of the population were almost continually oppressed by their Mohammedan rulers and were periodically engaged in bloody conflict with their Mohammedan neighbors. Secondly, while Crete was a separate Turkish vilayet, the Cretans, both Mohammedan and Christian, spoke the Greek language and were bound to Greece by a sense of common nationality. From these two circumstances resulted a long series of disastrous insurrections and massacres. Oddly enough, the Powers of Europe throughout the century persistently added to the confusion by coming to the aid of the Mohammedans as against the Christians, and by supporting the sultan's sovereignty as against the nationalist aspirations of the Cretan Hellenes.

Crete in 1800

When in 1821 the Greeks on the mainland revolted, the Greeks in Crete joined in the insurrection. But at the end of the war, the Powers decided that Crete should be left in the Ottoman Empire, instead of being joined to the new kingdom of Greece.[1]

[1] Crete was placed under the administration of Mehemet Ali, Turkish viceroy of Egypt. See below, p. 512.

For a time Crete was quiet, under the beneficent rule of an exceptionally statesmanlike governor, Mustafa Pasha (1832–1852),

Repeated Cretan Revolts against Turkey, 1821–1897 but he had hardly left the island when Crete again fell into anarchy. The Congress of Berlin (1878) vainly attempted to settle the question by establishing in Crete a sort of constitutional government, which had been promised by the sultan in the "Organic Statute" of 1868. The sultan, however, intended nothing of the kind, and in 1889 he placed Crete again under the despotic rule of a Mohammedan *vali* or governor. In 1896 a new insurrection compelled the sultan to promise reforms, but within a few

Græco-Turkish War, 1897 months the insincerity of his promises became apparent, and again civil war was the order of the day. This time the kingdom of Greece intervened, sending warships and an army to assist the Cretan insurgents (1897). On the mainland the Greeks were defeated by the Turks and compelled to abandon their enterprise. And the Powers, stubbornly and blindly, as ever, stepped in to declare that Greece must not annex Crete, that Crete must remain under the sultan's suzerainty. The Powers were willing, however, that the Cretans

The Autonomy of Crete, 1897 should have self-government in local affairs, and proclaimed the autonomy of Crete (December, 1897). Not yet were the Cretans satisfied. In 1905 insurgents led by Eleutherios Venezelos declared the union of their island with Greece, and the Cretan assembly assented, but the Powers again intervened to uphold the sultan's sovereignty. This time they conceded that, while Crete should remain an autonomous part of the Ottoman Empire, the king of Greece should appoint a high commissioner (1906) to rule the island, and Greek officers should drill the Cretan *gendarmerie* and militia. The desire of the Cretans for union with Greece was now irresistibly aroused. In 1908 they again voted union; but the question was left unsettled until in 1912 Cretan deputies were

Union of Crete with Greece, 1913 admitted to the parliament at Athens, the Turkish flag at Canea (in Crete) was hauled down, and by the treaty of London, 30 May, 1913, Turkey renounced all sovereignty over Crete. The national aspirations of Crete were at last satisfied when in December, 1913, Constantine, king of the Hellenes, took possession of the island at Canea and solemnly hoisted the flag of the Hellenic kingdom.

The first of the African provinces to be lost by Turkey was Egypt. The authority of the sultan's viceroy or "pasha" in Egypt had repeatedly been set at naught during the eight- Egypt in eenth century by the "beys" or commanders of the 1800 unruly soldiers called Mamelukes. Even more alarming than Mameluke conspiracies had been the invasion of Egypt in 1798 by Napoleon. To be sure, the French general insisted that he was merely fighting against the Mamelukes in order that the power of the sultan might be more firmly established; but the sultan sorely mistrusted Napoleon's motives, declared war, and, with the aid of the British forces, drove the French out of Egypt. The real danger was, however, neither from the Mamelukes nor from the French, but from an Albanian adventurer, Mehemet Ali by name. From his birthplace at Kavala, on the northern coast of the Ægean Sea, Mehemet Ali [1] first voyaged to Mehemet Egypt with a regiment of Albanian tribesmen who had Ali Pasha volunteered to fight for the sultan against Napoleon. of Egypt, 1805 Amidst the anarchy that followed the expulsion of the French, Mehemet Ali by lending the aid of his redoubtable Albanian warriors first to one faction and then to another, soon became the controlling factor in Egyptian politics, and induced the sultan to appoint him as " pasha " (1805). The Mamelukes who disputed his power were outwitted, defeated, and ruthlessly massacred. Mehemet Ali was as shrewd as he was unscrupulous and bold. During the first two decades of his rule as governor, he consolidated his power, reorganized his army on European lines with the aid of French military officers, created a navy, filled his treasury with tax receipts and revenues from governmental commercial monopolies, developed the cotton industry, and conquered Upper Egypt and the Egyptian Sudan. Then he was ready to extend his power abroad. The opportunity came in 1821, when the Greek revolt broke out, and the panic-stricken sultan called on his vassal, Mehemet Ali, for aid, promising as reward the " pashaliks " or governorships of Morea (part of the Greek mainland) and Syria. In response to the sultan's appeal, Mehemet sent his son Ibrahim with a splendid army to subjugate the Greek insurgents. As we have already seen, the Powers of Europe came to the aid of the Greeks, and Mehemet

[1] 1769–1849.

won neither Morea nor Syria, but only the island of Crete.
Between the Pasha Mehemet Ali, who was sorely disappointed
to be cheated of Syria, and the Sultan Mahmud II, who grew

Hostilities daily more jealous of his powerful and ambitious
between vassal, relations strained to the breaking point. In
Mehemet
Ali and the 1831 Mehemet Ali ambitiously sent his son Ibrahim
Sultan, with an Egyptian army to invade Syria. Angrily the
1831–1841 sultan declared Mehemet a rebel. In the war that ensued the well-trained Egyptian soldiers carried everything before
them and triumphantly marched on Constantinople. Despairing, the sultan accepted the aid of a Russian fleet and Russian
troops to defend his capital from the Egyptian army. Intricate
negotiations ensued between the sultan, the pasha, and Russia,
France, and Great Britain, with the result that Mehemet Ali
gained the governorship of Syria, Damascus, and Aleppo, together with the district of Adana (1833).

For a brief period the pasha of Egypt, while paying regular
tribute to the sultan was practically monarch of a vast empire,
                stretching from the upper reaches of the Nile river to
Mehemet
Ali " Hered- Antioch and Adana. But the Syrians presently rose
itary Gov- in revolt and in 1839 the sultan again attempted to
ernor " of
Egypt, 1841 crush the proud pasha. Again Mehemet's armies were
                victorious, and once more Russia interfered, this time
in concert with Great Britain on behalf of the sultan. Mehemet was now forced to relinquish Syria, Damascus, Aleppo,
and Adana. As compensation he was given the pashalik
of Egypt as an hereditary possession (1841). The dynasty of
Mehemet Ali thus became hereditary rulers of Egypt, virtually
independent, although paying tribute to the Ottoman sultan.
The defection of Egypt was accomplished.

Twenty-five years later (1866) a descendant of Mehemet Ali
" Khedive assumed the title of *khedive*, which was borne by the
of Egypt," ruler of Egypt until 1914, when he adopted the title
1866
                of sultan and was recognized by Great Britain and
France as absolutely independent of Turkey.[1]

Meanwhile Algeria, farther west on the African coast, was
passing under the control of France. Turkish power had never

---

[1] The history of Egypt from 1866 to 1914 will be taken up in the chapter on the
Partition of Africa. See below, pp. 626 ff.

been very secure in Algeria, for in the seventeenth century the Turkish pasha had been supplanted by a "dey" chosen by the lawless Barbary pirates of the Algerian coastland, who preyed on European commerce in the Mediterranean and made a regular business of capturing Christian voyagers for ransom or for slavery. Somewhat later, as piracy declined, the dey himself came under the domination of a military society — the janissaries — who elected and deposed him at will. Still Algeria was nominally a part of the Ottoman Empire.

Algeria under the Deys

In 1830 a French expedition was dispatched against Algiers to punish the insolence of the dey, who had not only fired on a French vessel in the harbor of Algiers, but had also struck the French consul in the face, thus adding insult to injury. French troops conquered Algiers, deported the dey, and expelled the janissaries. For the next few years the French were uncertain whether to conquer the whole country, or to withdraw altogether; they compromised by leaving garrisons in a few Algerian seaports and thus putting an end to the nuisance of Barbary piracy. When the French government finally decided to conquer Algeria, they were confronted by a tireless and formidable enemy in the person of Abd-el-Kader, a Mohammedan potentate who boasted the title of "amir" and commanded the loyalty of the restless Arab tribesmen in the interior. With ten thousand regular soldiers and five times as many untrained but courageous Arab horsemen, the amir in 1839 declared a holy war against the Christians. Once Abd-el-Kader was defeated and driven into Morocco but again he returned, eloquent and fearless as ever, to harass the French armies. He was fighting against fate, however; and at last in 1847 the gallant warrior surrendered. Algeria was a colony of France.[1]

French Conquest of Algeria, 1830–1847

The French next turned towards Tunis (or Tunisia), the province immediately east of Algeria, including the site of ancient Carthage. Tunis, like Algeria, had been conquered by the Turks in the sixteenth century, and had subsequently been ruled by leaders of the janissaries. In 1705 a Cretan adventurer, Hussein ben Ali, was set up by the troops

Tunis under the Beys

---

[1] For the subsequent history of Algeria, see below, pp. 629, 631.

as ruler of Tunis.   While Hussein remained nominally subject to
the sultan, he became practically an independent prince with
the title of " bey " of Tunis, and his dynasty still rules in name
French   if not in fact.   The French became real masters of
Occupation   Tunis in 1881 when a French army marched eastward
of Tunis,   from the Algerian frontier to the Tunisian capital, forc-
1881
              ing the terrified bey to accept the "protectorate" of
France, that is, to allow French officials to control his government.   In vain the indignant sultan might protest that Tunis
was by right a part of the Ottoman Empire; his protests were
ignored by the French government and Tunis remained a protectorate of France.

To the Ottoman Empire in Africa there remained thereafter
only the vilayets of Tripoli and Cyrenaica.[1]   Tripoli, including
Tripoli   Cyrenaica, which had been conquered by the Turks
Trans-   in the sixteenth century, was governed from 1714 to
formed into   1835 by hereditary princes, who, though in reality
the Italian
Colony of   independent, still called themselves pashas of the sul-
Libya, 1911– tan and paid tribute to the Ottoman government.   The
1912
              power of the Tripolitan pashas received a serious blow
early in the nineteenth century when the United States made
war on Tripoli to put an end to Tripolitan piracy.   Weakened by
the war with the United States, and by civil war as well, Tripoli
in 1835 was again brought under the direct control of the Ottoman government.   In 1875 the eastern part of Tripoli was
erected into a separate province, the vilayet of Cyrenaica.   A
quarrel between Turkey and Italy, however, resulted in the
annexation of both vilayets by a decree of the Italian government, 5 November, 1911, confirmed by the treaty of Ouchy,
18 October, 1912, which terminated the Turco-Italian War.
Tripoli and Cyrenaica became the Italian colony of Libya.
Obedient to the command of the Koran, which forbade the
cession to infidels of territory belonging to the *khalif*, the
Porte refused formally to recognize the annexation; but actually
the sultan retained in Tripoli only his religious authority.   The
dismemberment of Turkey in Africa was complete.

[1] Egypt was still a dependency of the empire in theory but hardly so in fact.

THE PROGRESS OF THE BALKAN NATIONS AND THE ATTEMPT TO REJUVENATE TURKEY, 1832-1912

By the disintegration of the Ottoman Empire in Africa and Europe, the historian's task is rendered more difficult, for, instead of one empire, he is confronted by half a dozen states, each making a history of its own. The affairs of Greece, of Rumania, of Serbia, of Montenegro, and of Bulgaria must, therefore, command attention, country by country; and then the course of events within the mutilated Ottoman Empire may be followed down through the bloody War of the Balkans (1912–1913) and to the outbreak of the War of the Nations. *The Balkan Nations Considered Separately*

First of all, let us turn to the nation which first won complete independence, — the kingdom of the Hellenes. We left the Greeks in 1832 bemoaning the small extent of the new Greek kingdom and lamenting the coronation as "king of the Hellenes" of an absolutist prince imported from Germany. Notwithstanding his unpopularity, King Otto kept his seat upon a shaky throne for thirty years. Then, in 1862, he was deposed by his rebellious subjects, and in the following year the Greek Assembly chose the second son of King Christian IX of Denmark to become king of the Hellenes with the title of George I. Shortly after his succession the new king, who firmly believed that his strength lay in cultivating the love of his subjects, consented to a thoroughly democratic constitution, the constitution of 1864, by which the entire legislative power was vested in a single representative chamber, the *Bulé*. *Modern Greece* *King Otto, 1832–1862* *Constitutional Greece under King George I, 1863–1913*

The *Bulé* consisted of 184 representatives, elected by universal manhood suffrage, for the term of four years. This constitution remained in effect until 1911, when a new constitution came into force, whereby a sort of second chamber or council of state was created.

After the achievement of democratic government in 1864, Greece made steady progress politically, intellectually, and, most of all, materially. As one prosperous decade succeeded another, population multiplied; hill and valley were once more covered with olive trees, with currant bushes, with the vine, and with

grain fields; a thousand miles of railway were built; a hundred
busy factories sprang up at Athens; a firm financial foundation
was assured to the young kingdom; and, most impressive of all,
enterprising Greek merchant vessels were plying in large numbers to Egypt, to Syria, to Asia Minor, among the Ægean Islands,
and even past Constantinople into the Black Sea.

Amazing as were these achievements of their little kingdom,
still greater aspirations filled the hearts of Hellenic patriots.
Nationalist Aspirations of the Greeks Less than half of all the Hellenes had been incorporated into the kingdom of the Hellenes; more than
four millions were yet to be emancipated from foreign rule and joined to Greece. In Epirus, in Salonica,
in the Ægean Islands, there were Greeks waiting to be freed from
Turkish oppression, and the Cretans more than once showed
themselves eager to form part of Hellas. Once, in 1897,
Greece waged an heroic but unsuccessful war against Turkey in
behalf of Crete. These nationalist ambitions went hand in
hand with economic motives: Crete and the Ægean Islands
were necessary to give Greek commerce supremacy in the Ægean
Sea; if the northern Greek frontier could be extended to include
Salonica, Greece would not only gain an advantageous seaport,
but would also be able to carry out the project — long thwarted
by Turkey — of linking up the Greek railway system with
Salonica and with the great railway to Belgrade, Vienna, and
the West. Crete, Salonica, and the Ægean Islands could be
wrested from Turkey only by war. For war Greece then
prepared.

What Bismarck did for Germany, and Cavour for Italy, was
accomplished for Greece by Eleutherios Venezelos (1864–   ),
Venezelos a wonderful organizer, an able statesman, and an
ardent patriot, who had won fame in Crete as a champion of union with Greece, and had been called to Greece first
as an adviser, then (in 1910) as prime minister of the Greek
government. With the help of French and British commissioners, army and navy were effectively reorganized. Public
finance was reformed. By skillful diplomacy Venezelos made
sure that in the next war against Turkey, Greece should not
fight hopelessly alone as in 1897 but with the united support of
Bulgaria and Serbia. His achievements need no other com-

mentary than the facts of the Balkan War of 1912–1913, in which Greece did fight shoulder to shoulder with Serbia, Bulgaria, and Rumania, and from which Greece finally issued triumphant, having almost doubled her territory by the acquisition of Crete, most of the Ægean Islands, southern Epirus (Janina), and a large slice of Macedonia. Salonica, the peninsula of Chalcidice, and the coast as far east as Kavala (opposite the island of Thasos) were hers. From 2,700,000 her population was increased to about 4,700,000. The puny state of 1832, struggling for existence, had become a strong nation, a greater Greece. *Expansion of Greece, 1913*

During the course of the war, King George I of Greece was struck down by an assassin's bullet while walking in the streets of Salonica, 18 March, 1913. His death was sincerely lamented by most Greeks; yet even in the dark hour of mourning a ray of light appeared; for the son who succeeded King George was adored by the nation as the successful leader of the Greek army in the Balkan War. By an odd turn of history, this new sovereign of Greece, who led his people triumphantly against the hated Turks, bore the name of Constantine I; as if indeed a new Constantine had been raised up to avenge that unhappy Constantine of the fifteenth century, the last of the Greek emperors, who, grievously wounded by Turkish weapons, fell fighting long ago in the streets of imperial Constantinople. *King Constantine, 1913–*

By the treaty of Berlin (1878), as we have seen, Rumania achieved independence, but on three irritating conditions. (1) Although Rumania had loyally assisted Russia in the Russo-Turkish War of 1877–1878, Rumania had to give up to the tsar that strip of Bessarabia which the Rumans since 1856 had considered their own. The compensation which Rumania received in the Dobrudja did not at all allay the smart of the wound inflicted by the tsar's ingratitude. (2) Another article of the Berlin treaty providing for religious equality in Rumania aroused even more resentment because the Rumans were unwilling to allow the Jews, who were already hated for their shrewdness as money-lenders, to own land. The Rumans pretended to obey, but in effect nullified the article, and only a few of the 260,000 Rumanian Jews were *Rumania an Independent Principality, 1878* ever endowed with the rights of citizens. (3) As a third condition of obtaining independence, Bismarck insisted that Rumania should buy the Rumanian railways which were owned by German speculators.

Reluctantly Rumania promised compliance with these provisions, and in return was recognized by the Powers as an independent

Rumania a Kingdom, 1881

principality. In 1881 the ministry decided to declare Rumania a kingdom.[1] Consequently Prince Charles,[2] —scion of the princely German family of Hohenzollern-Sigmaringen, and relative of the Prussian king, — who in 1866 had been elected prince of Rumania, received on 22 May, 1881, the new kingly crown, wrought of steel from Turkish cannon captured at Plevna.

The new-born kingdom had three chief problems to face. First of all, the Rumanians sadly remembered that four millions

Nationalist Aspirations of the Rumans

or more of their kinsmen were still in bondage, those in Bessarabia to the tsar, and those in Transylvania, Bukowina, and southeastern Hungary to the Habsburgs; the numerous Kutzo-Vlachs scattered throughout Macedonia were, moreover, supposed to be of Ruman nationality, and Rumanian nationalists bitterly resented the attempts of Greek enthusiasts to "Hellenize" Macedonia. More or less bound up with this "national problem," was an international difficulty. While the Rumans would gladly have annexed the portions of Russia and Austria-Hungary inhabited by their kinsfolk, they feared to offend either Power. Public opinion wavered between seeking the friendship of Russia or of Austria-Hungary, and remaining aloof from both.

Third, and most important, was the problem of developing Rumania into a prosperous, powerful, and progressive nation.

Material Progress of Rumania

For one thing, a thrifty and independent farmer-class had to be created. A beginning had been made in 1864 when Prince Cuza abolished feudalism, confiscated the vast estates owned by monasteries, and bestowed

---

[1] The constitution of the newly erected kingdom, originally drafted in 1866, and subsequently amended in 1879 and 1884, provided for a parliament, the two houses of which are elected by a class-system resembling somewhat the three-class-system of Prussia.

[2] Charles married Princess Elizabeth of Wied, who was famed in literature as "Carmen Sylva." Charles died in 1914 and "Carmen Sylva" in 1916.

upon each peasant family a farm ranging from 7½ to 15 acres in size. Four million acres were thus distributed to 400,000 peasant families. But the farms were so small that their owners still found it necessary to work part of the time for the wealthy men who owned large estates, and to borrow money from Jewish money-lenders. In 1889 the government sold off the state domains — one-third of the total area — in small parcels to peasants. As a result there were in 1912 about a million small landowners with less than 25 acres apiece, owning almost one-half the land; while a few thousand large proprietors owned the remaining half. Rich black soil, and the introduction of modern agricultural implements, — iron plows, steam threshers, and reaping machines, — gave Rumania high rank among the grain-growing countries of the world; but the peasantry still remained so poor that in 1907 an agrarian insurrection broke out. The government took warning and, after restoring order, passed new measures to better the lot of the farmer.

The prosperity of Rumania was also furthered by the development of rich mineral resources, of industry, and railways. Foreign capitalists (among them the Rockefellers) were encouraged to open up Rumanian oil-wells and coal-mines. Factories were founded and new industries fostered. The first short railway, opened in 1869, was the forerunner of the 2100 miles of railway owned by the state in 1913.

These and other economic reforms, such as the introduction of the gold standard, laid a sure foundation for the military power which the Rumanian government steadily sought to up-build. For its size, the little kingdom possessed an extremely formidable army, equipped with modern arms, and numbering in peace 100,000 men, in war 500,000. This was the largest army boasted of by any of the Balkan states, as Rumania also possessed the most numerous population.

Serbia's history as an independent state was less happy. Milan Obrenovich, who was recognized as an independent prince by the treaty of Berlin (1878), and later became King Milan (1882), was a nephew of that Prince Milosh Obrenovich who in 1830 had won autonomy for Serbia. Unfortunately the royal family was allied by tradition with the aristocratical faction in Serbia against the vastly more popular

Serbia, 1878–1914

Radical party. Moreover, plots against the king were continually being hatched by rival claimants to the throne, who sym-
Dynastic pathized with the Radicals and derived their name and
Feud claim from Karageorge — that "Black George," the
man of the people who had been prince of Serbia from 1804 to
1813. Throughout the nineteenth century the Obrenovich and
Karageorge families continually conspired against one another,
alternately in and out of power. To this dynastic feud, Serbia
owed the periodic political upheavals which retarded her growth,
and two brutal assassinations — one in 1868, the other in 1903
— which stained her history.

King Milan, then, was an Obrenovich. For a decade after
1878 he became steadily more unpopular. In order to redeem
Serbian finances from chaos he had to levy heavier taxes. Yet
more unfortunate than the taxes was his war on Bulgaria (1885).
The war was not only unjust, as a shameless attempt to ruin
or at least to extort concessions from Serbia's newly united
sister-state; the war was not even successful. Within two weeks
the Bulgars had repelled the attack and were advancing on
Serbia with an army of 55,000 men. Serbia was able to conclude
peace, without loss, thanks to the kindly intervention of Austro-
Hungarian diplomacy; but the fact remained that King Milan
had led the Serbian armies to defeat. Shrewdly enough, he
endeavored to regain favor by granting of his own free will a
very liberal constitution (1889), and abdicating the throne two
months later. Milan's son, Alexander, was a mere boy, unable
to cope with the situation. Once he had to call his father back
Assassina- from Paris to prevent a political crisis in Serbia. A
tion of the few years later Alexander made a sudden about-face,
Reigning exiled his father, and transferred his affections from
Family, 1903 Austria-Hungary to Russia. This bold move only
spurred on to greater activity the enemies of Alexander and of
his wife, Queen Draga, who was even more bitterly hated. Conspirators were already at work. The plot matured; king,
Accession queen, ministers of state, and fifty other persons were
of King murdered early in the morning of 11 June, 1903.
Peter The regicides placed Peter, grandson of Karageorge,
upon the throne, and restored the liberal constitution of
1889.

After the accession of King Peter, popular attention was once more centered upon nationalism. Serbia's "Great Idea" possessed the hearts and minds of patriots, who hoped to unite into one glorious empire the Serbs of Serbia, Montenegro, Bosnia, Herzegovina, Novi-Bazar, and northwestern Macedonia. To such patriots Austria-Hungary appeared as Serbia's arch-enemy, especially when in 1908 the Austro-Hungarian government annexed Bosnia and Herzegovina. Serbian patriotism would not be satisfied until Serbia had fought first with Bulgaria and Greece to despoil Turkey, then quarreled with Bulgaria over the spoils, and finally furnished the occasion for the War of the Nations.

National Ambition and Expansion of Serbia

The other Serb state, little Montenegro, secured by the treaty of Berlin in 1878 a bit of Adriatic coast land, including the port of Antivari, and recognition as an independent principality. Under the benevolent despotism of their monarch, Prince Nicholas, the Montenegrins advanced in prosperity, industry, and education, although they still remained for the most part intractable mountaineer-herdsmen. The progressive character of the Montenegrin government was well illustrated when in 1905 Prince Nicholas granted a democratic constitution and created a parliament, called the *Skupshtina*, as in Serbia, and elected by universal manhood suffrage. What he lost in autocratic power, Prince Nicholas gained in dignity, for on 28 August, 1910, he assumed the title of king.

Montenegro, 1878–1914

Although the Bulgars in northern Bulgaria were forced to wait until 1878 for autonomy, and until 1885 for national union with the Bulgars in Eastern Rumelia, their subsequent progress and prosperity was hardly inferior to that of Greece or Rumania. It is true that in 1912 the Bulgarian people were still a nation of peasants, among whom modern agricultural methods made slow progress; but the millions of small farmers were independent and had no great landlords to fear. Coal and iron mines were being developed, and infant industries showed signs of rapid growth. Commerce with other nations more than tripled in value between 1887 and 1911. With railways the advance was even more striking. There was in 1878 but a single line of railway, 137 miles long; in 1911 Bulgaria

Bulgaria an Autonomous Principality, 1878

Its Material Development

boasted 1200 miles of state-owned railways and 400 miles of telegraph. With the advance of commerce and railways the growth of population almost kept pace, with the result that the nation which in 1888 numbered less than 3,200,000 numbered in 1910 at least 4,300,000. The number of schools was much more than doubled between 1878 and 1910. Free public libraries were founded in the cities. Bulgaria was becoming a civilized European nation.

The greatest obstacle to internal progress in Bulgaria was the spirit of national patriotism. Patriotism demanded the main-

Nationalist Aspirations of the Bulgars tenance of an army which in times of peace (1911) numbered about 60,000 men, and necessitated an expenditure of more than eight millions of dollars a year. Patriotism held up the idea of a great Bulgaria, which would include Adrianople and Macedonia, and dominate the peninsula, — an ideal which kept Bulgaria in constant difficulties with foreign powers and brought about a disastrous war in 1913. The proud and independent spirit of the Bulgars also caused Russia, once the champion of Bulgaria, to adopt a decidedly unfriendly attitude. In 1883 Prince Alexander of Bul-

Russian Interference garia, by refusing to be the tool of Russian officials, first excited the anger of the tsar. Consequently Russia attempted two years later to prevent the union of Bulgaria and Eastern Rumelia. Though foiled in this attempt, Russian influence was used to foment rebellion against the obstinate Prince Alexander, with the result that a conspiracy was hatched and in 1886 the prince was forced at pistol's point to abdicate the throne. In choosing Prince Ferdinand of Saxe-Coburg-

Prince Ferdinand Gotha to succeed Alexander, the Bulgars opposed the desires and disregarded the advice of the tsar, who declared Ferdinand to be a usurper. Ferdinand, however, clung to his throne, and for almost seven years allowed his remarkable and domineering minister, Stefan Stambolov (1854–1895), to

Stambolov defy Russia. Unquestionably Stambolov was able; he has been called the "Bulgarian Bismarck"; but by his tyrannical methods of government he made himself so bitterly hated that he fell from power in 1894 and was assassinated in the following year. Stambolov had been the soul of Bulgarian nationalism in his refusal to be subservient to

Russia; with Stambolov dead, and Prince Ferdinand anxious to patch up his quarrel with the tsar, the Bulgarian government was able to sue for Russia's friendship with complete success. The reconciliation bore fruit some years later when Russia indulgently allowed Prince Ferdinand to cast off the sultan's suzerainty, to declare Bulgaria an independent kingdom on 5 October, 1908, and to style himself the "Tsar of the Bulgars." Of the catastrophe to which the inordinate patriotism of the Bulgars finally led — in the Balkan War of 1913 — we shall speak when we later consider that war.

Bulgaria an Independent Kingdom, 1908

While Rumania, Greece, Bulgaria, Serbia, and even little Montenegro were rapidly assimilating European civilization and becoming miniature reproductions of the great European nations, Turkey was making similar but pitiably feeble efforts. Yet in 1878 the future of Turkey seemed full of promise. The treaty of Berlin provided for an international commission to outline a program of reforms in European Turkey. German experts were to reorganize Ottoman finance; English officers were to reform the police and report abuses. And parliamentary government had been promised by the liberal constitution of 1876.

Plans for Reform of the Ottoman Empire, 1878

The dream of reform was soon dissipated. Sultan Abdul Hamid II had never been sincerely disposed to constitutional government. He was bent rather on exalting his own power. Although he had originally usurped the throne, Abdul Hamid was none the less emphatic in reasserting the religious character of his rule, as the sovereign intrusted by Allah with the military leadership of the Faithful, the successor on earth of Mohammed. Instead of imitating European monarchs, he became all the more an oriental, living in the royal park (Yildiz Kiosk), maintaining the customary harem, and punctiliously observing the rites of Islam. It was no marvel, then, that the wily Turk immediately nullified the reforms he had promised. The constitution of 1876 and the parliament of the Ottoman Empire had hardly been announced when they were suspended (1878). No parliament met again in Constantinople for thirty years. And meanwhile Abdul

Abdul Hamid II (1876–1909) and the Abandonment of Reform

Abrogation of the Constitution of 1876

Hamid continued to concentrate his autocratic power; he appointed personal favorites as ministers of state, and by means of wholesale corruption and systematic espionage endeavored to maintain his arbitrary rule.

Despite his wily diplomacy and unscrupulous cunning, Abdul Hamid was perpetually in difficulties. First, the public debt increased to such alarming proportions that in 1881 Turkey's European creditors, mostly French, stepped in to insure the payment of interest on their investments, and established an international commission to supervise Turkish finances. Next, Tunis was taken by France. Then the province of Eastern Rumelia was united to Bulgaria (1885). Then there were massacres in Asia Minor (1894–1895), where the Mohammedan Kurds hated their Christian neighbors, the Armenians. More than a hundred thousand, possibly two hundred thousand, Armenian villagers fell beneath the swords of Moslem fanatics; and even in Constantinople several thousands of Christians were slain. The wholesale slaughter of Armenian Christians was doubtless viewed by the sultan with satisfaction rather than with apprehension; but in the long run it aroused public sentiment in Europe against the Turks and hastened the downfall of the sultan. Armenia was still in uproar, when Crete was seized with revolutionary convulsions (1896), which resulted in a war between Turkey and Greece (1897). In the war Turkish armies were victorious, but a few years later Crete fell practically into the hands of the Greek kingdom. Arabia was in constant revolt. Anarchy reigned in Albania, where the sultan's officials found it all but impossible to enforce the laws and to collect the taxes. Worst of all was the ferment in Macedonia, where Greeks, Serbs, Bulgars, and Rumans were carrying on rival nationalist agitations and with their filibustering exploits kept the country in turmoil. An especially vigorous Macedonian upheaval, caused by the Bulgars in 1903, resulted in foreign intervention; and the sultan reluctantly consented to new reform schemes, which were never fully executed.

The Ottoman Empire in the first decade of the twentieth century seemed on the point of collapse, with mutiny in Arabia and anarchy in Albania, with Crete in the control of Greece,

Difficulties of Abdul Hamid's Régime

and foreigners interfering in the administration of Macedonia, with an enormous public debt, with railways, mines, and banks in the hands of foreign capitalists, with Balkan nations and European Powers greedily regarding the Ottoman provinces.

"The Sick Man of Europe," as Turkey had so often been called, was apparently tottering to his end. There was, however, a group of politicians who dared dream of rejuvenating Turkey. Some of their number were advanced in years, but all were "Young Turks" in the exuberance of patriotism. Many had studied in European universities, in Paris most commonly, and there under the influence of European civilization had conceived the project of modernizing Turkey. They would win parliamentary government for their home land. In education, in science, in industry, Turkey would be transformed into a progressive state, vying with European nations. Above all, they would induce their compatriots to forget religious differences in a spirit of national patriotism — that "fraternity" of allegiance to a common flag. Albanians, Armenians, Bulgars, Arabs, — all would be treated with justice, and all would become Turks, "Young Turks." It was a counterpart in Turkey of the nationalist agitations which had already created a Greece, a Serbia, a Rumania, and a Bulgaria.

Appearance of a Reforming Party within the Ottoman Empire: the "Young Turks"

Shrewdly enough, the Young Turks avoided all violence until they were absolutely sure that the army would support them. Then with swiftness and certainty they struck the blow, the *coup d'état* of 1908. On 23 July, 1908, the constitution of 1876 was proclaimed at Salonica by the central body of the Young Turks, the so-called Committee of Union and Progress, with Major Enver Bey at its head. Two army corps threatened to march on Constantinople if the sultan should deny the constitution. Terrified, Abdul Hamid hastily issued an imperial decree, officially restoring the constitution of 1876. A few opponents of the *coup* were assassinated, the press was emancipated, a Liberal statesman, Kiamil Pasha, was appointed grand vizier, and Turkey was a constitutional monarchy.

The Coup d'État of July, 1908; Establishment of Constitutional Government in Turkey

This disturbance was seized upon by Austria-Hungary as an occasion for the annexation of Bosnia and Herzegovina. By

Loss of
Bosnia and
Herzego-
vina, 1908
the treaty of Berlin (1878), Austria-Hungary had been given a protectorate over the two provinces and the right to station military garrisons in Novi-Bazar. The Austro-Hungarian government now proceeded to violate the treaty by announcing early in October, 1908, that the Dual Monarchy would annex Bosnia and Herzegovina and at the same time withdraw her garrisons from the sanjak of Novi-Bazar. On 7 October, 1908, the annexation was officially decreed by Emperor Francis Joseph. Almost simultaneously, Ferdinand of Bulgaria, who realized that Austria-Hungary's violation

Loss of
Suzerainty
over Bul-
garia, 1908
of the treaty would draw attention from his own action, declared Bulgaria (including Eastern Rumelia) entirely independent of Turkey and assumed the title of tsar. Helplessly but slowly the Turkish government acquiesced in what it could not prevent and recognized Bulgarian independence and the Austro-Hungarian annexation of Bosnia-Herzegovina as accomplished facts. Small comfort was derived from the indemnities which Turkey thereupon received — $11,000,000 from Austria-Hungary and $24,000,000 from Bulgaria.

To make matters worse for the constitutional government of Kiamil Pasha, Albania became more turbulent in the spring of

Continued
Disorders in
Turkey
1909 than ever, the Kurdish troops in Asia Minor revolted, fresh massacres of Armenians were reported, mutiny broke out in Arabia, and the quarrels of nationalities in Macedonia became so serious that the government decided to disarm the Macedonian population. The Christian portion of the population ceased to support the Young Turk Committee of Union and Progress and organized instead the Liberal Union. The grand vizier, who was a Liberal rather than a Young Turk, became increasingly hostile to the Committee. A counter-revolution against the Young Turks was set on foot in Constantinople and received the approbation of Sultan Abdul Hamid II. Then it was that the Committee of Union and Progress decided on a bold course. An army of 25,000 men was sent against Constantinople. After less than a day's fighting Shevket Pasha and his troops occupied the capital in

the name of the Committee, 25 April, 1909. The parliament, now calling itself a National Assembly, resolved on the deposition of Abdul Hamid, who was bundled off to Salonica. Mohammed V, Abdul Hamid's younger brother, was chosen to succeed to the throne, and on 10 May, 1909, received the famous sword of Othman.

Deposition of Abdul Hamid II, 1909

The revolution of 1909 established parliamentary government in the Ottoman Empire on the lines laid down by the constitution of 1876. Although Mohammedanism remained the state religion, and the sultan remained the chief of Islam, all Turkish subjects, Christian, Jewish, or Mohammedan, were guaranteed equal rights before the law and at the polls. The sultan was henceforth

New Nationalist Policies of the Young Turks

to be as much a constitutional monarch as King George of England; the government was to be carried on by a grand vizier (prime minister) and ministers responsible to a popularly elected parliament. But the revolution did not establish the liberties of the Christian nationalities. For it speedily became all too clear that constitutional government was a less important item of the Young Turk program than nationalism. By making the Turkish language official, by standardizing education, by planting new Moslem colonies in Macedonia, by using violence and bribery to influence elections, by forbidding public meetings, by repressing anti-Ottoman agitation, by practically excluding Christians from civil offices, by disarming the Macedonian villagers, — by these and numberless tokens the Young Turks signified their intention to weld all races into a Turkish nation, to "Ottomanize" the Turkish Empire. Resentfully the Bulgars, Greeks, and Serbs in Macedonia regarded the new policy of "Ottomanization," and, forgetting their own quarrels, they now made common cause against the Turk. Greece, Bulgaria, and Serbia began to draw more closely together with the object of protecting the Christians in Macedonia. On 13 March, 1912, a treaty of alliance was secretly signed by Serbian and Bulgarian plenipotentiaries; late in May, Greece and Montenegro were likewise bound in alliance

Opposition in Macedonia and the "Balkan Alliance"

to their sister Balkan states; and military conventions were drawn up, stipulating how many troops each state of the "Balkan Alliance" should put in the field if war should ensue.

Meanwhile the Turco-Italian War, coming like a thunderbolt from a clear sky, had caused consternation in Constantinople.

The Turco-Italian War, 1911–1912 On 28 September, 1911, the Italian government had announced its intention to seize Tripoli and Cyrenaica. The war that followed was confined mostly to irregular but fierce hostilities between the Italian expeditionary armies on the one hand, and on the other hand the Turkish garrisons and Arab tribesmen under the leadership of Enver Bey in Africa. During the course of the war, Italy seized Rhodes, Patmos, and ten other Ægean islands (the Dodecanesos), and, when peace was finally concluded by the treaty of Lausanne (signed at Ouchy, 18 October, 1912), Italy not only gained the African vilayets of Tripoli and Cyrenaica, but in addition acquired the right to hold the twelve islands until Turkey should have completed the evacuation of Tripoli and Cyrenaica.

THE BALKAN WARS, 1912–1913

It was during the spring and summer of 1912, while Turkey was still harassed and weakened by the war with Italy, that the Balkan states concluded the alliance referred to above,

The Question of Macedonia and Albania and began to press more vigorously for radical reforms in Macedonia. They were encouraged by mutinous outbreaks in Albania and by the seeming success of the Albanians in obtaining extensive concessions. Popular sentiment was inflamed by news that the Turks had massacred Christians in several Macedonian villages. When the mobilization of troops by the allies and by Turkey, early in October, 1912, gave warning that a conflict was at hand, the governments of the Great Powers [1] jointly informed the Balkan allies that they would be displeased by war, that they would persuade Turkey to carry out the reforms promised by the Berlin Treaty of 1878, that in any case the Balkan allies could gain no new territory by war, since the Powers "would not permit at the end of the conflict any modification of the territorial *status quo* in European Turkey." Nevertheless, Montenegro promptly declared war on Turkey and called on Serbia, Greece,

[1] For an account of the general attitude and alignment of the Great Powers, see below, pp. 706–710.

and Bulgaria to join in a "holy war against the cruel and infidel Turk." The reply of these states was the dispatch of a last
appeal — an ultimatum — to the Porte, demanding
autonomy for Macedonia under European governors. *Montenegro, Serbia,*
But the Turkish government, relying upon the pledge *Greece, and*
of the Great Powers, refused to relinquish control of *Bulgaria*
Make War
Macedonia, and angrily recalled the Turkish diplo- *on Turkey,*
matic representatives from Athens, Belgrade, and *October,*
1912
Sofia (October, 1912). Turkey, with perhaps 400,000
soldiers, was opposed by Bulgaria with an estimated war army
of 350,000, Serbia with 250,000, Greece with 150,000, and Montenegro with 30,000.

The first stage of the Balkan War was characterized everywhere by victories of the allied armies, superior to the Turks in
organization, in training, and in equipment. Insuffi- *The Cam-*
cient food provisions, cholera, and inability promptly *paign of the*
to put her armies in the field were hardly less fatal to *Bulgars*
Turkey than was the deadly artillery fire of the Bulgarians.
Nevertheless, the Turkish armies fought bravely and stubbornly.
In Thrace the fiercest battles were contested. There the Bulgarian army, advancing southward, encountered the Turkish
forces on a line stretching eastward from Adrianople to Kirk-
Kilisse. Adrianople, with its frowning fortresses, *Lule Burgas,*
long resisted capture. But at Kirk-Kilisse the Bulgars *1 November,*
triumphed and drove back the eastern wing of the *1912*
Turkish army. Leaving part of their forces to besiege Adrianople, the Bulgars again advanced south and administered a
decisive defeat to the enemy in the greatest battle of the war.
Four days the battle raged (29 October–1 Novem- *The Turks*
ber) along the front of twenty-two miles, stretching *on the De-*
from Lule Burgas to Bunar Hissar. Fifty thousand *fensive be-*
men fell on the field, wounded or dying. The Turks *fore Con-*
stantinople
retreated to Tchorlu, and thence to Tchataldja.
There, but a few miles distant from Constantinople, the shattered
Turkish forces drew up to make their last stand.

Meanwhile, the Greek navy had occupied the island of Lemnos, and an army led by the Greek crown prince had *The*
advanced north from Thessaly and had captured the *Western*
important city of Salonica early in November. Serbian *Campaign*

armies, coöperating with the Bulgar "army of the west," had
overrun Macedonia, capturing Pristina, Uskub, and Monastir

Successes
of Greeks
and Serbs
in rapid succession. Victorious Serbian and Montenegrin forces had occupied Novi-Bazar and Durazzo.
And the Montenegrins had begun the investment of
Scutari. Such was the desperate plight of Turkey when an
armistice was concluded, 3 December, 1912, preparatory to the
conclusion of peace.

At the peace conference, which met in London, three troublesome disputes arose : Turkey would not relinquish Adrianople

Unsuccess-
ful Negotia-
tions and
Renewed
Hostilities,
1913
as Bulgaria demanded; Turkey also refused to cede
all the Ægean Islands to Greece; and the allies by insisting on a war indemnity threatened to ruin both
the Ottoman treasury and the European creditors of
the Ottoman Empire. Despairing of an agreement,
the allies withdrew their deputies from the conference. With
urgent solicitation the Powers persuaded the Turkish government to yield on the question of ceding Adrianople to Bulgaria,
but on the very next day, 23 January, 1913, the Turkish government and the pacific Kiamil Pasha were violently overthrown
by the Young Turks, who set up a new cabinet with the motto
"no surrender." The *coup d'état* could have but one result,
the resumption of hostilities. On 3 February the conflict was
reopened. The Bulgars, camping all winter before the Tchataldja
line of trenches, were unable to advance farther on Constantinople, but at least they kept the main Turkish army bottled
up while the other armies of the allies besieged Adrianople, Janina
(in Epirus), and Scutari (in northern Albania). On 6 March,
Janina was captured by the Greeks; and on 26 March, Shukri
Pasha, the gallant defender of Adrianople, surrendered that city
with its garrison of 30,000 men to the Serbo-Bulgar army. In
April, Bulgaria, Serbia, and Greece agreed to an armistice with
Turkey. The plucky Montenegrins, however, continued to
besiege Scutari, despite pleas and threats, until that town was
surrendered on 23 April.

The fall of Scutari almost precipitated a great European war.
For the six Great Powers had already decided that Scutari
should be included in Albania, which they proposed to make an
autonomous state. Austria-Hungary and Italy had been so em-

phatic on this point that Serbia had been compelled regretfully to withdraw her troops from the coveted Adriatic port of Durazzo. Now, on 1 May, Austria-Hungary threatened war if Montenegro should retain Scutari, and her threat was backed by Italy and Germany. Loud cries went up in Russia, where enthusiastic Pan-Slavists called upon the tsar to protect the little Slav state against Austria-Hungary and to uphold Montenegro's occupation of Scutari. Just in time to avert war between Austria-Hungary and Russia, King Nicholas of Montenegro withdrew his troops peaceably from Scutari and an international force of marines marched into the disputed city. *Montenegro, Albania, and International Complications*

Peace negotiations were once more resumed, this time with greater success. On 30 May, 1913, a treaty was signed at London by representatives of all the belligerents. Turkey gave up all territory west of a line drawn from Enos on the Ægean Sea to Midia on the Black Sea, and likewise ceded Crete to Greece. The boundaries of autonomous Albania, the *status* of the Ægean Islands, and the final financial settlements were to be adjusted later by the Great Powers. *The Treaty of London (30 May, 1913): Turkey Shorn of Nearly All her European Possessions*

The treaty of London marked the triumph of the allied Balkan states over Turkey. Within eight months they had all but expelled the Turk from Europe. No sooner was their victory assured, however, than the allies fell to quarreling over the spoils, Bulgaria demanding the chief share, — two-thirds of the conquered territory, — Greece and Serbia protesting. Presently the public learned that the secret treaty of alliance signed by Serbia and Bulgaria in March, 1912, contained an agreement whereby Bulgaria was to annex the greater part of Macedonia, including even Monastir, while Serbia would content herself with a small slice of Macedonia and a large portion of Albania. But the Powers had blocked Serbia's designs on Albania, thus diminishing Serbia's gains. Bulgaria would receive more than had been contemplated at the time the treaty was signed, while Serbia would receive much less. In view of these facts, Serbia demanded a new apportionment. Pride in their recent spectacular feats-of-arms, and perhaps a vain hope *Quarrels among the Balkan Allies over the Turkish Spoils, 1913*

of obtaining Austro-Hungarian support, led the Bulgars to refuse the demand, and enthusiastically to embark on a new war.

In the ensuing second Balkan War—the war against Bulgaria — Serbia was joined by the Montenegrins, who were ever ready to assist Serbia, and by the Greeks, who were no less

Serbia, Montene-gro, Greece, and Ru-mania Make War on Bul-garia, June–July, 1913

jealous of Bulgaria. Shortly after the opening of hos-tilities, two more enemies attacked the Bulgarian kingdom. The Rumanian government had enviously watched the Balkan states dividing Macedonia among them; the Rumans had long been jealous lest the rapidly growing Bulgarian nation should overshadow Rumania; and they seized this occasion to gratify their greed for new territory and at the same time to attack their

Reëntrance of Turkey into the War against Bulgaria

rival. Finally, Turkey entered the arena against Bulgaria, hoping to regain at least a portion of what she had lost by the treaty of London, especially the city of Adrianople.

The fighting began late in June, 1913, between Greek and Bulgarian soldiers, although war was not officially declared until

Defeat of the Bulgars

5 July. In Macedonia occurred most of the engage-ments. The Greek armies in southern Macedonia pushed northward up the Struma River, aiming straight at Sofia, the Bulgarian capital; while Serbians and Montenegrins, west of the Struma, closed in upon the Bulgars at Kotchana and threatened to descend upon Sofia by way of the Bulgarian town of Kostendil. From the southeast advanced Enver Bey with a Turkish army, which reoccupied Adrianople on 22 July. Most alarming of all was the rapid triumphal march of the splendid Rumanian troops to within twenty miles of Sofia. Perceiving his enemies close in from every side, King Ferdinand of Bulgaria sued for peace, and the "July War," so disastrous for his coun-try, was ended.

Peace was concluded by the delegates of Bulgaria, Rumania, Serbia, Montenegro, and Greece, who signed the treaty at Bucharest on 10 August, 1913. Turkey was ignored. By the treaty of Bucharest, Bulgaria was compelled to relinquish her claims on the western part of Macedonia and to cede a strip of Bulgarian territory to Rumania. Rumania thus pushed her southern frontier southward to include Turtukai on the Danube and Baltchik on the Black Sea. Serbia enlarged her share of Macedonia by appropriating Monastir, Kotchana, and Istib; and, in addition, she annexed half of the sanjak of Novi-Bazar, and the Macedonian towns of Prisrend, Uskub, and Pristina. The rich prize of Salonica, together with all the Ægean coast west of the Mesta River, and the territory between Monastir on the north and Thessaly on the south, fell to Greece. Greece also extended her northwestern frontier to include Janina, the southern district of Epirus, and annexed the island of Crete. Montenegro's share in *The Treaty of Bucharest, 10 August, 1913, and the Partition of Macedonia among the Balkan States* the spoils was later determined; it embraced the western half of the sanjak of Novi-Bazar. Bulgaria's portion, although sadly diminished, was still considerable. To Bulgaria was allotted a strip of Macedonia with the town of Strumitza as its southwestern corner, and western Thrace with some seventy miles of seacoast on the Ægean between the Mesta and Maritza rivers.

It remained for Bulgaria to settle with Turkey the question of Adrianople and the position of Bulgaria's southeastern frontier. The Turks, having reoccupied Adrianople, were determined to retain it, despite Bulgaria's protests, despite the recent treaty of London, despite the unanimous but weak remonstrances of the Powers. Consequently Bulgaria, rather than risk a third war, yielded to the Turkish demands. By the treaty of London, the Turkish boundary had been fixed at a straight line from Enos on the Ægean to Midia on the Black Sea. By the Turco-Bulgarian treaty of Constantinople (29 September, 1913) the Enos-Midia line *The Treaty of Constantinople, 29 September, 1913, and the Turkish Recovery of Adrianople from the Bulgars* was made to bulge out so as to include Adrianople and Kirk-Kilisse. In consequence of this arrangement, Bulgaria had no access by railway to her new Ægean coast, except through Turkish territory *via* Adrianople, or by a roundabout route through Greek and Serbian country.

Albania and the Ægean Islands remained perplexing problems. As for the latter, Greece claimed and actually occupied all of the Ægean Islands except the twelve Sporades held by Italy. The reluctance of Turkey, however, definitely to renounce all claim on the islands, inspired *Question of the Ægean Islands* the Greeks with a fear that at the earliest opportunity Turkey would make war on Greece and recapture the islands. The Balkan Wars embittered the relations between Greece and Turkey and at the same time gave rise to a bitter rivalry between Greece and Italy.

As for Albania, the Powers had agreed, at the emphatic behest of Austria-Hungary and Italy, to erect that little state into an

Albania an Independent Principality
independent principality. They, therefore, in 1914 sent Prince William of Wied, a German prince and a relative of the queen of Rumania to rule as first prince or *mpret* of Albania. It was indeed a shaky throne that Prince William ascended. Half of the Albanians were Moslems, and so vigorously did they resent subjugation to a Christian prince . that they rose in armed rebellion. To add to his difficulties, the *mpret* was confronted on the north by Montenegro, ever anxious to regain Scutari, on the east by Serbia, ever longing for a port on the Adriatic, and on the south by Greece, ever desirous of Epirus, — three enemies who would gladly divide his little principality among them. Little wonder it was, then, that shortly after the outbreak of the Great War in 1914 Prince William fled from his turbulent realm.

The two wars of 1912–1913 constituted an epochal step in the solution of the Balkan question; they wrested from the Turk

Results of the Balkan Wars
four-fifths of his former European territory and divided it among the independent Christian nations,[1] giving to Greece 17,000 square miles, to Serbia 15,200, to Bulgaria 9600, to Montenegro 2100; forming 11,000 square miles into an independent Albania; and leaving Turkey in Europe less

1. Territorial Gains of Greece and the Balkan States
than 11,000 square miles, an area only slightly larger than Maryland. As regards population, Rumania with 7,500,000 inhabitants still remained greater than any Balkan state; Bulgaria with 4,800,000 inhabitants now had to count on the rivalry of Greece, with 4,700,000; Serbia with 4,500,000 was almost as important as Greece; Albania contained 800,000 unruly mountaineers, and Montenegro half a million; and, finally, Turkey-in-Europe could muster only 1,900,000 inhabitants, a population two-fifths

[1] Greece increased her territory by 68 per cent; Bulgaria, 29 per cent; Serbia, 82 per cent; Montenegro, 62 per cent.

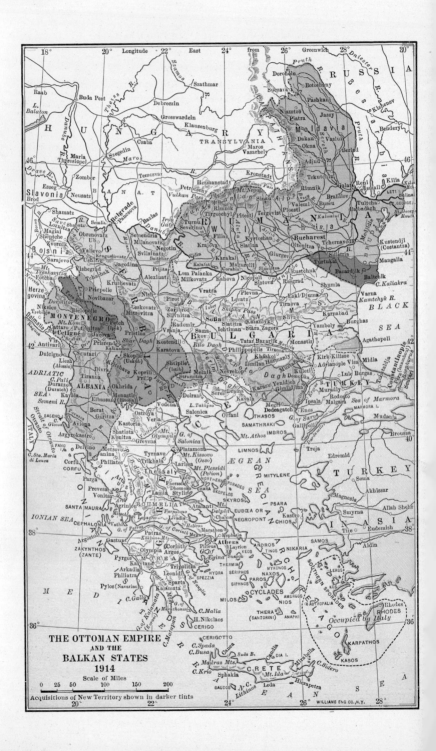

THE OTTOMAN EMPIRE
AND THE
BALKAN STATES
1914

Scale of Miles

0   25   50   100   150   200

Acquisitions of New Territory shown in darker tints

WILLIAMS ENG.CO.,N.Y.

that of Bulgaria. Against these gains must be balanced the terrible cost. At the very least, two hundred thousands of soldiers had laid down their lives in the two wars; **2. Loss in Men and Money** and the public moneys expended in maintaining and moving troops must have exceeded $1,500,000,000. Peaceful villagers, women, and old men had been wantonly butchered or cruelly abused by Greek as well as by Bulgarian soldiers. The Balkan nations emerged from the July War exhausted, yet hating each other with indescribable bitterness: the Bulgar now hated Greek or Serb more furiously than formerly he had detested the Turk.

Another result of the Balkan Wars was to emphasize the Asiatic, rather than the European, character of the Ottoman Empire. Though deprived of all real sovereignty in Africa and restricted in Europe to Constantinople, Adrianople, **3. The Ottoman Empire Largely Restricted to Asia** and a little surrounding territory, Turkey still embraced Asia Minor, Armenia, Kurdistan, Syria, Mesopotamia, and Arabia,—an aggregate Asiatic area of approximately 700,000 square miles and a population of about twenty-one millions. That the Turks retained any land in Europe was due not so much to their military prowess, although their armies were still formidable, as to the endless quarrels among the Balkan nations and to the support which several Great Powers continued to give, in their own interests, to the Ottoman Empire.

Throughout the nineteenth century, as we have seen, rival nationalist ambitions had embittered the relations among the Christian states of the Balkans. Temporarily repressed by the formation of the Balkan Alliance and **4. Intensification of National Rivalries among the Balkan States** the ensuing joint attack upon Turkey, these same ambitions naturally reasserted themselves as soon as Turkish power collapsed in Europe. The Balkan treaties of 1913 did not partition the conquered Turkish provinces — Macedonia and Thrace — along national cleavages. Indeed, it was quite impossible so to divide the country north of the Ægean, for Greek, Serb, Bulgar, Turkish, and even Vlach (Ruman) villages were scattered everywhere, and not infrequently it was difficult to distinguish the nationality of a Macedonian villager. Not only did the Bulgars hope in the future to add to their state some of the portions of Macedonia assigned in 1913 to Greece and Serbia, but the Greeks and Serbs likewise had but whetted their territorial appetites. The Greeks aspired all the more zealously to reclaim the Ægean Islands still held by Italy and to wrest from the Ottoman Empire at the earliest opportunity the coast of Asia Minor and possibly Constantinople. The Serbs began to talk more openly and more eloquently of taking from Austria-Hungary the Slav provinces of Bosnia, Herzegovina, Croatia-Slavonia, and Dalmatia, of uniting Montenegro with Serbia, and of establishing a Greater Serbia. Even the Rumans cherished more fondly their dream of incorporating their Ruman brethren of Bessarabia (in Russia) and of Transylvania, Bukowina, and southern Hungary (subject to the Habsburg Empire) into a Greater Rumania. For a time after the Balkan Wars, Serbia, Greece, and Rumania seemed to be able to coöperate, but Bulgaria was naturally indisposed to any further satisfaction of the nationalist aspirations of her rivals; and a pronounced success of any one was bound to provoke the jealousy of all the other Balkan states. And such a situation was favorable primarily to the Turks.

Likewise in the conflicting interests of the Great Powers the Turkish government found a certain amount of security for

5. Rival Interests of the Great Powers in the Near East itself. Of the Great Powers, Russia and Austria-Hungary had been since the seventeenth century the chief enemies of the Ottoman Empire, but their policies by 1913 were sharply antagonistic to each other. On the one hand was the ambition of Austro-Hungarian statesmen to extend the Habsburg Empire, at the expense of Serbia and Greece, from Bosnia to Salonica on the

Austria-Hungary Ægean. The Habsburgs, driven from Italy by Cavour and from Germany by Bismarck, would obtain compensation by reaching southward and building an empire of mixed races, in which Slavs would predominate. On the other

Russia hand was the magnificent dream of Russian Pan-Slavism. Russia, the Pan-Slavists declared, was bound to Serbia, Montenegro, and Bulgaria by the closest affection and sympathy, for Serbs, Bulgars, and Russians alike speak Slavic languages and adhere to the Orthodox Christian faith. This sentiment, becoming increasingly popular in Russia, threw that Power more and more into antagonism with Austria-Hungary. For if Russia should encourage the Slavic nations of the Balkans, Austro-Hungarian progress towards Salonica would be blocked by a strong Serbia. Worse still, if Russia should unite Serbia, Montenegro, and Bulgaria with herself in a Slavic confederation or in a Pan-Slavic empire, the Serbo-Croats, Czechs, and Poles in Austria-Hungary and the Poles in Germany might be attracted as Slavs to the great and powerful Pan-Slavic combination.

Athwart this major rivalry between Russia and Austria-Hungary lay peculiar interests of the other Great Powers. All of them had important financial investments to safe- Great guard in the Ottoman Empire and in the Balkan states, Britain for German and Italian capitalists had vied with British and French in making public loans to the governments in the Near East and in securing concessions for internal development. Throughout the nineteenth century Great Britain had repeatedly championed Turkey against Russian aggression, largely because of fear lest British merchants trading with India might be discomfited were a strong power like Russia to gain control of the Balkan peninsula, of the Dardanelles, and of Asia Minor. Similarly, France had long supported the Ottoman Empire France against Russia, not only because French speculators who held Turkish bonds desired to guarantee their investments by maintaining the Turkish government on a firm basis, but also because France was traditionally the protector of Roman Catholic Christians in the East. From the close of Germany the nineteenth century, Germany was taking a prominent position in the councils of the Ottoman Empire. The German government befriended the Porte and encouraged Austria-Hungary to checkmate Russia, and at the same time secured permission for German capitalists to build important railways in Turkey, as, for example, the Bagdad railway; and German officers drilled the Ottoman army. Although Italy Italy, like Germany, was an ally of Austria-Hungary from 1882 to 1915, Italians deprived Turkey of Tripoli and of several islands in the Ægean, obtained valuable concessions in Asia Minor and Syria, and made no secret of their wish to extend Italian influence over Albania.

By the time of the Balkan Wars (1912–1913), British and French interests in the East appeared to be menaced less by Russia than by Austria-Hungary and Germany. The latter Powers were working hand in glove: Germans were arming and drilling the Turkish troops and securing the major share of new concessions in the Ottoman Empire, while Austria-Hungary was curbing the Serbs and increasing her political and economic influence in Macedonia. In the course of the Balkan Wars, therefore, France and Great Britain tended, on the whole, to back Russia and the Balkan states against Turkey and Austria-Hungary. Between these clashing international interests and sympathies the results of the Balkan Wars afforded a temporary compromise. On one side, the Russians were proud of the expansion of the Balkan states at the expense of Turkey. On the other side, Austria-Hungary, with the support of her allies, succeeded in preventing the access of Serbia to the Adriatic and in creating a new principality under Austro-Italian influence.

Effect of the Balkan Wars upon the International Relations of the Great Powers

The compromise was only temporary, for with the almost complete disappearance of the Ottoman Empire in Europe there now loomed large in the minds of the Balkan peoples — especially Serbs and Rumans — the heterogeneous empire of the Habsburgs. Before the Balkan Wars the Near Eastern Question concerned the dismemberment of Turkey; henceforth it was connected with the dismemberment of Austria-Hungary. Rumans remembered that a dissolution of the Habsburg Empire might add populous territories to their kingdom. Serbs transferred their hatred from their former southern neighbors to their present northern neighbors and bestirred themselves to build the Greater Serbia out of the ruins of the Dual Monarchy. Even Italians who aspired to continue the work of Cavour and Garibaldi and to complete their national unification would have to wrest Trieste and Trent from Austria-Hungary. It was certainly a result of Austro-Hungarian policy in the Balkans, particularly during the Balkan Wars, that the Archduke Francis Ferdinand, heir to the throne of the Habsburg Empire, was assassinated at Sarajevo, the capital of Bosnia, on 28 June, 1914,

The Balkan Wars Tend to Turn Attention from the Dismemberment of the Ottoman Empire to the Possible Dissolution of the Habsburg Empire

by Serb conspirators possessed of the passion of nationalism. And most certainly it was as a phase of the Near Eastern Question that the Great War of 1914 began — Serbia, Montenegro, and Russia, with the support of France and Great Britain, in arms against Austria-Hungary backed by Germany. In view of the international situation created by the Balkan Wars it was well-nigh inevitable that both Turkey and Bulgaria should throw in their lot with Austria-Hungary and Germany, and that Italy should add her strength to that of the opposing combination in a patriotic hope of settling the fate not only of the Ottoman Empire but also of the empire of the Habsburgs.

Connection of the Eastern Question with the Great War

ADDITIONAL READING

The Near Eastern Question, Descriptive and Historical. Elementary narratives: C. D. Hazen, *Europe since 1815* (1910), ch. xxviii; J. H. Robinson and C. A. Beard, *The Development of Modern Europe*, Vol. II (1907), ch. xxix. More detailed accounts: *Cambridge Modern History*, Vol. X (1907), ch. xvii, on Mehemet Ali, Vol. XI (1909), ch. ix, on Russia and the Levant to 1852, and ch. xxii, on the Balkan lands to 1870, Vol. XII (1910), ch. xiv, on the Ottoman Empire and the Balkan peninsula, and ch. xv, on Egypt and the Sudan, 1841–1907; *Histoire générale*, Vol. X, ch. xxvi, Vol. XI, ch. vi, xv, Vol. XII, ch. xii, xiv, to 1900; William Miller, *The Ottoman Empire, 1801–1913* (1913), an excellent up-to-date account of the dismemberment of the Turkish Empire and of the rise of the Christian Balkan states; Édouard Driault, *La question d'orient depuis ses origines jusqu'à nos jours*, 6th ed. (1913), perhaps the clearest and best general history of the whole Eastern Question with its wide ramifications; J. H. Rose, *The Development of the European Nations, 1870–1900*, Vol. I (1905), ch. vii–x, valuable chapters on the Eastern Question, the Russo-Turkish War of 1877–1878, the Berlin Congress, and the making of Bulgaria; Luigi Villari (editor), *The Balkan Question : the Present Condition of the Balkans and of European Responsibilities* (1905), important studies of the situation at the opening of the twentieth century by a group of distinguished scholars and publicists representing many nationalities and interests; T. E. Holland (editor), *The European Concert in the Eastern Question: a Collection of Treaties and Other Public Acts* (1885); T. G. Djuvara, *Cent projets de partage de la Turquie, 1281–1913* (1914), the important contribution of a Rumanian diplomatist, contains among others many recent treaties and diplomatic documents; Sir Edward Hertslet, *Map of Europe by Treaty since 1814*, 4 vols. (1875–1891), embracing English translations of the major treaties from 1814 to 1891; Pierre Albin, *Les grands traités politiques,* *recueil des principaux textes diplomatiques depuis 1815 jusqu'à nos jours* (1912), especially useful for the later period; W. E. Curtis, *The Turk and his Lost Provinces* (1903); Heinrich von Treitschke, *Germany, France, Russia, and Islam,* Eng. trans. (1914); A. Schopoff, *Les réformes et la protection des chrétiens en Turquie, 1673–1904* (1904); Antonin Debidour, *Histoire diplomatique de l'Europe, 1814–1878,* 2 vols. (1891); Theodor von Sosnosky, *Die Balkanpolitik Oesterreich-Ungarns seit 1866,* 2 vols. (1913–1914).

Turkey in the Nineteenth and Twentieth Centuries. General histories: Stanley Lane-Poole, *The Story of Turkey* (1897), a well-organized and well-written summary in the " Story of the Nations " Series; Nicolae Jorga, *Geschichte des osmanischen Reiches,* Vol. V (1913), the best and most up-to-date account, part of a monumental work unfortunately not translated from the German; Sir Edward Creasy, *History of the Ottoman Turks from the Beginning of their Empire to the Present Time* (1877), based on the classical German work of Von Hammer, which is in ten volumes, and continued to 1876; E. A. Freeman, *The Ottoman Power in Europe: its Nature, its Growth, and its Decline* (1877). Recent descriptions: Richard Davey, *The Sultan and his Subjects,* new ed. rev. and cont. to date (1907); Sidney Whitman, *Turkish Memories* (1914), the outcome of several prolonged visits to Turkey, covering a period of twelve years, from 1896 to 1908, marked by sympathy for the Turks. On the Turkish Revolution of 1908–1909: C. R. Buxton, *Turkey in Revolution* (1909); G. F. Abbott, *Turkey in Transition* (1909); J. L. Barton, *Daybreak in Turkey,* 2d ed. (1908); Ernst Jäckh, *Der aufsteigende Halbmond* (1911), an extremely interesting German appreciation of the military and economic reforms of the Young Turks; René Pinon, *L'Europe et la Jeune Turquie: les aspects nouveaux de la question d'Orient* (1911). For an instructive series of sketches of the leaders and governors and foreign interests of Egypt, see A. E. P. Brome Weigall, *A History of Events in Egypt from 1798 to 1914* (1915); consult also the bibliography appended to Chapter XXIX, below.

Greece and the Balkan States. General: H. N. Brailsford, *Macedonia, its Races and their Future* (1906); William Miller, *The Balkans: Roumania, Bulgaria, Servia, and Montenegro,* 2d ed. (1908), a handy volume in the " Story of the Nations " Series; Nevill Forbes and others, *The Balkans: a History of Bulgaria, Serbia, Greece, Rumania, Turkey* (1915); André Chéradame, *Douze ans de propagande en faveur des peuples balkaniques* (1913), a review of Balkan history from 1900 to 1912. On Greece: William Miller, *Greek Life in Town and Country* (1905); Lewis Sergeant, *Greece in the Nineteenth Century: a Record of Hellenic Emancipation and Progress, 1821–1897* (1897); *Greece in Evolution,* studies prepared under the auspices of the French League for the Defense of the Rights of Hellenism, Eng. trans. ed. by G. F. Abbott (1909); R. A. H. Bickford-Smith, *Greece under King George* (1893); P. F. Martin, *Greece of the Twentieth Century* (1913). On Serbia: Alfred Stead (editor), *Servia by the Servians*

(1909), an estimate of Serbia and the Serb nationality from the pens of representative Serbs; Prince and Princess Lazarovich-Hrebelianovich, *The Servian People, their Past Glory and their Destiny*, 2 vols. (1910), encyclopedic, including history and description; W. M. Petrovitch, *Serbia, her People, History, and Aspirations* (1915). On Montenegro: F. S. Stevenson, *A History of Montenegro* (1912); P. Coquelle, *Histoire du Monténégro et de la Bosnie depuis les origines* (1895). On Bulgaria: Guérin Songeon, *Histoire de la Bulgarie depuis les origines jusqu'à nos jours, 485–1913* (1913), clear and succinct; Edward Dicey, *The Peasant State: an Account of Bulgaria in 1894* (1894), admirable both for society and for government; A. H. Beaman, *M. Stambuloff* (1895), a good biography of a famous Bulgarian statesman. On Rumania: Oscar Brilliant, *Roumania* (1915), an exhaustive description of present-day Rumania by a professor in the University of Bucharest; Nicolae Jorga, *Geschichte des rumänischen Volkes im Rahmen seiner Staatsbildungen*, 2 vols. (1905), a great national history; G. Benger, *Roumania in 1900*, Eng. trans. by A. H. Keene (1900); Sidney Whitman, *Reminiscences of the King of Roumania* (1899); Pompiliu Eliade, *Histoire de l'esprit public en Roumanie au XIXe siècle*, Vol. I (1905), *1821–1828*, and Vol. II (1914), *1828–1834;* Frédéric Damé, *Histoire de la Roumanie contemporaine depuis l'avènement des princes indigènes jusqu'à nos jours, 1822–1900* (1900); André Bellessort, *La Roumanie contemporaine* (1905).

The Tripolitan and Balkan Wars, 1911–1913. On the Tripolitan War of 1911–1912: Sir Thomas Barclay, *The Turco-Italian War and its Problems*, with appendices containing the chief state papers bearing on the subject . . . and with an additional chapter on Moslem Feeling by Ameer Ali (1912); W. K. McClure, *Italy in North Africa: an Account of the Tripoli Enterprise* (1913). On the Balkan Wars of 1912–1913: W. M. Sloane, *The Balkans: a Laboratory of History* (1914), a survey of the problems and diplomacy affecting the Great Powers as well as the Balkan States; J. G. Schurman, *The Balkan Wars, 1912–1913* (1914), an excellent summary; Hermenegild Wagner, *With the Victorious Bulgars* (1913), a newspaper correspondent's graphic picture of the Balkan lands and especially of the Bulgarian campaign against the Turks; Ellis Ashmead-Bartlett, *With the Turks in Thrace* (1913), the work of a special correspondent of the London *Daily Telegraph;* D. J. Cassavetti, *Hellas and the Balkan Wars* (1914); *Balkan Treaties, 1912–1913*, a valuable collection of the treaties of alliance and of peace, in the " American Journal of International Law," Vol. VIII, no. 1, supplement; *Report of the International Commission to Inquire into the Causes and Conduct of the Balkan Wars*, published by the Carnegie Endowment for International Peace (1914); I. E. Gueshoff, *The Balkan League*, Eng. trans. (1915), a Bulgarian statement. On the immediate results of the Balkan Wars: B. G. Baker, *The Passing of the Turkish Empire in Europe* (1913); G. M. Trevelyan, *The Servians and Austria* (1914), very partial to the Serb case; M. J. Bonn (editor), *Die Balkanfrage* (1914), a collection of ten articles by German professors on various phases of the new Balkan situation; R. W. Seton-

Watson, *The Southern Slav Question and the Habsburg Monarchy* (1911), a clear statement of the conflicting ambitions of Serbia and Austria-Hungary as they existed between the Habsburg annexation of Bosnia and the outbreak of the Balkan Wars; Marion I. Newbigin, *Geographical Aspects of Balkan Problems in their Relation to the Great European War* (1915).

PART V

NATIONAL IMPERIALISM

PART V

NATIONAL IMPERIALISM

THE general purpose of the preceding chapters has been to portray the development of democratic government and the rise of national patriotism among the peoples of Europe, and incidentally to furnish some account of the more significant events in the recent history of each European nation. Everywhere we have seen the Industrial Revolution at work, creating factories and railways, and adding to the wealth and importance of the bourgeoisie. Likewise the influence of the French Revolution has been universally apparent in the decline of the feudal nobility and in the ascendancy of the popular notions of nationalism and democracy. Both the Industrial and French Revolutions have combined to give business interests and bourgeois ideals a paramount position in the internal affairs of most European nations.

We are now in a position to study the operation of these same business interests and bourgeois ideals on a far grander scale, as they have determined in the nineteenth and twentieth centuries the course of international diplomacy and directed the current of European intercourse with Asia, Africa, and America.

CHAPTER XXVII

THE NEW IMPERIALISM AND THE SPREAD OF EUROPEAN CIVILIZATION IN ASIA

THE OLD COLONIAL MOVEMENT AND THE NEW IMPERIALISM

THE old colonial movement, dating from the epochal voyages of Columbus and of Vasco da Gama,[1] seemed to have lost much of its vitality in the early part of the nineteenth century. To be sure, the religious zeal which had figured so conspicuously in the earlier Spanish, Portuguese, and French colonization, continued to manifest itself in missionary endeavors, although no longer with energetic governmental support. But the other motive for colonization, the economic motive, had met with severe discouragement. The colonial rivalry of the sixteenth and seventeenth centuries, especially the contest between Holland and England,[2] and the world-conflict of France and Great Britain[3] in the eighteenth century had been largely inspired by the mercantilist doctrine that colonies were beneficial and necessary to the mother-country. Mercantilist statesmen[4] in the seventeenth and eighteenth centuries had confidently cultivated and carefully regulated colonial commerce with the two-fold object of creating a favorable balance of trade and rendering the nation economically independent of foreign countries. This mercantilist theory, however, was undermined late in the eighteenth century by the sharp criticisms of Turgot and Adam Smith. The new political economy taught by Turgot and Smith was summarized in the two French words, *laisser-faire*. Of course it took a goodly number of years for the doctrines of political

Decline of the Old Colonial Movement: Collapse of Mercantilism

[1] See Vol. I, ch. ii.   [2] See Vol. I, pp. 243 f., 278.
[3] See Vol. I, ch. ix.   [4] See Vol. I, pp. 63 f., 239 f., 322 ff., 338, 400 ff.

economists to bear fruit in practical politics; in fact, it may be stated that the long Revolutionary and Napoleonic struggle between Great Britain and France (1793-1815) was in the nature of a contest for mercantilist ends. But France was defeated, and in Great Britain the enthusiastic exponents [1] of *laisser-faire* subsequently became so influential that they were able to procure the repeal of the old Navigation Laws (1849), to sweep away multifarious customs duties, and triumphantly to proclaim the inauguration of an era of Free Trade.

Colonial revolts, moreover, seemingly proved mercantilism to be as disastrous in practice as it was unsound in theory. Great Britain lost her thirteen American colonies by attempting to enforce the mercantilist trade regulations of the "old colonial system." Early in the nineteenth century the Spanish colonies in America likewise revolted from the mother-country, and Brazil established its independence of Portugal (1822). These disasters, following in the train of long and expensive colonial wars, only confirmed the conviction in the minds of European statesmen that expending money and blood to acquire new colonies was unwise and unjustifiable. Richard Cobden, the famous English Free-Trade orator, even went so far as to declare (1849), "If we do not draw in our horns, this country, with all its resources, will sink under the weight of its extended empire." John Bright was no less outspoken in condemning imperialism and maintaining that the cost of acquiring and defending colonies was more than their worth. Gladstone was not so radical a "Little Englander," but he was decidedly reluctant to extend the British dominions.

In the first half of the nineteenth century, the old colonial movement seemed to be discredited. Let us briefly review what prior to 1815 had been its achievements. (1) Spain had overlaid with a veneer of Spanish Christian culture Mexico, Central America, most of South America (excepting Brazil), Cuba, Puerto Rico, and the Philippine Islands, — all of which she was to lose in the course of the nineteenth century. (2) Portugal not only had obtained footholds in southeast and southwest

Achievements of the Old Colonial Movement Prior to 1815

---

[1] Such men as Huskisson, Cobden, Bright, Peel, Gladstone. See above, pp. 82-85, 91 ff., 112 ff., 279 f.

Africa, but also had created a new Portuguese nation across the Atlantic in Brazil. (3) The Dutch were interested chiefly in exploiting East Indian Islands (Java, Sumatra, Borneo, Celebes, the Moluccas, and New Guinea); Dutch Guiana or Surinam (in South America) was comparatively unimportant; and the Dutch settlement of Cape Colony in South Africa,[1] like the Dutch settlement on the Hudson River,[2] had fallen into the grasp of Great Britain. (4) France had planted colonies in North America but had lost them, the French settlements in the Mississippi valley being absorbed by the United States,[3] and those in the St. Lawrence valley by Great Britain; of her once magnificent colonial empire, France retained only five posts in India to remind her of Dupleix's grandiose schemes, Guadeloupe and Martinique in the West Indies, French Guiana, and several small islands; and the creation of a new French empire was only faintly foreshadowed by feeble efforts in Madagascar and on the western coast of Africa. (5) Great Britain, having profited by the losses of Holland and France, had attained the proud position of the foremost colonial and maritime power. She had laid the foundations of empire in India, conquered Ceylon from the Dutch, and started the settlement of Australia; scant success had attended her colonizing enterprises on the African coast at Sierra Leone and Gambia, but in South Africa she had annexed the Dutch Cape Colony; Malta and Gibraltar insured her position in the Mediterranean; in South America she had taken part of Guiana from the Dutch (1803); she had a foothold on Honduras; Bermuda, the Bahamas, Jamaica, Trinidad, and other islands in the West Indies were hers, as well as New Brunswick, Nova Scotia, Newfoundland, and Prince Edward Island, Upper and Lower Canada, and the Hudson Bay Territory.

In summary, we may say that the most conspicuous achievement of the old colonial movement had been the discovery and Europeanization of the New World. Slight had been the progress, however, in the Europeanization of Asia. Russia had

---

[1] Cape Colony was conquered by Great Britain in 1806. See Vol. I, pp. 575 f.
[2] "New Amsterdam" was conquered by England in 1664. See Vol. I, pp. 243 f., 301.
[3] "Louisiana" was purchased by the United States, 1803.

long been groping her way eastward over the ice-fields and steppes of Siberia, but China and Japan had not yet been "opened up." Hardly any attempt had been made to penetrate the interior of Africa, the "Dark Continent." And even in America, the vast plains west of the Mississippi, the trackless Northwest Territory, and the tangled forests of the upper Amazon, were still left in the undisturbed possession of savage aborigines. To the "new imperialism" of the later nineteenth and early twentieth century was left the work of spreading the English language over Canada and all the United States, and the Russian tongue over all northern Asia, of exploring and partitioning Africa, opening up China, modernizing Japan, consolidating British India, developing Australia from an insignificant penal station into a thriving commonwealth, exploring the frozen polar regions, and founding the new French, German, and Italian colonial empires.

By the "New Imperialism" we mean the awakening of a new interest in colonization during the nineteenth century, especially

The New Imperialism and the Industrial Revolution
since 1870, and the marvelous progress which has since been made in the Europeanization of the world. It would not be far from the truth to say that the New Imperialism was the most significant feature in the history of the last half-century. The movement received its impulse from the Industrial Revolution and the French Revolution. The former produced the railway, the steamship, the telegraph, and the telephone, which annihilated distance and made the occupation of distant colonies infinitely more feasible, their commerce more valuable, their administration easier. The Industrial Revolution also enhanced the value of colonies as markets for manufactures and as sources of supply for raw materials and foodstuffs. In yet another way the Industrial Revolution imparted a mighty impetus to imperialism by creating a class of capitalists who were willing to invest their money in colonial enterprises; for the business men who had realized fortunes from their factories or railways at home were ever eager to increase their wealth by building railways, organizing industries, or developing mines in Africa, South America, or Asia.

The debt of the New Imperialism to the French Revolution

was twofold. In the first place, the French Revolution, and the subsequent insurrections inspired by the French Revolution, meant in a general way the victory of the bourgeoisie over feudalism and divine-right monarchy, and enabled the bourgeoisie to control the government for the benefit of its own interests, that is, business interests. These business interests, as we shall presently explain more fully, demanded colonial expansion. In the second place, the French Revolution led to the development of such an intense spirit of national patriotism that all classes were proud to assist in making any colonial acquisition which might add to the glory, extent, and power of their nation.

The French Revolution and the New Imperialism

In the latter half of the nineteenth century, when the harvest of the industrial and political revolutions was ripening to maturity, the new spirit of imperialism began to find expression. In England, Benjamin Disraeli heralded the new imperialist movement by buying for the British government 176,602 hundred-dollar shares in the Suez Canal (1875) and by proclaiming Victoria "empress of India" (1876). A generation later, Joseph Chamberlain put himself at the head of an enthusiastic party pledged to strengthen the British Empire. Meanwhile the Third French Republic had set itself with such zeal to seek compensation for the loss of Alsace-Lorraine that within thirty years three and one-half million square miles of territory, with twenty-six million inhabitants, had been added to its empire. Imperially-minded Hamburg merchants converted Bismarck to their views in 1884, and the recently-founded German Empire speedily acquired a million square miles and fourteen million subjects in Africa and Oceanica. Italy had no sooner achieved national unification than she, too, entered into the scramble for colonial dominion. Russia, Japan, the United States, Portugal, and Spain annexed new territories. Even the diminutive kingdom of Belgium acquired in the Congo a colonial empire eighty times as large as the mother-country.

The Contagion of Imperialism, 1871-1914

Before entering upon a detailed account of the foundation of these new colonial empires, it may be well to examine the economic, the patriotic, the missionary motives which explain the astonishing colonial activity of the hundred years from 1815 to 1915.

Motives for the New Imperialism, 1815-1915

Consider first the economic motives for acquiring colonies. We have seen how many Free Traders held that colonies were of little economic benefit to the mother-country. In the second half of the nineteenth century, however, a pronounced reaction set in against the thorough-going free-trade doctrines. Whereas the free traders had been chiefly anxious to emancipate business from restrictive and burdensome government regulations, the new school demanded that the government should positively protect and foster the infant industries of a nation, especially by imposing heavy customs-duties on imports, so as to give domestic manufactures an important advantage over imported foreign products in the home market. This idea of industrial "protection" was easily applied to colonies. The protectionists argued, in somewhat the same way as the seventeenth-century mercantilists had argued, that a colony would usually buy manufactures from and sell raw materials to the mother-country; hence, the more colonies a nation possessed, the wider market there would be for its manufactures; the wider the market for its manufactures, the greater would be the expansion of the nation's industries; and industrial expansion would bring wealth to the nation, earn profits for the manufacturer, and furnish employment for the laborer. According to these "neo-mercantilists," high protective tariffs and active colonial expansion would go hand in hand. The last quarter of the nineteenth century, which witnessed the adoption of high protective tariffs by every great industrial nation (with the exception of the United Kingdom),[1] was the very period in which colonial expansion proceeded most rapidly. One of the clearest illustrations of the connection between imperialism and tariff protection was afforded in 1898 when Canada, having previously adopted a high protective tariff, announced that henceforth the duties on imports from Great Britain would be a fourth[2] less than those on imports from other countries. Or, again, by

1. The Economic Motive

"Protection" and Colonial Markets

---

[1] It should be noted that, although Great Britain deemed it advantageous to adhere to free trade as far as the commerce of the United Kingdom was concerned, the British colonies established protective tariffs.

[2] In 1900, the preferential treatment was increased from a fourth to a third. It affected the whole British Empire, not merely the United Kingdom.

the French Tariff Act of 1892, while import duties were levied on foreign goods imported into French colonies, French goods were to be admitted free. These two concrete instances are sufficient to indicate the manner in which the possession of colonies might be advantageous to the trade and industry of a nation.

On the other hand, it is easy to prove by statistics that this advantage in colonial trade is much smaller than might be supposed. In 1913 Canada purchased only twenty per cent of her total imports from the United Kingdom; whereas Argentina, which is not a colony of Great Britain at all, obtained more than thirty per cent of her imports from the United Kingdom. France enjoyed less than a third of the total trade of her colony of Indo-China. The trade of Canada was more valuable to Germany than that of all the German colonies. In reply to this criticism, it is possible to instance a few colonies like the Dutch East Indies, the trade of which is largely in the hands of the mother-country. But the value of such trade was usually more than counterbalanced by the actual expenditure of the mother-country for the acquisition, administration, and defense of the colony. For example, when the total trade of Germany with German Southwest Africa in 1913 amounted only to 28,600,000 marks, it is difficult indeed to understand how the profit would make up the deficit of 12,140,000 marks which Germany had to pay for the government of the colony. Colonial trade, moreover, was a very small item in the total foreign trade of a nation. Thus Germany in 1913 exported to France alone almost fourteen times as much as to all the German colonies put together. From such figures the inference is plain that as far as commercial privileges were concerned, many colonies were of little or no advantage to the mother-country. In other words, the industrial and commercial prosperity of a nation could hardly be said to depend essentially upon the number of its colonies.

The real economic reason for imperialism was not so much the commercial advantage which colonies might afford to the mother-country, as the opportunities for gain which colonial enterprises offered to individuals in the mother-country. Investments in colonial mines, rubber forests, plantations, and railways yielded interest at anywhere from five to fifty per cent. The large profits to be gained from colonial investments natu-

Private Investments and Private Profits

rally attracted capitalists; and it is not surprising that men with their money invested in colonies should become eloquent advocates of a vigorous colonial and naval policy, especially when the expense of such a policy would be borne by the taxpayers of the nation at large. In every important nation there were to be found a group of bankers who were interested in colonial finance, liquor dealers who supplied the natives with alcoholic drinks often of an inferior grade, a handful of importers who specialized in colonial wares, and a larger number of bourgeois speculators who owned shares in some colonial mine or industry. All these people were ardent imperialists. The influence which investments have exercised in promoting imperialism were revealed in 1911, when the German government manifested great interest in Morocco, largely because the Mannesmann Brothers were financially interested in Moroccan mines. To cite another case, the beginnings of British rule in Egypt may be traced directly to the desire of the British government to safeguard the Egyptian investments of certain capitalists.

The comparatively small number of business men with actual economic interests at stake usually found it an easy matter to

2. The Patriotic Motive

gain popular support for a policy of imperial expansion. Patriotic to a fault, the vast majority of people were always ready to applaud the annexation of new territory. If the new territory happened to be a sparsely

Colonies for National Power and Prestige

settled region, it would serve as an outlet for emigration from the mother-country; if densely populated, the new dependency was probably sadly in need of European culture and orderly government; if only a barren island, the new colony would at least be a valuable coaling-station for the navy. And in any case, the average citizen felt a warm glow of satisfaction when he beheld the ever-larger blotch of red, or yellow, or purple that depicted on the map "our Empire." The American who was quite certain of the necessity of conferring the benefits of American civilization upon unwilling Filipinos, was inspired by the same patriotic egotism which convinced the German of Germany's world-mission, and moved the Englishman to talk of the "white man's burden." To every patriot it seemed obvious that the "manifest destiny" of his nation was to expand, to rule "inferior races," to become a World Power. Patriotic sentiment of this variety was invariably favorable to aggressive imperialism.

In this connection an additional word should be said about the popular argument for colonies as an outlet for surplus population. The problem of providing for "surplus population" became pressing in the nineteenth century with the rapid increase of population after the Industrial Revolution. Colonies for Surplus Population The population of Germany, for instance, increased from 41,058,792 in 1871 to 64,925,993 in 1910 — a gain of almost twenty-four millions. The appalling growth of the "slum" sections in most European cities and the misery of the working classes seemed to bear out the theory of the British economist, Malthus, that population tended to increase more rapidly than the means of subsistence. To prove conclusively that Europe was burdened with a surplus of population, one had only to point out the fact that in the second half of the century about nine million persons emigrated from the British Isles; that during the nineteenth century more than six million Germans became emigrants. To ardent nationalists it seemed a pity that these emigrants should be lost to the nation by settling in some foreign country, like the United States, abandoning their native language and surrendering their allegiance to "the old country." To remedy this sad state of affairs, each nation should provide itself with colonies, into which its surplus population might overflow, exactly as some of the superabundant population of Great Britain had overflowed to Canada and Australia. Some patriots went so far as to declare that a vigorous nation with a high birth rate had a moral right to conquer new territory for its rapidly enlarging population. Hence, imperialism, the conquest of more colonies, was justifiable if not morally necessary.

Although the "surplus population" argument still carries great weight with the public, in practice it has not worked out very well. In spite of the fact that Germany had acquired a million square miles of colonial territory, in 1913 out of a total of 25,843 German emigrants, 19,124 sought homes in the United

States, 5537 in Canada, 359 in Australia, 140 in Brazil. In that year more Germans were living in the British colony of Canada than in all the German oversea dominions. Clearly the German colonies had failed to attract German immigrants. Perhaps Germany had been particularly unfortunate in acquiring only tropical colonies, unfit for European habitation. But even Great Britain, with all her colonies in every climatic zone, still sent to the United States in the year 1913 more than 88,000 emigrants; and within twenty-five years after 1870 almost three million citizens of the United Kingdom settled in the United States rather than in the British colonies.

Along with the economic and patriotic motives for imperialism, there has pretty generally been a religious incentive. The desire to convert heathen peoples to Christianity has been a striking characteristic of the Christian Church in all ages. St. Paul, the apostle who evangelized Asia Minor and Greece; St. Patrick, the "apostle of Ireland" in the fifth century; St. Boniface, who carried Christianity to the Germans in the eighth century; St. Methodius, the pioneer of missionaries among the Slavs in the ninth century; the Franciscan friars who ventured into China as emissaries of the Catholic Church in the thirteenth century; St. Francis Xavier, the Spanish Jesuit of the sixteenth century, who converted thousands by his preaching in India and Japan, — these were only the more famous among thousands of zealous missionaries of the Christian Church. Missionary motives were at least in part responsible for the Commercial Revolution. Columbus, indeed, regarded himself as a missionary. The colonial expansion of Europe was accompanied, and to a considerable extent promoted, by the expansion of Roman Catholic missions, which were efficiently organized under the central control of the papal Congregation of the Propaganda, organized by Pope Gregory XV in 1622. The Jesuits, and the Dominican and Franciscan friars, preaching, baptizing, teaching, and, if need be, dying for the faith, converted most of the natives of Latin America, Christianized part of the Philippines, and established important Christian communities in India, China, Japan, in Africa, and in Polynesia. Among the numerous organizations for Catholic foreign missions, special mention

3. The Religious Motive

Roman Catholic Missions

should be made of the international Society for the Propagation of the Faith, which was founded at Lyons in 1822 and had collected for missions by the year 1910 more than $78,000,000. In 1910 there were more than 11,000 missionary priests (including some 5000 native priests) at work in Asia, Africa, and Australasia.

Until the nineteenth century, the various Protestant sects took comparatively little part in the conversion of the heathen. The Society for the Propagation of the Gospel in New England (1649), the isolated endeavors of a few clergy- men, the Society for the Propagation of the Gospel in Foreign Parts (1701), and the remarkable work of the Moravians (1731– 1732), foreshadowed but did not inaugurate the era of Protestant missionary enthusiasm. Just at the close of the eighteenth century, the formation by William Carey of a "Baptist Society for Propagating the Gospel among the Heathen" (1792), the organization of the London Missionary Society (1795) by Presbyterians and Congregationalists, and the establishment of the (Anglican) Church Missionary Society (1799), indicated the awakening interest in proselytism that was to characterize the nineteenth century. Thenceforward missionary societies, large and small, of every sect and of every nationality, numbering into the hundreds, were formed for the promotion of foreign missions. Mission study clubs and periodical publications sprang into existence for the purpose of disseminating information about the quaint customs or outlandish manners of the heathen folk to whom Bibles, missionaries, medicine, and civilized clothes were being sent.

Protestant Missions

The importance of this missionary movement in stimulating imperialism can hardly be exaggerated. Many earnest Christians, who might otherwise have disapproved colonial expansion, became enthusiastic when they considered that the propagation of the faith might be promoted by annexing the territory in question. In Africa, and in the islands of the South Sea, time and again an enterprising missionary-explorer led the way first for merchants and then for soldiers. "The first raising of the flag of Germany on the soil of Africa grew out of the need of protecting the Rhenish missionaries in Namaqualand (German Southwest Africa)." Again,

Missions and Imperialism

when Germany seized Kiao-chau in China, it was to avenge the murder of two German missionaries. Or, in the case of Great Britain, when the British East Africa Company was about to abandon its unprofitable territory in the region of Lake Victoria Nyanza, in 1891, the Church Missionary Society paid the Company £15,000 to hold the territory another year, in the hope — which was fulfilled in 1893 — that the British government might then be induced to assume responsibility for the country.

Missionaries have done much to further the work of imperialism, but it is doubtful whether imperialism has furthered the work of the missionaries. Not only have there been cases where missionary activity has been directly discouraged by the government, for fear that the awakening of religious antipathies might lead to political unrest, as in India and in Egypt; but far more harmful to the propagation of Christianity has been the shameless immorality and cruelty exhibited by European officials and traders in their dealings with the subject peoples. While the missionary was preaching the Christian precepts of charity, unselfishness, purity, and temperance, stern government officials were practicing ruthless severity, avaricious commercial corporations were enriching themselves by forcing the natives into virtual slavery, licentious soldiers were giving free rein to their vicious passions, European liquor agents were supplying the natives with cheap gin. The barbarous methods pursued by European rubber merchants in compelling the negroes of central Africa (notoriously, but by no means exclusively, in the Congo Free State) to collect rubber for commercial purposes, were calculated to inspire bitter hatred rather than grateful respect for Christian civilization.

The aim of this brief general discussion of the New Imperialism has been to suggest the underlying motives — economic, patriotic, and religious — which have been largely responsible **Summary** for the partition of Africa, the appropriation of the South Sea Islands, the spread of European civilization in Asia, and the development of the Americas in the century 1815–1915. In the course of the following chapters the thoughtful student will discern for himself many illustrations and new implications of the tendencies which have been outlined in this section.

As regards the moral justification or the alleged economic necessity for recent imperialism, the student must form his own conclusions. There is one reflection, however, without which this discussion would be incomplete, and with which this section may appropriately be closed,—namely, the effect of this imperialism upon the two cardinal principles of nineteenth-century politics,—nationalism and democracy. In an earlier paragraph we suggested that nationalism, or patriotic pride, was one of the causes of imperialism, and that triumph of national sentiment in Germany, in Italy, in France was accompanied by colonial aggrandizement. The very nations that had prized national freedom more highly than life itself, became destroyers of freedom in Africa and Asia. At the very close of the nineteenth century, which was preëminently the century of nationalism, Great Britain defied nationalism by her conquest of the two Boer republics in South Africa (1899–1902). Italy, having liberated herself from Austria-Hungary, attempted to subjugate the free nation of Abyssinia. It is a strange paradox that those who most cherished their own national independence, should least regard that of others. To this unhappy inconsistency we may trace not only the origin of a cynical attitude towards the ideal of Nationalism, but also the rise of that bitter imperial and militaristic [1] rivalry between the Great Powers, which culminated in the War of the Nations.

Imperialism and Nationalism

The effect of imperialism on Democracy has been no less deleterious. In dealing with their colonial possessions, even the most democratic nations have thrown Democracy overboard. The general type of modern colonial government has been the autocratic rule of a magistrate, or "governor-general," appointed by the home government and responsible to the home government rather than to the colony. The so-called "legislative councils" which existed in many colonies had no real control of the government, and were as a rule only partly elective. In most German colonies not even this shadow of representative government was found. The reason for this repudiation of democracy is obvious. The barbarous tribes of the South Sea Islands, the uncivilized negroes of Uganda, or the cannibal tribes of Dahomey, could hardly be

Effect of Imperialism on Democracy

[1] See below, pp. 687 ff.

intrusted with the ballot.   In India and in Egypt, where the
level of civilization was much higher, the illiteracy of the vast
majority of the population would furnish an excuse for undemocratic bureaucracy.   But even were it possible, through the diffusion of education, to overcome this practical obstacle, there
would still remain the fundamental difficulty, that if the inhabitants of the colonies had their way, beyond peradventure
of a doubt they would in almost every case put an end to the
domination of the "mother country." [1]

THE PARTIAL DISMEMBERMENT AND THE POLITICAL REGENERATION OF THE CHINESE EMPIRE

The narrative of the achievements of nineteenth-century
imperialism — the narrative to which the foregoing section was
an explanatory preface — may well begin with a study of the
effects of European imperialism upon Asia, the oldest and largest
of continents.   Throughout the ages European adventurers and
merchants had been attracted by the wealth, fascinated by the
civilization, and awed by the vastness of Asia; but the spread
of European civilization in the Far East had made small progress
prior to the nineteenth century.   Russia had appropriated the
bleak expanse of Siberia; portions of India had been brought
under British domination; Dutch traders had established themselves in the East Indies, and Spanish missionaries in the Philippine Islands.   Elsewhere the influence of Europe had not been
strongly felt.   In the nineteenth century, however, the powerful
pressure of European imperialism revolutionized China, Japan,
and Persia, and in effect reduced the whole of Asia to a position of either political or economic dependence upon Europe.
For convenience, we shall first depict the course of events in the
Chinese Empire and its dependencies, then the awakening of
Japan, the expansion of Russia, and the predicament of Persia.[2]

The greatest and probably the most ancient of Oriental states
was the Empire of China.   In territorial extent and in popula-

[1] To the sweeping generalizations of this paragraph, exception must be made in
respect of certain " self-governing colonies " in the British Empire, notably Canada,
Newfoundland, Australia, New Zealand, and South Africa.   See below, ch. xxix.
[2] For the British Empire in Asia — India and its dependencies — see below,
pp. 662–672.

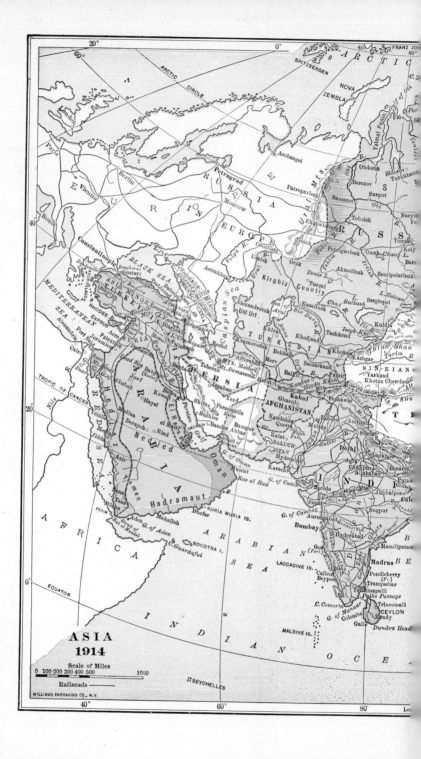

ASIA
1914

Scale of Miles
0 100 200 300 400 500   1000

Railroads ⎯⎯⎯⎯⎯

WILLIAMS ENGRAVING CO., N.Y.

tion the Chinese Empire was approximately equal to the whole
of Europe. The bulk of the three hundred millions of people
lived along the great river valleys of the Huang-ho The Ancient
and the Yangtsze-kiang, and were included within the Chinese
eighteen provinces of China proper, which territorially Empire
constituted about one-third of the entire empire. There for centuries — possibly forty or fifty centuries — the short, slant-
eyed yellow men had lived and labored, carefully cultivating
their tiny farms (three acres was considered a good farm), eating
their rice or millet, fishing in the great rivers, or sailing their
picturesque "junks," flying their kites for sport, weaving fabrics
of silk and cotton for the loose trousers and wide-sleeved jackets
which men and women alike wore, offering sacrifices at their
ancestral tombs, manufacturing exquisite porcelain, painting
curious and delicate pictures, and fashioning quaint vases of
bronze. The Chinese, proud of their own ancient culture, were
prone to despise all foreigners as barbarians. Of European civilization, of railways, of steam-engines, they were blissfully
ignorant, until comparatively recently. Before the nineteenth
century few Europeans could gain admission to the "Celestial
Empire." Only the bold missionaries of the Roman Catholic
Church and occasional enterprising traders had disturbed the
complacent stagnation of Chinese civilization.

Back in the thirteenth century, Marco Polo had sojourned at
the magnificent court of Kublai Khan, the Mongol emperor of
China. At an even earlier date, Franciscan friars Early In-
had been sent into the Far East by Pope Innocent IV, tercourse
and in the fourteenth century they had established with Europe
a Christian Church in Pekin, as well as in other Chinese
cities. From the sixteenth century, despite all obstacles, Roman
Catholic missionaries continued their work in China, making
many converts. In the sixteenth century, Portuguese merchants
had made their appearance in the China Sea and had built their
warehouses at Macao (south of Canton) for the trade in silks
and tea. The following century, the seventeenth, had seen
Dutch traders established on the island of Formosa, and British
at Canton. The Chinese trade was extremely precarious, however; it was only barely tolerated by the Chinese government.
The merchants who visited China were harassed by unfriendly

Chinese officials, burdened by heavy taxes, and not always secure in their lives and property. Until well into the nineteenth century, China remained practically closed to Europeans.

In the course of that century, and especially after 1870, China's self-sufficient isolation was disturbed in three ways. (1) The Chinese government found itself powerless to prevent European merchants from trafficking in Chinese seaports, Christian missionaries from preaching their gospel, and foreign capitalists from building railways, opening mines, and erecting factories within China. (2) Outlying provinces and tributary states of the Chinese Empire fell into the hands of foreign nations. (3) European ideas began to affect many of the Chinese people profoundly and to react powerfully upon the political life of the nation. Let us see how this came about.

In the first of these directions, *i.e.* in the opening up of China to European merchants and missionaries, an important stride

The Opening of China to Foreign Commerce: the Opium War, 1840–1842

was made in 1840, when the so-called Opium War was waged by Great Britain against China. It grew out of a quarrel between the Chinese government, which had prohibited the importation of opium, and the British traders at Canton, who insisted on smuggling opium from India into China. In June, 1840, a British fleet attacked the Chinese coast and captured the cities of Canton, Amoy, Ningpo, Shanghai, and Chin-kiang. Finally the emperor was compelled to sign the treaty of Nanking (1842), whereby the four ports of Amoy, Ningpo, Foochow, and Shanghai, in addition to Canton, were thrown open to foreign traders; the island of Hongkong (near Canton) was formally ceded to Great Britain; and China promised to pay $21,000,000 as a war indemnity. Curiously enough, the opium question which had occasioned the war was left unsettled. The fruits of Great Britain's victory were speedily shared by traders of other nations, — American, French, Belgian, Prussian, Dutch, and Portuguese, — who during the next decade gained the privilege of trading at the treaty ports. In fifteen years (1842–1856) China's tea-export doubled and the export of silk increased from 3000 to 56,000 bales.

The next step in the opening up of China was the Second Chinese War (1856–1860), waged by France and Great Britain, the former to avenge the murder of a missionary, the latter because the crew of a ship sailing under the British flag had been seized and jailed as pirates by a Chinese official. Canton was again taken by the British. French and English forces captured the Taku forts and proceeded up the Pei-ho River towards the imperial capital, Pekin, by way of Tientsin. At Tientsin they were met by commissioners of the emperor, with whom the treaty of Tientsin (1858) was negotiated. Hardly had the treaty been signed, however, when some British ships were treacherously fired upon by Chinese forts. Warlike operations were resumed by the allied forces, which now pushed their way up to the very gates of Pekin. There a brother of the emperor induced them to conclude peace (1860). China was to pay a war indemnity of 8,000,000 *taels*. The (modified) treaty [1] of Tientsin was now finally ratified, by which Great Britain received a foothold on the mainland next to Hongkong; six new ports (including Tientsin) were opened to trade, in addition to the five already existing treaty ports; foreign ministers might reside at Pekin; the privilege of traveling in the interior was conceded to Europeans; and Christian missionaries were not only to be tolerated, but even protected by the Chinese government. The traffic in opium, moreover, was legally recognized under a revised tariff.

The Second Chinese War (1856–1860); the Treaties of Tientsin

By the events of 1840–1860 China had been thrown open to European commerce [2] and to Christian missionaries. The invasion of China by European capitalists, and the beginnings in China of the Industrial Revolution, were to come at a later date. We shall, therefore, leave them for subsequent consideration, while we turn to the second phase of the Chinese question — the partial dismemberment of the Chinese Empire.

Within an empire so vast and so loosely knit together as that of China, there could not fail to be a tendency to disintegration, especially when energetic foreign nations were eager to hasten the process with a view to their own gain. The Chinese emperor was first of all sovereign of the eighteen Chinese prov-

---

[1] Or rather the treaties of Tienstin: one with France, one with Great Britain.
[2] Henceforth Chinese foreign trade was to advance with enormous rapidity, to the value of 188,123,877 *taels* in 1887; 437,959,675 *taels* in 1901; 674,988,988 *taels* in 1905; and in 1913 to 1,149,513,642 *taels* ($842,018,611).

inces, with their 1,500,000 square miles and 300,000,000 inhabitants: a vast realm stretching from Manchuria and Mongolia
The Extent on the north to Tonkin and Burma on the south,
of the and from the China Sea on the east to Tibet on the
Chinese west. In addition, the emperor was lord of Man-
Empire
about churia to the north of China proper. The three
1800 Manchurian provinces, extending over almost 400,000
square miles, and including some 12,000,000 inhabitants, had
been united to China when in the seventeenth century an
China ambitious Manchu chieftain had supplanted the na-
Proper tive dynasty of Chinese emperors. Since the seventeenth century, China had been ruled by Manchu emperors, who,
by the way, introduced the custom of wearing the
Manchuria
hair in a long queue or pigtail.

Besides the eighteen provinces of China and the three provinces of Manchuria, the Chinese emperor also exercised control,
The Fringe in varying degree, over a fringe of tributary and
of Quasi- subject states surrounding China proper. Korea, the
Independent peninsula between the Sea of Japan and the Yellow
States
Sea, had for many centuries been a kingdom tributary to China and partaking of Chinese civilization, a kingdom
somewhat smaller than Great Britain and about one-
Korea
third as populous. Still further north, the valley
of the Amur River was until 1860 claimed by China. To the
northwest was the vast territory of Mongolia, with
Mongolia
almost seven times as many acres as France, but with
fewer people than Paris. Inner Mongolia, bounded by the desert
of Gobi, China, and Manchuria, was under the direct control of
the Manchu emperors of China; Outer Mongolia, stretching
westward to the Tarbagatai Mountains, was too distant to be
easily ruled from Pekin, and, although a Chinese agent was
maintained at Urga, the hereditary khans were al-
Sin-kiang
most independent. South of Mongolia and with its
center directly west of Pekin, was the enormous province of Sin-
kiang (including Chinese Turkestan, Kuldja, Zungaria, and other
territories). Sin-kiang was administered by Chinese
Tibet
officials with native subordinates. Tibet, south of Sin-
kiang and west of China, was a region equally vast and sparsely
populated. At the capital city of Tibet, Lhasa (a little town of

15,000 inhabitants), dwelt the Dalai Lama, whom the Tibetans regarded as their supreme religious head and civil authority. Chinese authority in Tibet was represented by a few Chinese officials and by Chinese garrisons. Between Tibet and India were the two small states of Nepal and Bhutan, of which the latter was entirely independent and the former only occasionally sent envoys with presents to Pekin. Further southward lay the kingdoms of Burma, Siam, Cambodia, and Annam (including Cochin-China and Tonkin), all of which at the opening of the nineteenth century were practically independent states, although China still claimed Burma, Siam, and Annam as vassals. Finally, to the east of China lay the islands of Hainan, Formosa, and the Liukiu group. The first was part of the Chinese province of Kwangtung. Formosa had been conquered by the Chinese in the seventeenth century. And the Liukiu archipelago had been paying tribute to China since the fourteenth century. **Indo-China**

From all sides, Russia, Japan, and Great Britain pressed in on this fringe of states bordering China proper. From the north China was menaced by Russian expansion. Russian settlements were made on the island of Sakhalin. The region north of the Amur River, coveted by Russian statesmen since the middle of the seventeenth century, was finally annexed to Russian Siberia by the treaties of 1858 and 1860, when also the coast district south of the Amur, east of the Ussuri River, and north of Korea, was added to the Russian dominions. Russia next encroached on Chinese territory in the extreme west by annexing the fertile Kuldja district in the province of Sin-kiang, at a time when China was embarrassed by a revolt. **Foreign Aggression** **Russia**

Meanwhile the progressive little island empire of Japan was beginning to claim a share in the spoliation of the Chinese Empire. In 1874 Japan annexed the Liukiu archipelago and then turned covetous eyes toward Manchuria and Korea. First of all, Japan recognized Korea as an independent kingdom (1876). Then, by continual interference in Korean affairs, the Japanese embroiled China in a series of quarrels. Finally, when China sent troops to Korea, at the invitation of the king, and reasserted **Korea and the Chino-Japanese War, 1894–1895** her claims to suzerainty over the kingdom, a body of Japanese soldiers seized the king and prepared for war with China (1894). The war, known to history as the Chino-Japanese War of 1894–1895, was simply a succession of catastrophes for over-confident China. The "dwarfs," as the Chinese had contemptuously styled their foemen, in less than six months routed the Chinese forces in Korea, invaded Manchuria, captured Port Arthur, supposedly impregnable, demoralized the Chinese navy, and captured the naval stronghold of Wei-hai-wei. The triumphant

Treaty of Shimono-seki, 1895 Japanese forces were ready to advance on Pekin when peace was made by the treaty of Shimonoseki, 17 April, 1895. In addition to a war indemnity of $157,940,000, Japan obtained from China the title to the island of Formosa and to the Liao-tung peninsula, including the coveted naval base of Port Arthur, and important commercial concessions. Wei-hai-wei, moreover, was to be held by Japan until the treaty stipulations had been faithfully executed. China renounced all claim to the kingdom of Korea, which now gradually passed under the tutelage of Japan.

Japan's gains were Russia's grievance. For Russian expansionists had hoped eventually to annex Manchuria, Korea, and

Revision of the Treaty of Shi-monoseki by Russia, Germany, and France Port Arthur, thereby giving to Russia an ice-free outlet in the Far East and predominance in northern Asia. To this ambition the treaty of Shimonoseki spelled defeat. The Russian government, therefore, resolved to tear up the obnoxious treaty. It was not difficult to gain the coöperation of Germany and France, for both Powers were anxious to increase their prestige in the Far East, and both were jealous of the upstart Japan. Professing their alarm lest the cession of Port Arthur might lead to the ultimate disintegration of the ancient Chinese Empire, Russia, France, and Germany advised Japan to surrender her conquests on the mainland. This "friendly advice" Japan could not dare to ignore. Compliantly the Japanese government returned all except Formosa to China, receiving in return an additional indemnity of $23,700,000. But the Japanese were furiously disappointed, and they long remembered who had cheated Japan of the fruits of victory.

Japanese resentment was still further aroused when the three

Powers, who in order to despoil Japan had posed as the friends of China, now proceeded to help themselves to Chinese territory. The Germans in 1897 seized the bay of Kiao-chau in the province of Shan-tung, with the flimsy excuse that only in this manner could Germany obtain satisfaction for the murder of two German missionaries in China. The real intention of the Germans became clear, however, when they extorted a ninety-nine-year lease of Kiao-chau and began to fortify the place as a base for German power in the province of Shan-tung. France secured (1898) a similar lease of Kwang-chow Wan, a valuable bay on the mainland opposite the island of Hainan, which, it was believed, would also come under French rule eventually. But it was Russia that profited most richly by the *coup*. Russian influence became all-powerful in Pekin; and Russian capitalists loaned China $80,000,000. Russia secured the right to carry her trans-Siberian railway across Chinese Manchuria to Vladivostok, — a right which practically gave Manchuria into Russia's hands, since Russian infantry and cavalry would accompany the railway into Manchuria. Furthermore, Russia obtained a lease (1898) of Port Arthur and the neighboring harbor of Talien-wan, which were immediately linked up by railway with the trans-Siberian system. The telegraph lines of Korea were likewise connected with the Siberian lines. Obviously Russia once more regarded Manchuria, Korea, and the Liao-tung peninsula as her "sphere of influence."

Gains of Germany, France, and Russia, 1897–1898

These gains of Russia, France, and Germany excited British jealousy to such a pitch that the British government demanded and occupied (1898) the harbor of Wei-hai-wei, from which the British could keep a watchful eye upon the aggressive Russians in Port Arthur and the energetic Germans in Kiao-chau. A few years later Great Britain concluded an alliance with Japan (1902), to protect Manchuria and Korea from the ever more menacing Russian encroachments.

Intervention of Great Britain and the Anglo-Japanese Alliance, 1902

As it became ever clearer that the Russian government intended practically to annex Manchuria, the resentful Japanese resolved to check their rival by force of arms. The result was the Russo-Japanese War (1904–1905). Victory attended the Japanese. By the treaty of

The Russo-Japanese War, 1904–1905

Portsmouth (5 September, 1905) Russia acknowledged her complete defeat by surrendering to Japan the lease of Liao-tung, including Port Arthur, by recognizing Japanese inter- ests as supreme in Korea, and by yielding to Japan some 500 miles of railway.[1]   Manchuria, aside from the Liao-tung peninsula, was to be evacuated by both Japan and Russia,[2] restored to the civil administration of China, and preserved as a sort of neutral zone.

Treaty of Portsmouth: Russian Check and Japanese Gains

Not long after the war Japan and Russia came to an under- standing, and agreed to substitute a policy of coöperation for their former rivalry.   On the basis of this under- standing, Japan and Russia henceforth worked to- gether harmoniously.   With a free hand Japan pro- ceeded to assume control of Korea's foreign affairs, to force reforms upon the Korean government, to depose the Korean monarch, and finally to annex Korea (1910).   Russia, on the other hand, turned her attention to another portion of the Chinese Empire, the vast region of Mongolia.   Merchants, Cossacks, and filibusters rapidly weaned Outer Mongolia from its allegiance to China.   In 1912, while China was torn by a repub- lican revolution, the Outer Mongolians, with Russian encourage- ment, repudiated Chinese rule and sought the protection of Russia.   In vain Chinese patriots protested.   On 5 November, 1913, the Chinese government reluctantly agreed to a treaty with Russia, giving the Russians extensive privileges in Outer Mongolia and retaining for China only a hollow pretense of suzerainty over the province.

Japan in Korea and Russia in Mongolia

While Russia and Japan were encroaching upon the northern territories of China, Great Britain and France were making similar inroads upon the fringe of quasi-independent states in the south.   In 1862 France had secured a foothold on the Indo-Chinese peninsula, when, after making war upon the native king of Annam, who was ruler of Cochin-China and Tonkin, the French obtained three provinces of Cochin-China at the mouth of the Mekong River.   The very next year (1863) the French established their protectorate over the neighboring

The French in Indo- China

[1] For other provisions of the treaty of Portsmouth, as well as for a more detailed account of the Russo-Japanese war, see below, pp. 583 ff.

[2] With the exception of small railway guards.

kingdom of Cambodia, which had been hard pressed to maintain its independence against the Siamese on the west and the Annamese on the east. In 1867 the French annexed the three remaining provinces of Cochin-China. The kingdom of Annam, together with its dependency of Tonkin, was the next object of French ambition. To Tonkin, then, France sent her troops (1882), ostensibly to put down the piratical bands which infested the region, and presently announced that Tonkin was a French protectorate. Against this high-handed procedure, the Chinese government strenuously remonstrated, inasmuch as China claimed to be suzerain over Annam and Tonkin. Remonstrances proving of no avail, China took up arms. The war that followed was by no means a triumph for France; and when peace was concluded in 1885, China sustained her claim to suzerainty, although France was allowed to establish a protectorate over Annam and Tonkin. France had thus acquired between 1862 and 1885 sovereignty over Cochin-China and a protectorate over Cambodia and Annam (including Tonkin), — the entire eastern half of the Indo-Chinese peninsula. Her subsequent acquisition of Kwang-chow Wan (1898), in the Chinese province of Kwang-tung, pointed to the extension of French influence, if not ultimate French sovereignty, over the Chinese territory surrounding the gulf of Tonkin, *i.e.*, the island of Hainan, the southern part of the province of Kwang-tung, and possibly the province of Kwang-si.

Great Britain on the southwest completed the circle of foreign aggressors upon Chinese soil. Step by step the British had established their supremacy in India, until late in the The British nineteenth century they began to look eastward and in Burma northward for further conquests. To the east of and Tibet India lay the kingdom of Burma, rich in forests, in fertility, in minerals. To be sure, Burma was a tributary state of China; but no such consideration weighed upon the British when in 1885 they invaded the country, deposed King Theebaw, and annexed his dominions to the British crown. To the north of India lay the independent states of Nepal and Bhutan, and the vast Chinese dependency of Tibet, with its stores of salt, soda, potash, gold, iron, and borax, awaiting development. It was not necessary formally to annex Nepal and Bhutan: they

naturally became quasi-independent protégés of the British.
In Tibet, however, the British encountered obstinate opposition
on the part of the Chinese, who were determined not to let
Tibet slip out of their grasp. Nevertheless, China was unable
to prevent the British in 1904 from negotiating directly with
the Tibetan government at Lhasa for concessions to British-
Indian traders, and when in 1912 the Chinese government attempted to treat Tibet as a Chinese province, Great Britain
insisted that China was no more than nominal suzerain of Tibet.
Encouraged by Great Britain's attitude, the Tibetans rose in
rebellion against China, expelled all Chinese soldiers and officials
from their country, and defeated the small expeditionary armies
sent out from China. Diplomatic negotiations led to the formu-
lation of a convention in 1914, whereby Tibet was to be divided
into Outer and Inner Tibet, China retaining a mere fiction of
suzerainty over the whole territory and engaging not to interfere at all in the affairs of Outer Tibet. Upon the refusal of
the Chinese government to ratify this Convention, Great
Britain gave notice that China would be deprived of whatever
advantages remained to her in Tibet. The ultimate fate of
Tibet could hardly be in doubt; China would find her nominal
suzerainty but a thin thread whereby to secure Tibet against
the mighty attraction which had already drawn Burma into
the British Empire.

Let us briefly review the events thus far chronicled. The
ancient Empire of China was thrown open to merchants and
missionaries during the period from the beginning of
the Opium War in 1840 to the close of the Second
Chinese War in 1860, by which wars certain "treaty
ports" were opened to foreign commerce, missionaries
gained at least a theoretical claim to protection by
the government, and Europeans were given the right
to travel in China. During the next period, from 1860 to 1914,
China saw her dependencies one by one falling prey to aggressive foreign nations: — Amur to Russia (1860), the
Liukiu archipelago to Japan (1874), Kuldja to Russia
(1881), Annam to France (1885), Burma to Great Britain (1885),
Formosa to Japan (1895), the Liao-tung peninsula to Japan
(1895), then to Russia (1898), then to Japan (1905), Korea to

Summary of Foreign Encroach-ments on the Chinese Empire, 1840-1914

Territorial

Japan (annexed 1910), Outer Mongolia to Russia (1913), Outer Tibet to Great Britain (1914). Outer Mongolia and Tibet, to be sure, still remained formally under Chinese suzerainty, but there was little question that they would ultimately be appropriated, the one by Russia, the other by Great Britain. The "foreign devils" had, moreover, wrested from China a number of valuable seaports. Macao, long since occupied by the Portuguese, was in 1887 ceded to them; Hongkong in 1842 was ceded to Great Britain; Port Arthur was first ceded to Japan (1895), then leased to Russia (1898), then to Japan (1905); Kiao-chau was leased to the Germans, Wei-hai-wei to the British, and Kwang-chow Wan to the French.

Since 1840 the nature of the foreign interests in China had fundamentally changed. At first the European nations, while showing concern for the safety of Christian mission- Commercial aries in China, had been intent upon securing com- and mercial privileges. The Far Eastern Question had Industrial been simply a scramble in which each nation sought to obtain advantages for its merchants, believing that by increasing its trade, the nation as a whole would enrich itself. In the latter period, and especially after 1895, industrial interests began to take their place beside the commercial. For the Industrial Revolution was making itself felt even within the sacred precincts of the Celestial Empire. The "Son of Heaven," as the emperor was reverently styled, had so far lost his abhorrence of European civilization that he now disported himself in a steam yacht, and his ancient palace was radiant with the brilliance of electric lights. The first steam railway, constructed in 1875–1876, had been torn up by indignant Chinese officials and dumped in the mud on the forlorn shores of Formosa. But ten years had not elapsed before another and more successful railway was begun, and railway construction proceeded in such earnest that by 1914 China had 6000 miles of railway in operation, and 2300 miles under construction. Telegraphs, too, spread like a network over the country. Factories, as well, were being erected, since in 1895 China had granted foreigners permission to engage in the textile industry. At the end of 1914 there were forty-five textile mills, with 1,250,000 spindles, besides some 5000 power looms and numerous mills for grinding grain. Mines, moreover, were being exploited by British, Japanese, German, and Chinese capitalists, and were yielding treasures of coal, iron, tin, and copper.

To the wistful eyes of European capitalists, China appeared as an inexhaustible storehouse of wealth. Her soil was laden

"Spheres
of Influ-
ence " in
the Chinese
Empire

with minerals and oil, her countless inhabitants were sober, industrious, and accustomed to give great labor for small reward. To the Europeans who could build and own China's railways, who could set the Chinese masses to work digging in mines and toiling in factories, untold fortunes would accrue. Little wonder was it, then, that in each European country there appeared a group of wealthy men, eager to invest their capital in Chinese enterprises and insistent in urging their particular government to obtain for them special privileges in China. The decade of 1895–1905 was marked by the growth of this spirit. Concessions to build railways or to work mines were extracted from the Chinese government by various governments acting in behalf of their speculators. For a time it was assumed that in order properly to safeguard the railways, factories, and mines owned by its own citizens in China, each European Power would have to mark out a "sphere of influence" in the Chinese Empire. Great Britain would take the broad valley of the Yangtsze-kiang for British capitalists to develop; France would take Kwang-tung; Germany, part of Shan-tung; Russia and Japan would divide the north between them. Within its own "sphere of influence" each nation would maintain order, and protect and encourage its industrial capitalists in operating railways, mines, and mills. Perhaps the Powers would one day politically annex their spheres of influence, thus dividing China among them.

Aside from the financial advantage to be gained by European speculators, the most powerful argument for the partition of

Backward-
ness of the
Chinese
Government

China was the inefficiency, corruption, and unprogressive character of the Chinese government. The Manchu emperor was a divine-right monarch of the type which had gone out of fashion in Europe. The officials who actually conducted the imperial administration — they were called "mandarins" by Europeans — were, it is true, the foremost scholars of the realm, chosen through competitive written examinations on Chinese literature, ethics, and history.

To Europeans resident in China, however, the mandarins appeared to be dishonest, unprogressive, and absolutely hostile to western civilization. Therefore, it was urged, China would never become Europeanized while the mandarin bureaucracy and the Manchu monarchy remained in power.

In no respect was Chinese conservatism more disastrous than in the refusal of the Chinese government to adopt European methods of warfare. After a British officer, Major Charles George Gordon, had organized a body of Chinese troops into an "Ever Victorious Army," which crushed a serious rebellion [1] at Nanking (1853–1864), the emperor still was foolhardy enough to disband the "Ever Victorious Army" and continue in the old way. The overwhelming defeat of China by the Europeanized army of Japan in the Chino-Japanese War (1894–1895) demonstrated conclusively that, if China was to preserve her national existence, she must borrow European weapons and tools.

The lesson of the Chino-Japanese War was fully appreciated by Emperor Kwang-su.[2] With all the enthusiasm of youth — he was still in his twenties — Kwang-su espoused the cause of reform, and with the advice of liberal-minded philosophers endeavored to retrieve China's disgrace. In the year 1898 the young emperor issued a series of remarkable decrees, by which he commanded colleges to be established for European learning, the army and the civil service to be reorganized, the government to be reconstituted with ministerial departments of mechanics and railways, and means of internal communication to be extended. Kwang-su regarded himself as the Chinese counterpart of Peter the Great. Edicts, however, did not suffice to Europeanize China. They merely infuriated the powerful party of reactionaries who hated everything European and who now conspired with Kwang-su's aunt, the Dowager Empress Tzu-hsi, to overthrow the Europeanizing emperor. Yuan Shih-kai, leader of the army, gave military support to the conspirators. On the night of 20 Septem-

Reform Edicts of Emperor Kwang-su, 1898

---

[1] The T'ai-p'ing rebellion, instigated by the half-Christian fanatic Hung Hsin Ch'üan.

[2] Kwang-su, emperor of China, born, 1872; ascended the throne at the age of three years, 1875; began to govern, 1889; superseded by Dowager Empress Tzu-hsi, 1898; died, 1908.

ber, 1898, soldiers occupied the emperor's palace, and on the following day, Kwang-su, being practically a prisoner, resigned the government into the hands of his aunt.

The Dowager Empress Tzu-hsi,[1] who for the ensuing ten years (1898–1908) ruled in the stead of the retired emperor,

The Reaction under Tzu-hsi

was a woman of truly remarkable energy, ambition, and ability. She delighted in diplomacy and thoroughly enjoyed the business of governing. She was, moreover, the most powerful champion of the old order, the most formidable opponent of European innovations. One of her first acts as regent was to command six young reformers to be executed. Kwang-su's reform edicts she quickly cancelled. One of her edicts, appearing in the *Pekin Gazette*, declared with more truth than discretion that "the various Powers cast upon us looks of tiger-like voracity, hustling each other in their endeavors to be the first to seize upon our innermost territories," and exhorted the Chinese to "let no one think of making peace, but let each strive to preserve from destruction and spoliation his ancestral home and graves from the ruthless hands of the invader."

Encouraged by the dowager's attitude, reactionaries throughout China gave free vent to their hatred of foreigners. Taking

The "Boxer" Anti-Foreign Outbreak, 1900

the name of an earlier secret society — the "Order of Literary Patriotic Harmonious Fists" (*I ho Ch'üan*), or "Boxers," — the more violent reactionaries began an organized campaign against the Christian missionaries who would wean the Chinese from their ancient religion,[2] the foreigners who would run railways through grave-yards, the reformers who by adopting Western ideals would anger the gods of China. The growth of the Boxer movement could be measured during 1899 and 1900 by the increasing frequency of anti-Christian outbreaks, wholesale murders of missionaries, and plundering of Christian communities. The climax was reached in June and July, 1900, when the empress determined on "war to the knife" against foreigners. The German minister was shot down in the streets of Pekin. Scores

---

[1] The Dowager Empress, Tzu-hsi (1834–1908), consort of the Emperor Hsien-fêng (1850–1861), regent from 1861 to 1889 and from 1898 to 1908.

[2] In point of fact there were several religions in China, — ancestor-worship, Buddhism, and Taoism; but in the minds of the masses all three were blended, with a strong admixture of Confucian ethical teaching.

of Christian missionaries were murdered in the provinces. Pekin was for two months a battlefield, where foreigners, cooped up in the foreign legations, resolutely defended themselves against the attacking Boxers. To the relief of the foreigners besieged in Pekin came in August an international expedition (10,000 soldiers of Japan, 4000 Russians, 3000 British, 2000 Americans, and a smaller number of French and German troops), putting the Chinese troops to rout and the imperial court to flight. The victorious Europeans were now in a position to dictate terms. China was compelled to pay indemnities to the various Powers, amounting in all to something more than. $320,000,000; and additional privileges were conceded to European commerce.

The entry of foreign troops into Pekin in August, 1900, had registered the failure of reaction. The Empress Tzu-hsi, however reluctantly, admitted the necessity of reform. **Renewed Movement for Reform in China** The first decade of the twentieth century was, therefore, an era of reforms. A commission was sent abroad to study European governments. A parliamentary constitution for China was promised. The opium traffic was prohibited. The antiquated system of education for officials was swept away (1902–1906); many temples were converted into colleges; and careful attention was given to natural science, European history, geography, political economy, international law, and foreign languages.

Even these reforms were not radical enough to satisfy the Young China Party, a revolutionary organization strikingly similar to Mazzini's historic "Young Italy." Many **Sun Yat-sen and the Chinese Revolution** of these radicals had been educated abroad; some had embraced the Christian faith; and all hoped to make China a progressive republic. Their leader, Sun Yat-sen, a doctor of medicine and a Christian in religion, while compelled to live in exile, worked incessantly for the success of the republican movement. Alarmed by the progress of revolutionary propaganda, the imperial government offered sweeping concessions to the radical demands, called an Assembly in 1910, and promised to establish constitutional parliamentary government. But the followers of Sun Yat-sen would agree to no compromise with the odious Manchu autocracy. In October, 1911, they took up arms against the Manchus. They captured Nanking and made that city the capital of their provisional republic. Sun Yat-sen returned from exile to become president. The crowning success of the Revolution was achieved on 12 February, 1912, when the boy-emperor[1] abdicated the throne, putting an end to the Manchu dynasty which had ruled China for 267 years.

The new republic was organized not under the inspiration of Sun Yat-sen, who had engineered the Revolution, but rather under the influence of Yuan Shih-kai, who had upheld

Establishment of the Chinese Republic, 1912

the monarchy to the last — an able general and a shrewd politician. Yuan Shih-kai believed in a modern system of education, material progress, and a Europeanized army; as opposed to Sun Yat-sen, however, he wished so far as possible to conserve the spirit and forms of

Presidency of Yuan Shih-kai

the old monarchical régime. Superseding Sun Yat-sen as head of the provisional government, Yuan soon disclosed his distaste for parliamentary government and insisted that the National Assembly, which he had convoked to draft a constitution, should not make the president subordinate to parliament. He defied the National Assembly, moreover, by negotiating a loan of $125,000,000 with five foreign Powers (Great Britain, France, Germany, Russia, and Japan), and by agreeing that the five Powers should appoint advisers to superintend Chinese finances. The patriotic radicals, who strenuously resented Yuan's usurpation of power and accused him of truckling to foreign interests, angrily instigated a rebellion in the southern provinces during the summer of 1913. The rebellion failed, however, leaving Yuan more powerful than ever. Having been elected president of the republic for five years, 6 October, 1913, he shortly proceeded to dissolve the National Assembly, to abolish the provincial assemblies, and to inaugurate a series of conservative reforms. It was believed that China was drifting rapidly back toward monarchical absolutism, and there were repeated protests, riots, and insurrections on the part of republicans in the southern provinces, but the sudden death of Yuan Shih-kai in June, 1916, served to promote Vice-President Li Yuan-hung to the presidency and to promise that China would go forward as a frank and enthusiastic imitator of Western nations.

[1] The six-year-old Hsüan T'ung. His father, Prince Chun, had been regent.

THE AWAKENING OF JAPAN

Not far east of the Chinese coast lies a small island empire, the story of whose awakening affords both a violent contrast with, and an enlightening commentary upon, the Contrast with China disheartening disasters of China. For the Japanese awoke in time to the advantages of European civilization and easily became the successful imitators and rivals, instead of the miserable prey, of Western nations.

Modern intercourse between Japan and Europe began in the year 1542, when by chance a Portuguese sailing-vessel was blown to the coast of one of the smaller Japanese islands. Friendly Reception On board were three Portuguese adventurers, the of Foreign- first Europeans to visit Japan. To their surprise, they ers in the were welcomed with charming courtesy by the natives, Sixteenth Century who were in appearance under-sized Chinamen, alert, inquisitive, affable, and intensely interested in the foreigners' firearms. Later visitors to the Japanese islands were received in the same hospitable manner, whether they came, like the Portuguese merchants, for purposes of trade, or like Francis Xavier and other Jesuit missionaries, to convert the Japanese to Christianity. Within thirty-two years a hundred and fifty thousand had embraced Catholic Christianity.

Then suddenly the ruler of Japan, Hideyoshi, became alarmed at the number and power of the Christians and fearful lest the Christian converts might some day join with the The Closing foreigners in overthrowing what they regarded as a of Japan in the heathen government. Missionaries were curtly Seventeenth ordered out of the country (1587); in 1591 more than Century 20,000 converts were killed; yet the Christian sect temporarily increased. The statement that 280,000 native Catholic Christians suffered martyrdom in Japan between 1587 and 1635 is probably an exaggeration, but it gives some idea of the method by which Hideyoshi and his immediate successors attempted to stamp out the hated religion. Even Christian merchants fell under suspicion and were forbidden to enter Japan. Only a few Dutch traders were allowed to carry on commerce in Japanese goods, and that commerce was carefully limited. From the middle of the seventeenth century until the middle of the nineteenth century, Japan shut herself off from the world.

Japan's two long centuries of sullen seclusion came to an end in July, 1853, when Commodore Perry with four United States warships steamed into Uraga Bay near Yokohama, bringing sewing machines and other wonderful inventions as samples of what the West could offer to Japan, and bearing grim cannon, the like of which the Japanese had not yet seen. The islanders could not fail to be impressed by the advantages of European civilization; they could not blind themselves to the fact that in the arts of peace, and more especially in the arts of war, much was to be learned from the foreigners. Without much difficulty Perry was able to secure a treaty (1854) by which Japan promised (1) to shelter whatever American seamen might be driven by storm or shipwreck to the Japanese coast, (2) to permit foreign vessels to obtain provisions in Japan, and (3) to allow American merchantmen to anchor in the ports of Shimoda and Hakodate. Similar privileges were speedily obtained by Great Britain, Holland, and Russia. Four years later, another American, Townsend Harris, induced the ruler of Japan to sign a new treaty, throwing the port of Yokohama open to American commerce. Again Great Britain, Russia, Holland, and France followed suit.

The Second Opening of Japan to Western Civilization: Perry's Visit, 1853

The prince who signed these commercial treaties in the name of Japan was theoretically not the sovereign of the country, but only the hereditary chief-officer (shogun) of the emperor or mikado. Ever since 1336, however, — the space of more than five centuries — the shoguns had exercised almost regal powers, while the mikados, who were revered as the sacred descendants of Ninigi, grandson of the sun-goddess Amaterasu, resided in the imperial city of Kioto, sublimely indifferent to the actual government of the country. Many of the most eminent "daimios" (feudal princes), who had long been jealous of the shogun, would have been glad to assist the mikado in reasserting his long-dormant powers. Their hatred for the shogun was equaled by their detestation of foreigners. When, therefore, the shogun signed treaties opening Japan to foreign commerce, the daimios accused

Opposition of the Daimios

The Shogun vs. the Mikado

him of a double crime, of admitting "barbarians" upon the sacred soil of Japan, and of failing to obtain the mikado's consent for the exercise of sovereign power. So widespread was this sentiment that the shogun's prestige was hopelessly undermined. It was only a question of time before the mikado, who now personified Japanese patriotism, would cease being a puppet emperor and would resume the powers his fathers had delegated to the ancestors of the discredited shogun.

Two events were to effect a profound alteration in the attitude of the mikado's party towards foreigners. The first was the bombardment of the Japanese town of Kagoshima (1863) by a British squadron in retaliation for the murder of a British subject on Japanese soil. The second was the bombardment of Shimonoseki (1864) *Influence of Western Gunnery, 1863–1864* by a combined British, French, Dutch, and American fleet to punish a daimio who had fired on foreign vessels. The effectiveness of Western gunnery, as demonstrated on these two occasions, offered convincing proof that Japan would never be able to expel the foreigners, or even to protect herself from them, until the Japanese possessed cannon of equal caliber. Consequently, some of the daimios who had most bitterly reviled the "barbarians" suddenly reversed their former policy and declared that, since Japan could not possibly expel the Westerners, she must admit them freely, learn their secrets, and excel them in their own arts. Only in this fashion could Japan preserve her place as a nation. Thus it came about that a group of daimios, who had censured the shogun for concluding treaties with the foreigners, now most ardently advocated the opening up of Japan to European civilization. They retained, however, their enmity for the shogun and insisted that the powers of government wrongfully usurped by him should be restored to the mikado, the rightful sovereign of Japan.

The final step in the awakening of Japan — the Revolution of 1868 — resulted from (1) the agitation of the daimios against the shogun, (2) the conviction that Japan must assimilate Western civilization, and (3) a revival of Shintoism, which was regarded as the national religion, and which inculcated reverence for the divinely descended *The Japanese Revolution, 1867–1868* mikado. It was carried out by a small band of young reformers,

some of them great nobles, some of them without rank, but all
of them ambitious to carve out a glorious career for their country
and for themselves. The first stage of the Revolution was
End of the   accomplished peacefully in the year 1867, when
Shogunate   Yoshinobu, last of the shoguns, divining the weakness
of his position, voluntarily resigned the office which the members of his illustrious family (the Tokugawas) had held for two
hundred and sixty years. Yoshinobu's magnanimous action
enabled the youthful Mikado Mutsuhito, a boy fifteen years
old, who succeeded to the throne in 1867, to become actual as
well as titular monarch of Japan. The memorable reign of Mutsuhito (1867–1912), thus happily inaugurated, was fitly designated the "Enlightened Rule."

Yoshinobu's rivals were not yet satisfied; they desired so
completely to crush the ex-shogun that never again would he
Abolition of   be able to assert authority. In 1868, therefore, they
Feudalism   made war against him and against his vassals and so
successfully that he was forced to retire into private life, retaining only a portion of his lands and not a vestige of his former
greatness. Then, just as they had compelled Yoshinobu to surrender his privileges to the mikado, the chief daimios voluntarily
surrendered their own feudal rights, possessions, and honors
into the hands of the youthful ruler. Lesser lords followed.
By this remarkable act of patriotism, feudalism in Japan was
abolished, an imperial decree of July, 1871, announcing that
"The clans (or feudal jurisdictions) are abolished, and pre-
fectures are established in their place." In compensation for
their feudal rights, the great nobles received high governmental
offices and ample salaries. By the abolition of feudalism, three
fundamental reforms were made possible. (1) The peasants,
freed from servile dues, became the owners of the land they
tilled and, henceforth, paid regular land-taxes. (2) Fighting,
once the privilege of an hereditary warrior-caste, became now
the privilege and the duty of all. A truly national army and a
modern navy were created, recruited by compulsory military
service, drilled by European officers, and equipped with European arms. (3) Government, hitherto paralyzed by quarrels
between the shogun and the other daimios, was now concentrated
in the hands of the mikado's officials, becoming at once more

centralized and more efficient. From his quasi-religious seclusion in the sacred city of Kioto, the mikado now ventured forth as the enlightened ruler of a civilized Japan, and established his capital at Yedo, the former seat of the shoguns, which was now renamed Tokio.

His intention to make Japan a Europeanized nation and a World Power, the young mikado signified by the unprecedented act of freely receiving in audience the representa- Europeanitives of foreign Powers and by commanding his sub- zation of jects to treat all foreigners as friends. In every Japan respect the mikado and his advisers strove to make Japan the equal of Western states, — by patronizing Western learning, by creating a university at Tokio, by establishing public schools in which the English language formed part of the curriculum, by abolishing the privileged position of Buddhism, by granting liberty to all religions, by sending a commission abroad to inform foreign nations of Japan's change of heart and to study European institutions. Codes of civil and criminal law, based on French and German models, were adopted. What appeared to be the most advantageous characteristics of each European government were synthesized in a written constitu- Constitution, which was promulgated in 1889. Under the tional Government constitution, the first Japanese parliament, consisting ernment in of a popular and an aristocratic chamber, was con- Japan, 1889 vened in 1890. In order to insure a strong and stable government, the executive power, as also the deciding voice in legislation, was left to the emperor.

Meanwhile the Japanese were eagerly assimilating the material and martial civilization of Europe. The first railway line, covering eighteen miles, from Tokio to Yokohama, The Induswas officially opened in 1872; by 1914 there were trial Revo6000 miles of railway, almost entirely owned by the lution in state. Within fifteen years after the repeal of the law Japan which prohibited the construction of sea-going ships, Japan had 138 such vessels, and by 1914 her merchant marine included 2072 steamers, each above 20 tons (France then had only 1857 steamers) plying not only in her home waters, but also to Europe, to America, to Australia, to Bombay, and to China. Mining was developed, at first under the supervision of Western

experts, until in 1913 some 230,000 Japanese miners were annually producing coal, copper, iron, and other minerals to the
total value of $65,000,000.   The cotton industry, which had no
existence in Japan prior to 1880, developed so rapidly that in
1914 the cotton mills of Japan contained 2,402,573 busy spindles,
turned out annually 545,738,547 pounds of yarn, and gave employment to 22,000 men and 95,000 women.   Similarly in the
weaving industry, the introduction of power looms increased
the annual output eight hundred per cent between 1890 and
1901.   As one result of her industrial development, Japan's
foreign commerce, which in 1877 amounted to a meager $25,-
000,000, rose by 1890 to almost $70,000,000; by 1900 to almost
$250,000,000; by 1910 to more than $450,000,000; and by
1913 to $680,000,000, having been multiplied twenty-seven-fold
within thirty-six years.

The foregoing figures eloquently testify to the fact that in
the last quarter of the nineteenth century Japan became a

Social Effect
of the
Industrial
Revolution
in Japan

modern industrial nation.   And as the Industrial
Revolution in Europe had produced discontented factory-hands and prosperous capitalists, so also in Japan.
In 1906, for example, we know that there were in
Japan some 9000 joint-stock companies and partner-
ships, controlling paid-up capital to the amount of five hundred
millions of dollars.   The members of these 9000 companies
were Japan's capitalists, her bourgeoisie.   And just as the
capitalists of the British Isles fostered the idea of empire, so
also in the Japanese islands there were to be found wealthy
advocates of imperialism.   To the spirit of imperialism in Japan
two other factors contributed: namely, the extraordinary
patriotism of the Japanese people, and the fact that, to the
statistician at least, Japan's four principal islands (Nippon,
Shikoku, Kiushiu, and Hokkaidô), with their scanty area of
140,000 square miles, seemed to afford too little space for fifty
millions of people.   Consequently, Japan, imitating the Western
nations even in this respect, entered upon a career of territorial
expansion.

The Japanese naturally turned their eyes toward the peninsula
of Korea, just west of their islands.   We know already how the
Japanese, by recognizing Korea as independent of China and

by advocating a policy of reform and progress for the peninsula, came into conflict with China. In the resulting Chino-Japanese War (1894–1895) the newly organized Japanese army by its courage and training more than made up for some advantages which the Chinese possessed in equipment; and the remarkable success of the Japanese forces seemed ample vindication of the policy of imitating Europe. At the close of the war, Russia, France, and Germany compelled Japan to restore Port Arthur and the Liao-tung peninsula to China; but Japan still retained the island of Formosa (about four times as large as the island of Crete) and an indemnity of about $180,000,000 as the fruits of a victory which had cost her $100,000,000 and the lives of 4000 men. Korea, moreover, while not yet absorbed by Japan, was definitely detached from China.

Japanese Imperialism

1. War with China, 1894–1895

Annexation of Formosa

In the years that followed the Chino-Japanese War, it appeared that Russia forced Japan to restore Port Arthur to China only in order that Russia might later acquire the port herself; and it became painfully obvious that Man-churia and Korea would fall into Russian hands unless something radical was done. Therefore, Japan fought Russia. For this, her first struggle with a Western Power, Japan was well prepared. Since the establishment in 1868 at Tokio of an arsenal for small-arms, Japan had erected an arsenal at Osaka, powder-factories, military and naval colleges, iron-works at Nagasaki, a naval dockyard at Yokosuka, and factories capable of turning out twelve-inch guns. The army had been doubled since the Chinese War and its equipment improved, until in 1904 there were 180,000 men in arms, with more than 600,000 trained soldiers in reserve. To the first Japanese steam-gunboat, constructed in 1866, many had been added, so that Japan entered the war with 6 modern battleships, 8 armored cruisers, 80 torpedo boats, 19 destroyers, and 44 other cruisers. Japan's preparedness for war, together with the wonderful endurance and daring of the Japanese soldiers, and the ardent spirit of patriotism permeating the whole government and nation, determined the issue of the conflict.

2. The Russo-Japanese War, 1904–1905

Three days after the opening of hostilities (February, 1904) Vice-Admiral Togo surprised one Russian squadron, damaged it badly, and bottled it up in Port Arthur Bay. Six months later, this Russian squadron, venturing forth from Port Arthur, met a decisive defeat at the hands of Togo. Almost simultaneously, another Japanese squadron defeated the second Russian squadron, which had Vladivostok for its base. Meanwhile on land, General Kuroki with one Japanese army had crossed from Korea into the Liao-tung peninsula after a desperate struggle on the banks of the Yalu River (1 May, 1904); General Oku with a second army had landed just north of Port Arthur, defeating the Russians at Nanshan (26 May) and Telissu (14–15 June); and the combined Japanese forces under the supreme command of Marshal Oyama, by the battle of Liao-yang (2 September) forced the Russian commander-in-chief Kuropatkin to retreat on Mukden, considerably to the north of the Liao-tung peninsula. At Mukden, between 25 February and 10 March, 1905, was fought the greatest battle of the war. Three hundred thousand soldiers of Japan there met an equal Russian force. Though the Russian army was not surrounded and captured, as perhaps the Japanese general intended, nevertheless, it was forced to retreat thoroughly demoralized, and with a loss of almost 100,000 men. The Japanese losses were half as great.

Battle of Mukden, February–March, 1905

Meanwhile General Nogi had attacked the force of 47,000 Russians who were ensconced behind the formidable fortifications of Port Arthur. During three weeks in August, 1904, General Nogi had sacrificed 15,000 of his men in a vain attempt to carry Port Arthur by storm; but then, settling down to a siege, he had finally triumphed on 2 January, 1905, when Port Arthur capitulated, half of the Russian garrison having been killed, seriously wounded, or disabled by disease. Port Arthur cost the Japanese 58,000 in killed and wounded, besides 34,000 sick. In a last attempt to retrieve her fortunes, Russia sent her Baltic fleet to the Far East, but in a famed battle Admiral Togo met and completely annihilated the oncoming fleet in the Sea of Japan (27 May, 1905).

Siege and Capture of Port Arthur

Both combatants were ready for peace. Russia still had enormous resources, but was distracted by internal unrest and discouraged by the long list of defeats. Japan, while thus far victorious, was near exhaustion, and could not hope to invade the vast territory of her enemy.   At the suggestion of the president of the United States, Japan and Russia sent plenipotentiaries to Portsmouth, New Hampshire, where a treaty of peace was signed on 5 September, 1905.   The terms have already been noted in so far as they affected China; but besides gaining the lease of the Liaotung peninsula and freeing Korea and Manchuria from Russian influence, Japan obtained the payment of some $20,000,000 and the cession of the southern half of Sakhalin, an island north of Japan, which had been acquired by Russia from Japan in 1875. *(Victory of Japan: The Treaty of Portsmouth, 5 September, 1905)* *(Annexation of Sakhalin)*

The war with Russia gave Japan standing as a World Power. Within half a century the little island empire had learned what Europe had to teach, had entered upon a career of expansion, had defeated a European Power.   Yet another source of gratification was the alliance with Great Britain, formed first in 1902, and subsequently strengthened.   The Emperor Mutsuhito might well boast that his country was now received as a friend and an equal by a Western nation.   The Anglo-Japanese Alliance was later, as it will appear, to bear fruit in the War of the Nations. *(3. Japanese Alliance with Great Britain, 1902)*

So long as Japan and Russia were jealous rivals, neither would allow the other to appropriate Manchuria or Korea.   But after the Russo-Japanese War the two governments came to an amicable agreement, the details of which were not divulged: it appeared, nevertheless, to apportion Korea to Japan.   At any rate Japan annexed Korea in 1910 without protest from Russia.   The territory *(4. Japanese Annexation of Korea, 1910)* thus acquired, about twice as large as Ohio and almost three times as populous, was valuable not only as a granary to Japan, for Korea is a farming country, but also as a market for Japanese goods and a field of enterprise for Japanese capitalists.   In 1913 some twenty million dollars' worth of merchandise, constituting more than half of Korea's imports, were purchased from Japanese merchants.   Five banks in Korea had already been established by Japanese capitalists, and promising mines were being developed.   Korea was renamed " Chosen."

In taking leave of the progressive little island-empire of the East, it is impossible not to risk a comparison with the island

empire of the West.   Somewhat superior in area and population
to the British Isles, Japan is as yet greatly inferior to them
**Japan a
Europeaniz-
ing Nation** in economic and imperialistic development.   The
Japanese Empire controlled in 1913 a commerce worth
$680,000,000 annually, yet that was less than one-tenth
the magnitude of British commerce; the Japanese merchant
marine totaled more than two million tons, less than a ninth
that of the British Empire; and in territorial expansion Japan's
Empire is but in its infancy, compared to the greatest of modern
empires.   Nevertheless, Japan has made a remarkable beginning in territorial expansion, in commerce, in shipping, in industry.   Once for all, Japan has proved that an Oriental people
may assimilate the material civilization of Europe.   In one important respect Japan remains an Oriental nation — in respect of
religion; although by 1905 missionaries had won 60,000 converts to Roman Catholic Christianity, 27,000 to the Russian
Orthodox Church, 11,000 to the Anglican Church, and 39,000
to the various Protestant sects, in all about 137,000, a number
which has since been considerably increased.   On the material
side, however, Japan is to all intents and purposes a European
nation; her factories, her discontented working classes, her capitalists, her army, her navy, her government, her laws, — all
bear witness to the assimilation of Western civilization in Japan.

RUSSIAN EXPANSION IN ASIA

In many regions of Asia a national awakening like that of
Japan would be quite impossible.   For example, in the limitless
**Russian
Expansion
toward the
Pacific and
Indian
Oceans** half-frozen tracts of northern Asia, and in the rugged
mountain-country of Central Asia peopled by wandering semi-barbarian tribes, there could be little extension of European civilization except by the deliberate
purpose of some Great Power.   In this kind of imperialism — in gradually conquering and more or less civilizing
vast stretches of sparsely peopled territory — Russia stands
first.   Over the whole of northern and west-central Asia, the
Russian tsars have gradually extended their control, thus partially compensating themselves in Asia for their failure in Europe
to gain satisfying outlets to the seas.   Toward two oceans

Russian progress in Asia has been chiefly directed: straight eastward Russians have marched to the Pacific, occupying Siberia and menacing Mongolia, Manchuria, and Korea on their way; to the southeast the Russian frontier has less rapidly been pushed forward, at the expense of Turkey, Persia, and the independent tribes of Central Asia, only to find the British Empire blocking the path to the Indian Ocean.

The Russian progress through Siberia to the Pacific was begun in 1579, when the first Cossack adventurer crossed the Ural Mountains eastward, and it culminated when in 1638 Okhotsk was reached on the sea of Okhotsk opening out into the Pacific Ocean. It is needless here to repeat the story told in an earlier chapter.[1] Into the boundless territory thus claimed for Russia flocked roving bands of Cossack frontiersmen, gold-seekers, fur-hunters, traders, political outlaws, and discontented serfs. Siberia, they discovered, was not a land of "milk and honey." The north was an inhospitable expanse of marshes, frozen in winter; forests of central Siberia might delight the hunter but not the farmer; and while in the south farming was possible, extreme heat in summer and biting cold in winter made life unpleasant. Nor was the Russian desire for a Pacific port satisfied with Okhotsk, ice-bound in winter. Hoping to discover more fertile farm-lands and seeking for a better sea-port, Russian explorers, adventurers, and settlers began in the seventeenth century to invade the valley of the Amur River, in northern Manchuria, which was then held by the emperor of China. In the middle of the nineteenth century an adventurer planted the Russian flag at the mouth of the Amur; forts were built along the river's banks; and in 1860 China helplessly yielded the whole region north of the Amur, and in addition the coast province south of the Amur and east of the Ussuri River. At the southern point of her new territory, Russia now established Vladivostok, "Dominator of the East," looking out upon the Sea of Japan. In 1875 the island of Sakhalin, to the north of that sea, was acquired from Japan. From Bering Strait in the north to the border of Korea in the south, Russia controlled the Pacific coast.

Not yet were the Russians content. From Siberia they

[1] See Vol. I, p. 367

looked longingly southward. Korea, Manchuria, and Mongolia,
if they could be acquired, would afford access to the Yellow Sea
Looking   and to the precious trade of China. Even before the
Southward   close of the nineteenth century Russian merchants had
from   begun to settle in the cities of Chinese Manchuria.
Siberia
After 1895, when Russia intervened to keep Japan
out of southern Manchuria, it appeared inevitable that Manchuria, with its naval base at Port Arthur, and possibly Korea also,
would ultimately fall under Russian domination. Japan, however,
by the war of 1904–1905, forced the Russians to renounce Port
Arthur and Korea. By a different route Russia thenceforth
sought to reach the Yellow Sea. West of Manchuria and south
of Siberia, lay the great Chinese dependency of Mongolia, extending westward to Central Asia, and eastward almost to the Yellow
Sea. Possession of Mongolia would bring the Siberian frontier
close to Pekin. Into Mongolia Russian merchants and Cossacks
poured, with the result that in 1913 all Outer or Western Mongolia, while still recognizing China as overlord, had become practically a Russian protectorate, in which Russian merchants were
free to establish their warehouses exempt from customs duties.

While in northern Asia Russia had been constantly extending
her Siberian frontier, far to the west and south in the region of
Russian   the Caspian Sea and Turkestan another line of Rus-
Expansion   sian advance had been pursued. From the year 1554,
in the Cas-   when Ivan the Terrible gained in Astrakhan a foot-
pian Region   hold on the Caspian Sea, the Russians had been endeavoring to convert the Caspian into a Russian lake. On the
west of the Caspian, the half-independent tribes inhabiting
the fertile valleys of the Caucasus, some owing allegiance to the
shah of Persia, others to the Turkish sultan, had during the
course of the nineteenth century (prior to 1878) been conquered
and annexed by Russia, in spite of the heroic resistance offered
by the Circassian mountaineers on the northern slope of the
Caucasus range. On the eastern shore of the Caspian, Russia
had also advanced southward, compelling the shah of Persia
to renounce his claim to all territory north of Ashurada, Askabad,
and Sarakhs, which three towns were acquired by Russia in 1841,
1881, and 1885 respectively. Between Russia and the southern
ocean there remained only Persia.

Persia, the seat of an ancient empire, had been for centuries an independent Mussulman state, ruled by a *shah* or king.   During the nineteenth century the pressure upon Persia **Persia** from Russia on the north and from the British on the southeast ever increased.   Early in the twentieth century, Russian influence seemed to have gained the upper hand, inasmuch as Russian merchants in Persia were protected by a **Russian** favorable commercial treaty (1902), and Russian **Aggression** capitalists secured valuable investments.   For example, Russian capitalists in 1900 loaned $12,000,000 to Persia.[1]   Russian capitalists also undertook to construct roads in northwestern Persia.   The British merchants, on the other side, who traded in southern Persia and the gulf of Aden, as well as in India, feared lest Russia might gain control of all Persia and **British** impair their trade.   Consequently, British diplomacy **Aggression** was set in action, with the result that on 31 August, 1907, a convention or agreement was signed by the British and Russian governments, whereby the northern half of Persia was assigned as Russia's "sphere of influence," and the southeastern corner as that of the British.   In the Russian sphere of influence Great Britain would seek no commercial or political concessions ; similarly Russia would respect the British region ; between the two lay a "neutral" zone.   At the same time, Russia recognized the special interests of Great Britain in the Persian Gulf.

Meanwhile internal conditions in Persia had become alarmingly turbulent.   Bandits were everywhere, and brigandage was a regular business.   One shah had been assassinated in **The Persian** 1896.   Another, fearing that the patriotic party of **Revolution,** Persian Nationalists would revolt against his absolut- **1906–1909** ism, his misgovernment, and his subservience to foreign interests, had endeavored to conciliate the Nationalists by granting a constitution (5 August, 1906) which created a Persian parliament or *Mejliss*.   The Nationalists, however, remained recalcitrant, and in 1908–1909 engineered a revolution, deposed Shah Mohammed Ali Mirza, and set up his eleven-year-old son Sultan Ahmad Mirza as shah.   The new government was little better.   It could not prevent Russia from stationing

[1] Actually, only some $10,000,000, or 85 per cent of the face value, was advanced in cash.

troops (1911) in the northern Persian provinces of Azerbaijan and Khorasan; it signed away railway concessions and mining rights (1913) to British and Russian companies; it could not maintain order. Persia fell still more under foreign control when in 1912–1913 the government contracted new loans from Russian and British capitalists. A few brave souls still dared to hope that Persia like Japan would awake from her lethargy and embrace European civilization of her own accord; others deemed such an event impossible, since Russian and British interests kept Persia in bondage. Such was the view of Morgan W. Shuster, an American, who acted as financial adviser to the Persian government, and caused a great sensation in 1911 by declaring that anarchy and misgovernment in Persia were in no slight degree due to the selfish policies pursued by the British and Russian governments with regard to the "weakened, war-cursed country of Persia." Meanwhile, Persia continued to be a profitable field of investment for British and Russian financiers, and Russian merchants continued to monopolize three-fifths of Persia's foreign trade,[1] while most of the remainder fell into British hands.

Continued Russian and British Tutelage

Russian expansion southward, as a glance at the map will show, was not confined to surrounding the Caspian and infiltrating Persia; it spread out eastward into Central Asia, seeking to reach India and the Arabian Sea by encircling Persia to the eastward. Just east of Persia lay the independent state of Afghanistan; to the northeast extended the high plateaus of Western Turkestan, divided among numerous khanates or petty principalities, and merging into the mountainous western frontier of the Chinese Empire. By means of tactful diplomacy, and by dint of occasional hard fighting, the Russians during the nineteenth century won all of Western Turkestan for the tsar, including the basins of the Aral Sea and Lake Balkash, including also a part of Kuldja, appropriated from China (1881), and stretching south to Persia and Afghanistan. The two little states of Khiva and Bokhara, though they appear on the map to be independent, in reality formed part of the Russian Empire. The rapid progress of Russia into Central Asia gave the

Turkestan and the Anglo-Russian Frontier

---

[1] Amounting in 1913 to about $100,000,000.

British in India cause for alarm; for it had more than once been suggested that from Turkestan the Russians might advance southward into Afghanistan and the Punjab, to despoil the British of India. The British, therefore, endeavored to preserve Afghanistan as a buffer state between their empire and that of the Russians. After repeated interventions in Afghanistan, among them the disastrous expedition of 1841, which was annihilated by the Afghans, the British government set up in 1880 a prince or " amir " who agreed to let Great Britain control his foreign relations. Russian aggression, however, continued to threaten the outlying possessions of the Afghan amir in the northwest, where Russia captured Merv, Panjdeh, and Kushk (1885-1887), and in the northeast, where Russia gained a position on the commanding Pamir plateau in 1895. At last, in 1907, an agreement was reached, Russia receiving equal commercial opportunities in Afghanistan while allowing Great Britain to control Afghanistan's foreign affairs, and both Powers promising not to annex or occupy any part of the country. Thus the Russian advance toward the Indian Ocean was blocked by Great Britain, much as in the Far East the Russian designs on Manchuria were thwarted by Japan.

Despite these checks, the achievements of Russia in Asia are impressive in their very vastness. In Asia the tsar had gained an empire of six million square miles, three times the size of European Russia, or equal to all of Europe plus two-thirds of the United States. Of this huge territory the immediate value was less imposing. Only two per cent of Turkestan was under cultivation, and the Siberian grainfields were in 1913 less than a tenth as extensive as those of European Russia. Nor was the Asiatic empire of great commercial value; in 1913 the commerce carried on through Russia's Asiatic frontier amounted to less than $130,000,000. On the other hand, it is to be observed that Russian colonists, pouring into Siberia at the rate of 200,000 a year, may well reclaim great areas for agriculture; and in both Siberia and Turkestan rich mineral resources await development. More than a score of steam-power factories have already been erected in Turkestan. Of still greater significance for the future is the extension of railways. The Siberian railway, a tremendous undertaking, begun

The Russian Empire in Asia

in 1891, now links up Moscow and Petrograd with Vladivostok, Port Arthur, and Pekin. Another great Russian railway traverses Turkestan, sending off unfinished shoots toward Herat in Afghanistan and toward Chinese Sin-kiang. Still further extensions of the Russian railway system into Persia and across Mongolia are already in project. And railways, be it ever remembered, are the arteries of trade and the sinews of empire.

SURVEY OF THE RIVAL EMPIRES IN THE FAR EAST

Thus far we have seen how one ancient empire — the Chinese — began to crumble away; how another Asiatic empire — the Japanese — awoke to greatness; how an enormous Russian empire expanded over northern and Central Asia. The other great empire in Asia — the British — will be reserved for special treatment in a following chapter.[1] At this point, therefore, we may conveniently pause to survey the extent and position of these and lesser empires, — French, Dutch, German, American, and Turkish, — in the Far East on the eve of the outbreak of the Great War (August, 1914).

Imperialism in Asia and Australasia

Greatest in territorial extent was the Russian Empire, sweeping from the Ural Mountains east to Bering Strait and the Pacific, its northern borders washed by the icy waters of the Arctic Ocean, its southern frontier bordering on Korea, Manchuria, Mongolia, Afghanistan, Persia, and Turkish Armenia. For the future expansion of that mighty empire, Outer Mongolia and northern Persia were already marked.

1. Russian

Predominant in southern Asia and Australasia was the British Empire, beside whose wealth the bleak plains of Russian Siberia shrank into insignificance. To Great Britain belonged the populous peninsula of India, reaching northward to the Himalayas, with the Ganges valley on the east, the Indus on the west. To the west of India lay Baluchistan, partly appropriated; Afghanistan, still half-independent; and a "sphere of influence" in southeastern Persia. To the north, British merchants and British influence were penetrating the mountain principalities of Nepal and Bhutan, and crossing the Himalayas into Tibet. To the east, Burma had been annexed; the Feder-

2. British

[1] See below, pp. 662-672.

ated Malay States were under British protection; and the Straits Settlements, at the southern tip of the Malay peninsula, commanding the busy strait of Malacca, belonged to the British crown. In China, the British possessed Hongkong, leased Wei-hai-wei, and regarded the Yangtsze valley as a British "sphere of influence." Foothold also had been gained in Arabia at Aden. Of islands, the British possessed Ceylon, northern Borneo, a third of New Guinea, Australia, New Zealand, and Tasmania, not to mention a host of smaller ones.

Much smaller were the Asiatic possessions of France. In India, France still held five of her former trading posts — Pondicherry, Karikal, Chandarnagar, Mahé, and Yanaon — aggregating 196 square miles. The chief French col- **3. French** ony, comprising the eastern half of the Indo-Chinese peninsula, was Indo-China. The five states of Indo-China — Annam, Cambodia, Cochin-China, Tonkin, and Laos — were more than equal in area to the mother-country and were governed by a French governor-general, who, with the aid of some 10,000 European soldiers, kept the native population in order. Through the bank of Indo-China, with an authorized capital of 36,000,000 francs, French investors were engaged in financial, commercial, industrial, and mining enterprises. To the west of Indo-China lay the independent state of Siam, squeezed in as a buffer state between British Burma and French Indo-China. Northward there might be room for expansion, especially since France already occupied the port of Kwang-chow Wan on lease from China.[1]

The Dutch colonial empire — transferred from the Dutch East India Company to the government in 1798 — had suffered considerable losses during the Revolutionary and Napoleonic Wars, but still embraced a number of large **4. Dutch** and valuable islands lying southeast of Asia.[2] Java alone was almost four times larger than Holland and supported more than four times the population; Sumatra was larger than California, Celebes than Nebraska; Montana might be placed within the Dutch portion of New Guinea; and Borneo (of which the

---

[1] France also possessed the islands of New Caledonia and Tahiti in the Pacific.

[2] To these possessions near the Asiatic continent must be added the few remaining Dutch holdings in the New World — Dutch Guiana and Curaçao.

British owned only the northern coastland) was larger than all France. Of the total population of the islands, about equal to that of France, only some 80,000 were Europeans. Spices, coffee, cinchona, tobacco, sugar, and indigo made the Dutch East Indies exceedingly valuable possessions, and their commerce amounted in 1913 to more than $475,000,000. Although the Dutch imposed no burden on traders of other nations, Dutch merchants were able to monopolize the bulk of this lucrative trade.

Comparatively a newcomer, Germany had gained on the continent of Asia only 200 square miles about the bay of Kiao-chau in China. There the Germans had constructed a model town, a huge dry-dock, and first-class fortifications. Obviously Kiao-chau could be valuable only as a naval base, as a port (its commerce in 1913 exceeded $50,000,000), and as a center from which German influence might radiate in the Chinese province of Shan-tung. In the Pacific Ocean Germany had acquired the Bismarck Archipelago (1884), the Marshall Islands (1885), the Caroline Islands (1899), the Pelew Islands (1899), the Marianne or Ladrone Islands [1] (1899), and two of the Samoan Islands (1899), — all little better than coaling stations. Much more important was Kaiser Wilhelms Land, the northeastern section (70,000 square miles) of New Guinea, which was annexed to Germany at the same time that Great Britain annexed the southeastern third of the island (1884). At that time the island was quite wild and peopled by brown-skinned, frizzly-haired savages. Kaiser Wilhelms Land was given in charge to a German commercial company, which not only developed a promising commerce and introduced cotton and tobacco-growing, but received from the German government $100,000 when in 1899 the company surrendered its administrative powers. In 1913 the German Empire was paying some $400,000 a year to defray the cost of government in New Guinea and neighboring islands.

While disavowing any intention of gaining a Far Eastern empire, the United States of America had as a matter of fact gained colonial possessions in the Far East. The Hawaiian Is-

[1] Excepting Guam, the largest of the group, which was ceded by Spain to the United States (1898).

lands in the mid-Pacific, acquired in 1898, were a stepping stone to other tiny islands or "coaling stations" in the Pacific, and finally to the Philippine Islands, taken from Spain by the war of 1898. Over eight million native Filipinos, 6. American mostly Christians, the United States government forcibly extended its power, after two years of continuous fighting. In order to preserve the democratic traditions of the United States, in 1907 a Philippine Assembly was instituted; but its upper chamber was appointed by the United States government, and, although the lower chamber was supposed to be representative, it was elected by 100,000 voters out of a population of 8,000,000.

It was often declared in the United States that eventually the Filipinos would be granted their independence; on the other hand it may be observed that the American merchants, who in 1913 possessed the lion's share ($52,000,000) of Philippine trade, would not lightly renounce their profits in order to gratify the Filipinos' desire for independence. To these merchants, and to those who engaged in Chinese commerce, might be ascribed the growth of an imperialistic spirit which regarded the Philippines as an American colony, demanded protection for "American interests" in the Far East, and insisted that China should have an "open door" to merchants of all nations, especially to those of the United States.

Finally, it is not inappropriate here to call attention once more to the fact that the imperialistic ambitions of Western nations inevitably conflicted with the national sentiments of Asiatic peoples. The Japanese, tremendously patriotic, 7. Asiatic had made sufficient progress in the arts of peace and of war to repel aggression. The Chinese resented but were scarcely able to prevent attacks on their territory and interference with their liberty; and the party of progress and reform in China, which would fain emulate Japan, found its task of renovating China enormously increased by the vexatious interference of European capitalists, who insisted on supervising Chinese finances, and by the attempts of European diplomats to detach China's outlying provinces. Persia, too, was held more or less in leading-strings, or rather in harness, by Russia and Great Britain. The insignificant states of Siam, Nepal, Bhutan, Afghanistan, and Oman, while retaining nominal independence, had mostly fallen under the shadow of European influence. Last of all, and not to be forgotten, was the Ottoman Empire in Asia, including Asia Minor, reaching east through Armenia and Kurdistan to the Trans-Caucasian provinces of Russia, extending down the valley of the Euphrates to the Persian Gulf, and stretching another arm southward to include Syria and Palestine and the eastern shore of the Red Sea, thus half-encircling the desert plateau of Arabia, which was peopled by independent and wandering tribes. The southern end of the Arabian peninsula, it may be remarked, from Aden (which the British occupied in 1839) to Oman, was regarded as a British "sphere of influence."

ADDITIONAL READING

The New National Imperialism. General. J. H. Robinson and C. A. Beard, *The Development of Modern Europe*, Vol. II (1907), ch. xxx, an elementary but useful survey of the expansion of Europe in the nineteenth century; *Cambridge Modern History*, Vol. XII (1910), ch. xxv, a clear account of recent geographical explorations and discoveries; P. S. Reinsch, *World Politics at the End of the Nineteenth Century* (1900), an illuminating study of certain economic and diplomatic forces underlying the new imperialism, with special reference to the Far Eastern Question, and, by the same author, *Colonial Government* (1902) and *Colonial Administration* (1904), convenient handbooks of the political institutions of the new imperialism; J. A. Hobson, *Imperialism: a Study* (1902), a suggestive criticism of modern imperialism on economic grounds; S. P. Orth, *The Imperial Impulse* (1916), essays on the new imperialism as exemplified by Germany, Great Britain, France, Belgium, and Russia; D. S. Jordan, *Imperial Democracy: a Study of the Relation of Government by the People, Equality before the Law, and Other Tenets of Democracy, to the Demands of a Vigorous Foreign Policy and Other Demands of Imperial Dominion* (1899); W. C. Webster, *A General History of Commerce* (1903); J. W. Root, *Colonial Tariffs* (1906), good for the study of colonial economics; H. C. Morris, *The History of Colonization*, 2 vols. (1908), a convenient comprehensive outline; E. A. Pratt, *The Rise of Rail-Power in War and Conquest, 1833–1914* (1916); A. G. Keller, *Colonization, a Study of the Founding of New Societies* (1908); M. B. Synge, *A Book of Discovery: the History of the World's Exploration, from the Earliest Times to the Finding of the South Pole* (1912); Alexander Supan, *Die territoriale Entwicklung der europäischen Kolonien* (1906), a brief German survey; Veit Valentin, *Kolonialgeschichte der Neuzeit* (1915), another brief sketch from the German point of view; Alfred Zimmermann, *Die europäischen Kolonien*, 5 vols. (1896–1903), an elaborate history of the colonial undertakings of Spain, Portugal, Great Britain, France, and Holland, well supplied with maps and bibliographies; Paul Leroy-Beaulieu,

De la colonisation chez les peuples modernes, 6th ed., 2 vols. (1908), a standard French history; and, particularly for British imperialism in the nineteenth and twentieth centuries, consult the bibliography appended to Chapter XXIX, below. For the relation of Protestant missions to imperialism see the important work of J. S. Dennis, *Christian Missions and Social Progress*, 3 vols. (1897–1906), and the suggestive survey of R. E. Speer, *Missions and Modern History, a Study of the Missionary Aspects of some Great Movements of the Nineteenth Century*, 2 vols. (1904); the *Catholic Encyclopædia* contains a vast amount of reliable information on the similar relationship of Roman Catholic missions.

The Far Eastern Question. General. C. D. Hazen, *Europe since 1815* (1910), ch. xxx, a clear political outline; *Cambridge Modern History*, Vol. XI (1909), ch. xxviii, on China and Japan from 1815 to 1871, Vol. XII (1910), ch. xvii–xix, on the Far East, the regeneration of Japan, and the Russo-Japanese War; *Histoire générale*, Vol. X, ch. xxvii, xxviii, Vol. XI, ch. xx, Vol. XII, ch. xxiv, xxv; Sir R. K. Douglas, *Europe and the Far East, 1506–1912*, new ed. rev. and cont. by J. H. Longford (1913), the best historical summary; Édouard Driault, *La question d'extrême Orient* (1908), an admirable French book, stating the question clearly and fairly; P. S. Reinsch, *Intellectual and Political Currents in the Far East* (1911), devoted largely to educational and political matters in China and Japan; T. F. Millard, *America and the Far Eastern Question* (1909), an examination of those elements in the Eastern Question which seemed to concern the United States; Pierre Leroy-Beaulieu, *The Awakening of the East —Siberia, Japan, China*, Eng. trans. by Richard Davey (1900), a readable narrative; Alexis Krausse, *The Far East: its History and its Questions*, 2d ed. (1903), with appendix of important documents; G. N. C. (Earl) Curzon, *Problems of the Far East*, rev. ed. (1896), a well-known work on Japan, China, and Korea; Lancelot Lawton, *Empires of the Far East, a Study of Japan and of her Colonial Possessions, of China and Manchuria, and of the Political Questions of Eastern Asia and the Pacific*, 2 vols. (1912).

China. The best introduction to the study of China is afforded by the writings of H. A. Giles, a very eminent authority on all things Chinese, *China and the Chinese* (1902), *China and the Manchus* (1912), and *The Civilization of China* (1911) in the " Home University Library." Brief but already out-of-date histories are those of E. H. Parker, *China, her History, Diplomacy, and Commerce, from the Earliest Times to the Present Day* (1901), and Sir R. K. Douglas, *The Story of China* (1901) in the " Story of the Nations " Series. Special studies of importance: H. B. Morse, *The International Relations of the Chinese Empire: the Period of Conflict, 1834–1860* (1910); Henri Cordier, *Les expéditions de Chine de 1857–58 et de 1860: histoire diplomatique, notes et documents*, 2 vols. (1905–1906), and, by the same author, a famous French student of the languages and history of the Oriental peoples, *Histoire des relations de la Chine avec les puissances occidentales*, 3 vols. (1901–1902), covering the period from 1861 to 1902; J. O. P. Bland and E. Backhouse, *China under the Empress Dowager*, *being* *the History of the Life and Times of Tzŭ Hsi* (1910); P. W. Sergeant, *The Great Empress Dowager of China* (1910); W. F. Mannix (editor), *Memoirs of the Viceroy Li Hung-Chang* (1913), suggestive but not very informing; Vladimir (*pseud.*), *The China-Japan War* (1895); A. R. Colquhoun, *China in Transformation* (1898); P. H. Clements, *An Outline of the Politics and Diplomacy of China and the Powers, 1894-1902* (1915), an admirable review of the causes and suppression of the Boxer Rebellion; several memoirs of missionaries in China, such as A. J. Brown, *New Forces in Old China* (1904), A. H. Smith, *China in Convulsion*, 2 vols. (1901), and W. A. P. Martin, *The Awakening of China* (1907); H. B. Morse, *The Trade and Administration of the Chinese Empire*, new. ed. (1913), a useful work by a Commissioner of Customs for the Chinese government; P. H. Kent, *The Passing of the Manchus* (1912), a history of the outbreak of the republican revolution related with great fairness; J. O. P. Bland, *Recent Events and Present Policies in China* (1912); J. S. Thompson, *China Revolutionized* (1913); James Cantlie and C. S. Jones, *Sun Yat Sen and the Awakening of China* (1912); Edmond Rottach, *La Chine en révolution* (1914). Useful for most recent events in China is *The China Year Book*, ed. by H. T. M. Bell and H. G. W. Woodhead (1912 *sqq.*).

Japan. The best general history in English is that of F. Brinkley and Baron Kikuchi, *A History of the Japanese People from the Earliest Times to the End of the Meiji Era* (1915), containing, as appendices, the Japanese Constitution of 1889, the Anglo-Japanese Agreement of 1905, and the Treaty of Portsmouth. Briefer and less satisfactory histories are those of J. H. Longford, *The Evolution of New Japan* (1913), and David Murray, *The Story of Japan* (1904) in the " Story of the Nations " Series. W. E. Griffis, *Matthew Calbraith Perry: a Typical American Naval Officer* (1887) is an interesting biography of the American who " opened up " Japan. On Japanese government: Toyokichi Iyenaga, *The Constitutional Development of Japan, 1853-1881* (1891), brief but scholarly; P. S. Reinsch, *Intellectual and Political Currents in the Far East* (1911), including an excellent chapter on political parties and parliamentary government in Japan; *Japanese Government Documents, 1867-1889*, published by the Asiatic Society of Japan (1914), presenting English translations of all the essential documents — laws, constitutions, ordinances, rescripts — for the history of the transition from the feudal to the modern and representative system; Théophile Gollier, *Essai sur les institutions politiques du Japon* (1903). Discussion of social and political life: G. W. Knox, *Japanese Life in Town and Country* (1904); W. E. Griffis, *The Mikado's Empire*, 10th ed. (1903), and, by the same author, *The Japanese Nation in Evolution: Steps in the Progress of a Great People* (1907); Henry Dyer, *Japan in World Politics* (1909); Count Okuma (editor), *Fifty Years of New Japan*, Eng. trans. ed. by M. B. Huish, 2 vols. (1909), an encyclopedic work prepared by foremost native authorities. An elaborate history of Japan is now (1916) in preparation, by James Murdoch, of which two volumes have appeared — Vol. I, *From the Origins to the Arrival of the Portuguese in 1542* (1910), and Vol. II,

The Century of Early Foreign Intercourse, 1542–1651 (1903); another important history is that in French, by the Marquis de La Mazelière, *Le Japon: histoire et civilisation*, 5 vols. (1907–1910), from earliest times to 1910. Useful for most recent events in Japan is *The Japan Year Book* (1905 *sqq.*).

The Russo-Japanese War of 1904–1905. Kanichi Asakawa, *The Russo-Japanese Conflict, its Causes and Issues* (1904), an excellent statement, favorable to the Japanese; A. S. Hershey, *The International Law and Diplomacy of the Russo-Japanese War* (1906); Charles Ross, *The Russo-Japanese War, 1904–1905*, Vol. I (1912); A. N. (General) Kuropatkin, *The Russian Army and the Japanese War*, partial Eng. trans. by A. B. Lindsay, 2 vols. (1909), the apology of the Russian commander; Sir Ian Hamilton, *A Staff Officer's Scrap-Book during the Russo-Japanese War*, 2 vols. (1905–1907); *The Russo-Japanese War*, prepared by the Historical Section of the German General Staff and translated into English by Karl von Donat, 5 vols. in 6 (1908–1910), a technical and truly monumental work.

Russia in Asia. F. H. Skrine, *The Expansion of Russia*, 3d ed. (1915), an accurate survey of the Russian advance in Asia since 1815; J. H. Rose, *The Development of the European Nations, 1870–1900*, Vol. II (1905), ch. ii, iii, ix, on the Central Asian Question, the Afghan and Turkoman campaigns, and Russia in the Far East; G. F. Wright, *Asiatic Russia*, 2 vols. (1902), a standard work on the geography, society, and political organization of the Russian conquests and occupations; Alexis Krausse, *Russia in Asia: a Record and a Study, 1558–1899* (1899), a severe indictment of Russian policies and methods; Vladimir (*pseud.*), *Russia on the Pacific, and the Siberian Railway* (1899); Alfred Rambaud, *The Expansion of Russia: Problems of the East and Problems of the Far East*, 2d ed. (1904); J. F. Baddeley, *The Russian Conquest of the Caucasus* (1908); H. G. C. Perry-Ayscough and R. B. Otter-Barry, *With the Russians in Mongolia* (1914); Ármin Vámbéry, *Western Culture in Eastern Lands: a Comparison of the Methods adopted by England and Russia in the Middle East* (1906).

Miscellaneous. On French Indo-China: J. G. Scott, *France and Tongking: a Narrative of the Campaign of 1884 and the Occupation of Further India* (1885); J. M. A. de Lanessan, *La colonisation française en Indo-Chine* (1895); Albert Gaisman, *L'oeuvre de la France au Tonkin* (1906). On Persia: P. M. Sykes, *A History of Persia*, 2 vols. (1915), an excellent account by one thoroughly familiar with present-day Persia; W. M. Shuster, *The Strangling of Persia: a Record of European Diplomacy and Oriental Intrigue* (1912); E. G. Browne, *The Persian Revolution of 1905–1909* (1910), good also, incidentally, on the Turkish Revolution of 1908. For the Ottoman Empire, see bibliography appended to Chapter XXVI, above, and for the British Empire in Asia consult the bibliography accompanying Chapter XXIX, below.

CHAPTER XXVIII

THE SPREAD OF EUROPEAN CIVILIZATION IN AMERICA AND IN AFRICA

THE religious, economic, and patriotic motives which sent out Christian missionaries, merchant adventurers, and conquering armies from Europe to Asia, and the amazing rapidity with which these emissaries of Western civilization made their way among the highly-civilized but unprogressive peoples of the Orient, furnished the theme of the foregoing chapter. In the present chapter, the actors remain the same — missionaries, capitalists, settlers, and soldiers; but the scene shifts, first to America, which has been known to Europe for more than three centuries, and later to Africa, which continent, all except the Mediterranean coastland, was until the nineteenth century largely uncivilized and unexplored.

THE EUROPEANIZATION OF AMERICA

In the history of America no fact is more important than this — that whereas in the year 1500 the two American continents were inhabited by tribes of red-skinned "Indians," some of whom were savages roaming the wilderness, some were cannibals, while others of less primitive habits dwelt in well-built cities; in the year 1914 we find the same two continents peopled by civilized nations, European in manners, in culture, in language, and largely European in descent. The New World has become a "New Europe." Instead of merely conquering America, as they conquered Burma, the British had come by hundreds of thousands to make their homes in America, to create a New England on the western shore of the Atlantic. Similarly, the Frenchmen and Spaniards had tried to create a "New France," or a "New Spain." This was the old colonialism.

Contrast between 1500 and 1914

Its results are a familiar story. (1) North of the Great Lakes was established a British dominion,[1] with almost five millions of English-speaking inhabitants, about 1,800,000 speaking French, and only about one hundred thousand representatives of the Indian tribes from whom the country had been taken. (2) The country south of the Great Lakes and north of the gulf of Mexico was settled by men of many nations — Frenchmen, Spaniards, Swedes, Dutchmen, Scotchmen, and Englishmen; later it received millions of negro slaves from Africa, and immigrants from Germany, Ireland, Italy, Poland, Bohemia, Scandinavia, and Greece; yet it was united under one federal government and its many races were fused into one nation, a nation predominantly English in speech, customs, and law. (3) The eastern portion of South America, once a colony of Portugal, remained Portuguese in culture, although politically it became the separate nation of Brazil. (4) The rest of the New World, including Mexico, Central America, most of the West Indies, and all of South America except Brazil and Guiana, was colonized by Spaniards; and its Indian population for the most part became Catholic Christian and mingled with the Spanish. Spanish America together with Brazil, — that is, nearly all of the New World south of 30° north latitude, — inherited "Latin" or "Romance" languages (Spanish and Portuguese), embraced the faith of the Roman Catholic or Latin Church, and, therefore, has been aptly styled "Latin America," just as France, Belgium, Spain, Portugal, and Italy collectively have been designated "Latin Europe."

Results of the Old Colonialism in America

The achievement of the old colonialism of the sixteenth, seventeenth, and eighteenth centuries was, briefly, to plant in America off-shoots of European nations. Far different are the fruits of the new imperialism, for the essence of modern imperialism is the quest of profitable investments for capital, rather than of farms and new homes for settlers. What fruits this new imperialistic movement of the last half-century may have borne in America, and what may be

The New Imperialism in America

---

[1] As a part of the British Empire, Canada receives attention in the following chapter. See below, pp. 643 ff. Northeast of the great British dominion lay the Danish settlements of Greenland and Iceland.

the outstanding features of the histories of the several European-American nations, we shall attempt concisely to indicate.[1]

As regards the United States, mention may here be made only of three significant features : territorial expansion, economic expansion, and the beginnings of world imperialism. The course of territorial expansion was amazingly rapid. The United States which in 1783 won independence from Great Britain, spread westward into the broad plains of the Mississippi (purchased from France in 1803), annexed Florida in 1821, took possession of Texas in 1845, acquired undisputed possession of the Oregon country in 1846, and (1848–1853) wrested from Mexico [2] that expanse of territory which now constitutes the states of California, Nevada, Utah, Arizona, New Mexico, and a part of Colorado. Into the fertile plains of the Middle West, and on to the wonderful gold-lands of the Pacific coast flowed westward a constant stream of caravans, until from the Atlantic to the Pacific was one nation. Many of the Indians were killed, many succumbed to the white man's "fire-water," and most of the rest were cooped up in reservations.

Territorial Expansion of the United States, 1803–1853

Meanwhile, since 1830, McCormick reapers, steam railways, iron foundries, and cotton factories had been working mightily to expand the industries of the growing nation and to link together its extensive and diversified territories. A never-failing influx of immigrants from Europe furnished an abundant supply of cheap labor for the new factories and mines. Fortunes were made almost overnight, millionaires appeared, then multi-millionaires. The United States emerged in the second half of the nineteenth century as a great industrial nation, with infant industries growing to gigantic proportions, with business men seeking the most profitable investment for vast masses of capital. As in European countries certain types of business men had raised the cry for imperialism, so also in the United States there began to be heard a clamor for the acquisition of new territories. The new expan-

The Industrial Revolution in the United States

---

[1] Reference to the British possessions in America will be omitted in this chapter, being reserved for Chapter XXIX.

[2] A small strip of the territory was purchased in 1853, but the greater part was taken from Mexico by the war of 1846–1848.

sion was not to be a matter of colonizing lands adjacent to the United States, but of acquiring distant possessions in a climate which rendered extensive European civilization more difficult.

Alaska, purchased from Russia in 1867, was the first distant territory to be annexed, but can hardly be taken as the beginning of imperialism, for Alaska became a genuine colony with white men in the majority. The real start was made in 1898. In that year the United States annexed the Hawaiian Islands, lying some 2000 miles off the western American coast and constituting a convenient station on the way to the Far East. In that year also the United States made war on Spain, with the result that in 1898 Spain was forced to cede Puerto Rico, Guam, and the Philippine Islands to the United States, and to withdraw from Cuba. At one stroke the United States became a power in the West Indies and in the Far East. *The United States and the New Imperialism*

The government at Washington now took new interest in Chinese affairs, asserted that for American commerce an "open door" in China must be maintained, and that the Chinese Empire must not be dismembered. The acquisition in part of the Samoan Islands (1899–1900) still further strengthened the position of the United States in the Pacific. With ever greater ardor imperialists demanded that the United States should protect "her interests in the Pacific," that she should retain the Philippines as the nucleus of a future empire in the Far East, that she should enter unreservedly into the costly game of imperialistic rivalry and world politics. *The United States a World Power*

While acquiring new domains for herself in the Far East, the United States continued to deny the right of European nations to acquire new territory in the Western Hemisphere. This policy had been formulated in 1823 by President Monroe, who declared that the American continents were "henceforth not to be considered as subjects for future colonization by any European Powers." The famous Monroe Doctrine [1] was first designed to pre- *The Monroe Doctrine and the Imperialism of the United States*

[1] See above, pp. 25 f. It was reasserted in an emphatic manner by President Cleveland in order to prevent alleged British encroachment on the Venezuelan frontier of British Guiana (1895).

vent the re-conquest of the Latin-American colonies which had revolted from Spain.[1] Subsequently, while the government continued to pose as the benevolent protector of the weaker nations in the New World, business men of the United States invested ever more heavily in Latin-American countries, buying bonds of Nicaragua, obtaining possession of Mexican silver-mines, building up huge business enterprises, such as the banana trade in Costa Rica, and purchasing broad plantations, as in the tobacco-lands of Cuba. Their business activities and their claims as creditors inevitably involved these business men in Latin-American politics, and, in order to protect their property from rioters or insurgents, they had frequently to call upon the navy and army of the United States. For example, in 1913–1914, when revolutionary disorders menaced their property in Mexico, the Dominican Republic, and Haiti, American investors insistently demanded that United States warships and soldiers be sent to "restore order" in the troubled states. In Cuba, which after the Spanish-American War of 1898 was created a republic under American protection, the United States not only stepped in (1906) to prevent a revolution but actually governed the island for three years. Again, in Nicaragua, where New York bankers had heavily invested, the United States established a virtual protectorate.

Even more significant was the construction of the Panama canal. The right to dig a canal[2] across the isthmus of Panama **The Panama Canal** had been acquired from the republic of Colombia by a French syndicate, which offered in 1902 to sell its equipment and right of way to the United States for $40,000,000. To this arrangement the Colombian government refused its assent (1903), thus blocking the whole project. Then suddenly a revolution broke out on the isthmus of Panama against Colombia, a revolution which the United States warships prevented Colombia from crushing, and which resulted in the establishment

---

[1] It was also directed against the further extension southward of the Russian territory of Alaska.

[2] By the Clayton-Bulwer treaty (1850) the United States and Great Britain had agreed not to construct any canal between the Atlantic and Pacific oceans except as a joint enterprise; this treaty was superseded in 1901 by the Hay-Paunce-fote treaty, which enabled the United States alone to construct a canal, but provided that the canal should be open to ships of all nations on equal terms.

of a diminutive republic of Panama under the protection of the United States. From the new republic, the United States immediately obtained the coveted "canal zone," for the sum of $10,000,000 and an annual payment of $250,000. Work on the canal, begun in 1907, proceeded so rapidly that in 1914 all was complete. By constructing the canal, the United States had given to world commerce an invaluable short-cut from the Atlantic to the Pacific; but in admiring the achievement it is well to remember that the canal was also designed to facilitate the passage of American warships to the Pacific in case of a war in the Far East, that possession of the canal still further excited the ambition of American imperialists for aggrandizement in Central America, that the republic of Colombia resentfully regarded the United States as having encouraged, if not as having instigated, the secession of Panama, and that the canal had cost the taxpayers of the United States almost $400,000,000.

The Latin-American states developed less rapidly than their great northern neighbor, for they were handicapped by three circumstances: (1) there were not enough European settlers in Latin America; (2) for this and for geographic reasons, Latin America was saddled with a landed aristocracy; and (3) lacking capital, as well as population, much of Latin America became financially dependent upon Europe and the United States. These three conditions deserve a little closer attention. *Slower Development of Latin America*

Once again let it be repeated, not settlers seeking homes had come in the sixteenth and seventeenth centuries to Spanish and Portuguese America, but missionaries seeking converts, adventurers seeking wealth, and soldiers of fortune eager for glory. The soldiers had performed a number of brilliant exploits in the sixteenth century, such as the conquest of Mexico and the conquest of Peru, *Impress of the Old Colonialism on Latin America* earning fame by their hardihood and shame for their cruelty. The adventurers had acquired rich gold and silver mines in which they compelled unwilling natives to work, and fertile plantations which were often cultivated by negro slaves imported from Africa. The missionaries, on the other hand, with the aid of higher Spanish officials had endeavored to shield the Indians from the cruelty of fortune-hunters and so genuine had been their

missionary zeal that the bulk of the natives had embraced the
Roman Catholic Christian faith. One of the converted Indians
had even attained the dignity of a saint in the Catholic Church —
Saint Rose of Lima; many had adopted, along with the religion
of the white man, his manners and customs, and had intermarried freely with the Spaniards and Portuguese; others had
remained half-savage and were but half-hearted Christians;
still others were complete savages, untamable and wild. These
facts, already familiar to us, have once more been rehearsed
because they explain a fundamental feature of Latin-American
society, — the existence of half-civilized negro and Indian lower
classes side by side with highly civilized upper classes of pure
European, or, more frequently, of mixed descent.

That the Spaniards who came to the New World were not
inferior in culture to the English colonists of Massachusetts, we
*European
Culture in
Latin
America*
may infer from the facts that the first universities in
America were founded by the Spaniards, that the first
printing-press in the New World was set up in Mexico
(1535), that even before 1800 astronomers of Mexico
City had won world-wide fame. In art, in literature, in architecture, in all the graces and refinements of polite society, Latin
America has given proof of a high degree of civilization. But
the comparatively large proportion of ignorant natives and
shiftless negroes in Latin-American countries operated to re-
tard political and economic progress.

In achieving political independence, for example, the Latin-
American nations lagged behind the United States by almost half
*Achieve-
ment of
Political
Independ-
ence in
Latin
America,
1810-1903*
a century. The revolt of Brazil from Portugal, and of
the Spanish colonies from Spain, did not take place
until the decades of 1810–1830. During these historic decades were established nine independent nations: the United Mexican States, the Central
American Federation, Great Colombia, Peru, Bolivia,
the empire of Brazil, Paraguay, the United Provinces
of the Rio de la Plata (Argentine Confederation), and Chile.
In the West Indies, Haiti had already revolted from France (1804)
and conquered Santo Domingo (1822), the other part of the
Haitian island, once a Spanish colony. These states, comprising nearly all of America south of the United States,

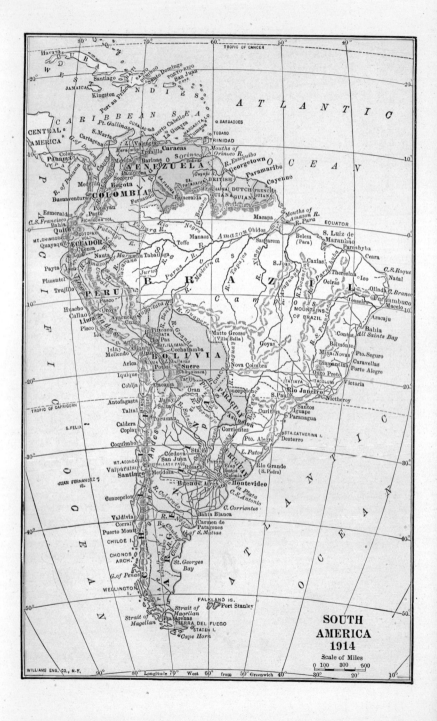

SOUTH
AMERICA
1914

Scale of Miles

0   100   300   500

were subsequently split up and reorganized until the map of Latin America assumed its present appearance, with twenty independent republics. First of all, Uruguay, a state slightly smaller than Nebraska, after a bitter struggle won its independence (1828) from the United Provinces of the Rio de la Plata, resisted the aggression of Brazil, and was constituted a free republic in 1830. Next came the break-up of the Great Colombia which had been established in 1819 by the heroic efforts of Simon Bolivar,[1] the great revolutionary hero. Bolivar, sadly enough, lived just long enough to see his Great Colombia split up into the three states of Venezuela (1829), Ecuador (1830), and Colombia.[2] Had he lived 73 years longer, he might have witnessed the secession of yet another state from Colombia, the little republic of Panama (1903). The Central American Federation showed a similar tendency toward disintegration, and in the years 1838–1847 became divided into the five diminutive republics of Guatemala, Honduras, Nicaragua, Salvador, and Costa Rica. In 1844, also, the eastern part of Haiti became the Dominican Republic (Santo Domingo). The Cuban republic, established in 1902, and Panama, in 1903, complete the roll-call of twenty Latin-American nations. There remained on the South American continent the three small sections of Guiana, belonging respectively to Great Britain, Holland, and France; in Central America, British Honduras still obeyed foreign rule; and in the West Indies the Bahamas, Jamaica, Barbados, the Leeward and Windward islands, Trinidad, and Tobago, all belonged to Great Britain; France retained Martinique and Guadeloupe; the Dutch had Curaçao and a few islets; while St. Thomas, St. John, and St. Croix were possessed by the Danes; and Puerto Rico, larger than Delaware, was ruled by the United States.

The Ten Latin-American States of 1830

The Twenty Latin-American States of 1914

Remnants of European Holdings in Latin America, 1914

[1] 1783–1830.

[2] Colombia was successively called "the Republic of Colombia" (1819–1831), "the Republic of New Granada" (1831–1858), "the Granadine Confederation" (1858–1861), "the United States of New Granada" (1861–1863), "the United States of Colombia" (1863–1886), and "the Republic of Colombia" (since 1886).

Independence achieved, the real troubles of the Latin-American nations began. The masses of half-Europeanized natives and negroes, lacking the traditions of self-government, and very imperfectly comprehending the principles of democracy and of law, fell easily under the domination of politicians and military dictators. Especially in the smaller countries politics was simply a lucrative game of a handful of men. Changes in government were effected more often by "revolutions" than by regular balloting. In the negro republic of Haiti, which by the way received its culture from France rather than from Spain, "revolution" succeeded "revolution" ever since the time of Jean Pierre Boyer, who ruled the island despotically until 1843. Turbulent have been the politics of Santo Domingo, also, except during the enlightened but autocratic rule of President Ulises Heureaux (1882–1899). In the five Central American republics of Guatemala, Honduras, Salvador, Nicaragua, and Costa Rica, frequent revolutions and wars attended the struggles between the Conservatives and Liberals, between the Clericals and Anti-Clericals. Again and again ill-starred attempts were made to revive the federation of the five states. These troubles were increased by the intrigues of foreign adventurers in Central America. For instance, in 1855 a California journalist by the name of William Walker, with fifty-six American "soldiers of fortune," made himself practically master of Nicaragua, and was financially supported by a group of American capitalists who had business interests in Nicaragua. Agents of another American capitalist, Cornelius Vanderbilt, aided combined forces from the other Central American states to expel Walker. Another upheaval occurred in 1885, when Rufino Barrios, the Liberal president of Guatemala, attempted unsuccessfully to gain control of all Central America. Again in 1906 Central America was disturbed by a civil war in which foreigners again played a prominent part. It is only fair to remark that while intrigue and factional strife were distressing Honduras, Nicaragua, Salvador, and Guatemala, comparative peace and prosperity settled down in Costa Rica, the one Central American state in which the Spanish element was not hopelessly outweighed by the Indian population.

[marginal notes: Governmental Problems in Latin America · "Revolutions" · Haiti · Santo Domingo · Central America]

In South America, as in Central America, some of the states, where the Indian aborigines had been imperfectly assimilated to Spanish civilization, were kept in constant turmoil by the mimic warfare between politicians and by so-called "revolutions" in which little blood was usually spilled, but much excitement was manifested. In Colombia the chief disturbances were caused by the Liberals and Anti-Clericals, who continually plotted to overthrow the government. Venezuela was torn by civil strife between the advocates of a centralized government and the supporters of a loose federal system, — the latter triumphing. Although possessing the forms of democratic government, Venezuela was ruled by a few unscrupulous military leaders, one of whom, Antonio Guzman Blanco, maintained himself almost twenty years (1870–1889), sometimes as president and sometimes as the power behind the president. Following the overthrow of Blanco (1889), a series of "revolutions" occurred, until in 1900 the notorious General Cipriano Castro came into power. After eight years he too was ousted, and new disturbances were precipitated. In Ecuador, where a comparatively small percentage of the population was thoroughly imbued with Spanish civilization, civil wars were frequent and military leaders were able to make themselves practically dictators. Although a few of these dictators were pronounced Clericals, notably Garcia Moreno, the greater number were Anti-Clericals, who introduced divorce, civil marriage, and religious equality, who forbade the establishment of new monasteries or convents, and who confiscated for the state all church property.

Peru, the land of gold, silver, and copper, was for a time ruled by commanders who had fought in the war of independence, and who by their rivalries caused occasional disturbances. Twice Peru was engaged in war with Chile. The first time Chile intervened to break up a confederation which had been formed by Peru and Bolivia under the latter's remarkable president, Andres Santa Cruz, who proudly boasted his descent from the Incas, ancient Indian rulers of Peru. The second war was waged in 1879–1883 with the help of Bolivia against Chile, and resulted in a complete triumph for the Chileans, the cession to Chile of Bolivia's seacoast, as well

Marginal notes: Colombia · Venezuela · Ecuador · Peru

as the annexation by Chile of the Peruvian province of Tara-
pacá, also rich in guano and nitrate, and the occupation by
Chile of the Peruvian provinces of Tacna and Arica.

Bolivia   Bolivia, uneven country of mountains, swamps, and
plains, deserves little mention; we may observe simply that
political disturbances, frequent from 1825 to 1884, thereafter
became rare. Southeast of Bolivia lies the smaller inland state
of Paraguay, in which the proportion of white inhab-
Paraguay   itants and the degree of civilization were probably
lower than in any other region of South America. Between 1814
and 1870 Paraguay was despotically ruled by a single family,
one member of which, Francisco Lopez, involved his country in
a disastrous war with Brazil, Uruguay, and Argentina (1864–
1870), a war which exterminated the majority of Paraguay's
population and saddled the country with a huge war debt of
$200,000,000. Lopez was killed in battle (1870), and a demo-
cratic constitution was then adopted. Since that time Paraguay
has slowly recuperated, though repeatedly disturbed by revolutionary agitation. Uruguay, the smallest inde-
Uruguay   pendent state in South America, was long dominated
by contending cliques of more or less unscrupulous politicians,
but more recently has grown very prosperous and has tried many
interesting experiments in social reform and political democracy.

The greatest of the Latin-American states, the most prosperous, and probably the best governed, are the Argentine
The   Republic, Brazil, and Chile — the so-called "A-B-C"
"A-B-C"   Powers. Although during its first half-century of
Powers   independence Argentina was vexed by foreign war as
well as by internal dissensions, since 1825 the republic, with a
constitution copied from the United States, has made amazing
advances in material prosperity, in orderly govern-
Argentina   ment, in population (from 1,830,000 in 1869 to
7,500,000 in 1913), in art, in science, in military and naval
power; and its capital, the beautiful Buenos Aires, has become
in size the metropolis of the southern hemisphere, in culture a
second Paris.

Brazil, after enjoying for five decades (1840–1889) the benevolent rule of the kindly Emperor Pedro II, was constituted a
federal republic, — the United States of Brazil. Against Presi-

dent Peixoto, who attempted to rule despotically, and whose administration was marred by scandalous corruption, an insurrection broke out in 1893, but was suppressed with stern severity. Since then Brazil has prospered in peace and has welcomed immigrants from Europe by thousands, especially Portuguese, Italians, and Germans. **Brazil**

Chile, the long, narrow country west of the Andes, early achieved political stability. In 1833 the Chileans formed a strongly centralized republican government, which under Conservative auspices promoted education, arts, and financial prosperity. Two Liberal presidents — Santa Maria (1881–1886) and José Balmaceda (1886–1891) — introduced radical reforms and attacked the privileges of the Roman Catholic Church, but by establishing a virtual dictatorship Balmaceda provoked a revolution in 1891, which ended in his defeat and suicide. Admiral Montt, leader of the insurgents, was almost unanimously chosen in a free election as the next president, and the subsequent history of Chile was distinguished by peace, order, and prosperity. **Chile**

. Not only did the "A-B-C" Powers appear by 1914 to have achieved domestic tranquillity, but in their international relations, complicated by vexatious boundary disputes, they had given evidence of a very real desire to substitute arbitration for war. For example, a boundary dispute between Argentina and Chile in 1898 might well have caused a bloody struggle, had not the two nations amicably agreed to submit their conflicting claims to peaceful arbitration. The pacific influence of the "A-B-C" Powers was splendidly exemplified in 1913 when they offered themselves as peacemakers to avert a threatened war between the United States and Mexico.

A few pages back we referred to three circumstances as hindrances to the peace and prosperity of Latin America, the first being the large proportion of imperfectly civilized Indians, negroes, and half-breeds, which rendered democratic government exceedingly difficult. It is now high time to take up the second of these circumstances, the persistence of a landed aristocracy. Partly because most of the country was better suited either to stock-raising on a large scale, or to raising coffee, cotton, and tobacco on large **The Plantation System in Latin America** plantations, than to division into small farms; partly because it was easy to obtain the cheap labor of Indians and the slave labor of imported African negroes on great ranches and plantations; and partly because many influential families had obtained the grant of vast estates in colonial times, there grew up in Latin America a powerful and wealthy land-holding aristocracy, on whose estates labored negroes, Indians, and the poorer class of mixed race. Where negroes were numerous, as in Brazil and in the West Indies, they were generally emancipated during the nineteenth century. In other countries the farm-laborers or "peons," being mostly ignorant Indians, were held in a position somewhat similar to that of the medieval serf. They worked on the estates of great land-holders; they possessed for themselves no land or only a little patch of poor soil; they frequently were obliged to remain on the same estate whether they would or no; they were often saddled with debts handed down from generation to generation; they were always extremely poor; and quite commonly they were improvident, inclined to vice, and easily led into armed revolt.

Such was preëminently the case in Mexico. Being discontented with their miserable lot, the peons were in a state of chronic rebellion. Under the leadership of Benito Juarez, a full-blooded Indian, they had rallied to expel Emperor Maximilian and his French soldiers from Mexico in the 'sixties;[1] but Juarez had shown more energy in attacking the Catholic Church than in caring for the welfare of the peon. Porfirio Diaz, the successor of Juarez, who by military force made himself supreme in Mexico and by ruthless severity maintained himself as president, really as dictator, of Mexico almost continuously from 1877 to 1911, was less hostile to the Catholic Church and not at all interested in the peon. Under Diaz agrarian revolts were sternly suppressed. But when age loosened his grip on the government, the peons again began to stir. Their successful revolution in 1911 put into the presidential chair Francisco Madero, who was a wealthy man himself but pledged to better the lot of the poor agricultural laborers. A nephew of Porfirio Diaz, however, took up arms against Madero; a new revolution was started; and, after the

The Situation in Mexico

[1] See above, pp. 177 f.

execution or murder of Madero, one of Madero's generals, Victoriano Huerta, who had joined young Diaz, became provisional president. A bloody and protracted civil war then ensued between Provisional President Huerta's forces and the so-called "Constitutionalists," led by Venustiano Carranza and by the dashing Indian bandit, Francisco Villa, claiming to represent the down-trodden peons and denouncing Huerta's violations of the constitution. In 1914 the Constitutionalists triumphantly entered Mexico City, but instead of granting the promised land reforms the two leading "reformers," Villa and Carranza, shortly fell to quarreling and plunged their country again into disgraceful civil wars.

The case of Mexico is cited as an extreme example of Latin America's land problem. The third difficulty under which Latin America labored — her lack of financial re- Economic sources — remains to be considered. For various Dependence reasons, some of which may already be clear, South of Latin and Central America failed to keep pace with Europe America and the United States in industrial development, in business organization, and in banking; consequently when railways were to be built, industrial enterprises launched, warships purchased, canals constructed, or an extraordinary expenditure incurred, there being insufficient funds at home, the Latin-American governments necessarily borrowed money in London, Foreign New York, or Paris. For example, Nicaragua bor- Loans to rowed in France 12,500,000 francs in 1905; the Latin central government of Brazil owed London creditors America (1913) some £91,600,000; Honduras borrowed between 1867 and 1870 some $25,000,000, and, being unable to pay the annual interest, allowed interest-arrears to accumulate to the amount of $35,000,000. Altogether the Latin-American states officially owe several billions of dollars to Europe, that is, they pay annually many millions of dollars interest or tribute to European financiers. Should any country refuse to pay its debt, warships from Europe or from the United States would be sent to enforce payment as they did in the case of Venezuela in 1903; or officials from the United States might assume the right to collect customs duties and therewith pay the interest, as in the case of the Dominican Republic (1904).

Yet more staggering sums were invested and more enormous profits realized by foreign business men, who, instead of loan-

Foreign Investments in Latin America ing money to Latin-American governments, obtained from those governments the right to work mines, build factories, construct railways, collect rubber, cut timber, or export bananas. For example, the fabulous wealth of many Mexican mines went to swell the profits of mine-owners in New York City; the great oil-wells of Vera Cruz, Mexico, produced enormous quantities of petroleum but to enrich certain business men in the United States and Great Britain; from the gold mines of Esmeraldas, Ecuador, $250,000 worth of precious metal was dug out in 1910 for a few investors of the United States; in the rubber forests of the upper Amazon there were toiling an army of Indians, collecting rubber for the English speculators who owned stock in the Peruvian Amazon Company. A British syndicate, *Pearson and Son Ltd.*, was in 1913 endeavoring to obtain the very important privilege of exploiting the oil-wells of Costa Rica, Colombia, and Ecuador. Then, too, there were the banks. In Argentina, for instance, there were British, Spanish, German, French, and Italian banks, with a total capital which certainly would exceed $60,000,000. Such facts, so often overlooked, most eloquently bespeak the economic dependence of Latin America upon the United States and Europe; beyond the shadow of a doubt they prove that South America, although politically independent, is paying heavy tribute to financiers in London, in Paris, and in New York. British investors, it was asserted in 1914, annually realized $160,000,000 in South America on capital investments totaling more than three billion dollars. The domination of Latin America by foreign capitalists, who controlled a great part of her economic activities, who were not without a powerful influence upon her politics, and who were backed by the might of their several governments, constitutes the effect upon Latin America of the new capitalistic imperialism.

THE PARTITION OF AFRICA

From America we turn to Africa, the other great continent discovered by Europeans in the fifteenth century, and colonized in more recent times. Of course the Mediterranean coast and Egypt, which had formed part of the ancient Roman Empire, had long been known to Christendom, and feared too, be- Africa in the Middle Ages cause since the Arab conquest of the seventh century all the northern edge of Africa had become a strong- hold of Mohammedanism, and, in the sixteenth century, of piracy. Not only the northern coastland but also the eastern shores of Africa had been visited in the Middle Ages by Arab traders and warriors, who communicated their Mohammedan religion and in some cases their language, customs, and costume to the native whites ("Libyans" or "Berbers") of northern Africa, and to the brown-skinned, frizzly-haired "Hamites" of Somali- land on the East African coast. Even as far south as Sofala, on the east coast, and as far inland as Timbuctu,[1] in the Sahara, Arab tribesmen carried their culture. But of this, Europe was ignorant.

The vast continent which lay south of Egypt, Tripoli, Tunis, Algeria, and Morocco was first made known to Europe by Portu- guese explorers in the fifteenth century. The roman- The Portu- guese in Africa tic story of Portuguese exploration needs not to be retold here.[2] Suffice it to say that the Portuguese were amazed at the size of the continent, and astonished to find naked, savage, black or brown men who hunted strange beasts in the tropical African forests. In the extreme south were short yellowish-brown people (Bushmen and Hottentots) who made crude attempts to till the soil and to raise cattle. Coming up the east coast, after rounding the Cape, the Portuguese were no less astounded to meet Arab traders, and delighted to discover the Coptic Christian kingdom of Abyssinia, which they helped to defend against Mohammedan onslaughts. Heroic Portu- guese explorers and missionaries, undaunted either by the deadly fevers of the tropics or by the cannibalistic customs of many negro tribes, explored the Zambesi and Congo rivers. They intro- duced the pineapple, tobacco, arrowroot, the sweet-potato, sugar-cane, onions, guava, pigs, ducks, and many other things useful and pleasant. Trading-posts were founded in many ports.

---

[1] Timbuctu, first visited by an Arab traveler in 1352, became a Moslem city in 1591.

[2] See Vol. I, pp. 49 ff.

But try as it might, the petty Portuguese kingdom could not monopolize or effectively control so enormous a continent.

Great Britain, France, and Holland became the successful rivals of Portugal in Africa. By 1870 the Portuguese could claim only: (1) Portuguese East Africa (Mozambique and Zambesia), a fertile territory eight times as large as Portugal, rich in coal, gold, ivory, and rubber; (2) Angola or Portuguese West Africa, with 900 miles of coast, south of the Congo River, and valuable for its rubber; (3) Portuguese Guinea, a small district in the extreme west; and (4) the island of St. Thomas, Prince's Island, the Cape Verde Islands, the Azores, and the Madeira Islands, lying off the west coast of Africa.

The Dutch began seriously to compete with the Portuguese in Africa in the seventeenth century, when they acquired various The Dutch posts along the coast from Cape Blanco to the gulf of in Africa Guinea, and established a colony at the Cape of Good Hope in South Africa. The West African posts proved valuable in the seventeenth and eighteenth centuries as depots for the slave trade; from them the Dutch exported four or five millions of negro slaves for servile labor in America. Into South Africa, however, the Dutch came as settlers rather than as slavers, and instead of exporting slaves actually imported negroes from the Gold Coast for service on South African farms.

The number of Dutch farmers or "Boers" was probably more than 10,000 [1] when the colony was conquered from Holland by Great Britain (1806) [2] in the course of the Napole- The British onic wars. The Boers were so sorely dissatisfied under and the Dutch in British rule — they bitterly resented the emancipation South Africa of their negro slaves in 1834 — that they abandoned before 1870 Cape Colony in thousands and sought new homes north of the Orange River, or in Natal, northeast of Cape Colony. This wholesale migration of 1836–1840 has become famous in history as the "Great Trek." Even in Natal and the region north of the Orange River the shadow of the British flag fell upon them, for in 1843 Natal was annexed by Great Britain, and in 1848 the Orange

[1] There were also small minorities of Germans and French Huguenots.

[2] The British first seized Cape Colony in 1795, but returned it in 1803; they occupied the colony again in 1806, and in 1814 paid £6,000,000 as compensation to the Dutch.

River State (between the Orange and Vaal rivers). In the following decade, however, the Boer settlement in Transvaal (north of the Vaal River) and the Orange River State obtained their independence. The situation in 1870, then, was this: the Boer republics of Transvaal and Orange Free State were independent, and the former Dutch settlements of Natal and Cape Colony were under British rule.

Besides South Africa, Great Britain had acquired very little African territory prior to 1870. The British posts on the Gold Coast and at the mouth of the Gambia River in western British Posts in West Africa Africa had been important chiefly as centers of the slave-trade in the seventeenth and eighteenth centuries. Sierra Leone had originated as a colony for freed slaves.

France likewise had established posts for the slave traffic on the West African coast, near the mouth of the Senegal River, and had seized neighboring Dutch establishments in The French in Africa before 1870 the seventeenth century. Louis XIV, moreover, had nominally annexed the large island of Madagascar; but before 1870 the French had practically abandoned the island. In the early part of the nineteenth century France was interested in Egypt, not only because Napoleon had made an attempt to conquer the country, but also because the Turkish viceroy, Mehemet Ali, allowed French officers to organize his army and navy; but Egypt was in no sense a French colony. Between 1815 and 1870, however, France did acquire two important African colonies. The lesser of these was Gabun, now a part of French Equatorial Africa. The greater was Algeria.

French rule in Algeria dated from the last year of the reign of Charles X (1830), when an insult administered by the native dey to the French minister had evoked a punitive ex- French Conquest of Algeria pedition from France and had led to a French military occupation of Algiers and the deposition of the dey. Thenceforth, despite the native resistance brilliantly led by Abd-el-Kader, which cost France heavily throughout the reign of Louis Philippe, and despite subsequent bitter revolts which lasted almost continuously from 1864 to 1871, the French were steadily pressing their conquests and bringing the whole of Algeria under subjection.[1]

[1] For further details of the French conquest of Algeria, see above, p. 513.

The foregoing paragraphs must have made it clear that before the last quarter of the nineteenth century comparatively little progress had been made in the partition of Africa.

Abolition of the African Slave-Trade, 1807–1850

This was in no small part due to the fact that the slave-trade, which flourished in Africa until the nineteenth century, did not encourage Europeans to penetrate into the interior, since they might better establish trading stations on the coast, where they could purchase the negroes from Arab slave-dealers. In 1807, however, Great Britain, the greatest slave-trading nation, abolished the shameful traffic.[1] Other countries followed the British example, until before 1850 the wholesale shipping of negro slaves from Africa by European traders had practically ceased. The abolition of the slave-trade was extremely important in its results. Henceforth the interest of Europe in Africa was to be in material commodities rather than in human beings.

The abolition of the slave-trade, moreover, was accompanied by an awakening of religious and humanitarian zeal for the welfare of the natives.

Exploration

Africa must be explored, the war against the slave-trade must be carried even into the darkest recesses of the Dark Continent, and the negroes must be reclaimed for Christianity, civilization, and commerce. Missionaries and intrepid explorers penetrated to the very heart of the Dark Continent, bringing back romantic tales of trackless forests traversed, of mighty lakes and rivers discovered, of brown-skinned "Pygmies" four feet tall, of cannibal orgies, of elephants, zebras, crocodiles, of monstrous snakes, and of gigantic apes. Many missionaries, Catholic and Protestant, with great zeal made their way where never white man had been seen before, and preached to the natives; but the great work of exploration in the middle of the nineteenth century was inspired by other than missionary motives. David Livingstone, a famous Scotch explorer, was, it is true, sent to Africa in 1840 by a Protestant missionary society; but he speedily became more explorer than evangelist; instead of converting the negroes he would "open up the country" for others; and in 1857 he severed his connection with the missionary society. By his wonderful transcontinental journey through the upper Zambesi valley, by his courage in

[1] Denmark had previously taken a similar step.

facing danger, by his kindliness to the natives, by his stirring·
denunciations of the slave-trade, and finally by his mysterious
disappearance in the very heart of the African wilderness, Livingstone aroused the sympathetic interest of the entire world.
Public opinion was still more excited when James Gordon Bennett,
a New York newspaper man, sent out his cleverest reporter to
look for Livingstone, and when that reporter, Henry Morton
Stanley, not only found Livingstone, but discovered the course
of the Congo River and explored the great lakes of Central Africa
(1871-1877). The thrilling story of Stanley's trip *Through the
Dark Continent*, published in book form, enthralled the imagination and decorated the center-table of many a bourgeois in England and America. In person Stanley urged upon business
men, in England, in Germany, the value of Central Africa
(Congo) as a field for commercial enterprise.

No one understood Stanley so well as did Leopold II, king
of the Belgians, nor did any one act with such quick decision
to seize the opportunity for gain. In 1876 Leopold
held an informal conference of all the Powers at
Brussels, explained the commercial possibilities of
Central Africa, and formed an "International Association for the Exploration and Civilization of Africa," with committees in each country and headquarters at Brussels. The
Belgian committee, however, was the most active, and in 1878
a new committee, practically a Belgian commercial company, was
formed for the development of the Congo valley. This committee, financed by the shrewd Leopold, became the so-called "International Association of the Congo"; it employed Stanley to
found Belgian stations and to make treaties with the native
chieftains of the Congo (1880-1884). In spite of the rival claims
of Portugal and France, King Leopold obtained for his "International Association" complete control of the Congo region and
a recognized status as an independent neutral state, although the
conference of the Powers which met in Berlin during the winter
of 1884-1885 stipulated for the free navigation of the Congo
River, free commerce, the suppression of slave-trading, and the
protection of missionaries, scientists, and explorers in the Congo.
In 1885 Leopold became personal sovereign of the new state, called
"Congo Free State," towards the development of which he con-

Leopold II and the Belgian Congo

tributed millions from his personal estate. Presently he reaped his reward. For himself and his family he carved out a vast estate, the *Domaine de la couronne*, almost ten times as large as Belgium, embracing the choicest "rubber country" of the Congo River, and yielding rich returns from the forced labor of the natives who collected the rubber. Other lands, too, were seized by the state as "vacant lands," and exploited for rubber, ivory, and palm-oil, either directly or through *concessionaire* [1] companies in which Leopold's associates were heavily interested. Some idea of the increasing value of these enterprises may be gained from the fact that the rubber exported from the Congo was worth in 1886 some $30,000 and in 1910 some $10,000,000 a year, not to speak of ivory and palm-oil. All this while, however, the natives of the Congo, instead of being "civilized," were being forced to work practically as slaves collecting ivory and rubber for the enrichment of Leopold and his fellow-investors. To be sure, several hundred Christian missionaries were endeavoring to win converts, but the state authorities seemed to show greater interest in promoting business than in furthering Christianity. Finally, after the scandalous condition of the Congo had aroused violent criticism in Belgium and evoked stern warnings from Sir Edward Grey, the British foreign minister, reforms were introduced, the territory of the Congo Free State was annexed to Belgium (1908) and placed under control of the Belgian parliamentary government, and Leopold surrendered his vast Congo estate in return for liberal compensation.

Meanwhile, France, Great Britain, Germany, Italy, and Spain had been drawn into the game of founding empires in Africa and were following Leopold's lead. Ardent Christians hoped that Africa might thus be more easily reclaimed from paganism; other altruistic citizens, whose faith was more in "civilization" than in Christianity, talked enthusiastically about the mission of Europe in bringing civilization to the Dark Continent; still other and less thoughtful people found pleasure in seeing great blocks of the

Motives and Men in the Partition of Africa

---

[1] A *concessionaire* company is a business corporation which has received as a "concession" from the government the special and monopolistic right of carrying on a certain industry, collecting rubber, or mining for a certain metal, in a specified district.

African map labeled "British" or "German," and referring with swelling pride to "our African Empire." But the prime movers were business men, who knew that the opening up of Africa meant big business opportunities, who formed companies for the development of African colonies, and who not infrequently made fortunes in African enterprises. Such an one was Cecil Rhodes (1853–1902). As a young man he had found riches in the famous Kimberley diamond fields of South Africa; he had acquired a controlling interest in several big South African mining companies; and he had conceived the project of extending British rule from Cape Colony northward to the Mediterranean. It was Cecil Rhodes who gained Bechuanaland for Great Britain; it was Cecil Rhodes who controlled the British South Africa Company which ruled over the extensive territory now called in his honor Rhodesia. During his lifetime he enjoyed power as the leading man in South Africa, as well as enormous wealth derived from South African mines; and at his death he left provision for 175 scholarships at Oxford to be bestowed upon select young men of America, Germany, and the British colonies, thus fostering the idea of the British empire and perpetuating his own name as the donor of the "Rhodes Scholarships."

Cecil Rhodes

Cecil Rhodes may serve as type of the men who gained African empires for European nations. As an example of the manner in which such empires were gained, the case of German Southwest Africa is typical. With the exception of Walfisch Bay, which was occupied by the British in 1878, the southwestern coast of Africa from Cape Frio to the Orange River was until 1883 still under the sway of independent chieftains. In that year a German merchant, Lüderitz by name, with Bismarck's consent, sent an agent to establish a trading-post at Angra Pequeña or "Lüderitz Bay." Quietly and quickly the agent persuaded the native chieftains to make treaties with him and to cede to him large sections of coastland. Meanwhile German diplomats had made sure that Britain would not seriously object to the formation of a German colony in Southwest Africa. In 1884, therefore, the German government took over the territories which Lüderitz had privately acquired, from the Orange River northward to 26° S. latitude; and the adjoining territory from 26° S. latitude northward to Cape Frio

Lüderitz and German Southwest Africa

was declared to be a German protectorate, excepting the British
district around Walfisch Bay.   In this manner German Southwest
Africa was founded.   In a similar manner other colonies were acquired by Germany, and by Italy, France,
and Great Britain.   On the gulf of Guinea, Kamerun
and Togoland, for instance, were obtained for Germany in 1884 by the adventurous traveler, Dr.
Nachtigal, who journeyed along the coast making "treaties"
whereby native chieftains placed themselves under the "protection" of Germany.   Hot on Dr. Nachtigal's trail followed a
British consul, who in the same way acquired the region around
the Niger delta for Great Britain.   Again, in eastern Africa,
there landed in 1884 three enterprising young Germans with
plenty of German flags and blank treaty forms, to lay the foundations of German East Africa.   In almost every case, territory
thus acquired was given over into the hands of a chartered company, and among the prominent members of the company were
usually to be found the few individuals — like Rhodes and
Lüderitz — who had been active in winning the territory.

Acquiring African territories in this manner was so easy that
ambitious Englishmen began to talk of extending the British
Empire from the Cape of Good Hope in the south to
Cairo at the mouth of the Nile in the north, and
started to build a "Cape to Cairo" railway; French
expansionists began to dream of a French Empire,
stretching in a broad belt across the Sahara from ocean to ocean;
and German enthusiasts to think how they might carve out large
slices of Africa for Germany.   Obviously these conflicting ambitions could not all be realized; compromise was necessary, and a
friendly agreement between the nations concerned as to how they
should partition Africa among themselves.   A number of such
compromises and agreements or "deals" were made, assigning
great blocks of half-explored territory to one nation or to another
as spheres for conquest.   Several deserve mention.

First of all should be noted the international conference at
Berlin (1884–1885), which practically recognized the possession of
the Congo region by Leopold II and his "International Association"; the same conference laid down the rule that any Power,
in annexing African territory, must notify the other Powers of

Rapid Partition of Africa in the 'Eighties

Colossal "Deals" in African Territory

the fact.   The next important move in the game was made by
Germany and Great Britain in 1890, when they agreed that
(1) Great Britain should be allowed to connect her
spheres of influence in the Nile valley with her already   The Anglo-
existing colony on the coast of East Africa, by assum-   German
ing a protectorate over the domains of the negro   Agreement,
king of Uganda.   A glance at the map will show how   1890
Egypt, the Anglo-Egyptian Sudan, or upper valley of the Nile,
Uganda, and British East Africa, all destined to be dominated by
Great Britain, formed a magnificent empire, sweeping from the
Mediterranean up the Nile to Lake Victoria Nyanza and opening
out upon the Indian Ocean.   But the British ambition to obtain
a continuous stretch of territory from Egypt to South Africa
had to be renounced, since German East Africa was extended
inland to the border of Belgian Congo, thus effectually separating
British South Africa and Rhodesia from British East Africa and
Uganda.   (2) Great Britain also obtained by the agreement of
1890 a protectorate over the islands of Zanzibar and Pemba,
which lay off the coast of German East Africa and which belonged
to the sultan of Zanzibar, Germany receiving in return the
island of Heligoland in the German corner of the North Sea.
(3) By this same "deal" of 1890 the boundary was adjusted in
Western Africa between the German protectorate of Kamerun
and the British district of Nigeria; the Kamerun was extended
inland to Lake Chad, and Germany was given a free hand in the
central Sudan northeast of Kamerun, with the understanding that
Germany would seek no territory in the western upper Nile
valley.   (4) Yet another article of the agreement gave German
Southwest Africa a narrow arm of territory reaching eastward
to the Zambesi River.

Hardly less important than the Anglo-German arrangement
of July, 1890, was the Anglo-French understanding
of August, 1890, whereby France was allowed to es-   The Anglo-
tablish a protectorate over the island of Madagascar [1]   French
— larger than all France; French influence was recog-   African
nized as supreme in the burning Sahara; and the   Agreement
territory of northern Nigeria between the Niger River and Lake   of 1890

---

[1] Madagascar became a French colony in 1896, and the native queen was deported.

Chad was allotted to Great Britain. This agreement, however, by no means ended the rivalry of French and British in northern and central Africa; for the French, having conceived the idea of a vast North African empire, were anxious to dominate the Sudan — as the region south of the Sahara is called — throughout its entire sweep from Cape Verde on the west to the mountains of Abyssinia on the east. Most of the western Sudan the French had already overrun; in 1894 they induced Germany to leave the central Sudan to France; they then turned to the eastern Sudan, which constitutes part of the Upper Nile basin. The British, on the other hand, regarded this region, the "Anglo-Egyptian Sudan," as their own preserve,[1] although it had not yet been conquered. Consequently, when in 1898 a French expedition from French Congo, under the lead of Captain Marchand, entered the Upper Nile valley and raised the French flag at the famous but swampy post of Fashoda on the Nile, the British were highly indignant. A British-Egyptian force hurried south to Fashoda from Khartum. War was in the air. Then gracefully France gave way, renouncing her claim to Fashoda and to the Anglo-Egyptian Sudan, giving up the idea of a transcontinental empire, but receiving in return the undisputed right to occupy the kingdom of Wadai in the central Sudan, and thus to link up French Congo with the French possessions in northwestern Africa. This was the famous Anglo-French declaration of 1899, which paved the way for more cordial relations between the French and British in Africa and likewise in Europe.

The Fashoda Incident and the Anglo-French Agreement of 1899

A further understanding was reached by Great Britain and France in 1904, when France allowed Egypt to become practically a British protectorate, and in return Great Britain designated Morocco as a proper sphere for French ambition. Italy had already agreed (1901) that France should have a free hand in Morocco, provided that Italy should have Tripoli. Germany, however, in 1905 raised a protest, and in order to settle the "Moroccan Question"

The Anglo-French Agreement of 1904

---

[1] King Leopold of Belgium also coveted possession of the Upper Nile, and in 1892 sent expeditions from Congo Free State, hoping to gain the province of Bahrel-Ghazal; but in the end he, too, gave way before his more powerful competitors — the British.

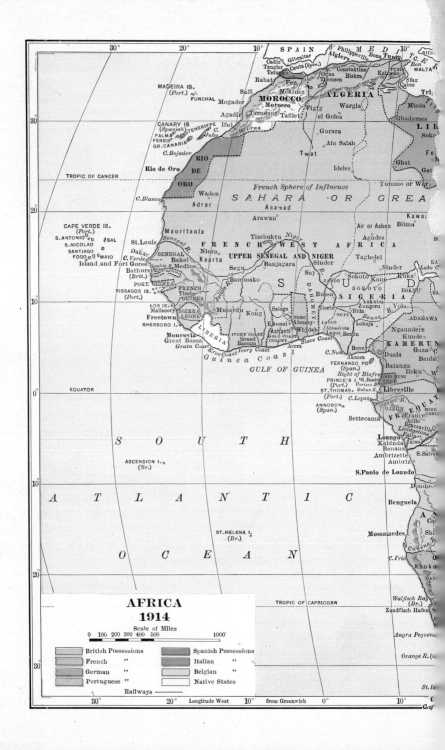

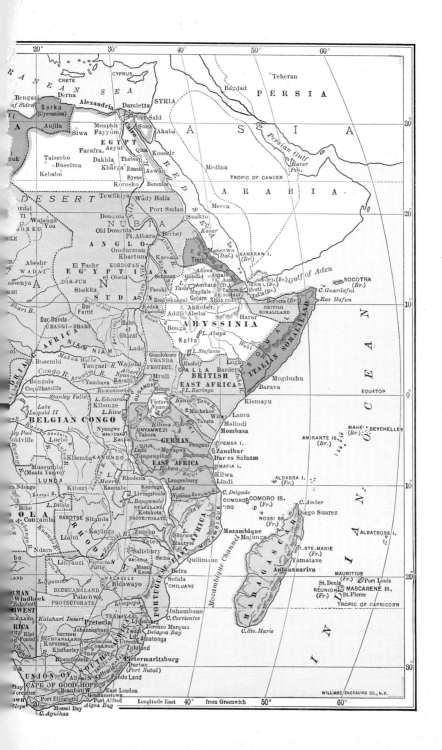

a general international conference met at Algeciras in 1906. The next year French armies in Morocco endeavored to quell a native insurrection. Claiming that some German The residents in Morocco were endangered, Germany in Moroccan 1911 suddenly dispatched the cruiser *Panther* to Question Agadir, on the coast of Morocco, to protect German interests. The French were angered by this interference; but by ceding to Germany a large section of French Equatorial Africa, the French government averted war and obtained Germany's consent to the establishment of a French protectorate over Morocco. Next France had to come to an agreement with Spain, for Spain was also interested in Morocco. Finally in 1912 the affair was settled, Spain retaining a narrow strip along the northern coast and a small inclosure or "enclave" on the southwestern coast at Ifni, France establishing a protectorate over the remainder — the greater part of Morocco, — and 140 square miles at Tangier being erected into an "international zone."

One other international transaction in African territory deserves mention, and that is the Anglo-Portuguese treaty of 1891. For years Portuguese imperialists had planned to push the boundaries of Portuguese West Africa (Angola) The Anglo-Portuguese and Portuguese East Africa (Mozambique) inland until African they should meet, thus forming a broad band quite Agreement, across the continent. For this scheme Portugal had 1891 in 1886 obtained the consent of France and Germany. But the British protested, and Cecil Rhodes, who for patriotic and business reasons was eager to extend the British dominions, founded the British South Africa Company to gain control of the upper Zambesi valley, just west of Portuguese East Africa. Unable to resist, Portugal reluctantly consented to the British occupation of the country now known as Rhodesia, lying between Angola and Mozambique, and extending north to Lake Tanganyika.

Having familiarized ourselves with a few typical men and instances in the partition of Africa, which European took place in the last quarter of the nineteenth cen- Holdings in Africa in tury, we are now in a position to review the results 1914 of the partition, and to take up in turn the African empires of Great Britain, France, Italy, Germany, Portugal, Spain, and Belgium. First comes the British Empire.

As a result of her participation in the scramble for African possessions, Great Britain could boast in 1914 that one-third of

1. The British Possessions in Africa

Africa, with a population of fifty millions, was under British domination.[1] The value, the government, and something of the nature of these possessions will be considered in detail in the following chapter on the British Empire; only their location and extent concern us at present. At the southern end of the continent were the four

Union of South Africa

thriving colonies of the Cape of Good Hope, Natal, Transvaal, and Orange River Colony, self-governing, united (since 1910) in the "Union of South Africa," embracing an area twice as large as France, and supporting a population of about 1,300,000 white and 4,700,000 colored inhabitants. Two of these four provinces — Transvaal and Orange River Colony — had been colonized, as we have seen, by Boers who had "trekked" northward from the Cape in order to escape British rule, who had fought valiantly in 1899–1902 for their independence, and who finally had been defeated and

Bechuana-land

incorporated in the British Empire. North of the South African Union extended Bechuanaland, — part colony, part protectorate, — a vast tableland of 275,000 acres, with more than two square miles to each inhabitant, and more

Rhodesia

than 70 natives to every European. Stretching still farther northward across the Zambesi valley was Rhodesia, bounded on the north by Belgian Congo and German East Africa, comprising a territory three and one-half times as large as the British Isles, inhabited by some 26,000 white pioneers and sixty times as many uncivilized negroes. The foregoing colonies, together with the smaller crown colonies of Basutoland and Swaziland, and the Nyasaland Protectorate, gave Great Britain an unbroken sweep of territory in southern Africa from the Cape of Good Hope to Lake Tanganyika.

A second colossal slice of Africa allotted to Great Britain was the Nile valley. British interest in this region had been excited

Egypt

by Napoleon's ill-starred Egyptian expedition (1798), and stimulated in the latter part of the nineteenth century by British explorers who traced the hitherto unknown

---

[1] These figures include Egypt and the Anglo-Egyptian Sudan. For a more detailed account of the British Empire, see below, ch. xxix.

course of the Upper Nile. But while Egypt, as a practically independent part of the Ottoman Empire, had been ruled by the able Mehemet Ali (pasha of Egypt from 1811 to 1848) and his descendants, the "khedives" of Egypt, Great Britain had allowed the French to become influential in Egypt. So it happened that the Suez Canal (1869), that monumental feat of engineering, was constructed by French rather than by British capitalists. British statesmen, notably Disraeli, argued that since the Suez Canal commanded the all-sea-route by way of the Red Sea to India, Great Britain as mistress of India should also be mistress of the canal; and when in 1875 the hard-pressed khedive, who held a large block of the canal company's stock, offered to sell, the British government purchased his canal shares for about $20,000,000. The Suez Canal itself was later declared to be equally open to all nations (1888). But meanwhile Great Britain had gained control of Egypt so that the waterway ran practically through British territory. It came about in this way. Discovering the Egyptian treasury to be about bankrupt, France and Great Britain in 1877 established a "Dual Control" over Egypt, *i.e.* a Frenchman supervised Egyptian public expenditures while an Englishman took charge of the revenues. Ismail, the then khedive, so bitterly opposed this interference with his affairs that British and French diplomats induced the Turkish sultan to exert his authority as overlord of Egypt and depose Ismail (1879). Ismail's son, Tewfik, submitted more tamely to the Dual Control. Presently, however, a new and fierce anti-foreign movement of the Arab soldiers, led by Arabi Pasha, furnished an excuse for armed intervention; and while the French government remained inactive, Great Britain sent forces which crushed the insurrection (1882). Henceforth the British were supreme in Egypt; the Dual Control was replaced by an English financial "adviser"; and the khedive of Egypt, although remaining in theory a vassal of the Turkish sultan, was in practice the puppet of British commissioners.

The 12,000 square miles of fertile land on the banks and delta of the Lower Nile, and the 390,000 square miles of surrounding desert, which together constitute Egypt, were not enough for Great Britain. South of Egypt lay even vaster stretches of desert, traversed by the thin ribbon of rich Nile-land; still farther south where the mighty river branched out east and west, comparatively productive regions were still unconquered.

The Anglo-Egyptian Sudan   All this country from Egypt south to Uganda was conquered between 1882 and 1900 by combined British and Egyptian forces, brought under the joint rule or "condominium" of Great Britain and Egypt, and labeled "the Anglo-Egyptian Sudan," but only after much blood was spilled in subduing the fanatical Mohammedan Arabs (led by their monks or "Dervishes"), and after much diplomacy was expended in removing the rivalry of the French, who had also coveted the region of the Upper Nile.

The main source of the Nile is Lake Victoria, or Victoria Nyanza.   Just north of Victoria Nyanza, and south of the Anglo-Egyptian Sudan, lay the negro kingdom of Uganda, **Uganda** which was allotted to the British in 1890 and established as a British protectorate a few years later.   While the native king — "His Highness the Kabaka" — still retained his throne, justice and finance were controlled by the British governor.   Uganda was the connecting link between the Anglo-Egyptian Sudan on the north and British East Africa **British East Africa** on the southeast.   The British East Africa Protectorate, including an area larger than France, gave Great Britain a splendid front upon the Indian Ocean — a front which was still further strengthened by Great Britain's protectorate (1890) over the East African islands of Zanzibar and Pemba, and by British possession (1810) of the Seychelles Islands, Mauritius, and Rodriguez.   The corner of Africa which juts out east from the Nile-Uganda-East Africa line of British possessions was in the main occupied by the independent Christian kingdom of Abys-**British Somaliland** sinia and the Italian colonies of Eritrea and Somaliland; but a portion about as large as Missouri was held by Great Britain, including almost the whole southern shore of the gulf of Aden.

In western Africa the British possessions were detached and scattered.   Farthest north was British Gambia, a mere foothold where the Gambia river enters the Atlantic just **Gambia** south of Cape Verde.   Farther down the coast lay the small territory of Sierra Leone, governed partly as a crown colony and partly as a protectorate.   On the northern coast of the gulf of Guinea were two larger British colonies. The westernmost, Gold Coast, included 334 miles of the shore line. Sierra The easternmost, Nigeria, was a loosely organized Leone protectorate over some seventeen millions of negroes and over an area almost equal to the combined area of Gold Coast Washington, Oregon, and California. Along the whole stretch of coast from Nigeria south to British South Africa, there was no British colony, except a few hundred Nigeria square miles around Walfisch Bay, surrounded by German Southwest Africa.

One is tempted to say that Great Britain was the greatest gainer by the partition of Africa. But in sheer territorial expanse the French dominion [1] in the Dark Continent 2. French was even more imposing. For every square mile in the Possessions mother-country, France could point to twenty square in Africa miles in Africa. As we are aware, the French at the opening of the nineteenth century had to their credit a foothold at the mouth of the Senegal River, a shadowy claim to the immense island of Madagascar, the small island of Mauritius, and a disastrous expedition to Egypt. In 1810 Mauritius was surrendered to Great Britain. As the nineteenth century wore on, however, Frenchmen began to take a more active interest in African enterprises. During the reign of Louis Philippe (1830–1848) Algeria was painfully conquered for France. Algeria French explorers scoured western Africa, and French settlements were established along the Ivory and Guinea coasts (1843). The great development came after the Franco-Prussian war when conspicuous Republican politicians sought in Africa to retrieve the misfortunes of France in Europe. In 1881 Tunis Tunis,[2] just east of Algeria, was occupied by French troops. In the region of the Senegal, expeditions were sent inland as far as Timbuctu (1893), with the aim of claiming both the Senegal and the Niger valleys for France. From French the Ivory Coast the French dominion was pushed north- West Africa ward, across dense forests, to connect with the Niger valley, French Guinea, and Senegal. Dahomey, a narrow wedge between British Nigeria and German Togoland, conquered in 1892, gave

---

[1] For the French Empire in Africa, see also above, pp. 160, 347 f., 512 ff.
[2] See above, pp. 513 f.

yet another arm reaching from the Niger to the sea. Between
German Kamerun and the Congo River another French trading
colony, at first confined to the coast at Gabun, had expanded
towards the interior until in 1899 French Congo
**French
Congo** reached the Shari River and Lake Chad. French
Congo, Dahomey, Ivory Coast, French Guinea, Sene-
gal, Algeria, and Tunis, — all were the seaward-stretching arms of
the great French West African empire, with its heart in the burning sands of the Sahara. From Algiers one could travel southward over the Algerian hills, across the desert wastes of Sahara,
over the dreary plains and woodlands of Wadai in the central
Sudan, and into the tropical forests of French Congo,[1] — all was
Morocco French territory. Last of all, the independent Mohammedan state of Morocco was mostly swallowed up by
the mighty French empire; in 1912 the sultan of Morocco submitted to a French protectorate, *i.e.* allowing a French official, a
"resident-general," to rule his country.

French dominion in Congo and West Africa did not mean any
rapid spread of Christianity; for the French government, hostile
to the Church at home, hindered rather than helped
**Some
Character-
istics of
French
West Africa** the missionaries in the colonies. Nor did it mean
immediate "civilization"; for the savages of the Ivory
Coast still occasionally indulged their cannibalistic
tastes. Nor could the possessions be said to be
"colonies," when, for example, in French Guinea there were
hardly more than a thousand Europeans, and those mostly
officials and traders rather than colonists. Only in the three
northern territories was the climate attractive to French settlers.
Algeria, the best developed of French colonies, had almost 450,000
inhabitants of French descent, and 230,000 of Spanish, Italian,
Maltese, and Jewish descent; but even in Algeria the natives
(Berbers and Arabs) outnumbered the colonists almost six
to one. French rule did mean exploitation — industrial and
commercial. The external trade of French West Africa, including the colonies of (1) Senegal, (2) Upper Senegal and
Niger, (3) Guinea, (4) Ivory Coast, (5) Dahomey, and (6) Mauri-

---

[1] Before 1911. It is important to note that in 1911, however, by ceding a large
section of French Congo to Germany, the territorial connection between lower
French Congo and the interior was severed.

tania, doubled in the ten years 1895–1904. The trade of Tunis almost tripled in twenty years. To France — for most of the trade was with France — the colonies sent fruits, palm-oil, peanuts, rubber, mahogany; from French merchants they bought cotton clothing, spirits, and various manufactured articles. French capitalists established the Bank of West Africa with millions of capital to make loans for the construction of railways and development of industries. Thousands of miles of railway and telegraph were constructed by French financiers, with interest on their capital guaranteed by the government. In Algeria and Tunis, and to a lesser degree in Morocco, where climate and natural resources were inviting, a more advanced development was attained. The waving fields of grain, the hillside vineyards, the luxuriant olive-groves might remind the colonist of his former home in France. Oranges and pomegranates, dates and figs, were likewise Algerian products. Nor should we forget the ninety-odd mines of Algeria, which annually yielded to *concessionaire* companies ten million dollars' worth of iron, zinc, lead, and phosphates. All this meant profits for certain French speculators and business men; while the French people at large paid in taxes some four million dollars a year to maintain troops in West Africa, and an even larger amount to support troops in Algeria and to pay interest to stock-holders of the Algerian railways.

French occupation also meant strong undemocratic government. Tunis was autocratically ruled by a representative of the French foreign office. Senegal, Guinea, Ivory Coast, Dahomey, Upper-Senegal-and-Niger, were under non-elective French lieutenant-governors, subject to a governor-general. Even in Algeria, which regularly sent three senators and six deputies to the French National Assembly, only a small minority of the population had a voice in choosing its "representatives"; and, although "Delegations" or chambers representing natives as well as colonists regularly met at Algiers to discuss local affairs, they had little control over the powerful governor-general. The natives of Africa, it seemed, were unfit to enjoy democracy. If the French rule was despotic, it at least had the merit of being fairly firm. It took almost half a century (1830–1871) thoroughly to subjugate Algeria; much blood was shed in Wadai; constant warfare was being waged in 1914 against the rebellious natives of Morocco;

but wherever the French established their power, they endeavored with success to prevent tribal wars, to maintain order, and to encourage the arts of peace.

Besides her vast territories in northwestern Africa, with which we have just now been concerned, France had also impor-
French   tant possessions on the eastern side of Africa.   French
Somaliland   Somaliland (acquired 1864–1884) at the head of the gulf of Aden, and commanding the entrance to the Red Sea, was very small in area, but great in strategic value.   The island of Madagascar, on the other hand, lying 260 miles off the East
Mada-   African coast, was greater in size than in value.
gascar   Although the island is almost a thousand miles in length, its population amounted (1913) to only 3,250,000 and its commerce to $20,000,000.   Madagascar, we may observe, was never officially occupied by the French until 1894–1895, when victorious French arms enforced a French protectorate, which was subsequently (1896) converted into a formal colony.

Italian imperialism began in a very modest way in 1870 when an Italian steamship company purchased the port of Assab, on
3. Italian   the southwestern shore of the Red Sea, just north of
Possessions   what is now French Somaliland.   Twelve years later
in Africa   the Italian government took Assab over as a colony ; and with Assab as a nucleus, Italy built up the colony which is now called Eritrea.   The lowlands of Eritrea made good pas-
Eritrea   ture, the plateau in the northern part was fertile, and pearl fisheries were profitable ; nevertheless, instead of bringing in revenue, Eritrea cost the Italian taxpayers each year more than a million dollars.   A second Italian colony was estab-lished in 1889 further south on the coast, east and southeast of
Italian   Abyssinia.   This was Italian Somaliland, larger than
Somaliland   Italy.   Pushing inland, both Eritrea and Italian Somaliland encroached upon the Christian but primitive kingdom of Abyssinia (Ethiopia).   The Italians made no secret of their eagerness to gain control of the attractive Abyssinian highlands, the altitude of which rendered the climate almost temperate, although the country lay wholly within the torrid zone.   Between 1889 and 1896 Italy even claimed that Abyssinia was an Italian protectorate.   To such a pretension, however, the Abyssinians would not submit, and under the leadership of their emperor

(or *negus*) Menelek, they made war against Italy. At Adowa (1896) Menelek inflicted such a crushing defeat on the Italian forces that in the same year Italy gave up her attacks on the independence of Abyssinia. In 1906, we should observe, Italy, France, and Great Britain agreed to respect Abyssinia's freedom.

Defeated in her designs on Abyssinia, Italy next turned to Tripoli, a Turkish province, on the northern coast of Africa. In 1901 the French government agreed not to oppose this new ambition. Consequently, in 1911 an Italian army invaded Tripoli, and, after a year of fighting, Turkey was forced to surrender both Tripoli and Cyrenaica, which two pro- Libya vinces became the Italian colony of Libya.[1] But even after the war between Turkey and Italy was ended, Italy still had to maintain armies in Libya; for the Arab tribesmen of the interior — superb horsemen, daring warriors, and zealous Mohammedans — continued a kind of irregular warfare against the Italians. Supporting troops in Libya was tremendously expensive; it was said to cost something like $200,000 a day. The total expense of acquiring the new colony soon surpassed the $200,000,000 mark; and, in addition, new millions had to be spent on harbor improvements, docks, and railways, before Libya could become a valuable possession. Some parts of Libya were indeed fertile and fruitful; but most of the interior was little more than an expanse of desert, dotted here and there with palm-trees and oases, and traversed by merchant caravans, but not at all adapted to colonization.

Although Great Britain, France, and Italy, — not to speak of Holland, Spain, and Portugal, — had all entered the field before Germany, so energetically did Germany push her 4. German claims that within six years (1884-1890) four impor- Possessions tant sections of Africa were won for the German in Africa Empire. Even the smallest of the German colonies in Africa — Togo — was larger than the American state of Togo Maine. Togo was too near the equator to attract German colonists, but it gave German commerce a convenient post on the northern bank of the gulf of Guinea, and annually exported more than $900,000 worth of palm-products and cotton. Kamerun, just at the bend of the gulf of Guinea, was a more im-

[1] See above, pp. 514, 528.

portant colony.   Gradually its boundaries were extended back
into the richly forested mountain-country until Lake Chad and
Kamerun   the Shari River were reached ; and a hundred thousand
               square miles of French Congo were added to Kamerun
in 1911, giving Germany a foothold on the Ubangi and Congo
rivers.   The most important product of Kamerun, as of Togo,
was palm-oil; but rubber was also obtained from its tropical
forests, and a considerable amount of ivory; moreover the
Germans were beginning to establish plantations for the cultivation of cocoa, coffee, rubber, and spices, by negro-labor.

Further down along the western coast was German Southwest
Africa, acquired in 1884.   In 1890 Germany gained an additional
German   strip of territory which connected German Southwest
Southwest   Africa with the Zambesi River, thus enabling German
Africa   merchants to tap the trade of the Zambesi valley.
German Southwest Africa was from the first an expensive colony,
requiring an expenditure by Germany of more than a million dollars every year.   It is estimated that Germany spent $75,000,000
and sacrificed the lives of 5000 German soldiers and settlers
in order to crush a native rebellion in 1903–1907.   This was all
the more discouraging because the lack of rain made the whole
southern part of the colony a desert land, and this was the only
part of German Africa outside the tropics.   But German Southwest Africa suddenly rose in value when diamonds were discovered
near Lüderitz Bay in 1908 in sufficient quantities to yield about
$5,000,000 a year.

The largest and most populous of the four German colonies
was German East Africa, with a population fifty per cent larger
German   than that of New England, and an area eight times
East Africa   that of New York State.   Wedged in between British
East Africa and Portuguese East Africa, the Germany colony was
naturally bounded on the east by the Indian Ocean and on the
west by the three great lakes of Victoria, Tanganyika, and Nyasa.
German East Africa was acquired through the enterprise of three
young Germans who made treaties in 1884 with the native
chieftains, and was taken under protection of the German government in 1885 ; a strip along the coast had to be purchased from
the sultan of Zanzibar at the price of $1,000,000 ; and the bound-
aries were fixed by agreement with Great Britain, Portugal,

and the Congo Free State. In East Africa, as in Southwest Africa, the Germans encountered fierce resistance and frequently resorted to cruel measures. One governor did not hesitate to put women to death, but he was later condemned for misusing his authority. Matters reached a crisis in 1905, when the natives, who resented being forced to labor on German plantations, rose in a general rebellion. More than 100,000 perished before the rebellion was crushed. This attitude of the negroes and Arabs in German East Africa is worth noticing because this was a typical tropical colony, largely unfit for colonization, and could be developed only by hiring or forcing the natives to work at the rubber-trees, coffee-plantations, and banana-groves.

In general, four aspects of the German rule in Africa may well be noticed. (1) First of all, the German territories were not suitable for colonization, because they were either too hot, as Kamerun, or too dry, as German Southwest Africa. (2) Secondly, the value of these possessions lay chiefly in their mines, their rubber, their rare timber, their ivory, their palm-oil; and also in the possibility that in the future they might produce great quantities of cotton, coffee, cocoa, tobacco, and other tropical products which had become veritable necessities in Europe. In this hope the German government established experimental stations to promote the cultivation of such products; and many private individuals established large plantations with negroes to do the work. It thus became clear above all that the Germans must transform the negroes from lazy savages into industrious and obedient toilers. (3) Thirdly, as might be expected in territories where a handful of white men had to rule millions of discontented negroes, the government was absolutely undemocratic. In each colony the supreme authority was vested in an imperial governor, responsible not to the people but to the colonial office at Berlin. It was government primarily in the interest of German imperialism, and secondarily for the protection of German merchants and investors; the interests of the natives were least considered. (4) Fourthly, as for "civilizing" the natives, the government established a few schools in each colony; in Togo, for example, there were two government schools with 312 pupils. At that rate, it would be slow work civilizing a million natives. The

Some Aspects of German Imperialism in Africa

missionaries, however, were doing somewhat better; in Togo they had 368 schools with 14,600 pupils. And in all German Africa there were in 1913 about 160,000 negro children receiving some kind of an education.

Portugal, Belgium, and Spain also possessed territories in Africa. We have already treated the Belgian Congo, as well as the Portuguese colonies of Guinea, Portuguese West African Africa, and Portuguese East Africa. Only Spain Possessions of Portugal, remains. Spain in 1885, at the time of the Berlin conBelgium, and Spain ference, declared a Spanish protectorate over a portion of the coast between Cape Bojador and Cape Blanco; later the coast between Bojador and Morocco was included; this territory now constitutes the Rio de Oro and Adrar colonies, and is administered by the Spanish governor of the Canary Islands. Spain also claimed part of the Guinea coast, and after long disputes secured a small strip of territory (Rio Muni), which since 1911 has been surrounded on the land side by German Kamerun. In Morocco, also, Spain obtained the northern coast and a small district on the western coast at Ifni.

There yet remained two independent states in Africa, unappropriated by Europeans. One was the ancient empire of Remaining Abyssinia or Ethiopia, Christian since the fourth cenIndependent tury, and now hemmed in on every side by British, States in French, and Italian possessions. By an agreement beAfrica tween France, Great Britain, and Italy, the independ1. Abyssinia ence of Abyssinia was assured, although in the spheres of industry and finance the Abyssinians became more or less dependent upon British and French capitalists. The other 2. Liberia independent state, Liberia, was established in the nineteenth century by the settlement of former negro slaves, mostly from the United States, and was organized in 1847 as a free republic like the United States. In this remarkable negro republic — approximately the size of Virginia — were included about 50,000 civilized, Christian, English-speaking negroes, together with about two millions of uncivilized negroes, some of whom still roamed as naked cannibals through the tropical forests in the heart of Liberia. The Liberians had such vexatious boundary disputes with the neighboring French and British colonies that in 1910 President Taft offered to send American officials to take charge of the Liberian army, to collect the customs, to settle boundary disputes, and to supervise finance, with the coöperation of British, French, and German officials, so that Liberia was placed partially under foreign tutelage without becoming a mere dependency of any single empire.

ADDITIONAL READING

Latin America. General works of history and description: W. R. Shepherd, *Latin America* (1914), in the " Home University Library," the best survey, clear and accurate; *Cambridge Modern History*, Vol. XII (1910), ch. xxi; F. García Calderón, *Latin America : its Rise and Progress,* Eng. trans. by Bernard Miall (1913), a valuable work, written from the standpoint of a scholarly Peruvian diplomatist; R. P. Porter, *The Ten Republics* (1911); W. H. Koebel, *The South Americans* (1915); Arthur Ruhl, *The Other Americans : the Cities, the Countries, and especially the People of South America* (1908), impressions of an alert traveler; C. R. Enock, *The Republics of Central and South America, their Resources, Industries, Sociology and Future* (1913); T. C. Dawson, *The South American Republics,* 2 vols. (1903-1904), a popular historical and geographical study of each of the South American countries in turn, published in the " Story of the Nations " Series; C. E. Akers, *A History of South America, 1854-1912,* 2d ed. (1912), sincere but ill-balanced and poorly written; James (Viscount) Bryce, *South America: Observations and Impressions* (1912), a readable account of the impressions produced by a brief visit. An indispensable book of reference for the student of political institutions is J. I. Rodriguez, *American Constitutions : a Compilation of the Political Constitutions of the Independent Nations of the New World, with short historical notes and various appendixes,* 2 vols. (1906-1907), in the language of the originals with Spanish or English translation in parallel columns. Trenchant criticism of the policy of the United States toward the Latin-American republics is supplied by Hiram Bingham, *The Monroe Doctrine: an Obsolete Shibboleth* (1913).

For more detailed information concerning the history and the political, social, and economic conditions of the several Latin-American countries, the volumes in the " South American Series," edited by Martin Hume, will be found generally reliable: W. A. Hirst, *Argentina* (1910); Paul Walle, *Bolivia,* Eng. trans. by Bernard Miall (1914); Pierre Denis, *Brazil,* Eng. trans. by Bernard Miall (1911); G. F. S. Elliot, *Chile* (1909); P. J. Eder, *Colombia* (1913); C. R. Enock, *Ecuador* (1914); James Rodway, *Guiana, British, Dutch, and French* (1912); C. R. Enock, *Mexico* (1909); C. R. Enock, *Peru,* 2d ed. (1910); W. H. Koebel, *Uruguay* (1911); and L. V. Dalton, *Venezuela* (1912). Other volumes of some special significance: Forbes Lindsay, *Cuba and her People of To-Day* (1911), interesting description with an historical introduction and with appendices of important documents; A. G. Robinson, *Cuba, Old and New* (1915); Stephen Bonsal, *The American Mediterranean* (1912), a breezy account of the republics in and around the Caribbean Sea; Alcée Fortier and J. R. Ficklen, *Central America and Mexico* (1907), being Vol. IX of *The History of North America*, ed. by G. C. Lee and F. N. Thorpe; P. F. Martin, *Mexico of the Twentieth Century*, 2 vols. (1907), superficial though not without interest; Arthur Bullard, *Panama, the Canal, the Country, and the People*, new ed. (1914), popular and journalistic; Richard Villafranca, *Costa Rica* (1895); W. H. Koebel, *Argentina, Past and Present* (1910). For the earlier history of Latin America see Chapters II and XVII, above, and the accompanying bibliographies. For additional titles consult the helpful pamphlet of P. H. Goldsmith, *A Brief Bibliography of Books in English, Spanish, and Portuguese relating to the Republics commonly called Latin American, with comments* (1915).

The Partition of Africa. Brief general narratives: C. D. Hazen, *Europe since 1815* (1910), ch. xxiii; J. H. Rose, *The Development of the European Nations, 1870–1900*, Vol. II (1905), ch. iv–viii, especially good on Egypt, the Sudan, and the Congo Free State; *Histoire générale*, Vol. XII, ch. xxvi, *Le partage de l'Afrique, 1870–1900*, by R. de Caix de St. Aymour; Sir H. H. Johnston, *The Opening Up of Africa* (1911), an excellent summary in the " Home University Library." Standard treatises: Sir Edward Hertslet, *The Map of Africa by Treaty*, 3d edition, completed to 1908, 3 vols. (1909), a collection of treaties in English, showing how the " Map of Africa " has been changed by treaties or by other international arrangements; Sir H. H. Johnston, *A History of the Colonization of Africa by Alien Races*, new rev. ed. (1913); J. S. Keltie, *The Partition of Africa* (1895); N. D. Harris, *Intervention and Colonization in Africa* (1914), not so authoritative as Johnston or Keltie but more detailed on the period since 1870. On the explorations: *Great Explorers of Africa*, 2 vols. (1894), an interesting compilation; Thomas Hughes, *David Livingstone* (1889), a brief biography in the " English Men of Action " Series; W. G. Blaikie, *Personal Life of David Livingstone* (1881); David Livingstone, *Missionary Travels and Researches in South Africa*, 25th ed. (1860), and *Last Journals in Central Africa from 1865 to his death*, ed. by Horace Waller (1875); and the writings of Sir H. M. Stanley, *How I found Livingstone: Travels and Adventures in Central Africa* (1872), *Through the Dark Continent, or the Sources of the Nile*, 2 vols. (1878), *In Darkest Africa*, new ed. (1897), *Congo and the Founding of its Free State*, 2 vols. (1885), and *The Autobiography of Henry M. Stanley*, ed. by Dorothy Stanley (1909). On the African Empire of the French: Roy Devereux, *Aspects of Algeria: Historical, Political, Colonial* (1912); Victor Piquet, *La colonisation française dans l'Afrique du nord: Algérie — Tunisie — Maroc* (1912); Maurice Wahl, *L'Algérie*, 4th ed. (1903); Ellis Ashmead-Bartlett, *The Passing of the Shereefian Empire* (1910), a popular account of Morocco; André Tardieu, *Le mystère d'Agadir* (1912), a French view of Franco-German rivalry in Morocco and

Congo; *Annuaire colonial*, an official French publication, annual since 1888, gives valuable information concerning the French colonies. For other works on French imperialism see the bibliography appended to Chapter XXIII, above. In addition to works on German imperialism cited in the bibliography of Chapter XXIV, above, consult P. E. Lewin, *The Germans and Africa, their Aims on the Dark Continent and How they Acquired their African Colonies* (1915). For the British colonies in Africa, refer to the next chapter and its bibliography.

CHAPTER XXIX

THE BRITISH EMPIRE

In 1914 approximately one-fourth of the earth's habitable area and a fourth of the world's population were embraced by the British Empire. No better sequel could be found to the foregoing chapters on modern imperialism than a study of this most gigantic product of colonialism with its perplexing political and economic problems. Larger than any other state in the world, nine times the size of the German Empire (including colonies), and considerably more than three times the size of the United States, by its very vastness the British Empire merits attention. Its closest rival, the Russian Empire, boasted in 1914 only three-quarters the area and three-tenths the population.

The Greatest World Empire

The size of the British Empire becomes even more impressive when compared with the smallness of the mother-country. In area, the United Kingdom constituted less than a hundredth part of the empire; in population, about one-tenth. Shorn of its colonies, Great Britain would have been a comparatively small state, less than half the size of Texas, with less than three-quarters the population of Germany, or about one-half that of the United States. Indeed, the entire English-speaking people, if we exclude the United States, numbered no more than sixty millions, whereas there were sixty millions speaking French, eighty millions speaking German, and ninety millions speaking Russian. The comparatively small size of the British nation proves that the colossal empire was not produced by the normal increase of the English-speaking people. In the entire empire, there were only sixty million white inhabitants, three-fourths of whom lived in the British Isles. From the remaining fifteen million white inhabitants there must be deducted 1,800,000 Canadians of French origin, 500,000 Cana-

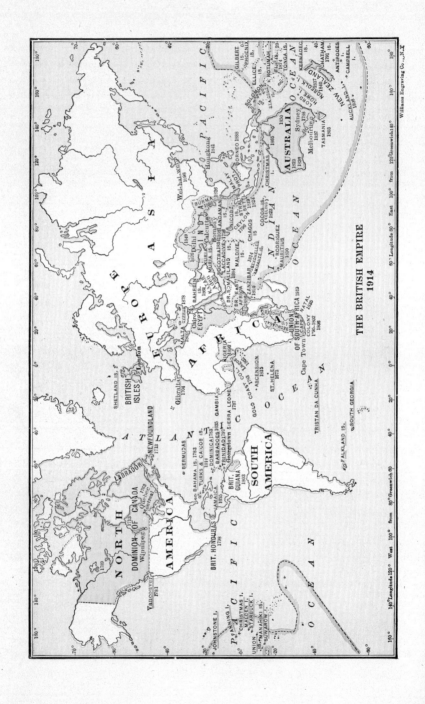

THE BRITISH EMPIRE
1914

dians of other nationalities, 700,000 South Africans of Dutch and German extraction. It appears, then, that there were hardly more than twelve millions of really British settlers in all the British "colonies." For every one of the British colonists there were more than thirty dusky-skinned "natives" subject to British rule. Three hundred and fifteen million Asiatic "Indians," forty million blacks, six million Arabs, six million Malays, a million Chinese, a million Polynesians, and a hundred thousand red (Canadian) Indians, overwhelmingly outnumbered the British in the empire.

The British Empire was a heterogeneous collection of people of every race, representing every phase of culture from cannibalism to Cambridge, inhabiting lands of the most diverse climates, professing five great and innumerable lesser religions, and inhabiting important territories in five of the world's six continents.[1] By its very nature such an empire must be a highly complex and inharmonious organization, the more so, since its constituent parts were added one by one, some by conquest, some by mere occupation, some by settlement. The expansion of "Greater Britain" was guided by no consistent policy, unless the constant shifting of policies be itself a policy. It has indeed been well said that the British Empire was built up in a fit of absence of mind. So it is hardly surprising that instead of conforming to a single standard type, the British possessions were of many varieties, and could be classified only with considerable difficulty in three major groups — (1) the self-governing colonies; (2) the crown colonies, possessing few or no rights of self-government, the chartered companies, and the protectorates; (3) India. We shall treat each of the three classes in turn.

SELF-GOVERNING COLONIES

The self-governing colonies included a trifle more than half of the territory possessed by Great Britain. It would be most misleading, however, to say that half of the British colonies enjoyed the proud privilege of governing themselves; for in respect of population the self-governing colonies constituted only

[1] Asia, Africa, Australasia, North America, and Europe. Even in South America there was the small colony of Guiana.

a twentieth part of the British colonial empire.   Self-government
was a special privilege conferred by Great Britain upon a very
small minority of her colonial subjects, not a natural
right granted freely to all.   Moreover, one cannot
fail to be impressed by the fact that this privileged
minority was exclusively of European stock : that
the colonies enjoying home rule were precisely the
colonies in which large numbers of Europeans had settled —
Canada, Newfoundland, Australia, New Zealand, and the Union
of South Africa.   In none of these colonies did the native population amount to more than five per cent of the whole, except
in South Africa ; and even South Africa had over a million white
inhabitants.[1]   Outside of the self-governing colonies, there were
but a few thousand white men in all the British dominions.[2]
Self-government, in short, was enjoyed by almost all the
"white" colonies, and by none other.   And since Great Britain
alone of all the European Powers possessed "white" colonies,
colonial self-government existed only within the British Empire.[3]

*Self-Gov-
ernment the
Exclusive
Privilege of
"White"
Colonies*

In order to understand how the white colonies of Great Britain
obtained the right of ruling themselves, it is necessary to refer
once more, let us hope for the last time, to the old
colonial system.   Before the American Revolution,
the British colonies had developed a mixed form of
colonial government, in which the royal governor of
each province or colony was the appointee and official
representative of the British Crown, and the elective
assembly was the champion of local, colonial interests.   There
was usually also a legislative council, which constituted the
upper house of each colonial legislature, and was as a rule both
appointed and controlled by the royal governor.   The colonial
assembly, like the English House of Commons, had originally
held the purse-strings of the government and had attempted to
use its financial powers for the purpose of asserting the right to
frame the laws and to control the administration.   As a result,

*The Royal
Governor
and the
Colonial
Assembly
under the
Old System*

[1] They formed more than 20 per cent of the population.
[2] The Falkland Islands and the Mediterranean colonies were "white" but not
self-governing; in the West Indies also there were a fairly large number of white
settlers.
[3] Except in the Danish colony of Iceland.

there had been constant quarrels between governor and assembly. The struggle had ended in the complete triumph of the colonial legislatures in the thirteen American colonies which revolted from the mother-country. But in the other colonies, in Canada for example, the contest continued until the middle of the nineteenth century.

Canada had not been given an elective assembly by the Quebec Act of 1774, but only a council appointed by the crown, for the reason that the people of Canada were then mostly French and were presumably neither accustomed to representative government nor loyal to Great Britain. After the American Revolution, however, Ontario received such large numbers of Scotch and Scotch-Irish immigrants in addition to Loyalist refugees from the United States, that William Pitt thought it necessary to pass a Constitutional Act in 1791, separating Upper Canada (or Ontario), which was entirely British, from Lower Canada (or Quebec), which was overwhelmingly French, and establishing an elective assembly in each of the two provinces. Pitt's scheme failed. Not only were the French and British elements in Canada inflamed against each other, but also in each of the provinces the old quarrel arose, whether the royal governor or the colonial assembly was to control the ministers who conducted the government.[1] In Lower Canada, where the antagonism was intensified by the fact that the Assembly was mainly French and the governor English, the arbitrary acts of the governor infuriated the French or popular party and brought about the Rebellion of 1837. Almost simultaneously the reform party in Upper Canada resorted to arms. The rebellion was easily crushed, but it succeeded in calling attention to Canada's grievances and aroused the British government to send a High Commissioner to redress them. Lord Durham, who was selected for this difficult mission, perceived at once that radical reforms were needed, and with characteristic impetuosity he started out to exercise all the arbitrary powers of a dictator in pacifying Canada. When the British government

Canadian Government, 1774–1837

The Canadian Rebellion of 1837

[1] In Lower Canada the upper chamber of the legislature was appointed by the governor and joined with him in opposing the lower, elective chamber. In Upper Canada the upper chamber sympathized with the lower.

refused to uphold him in this course and revoked his ordinance banishing certain rebel leaders, Lord Durham angrily resigned, Lord Durham's Report, 1839 returned home in a huff, and published a lengthy report. The report is famous in British colonial history, because in it two fundamental principles of Great Britain's later policy were clearly enunciated. In the first place Lord Durham contended that the colonies already possessing representative institutions should be granted responsible governments, *i.e.* should be permitted to manage their own affairs through ministries responsible to the several colonial assemblies. Lord Durham realized that his plan for conferring responsible government on the colonies would emancipate them from the control of the royal governor and of the mother-country, except in a few matters like foreign policy, over which the colonial government would have no power. But he maintained that with self-government the colonies would be more loyal, having fewer causes of complaint against the mother-country. In the second place, Lord Durham pleaded for the unification of Upper and Lower Canada, so that French Lower Canada would be dominated by British Upper Canada. Ultimately, he hoped, all of British North America might be confederated into one united colony. These two principles — responsible self-government and colonial confederation — were destined to triumph not only in Canada, but in far-off Australia and South Africa as well.

In accordance with Lord Durham's recommendation, Upper and Lower Canada were at once united (1840). Seven years Responsible Government granted to Canada and Other Colonies later his son-in-law, Lord Elgin, became governor of Canada and put into practice the other recommendation, that the royal governor should choose his cabinet from the majority party in the assembly, thus recognizing the principle of responsible government. It is significant that Lord Elgin gave Canada responsible government (which amounted to self-government) just a year or so after the Free Traders in England had repealed the Corn Laws (1846) and dealt a staggering blow to the old mercantilist theory of trade and colonies. Almost immediately the same freedom to control their own government was granted to the other North American colonies of New Brunswick, Nova Scotia, and Prince

Edward Island. Before 1860, Newfoundland, and the Australasian colonies of New South Wales, Victoria, Tasmania, South Australia, and Queensland had likewise been accorded responsible governments. Subsequently Cape Colony (1872), Western Australia (1890), Natal (1893), Transvaal (1906), and the Orange River Colony (1907) were added to the list of self-governing colonies, the two last-mentioned provinces having been promised self-government by the terms of the Boer capitulation at the close of the Boer War (1899–1902).

Pessimistic patriots saw only a foolhardy altruism in this extension of responsible self-government to all of Great Britain's important white colonies in the years from 1847 to 1907, especially when the colonies used their freedom, as did Canada in 1859, to lay taxes on imports from the mother-country. But the Liberal statesmen who had definitely committed Great Britain to Free Trade in the momentous years 1846–1849, looked upon colonial autonomy as no more than the logical consequence of Liberal, *laisser-faire* principles, and prophesied that the extension of freedom would only magnify the greatness and promote the prosperity of the Empire. Self-government, as a matter of fact, did have just this effect in stimulating the patriotism of the white colonies. Now that the mother-country no longer irritated them by interfering in their local affairs, Canada and Australasia became enthusiastically loyal to the British crown, and realized as never before that they were indeed fortunate at so little cost to themselves to enjoy the protection of the world's mightiest Empire and to share in its prestige.

As Canada had been the first colony to obtain a responsible government, so also Canada was the pioneer in another important movement, the formation of confederations among the self-governing colonies. In 1867 the hitherto separate colonies of New Brunswick and Nova Scotia joined with Quebec and Ontario to form a confederation with the style of the " Dominion of Canada." The Dominion was formally organized under the British North America Act of 1867, passed by the British Parliament at Westminster; but the plan had originated in Canada and had been fully formulated by a convention at Quebec in 1864. The government of

Establishment of the Dominion of Canada, 1867

the Dominion was a rough copy of the British government, with the governor-general instead of the king, a senate (appointed by the governor-general for life) in place of the House of Lords, and an elective House of Commons, to which the cabinet of ministers was responsible. Although each of the four provinces preserved its separate legislature, there was little question of "states' rights" in Canada. With the terrible example of the United States in civil war close at hand, the framers of the Canadian constitution carefully limited the powers of the provinces, in order that the supremacy of the federal government might never be challenged. Nova Scotia, to be sure, desired to withdraw from the Dominion, but the British government firmly refused to countenance any such secession, and the unity of the Dominion was maintained.

Under the auspices of the Conservative Party, whose leader, Sir John Macdonald, was premier from 1867 to 1891 (excepting the five years 1873–1878), the militia, postal system, civil service, banking, and currency of the Dominion were placed upon a sound basis; a protective tariff was established for the benefit of Canadian industries; and the westward expansion of Canada to the Pacific was accomplished. The growth of the Dominion was amazingly swift. First from the Hudson's Bay Company extensive territories west of Ontario were purchased (1869), out of which the new province of Manitoba was carved; then British Columbia (1871) and Prince Edward Island (1873) were brought into the Dominion; finally a decree of 1878 proclaimed that all British North America — with the sole exception of stubborn Newfoundland, which remains to this day a separate colony, — belonged to the Dominion. The rich mines and fertile prairies of western Canada attracted a steady stream of settlers, particularly after the construction of the Canadian Pacific Railway (1886), and the resulting marvelous economic development of the west received political recognition by the creation of two new prairie provinces, Alberta and Saskatchewan, in 1905.

Notwithstanding the evident success of the confederating movement in Canada, the Australian colonies hesitated a long time before they finally decided to form a similar federal union. During the course of the nineteenth century, six self-governing colonies had appeared in Australasia besides the original colony of New South Wales, which had been established as a penal station[1] in 1788, and had since developed into a free, prosperous community of sheep-farmers, mechanics, and miners, endowed with self-government (1855). *The Australasian Colonies* Two daughter-colonies had been separated from New South Wales, — on the north, Queensland (1859), and, on the south, Victoria (1851). Two other colonies, South Australia (1836) and Western Australia (1829), had been founded independently, thus making five colonies on the island continent. A sixth colony was the neighboring island of Tasmania or Van Diemen's Land (separated from New South Wales in 1824). And the more distant islands of New Zealand, colonized in the nineteenth century, might count as a seventh. At the opening of the nineteenth century the introduction of sheep-raising, and in the middle of the century the discovery of gold, had enabled these island-colonies of the South Pacific to spring almost instantaneously into maturity.

The Australian colonies would no doubt have been consolidated as early as 1885, had they not been divided on the tariff question. Victoria and the other colonies had adopted a protective tariff, while New South Wales clung stubbornly to free trade. The younger colonies, moreover, were reluctant to surrender the revenues *The Australian Commonwealth Act, 1900* they obtained from their separate customs duties. But the advantages to be gained by confederation — especially the advantage of concerted action in excluding Chinese immigrants and in maintaining British supremacy in the South Pacific .against French and German intruders [2] — finally outweighed the disadvantages. After long discussion, the colonists agreed upon a plan of confederation which was enacted by the British Parliament as the Commonwealth of Australia Act, 1900. New Zealand, being separated from Australia by 1200 miles of water, refused to join the Commonwealth, just as the island of Newfoundland had held aloof from the Dominion of Canada. The

---

[1] No more convicts were shipped to New South Wales after 1840.

[2] Germany, it will be recalled, was pursuing an ambitious policy in Oceanica, having acquired Kaiser Wilhelms Land, the Bismarck Archipelago, and the Marshall Islands (1884–1885).

other six colonies became States in the Commonwealth,[1] under
a constitution strongly resembling that of the United States of
America.   The federal or Commonwealth legislature, like the
United States Congress, was composed of a Senate, in which
each state had the same number (six) of seats, and a House of
Representatives, in which the seats were distributed according
to population.   The High Court of the Commonwealth, like
the American Supreme Court, was the guardian of the Constitution.   In delegating only limited powers to their federal government, moreover, the Australians imitated the federal structure
of the United States rather than the unitary policy of Canada.
In two important respects, however, the Australian Commonwealth was essentially British.   Its highest magistrate was a
governor-general, appointed theoretically by the British crown,
really by the ministry of the United Kingdom.   And its cabinet of
ministers was responsible to parliament rather than to a president.   It is also worth observing that Australia was more democratic than the United States, in allowing women to vote and
in providing for constitutional amendment by referendum.

The history of the Commonwealth may be summed up as
the search for solutions to five problems.   (1) The problem of
Australian   defense, which will be considered later.   (2) The ques-
Problems   tion of states' rights has proved troublesome, especially
in respect of the financial relations between the Commonwealth
and the States, in the matter of industrial legislation, and in
regard to the State railways, which were built on a different
gauge in the different States.   (3) Difficulty has been encountered with the bicameral form of legislature, both in the federal
and in the State governments, when the upper chamber has
happened to oppose the lower.   (4) Rural development has been
a primary concern of the Government.   Irrigation works have
been constructed, railways built into the interior, and all manner
of inducements offered to farmers, in the hope not only of bringing undeveloped land under cultivation, but also of creating
a rural population commensurate with the overgrown and
trouble-giving towns.   (5) Most interesting of all has been the
effort of Australia to cope with the problem of poverty.   After

[1] Subsequently the Commonwealth took over the government of the Northern
Territory of Australia (1911) and Papua or British New Guinea (1905).

a furious but futile fight for the principle of the "closed shop" (in the Great Strike of 1890), the workingmen had become convinced that they must use the ballot-box as well as the trade union to achieve their economic demands. Labor parties in the several States demanded socialistic legislation. Between 1890 and 1910 Victoria passed a series of laws providing, amongst other things, for the creation of trades boards to regulate the wages and hours of industrial labor; Queensland and South Australia followed suit, while New South Wales borrowed a somewhat different scheme [1] from New Zealand. The federal government followed the lead of the States, establishing a Federal Arbitration Court in 1904 for the peaceful settlement of interstate industrial disputes, and in 1908 providing old age pensions (ten shillings a week) for poor people over sixty-five years of age or invalids over sixty. Possibly one reason for the willingness of the Australians to experiment with social legislation was the fact that the Australian railways had been constructed and operated from the first as socialistic enterprises. Other branches of industry would doubtless have been taken over by the government and a much more effective regulation of business would have been introduced by Andrew Fisher, a former Scotch coal-miner, who became Commonwealth prime minister in 1910 [2] with a Labor cabinet and a large Labor majority behind him; but he could not induce the people to pass the constitutional amendments which would give the Commonwealth government power to enact the Labor party's socialistic program.

Social and Labor Legislation in Australia

The other Australasian colony, New Zealand, which remained apart from the Commonwealth, might be regarded as a confederation in itself; geographically New Zealand is a group of islands (two large and numerous small islands); while politically, New Zealand was divided until 1876 into six provinces, each having a legislature. In 1907, at any rate, New Zealand was styled a "Dominion" and classed with the confederations of Canada and Australia. During the last quarter-century New Zealand has attracted world-wide atten-

The Dominion of New Zealand

[1] An arbitration court to prevent strikes, to fix minimum wage rates, and to determine the number of working hours.

[2] He had held the office six months in 1908.

tion by its radical experiments in political and economic democracy. New Zealand's radicalism dates from the year 1890,

Political and Social Democracy in New Zealand

when the trade unions, excited by the Great Strike of that year, entered politics with the purpose of using their powerful organization as a political machine in the interests of labor and democracy. The trade unions elected few "Labor" representatives to parliament, but they wielded a most potent influence over the "Liberal" Party, which, thanks to workingmen's votes, held office from 1891 to 1912. Under the impulse of this radical movement, New Zealand extended the franchise to adult women and thus stood forth as one of the pioneers of universal suffrage. Another constitutional reform was the democratization of the Upper House of the legislature, whose members had originally been appointed for life; first the term was reduced to seven years (1891), and finally the Upper House was made elective on the broad basis of popular suffrage and proportional representation. More remarkable than these democratic reforms, however, were the socialistic enterprises of the government. Government-owned railways, government life-insurance, accident-insurance, and fire-insurance offices, and government coal-mines were some of New Zealand's experiments in state-socialism. Notable also was the land-tax, which was graduated so as to fall chiefly on great landlords, and the Advance to Settlers Act (1894), which provided government loans to farmers. An Industrial Conciliation and Arbitration Act (1895) created a court to settle disputes between trade unions and capitalists. Pensions were given to aged working-people (1898), and compensation to workingmen injured by accident (1900).

The confederation of four British colonies in South Africa followed nine years after the creation of the Australian Common

South Africa

wealth. The previous chapter has already told the story how Cape Colony, the oldest of the South African settlements, was wrested by Great Britain from the Dutch (1806), and how the unsubmissive Dutch farmers or Boers, feeling that the British government was more kindly disposed toward the negroes than toward themselves, "trekked" to Natal, to Orange Free State, and to the Transvaal. Cape Colony had been given responsible government in 1872, a year after the discovery of fabulous wealth in diamond mines. Natal had been annexed by Great Britain in 1843, separated from Cape Colony ten years later, and granted self-government in 1893; by the close of the century the British settlers in Natal outnumbered the Boers. Meanwhile the Boer republic of Orange Free State,[1] since the recognition of its independence in 1854, prospered under the rule of its president, John Brand, although the valuable Kimberley diamond fields, discovered in Free State territory, were annexed by Great Britain (1871) and Orange Free State received therefor only £90,000 indemnity. The other Boer republic, the "South African Republic," was organized in the Transvaal country as a result of a further "trek" on the part of the Boers (1848–1852), and its independence was recognized by Great Britain in a treaty known as the "Sand River Convention" (1852); in 1877 it was annexed by a British commissioner; but four years later, after the Transvaal Boers had revolted and defeated a small British force at Majuba Hill (1881), Gladstone virtually restored their independence.[2] Unfortunately the Transvaal Boers interpreted Gladstone's benevolent concession as a cowardly confession of Great Britain's weakness, and henceforth they regarded the British with more of scornful hatred than of respectful fear. The Boers even dreamed of regaining Cape Colony and establishing Boer supremacy in all South Africa. The *Afrikander Bond* was formed to promote Boer interests. The relations of the Boers with the British were not improved when the Transvaal was invaded by hordes of eager British fortune-hunters after the discovery of the world's richest gold mines in the Rand region of the Transvaal (1886), or when the British shut the Transvaal off from all access to the ocean by annexing Zululand and the territory just south of Delagoa Bay (which was Portuguese), or when Dr. Jameson with a band of British mounted police rashly attempted a filibustering expedition against the Transvaal (1895). The "Jameson Raid," as

British and Boers

---

[1] Founded, 1836; annexed by Great Britain, 1848; independent again, 1854–1900.

[2] The Pretoria Convention (1881) gave the Transvaal autonomy under British suzerainty; even suzerainty seemed to have been abandoned by the London Convention of 1884.

the invasion was called, failed miserably, but it warned the Boers to be on their guard. From 1895 to 1899 the Transvaal government, headed by that hardy old Dutch pioneer, President Paul Kruger, became steadily more hostile to the British; while the "Uitlanders," or British miners who had settled in the Transvaal, cried out ever more loudly against the unfriendly and oligarchical Boer government. The refusal of the Boers to enfranchise the "Uitlanders" (except after seven years' residence) was one of the greatest grievances.

The final struggle between the British and the two Boer Republics began in 1899 with the outbreak of the South African **The Boer War, 1899-1902** War (1899-1902). At the outset the Boers took the offensive, invading Natal and striking at the Kimberley diamond fields of Cape Colony; but British reënforcements poured into South Africa until finally no fewer than 350,000 men had been put into the field under the able command of Lord Roberts (1832-1914) and Lord Kitchener (1850-1916). The Boers probably never had more than 40,000 men in the field together. Overwhelmed by sheer force of numbers, the republican troops had to retreat and on 5 June, 1900, surrender their capital city of Pretoria. Nevertheless two years of guerrilla warfare were required before the last irregular bands of Boer riflemen were broken up. At last peace was made in May, 1902. By the terms of peace, Great Britain promised to grant responsible government to the two Boer Republics (Orange Free State and the Transvaal) which had been annexed during the war. The promise was carried out in 1906 as regards the Transvaal and in 1907 as regards the Orange Free State.

The way was now clear for the confederation of South Africa. Earlier projects of union had met shipwreck either by reason of **The Union of South Africa, 1909** British disapproval or because of Boer nationalism. But Britain was now willing, Boer resistance had been crushed, and union was imperatively necessary for the establishment of uniform tariffs, for the administration of interstate railways, and for the adoption of a vigorous native policy. An intercolonial convention for the discussion of tariff questions was speedily followed by agreement upon a plan of consolidation which was ratified by the British Parliament in September, 1909. Cape Colony, Natal, the Transvaal, and

Orange Free State became provinces in the Union of South Africa, a union even more strongly centralized than Canada. As the Boers received equal rights with the British in the new Union, both in respect of language and in respect of political privileges, the Union Parliament and the ministry responsible to it at once fell under the control of the "South African" or Boer party. General Louis Botha, who had so valiantly fought against Great Britain, became the first premier of the Union, and the British or Unionist party fell naturally into the position of a minority.

Animosity between Boer farmers and British business men continued to vex the Union of South Africa; but with the rapid development of the mining industry still more serious problems pressed for solution. In the first place, the government had to cope with a violent Syndicalist agitation among the British-born skilled laborers, an agitation which grew even more violent after the Rand strike of 1913, when government troops had ruthlessly shot down strikers in the streets of Johannesburg. In the second place, the Union lived constantly in fear of native uprisings. In a colony where the white population had been forced to fight almost continuously against warlike native tribes, and where the whites were still outnumbered by the negroes almost four to one, riotous struggles between capital and labor and division between Boers and British might easily lead to serious native insurrections. The situation was complicated, furthermore, by the presence in South Africa of over two hundred thousand discontented Asiatic laborers who had been imported from India.

If we count the smaller self-governing colonies of Newfoundland and New Zealand together with the confederations of Canada, Australia, and South Africa, Great Britain was now mistress of five "colonial nations" whose vast territorial extent and enormous natural resources gave promise of great future development. Canada and Australia were rapidly becoming nations in a very real sense; each had its national flag, its national army, its national tariff, its national government. The authority of the mother-country over her buxom daughters was steadily declining. Since the introduction of responsible government, the

Slight British Control over the Dominions

royal governor appointed by the British Crown was less likely to be an energetic politician than a distinguished and disinterested nobleman, and the governor tended to assume in the colony somewhat the same honorary position that the king himself occupied in the United Kingdom. The right of the mother-country to veto the acts of colonial parliaments, the right of the mother-country to control foreign relations, and the right of the Judicial Committee of the Privy Council to hear appeals from colonial courts, were still maintained in theory; but in practice Great Britain rarely interfered with the legislative liberty of the self-governing dominions and frequently permitted them to negotiate independent commercial and other treaties with foreign nations; and the right of judicial appeal was severely curtailed by Canada, Australia, and South Africa. In short, the political connection between Great Britain and her self-governing colonies was very slight.

With the general awakening of the imperialistic spirit toward the close of the nineteenth century, there appeared in Great Britain a movement to bring "The Dominions," as the self-governing colonies later came to be styled, into closer union with the mother-country. "Imperial Unity" became the battle-cry of Unionist statesmen who hoped to strengthen the Empire against rival imperial Powers, especially Germany; the cry was taken up by British business men who were engaged in colonial trade, and echoed by loyal British hearts in mother-country and colonies alike. Imperial unity, as Joseph Chamberlain [1] pointed out, could be secured only through "Imperial Federation," that is, through the recognition of the Dominions as copartners with the United Kingdom in a sort of federal empire. This ideal of Imperial Federation could be approached by three main avenues: imperial preference, imperial conference, and imperial defense.

Imperial preference meant simply that by mutual agreement the United Kingdom as well as the Dominions should establish a protective-tariff system by which heavier duties would be placed on imports from foreign countries than on imports from British lands. Such an arrangement would prevent British trade from falling into foreign hands,

The Movement for Imperial Federation

Imperial Preference

[1] See above, pp. 300 ff.

and would cement the British Empire into the most gigantic economic unit in the world. British industries would be delivered from German competition in supplying the colonial demand for manufactures. Grain, meat, and the raw materials so vital to manufacturing England would flow in a plenteous stream from Great Britain's own colonies. England would be assured of her food supply, and the Dominions would be certain of à market for their agricultural products. The first step toward the realization of this roseate dream was taken by Canada in 1897, when the Dominion allowed imports from the United Kingdom a reduction of one-eighth of the "general" Canadian customs tariff. Canada subsequently increased this preference to one-fourth (1898), and even to one-third (1900). South Africa, Australia, and New Zealand followed Canada's example. But the United Kingdom, firmly intrenched in her free-trade policy, absolutely refused to meet the Dominions halfway. Joseph Chamberlain, the great imperialist, with all his incisive argument, could not convert England from Free Trade, he could not even convert his own Unionist party entirely. The advent of the Liberal ministry in 1905 marked the failure of Chamberlain's agitation in Great Britain for imperial preference.

Better progress was made along the second route to Imperial Federation, namely, imperial conference. It was demanded that the United Kingdom should give the Dominions *Imperial Conference* a voice in imperial affairs. Although each had a "high commissioner" to represent its interests in London, the Dominions considered it humiliating to deal with their "co-partner" through the latter's Colonial Office, and they resented the fact that imperial defense and foreign policy were determined by the cabinet of the United Kingdom rather than by a body representing the empire. The Dominions were not content to be silent partners. At least a partial remedy for this complaint was found in the Imperial Conference. The first Imperial Conference was a meeting of representatives of the self-governing colonies held at London on the auspicious occasion of Queen Victoria's Jubilee in 1887. Similar conferences were held at Ottawa in 1894, and at London in 1897, 1902, 1907, and 1911. Especially noteworthy was the Conference of 1907, which arranged for regular quadrennial sessions of the Imperial

Conference, and for subsidiary conferences on particular matters. The United Kingdom was to be represented in the Imperial Conference no longer by its secretary of state for the colonies, but by its prime minister, just as the Dominions were represented by their respective premiers.[1] Since the Imperial Conference possessed no constitutional powers, it resembled a congress of diplomats rather than an imperial representative assembly; nevertheless, this periodical meeting of premiers could not fail to exercise a powerful influence in harmonizing the interests of Great Britain and her Dominions. Bolder schemes for the regular representation of the Dominions in a special "Imperial Parliament" or in the Parliament of the United Kingdom met with discouragement because no basis of representation was discoverable which would satisfy both the Dominions and the mother-country, nor could the powers of such an Imperial Parliament be easily defined.

One of the chief concerns of the Imperial Conferences was imperial defense. Great Britain at the opening of the twentieth **Imperial** century was fairly staggering under the load of an **Defense** enormous naval expenditure, due partly to acceleration of naval construction necessitated by the rapid growth of foreign navies, and partly to the higher cost of battleships.[2] Here was an opportunity for the Dominions to prove their loyalty and to show themselves true partners in the Empire by sharing the burden of imperial defense. New Zealand responded by contributing a battle-cruiser, the *New Zealand*, to the British North Sea Fleet. South Africa contented herself with a small annual money contribution. Australia, actuated as much by local as by imperial patriotism, started to construct a separate Australian fleet unit, including one first-class battle-cruiser and smaller craft. Canada wavered. While the French-Canadian Liberal leader, Sir Wilfrid Laurier, was in power (1896–1911), Canada aspired to have a Dominion navy, built in her own shipyards, manned by her own seamen, controlled by her own government. But the Conservative cabinet of Sir Robert Borden, coming into power in 1911, decided instead of building a separate fleet to contribute £7,000,000 for the addition of three battle-

[1] Other ministers were also permitted to attend.
[2] The first *Dreadnought*, launched in 1906, cost about $9,000,000.

ships to the British navy. As this plan was vetoed by the Canadian Senate, Canada did nothing. Thus the Dominions were of some assistance, but not of much importance, in bearing the burden of imperial naval defense. The chief difficulty seemed to be that Great Britain wanted a concentrated navy for use against Germany, whereas the Dominions were strongly inclined to prefer local navies for the gratification of local pride, for the protection of local commerce, for the profit of local shipbuilders.

In military matters there was less disagreement. The Dominions required little urging to establish local armies. In the Boer War, Canada, Australia, and New Zealand zealously dispatched troops to fight for Great Britain in South Africa. Thanks to systems of military training installed after the Boer War, the Dominions were able to render even more material aid to the mother-country in the War of the Nations.

THE CROWN COLONIES

The second group of British dependencies — the Crown Colonies — stood in marked contrast to the first in three respects. First, whereas in the group of colonies just considered the elective colonial assemblies had obtained virtually complete control of the government through responsible ministries, in the Crown Colonies representative assemblies were either entirely lacking or quite power-less. Secondly, whereas the self-governing colonies were settled largely by people of British, or, at any rate, of European stock, the Crown Colonies, on the other hand, contained relatively few British inhabitants. Thirdly, the self-governing colonies were situated mostly in the temperate zones and were suitable for important agricultural and industrial development by Europeans ; most of the Crown Colonies, on the contrary, were situated within the tropics, and many were small island naval posts or coaling stations.

How Different from Self-Governing Colonies

A considerable number of British Crown Colonies were located in the West Indies. Some of these, notably Barbados and the Bahamas, still preserved the old form of colonial government, in which the lower house of the legislature was elected but could

not control the "executive council" or ministry. Similar representative bodies had formerly existed in Jamaica, and in
The British British Honduras, but they had been abolished in
West Indies 1866 and 1870 respectively, and the modern form of
Crown Colony government installed, with a "legislative council"
wholly or partly appointed by the crown. Whether this legislative council included some members elected by the colony, as in
Jamaica, in the federated Leeward Islands, and in British Guiana,
or was entirely nominated, as in Trinidad, British Honduras, and
the various Windward Islands, it was plain that the balance of
power rested with officials of the British government, rather
than with the colonists. Possibly the negroes who labored on
the sugar-plantations of the West Indies under the direction
of a few thousand wealthy white plantation-owners were not
fit for self-government; or perhaps Great Britain was more
anxious to retain direct control over the West Indies — valuable
both as plantation-colonies and as coaling-stations — than to
satisfy the political aspirations of the islanders.

The Crown Colonies in Africa were inhabited entirely by
negroes, and none of them enjoyed representative government.
British   The legislative councils in the torrid West-African
Crown   colonies of Gold Coast, Nigeria, Gambia, and Sierra
Colonies in   Leone were wholly appointive; and Basutoland and
Africa and   Swaziland in South Africa were autocratically ruled
Asia   by British commissioners without legislative councils.
In the Asiatic Crown Colonies as a rule a few members of the
legislative council were elected either by the colony at large,
as in the populous island of Ceylon, or by the chambers of com-
merce, as in Hong Kong or in the Straits Settlements.

The list of Crown Colonies also included a number of small
islands like Mauritius, valued as coaling-stations or naval
Naval   bases.[1] Five of these were situated in the temperate
Stations   zones and inhabited by whites, thus forming exceptions
to the general rule that Crown Colonies were torrid regions with
colored inhabitants. The five included (1) the impregnable rock-
fortress of Gibraltar with its adjacent town of about twenty
thousand Spanish-speaking inhabitants; (2) the mid-Mediter-

[1] Some of these posts were not regular Crown Colonies, but were administered
by the naval authorities, — Ascension, for example.

ranean naval station of Malta with its 200,000 peasants and townspeople speaking an Italian dialect; (3) the Mediterranean island of Cyprus,[1] with its quarrelsome population of Greeks and Turks; (4) the Falkland Islands (southeast of South America) with their Scottish settlers; and (5), no less important as a naval base than as a winter-resort, the Bermuda Islands with 12,000 colored and 7000 white inhabitants. Although the white inhabitants of these five colonies might have been capable of self-government, they were not granted that privilege. In Gibraltar the governor was an autocrat; in the Falkland Islands he was restrained merely by an appointive legislative council; in Malta only a minority of the legislative council was elective (since 1849), and in Cyprus only two-thirds; in the Bermudas the house of assembly was elective, to be sure, but the upper chamber of the legislature was appointive, and the ministry took its orders from the governor.

In the same general class with the Crown Colonies we may place the protectorates and the territories administered by Chartered Companies, which, like the Crown Colonies, **Chartered** were usually tropical in climate, non-European in re- **Companies** spect of population, and non-representative in government. The Chartered Company was a favorite form of colonial organization in the last quarter of the nineteenth century, as in the seventeenth century, but it was better suited for the acquisition of new territories than for the government of old, and consequently many chartered colonies were transformed into Crown Colonies, so that by the year 1914 the only British colonies remaining under Chartered Companies were Rhodesia and North Borneo. Rhodesia, a vast tract of undeveloped territory north of the Transvaal, including some good agricultural land and promising gold-fields, was originally acquired for Great Britain, thanks to the energy of Cecil Rhodes, who organized the British South Africa Company (1889), and in whose honor the company's territory was named Rhodesia. The British North Borneo Company was slightly older, having been chartered in 1882; and it had continued to govern North Borneo even after the

---

[1] Formerly a Turkish possession, "occupied" and governed by Great Britain, while nominally remaining part of the Ottoman Empire, from 1878 to 1914, and formally annexed by Great Britain in 1914.

territory was declared a British protectorate (1888). The actual
government in both Rhodesia and North Borneo strongly
resembled that of a Crown Colony, with partially representative
legislative councils, and with governors appointed by the company in place of royal governors.

The protectorates were more numerous than the chartered
colonies. As a rule, a protectorate was established wherever
Protecto- Great Britain found it easier to adapt native institu-
rates tions to British rule than to destroy them. The
scepter was left in the hand of the native potentate, but it
was wielded in behalf of British interests and at the behest of
an all-powerful British Resident Commissioner. Thus the
Malay States (on the Malay peninsula in southeastern Asia),
placed under British "protection" in the nineteenth century,
were still ruled by their sultans, who were bound to follow the
"advice" of British Residents. Similar protectorates, as the
next section will make clear, still existed in India. The most
extensive, however, were in Africa. British East Africa (including Uganda, Zanzibar, and Pemba), Nyasaland, Somaliland,
Bechuanaland, and the extensive "hinterlands" (inland regions)
of Nigeria, Gambia, and Sierra Leone, were all protectorates.
Some of these had become practically Crown Colonies, while
others preserved their former governments, as Zanzibar its Arab
sultan, Bechuanaland its native chieftains, and Buganda (in
Uganda) its king — "His Highness the Kabaka." These tropical African protectorates, mostly unfit for white settlement, were
important chiefly on account of the rubber, the ivory, the palm-
oil, and the cloves which they produced.

Egypt, probably the most important of Great Britain's African
possessions, did not become formally a British protectorate
Egypt until the outbreak of war between Great Britain and
Turkey in 1914. For more than thirty years, however,
Egypt had been practically a British protectorate, while remaining theoretically a vassal state of the Ottoman Empire. During
the course of the nineteenth century, as was explained in the
foregoing chapter,[1] the Turkish viceroys of Egypt had become
virtually independent monarchs and assumed the title of Khedive; then a reckless Khedive by plunging his country into

[1] See above, pp. 626 ff.

bankruptcy had given his French and English creditors an excuse for establishing the so-called Dual Control of France and Great Britain over Egyptian finances; a few years later, British troops had been landed to suppress a rebellion in Egypt (1882), and the Dual Control had been replaced by the single control of a British Financial Adviser (1883). From 1883 to 1914 Egypt was to all intents and purposes a British protectorate. At first the British government, under Gladstone's leadership, was inclined to regard the occupation of Egypt as a temporary affair; but in time British statesmen came to believe that the possession of Egypt was absolutely essential to the British Empire, because the main artery of the Empire, the route to India and Australasia, passed through Egypt by way of the Suez Canal, which was constructed by a French company between 1859 and 1869. Great Britain had purchased a controlling interest in the canal in 1875.

Under the energetic administration of able British financial advisers, such as Lord Cromer and Lord Kitchener, many abuses were done away with, praiseworthy reforms were instituted for the benefit of the downtrodden *fellahin* or peasantry, finances were put on a solid footing, the administration of justice was reformed, and profitable irrigation works were undertaken, culminating in the construction of the magnificent Assuan Dam (1898–1902). A representative assembly, moreover, was created (1883), and in 1913 legislative powers in addition to a veto on new taxes were intrusted to the assembly. Notwithstanding this enlightened and comparatively liberal treatment, the Egyptians were discontented. Like the Germans, like the Italians, like the Turks, the educated Egyptians, especially the young men who had studied abroad, felt the stirrings of a national patriotism. Arabi Pasha's insurrection of 1882 had been crushed to the ground, but the echoes of his slogan, "Egypt for the Egyptians," had never died away. British rule might be benevolent, but it was foreign rule and therefore intolerable. This was the spirit which inspired the Egyptian Nationalist agitators to present a petition for liberty to the Prince of Wales at Cairo in 1906. But petitions and propaganda were alike useless, as long as Great Britain could maintain a sufficient army in Egypt.

One of the results of the British occupation of Egypt was the re-conquest of the Sudan, that vast region to the southward, which had been incited to revolt by a Mohammedan religious fanatic, the "Mahdi" or "Messiah," and was independent of Egypt from 1885 to 1898. The Sudan was won back by Sir Herbert (later, Lord) Kitchener, "Sirdar" or commander of the reorganized Egyptian army, between 1896 and 1898. The joint rule or "Condominium" of Great Britain and Egypt was imposed upon the Sudan in 1899. The Anglo-Egyptian Sudan was not a valuable territory, but its possession, implying the control of the Upper Nile, was considered vitally necessary for the prosperity and safety of Egypt.

THE EMPIRE OF INDIA

The greatest of all British possessions remains to be considered. Although less than half the size of Canada, India was Importance justly entitled to rank first, because it contained forty of India times the population of Canada; because four-fifths of the population of the entire British colonial empire were included within this one Asiatic dependency; because India's trade with the United Kingdom, worth more than half a billion dollars a year, far exceeded that of any other colony.[1] For every square mile of territory in the United Kingdom, India could show fifteen; and as the British Isles had only 45,000,000 inhabitants as against India's 315,000,000, every man, woman, and child in the United Kingdom might have been said to possess seven subjects in India. North and South America put together had only half as many people as India.

The conquest of this tremendous empire by a handful of British merchant-adventurers would have been absolutely impossible Geographi- but for two facts. In the first place, Great Britain cal Divisions had the advantage of a more aggressive and progres- of India sive civilization, which implied, among other less obvious things, the possession of deadly firearms, marvelous

---

[1] In 1913 the total commerce (excluding shipments of treasure) between India and Ceylon and the United Kingdom amounted to $650,000,000. No other colony or country in the world purchased so large an amount of British merchandise as India.

machines, and medical science. In the second place, India was divided. Geographically India fell into three well-defined regions — the triangular peninsula-plateau of southern India (usually called the Deccan), the broad belt of lowlands formed by the Ganges and Indus river valleys to the north of the Deccan, and still further north the mountainous region of the lofty Himalayas. Racial divisions corresponded roughly to the geography, the so-called Dravidians dwelling in the Deccan, the Hindus in the lowland belt ("Hindustan"), and the descendants of Mohammedan (Arab, Afghan, and Persian) invaders in the mountainous north; but in many localities the different races lived side by side in neighborly hostility. There were dozens of distinct vernacular languages. Religious antagonisms accentuated the racial and geographical divisions. About two-thirds of the entire population followed the Brahmanic or orthodox Hindu religion, with its polytheistic theology, its reverence for the sacred cow, its pilgrimages, its Brahmanical hierarchy, its rigid caste system. Three heretical sects — the Buddhists (10,700,-000,[1] mostly in Burma), the Jains (1,250,000), and the Sikhs (3,000,000, in the Punjab province) — had split off from Hinduism just as the Protestant sects from Roman Catholicism, though much earlier. Orthodox and heretical Hindus alike, as well as the more primitive pagan tribesmen (10,000,000), were constantly coming into contact with the Mohammedans, whose strongholds were the northern fringe of provinces — Sind, the Punjab, the Frontier Province, Kashmir, East Bengal, and Assam, — but whose energetic and ambitious emissaries had penetrated almost every part of the peninsula. The Mogul Emperors of India, as will be remembered, were descendants of a Mohammedan invader of the sixteenth century, and their provincial lieutenants (nawabs) were likewise Mohammedans. The Mogul's viceroy in the Deccan, the nizam of Hyderabad, was also a Mohammedan prince. But long before the nineteenth century, the Mogul's power had declined; his nawabs and nizams no longer respected his authority, and the numerous Hindu rajas who had once been his vassals became independent princelings. Particularly the confederated Mahratta princes, commanding a

Races

Religions

Political Dissensions

[1] Census of 1911.

powerful Hindu nation of central India, in the eighteenth century mocked and menaced the Mogul's lordship. Thus, political dissensions reduced India to impotence and enabled the
British to extend their dominion over the country little by little,
by subtle intrigue or by piecemeal conquest.

Previous chapters [1] have traced the rise of the first English
establishments in India, notably the trading-posts at Surat

Career of
the East
India
Company

(1612), at Madras (1640), at Bombay (1662), and at
Calcutta (1686), and the bitter conflict between the
French and the British, culminating in the decisive
defeat of the French in the Seven Years' War (1756–
1763). After the Seven Years' War, being rid of French rivalry,
the English East India Company embarked on a career of constant warfare and conquest.

A succession of able and ambitious empire-builders, acting
in the Company's interest, built up story by story the stupen-

Empire-
Builders

dous structure of the British Indian Empire. Robert
Clive (governor of Bengal from 1758 to 1760, and
from 1765 to 1767), a man whose melancholy moods alternated
with fits of fierce energy, was the real founder of the empire.

Clive

He established British prestige on a sure footing in
Bengal, the province at the mouth of the Ganges, by
defeating at Plassey (1757) the monstrous army mustered
against him by the local nawab. In Clive's time, too, the
Mogul emperor was defeated, captured, and compelled to cede
to the Company the revenues of Bengal, Behar, and Orissa

Warren
Hastings

provinces (1765). Warren Hastings (governor-general from 1774 to 1785), that somewhat unscrupulous
but undoubtedly capable successor of Clive, fought the Mahrattas, who were aided by French soldiers of fortune, and fended off
the attacks of Hyder Ali, the warlike Mohammedan sultan of

Cornwallis

Mysore, who threatened to wipe out the British posts
in the south. Lord Cornwallis (1786–1793), of
American fame, continued the war against Mysore, now ruled
by Hyder Ali's son, Tippoo.

From 1798 to 1805 the military genius of the marquess of
Wellesley (elder brother of the duke of Wellington) was employed in India. Tippoo met defeat and death at his hands

[1] See Vol. I, ch. ii, ix, x.

(1799) and an infant Hindu raja was substituted on the throne of Mysore as the puppet of the British. Next, Wellesley concluded an alliance with the nizam of Hyderabad, Mohammedan viceroy of the Deccan, and brought **Wellesley** under British administration the Carnatic and Tanjore (on the coast, opposite Ceylon), as well as the districts of Rohilkhand and the Doab, on the upper Ganges. Wellesley also defeated the Mahrattas and annexed Orissa. Such extensive — and expensive — military operations were highly distasteful to the businesslike directors of the Company, and they ordered the next governors to be less aggressive. But the mar- **The** quess of Hastings (governor from 1813 to 1823) was **Marquess of** compelled to adopt a martial policy in defense of the **Hastings** Company's territory. He fought and subdued the brave Gurkha nation of Nepal. He finally (1817–1818) shattered the troublesome Mahratta confederacy of central India, and annexed part of its lands (around Bombay). He made the Hindu rajas of Rajputana (just east of the Indus) his vassals. When Lord Hastings returned to Europe, all India from the Indus to the Ganges was dominated if not actually governed by the East India Company, excepting Sind and the Punjab in the northwest. Sind was conquered in 1843. The Punjab was annexed in 1849 by Lord Dalhousie,[1] the last of the great **Dalhousie** empire-builders, after its gallant defenders, who belonged to the Hindu sect of Sikhs, had been defeated in two bloody wars. Under British rule, the Punjab enjoyed great prosperity, and the Sikhs became the most loyal British soldiers.

The Deccan and the lowland belt of India formed a compact empire. But the third geographical region, the northern fringe of mountains, was deemed necessary for protection against invasion from the north, particularly for protection against Russia. On the northeast, Assam was wrested from Burma (1824), then Lower Burma (1852) and finally Upper Burma (1886) were conquered. The mountain-states of Bhutan and Nepal, while not actually annexed, virtually became vassals of British India. Tibet, further north, although nominally belonging to China, accorded special privileges to the British by a treaty of 1904, and was clearly included within the British

---

[1] Governor-general from 1848 to 1856.

sphere of influence.[1] West of Tibet, the province of Kashmir
became a British protectorate (1846). The North West Frontier
Province was organized in 1901. Afghanistan, after two wars[2]
with the British, was left as a dependent buffer-state between
the British and Russian Empires; in its foreign relations Afghanistan was placed under British tutelage and protection,
but in domestic affairs the Afghan ameer remained an independent despot. Baluchistan, lying between India and Persia,
was brought more definitely under British domination. In
1854 the khan of Baluchistan promised always "to act in subordinate coöperation" with India; a considerable part of Baluchistan was formally incorporated into British India (1887), the
rest remaining under native rulers, who were controlled by British agents. Thus from Burma to Baluchistan India was protected by an almost unbroken line of mountain ramparts.

Having acquired an empire in India, the British had to invent
a government for it. Originally, as we remember, England was
represented in India by a simple trading corporation,
the East India Company. When the officials of that
company, in the second half of the eighteenth century,
began to behave like Indian nawabs, interfering in
Indian politics, accepting or extorting huge sums of
money[3] from native potentates, organizing armies, fighting
wars, and exercising despotic power in quite an Oriental fashion,
British statesmen at home raised loud protests, and demanded
that the shamefully corrupt administration of the East India
Company should be reformed and regulated. By the
Regulating Act of 1773 a council of four members,
nominated by Parliament, was established at Calcutta to restrain the company's representative, the governor-
general, from arbitrary, immoral, or indiscreet action. This
scheme simply resulted in quarrels between the governor-general
(Warren Hastings) and the council; and William Pitt, who became prime minister in 1783, drew up a more effective measure, the
famous India Act of 1784. Not only were the governor-general
and higher officials of India henceforth to be nominated by the

*Indian Gov-
ernment
under the
British East
India
Company*

*The Regu-
lating Act
of 1773*

[1] See above, pp. 569 f.
[2] The first Afghan war from 1838 to 1842, the second from 1878 to 1880.
[3] Robert Clive thus made himself a millionaire.

British ministry, but furthermore a special State Department or Board of Control, with a cabinet minister at its head, was to supervise Indian affairs from London. On these lines India continued to be governed until 1858, with the ministerial "India Office" at London exercising a more or less rigorous control over the otherwise autocratic governor-general. Between 1784 and 1858 a series of far-reaching reforms were achieved by enlightened governors-general. Lord Cornwallis put an end to the extortions of revenue-collectors in Bengal by fixing the rates of the land-tax permanently at a moderate figure. The marquess of Hastings began the organization of native education and smiled benevolently on the first native newspaper. Lord William Bentinck (governor-general from 1828 to 1835), who attempted to abolish the practice of "suttee," [1] has been praised as a reformer who "infused into Oriental despotism the spirit of British freedom." [2] Lord Dalhousie placed the civil service on a competitive basis, granted government aid to schools, and organized a public works department to carry out far-reaching plans for railway and canal construction.

The India Act of 1784

The British were complacently congratulating themselves upon the benevolent, enlightened character of their rule in India, when of a sudden there burst forth in the vicinity of Delhi a fierce rebellion, which spread like wildfire throughout the length and breadth of the Ganges valley, jeopardizing the very existence of the British power in Hindustan. Several reasons might be assigned for the insurrection. Bitter discontent had been caused by British interference with Indian social and religious customs. Reforms that suited British ideas of progress and justice were odious to Oriental minds. Native princes, moreover, who had been deposed from their thrones, and the Great Mogul, who still forlornly pretended to hold court at Delhi, longed for revenge. Then, too, the native troops — there were less than 40,000 British soldiers and more than 250,000 native troopers or "Sepoys" in the East India Company's employ — were infuriated by insults to their reli-

The Sepoy Mutiny, 1857

---

[1] "Suttee" is the word applied to the Hindu practice of widows' cremating themselves on the funeral piles of their husbands.

[2] Quoted from the extravagant panegyric composed by Macaulay and graven on Bentinck's statue at Calcutta.

gious prejudices. The Hindu Sepoy had a superstitious repugnance to sea-voyages, but he was sometimes compelled to cross
the sea to fight in Burma and in China. Furthermore, a new
kind of greased cartridge was introduced which had to be bitten
before it was used. The Hindus believed the grease contained
the fat of cows and could not be used without sacrilege, since the
cow was a sacred animal. The Mohammedans, who abhorred
swine, suspected that the grease was pig's fat and feared to bite
the cartridges lest they should be defiled thereby. Hindus
and Mohammedans alike were furious.

The great mutiny began on 10 May, 1857, when a native
cavalry regiment at Meerut, rather than use the greased cartridges, rebelliously left its barracks and galloped off to the ancient
imperial capital of Delhi to offer the Mogul their services in
overthrowing the British. Quickly the mutiny became general
throughout the Ganges provinces and central India. In many
places the populace made common cause with the Sepoys. At
Cawnpore hundreds of European residents and British soldiers
were treacherously massacred. At Lucknow the English garrison was besieged by a host of rebels. At Delhi the aged Mogul
was triumphant. As soon as the gravity of the situation was
realized, the British government hurried reënforcements to India,
and the British troops, with the aid of loyal Sikh and Gurkha
regiments, undertook to reconquer the country. Delhi, Cawnpore, Lucknow, were won back. By the summer of 1858 the
mutiny was practically crushed, although not completely until
April, 1859. Terrible punishment was meted out to the muti-
neers. Many were shot from the mouths of cannon. The
feeble old Mogul emperor was exiled to Rangoon, and his sons
were shot down in cold blood by a British officer. "No muti-
neer," said one of the leading British officials at the time, "ever
surrenders; for directly he is caught he is shot or hanged."

The disastrous Sepoy mutiny sealed the doom of the antiquated East India Company. After 257 years of existence,
the Company had outlived its usefulness. It had already been
shorn of many of its powers, and had lost its monopoly of
Oriental commerce.[1] Now, in the year 1858, the Company's

[1] The Company had been deprived in 1813 of its monopoly except with regard
to tea and the Chinese trade; even these vestiges of commercial monopoly had
been swept away by the Charter Act of 1833.

remaining powers were taken over by the British Government, India became a Crown dominion, and the East India Company ceased to exist, except solely for the function of receiving from the government and distributing to the stockholders the $10\frac{1}{2}$ per cent of yearly dividend on its capital stock of £6,000,000.

India Transferred from the Company to the Crown, 1858

The same Act of Parliament — the Better Government of India Act, 1858 — vested the supreme control of Indian affairs in a cabinet officer, the Secretary of State for India, assisted by a small council sitting in London. The actual administration was henceforth to be conducted by a viceroy, appointed by the British ministry to represent the Crown in India, and assisted by an Executive Council or cabinet and a Legislative Council. Subordinate to the central government, which had its seat at Calcutta,[1] there were provincial governments, some with governors and nominated councils, some with chief commissioners and no councils. There were also more than six hundred native states, comprising two-fifths the area and two-ninths the population of India, ruled by their Hindu and Moslem potentates, under British protection and supervision, but not under direct British administration.

Government of India

For half a century this system continued in force, with few changes, except that the Queen was in 1877 proclaimed Empress of India. Toward the close of the nineteenth century, however, a Nationalist movement appeared in India, which enlisted the sympathies of those educated natives who had studied the European political ideal of national democracy, and demanded representative government for India. As a concession to this agitation, two Indians were appointed on the council of the Secretary of State, and one on the Executive Council of the viceroy. The Indian Councils Act (1909) was an attempt to reconcile the Indian desire for representative government with the British determination to rule. Twenty-five of the sixty-eight members of the viceroy's legislative council were to be elected; in six of the nine great provinces, into which India was then divided,[2] the provincial

Political Unrest in India and the Indian Councils Act of 1909

---

[1] Until 1912, when the seat of government was transferred to the ancient capital-city of Delhi.

[2] In consequence of administrative changes in 1912, India is now (1916)

councils were to contain majorities of non-official members, in some cases appointed, in others elected, to represent the natives; the three remaining provinces were to be ruled by British chief commissioners without councils.

Notwithstanding these seemingly liberal concessions, the Indian Councils Act failed to satisfy the Hindu agitators, who complained because the provincial councils had no more power than debating clubs, because the majority of the viceroy's council was still composed of appointed members and officials, because Mohammedans were given separate representation. Only a sham of representative government was being granted to India, they said. In order to stifle the rancorous fault-finding which filled the native newspapers, the government resorted in 1910 to stern measures curtailing the freedom of the press, subjecting the mails to censorship, and forbidding seditious meetings. Still the Hindu and Moslem malcontents continued to hold their separate national congresses and to agitate for constitutional reform; riots, assassinations, and rumors of conspiracies continued to disquiet the British bureaucracy; and although in 1911 the Durbar or ceremonial coronation of King George V as Emperor at Delhi passed off without untoward incident, one year later the viceroy barely escaped assassination.

In all the preceding paragraphs we have well-nigh lost sight of the economic considerations which inspired the British to cherish their Indian Empire, and the economic development which constituted the most striking feature of British rule. While cunning Indian artificers continued to produce the fine fabrics, the filmy shawls, and the quaint trinkets of wrought metal or carved ivory, which were so eagerly sought by Europeans, these artistic manufactures, gems, spices, and gold were overshadowed in importance by staple products of the soil. Under British auspices colossal irrigation canals were dug, so that the fertile soil could regularly be utilized where the rainfall was slight or irregular. One-sixth of the total crop area was

Economic Advantages of India to Great Britain

Agricultural

divided into fifteen provinces: Madras, Bombay, Bengal, United Provinces of Agra and Oudh, the Punjab, Burma, Bihar and Orissa, Central Provinces and Berar, Assam, North West Frontier Province, Ajmer-Merwara, Coorg, Baluchistan, Delhi, and the Andaman and Nicobar Islands. The first nine have provincial councils.

irrigated land. The country was covered with a network of railways — more than thirty-three thousand miles in all — making it possible for inland provinces to market their crops. Besides millet, pulse, and sugar-cane, which were largely consumed at home, India began to produce enormous quantities of rice, coffee, tea, opium,[1] cotton, and jute, for export to foreign countries. The Punjab province became a great wheat-country, so that in 1912 the annual exports of wheat exceeded $40,000,000. As most of the wheat went to the United Kingdom, India was accounted one of the foremost sources of Great Britain's food supply.[2]

The wheat-supply in itself furnished — for many British statesmen — a sufficient reason why Great Britain should rule India. Other economic interests there were, too, **Commercial** hardly less influential in confirming the same conclusion. Of India's rapidly growing commerce, which had increased by four or five hundred per cent since the Sepoy Mutiny, Britain enjoyed almost a monopoly.[3] The United Kingdom exported to India almost ten times as much merchandise as did the rival industrial nation of Germany.[4] Three-fourths of India's sea-borne trade was carried under the British flag. The merchants and shippers engaged in this commerce were naturally enthusiastic in favor of British political supremacy in India, which insured British commercial supremacy.[5]

Moreover, certain industries in Great Britain depended materially upon the command of the Indian market. Cotton manufacturers and the iron industries were chiefly concerned, inasmuch as India purchased annually $200,000,000 [6] worth of cot-

[1] Opium, a government monopoly, brought a net revenue of £4,500,000 into the Indian treasury in the year 1912–1913.

[2] In 1912 the United Kingdom imported over 25,000,000 cwt. of wheat from India, more than from any other country. In 1913, however, Canada and the United States surpassed India as wheat-providers.

[3] Sixty-four per cent of the private merchandise imported by India in 1913 was from the United Kingdom.

[4] 1910.

[5] India's tariff did not show a preference to British goods. That would hardly have been necessary, for British supremacy was secured by the presence of so many British officials and merchants in India, the preëminence of English over other foreign languages, and possibly government influence.

[6] Figures for 1913–1914. That India, instead of selling cotton goods to Europe as in past centuries, should now be importing such enormous quantities from

ton goods, and $125,000,000 worth of iron and steel, machinery, and railway materials, mostly from Great Britain. Little wonder then that cotton and iron magnates were interested in British India. Furthermore there were the capitalists, large and small, who had invested in Indian government securities (of which some $600,000,000 were held in England), or in Indian railways (which represented a capital of over $1,500,000,000, partly held by the government, however), or in some of the 241 cotton factories, the 61 jute mills, or the 22 breweries in India, or in the promising oil-fields and coal-mines (which produced 16,000,000 tons in 1913). Such speculators were very prone to dilate upon the civilizing mission of England in India. Aglow with altruism, they recounted the benefits conferred upon India by her British masters, the abolition of widow-suicide ("suttee"), the prevention of infanticide, the codification of law, the relief of famines, the improvement of sanitation, the irrigation of parched fields, the construction of splendid roads and railways, the hushing of inter-tribal wars under the beneficent régime of the *Pax Britannica*. Some even persuaded themselves that Great Britain was a sort of kindly schoolmistress, teaching civilization to her class of rather backward Hindu scholars and preparing them for the noble but difficult task of governing themselves according to Anglo-Saxon notions. In justice to India, however, it should be remarked that Great Britain as yet appeared more anxious to promote her own economic interests than to educate the native population; in 1912-1913, the government of India was spending almost $60,000,000 on railway and canal construction and almost $100,000,000 on the army, but only some $30,000,000 was appropriated for schools. It was hardly surprising, therefore, that of the total population of the great Indian Empire more than 94 per cent could neither read nor write.

CONCLUSION

The remarks just passed on India naturally suggest some reflections upon the subject of British imperialism as a whole.

Great Britain, may be ascribed in part to the British policy of taxing Indian exports of cotton cloth. The decline of the cotton industry in India, it need hardly be observed, has spelled ruin to thousands of Indian hand-loom weavers.

In the first place, it cannot be denied that, excepting the one disaster of 1776, Great Britain had been wonderfully successful as an imperial Power. No other colonizing nation owned such vast areas suitable for European settlement. No other empire boasted such populous dependencies. From the economic point of view, the British Empire was the most colossal combination in all history. It controlled one-half the world's annual production of gold, a third of the world's wool supply, a third of the coal, a fourth of the cotton, a fifth of the wheat, a sixth of the pig iron. Its navy and its merchant marine were by far the largest in the world, the latter being equal to twice the sum of its two most formidable rivals — Germany and the United States.

British Success in Empire-Building

Of course, this economic preëminence of the British Empire was not entirely due to the colonies. But at least thirty per cent of the United Kingdom's external trade was with the colonies; and the colonies furnished a market for considerably more than a third of British exports. Believing that the loss of the colonies would mean the loss of a large part of the colonial trade, and hoping that the acquisition of new colonies would augment the colonial trade, British manufacturers felt that the possession of an enormous empire was vital to their prosperity. Imperialists furthermore pointed out that about a quarter of industrial England's food-imports and almost a third of her imports of raw-materials came from British possessions. The colonies appeared as necessary to England as the tender to a locomotive.

Advantages to British Manufacturers

A less obvious advantage, but not less important, was that enjoyed by British bankers and investors. In a sense, the British Indian Empire, as we have already seen, was a huge business enterprise in which British capitalists held the shares. During the nineteenth century, and more especially in the twentieth, London bankers invested literally billions of dollars in the British colonies. Billions of British capital were also invested in foreign countries, but the British colonies offered a more favorable field for investment, not only because as a rule richer rewards were to be reaped, but also because interest was oftentimes guaranteed by the government, whereas interest on loans to the independent Latin-American

Advantages to British Capitalists

countries, for example, was sometimes difficult to collect. The total annual income from British capital invested abroad could, of course, be only roughly estimated, but it was computed at over one and one-half billion dollars.

Thus, although the British government derived no tribute from its imperial dominions, nevertheless certain private citizens of the United Kingdom drew enormous profits from the colonies. These investors have been called by a brilliant British economist "the parasites of imperialism." There were other classes, too, which, like parasites, obtained their living from imperialism. First and foremost, in honor and dignity, were the officials sent out from London to act as governors, commissioners, councilors, and petty magistrates. Men of university training, cultured and talented, found in this imperial bureaucracy comfortable salaries and honorable careers. The army and navy offered an equal opportunity for ambition, along with greater excitement. And all the British manufacturers who specialized in the production of military supplies, soldier's clothing, battleships, rifles, bullets, flags, and a thousand and one other imperial necessities, — they too might be reckoned parasites of imperialism.

"Parasites" of British Imperialism

Enough has been said to bring out the importance of economic motives in British imperialism. They must not be exaggerated. The average Englishman probably had no direct profit to gain from the Empire. He believed it to be true, in a vague way, as he had so insistently been told, that upon the Empire the nation's prosperity depended — although he had no thorough understanding of economic theories. At any rate, it seemed a glorious thing to have an Empire upon which the sun never went down, the greatest Empire in the world.

One other aspect of British imperialism is worthy of notice — its dependence on sea-power. One has only to glance at the map, and the dependence of British imperialism upon sea-power becomes clear. The five greatest states of the Empire lie in five separate continents, with the trackless ocean between. Repeatedly, as in the Indian Mutiny or in the South African War, Great Britain has had to hurry troops by sea to subdue a rebellious colony or to crush a stubborn enemy. If a Great Power at war

Importance of "Sea-Power" to the British Empire

with the British Empire could sink the British navy, it would be a simple matter to starve out England, and to capture the separate colonies, few of them strongly defended. Realizing this, the British government was careful to maintain the most powerful navy of any nation. In addition, Great Britain provided her Empire with coaling stations and naval bases, linking up her major possessions. The route through the Red Sea to India and Australasia was guarded by Gibraltar, Malta, Cyprus, Egypt, Aden, Sokotra. In every corner of the seven seas, Great Britain had a station for her fleet.

The cost of such a naval establishment was staggering. But it was considered necessary in order to preserve the Empire. The Empire, indeed, was otherwise a frail structure. Its only really loyal parts were the "white" Dominions, and they were the very colonies which were most independent of the mother-country. In Africa and in India Great Britain had built railways, roads, canals, and dams, but had not made her subject races British in civilization or in loyalty. If by rebellion or by foreign war the British were expelled from Egypt or from India, the historian might safely turn prophet in predicting that time would soon leave fewer traces of British rule there than imperial Rome has left in England.

ADDITIONAL READING

General. Brief outlines: J. H. Robinson and C. A. Beard, *The Development of Modern Europe*, Vol. II (1907), ch. xxvii; C. D. Hazen, *Europe since 1815* (1910), ch. xxii; Oscar Browning, *A History of the Modern World*, Vol. II (1912), Book IV; A. L. Lowell, *The Government of England* Vol. II (new ed., 1912), ch. liv–lviii. Good one-volume narratives: W. H. Woodward, *A Short History of the Expansion of the British Empire, 1500–1911*, 3d ed. (1912); E. G. Hawke, *The British Empire and its History* (1911); H. E. Egerton, *A Short History of British Colonial Policy* (1897); W. P. Greswell, *Growth and Administration of the British Colonies, 1837–1897* (1898); W. J. Ashley (editor), *British Dominions: their Present Commercial and Industrial Condition* (1911); A. F. Pollard (editor), *The British Empire: its Past, its Present, and its Future* (1909); Sir Charles Lucas, *The British Empire* (1915). Standard series: C. P. Lucas, *A Historical Geography of the British Colonies*, comprehensive and accurate, appearing first in 1888 and subsequently enlarged and revised by various authorities so as to comprise (1916) 6 volumes in 12 — Vol. I, *The Mediterranean and Eastern Colonies*, Vol. II, *The West Indies*, Vol. III, *West Africa*,

Vol. IV, *South Africa* (3 parts), Vol. V, *Canada and Newfoundland* (4 parts), Vol. VI, *Australasia* (2 parts) ; A. J. Herbertson and O. J. R. Howarth (editors), *The Oxford Survey of the British Empire*, 6 vols. (1914), descriptive rather than historical, embracing Vol. I, *The British Isles and Mediterranean Possessions*, Vol. II, *Asia*, Vol. III, *Africa*, Vol. IV, *America*, Vol. V, *Australasia*, Vol. VI, *General Survey;* A. W. Tilby, *The English People Overseas*, 6 vols. (1912–1914), including Vol. I, *The American Colonies, 1583–1763*, Vol. II, *British India, 1600–1828*, Vol. III, *British North America, 1763–1867*, Vol. IV, *Britain in the Tropics, 1527–1910*, Vol. V, *Australasia, 1688–1911*, Vol. VI, *South Africa, 1486–1913; British Empire Series*, 5 vols. (1899–1902), popular descriptions ; *All Red Series*, 5 vols. (1909–1912), another series of popular descriptions by competent authorities.

Colonial Government and Colonial Federation.   Sir Henry Jenkyns, *British Rule and Jurisdiction beyond the Seas* (1902) ; Bernard Holland, *Imperium et Libertas : a Study in History and Politics* (1901) ; E. J. Payne, *Colonies and Colonial Federation* (1905) ; Sir Charles Dilke, *Problems of Greater Britain* (1890), and, by the same author, *The British Empire* (1899) ; Alpheus Todd, *Parliamentary Government in the British Colonies*, 2d ed. (1894) ; Richard Jebb, *Studies in Colonial Nationalism* (1905), and, by the same author, *The Imperial Conference*, 2 vols. (1911), and *The Britannic Question : a Survey of Alternatives* (1913) ; J. W. Root, *Colonial Tariffs* (1906) ; C. J. Fuchs, *The Trade Policy of Great Britain and her Colonies since 1860*, trans. from German by Constance Archibald (1905) ; H. E. Egerton, *Federations and Unions within the British Empire* (1911) ; C. E. A. Bedwell (editor), *The Legislation of the Empire : being a Survey of the Legislative Enactments of the British Dominions from 1898 to 1907*, 4 vols. (1909) ; Sir Charles Bruce, *The Broad Stone of Empire: Problems of Crown Colony Administration*, 2 vols. (1910).   See also Sir C. P. Lucas, *Greater Rome and Greater Britain* (1912) ; and the suggestive essays of James (Viscount) Bryce on *The Ancient Roman Empire and the British Empire in India*, and *The Diffusion of Roman and English Law throughout the World*, originally published in his *Studies in History and Jurisprudence*, but now brought out in a separate little volume (1914).   The " Round Table " is an organization devoted to the cause of imperial federation and to the study of problems confronting the self-governing colonies : it publishes scholarly studies and an admirable journal.

Special Works on Canada.   A. G. Bradley, *Canada* (1912), a convenient volume in the " Home University Library " ; Agnes C. Laut, *The Canadian Commonwealth* (1915), in " Problems of the Nations " Series ; W. L. Griffith, *The Dominion of Canada* (1911), in the " All Red " Series ; Sir J. G. Bourinot, *Canada under British Rule, 1760–1900* (1900), and, by the same author, a competent writer on the subject, *Manual of the Constitutional History of Canada from the Earliest Period to 1901*, new ed. (1901) ; C. G. D. Roberts, *History of Canada* (1897), well-written, compact, and valuable ; William Kingsford, *History of Canada*, 10 vols. (1887–1897), an exhaustive painstaking work covering the years from 1608 to 1841 ; H. E. Egerton and

W. L. Grant, *Canadian Constitutional Development, shown by Selected Speeches and Despatches* (1907); William Houston (editor), *Documents illustrative of the Canadian Constitution* (1891); Frederick Bradshaw, *Self-Government in Canada and How it was Achieved: the Story of Lord Durham's Report* (1903); S. J. Reid, *Life and Letters of the First Earl of Durham*, 2 vols. (1906), very laudatory, but informing; *Lord Durham's Report on the Affairs of British North America*, ed. by Sir C. P. Lucas, 3 vols. (1912); E. S. Montague and Bron Herbert, *Canada and the Empire, an Examination of Trade Preferences* (1904); J. C. Hopkins (editor), *The Canadian Annual Review of Public Affairs* (1901 *sqq.*).

Special Works on Australasia. G. W. Rusden, *History of Australia*, 3 vols. (1883), and, by the same author, *History of New Zealand*, 3 vols. (1883), standard works; J. G. Grey, *Australasia Old and New* (1901); B. R. Wise, *The Making of the Australian Commonwealth, 1889–1900: a Stage in the Growth of Empire* (1913); H. G. Turner, *The First Decade of the Australian Commonwealth: a Chronicle of Contemporary Politics, 1901–1910* (1911); W. H. Moore, *Constitution of the Commonwealth of Australia* (1902); A. I. Clark, *Studies in Australasian Constitutional Law*, 2d ed. (1905); Frank Parsons, *The Story of New Zealand* (1904); V. S. Clark, *The Labor Movement in Australasia: a Study in Social Democracy* (1906); W. P. Reeves, *State Experiments in Australia and New Zealand*, 2 vols. (1902); H. D. Lloyd, *Newest England* (1900).

Special Works on South Africa. F. R. Cana, *South Africa from the Great Trek to the Union* (1909); G. E. Cory, *The Rise of South Africa: a History of the Origin of South African Colonization and of its Development Towards the East from the Earliest Times to 1857*, a scholarly work projected in 4 vols. (1910 *sqq.*); G. M. Theal, *South Africa* (1900) in "Story of the Nations" Series; R. H. Brand, *The Union of South Africa* (1909), containing the constitution and an account of its adoption; W. B. Worsfold, *The Union of South Africa* (1912), history and description, in the "All Red" Series. On the Boer War: James (Viscount) Bryce, *Impressions of South Africa* (1897), useful for conditions on the eve of the struggle; Sir A. Conan Doyle, *The War in South Africa, its Cause and Conduct* (1902), a popular narrative from the British standpoint; J. A. Hobson, *War in South Africa, its Causes and Effects* (1900), an Englishman's bitter indictment of the policy of his own government; L. S. Amery (editor), *The Times History of the War in South Africa, 1899–1902*, 7 vols. (1900–1909), the most detailed account; *Briton and Boer: Both Sides of the South African Question* (1900), an interesting collection of papers by James (Viscount) Bryce, Sydney Brooks, and other eminent persons; *The Memoirs of Paul Kruger, Four Times President of the South African Republic, Told by Himself*, ed. by A. Schowalter, and Eng. trans. by A. Teixeira de Mattos (1902). For a more complete bibliography of the Boer War, consult the *American Historical Review*, Vol. XII, pp. 299–321.

Special Works on India. Sir T. W. Holderness, *Peoples and Problems of India* (1912), an excellent brief treatise in the "Home University Library "; Sir Henry J. S. Cotton, *New India* (1907); Sir J. B. Fuller, *The Empire of India* (1913); *Cambridge Modern History*, Vol. XII (1910), ch. xvi, a summary of political and military events since 1870, written by P. E. Roberts; *Cambridge History of India*, projected (1916) in 6 vols.; *The Imperial Gazetteer of India*, 3d ed., 26 vols. (1907–1909), a comprehensive survey of all Indian interests, the coöperative work of a number of specialists; Ramsay Muir, *The Making of British India* (1915), covering the years 1775–1858, mostly documentary; D. C. Boulger, *India in the Nineteenth Century* (1901); F. S. (Earl) Roberts, *Forty-one Years in India: from Subaltern to Commander-in-Chief*, 29th ed. (1898); G. W. Forrest, *History of the Indian Mutiny, reviewed and illustrated from Original Documents*, 3 vols. (1904–1912), full and accurate, but dry and poorly arranged; McLeod Innes, *Sepoy Revolt, a Critical Narrative*, 2d ed. (1897), brief and clear; Sir J. W. Kaye, *History of the Sepoy War, 1857–1858*, completed by G. B. Malleson, 3 vols. (1879–1880), a standard work; Sir John Strachey, *India: its Administration and Progress*, 3d ed. (1903), an official account and apology; Sir Courtney Ilbert, *The Government of India*, 3d ed. (1915), an authoritative digest of the constitutional law with historical introduction and valuable comments; Panchanandas Mukherji (editor), *Indian Constitutional Documents, 1773–1915* (1915); R. C. Dutt, *Economic History of British India, 1757–1837* (1902); Sir Theodore Morison, *The Economic Transition in India* (1911); William Digby, ' *Prosperous* ' *British India: a Revelation from Official Records* (1901), a bitter arraignment of British rule in India; Lovat Fraser, *India under Curzon and After* (1911), an important contribution to recent Indian history.

Special Works on Egypt. Earl of Cromer, *Modern Egypt*, 2 vols. (1908), a masterly exposition of Egyptian history and problems since 1876 by a scholar who was the British official representative in Egypt for 27 years; A. E. P. B. Weigall, *A History of Events in Egypt from 1798 to 1914* (1915); Edward Dicey, *Story of the Khedivate* (1902), and, by the same author, *Egypt of the Future* (1906), popular accounts; G. W. Steevens, *With Kitchener to Khartum*, 4th ed. (1898); W. S. Blunt, *Secret History of the English Occupation of Egypt* (1907), and, by the same author, a severe critic of British rule, *Gordon at Khartoum* (1911).

Special Works on Malaysia. Sir F. A. Swettenham, *British Malaya: an Account of the Origin and Progress of British Influence in Malaya* (1907); Arnold Wright and T. H. Reid, *The Malay Peninsula: a Record of British Progress in the Middle East* (1912).

CHAPTER XXX

INTERNATIONAL RELATIONS (1871–1914) AND THE OUTBREAK
OF THE WAR OF THE NATIONS

THE CONCERT OF EUROPE

PEACE — international and permanent — became an ideal of many distinguished statesmen of the nineteenth century whether Liberals or Reactionaries. Had all Europeans been devout adherents of the Catholic Church, it might have been possible to have realized that ideal under the guidance of the pope, for the Catholic Church was always preaching the doctrine of "peace on earth to men of good will," but the disruption of the Church in the sixteenth century, to say nothing of the defection of the Eastern Christians in earlier ages, prevented the pope in the nineteenth century from maintaining universal peace. Or, had all civilized men been under the temporal authority of a single sovereign, such as a Roman emperor, a real *Pax Romana* might have been revived, but with the long decline and final extinction in 1806 of the Holy Roman Empire, the last state that even vaguely laid claim to universal secular predominance, hope of peace by means of an international empire vanished.

Inability of Church or Empire to Secure Peace

What the Catholic Church and the Holy Roman Empire failed to do, the Tsar Alexander I and his fellow monarchs sought to achieve by means of the European agreements framed at the time of the downfall of Napoleon, in the early part of the nineteenth century. These agreements constituted a "Concert of Europe," which formally recognized that the various nations of Europe were united as one family by ties of religion, institutions, and culture, and which solemnly pledged its members to the preservation of "public peace, the tranquillity of states, the inviolability of possessions, and the faith of treaties." The "Concert of Europe" in theory embraced all the Christian

"The Concert of Europe": an Attempt to Secure Peace by Coöperation of Sovereign States

states of the entire Continent, but in practice it was dominated and directed by five Great Powers — Austria, Russia, Prussia, Great Britain, and France. How the Concert of Europe operated from 1815 to 1830 has been related in an earlier chapter [1] and likewise how it came to grief through British secession and through its own inability to reconcile the principles of international peace and the sanctity of treaties with the maintenance of order and tranquillity within the several sovereign states.

The "Great Powers"

Despite the rather early lapse of the formal agreements upon which the Concert of Europe was based, the idea of the Concert was never wholly lost. With greater, rather than with less, repugnance did rulers and peoples view the possibility of European war, especially the possibility of war between the Great Powers. On only four brief occasions in the whole century from 1815 to 1914 were wars actually fought by the Great Powers of Europe with one another: (1) Great Britain and France, on one side, against Russia, on the other (1854–1856); (2) France against Austria (1859); (3) Prussia against Austria (1866); and (4) Prussia against France (1870–1871). After the wars of 1866 and 1870, Germany naturally fell heir to Prussia's membership in the Concert of Great Powers, and new Italy became a sixth Great Power. Early in the twentieth century the non-European nations of Japan and the United States, by reason of their growing importance in world politics, were accorded by most writers the honorary designation respectively of seventh and of eighth Great Power, and were admitted for many purposes to the counsels of the six Great Powers of Europe.

Permanence of the Idea, if not the Organization, of a Concert of Europe

Meanwhile the more or less informal Concert of Europe was performing valuable service in crystallizing international solidarity and in seeking to prevent war or to alleviate its miseries. Thus the representatives of the Great Powers and of Turkey, assembled in the Congress of Paris to conclude the Crimean War, signed the so-called Declaration of Paris (1856) for the protection of neutral trade in times of war. The Declaration, which was subsequently adopted by

Services of the Concert of Europe

[1] See above, ch. xvii, especially pp. 10–14, 46–57.

most civilized governments,[1] consecrated the following principles:
" 1. Privateering is and remains abolished; 2. The neutral flag
covers enemy's goods, with the exception of contra- Declaration
band of war; 3. Neutral goods, with the exception of of Paris,
contraband of war, are not liable to capture under 1856
the enemy's flag; 4. Blockades, in order to be binding, must
be effective, that is to say, maintained by a force sufficient really
to prevent access to the coast of the enemy."

In 1864 the Great Powers signed a Convention at Geneva,
Switzerland, by the terms of which, subject to certain regulations,
not only wounded soldiers in the field but also the offi- The Geneva
cial staff of ambulances and their equipment were Convention
rendered neutral, the former, therefore, no longer being and the Red
liable to be retained as prisoners of war, nor the latter Cross
to be taken as prize of war. For the execution of the Geneva
Convention, an International Red Cross Society was organized,
with headquarters at Geneva, with branches in all European
countries, and with an international flag — the Swiss flag with
colors reversed. In 1882, largely through the enthusiasm
and energy of Clara Barton, a distinguished American philanthropist, the United States ratified the Geneva Convention; and
later both Turkey and Japan established local branches of the
Red Cross Society, though under flags slightly modified so as to
satisfy the religious scruples of their non-Christian inhabitants.

In 1878 the principle of the Concert of Europe was invoked
in order to prevent the Russo-Turkish War from precipitating
a much vaster struggle, in which Great Britain and The Con-
Austria-Hungary might easily have become involved. gress of
The resulting Congress of Berlin,[2] attended by diplo- Berlin
mats of the Great Powers and of Turkey, effected a the Concert
compromise between conflicting national interests in the Near
and exercised a sort of joint oversight of the domestic East
affairs of Turkey, Greece, and the Balkan states. From 1878
to 1914 the Concert of Europe managed to maintain some sem-

---

[1] All maritime states of any importance, except the United States and Spain,
acceded to the Declaration of Paris. Even Spain acceded to the Declaration in
1907, and the United States acquiesced in a Hague Convention of 1907 which was
of the same general tenor.

[2] See above, pp. 505 ff.

blance of harmony in dealing with successive phases of the Near
Eastern Question.   In 1885 Austria-Hungary was allowed to put
a stop to Bulgarian aggression against Serbia.   In 1897 the Great
Powers arrested Turkish aggression against Greece; and at the
same time Russia, Great Britain, France, and Italy coöperated
to secure autonomy for Crete under their common protection.
Repeatedly the Great Powers acted together in presenting protests to the sultan against massacres of Christians, in pressing
upon him demands for internal reforms, and in collecting debts
from him or obtaining financial concessions.   It was under the
auspices of the European Concert of Great Powers that the Balkan
states drew up their treaty with Turkey at London in 1913 and
that the autonomous principality of Albania was erected.

Southeastern Europe was not the only field of concerted action
by the Great Powers.   In central Africa the Congo Free State

**The Con-
cert in
Africa and
Asia**

was organized in the 'eighties under joint guarantees.
In China, troops of Russia, Germany, France, Great
Britain, and Italy coöperated in 1900 with those of
Japan and the United States to suppress the Boxer
insurrection;[1]   and subsequently the Great Powers arranged
among themselves "spheres" of economic interest in eastern
and central Asia.

It should be remembered that these examples of international
accord on the part of the Concert of Europe were but a token of

**Growth of
Popular In-
ternation-
alism**

a very deep popular interest in international solidarity.   As the nineteenth century advanced and the
Industrial Revolution progressed and the most different nationalities and the most diverse localities were
knit together by railways, steamships, telegraphs, and cables,
the number and importance of international undertakings
rapidly increased.   There was the prodigious increase of foreign
travel and foreign trade.   There was the remarkable growth of
science and popular education, restricted to no one land and to
no one nation.   There was the marked tendency everywhere to
adopt uniform standards of clothing, food, and architecture, as
well as of literature, science, and politics.   There was the multiplication of international societies and congresses.   Thirty
nations formed the Universal Telegraph Union (1875); twenty-

[1] See above, pp. 574 f.

three adopted a convention regarding the common use of the metric system of weights and measures (1875); sixty adhered to the Universal Postal Union, which was formed in 1878, with headquarters at Bern in Switzerland; five joined the Latin Monetary Union (1865) for the regulation of an interchangeable coinage for the countries of Latin Europe; twenty ratified the Bern Convention of 1883 for the standardizing of patent laws; and twelve signed the Bern Convention of 1887 providing for practically uniform copyright laws.

The international character of the problems and interests of workingmen throughout the world was stressed not only by the International Congresses of the Socialists, but also by international organizations of the several coöperative societies and of trade unions. Similarly, earnest advocates of democracy organized the International Parliamentary Union (1889), and agitators of woman suffrage and feminism held international women's congresses. Religion felt the general impulse : Protestant Christians of a hundred divergent creeds and of a thousand shades of individual opinion met in world congresses and made amicable agreements for the parceling out of heathen lands among their several local bodies for missionary purposes; among the Roman Catholics a series of annual Eucharistic Congresses was instituted in 1881 and drew large numbers of clergymen and laymen now to Paris, now to London, now to Jerusalem, now to Montreal; even a World's Parliament of Religions was projected and actually convened. For the advancement of learning there were periodical world conventions of distinguished physicists, chemists, biologists, historians, and economists; there were "exchange professors" between the universities of different countries; there was developing around the globe a community of intellectual interests, the product of what a distinguished American scholar has termed "the international mind."

It was natural under these circumstances that to many thoughtful persons the idea of war between nations should seem intolerable. An English Peace Society was organized as **Growth of** early as 1816 and an American Peace Society — a **Popular** national federation of local and state societies — as **Pacifism** early as 1828. The first peace society on the continent of Europe was founded at Geneva in 1828 and the second at Paris in 1841. Thenceforth, especially after 1878, the number of peace societies increased steadily, until in 1914 there were about 160 with many branches and large membership. International Peace Congresses, assembling intermittently and spasmodically between 1843 and 1889, became regular annual events after the latter date, and in 1891 permanent headquarters of the international peace movement were established at Bern. Philanthropic gentlemen throughout the world, such as the Swedish Alfred Nobel,[1] and the Scotch-American Andrew Carnegie,[2] the Frenchman Baron D'Estournelles de Constant,[3] and the Russian Count Leo Tolstoy,[4] freely gave pen or purse to the propaganda of pacifism. A host of pacifists arose, denouncing war as a relic of barbarism, immoral, un-Christian, and inimical to modern culture, to sound economics and sound politics. To the new generation of pacifists, with which the twentieth century opened, it appeared that war was a thing of the past: the capitalists of

Anti-Militarism

every country had too many foreign investments or too much foreign commerce to allow their governments to precipitate war; the laboring classes had too much to lose from a state of war in the way of employment and wages, and, moreover, many of them were identified with international Socialism; the intellectual classes were too "enlightened" and too internationally minded not to perceive the fallacies in all arguments and pretexts for war; the Christian bodies were traditionally committed to the inculcation of the principle of universal peace.

It was, therefore, the pacifists who backed the Concert of Europe in its efforts to prevent war or to mitigate its horrors. It was the pacifists who encouraged and lauded the newer tend-

[1] Alfred Bernhard Nobel (1833–1896) was a chemist and engineer, whose invention of dynamite, cordite, and other high explosives enabled him to amass an immense fortune, the bulk of which he left in trust for the establishment of five prizes, each worth a goodly sum and awarded annually without distinction of nationality; the first three of these prizes are for eminence in science, the fourth for excellence in idealistic literature, and the fifth for the greatest service to the cause of international peace.

[2] Andrew Carnegie (1837–   ) drew liberally upon the fortune that he had accumulated in the iron and steel business in order to endow peace societies and to build a Temple of Peace at the Hague and a Pan-American Palace at Washington.

[3] Born in 1852, a Senator of the French Republic, and a prominent publicist in behalf of peace.

[4] The famous novelist and social reformer (1828–1910).

encies of nations to submit their quarrels to international arbitration. Repeatedly Great Britain and the United States showed their willingness to arbitrate their disputes, as in the Inter-case of the Alabama claims (1871–1872), of the Bering national Arbitration Sea controversy (1892), and of the Alaskan boundary (1903), with such success that there seemed to be no need of fortifications along the Canadian frontier and the possibility of war between the two great English-speaking countries appeared more and more remote. To mention but a few of the many cases of international arbitration, — the pope successfully arbitrated a colonial controversy between Germany and Spain (1886) ; Germany, Great Britain, and the United States amicably composed their differences in Samoa (1899) ; Argentina and Chile submitted their long-standing boundary dispute to the arbitration of the British king, who gave judgment in 1902 ; France and Germany settled the Moroccan crisis of 1909 by arbitration.

At the same time the pacifists had to face the fact that since 1860 there had been an astounding growth of military and naval armaments in almost every nation. Of course Opposition most advocates of national armament, themselves in- to Heavy fluenced by the pacific spirit of the age, insisted that Armaments such armaments were strictly defensive, that they constituted mere preparedness against dreadful but possible eventualities and were the surest and safest pledge of lasting peace. Nevertheless, foremost pacifists scented danger in military and naval "preparedness," and other persons who were not professionally pacific complained of the growing burdens of taxation which this "peace insurance" policy necessitated. A conspicuous plank in the pacifist platform, therefore, was the demand for the limitation of armaments by international agreement, coupled with the plea for the establishment of an international court of arbitration. Such a program seemed capable of realization in the light of the increasingly pacific mutual relations of the republics on the American continents, especially after the inauguration of the series of Pan-American Conferences (1889). And such a program appealed strongly to various European statesmen, harassed by the constant necessity of providing funds to maintain the positions of their respective nations in the fiercely competitive race of armaments.

In August, 1898, the Tsar Nicholas II of Russia, imitating the pacifist sentiments of the Tsar Alexander I, addressed a famous rescript to all independent and sovereign states
The First Hague Peace Conference, 1899
of Europe and Asia and to the United States and Mexico, inviting them, with the concurrence of Queen Wilhelmina of Holland, to send representatives to The Hague in the following year in order to promote in-
ternational peace. In January, 1899, the tsar's government defined the object of the proposed conference as an attempt to arrive at an "understanding not to increase for a fixed period the present effectives of the armed military and naval forces, and at the same time not to increase the budgets pertaining thereto; and a preliminary examination of the means by which even a reduction might be effected in future in the forces and budgets above mentioned." The conference, known as the First Hague Conference, was attended by representatives of twenty-six states — 20 European, 4 Asiatic, and 2 American — and sat from 18 May to 29 July, 1899. The Conference was important in two ways. First, it showed that the pacifists were mistaken in supposing that all governments were opposed to militarism; apparently the spirit of national and racial rivalry was still much stronger than the consciousness of common interests; and the determined attitude of several delegates, notably those of Germany, blocked every attempt of the Conference to arrive at an understanding regarding the limitation of armaments. Secondly, the Conference did achieve some noteworthy results, though of less immediate importance. It established a regular tribunal at The Hague to which international disputes might be referred for adjudication. It directed a systematic codification of the laws and customs of war. It adapted the principles of the Geneva Convention of 1864 to the newer possibilities of maritime warfare. Moreover, some — but not all — of the Powers represented in the Conference signed promises that in warfare they would not use asphyxiating gases or poisoned bullets or bullets ("dumdum") which inflict needlessly torturing wounds, and that they would not launch projectiles and explosives from balloons.

In 1907, upon the suggestion of President Roosevelt of the United States and the formal invitation of the Tsar Nicholas II, a Second Peace Conference was held at The Hague, this time representing forty-four states, including nineteen American.   Again it was impossible to reach any sort of agreement on the much-mooted question of the limitation of armaments, but many humane amendments were made to the laws of maritime and land war, an international prize court was provided for, and conventions were adopted requir- *The Second Hague Peace Con- ference, 1907* ing a formal declaration of war before the opening of hostilities and restricting the employment of force for the recovery of for-eign debts.   Finally, the Conference recommended to the Powers the convocation of a Third Peace Conference.

It began to look to optimistically minded pacifists as if here was a real beginning of an organized international state, with its capitol in The Hague, with its regular congresses, with its statutes and codes, with its permanent court of arbitration.   If the German Empire, the United *The Pacifist Ideal* States, and Switzerland were successes as federal states, why should not an International Federation of the World be practical and successful?   Certainly, the Hague Conferences did a good deal to strengthen public opinion in favor of peaceful methods in the solution of international problems.   The court of arbitration was duly instituted, and to it were referred between 1901 and 1914 for peaceful adjustment several misunderstandings which a hundred years earlier would assuredly have led to war.

But the view of the pacifists was too roseate.   They saw the first flushes of a glorious dawn of human justice and universal peace and failed to perceive the long gruesome shadows which stretched close to them from a miserable mass of earthly obstructions athwart that dawn.   The chief *Obstacles to Inter- national Pacifism* obstacles to the full realization of the pacifists' pro-gram were five in number.   The first was the stubborn and persistent growth of the spirit of nationalism — the notion that people speaking the same language and sharing the same general customs should be politically united as nations, — a growth not arrested in the nineteenth century, when Germany or Italy was unified, but continuing in the twentieth century, by means of literature and public *1. Intense Nationalism and Uncriti- cal Patriot- ism* school systems, to affect French, English, Norwegians, Greeks, Serbs, Poles, Irish, Czechs, and many other nationalities, great and small.   Nationalism emphasized what was peculiar to a given people rather than what was common to all peoples. It was exclusive rather than inclusive. And when nationalism was embodied in a state, it usually gave rise to a dogmatic patriotism which rendered such a state not only intolerant of any diminution of its internal authority but extremely jealous of external encroachments upon its sovereignty. The national state was becoming an end in itself, and for the old adage that "the king can do no wrong" was being substituted the popular belief that "the state can do no wrong." Many a patriot talked about "rights," "dignity," and "honor," just as duelists used to talk; and it is unnecessary to point out the incompatibility of such language with the principle of compulsory arbitration of international disputes.

Secondly, there was the survival from earlier times of grave territorial questions, which could hardly be submitted to peaceful arbitration. Such was the question of Alsace-Lorraine, the provinces which had been wrested from France by German prowess in 1871, which Frenchmen demanded back, and which Germans would not think of restoring. Such, too, was the question of the reëstablishment of an independent or autonomous Poland, ardently longed for by all Polish patriots, but bound to produce the gravest consequence to the interrelations of Russia, Germany, and Austria. Such, likewise, was the question of the dismemberment of the Ottoman Empire, for the traditional interests of the Great Powers were notoriously at variance with one another and also with the national sentiments of the Balkan peoples. Such, finally, was the question of the disposal, on some national basis, of the heterogeneous population of the Dual Monarchy of Austria-Hungary. There was hardly a single Power, great or small, which was not vitally concerned in the solution of some territorial problem.

2. Survival of Grave Territorial Problems

Thirdly, the rivalries of sovereign states, inspired by the sentiment of nationalism and intensified by material questions of territorial boundaries, were rendered even more acute by the agitation of interested capitalists and business-men, who demanded and received from their several national governments protection for their foreign trade and foreign investments, or who loaned money to their governments, or who, like the Krupps in Ger-

3. Militaristic Agitation of Particular Classes

many or the Armstrongs in Great Britain or the Schneiders in France or the Du Ponts in the United States, manufactured munitions of war. It was the ambition and to the personal advantage of these able and influential citizens to make their several national states powerful enough to inspire fear and respect at home and abroad.

Out of the foregoing obstacles to pacifist propaganda proceeded a fourth obstacle — the prevalence of militarism. Prussia, always a military state *par excellence*, had set a new pace in land armaments in 1862, when, thanks largely to King William I and Bismarck, she introduced compulsory military service for every able-bodied male citizen. The success of the new Prussian military machine in effecting the political unification of Germany between 1866 and 1871 not only convinced Germans that the preservation of their national union depended upon the continuance of the principle of compulsory military training and accordingly saddled the German Empire from 1871 to 1914 with an ever-growing burden of armaments, but also helped to impress like convictions and like practices upon most Great Powers and upon many lesser states. Austria-Hungary followed the German example in 1868, France in 1872, Japan in 1873, Russia in 1874, and Italy in 1875. What Germany did for militarism on land, Great Britain did for navalism. Great Britain, long the foremost maritime Power, did not introduce conscription or maintain a large standing army, but she built an enormous fleet, larger than any two other navies put together. Gradually other Powers strove to imitate the British example on the high seas, and even the United States entered into the competition, until in 1914 the American navy ranked close to Germany's and ahead of the French and Japanese. The new militarism was represented by statesmen and publicists as making for peace — "national defense" — but it certainly rendered the diplomatists of the Great Powers more truculent in asserting the claims of their nations to a lion's share in the spoils of the world; it fed the spirit of nationalism and encouraged the activities of parasitic manufacturers of military supplies; and it produced a whole crop of professional militarists — many of them military officers or ex-officers — who by pointing out the armed strength of their nation's neighbors

4. Rapid Growth of National Armaments after 1862

"National Defense"

caused alarm and apprehension at home, and at the same time by bellicose utterances and by confident references to "the next war" inspired distrust and hostility abroad.

Finally came numerous philosophers, scientists, poets, historians, and sociologists, who set forth an intellectual justification of nationalism and militarism. Gradually they took over the scientific hypothesis of evolution, which had been advanced by Darwin and popularized by Huxley and Spencer just about the time of the political unifications of Germany and Italy, and applied it not only properly to the field of biology but also improperly to the field of sociology, asserting that Spencer's fine phrase of "the survival of the fittest" was particularly applicable to the rise of *nations*. Militarists were not slow to utilize a supposedly scientific doctrine that was enunciated by scholars and that was sure to secure a large following among the ignorant and half-educated masses in an age in which "science" was fast becoming a popular fetish. Prominent European militarists, with the authority of their newly discovered philosophy, commenced to talk less of the defensive character of armaments and more of "the struggle for existence" and of the advantages, nay the downright necessity, of waging war. Persons in Great Britain, in France, in Italy, in Russia, even in the United States, preached a cult of war — a veritable religion of valor — but it was reserved to a retired German cavalry-general[1] in 1912 to state most clearly the militarist's conception of war in the light of the new philosophy and science. "'War is the father of all things,'" he quoted, and then went on to say, "The sages of antiquity long before Darwin recognized this. The struggle for existence is, in the life of Nature, the basis of all healthy development. All existing things show themselves to be the result of contesting forces. So in the life of man the struggle is not merely the destructive, but the life-giving, principle. . . . War gives a biologically just decision. . . . The knowledge, therefore, that war depends on biological laws leads to the conclusion that every attempt to

5. "Scientific" Justifications of Nationalism and Militarism

[1] General Friedrich von Bernhardi (1849-   ), whose book *Germany and the Next War*, though by no means representative of the opinion of all classes in Germany, attracted much attention abroad as the work of a conspicuous member of that military caste which seemed to be urging Germany to war.

exclude it from international relations must be demonstrably untenable. But it is not only a biological law, but a moral obligation, and, as such, an indispensable factor in civilization." Thus modern science, with the manifold and unquestionable blessings which it has conferred upon the world, contributed directly to raising a fifth and peculiarly fateful obstacle to pacifism. Even the intellectual classes now fell to quarreling as to the biological necessity of war, and while they quarreled real war of proportions hitherto undreamed of was preparing. The Concert of Europe was passing from a practicality to an ideal, and from an ideal to a memory.

In order to understand the immediate causes of the Great War of the Nations, which in 1914 destroyed at least temporarily even the semblance of a Concert of Europe, and to appreciate the alignment of the Great Powers in the war and the questions at stake, it is necessary at this point to turn aside from our review of the development of pacifism and militarism and to take up in chronological order the shifting diplomatic history of *Menace to the Concert of Europe in Diplomatic Developments, 1871–1914* the Great Powers of Europe from 1871 to 1914. During approximately half of this period, the chief interest of international politics centered in the hegemony of Germany; during the second half of the period it was divided between two rival alliances which managed to maintain a more or less precarious "balance of power."

THE HEGEMONY OF GERMANY, 1871–1890

The Franco-German War of 1870–1871 was the starting-point of a new era in European diplomacy. Great Britain, it is true, was not directly or immediately affected by the war: she continued to hold her position as the chief commercial, colonial, and industrial Power in the world; and the prestige and overwhelming numerical supremacy of her navy still guaranteed her that proud title of "mistress of the seas" which she had won for herself in the long series of maritime wars against Spaniards, Dutch, and Frenchmen. But on the Continent the war had far-reaching consequences. France was abased. Germany was united and exalted. In fact, *After 1870 Great Britain Remains Chief Maritime Power* *Germany Becomes Chief Military Power* from the very moment of its birth the German Empire was the strongest military state in the world.

Bismarck, who served as chancellor and foreign secretary of the German Empire from 1871 to 1890, was undoubtedly the leading statesman and diplomat of Europe through-

Bismarck's Foreign Policy, 1871–1890

out those twenty years. His international policy, in its broad outlines, was simple : he would maintain and develop the military superiority of his country; he would preserve what had been won in the wars of 1866 and 1870–1871, but he would oppose further German conquests ; he would resist any German aggrandizement in southeastern Europe which might arouse the hostility of Russia, or outside of Europe which might provoke colonial and maritime rivalry with Great Britain ; he would keep the peace and he would compel France to keep the peace.

France was the one country which Bismarck could afford to fear. In France the popular feeling for a war of revenge against

The Necessity of "Isolating" France

Germany was particularly acute in the years immediately following the disastrous events of 1870–1871 ; and Bismarck was amazed at the rapidity with which the French paid off the enormous war indemnity that he had imposed on them, and at the zeal with which they reformed their army, erected powerful new fortifications, and introduced compulsory military service. It was not that Bismarck feared an attack upon Germany by France single-handed, for the relative population of Germany was steadily increasing while that of France was waning, but he did clearly perceive the possible dangers to the newly created German Empire of a war of revenge waged by France with the active assistance of one or more Great Powers. In the war of 1870–1871, despite lack of efficient leadership and organization, the French had fought valiantly and stubbornly, but they had fought alone. Were they in the future to secure military support from Russia, or Austria-Hungary, or Italy, the outcome of a second Franco-German War might be quite different from the first.

So Bismarck, to prevent a French war of revenge, set out to isolate France diplomatically, to deprive her of potential allies and supporters. And so long as he remained chancellor, success invariably attended German diplomacy. The international situation from 1871 to 1890 was peculiarly favorable to Germany, and the astute, and not too high-principled, chancellor took full advantage of it.   First of all, he adopted a most con- *The Means* ciliatory attitude toward Austria-Hungary.   He had *of Isolating* purposely been lenient in dictating terms of peace to *France* the Habsburg emperor in 1866; and now after 1871 the internal exigencies of the Dual Monarchy, and the desire of the Habsburg family to recoup their losses in Italy and *Bismarck's* in Germany by means of a vigorous policy in the *Conciliation* Balkans, caused the governing classes of Austria-Hun- *of Austria-Hungary* gary to lean more and more heavily upon the strong military arm of Germany and the dexterous diplomatic hand of Bismarck.   Then, too, Bismarck could count upon the friendship of the newly formed kingdom of Italy.   Many Italians had not forgotten how the French left them in the lurch in the *Italy* campaign of 1859, and all Italians remembered that it was through an alliance with Bismarck's Germany that their kingdom had been able to wrest Venetia from Austria in 1866. Moreover, Italy had a bitter quarrel with the papacy, and so did Germany in the 'seventies — the *Kulturkampf*, — while France throughout that decade was governed by Clericals, many of whom declared it a national French duty to intervene in Italy for the purpose of restoring the temporal rule of the pope.   Under these circumstances the Italian government was naturally inclined in foreign relations to favor Germany rather than France.

In respect of Great Britain, Bismarck was quite willing to let well enough alone.   He was aware of the spasm of jealousy that passed through English newspapers and periodi- *Great* cals as the result of the unexpectedly sudden emergence *Britain* of Germany as a Great Power, but he sedulously avoided giving offense to British susceptibilities.   He insisted during the war of 1870–1871 upon the scrupulous observance of Belgian neutrality — an object always dear to the British foreign office, — and he long opposed the entrance of Germany into the domain of colonialism [1] — a domain always considered by the British public to be their own private sphere.   He knew that Great

---

[1] In the 'eighties Bismarck yielded to the entreaties of German imperialists and patronized the acquisition of colonies for Germany, though always seeking to avoid quarrels with Great Britain.   See above, pp. 412, 621 ff.

Britain had constantly recurring quarrels with Russia over the Near Eastern Question and over their respective imperialistic policies in Asia, and likewise with France over commercial relations and over colonial expansion in Africa and Indo-China. He knew that the British Liberals were much interested in Italy : in its Liberal politics and its conflict with the Catholic Church and in the opportunities it offered to British trade and investment.   He knew that many English professors admired the German people and extolled the "Teutonic race" that had produced the two leading states of modern Europe — Germany, the master of the Continent, and Great Britain, the mistress of the seas. He knew that it was a tradition of the British foreign office to avoid entangling alliances upon the continent of Europe so long as British maritime supremacy was unquestioned.   From all this knowledge Bismarck convinced himself that Germany need not fear an alliance between Great Britain and France.

Russia was more doubtful.   Just as France had striven for northeastern expansion, so Russia had sought southwestern extension; and now the erection of a powerful military **Russia** state in intervening Germany placed an effective check upon French and Russian policies alike.   Bismarck perceived that the new international situation created by the establishment of the German Empire rendered Russia a natural ally of France in any attempt to weaken that empire.   But several circumstances enabled the clever German chancellor to forestall a Franco-Russian alliance.   Politically, autocratic Russia had much more in common with conservative Germany than with republican and revolutionary France.   Alexander II, the Russian tsar (1855–1881), was mortally afraid of Nihilists and Anarchists and Socialists, who were reputed to have learned their doctrines in France; and he remembered with all the gratitude of a sentimental soul how Bismarck had offered him Prussian aid for the suppression of the Polish insurrection of 1863,[1] and how again in 1871 Bismarck had graciously acquiesced in his high-handed recovery of the right to maintain a Russian battle-fleet on the Black Sea.[2]   Russia felt the need of German support to achieve her ambition in the Balkans and to overcome British opposition to the expansion of her Asiatic empire.

[1] See above, pp. 188, 456 f.   [2] See above, p. 204.

Of these factors Bismarck took canny account. And in September, 1872, a meeting at Berlin of the Emperor William I, the Emperor-King Francis Joseph, the Tsar Alexander II, and their several ministers, served to announce to the world the intimate and cordial relations existing between Germany, Austria-Hungary, and Russia. Though no formal treaty of alliance appears to have been concluded, the members of this so-called "Three Emperors' League" held frequent conferences between 1872 and 1876 and repeatedly expressed sentiments of devotion to one another. In 1875 the members of the German general staff, especially Moltke, took fright at the military increases in France and demanded that Germany at once make war upon France before the French increases should become effective, but Bismarck dismissed their importunities with a sneer. French publicists and one distinguished Russian diplomat insisted that Bismarck himself had been dissuaded from attacking France only by Russian threats, but this was emphatically denied by Bismarck. At any rate the "Affair of 1875" made no appreciable ripple on the serene surface of the Three Emperors' League.

The Three Emperors' League, 1872

A more serious difficulty for Bismarck's diplomacy was presented by the Russo-Turkish War of 1877–1878. The triumph of Russia and her seeming ability to dictate a settlement of the Balkan Question provoked the liveliest apprehension in Austria-Hungary as well as in Great Britain, and at the ensuing Congress of Berlin (1878) Bismarck undertook to play the rôle of "honest broker" in apportioning the Turkish spoils.[1] By reducing the Russian share and by handing over Bosnia-Herzegovina to the Dual Monarchy, Bismarck kept the balance of power in the Balkans nicely adjusted between Russia and Austria-Hungary, and thereby he aroused the enmity of Russia while he strengthened the friendship of Austria-Hungary. The Three Emperors' League was imperiled.

The Congress of Berlin (1878) and Temporary Waning of Russo-German Friendship

In order to guard Germany against untoward results of Russian ill-feeling, Bismarck in October, 1879, concluded a formal though secret treaty of defensive alliance[2] between Austria-Hungary

---

[1] On the Russo-Turkish War and the Congress of Berlin, see above, pp. 504 ff.
[2] The treaty, concluded in 1879, was not published until 1888.

and Germany, in accordance with the terms of which each

Defensive party bound itself to support the other with all the
Alliance military forces at its command if either party or
between both should be attacked by Russia or by another
Germany
and Austria- Power backed by Russia.
Hungary,
1879   Then, in order still further to offset the threatened
          defection of Russia from the Three Emperors' League,
Bismarck turned his attention to Italy. Italy, as has been remarked, was already naturally well disposed toward Germany,

Italian but she was traditionally hostile to Austria-Hungary,
Hostility and it seemed an almost impossible task to bring her
to France into close alliance with the two Teutonic states so long
as the Italian-speaking communities of Trent and Triest remained
subject to the Habsburg emperor and so long as Italy and the
Dual Monarchy entertained rival ambitions of mastery in the
Adriatic and in Albania. Nevertheless, the Italian government
was fearful of the effects of the internationally isolated position
of their country and anxious to prevent foreign intervention
in behalf of the pope; and in 1881 the Italian people were
astounded and angered by French occupation of Tunis, the region of ancient Carthage, just across from Sicily, which patriots
had marked as the most appropriate field for Italian imperialism.[1] In the midst of the Franco-Italian quarrel, Italy responded
cordially to the overtures of Bismarck, agreed to banish
anti-Austrian propaganda, and in May, 1882, signed secret
treaties of alliance with Germany and with Austria-Hungary.
          These treaties created the famous Triple Alliance.

Formation Their terms have never been published in full, but it
of the Triple is safe to say that they were defensive in character,
Alliance
(1882): each party promising the others military assistance
Germany, against attacks by outside Powers, that they were
Austria- directed mainly against fears of French or Russian
Hungary,
and Italy aggression, and that they were binding for only a speci-
          fied term of years. The Triple Alliance, first formed
in 1882 for five years, was subsequently renewed for continuous
periods in 1887, in 1891, in 1902, and in 1912, lasting at least on
paper until May, 1915, when Italy denounced her alliance with
Austria-Hungary though still preserving the formal agreement

[1] See above, pp. 514, 629.

with Germany.   Certainly for a generation after 1882 the Triple
Alliance preserved the peace of central Europe and restrained
France from embarking on a war of revenge against Germany.
Bismarck considered it a diplomatic masterpiece.

In the meantime, relations between Germany and Russia
sensibly improved.   The assassination of the Tsar Alexander II
by Nihilists in 1881 and the accession of the ultra-
reactionary Alexander III precluded any immediate   Improved
understanding between Russia and democratic France.   Russo-
German
Meetings of the Three Emperors' League accordingly   Relations,
went on as before, and in 1884 Russia and Germany   1881–1890
actually concluded a secret three years' convention by which
they mutually promised a friendly neutrality in case one or the
other should be assailed.   Though difficulties in the Balkans
between Russia and Austria-Hungary in 1885–1886 [1] caused the
tsar to withdraw from the informal Three Emperors' League,
nevertheless Russia made no immediate advances to France
and in 1887 renewed her military convention with Germany
for another three years.   In fact, the tsar quite sternly frowned
upon the attempt of General Boulanger [2] in 1887–1888 to incite
the French people to undertake their long-heralded war of revenge
against Germany.

Thus between 1871 and 1890, by means of the Three Emperors'
League and the Triple Alliance, and thanks to the detached posi-
tion of Great Britain, Bismarck had been able to isolate
France diplomatically and to secure the hegemony of   Bismarck's
Germany in international politics.   Success

THE BALANCE OF POWER, 1890–1914

The date of Bismarck's retirement from office (1890) marked
a change in the international position of Germany.   Caprivi,
who succeeded him as imperial chancellor, did not   Reasons for
think it advisable to preserve the Three Emperors'   Lessened
League or to continue the special Russo-German con-   Friendship
between
vention.   He feared that Germany's freedom of ac-   Russia and
tion would be seriously restricted by her obligations,   Germany
on the one hand to Austria-Hungary and to Italy, and on the

[1] See above, pp. 520, 522.   [2] See above, pp. 352 f.

other hand to Russia, especially since the rivalry between Austria-Hungary and Russia was becoming ever more acute in the Balkans. He also feared that by supporting Russia, Germany would be dragged into colonial quarrels with Great· Britain.

The Russian government, likewise, was averse from continuing the friendly understanding with Germany. The decade of the

Formation of the Dual Alliance between Russia and France, 1891–1895 'nineties was characterized in Russian history [1] by the rapid growth of Pan-Slavism, the leading exponents of which, championed by the Tsars Alexander III and Nicholas II, were determined to purge "holy Russia" of Teutonic influence, and by the simultaneous development of the Industrial Revolution. Russian citizens both in public and in private life began now to borrow large sums of money from French capitalists in order to build railways, erect factories, or open mines. Financial needs gradually overcame Russian antipathy to the democratic politics of France, and little by little democratic France and autocratic Russia drifted into an alliance. A French squadron paid a visit to Cronstadt in 1891 : the tsar ordered the *Marseillaise* to be played, and listened to it standing. In 1893 a Russian squadron made a return visit at Toulon : the tsar and the president exchanged felicitous telegrams, the tsar referring to "the bonds that unite the two countries." In 1896 Nicholas II was received in Paris with much honor and rejoicing, and in 1897 the French president visited the tsar at Petrograd. Of the exact steps by which the friendship of the two nations was transformed into a defensive alliance between the two governments little is actually known, but it appears that a diplomatic protocol for an alliance was signed in 1891 and that a military convention was agreed upon in 1894. At any rate, in 1895 the French premier spoke publicly of an alliance existing between France and Russia. Though the precise terms of the so-called Dual Alliance have never been published, there is no doubt that close friendly relations were established between the two Powers and that in all important international affairs in Europe they sought to act in accord with each other. It is equally certain that for some years Russia was the predominant partner, and

---

[1] See above, pp. 460, 465–469, 473 f.

that, in accordance with the pacific tendencies of the tsar, she systematically exerted a restraining influence on France.

Thus, in the 'nineties, a sort of balance of power was substituted in international politics for the earlier hegemony of Germany and isolation of France. Henceforth, for several years, there were, on the one side, the Triple Alliance of Germany, Austria-Hungary, and Italy, and, on the other side, the Dual Alliance of Russia and France, with Great Britain inclined to pretty strict neutrality between the rival combinations. *Balance of Power between Triple and Dual Alliances*

As the 'nineties advanced, it became increasingly obvious that Germany could no longer count on any particularly friendly coöperation with Great Britain. The British government from 1895 to 1905 was controlled by the Conservative party, the party that traditionally extolled imperialism, a big navy, and a vigorous foreign policy. *Aloofness of Great Britain, 1890-1904* It was the time when the marquess of Salisbury, as foreign secretary, was furthering British colonial and economic interests throughout the world; when Joseph Chamberlain was carrying on his agitation within the United Kingdom for imperial expansion and federation; when Cecil Rhodes was engaged in colossal empire-building in Africa; when Rudyard Kipling, the priest and psalmist of the new dispensation, was chanting songs about "Tommy Atkins" and "The White Man's Burden." These British Conservatives and Imperialists took fright at the great growth of German industry and commerce in the 'eighties and 'nineties, a fright which the simultaneous emergence of Germany as a colonial Power naturally did not moderate.[1] Then, too, when Germany under the influence of Emperor William II began at the close of the nineteenth century to construct a large navy and *Reasons for Growing Rivalry between Great Britain and Germany* to compel Great Britain, if she was to maintain her maritime supremacy, to quicken her naval construction and enormously to increase her expenditure, the former amicable relations between Great Britain and Germany gave way to popular jealousy, recriminations, and fear. During the Boer War[2] (1899-1902) the British were especially aroused by the more or less

---

[1] On these aspects of German history, see above, pp. 421 ff.

[2] See above, p. 652.

open favor and sympathy which the emperor and official classes of Germany showed to the Boers. Thenceforth, despite constant efforts on the part of peace advocates both in Germany and in Great Britain, the two peoples drifted further and further apart. Too many Germans called England the "robber-state" and imputed to her government a desire to isolate Germany and to prevent Germany from exercising an influence in world politics. On the other hand, too many Englishmen suspected the German government of an ambition to rule the world and to oppose, as Spaniards, Dutch, and French in earlier centuries had tried to oppose, the maritime interests of Great Britain.

Nevertheless, the strained relations between Germany and Great Britain did not make at once for any special cordiality

Rivalry between Great Britain and Russia

between Great Britain and the Dual Alliance. One of the chief reasons why Russia had allied herself with France was a desire to secure French support in her almost incessant quarrels with Great Britain over the Ottoman Empire, Persia, Afghanistan, and the partition of China. In fact, it was against Russian aggression in

Formation of the Alliance between Great Britain and Japan, 1902

China, rather than against German ambitions, that Great Britain concluded in 1902 the defensive alliance with Japan.[1] Nor did any *rapprochement* seem possible between Great Britain and France. These two Powers were traditional rivals in commerce and industry; and the vigorous acquisition of colonies by the Third Republic since 1880 served to accentuate imperialistic

Rivalry between Great Britain and France

rivalry between them and to raise many serious territorial questions in Africa and in Indo-China. As late as 1898 France and Great Britain were on the verge of war over a dispute as to their respective spheres of influence in the Egyptian Sudan.[2]

Continental publicists were not lacking in 1899–1900 who advocated a grand alliance of Germany, Russia, and France — a welding of the Triple and Dual Alliances — in order to give aid to the Boers and to set limits to the further expansion of the British Empire; and there were rumors that the German gov-

[1] See above, p. 585. The Anglo-Japanese Alliance was strengthened in 1905, and renewed, with minor changes, in 1911.
[2] The so-called Fashoda Incident. See above, p. 624.

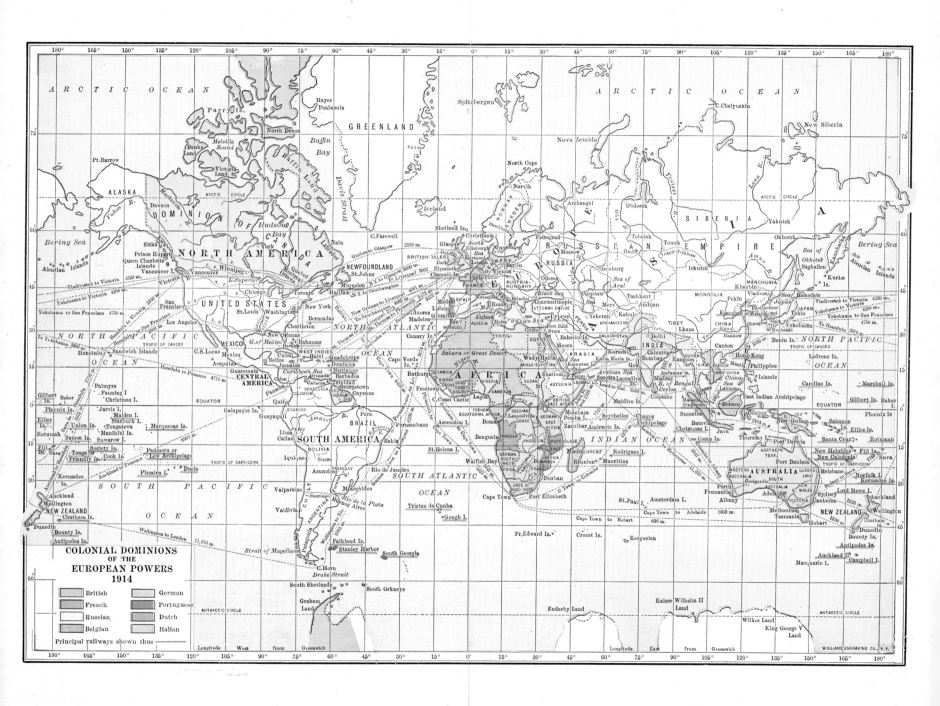

COLONIAL DOMINIONS
OF THE
EUROPEAN POWERS
1914

British
French
Russian
Belgian
German
Portuguese
Dutch
Italian

Principal railways shown thus ——

WILLIAMS ENGRAVING CO., N.Y.

ernment had opened negotiations looking toward such an end. Whatever may be the truth concerning the rumors, nothing came of them. Germany would not restore Alsace-Lorraine to France as the price even of a grand alliance against Great Britain, and without Alsace-Lorraine France would not listen to German proposals. Under these circumstances, Great Britain was enabled to reap the reward of her struggle with the Boers, but rightly or wrongly British ill-feeling was thenceforth directed rather against Germany than against France.

Impracticability of a Grand Alliance against Great Britain

At this point appeared on the stage of international politics a famous French statesman and diplomat, Théophile Delcassé, who, taking nice advantage of changed circumstances, became the guiding spirit between 1898 and 1907 in altering the balance of power and in effecting an isolation of Germany almost as complete as the isolation to which Bismarck formerly had condemned France. Delcassé proved himself a veritable Nemesis of Bismarck.

Delcassé the Nemesis of Bismarck

Théophile Delcassé was connected with the French colonial office from 1893 to 1898, and served as French minister of foreign affairs continuously from 1898 to 1905. In the former capacity he showed himself an ardent and able imperialist, and in the latter capacity a shrewd and far-sighted diplomatist. He was a warm friend of the Dual Alliance and always enjoyed the trust and respect of the tsar. He hated Germany with all the ardor of a French nationalist, and repudiated every suggestion of a possible Franco-German *rapprochement* so long as Alsace-Lorraine was held by Germany. To recover Alsace-Lorraine was the one great object of his diplomacy. To realize this ambition he believed that France would need the support, or at least friendly neutrality, of some Great Power in addition to Russia. Accordingly, while remaining most loyal to the Russian alliance, he adopted a conciliatory attitude toward Great Britain. Becoming foreign minister of France in the midst of the crisis in Franco-British relations occasioned by the Fashoda Incident, he promptly and courageously averted the danger of war by surrendering all French claims in the Egyptian Sudan to Great Britain. Then, taking advantage of the increasing strain in the relations between

His Diplomatic Work for France

Great Britain and Germany, he opened negotiations with Great Britain in 1903 for the settlement of all outstanding colonial and commercial disputes between the two Powers. His overtures were welcomed by the British government, especially
by King Edward VII, who incidentally was fond of Paris and whom Frenchmen liked, and resulted in the conclusion in April, 1904, of several conventions affecting Franco-British relations in Egypt, Morocco, Newfoundland, Siam, Nigeria, and the New Hebrides. These conventions not only gave Great Britain free rein in Egypt and France in Morocco, but marked the end of several centuries of intense colonial rivalry and paved the way for the development between 1904 and 1914 of particularly friendly relations between the peoples and governments of France and Great Britain, — the so-called *Entente Cordiale.*

Conclusion of the Entente Cordiale between France and Great Britain, 1904

The Franco-British *Entente*, as inaugurated in 1904, was not an alliance in the strict sense of the word, for there were no
formal promises of military or naval support ; but, by removing the causes of friction between the two countries, the conventions of 1904 made it possible for the British and French governments thenceforth to conduct their foreign policies in harmony. The Russo-Japanese War of 1904–1905 [1] put a severe strain on the *Entente* and on Delcassé's diplomacy, because it was a war between Russia, the ally of France, and Japan, the ally of Great Britain. But in fact the outcome of the war proved to be advantageous to the *Entente*. The defeat of Russia caused most Englishmen to lose their former fear and distrust of the Slavic Great Power, and increased the desire of the French to strengthen their foreign alliances. Consequently, in 1907, after Delcassé's
retirement from the French foreign office, though quite in accord with his policy, the British and Russian governments managed to arrive at a mutual understanding [2] concerning their disputed spheres of influence in Persia, Afghanistan, and China, and to sign conventions which practically transformed the *Entente Cordiale* between France and Great Britain into the Triple Entente between Russia, France, and Great Britain.

International Effects of the Russo-Japanese War, 1904–1905

Conclusion of the Triple Entente (1907): France, Russia, and Great Britain

[1] See above, pp. 583 ff.   [2] See above, pp. 589, 591.

Japan, also, was brought into harmonious relations with the Entente Powers, not only by means of the renewal in 1911 of the treaty of alliance between Japan and Great Britain, but also by means of the amicable Russo-Japanese convention of 1910 respecting Manchuria.[1] *Japan's Agreement with the Triple Entente*

One other diplomatic policy of Delcassé's deserves mention — the policy of reconciling French foreign interests with those of Spain and Italy. The astute French foreign minister negotiated with the Spanish government the delimitation of Franco-Spanish spheres of influence in Morocco, and secured from Italy full recognition of the French protectorate over Tunis on condition that Italy should be accorded by France free rein in Tripoli and Cyrenaica.[2] *French Conciliation of Italy*

Meanwhile German publicists, army officers, and other patriots were viewing with alarm the growing international isolation of their country. Italy was suspected of lukewarmness in her friendship for Germany and Austria-Hungary. Russia was in formal alliance with France. Great Britain was in an *Entente Cordiale* with France and with Russia. Japan was in formal alliance with Great Britain. Only Austria-Hungary remained a stanch friend and ally of Germany. *Isolation of Germany and Austria-Hungary*

Under these circumstances the German government labored from 1907 to 1914 to break up the Triple Entente by diplomatic maneuvers, to strengthen Austria-Hungary and increase her prestige in southeastern Europe, to win the Ottoman Empire as a friend and ally, and, by means of military threats, to insist upon Germany's right to participate on the same basis as other Great Powers in world commerce and foreign investment. The new German policy did not undo Delcassé's work, but it produced periodic crises in the relations between the Triple Entente and the Teutonic Powers — crises which grew more and more threatening to the preservation of any semblance of a Concert of Europe and more and more indicative of an impending war of huge dimensions. These crises had to do alternately with the Moroccan Question and with the Near Eastern Question. *German Policy and Resulting International Crises, 1905–1914*

[1] See above, p. 585.   [2] See above, p. 633.

In the case of Morocco [1] the German government felt itself aggrieved that Delcassé had taken it upon himself to arrange
The Moroccan Question for the political and economic control of that tempestuous and brigand-ridden country simply by agreements between France and Spain and Great Britain, without consulting Germany. To be sure, Morocco was contiguous to the French Empire in Africa and to Spanish posts on the Mediterranean, and it seemed to Delcassé that the preservation of order within Morocco was therefore a practical concern only of Spain and France. But despite the fact that most of the foreign commerce of Morocco was with Great Britain, France, and Spain, German capitalists had secured economic concessions within the sultanate, and they enlisted the support of their government in an endeavor to prevent France from establishing a political protectorate over Morocco that might confer economic privileges upon French capitalists to the exclusion of themselves.

The first Moroccan crisis was precipitated on 31 March, 1905, — exactly three weeks after the decisive defeat of the Russians by the Japanese in the battle of Mukden,[2] — when
First Moroccan Crisis: William II at Tangier, 1905 the Emperor William II landed at Tangier and in a vigorous speech declared that he came to visit the sultan of Morocco as an independent sovereign in whose lands all Powers were to hold the same footing and enjoy the same rights. France, against whom the speech was directed, could not then hope to oppose German pretensions because of the military collapse of her ally, Russia; and accordingly she surrendered to Germany, sacrificed her able foreign minister Delcassé, and agreed to submit the whole Moroccan Question to an international congress. The Congress, meeting
The Algeciras Congress, 1906 at Algeciras in Spain from January to April, 1906, reached a compromise whereby the territorial integrity of Morocco and the sovereignty of the native sultan were affirmed, certain internal reforms were devised of an administrative and financial nature, the "open door" was guaranteed to the merchants and investors of all the signatory Powers, and France and Spain were authorized to instruct and officer a native police force.

[1] See above, p. 630.   [2] See above, p. 584.

Civil war in Morocco and outrages against foreigners, especially Frenchmen, caused the French government to land marines at Casablanca in August, 1907. Germany repeatedly Second expostulated against the continued presence of French Moroccan Crisis: the troops in Morocco; and in September, 1908, an attempt Affair of on the part of the German consul at Casablanca Casablanca, to protect from arrest a number of deserters from the 1908 French foreign legion precipitated a second grave crisis, which was successfully passed in 1909 by reference of the questions at stake to the Hague Tribunal. The conclusion of a special Franco-German convention in February, 1909, seemed to preclude future misunderstandings between these Powers: The Franco- Germany put on record that her interests in the sul- German tanate were "only economic," and, France agreeing Convention of 1909 to "safeguard economic equality," Germany undertook not to impede the political interests of France in Morocco.

But the Franco-German agreement of 1909 was so distasteful to German patriots that Prince von Bülow, the German chancellor who had negotiated it, was forced out of office, and his successor, Bethmann-Hollweg, sought the Third earliest opportunity to nullify it. The opportunity Moroccan Crisis: the was afforded by the military occupation of Fez, the Agadir Incident, 1911 Moroccan capital, by the French in 1911. In July, the German government dispatched a warship to the Moroccan port of Agadir, ostensibly to safeguard the mining property of German capitalists, but with a significant hint that the warship would be withdrawn as soon as conditions were sufficiently settled to admit of French withdrawal from Fez. The gravity of the international situation was felt throughout Europe, and military preparations were hurried forward both in Germany and in France. Russia was not yet sufficiently recovered from the Japanese War to be of much assistance to France, but Sir Edward Grey, the British foreign secretary, declared that his country would support France. The German govern- The Franco- ment apparently did not desire war and contented it- German self with concluding a second Franco-German conven- Convention of 1911 tion (November, 1911), whereby Germany promised not to oppose the establishment of a French protectorate over Morocco and France agreed to maintain the "open door" in

Morocco and to cede two strips of the French Congo to Germany. Although France was thus enabled in 1912 to settle the political question of Morocco satisfactorily to herself and to Spain, the Agadir crisis of 1911 served to increase the fear and hatred of the French for the Germans, who, in their opinion, had "blackmailed" them out of rich portions of the French Congo, and at the same time it served to consolidate the friendship of France and Great Britain. On their side, the Germans believed that their legitimate interests in Morocco had been prejudiced and their position as a World Power jeopardized by the joint machinations of the French and the British.

Bitterness between France and Germany

Even more disquieting to pacifists than the Moroccan crises were the almost simultaneous crises in the Near East, where Russia and Austria-Hungary, instead of France and Germany, were the protagonists. But while in the case of Morocco, Russia, on account of her weakened military position, was able to give but little effective support to her French ally, in the case of the Near Eastern crises Germany had economic motives and powerful military means for backing Austria-Hungary. There was little doubt from the opening of the twentieth century that various Austro-Hungarian capitalists and patriots favored the political and economic expansion of the Dual Monarchy in a southerly direction through Bosnia and Macedonia to Salonica on the Ægean, or that German patriots and capitalists cherished the idea of "Germanizing" the Balkan states and the Ottoman Empire. So Germany and Austria-Hungary, acting in perfect harmony, gradually extended their political and economic influence in southeastern Europe. In 1898 the Hohenzollern king of Rumania conceded direct railway communication through his territories from Berlin and Vienna to Constantinople. In 1899 Emperor William II ostentatiously visited the sultan of Turkey, and a German company obtained a concession for the construction of a railway across Asia Minor, Armenia, and the fertile valleys of the Tigris and Euphrates, to Bagdad and the head of the Persian Gulf. Austrian influence was paramount at the Serbian court from the Congress of Berlin (1878) to the assassination of King Alexander in 1903; and

The Near Eastern Question, 1898–1914

Teutonic Policy in the Near East

Prince Ferdinand of Bulgaria, a German by birth, was long estranged from Russia and dependent upon Austria-Hungary. The king of Rumania was a kinsman of the German emperor, and the wife of the future King Constantine of Greece was a sister of William II. In a word, the Teutonic Powers began to stand in the way of the Russian ambition of ousting the Turks from Europe and ruling at Constantinople; the Teutonic Powers began to buttress the Turk, to train his army, to exploit his country, and to seek to minimize both Russian and British influence in southeastern Europe.

In 1903 the Balkan policy of Germany and Austria-Hungary received a check. A palace revolution at Belgrade put an end to the rule of the pro-Austrian dynasty in Serbia and brought to the throne the King Peter who vigorously supported the nationalist propaganda of the Serbs and loyally depended upon Russia.[1]

The first serious crisis in the Near Eastern Question affecting the new Balance of Power between the Triple Alliance and the Triple Entente occurred in 1908, when Austria-Hungary, taking advantage of an internal revolution in Turkey, formally incorporated the Serb-speaking provinces of Bosnia and Herzegovina, thereby violating a provision of the treaty of Berlin of 1878 and arousing a storm of wrath and indignation in the Serb countries of Serbia and Montenegro.[2] Russia immediately took steps to back the Serb states and to resist the Austro-Hungarian aggression, but in the midst of Russian mobilization Germany announced (1909) her firm intention of giving full military support to Austria-Hungary. Russia, still not fully recovered from the Japanese War and her own internal revolutionary movement,[3] thereupon gave way, acquiescing in the high-handed treaty-violation and even obtaining from Serbia a solemn promise in the future not to tolerate any anti-Austrian demonstrations or propaganda. Nevertheless, the Pan-Slavists of Russia did not forget the humiliation of their country at

First Near Eastern Crisis: Annexation of Bosnia-Herzegovina by Austria-Hungary, 1908

Submission of Russia and Serbia, 1909

---

[1] For the Balkan policy of Russia, see above, p. 536. In recent times, Russian policy in the Balkans has been intimately associated with the growth of Pan-Slavism, which is briefly discussed on pp. 465 ff., above.

[2] See above, pp. 521, 526.

[3] See above, pp. 478 ff.

Teutonic hands in 1908–1909; under their influence the Russian government began to reorganize its army, to construct strategic railways, and to do everything in its power to insure Russia against a like humiliation in the future.

A second crisis in the Near East was at least threatened by the Tripolitan War, which Italy waged against Turkey in 1911–1912.[1] Russia was not directly concerned in the struggle, but it was obvious to students of international politics that the war was distasteful to Germany as well as to Austria-Hungary, both of which were endeavoring to bolster up Turkish power, and that it was bound sooner or later to produce the gravest consequences, not only in the Near East but throughout Europe. In the first place it increased the desire of Italian imperialists for the further economic and political expansion of their country in Albania, in the Ægean, and in Asia Minor, thereby bringing Italy's policy in the Near East into sharp conflict with that of Austria-Hungary and weakening Italy's adherence to the Triple Alliance. Secondly, and quite naturally from the foregoing, the war showed a possible community of world interests between Italy and the Powers of the Triple Entente. And thirdly and most significantly of all, the Tripolitan War was the immediate forerunner, and in a measure the cause, of the Balkan War of 1912–1913, out of which emerged the gravest international crises that had ever confronted the European Balance of Power.

Second Near Eastern Crisis: the Tripolitan War between Italy and Turkey, 1911–1912

Resulting International Dangers

In the course of the Balkan War Austria-Hungary adopted a most unyielding attitude toward Serb ambitions.[2] On threat of war, in which she was backed by Germany, she deprived Montenegro of the important town of Scutari and obliged Serbia to evacuate various Adriatic towns which the Serbs had conquered from the Turks. Also, by securing the sanction of the Great Powers for the erection of an autonomous Albania under a German prince, she effectually prevented Serbia from obtaining any outlet to the sea. Only the positive refusal of Italy to coöperate with her caused Austria-Hungary to abandon a project to attack Serbia forthwith.

Third Near Eastern Crisis: the Balkan War, 1912–1913

Anti-Serb Policy of Austria-Hungary

[1] See above, pp. 514, 528, 633.   [2] See above, pp. 530 f., 534.

The year 1913 — the year of the conclusion of the Balkan War — witnessed an unprecedented outburst of national militarism. Germany put all Europe in a panic [1] by preparing an army bill which proposed to raise the peace footing of the empire from 656,000 men to 870,000 and to make an extraordinary military expenditure of almost a billion marks. Immediately France replied to the German challenge by increasing the term of active military service from two to three years. The German bill was accepted by the *Reichstag* on 30 June, 1913, three weeks before the passage of the counter-measure by the French parliament. Russia, the ally of France, and Austria-Hungary, the ally of Germany, likewise gave attention to military "preparedness." In July, 1913, the Russian Duma authorized a new army budget and the lengthening of active military service from three to three and a quarter years; General Joffre, the French commander-in-chief, visited Russia in August, 1913, to confer on the reorganization of the Russian army. Austria-Hungary introduced a new scheme whereby her peace footing was increased from 463,000 to 560,000; and enormous sums were appropriated for the provision of up-to-date artillery. Italy introduced many military reforms and Great Britain greatly increased her expenditures for naval purposes. Even the smaller states of the Low Countries and of the Balkan, Iberian, and Scandinavian peninsulas caught the contagion of the army fever. The most ominous feature of all this military preparation was the fear and hatred it inspired. France introduced three-year service because she feared the German army, with its splendid corps at strategic points on the Alsace-Lorraine frontier. When little Belgium introduced universal military service and planned to create a field army of 150,000 in addition to garrisons of 130,000 men, the argument was advanced that the recent construction of German railways leading to the Belgian frontier, without obvious economic purpose, signified that Germany was preparing to transport troops into and through Belgium in case of a Franco-German

Marginal notes: Fear Engendered by Recurring International Crises — The Year of Military Preparations, 1913

---

[1] It should be remarked that many Germans were undoubtedly panic-stricken themselves by the contemporaneous activity of Russian Pan-Slavists. See above, pp. 425 f., 468 f., 485, 487.

war. Similarly Germany was alarmed by the projection of new Russian railways which would facilitate Russian mobilization against Germany. And in the spring of 1914 a veritable panic was created in the German and Austro-Hungarian press by a series of newspaper articles commenting on the Russian preparations which would be perfected in 1916 or 1917. On the other hand, a prominent Petrograd journal declared in June, 1914, that "France and Russia do not desire war, but Russia is prepared and hopes that France will likewise be prepared."

Slowly but surely the trend of international relations between 1890 and 1914 showed that the principle of the balance of power between two great combinations — the Alliance Powers and the Entente Powers — was incompatible, not only with the claim to European hegemony which Germany had put forth and in large part substantiated between 1871 and 1890, but also with the older theory and effective operation of a Concert of Europe. The diplomatic grouping of the Powers in two mutually hostile coalitions by 1914 had greatly intensified the nationalism and the militarism of every European state, had given vindictive color to the economic and colonial rivalries of the Great Powers, and had placed the nations of Europe in such a perilously delicate position that a comparatively trivial occurrence was sufficient to tip the balance of power and to precipitate an almost universal war.

Upsetting the Balance of Power

THE OUTBREAK OF THE WAR OF THE NATIONS, 1914–1915

At the beginning of 1914 the powder-magazines throughout Europe were pretty well stocked, and the tiny spark which set them off was the assassination by Serb conspirators, on 28 June, of the Archduke Francis Ferdinand, nephew of the Emperor-King Francis Joseph and heir to the Habsburg throne, together with his wife, while on the archduke's first official visit to Sarajevo, the capital of Bosnia. The assassination caused a tremendous outburst of indignation throughout Austria-Hungary and Germany. For on Francis Ferdinand many hopes had been pinned. His piety had made him a favorite with the Roman

Assassination of the Archduke Francis Ferdinand, 28 June, 1914

Catholics; his loyalty to the German alliance augured well for the future maintenance of the international solidarity of the two great Teutonic Powers; his vigorous patriotism and his conscientious fulfillment of administrative duties Its Significance were guarantees of the continued integrity and stability of the Dual Monarchy after the demise of the aged Francis Joseph. Moreover, Francis Ferdinand was supposed to favor a special policy on the part of Austria-Hungary toward the Slavs of southeastern Europe: to him was attributed the leadership in a scheme to transform the Dual Monarchy into a Triple Monarchy, in which the Serbs of Bosnia and the Serbo-Croats of Croatia-Slavonia and probably the Slovenes would constitute an autonomous entity resembling Austria and Hungary; and to him, therefore, was imputed by patriotic Serbians and Montenegrins the inspiration of the hostile attitude which Austria-Hungary had taken, especially since 1908, toward the territorial expansion of the two independent Serb kingdoms.

Certainly the Serbs disliked Francis Ferdinand immensely and certainly from 1908 to 1914 they organized secret societies in Bosnia as well as in Serbia and Montenegro and conducted a deliberate propaganda with the more or less avowed object of disrupting the Habsburg Empire.[1] Naturally, then, when the official investigation of the Sarajevo assassination indicated that the plot Tension between Austria-Hungary and Serbia had been carried out by youthful Bosnians, inspired by the revolutionary secret societies of the Serbs and with the connivance of at least two officials of the kingdom of Serbia, the indignation of Germans and Magyars against Serbia knew no bounds. The government of Austria-Hungary solemnly affirmed that the very existence of the Dual Monarchy depended upon putting an end once for all to Serbian machinations, and with practical unanimity the press of Germany declared that Austria-Hungary's welfare was Germany's welfare. But by the same token and with equal unanimity the press of Russia declared that Serbia's welfare was Russia's welfare. A new crisis — and a most serious one — had arisen in the Balkans.

[1] On the feeling of the Serbs against the Dual Monarchy, see above, p. 538. Many Germans and Magyars insisted that the Serb propaganda was inspired and directed by Russian Pan-Slavists with the connivance of the Russian government. On Pan-Slavism, see above, pp. 468 f.

On 23 July, 1914, Austria-Hungary presented an ultimatum to Serbia, couched in the most peremptory terms: its spirit was that of an outraged government, exasperated beyond endurance and determined to crush all Pan-Serb plotting regardless of international usage or of constitutional formalities. The ultimatum alleged that, by failing to suppress anti-Austrian conspiracies, Serbia had violated her promise of 1909 to "live on good neighborly terms" with Austria-Hungary, and had compelled the Austro-Hungarian government to abandon its attitude of benevolent and patient forbearance, to put an end "to the intrigues which form a perpetual menace to the tranquillity of the monarchy," and to demand effective guarantees from the Serbian government. As definite guarantees of good behavior Serbia was called upon to suppress anti-Austrian publications and societies, to discharge such governmental employees as the Austro-Hungarian government should accuse of anti-Austrian propaganda, to discard anti-Austrian text-books from the Serbian educational system, "to accept the collaboration in Serbia of representatives of the Austro-Hungarian government for the suppression of the subversive movement directed against the territorial integrity of the monarchy," and to signify unconditional acceptance of these and the other Austro-Hungarian demands within forty-eight hours.

The Peremptory Ultimatum of Austria-Hungary to Serbia, 23 July, 1914

Thenceforth events marched rapidly. Russia, France, and Great Britain at once coöperated in requesting Austria-Hungary to extend the time-limit of the ultimatum in order that the whole question might be submitted to general international negotiation, but this joint request Austria-Hungary promptly declined. On 25 July Serbia replied to the Austro-Hungarian ultimatum, promising to comply with such demands as did not seem to impair her independence and sovereignty, and offering to refer all disputed points to the Hague Tribunal or to the Great Powers. Austria-Hungary pronounced the reply evasive and unsatisfactory, broke off diplomatic relations with Serbia, and started the mobilization of her army. The Serbians removed their capital from Belgrade to Nish and began a counter-mobilization. War was clearly impending between Austria-Hungary and Serbia.

The Serbian Reply Unsatisfactory to Austria-Hungary

But a much vaster and more terrible war was also impending. The Russian government professed to believe that Austria-Hungary was planning to impair the sovereignty, if not to reduce the territory, of Serbia, and that an Austro-Hungarian campaign against Serbia would consolidate Teutonic power in the Balkans and deprive Russia of all influence in southeastern Europe. On the other hand, Germany insisted that the quarrel was one which concerned Austria-Hungary and Serbia alone : she consistently opposed the repeated efforts of Russian, British, French, and even Italian, diplomats, to refer the quarrel to an international congress or to the Hague Tribunal, and, mindful of the success of her former military threats in 1909 and in 1912–1913, she again in July, 1914, declared unequivocally that if Russia should come to the assistance of Serbia, she would support Austria-Hungary with all the armed forces at her command. Probably the chief reason that actuated Germany to assume such a determined position was a belief that Russia in 1914 would yield without fighting, as she had done in the earlier Balkan crises in 1909 and in 1912–1913. It was known in Germany that the Russian military reforms were not yet completed; and it was likewise known that each one of the Entente Powers was embarrassed by domestic difficulties — Russia by a serious and violent strike in Petrograd, France by an alarming popular opposition to the new three-year military law and by a scandalous murder trial of political importance at Paris, and Great Britain by the menace of civil war in Ireland. Under these circumstances, Austria-Hungary formally declared war against Serbia (28 July, 1914).

Serbia Backed by Russia

Austria-Hungary Backed by Germany

Outbreak of War at Time Unfavorable to the Triple Entente

Austria-Hungary vs. Serbia, 28 July, 1914

But this time Teutonic diplomacy appeared to have misjudged the temper of Russia and to have overreached itself. The Russian government refused to be intimidated, and on the day following the Austro-Hungarian declaration of war against Serbia the mobilization of the Russian army was begun. On 1 August the frantic endeavors of various diplomats to arrive at some peaceful solution of the Serbian problem were suddenly and rudely arrested

Germany vs. Russia, 1 August, 1914

by the outbreak of war between Germany and Russia. Germany had presented a twelve-hour ultimatum to Russia, demanding immediate and complete demobilization; Russia had refused to comply; and Germany had declared war.

Germany knew that war with Russia was practically certain to involve France. She knew that France was the sworn ally of Russia. She appreciated the popular feeling in France that common cause must be made with Russia in order to preserve international prestige and to recover Alsace-Lorraine. Accordingly, on the very day of delivering the ultimatum to Russia, Germany demanded to know within eighteen hours what would be the French position. France gave a non-committal answer and began mobilization. And on 3 August, 1914, Germany declared war against France.

Germany vs. France, 3 August, 1914

Thus, within a week of the declaration of hostilities by Austria-Hungary against Serbia, four Great Powers were in a state of war — Germany and Austria-Hungary opposed to Russia and France. The attitude of the other two Great Powers of Europe — Great Britain and Italy — did not long remain in doubt. Italy promptly proclaimed her neutrality, on the ground that the war was not defensive on the part of Austria-Hungary and Germany, but offensive, and that therefore she was not bound to give assistance to her allies. Great Britain, however, appeared more hesitant. The British people certainly had sympathy for France and little love for Germany, and the British government had already informed Germany that, while their country was not bound by treaty obligations to help France or Russia, they could not promise in case of war to observe neutrality. By 2 August the British government had gone further and had announced that they would not tolerate German naval attacks on the unprotected western coast of France. And on 4 August occurred an event which decided Great Britain to enter the war on the side of Russia and France.

Italy Proclaims Neutrality

Hesitation of Great Britain

On 2 August — twenty-four hours before the formal declaration of war by Germany against France — German troops were set in motion toward the French frontier, not directly against the powerful French border fortresses of Verdun, Toul, and Belfort, but toward the neutral countries of Luxemburg and Belgium, which lay between Germany and less well-defended districts of northern France. Both Germany and France had signed treaties to respect the neutrality of these "buffer states," and France had already announced her intention of adhering loyally to her treaty engagements. But on 2 August German troops occupied Luxemburg, despite protests from the grand-duchess; and on the same day the German government presented an ultimatum to Belgium demanding the grant within twelve hours of permission to transfer German troops across that country into France, promising, if permission were granted, to guarantee Belgian independence and integrity and to pay an indemnity, and threatening that, if the little state should in any way resist, Germany would treat her as an enemy and that "the decision of arms" would determine the future relations of Belgium to Germany. The Belgian government characterized the ultimatum as a gross violation of international law and not only refused categorically to grant Germany's request but appealed at once to Great Britain to assist in upholding the neutrality of Belgium.

Germany's Violation of Belgian Neutrality

Germany vs. Belgium, 4 August, 1914

The neutrality of Belgium had always been a cardinal point in the foreign policy of Great Britain. The British had fought against Napoleon I in part because of the annexation of Belgium by France, and they had opposed the threatened aggression of Napoleon III against the little kingdom; they were not likely to view with pleasure German attacks on Belgium or its possible incorporation into the German Empire. On 4 August, therefore, when news was received in London that German troops had actually crossed the border into Belgium, Sir Edward Grey, the British foreign secretary, dispatched an ultimatum to Germany, requiring assurances by midnight that Germany would respect Belgian neutrality. Germany refused, on the ground of military necessity, and Bethmann-Hollweg, the German chancellor, with evidence of anger and disappointment, rebuked Great Britain for making war just for "a scrap of paper." The next day, Mr. Asquith, the British prime minister, announced that a state of war existed between Great Britain and Germany.

Great Britain vs. Germany, 4 August, 1914

On 7 August little Montenegro joined her fellow-Serb state of Serbia against Austria-Hungary. Then Japan became a
Montenegro vs. Austria-Hungary, 7 August, 1914 party to the war, partially to fulfill her treaty obligations to Great Britain and partially to avenge herself on Germany, for the Japanese had not forgotten the German Kaiser's slighting references to them in the past, nor the part Germany had played in preventing Japan from retaining Port Arthur in 1895 after the Chino-Japanese War. Accordingly, on 17 August, Japan presented an ultimatum to Germany, demanding that the latter Power should immediately withdraw all warships from Chinese and Japanese waters and deliver up the entire leased territory of Kiao-chau before
Japan vs. Germany, 23 August, 1914 15 September, "with a view to the eventual restoration of the same to China." Upon the refusal of the German government to comply with the terms of her ultimatum, Japan forthwith declared war (23 August, 1914).

Against the combination of so many foes, Germany and Austria-Hungary welcomed support from the Ottoman Empire.
Entrance of Turkey as Teutonic Ally, November, 1914 Turkey, having purchased two fugitive German warships and being inspired by the Young Turk faction with a hope of recovering at least part of what she had lost in the Balkan War, bombarded Russian Black Sea ports on 29 October, 1914; consequently a state of war was proclaimed between Russia and Turkey; and on 5 November France and Great Britain declared war against Turkey.

As the war progressed popular feeling in Italy reached a high pitch. Italian patriots felt that their country should take advantage of the embarrassments of Austria-Hungary
Italy vs. Austria-Hungary, 23 May, 1915 in order to wrest from the latter country the Italian-speaking districts of Trent and Triest, and they brought such pressure to bear on their government that at length on 4 May, 1915, Italy, despite the eager activity of German diplomats, denounced her treaty of alliance with Austria-Hungary and on 23 May declared war against her former ally.

Further formal declarations of war between the nations already engaged in hostilities completed the alignment, at the

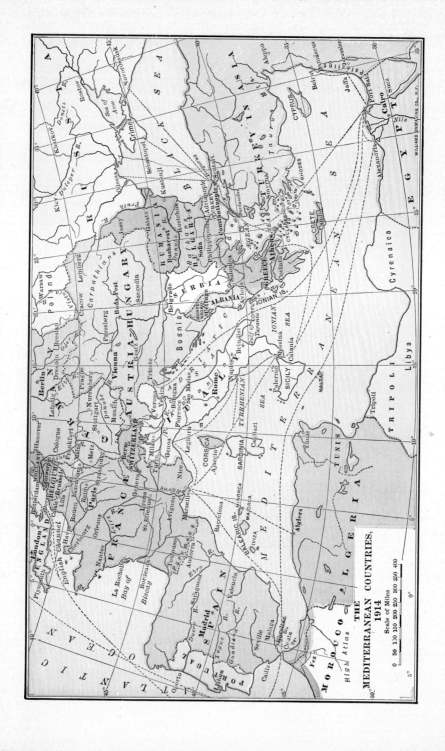

THE
MEDITERRANEAN COUNTRIES,
1914

Scale of Miles

0 50 100 150 200 250 300 350 400

close of the first year of the huge struggle, of Germany, Austria-Hungary, and Turkey against Russia, France, Great Britain, Italy, Japan, Belgium, Serbia, and Montenegro.[1] Moreover, in August, 1915, popular factions both in Greece and in Rumania were urging their Germanophile sovereigns to enter the war against the Teutonic allies, and Bulgaria appeared willing to sell her national support to whichever side would best secure territorial gains to her in Thrace and Macedonia. Even neutral states like Switzerland, Holland, and the Scandinavian kingdoms found it necessary or expedient to keep large bodies of troops under arms and ready for any emergency.

Alignment of Powers at War in August, 1915

Such was the international situation created by the War of the Nations. The military and naval operations during the first year of the struggle gave evidence that the two opposing combinations were fairly evenly matched in resources, in prowess, and in determination, and that the war would be not only terribly expensive but horribly destructive and long drawn out. There was no sign that either Germany or Austria-Hungary would consent to make peace separately; and on the other side, Great Britain, France, and Russia mutually engaged on 5 September, 1914, not to conclude peace separately nor to demand terms of peace without the previous agreement of each of the others. To this engagement Japan became a party on 19 October, 1914, and Italy announced her adherence on 1 December, 1915, thus creating virtually a new Quintuple Entente.

Agreements to Make Peace Only Jointly

Over the military and naval operations of the Great War it is not our purpose to tarry. No one could predict with any accuracy when they would be brought to a close, and only with their close could the historian properly review them and sort out the important from the unimportant. No one could doubt, however, that on the ruins of the Great War would be builded a new Europe and perhaps a new world. As the War of the Nations marked the close of one period of the world's history, so it was bound to mark the beginning of another.

The Great War the Close of One Era and the Beginning of Another

---

[1] Subsequently, Bulgaria entered the war on the Teutonic side (14 October, 1915), and Portugal joined the opposing combination (9 March, 1916).

And here is the proper place to set limits to our present study. Since those days at the opening of the sixteenth century we have followed the long and involved story of Europe down to the War of 1914. We have watched the development of a remarkable state-system: Great Britain, slowly but steadily forging ahead to a preëminent position in maritime and colonial dominion; Germany, painfully consolidating her lands and exalting her military power on the Continent; Austria-Hungary, apparently ever defeated and ever rallying from defeat to obtain new prestige for the hoary Habsburg family; France, risen to sudden greatness on the Continent, on the seas, and in colonial enterprise, as suddenly put down, and again in the nineteenth and twentieth centuries rising to new greatness with a strange youthful exuberance; Russia, coming out of the East to learn of the West and to assume a mighty position in the councils of the world; Italy, shaking off her centuries-old foreign masters, gathering herself together, and essaying to play the rôle of a Great Power; the slow waning of the Ottoman Empire before the waxing power of lesser nationalities; Spain and Sweden, regretfully abandoning world careers for which they were not naturally suited to follow the gentler but no less fruitful paths of peace. We have likewise watched the long drama of European expansion: the explorations and discoveries, the trade and missions, the erection of a mercantilist colonial system and its destruction, the rapid growth in the nineteenth century of a new imperialism, the Europeanization of America, of Asia, of Africa, and of the isles of the seven seas. We have witnessed the constant shifting of social distinction from clergy and nobility to bourgeoisie — the middle class — that enriched itself from the Commercial Revolution, that helped to unfrock priests in the sixteenth and seventeenth centuries and to dethrone kings in the seventeenth and eighteenth centuries, that reaped the richest profits from the Industrial Revolution, and that placed its own peculiar impress on the whole civilization of the nineteenth and twentieth centuries. Also we have heard from peasants and particularly from town laborers murmurings and mutterings that in the nineteenth century grew in frequency and dissonance and that might in the twentieth century bode no good to the bourgeoisie. We have observed the breakdown of divine-right monarchy and the lessening frequency of wars waged solely for dynastic aggrandizement, as the thunders of the French Revolution reverberated throughout Europe and its lightnings smote all peoples with the electric fire of democracy and nationalism. And if we have been alive to intellectual developments, we have noticed the disruption of the Catholic Church in the sixteenth century, the subsequent disintegration and revolutionizing of Protestantism, the rise of deism and skepticism, of religious indifference and toleration, the continued exertions of Catholics to repair the ravages of the faithless, the growth of a spirit of progress in material well-being, the increasing popular devotion to experimental and applied science and to those philosophical speculations about science, such as Darwinism, which in the nineteenth and twentieth centuries gave new complexion to man's ideas concerning the physical and spiritual world about him.

Out of all these factors in the evolution of European civilization during the span of some four hundred years has come the War of the Nations. It is the product, at once inevitable and ironical, of materialistic science, of rivalries in the state-system, of conflicting ambitions of divers social classes, and of the potent operation everywhere of the principles of democracy and nationalism. The past has made the present war. But as inevitably will the present war contribute new factors and modifications of the old to generations yet unborn. The war is not a perfect break in human history, though it substitute a "new régime" for an "old régime"; and in all probability the problems of the future will be fully comprehended only in connection with the history of the four hundred years that has constituted the subject-matter of this book.

ADDITIONAL READING

Internationalism and Pacifism. C. D. Hazen, *Europe since 1815* (1910), ch. xxxii, a brief, clear statement of the rise of internationalism; J. B. Scott, *The Hague Peace Conferences of 1899 and 1907*, 2 vols. (1909), texts and comment, elaborate and authoritative; W. I. Hull, *The Two Hague Conferences and their Contributions to International Law* (1908), less pretentious than the preceding, but useful; A. P. Higgins, *The Hague Peace Conferences and Other International Conferences concerning the Laws and Usages*

720 HISTORY OF MODERN EUROPE

of War (1909), a convenient résumé of the achievements of various international conferences from that of Paris in 1856 to that of London in 1909; J. W. Foster, *Arbitration and The Hague Court* (1904), a suggestive essay; G. G. Wilson (editor), *The Hague Arbitration Cases* (1915), containing the complete text of the fifteen cases decided before the Tribunal of Arbitration at The Hague since 1899, with English translation; *Cambridge Modern History*, Vol. XII (1910), ch. xxii, by Sir Frederick Pollock, on the modern law of nations and the prevention of war; N. M. Butler, *International Mind: an Argument for the Judicial Settlement of International Disputes* (1913), temperate and illuminating; E. B. Krehbiel, *Nationalism, War and Society* (1916), a scholarly and clear syllabus of the growth of internationalism; R. N. A. Lane (pseud. Norman Angell), *The Great Illusion*, new ed. (1914), a brilliant defense of the thesis that " it has become a physical impossibility for any nation to benefit by military conquest "; George Nasmyth, *Social Progress and the Darwinian Theory* (1916), an attack upon the "scientific" justification of war; G. H. Perris, *A Short History of War and Peace* (1911), a handy volume in the " Home University Library "; H. N. Brailsford, *The War of Steel and Gold, a Study of the Armed Peace* (1914); F. W. Hirst, *The Political Economy of War* (1915), a cursory economic history of the chief wars of the world from the seventeenth to the twentieth century, with special attention to war-debts and to the trade in armaments; D. S. Jordan, *War and Waste: a Series of Discussions of War and War Accessories* (1913); D. S. and H. E. Jordan, *War's Aftermath* (1914), a study of the effect of the American Civil War and of the Balkan Wars on the quality of subsequent generations; Charles Plater (editor), *A Primer of Peace and War: the Principles of International Morality* (1915), a clear statement of the Catholic position; Clara Barton, *The Red Cross: a History of this Remarkable International Movement in the Interest of Humanity* (1898); P. H. Epler, *The Life of Clara Barton* (1915), laudatory and interesting. Helpful for the further study of pacifism are the numerous pamphlets published by the " American Association for International Conciliation " (New York) and by the " World Peace Foundation " (Boston).

Militarism. Typical pleas for military might: Homer Lea, *The Day of the Saxon* (1912); J. A. Cramb, *Germany and England* (1914), and, by the same author, *The Origins and Destiny of Imperial Britain and Nineteenth-Century Europe* (1915); Friedrich von Bernhardi, *Germany and the Next War*, Eng. trans. by A. H. Powles (1912). For refutations, or attempted refutations, of the doctrines of Norman Angell and F. W. Hirst, cited above, consult A. T. Mahan, *Armaments and Arbitration, or, The Place of Force in the International Relations of States* (1912); J. H. Jones, *The Economics of War and Conquest* (1915); and G. G. Coulton, *The Main Illusions of Pacificism* (1916). For a scientist's justification of war on the basis of biology, see Karl Pearson, *National Life from the Standpoint of Science* (1901).

International Relations, 1871–1914. An illuminating little volume, setting forth the basic correlation of modern patriotism, business, and diplomacy, is Walter Lippmann, *The Stakes of Diplomacy* (1915). On the general history of international relations since 1871 : Charles Seignobos, *A Political History of Europe since 1814*, Eng. trans. ed. by S. M. Macvane (1900), ch. xxvii, xxviii; J. H. Rose, *The Development of the European Nations, 1870–1900*, Vol. II (1905), ch. i, and, by the same author, *The Origins of the War* (1914) ; *Histoire générale*, Vol. XII, ch. xiii, xv; W. M. Fullerton, *Problems of Power: a Study of International Politics from Sadowa to Kirk-Kilissé* (1913); Gottlob Egelhaaf, *Geschichte der neuesten Zeit 1871–1912*, 4th ed. (1913), Book I, ch. vii–x, Book II, ch. xiii, xv, xvii; Arthur Singer, *Geschichte des Dreibunds* (1914); André Tardieu, *France and the Alliances: the Struggle for the Balance of Power* (1908); Ernest Lémonon, *L'Europe et la politique britannique, 1882–1911*, 2d ed. (1912); Ernst (Count) zu Reventlow, *Deutschlands auswärtige Politik, 1888–1913* (1914); Bernhard von Bülow, *Imperial Germany*, Eng. trans. by Marie A. Lewenz (1914), pp. 3–123 ; Francis Delaisi, *The Inevitable War* (1915) ; Pierre Albin, *Les grands traités politiques: receuil des principaux textes diplomatiques depuis 1815 jusqu'à nos jours*, 2d ed. (1911). Special phases: René Pinon, *France et Allemagne, 1870–1913*, new ed. (1913) ; Albert Billot, *La France et l'Italie: histoire des années troubles, 1881–1899*, 2 vols. (1905) ; Sir Thomas Barclay, *Thirty Years: Anglo-French Reminiscences, 1876–1906* (1914) ; G. H. Perris, *Our Foreign Policy and Sir Edward Grey's Failure* (1912), a pacifist's protest against England's entangling ententes ; Sir Harry Johnston, *Common Sense in Foreign Policy* (1913) ; Valentine Chirol, *The Middle Eastern Question* (1903) ; E. G. Browne, *The Persian Revolution of 1905–1909* (1910), containing a critical account of the Anglo-Russian agreement of 1907 in regard to Persian affairs ; André Tardieu, *La conférence d'Algésiras: histoire diplomatique de la crise marocaine*, 3d ed. (1909), and, by the same author, *Le mystère d'Agadir* (1912) ; Gustav Diercks, *Die Marokkofrage und die Konferenz von Algeciras* (1906) ; Gabriel Hanotaux, *La politique de l'équilibre, 1907–1911* (1912) ; Pierre Albin, *La guerre allemande: d'Agadir à Sarajevo, 1911–1914* (1915) ; H. A. Gibbons, *The New Map of Europe, 1911–1914: the Story of the Recent European Diplomatic Crises and Wars and of Europe's Present Catastrophe* (1914) ; R. W. Seton-Watson, *The Southern Slav Question and the Habsburg Monarchy* (1911), and, by the same author, *The Balkans, Italy, and the Adriatic* (1915) ; A. R. and Mrs. E. M. C. Colquhoun, *The Whirlpool of Europe, Austria-Hungary and the Habsburgs* (1907) ; Theodor von Sosnosky, *Die Balkanpolitik Oesterreich-Ungarns seit 1866*, 2 vols. (1913–1914) ; *European Politics during the Decade before the War as Described by Belgian Diplomatists* (1915), selections from the reports of Belgian representatives in London, Berlin, and Paris, to the minister of foreign affairs in Brussels, 1905–1914, issued in original French and in English translation by the German Foreign Office.

The War of the Nations. Bibliographies: F. W. T. Lange and W. T. Berry, *Books on the Great War* (1914 *sqq.*) ; A. Maire and A. Pereire, *Les sources de l'histoire de la guerre européenne* (1915 *sqq.*) ; *Die deutsche Kriegsliteratur*, pub. by Hinrichs, Leipzig (1914 *sqq.*). Of the countless books, pamphlets,'and articles which have been written about the war, only time and thorough criticism will prove the relative worth. The following bibliography is offered not as an exhaustive catalogue but simply as a select list which may be found useful alike by teachers and by students. It is perhaps needless to add that every reader must guard against generalizations and uncritical comments in which even reputable historians are likely to indulge at a time in the world's history so fraught with extreme national passions as the present.

Diplomatic History of the War. A handy volume published by Harrison and Sons, London, contains the *Collected Diplomatic Documents Relating to the Outbreak of the European War*, including the British *White Paper*, the French *Yellow Book*, the Russian *Orange Book*, thè Belgian *Grey Book*, the Serbian *Blue Book*, the German *Denkschrift*, the Austro-Hungarian *Red Book*, and other material, carefully indexed. In addition to these earlier diplomatic documents, the New York *Times* and the " American Association for International Conciliation " have made available to the American public the Italian *Green Book*, the Second Belgian *Grey Book*, the correspondence of the United States government with the belligerents, etc. For English readers, more or less partisan, but fairly reliable, accounts of the diplomatic maneuvers preliminary to the war have been written by J. W. Headlam, *History of Twelve Days, July 24–August 4, 1914* (1915); J. H. Rose, *The Origins of the War* (1914); Arthur Bullard, *The Diplomacy of the Great War* (1916); and E. C. Stowell, *The Diplomacy of the War of 1914*, Vol. I (1915). The German version of the diplomacy that led up to the conflict has been ably presented by H. F. Helmolt, *Die geheime Vorgeschichte des Weltkrieges* (1914); Paul Rohrbach, *Germany's Isolation*, Eng. trans. by P. H. Phillipson of the original German work, *Der Krieg und die deutsche Politik* (1914); H. Frobenius, *Germany's Hour of Destiny* (1914); and Edmund von Mach, *Germany's Point of View* (1915) and *What Germany Wants* (1914). A striking indictment of the German government purports to have been written by a German: the volume was originally published in Switzerland with the title, *J'accuse: von einem Deutschen*, and has since been translated into French and into English. The best general statement of the German position is *Deutschland und der Weltkrieg* (1915), containing contributions from the pens of such well-known German scholars as Otto Hintze, Friedrich Meinecke, Hermann Oncken, and Hermann Schumacher: excepting one chapter, it has been translated into English by W. W. Whitelock under the title of *Modern Germany in relation to the Great War* (1916). On the English side: E. P. Barker and other members of the Oxford Faculty of Modern History, *Why We Are at War: Great Britain's Case* (1914); H. A. L. Fisher, *The War, its Causes and its Issues* (1914); Ramsay Muir, *Britain's Case against Germany* (1914). For opposing views of the German invasion of Belgium, consult Alexander Fuehr, *The Neutrality of Belgium* (1915), and Charles Sarolea, *How Belgium Saved Europe* (1915).

General Histories of the War. Pretentious continued histories of the war and monumental collections of war-material have already begun to make their appearance. Of those published in the United States, probably the best-known are the (New York) *Times Current History of the War*, a heterogeneous collection, published in monthly installments, containing many valuable historical documents as well as a number of unimportant articles; F. H. Simonds, *The Great War* (1914 *sqq.*), an analytical interpretation, rather than a detailed narrative, of the war's most significant events; and G. H. Allen and H. C. Whitehead, *The Great War* (1915 *sqq.*). In England, the leading newspapers are publishing weekly and fortnightly " histories " of the war : the best are the *Manchester Guardian History of the War* (fortnightly) and the (London) *Times History of the War* (weekly). F. A. Mumby (editor), *The Great World War* (1915 *sqq.*), gives a concise discussion of the principal features of the conflict; Hilaire Belloc, *General Sketch of the European War* (1915 *sqq.*), is characterized by illuminating, but frequently too optimistic, analyses of geographical and numerical factors in favor of the Entente Powers; one of the clearest and most accurate narratives yet written is John Buchan, *Nelson's History of the War* (1915 *sqq.*). One of the leading French serial histories of the war is edited by Gabriel Hanotaux, *Histoire illustrée de la guerre de 1914;* but at present the most valuable French work is the official *Guerre de 1914: documents officielles, textes législatifs et réglementaires* (1914 *sqq.*). Of the many excellent German works mention should be made of C. H. Baer, *Der Völkerkrieg, eine Chronik der Ereignisse seit dem 1 Juli 1914* (1915 *sqq.*), and H. F. Helmolt, *Der Weltkrieg in Bildern and Dokumenten.* The (London) *Daily Chronicle* and the (London) *Daily Telegraph* have each published dozens of pocket-edition books on war-topics; and many eminent British scholars have contributed monographs to the *Oxford Pamphlets*, criticizing the policy and impugning the motives of the German government. On the other hand, the *Deutsche Kriegschriften* (*German War Pamphlets*), the *Politische Flugschriften* (*Political Pamphlets*), *Zwischen Krieg und Frieden* (1915 *sqq.*), and the *Deutsche Vorträge hamburgischer Professoren* (1914), in a controversial spirit, lay the burden of guilt upon the Entente Powers, especially on Great Britain. Useful for French opinions and contentions are two extensive series of similarly controversial pamphlets : *Pages d'histoire* (pub. by Berger-Levrault, Paris) ; and *Pages actuelles* (pub. by Bloud & Gay, Paris).

Special Aspects of the War. On Socialism and the war: W. E. Walling, *The Socialists and the War* (1915), authoritative and useful; H. G. Wells, *The War and Socialism* (1914). On nationalism in the war: A. J. Toynbee, *Nationality and the War* (1915) ; and for a broader survey, J. H. Rose, *Nationality in Modern History* (1916). On Catholicism and the war: Alfred Baudrillart (editor), *La guerre allemande et le catholicisme* (1915) ; Gabriel Langlois, *Le clergé, les catholiques, et la guerre* (1915) ; Alfred Loisy, *The War and Religion*, Eng. trans. by Arthur Galton (1915), anti-clerical in tone. For Russia's part in the war, from the standpoint of a Russian Social Democrat, an ex-member of the Duma, see Grégoire Alexinsky, *La Russie et la guerre* (1915), Eng. trans. by Bernard Miall.

AIDS IN LINKING CURRENT NEWS WITH MODERN HISTORY

Annual Historical Surveys. Beginning in September, 1916, the *Political Science Quarterly*, which has long published a " Record of Political Events " semi-annually, will publish such record annually as a separate supplement: procurable at moderate expense, this *Record of Political Events* promises to provide American students with convenient little summaries of the chief political events throughout the world, country by country, and thereby to furnish a valuable means of supplementing such histories as the foregoing and of keeping them up-to-date. More exhaustive American annuals, useful for reference, are the encyclopedic *International Year Book*, ed. by F. M. Colby (1899–1902), continued under the same editorship since 1907 as *The New International Year Book;* and *The American Year Book : a Record of Events and Progress*, ed. by S. N. D. North (1910 *sqq.*). The *Annual Register* is an annual résumé of political happenings, which has been appearing in England since 1758, half the space in each of the rather large volumes being devoted to Great Britain and the other half to " Foreign and Colonial History." What corresponds to The Annual Register for France is the *Annuaire historique universel* (1818–1861), continued by *L'année politique*, pub. by André Lebon (1874–1905), and *La vie politique dans les deux mondes*, ed. by Achille Viallate (1906 *sqq.*). Similar German works of recognized value: *Europäischer Geschichtskalender*, ed. by H. K. L. Schulthess (1861–1884) and continued since 1885 by other editors; *Das Staatsarchiv: Sammlung der offiziellen Aktenstücke zur Geschichte der Gegenwart* (1861 *sqq.*), ed. by Alfred Klauhold (1872–1890), now ed. by Gustav Roloff; *Jahrbuch des öffentlichen Rechts der Gegenwart*, ed. by Georg Jellinek, Paul Laband, and Robert Piloty (1907 *sqq.*). There is also an admirable Austro-Hungarian work of a semi-official character, published monthly and edited by Karl Neisser, *Politische und Volkswirtschaftliche Chronik* (1912 *sqq.*).

Special Reference Annuals. *The Statesman's Year Book*, since 1864, a statistical and descriptive annual of the countries of the world; *Hazell's Annual*, since 1886, containing lists of principal officials in all countries, together with brief reviews of main political events and much miscellaneous information; Joseph Whitaker, *An Almanack* " containing an account of the astronomical and other phenomena . . . information respecting the government, finances, population, commerce, and general statistics of the British Empire," since 1868; *Almanach de Gotha : annuaire généalogique, diplomatique, et statistique*, a famous work issued annually since 1818 and valuable for relationships of royalty and of great noble families; *The Year Book of Social Progress*, published in London since 1912, a summary of recent legislation, official reports, and voluntary effort, with regard to the welfare of the people; *Annuaire de la législation du travail*, an annual digest of social legislation in all countries, pub. by the Belgian Office of Labor since 1897. *The British and Foreign State Papers*, published annually since 1812, constitute a store-house of information concerning international relations and the general history of Europe. See also the various other year-books cited in the bibliographies appended to Chapters XXVII–XXIX, above.

Other Current Publications. The London *Times* publishes extremely valuable and convenient monthly and yearly indices; and from American newspapers is gathered the material which is summarized, arranged in alphabetical order, and published in the recently established monthly and cumulative *Information.* A moderately sized library of recent history might well include files of the following periodicals: American — *New Republic, Independent, Survey, Current Events, America, Review of Reviews, North American, American Journal of International Law, New Review, Pan-American Magazine;* British — London *Times* (weekly), *Westminster Gazette* (weekly), *Spectator, Nation, Tablet, Fortnightly, Contemporary, Nineteenth Century, Westminster, Edinburgh Review, Quarterly Review, National Review, Near East, Far East, Russian Review, Dublin Review, Hibbert Journal;* French — *Journal des débats* (weekly), *Revue politique et parlementaire, Le Correspondant, Revue de Paris, Revue bleu;* Belgian — *Revue de droit internationel et de législation comparée;* Italian — *Rivista d'Italia;* German — *Das Echo, Frankfurter Zeitung* (weekly), *Preussische Jahrbücher, Zeitschrift für Völkerrecht und Bundesstaatsrecht.* The best libraries contain, likewise, hundreds of volumes of stenographic reports of the proceedings of parliamentary bodies throughout the world, which, while altogether too voluminous for ordinary use, are indispensable aids to the mature and painstaking scholar in studying particular governmental actions in the nineteenth and twentieth centuries.

APPENDIX

RULERS OF THE CHIEF EUROPEAN STATES SINCE THE OPENING OF THE SIXTEENTH CENTURY

AUSTRIA-HUNGARY

(Archdukes of Austria since 1453; Kings of Hungary and Bohemia since 1526; Emperors of Austria since 1804)

Maximilian I, 1493–1519
Charles I (*V as Holy Roman Emperor*), 1519–1520
Ferdinand I, 1520–1564
Maximilian II, 1564–1576
Rudolph V (*II as Holy Roman Emperor*), 1576–1612
Matthias, 1612–1619
Ferdinand II, 1619–1637
Ferdinand III, 1637–1657
Leopold I, 1658–1705
Joseph I, 1705–1711

Charles II (*VI as Holy Roman Emperor, III as King of Hungary*), 1711–1740
Maria Theresa, 1740–1780
Joseph II, 1780–1790
Leopold II, 1790–1792
Francis I (*II as Holy Roman Emperor*), 1792–1835
Ferdinand I (*V of Hungary*), 1835–1848
Francis Joseph, 1848–1916
Charles I (IV of Hungary), 1916–

BELGIUM

Leopold I, 1831–1865
Leopold II, 1865–1909

Albert, 1909–

BULGARIA

Alexander, *Prince*, 1879–1886

Ferdinand I, *Prince*, 1887–1909, *King*, 1909–

DENMARK

John, 1481–1513
Christian II, 1513–1523
Frederick I, 1523–1533
Christian III, 1533–1559
Frederick II, 1559–1588
Christian IV, 1588–1648
Frederick III, 1648–1670

Christian V, 1670–1699
Frederick IV, 1699–1730
Christian VI, 1730–1746
Frederick V, 1746–1766
Christian VII, 1766–1808
Frederick VI, 1808–1839
Christian VIII, 1839–1848

DENMARK — *Continued*
  Frederick VII, 1848-1863
  Christian IX, 1863-1906

  Frederick VIII, 1906-1912
  Christian X, 1912–

FRANCE
  Louis XI, 1461-1483
  Charles VIII, 1483-1498
  Louis XII, 1498-1515
  Francis I, 1515-1547
  Henry II, 1547-1559
  Francis II, 1559-1560
  Charles IX, 1560-1574
  Henry III, 1574-1589
  Henry IV, 1589-1610
  Louis XIII, 1610-1643
  Louis XIV, 1643-1715
  Louis XV, 1715-1774
  Louis XVI, 1774-1792
  The First Republic, 1792-1804
    The Convention, 1792-1795
    The Directory, 1795-1799
    The Consulate (Napoleon Bonaparte as *First Consul*), 1799-1804
  Napoleon I, *Emperor of the French*, 1804-1814
  Louis XVIII, 1814-1824
  Charles X, 1824-1830
  Louis Philippe, 1830-1848

  The Second Republic, 1848-1852
    (Louis Napoleon as *President*)
  Napoleon III, *Emperor of the French*, 1852-1870
  The Third Republic, 1870–
  Government of National Defense, 1870-1871
  Adolphe Thiers, *President*, 1871-1873
  Marshal MacMahon, *President*, 1873-1879
  Jules Grévy, *President*, 1879-1887
  F. Sadi Carnot, *President*, 1887-1894
  Casimir Perier, *President*, 1894-1895
  Felix Faure, *President*, 1895-1899
  Émile Loubet, *President*, 1899-1906
  Armand Fallières, *President*, 1906-1913
  Raymond Poincaré, *President*, 1913–

GERMAN EMPIRE
  William I, 1871-1888
  Frederick III, 1888

  William II, 1888–

GREAT BRITAIN
  Sovereigns of England, 1485-1707
    Henry VII, 1485-1509
    Henry VIII, 1509-1547
    Edward VI, 1547-1553
    Mary I, 1553-1558
    Elizabeth, 1558-1603
    James I (*VI of Scotland*), 1603-1625
    Charles I, 1625-1649
    The Commonwealth, 1649-1660 (Oliver Cromwell)
    Charles II, 1660-1685

  Sovereigns of Scotland, 1488-1707
    James IV, 1488-1513
    James V, 1513-1542
    Mary, 1542-1567
    James VI, 1567-1625 (*I of England*, 1603-1625)
    [Succession as in England, 1603-1707]

GREAT BRITAIN — *Continued*

> James II (*VII of Scotland*),
> 1685–1688
> William III and Mary II,
> 1689–1694
> William III, 1694–1702
> Anne, 1702–1714 (*Queen of
> Great Britain after 1707*)

Sovereigns of Great Britain, 1707–1801

Anne, 1707–1714
George I, 1714–1727
George II, 1727–1760

George III, 1760–1820 (*King
of Great Britain and Ireland
after 1800*)

Sovereigns of the United Kingdom of Great Britain and Ireland, 1801–

George III, 1801–1820
George IV, 1820–1830
William IV, 1830–1837

Victoria, 1837–1901
Edward VII, 1901–1910
George V, 1910–

Chief Ministers in Great Britain since 1721

> Sir Robert Walpole, 1721–1742
> John Lord Carteret (Earl Granville), 1742–1743
> Henry Pelham, 1743–1753
> Thomas Pelham, Duke of Newcastle, 1754–1756
> William Cavendish, Duke of Devonshire, 1756–1757
> Duke of Newcastle, 1756–1761 (William Pitt, Secretary of State)
> John Stewart, Earl of Bute, 1762–1763
> George Grenville, 1763–1765
> Charles Wentworth-Watson, Marquess of Rockingham, 1766
> Augustus Fitzroy, Duke of Grafton, 1766–1769
> Frederick Lord North (Earl of Guildford), 1770–1782
> Marquess of Rockingham, 1782
> William Petty, Earl of Shelburne (Marquess of Lansdowne), 1782–1783
> William Bentinck, Duke of Portland, 1783
> William Pitt, 1783–1801
> Henry Addington (Viscount Sidmouth), 1801–1804
> William Pitt, 1804–1806
> William Lord Grenville, 1806–1807 (Charles James Fox, Foreign
>   Secretary)
> Duke of Portland, 1807–1809
> Spencer Perceval, 1809–1812
> Robert Banks Jenkinson, Earl of Liverpool, 1812–1827
> George Canning, 1827
> Frederick John Robinson, Viscount Goderich (Earl of Ripon), 1827
> Arthur Wellesley, Duke of Wellington, 1827–1830
> Earl Grey, 1830–1834
> William Lamb, Viscount Melbourne, 1834

Great Britain — *Continued*

Sir Robert Peel, 1834–1835
Viscount Melbourne, 1835–1841
Sir Robert Peel, 1841–1846
Lord John Russell (Earl Russell), 1846–1852
Edward Stanley, Earl of Derby, 1852
George Hamilton-Gordon, Earl of Aberdeen, 1852–1855
Henry J. Temple, Viscount Palmerston, 1855–1858
Earl of Derby, 1858–1859
Viscount Palmerston, 1859–1865
Earl Russell, 1865–1866
Earl of Derby, 1866–1868
William Ewart Gladstone, 1868–1874
Benjamin Disraeli (Earl of Beaconsfield), 1874–1880
W. E. Gladstone, 1880–1885
Robert Cecil (Marquess of Salisbury), 1885–1886
W. E. Gladstone, 1886
Marquess of Salisbury, 1886–1892
W. E. Gladstone, 1892–1894
Archibald P. Primrose (Earl of Rosebery), 1894–1895
Marquess of Salisbury, 1895–1902
Arthur James Balfour, 1902–1905
Sir Henry Campbell-Bannerman, 1905–1908
Herbert Henry Asquith, 1908–

Greece

Otto I, 1833–1862
George I, 1863–1913

Constantine I, 1913–

Holy Roman Empire

Maximilian I, 1493–1519
Charles V, 1519–1558
Ferdinand I, 1558–1564
Maximilian II, 1564–1576
Rudolph II, 1576–1612
Matthias, 1612–1619
Ferdinand II, 1619–1637
Ferdinand III, 1637–1657

Leopold I, 1658–1705
Joseph I, 1705–1711
Charles VI, 1711–1740
Charles VII, 1742–1745
Francis I, 1745–1765
Joseph II, 1765–1790
Leopold II, 1790–1792
Francis II, 1792–1806

Hungary (see Austria-Hungary)

Italy

Kings of Sardinia

Victor Amadeus II, 1720–1730
Charles Emmanuel III, 1730–1773
Victor Amadeus III, 1773–1796
Charles Emmanuel IV, 1796–1802

Victor Emmanuel I, 1802–1821
Charles Felix, 1821–1831
Charles Albert, 1831–1849
Victor Emmanuel II, 1849–1878 (*as King of Italy after 1861*)

ITALY — *Continued*

Kings of Italy

Victor Emmanuel II, 1861–1878
Humbert, 1878–1900

Victor Emmanuel III, 1900–

MONTENEGRO

Danilo (*Prince-Bishop*), 1696–1735
Sava and Vasilije, 1735–1782
Peter I, 1782–1830

Peter II, 1830–1851
Danilo I, *Prince*, 1851–1860
Nicholas I, *Prince*, 1860–
(*as King since 1910*)

NETHERLANDS

William the Silent, 1581–1584
Maurice, *Stadholder*, 1584–1625
Frederick Henry, *Stadholder*, 1625–1647
William II, *Stadholder*, 1647–1650
John De Witt, *Grand Pensionary*, 1653–1672
William III, *Stadholder*, 1672–1702 (*King of England and Scotland, 1689–1702*)
John William Friso, *Nominal Stadholder*, 1702–1711

William IV, *Nominal Stadholder*, 1711–1747, *Hereditary Stadholder*, 1747–1751
William V, *Hereditary Stadholder*, 1751–1795
The Batavian Republic, 1795–1806
Louis Bonaparte, *King*, 1806–1810
Napoleon I, *Emperor of the French*, 1810–1813
William I, *King*, 1813–1840
William II, 1840–1849
William III, 1849–1890
Wilhelmina, 1890–

NORWAY

Same Sovereigns as in Denmark, 1450–1814
Christian Frederick, 1814

Same Sovereigns as in Sweden, 1814–1905
Haakon VII, 1905–

POLAND

John I Albert, 1492–1501
Alexander, 1501–1506
Sigismund I, 1506–1548
Sigismund II, 1548–1572
Henry of Valois, 1573–1574 (*Henry III of France*)
Stephen Báthory, 1575–1586 (*Prince of Transylvania*)
Sigismund III Vasa, 1587–1632
Ladislaus IV, 1632–1648
John II Casimir, 1648–1668
Michael Wisniowiecki, 1669–1673

John III Sobieski, 1674–1696
Augustus II, 1697–1704 (*Elector of Saxony*)
Stanislaus Leszczynski, 1704–1709
Augustus II (*restored*), 1709–1733
Stanislaus Leszczynski (*restored*), 1733–1734
Augustus III, 1734–1763 (*Elector of Saxony*)
Stanislaus II Poniatowski, 1764–1795

THE POPES

Alexander VI (Rodrigo Borgia), 1492–1503

Pius III (Francesco Todeschini), 1503

Julius II (Giulio della Rovere), 1503–1513

Leo X (Giovanni de' Medici), 1513–1521

Adrian VI (Adrian Boyers), 1522–1523

Clement VII (Giulio de' Medici), 1523–1534

Paul III (Alessandro Farnese), 1534–1549

Julius III (Giovanni del Monte), 1550–1555

Marcellus II (Marcello Cervini), 1555

Paul IV (Giovanni Caraffa), 1555–1559

Pius IV (Gian-Angelo Medici), 1559–1565

Pius V (Michele Ghislieri), 1566–1572

Gregory XIII (Ugo Buoncompagno), 1572–1585

Sixtus V (Felix Peretti), 1585–1590

Urban VII (Giambattista Castagna), 1590

Gregory XIV (Niccolò Sfondrato), 1590–1591

Innocent IX (Gian-Antonio Facchinetto), 1591

Clement VIII (Ippolito Aldobrandini), 1592–1605

Leo XI (Alessandro de' Medici), 1605

Paul V (Camillo Borghese), 1605–1621

Gregory XV (Alessandro Ludovisi), 1621–1623

Urban VIII (Maffeo Barberini), 1623–1644

Innocent X (Giambattista Pamfili), 1644–1655

Alexander VII (Fabio Chigi), 1655–1667

Clement IX (Giulio Rospigliosi), 1667–1669

Clement X (Giambattista Altieri), 1670–1676

Innocent XI (Benedetto Odescalchi), 1676–1689

Alexander VIII (Pietro Ottobuoni), 1689–1691

Innocent XII (Antonio Pignatelli), 1691–1700

Clement XI (Gianfrancesco Albano), 1700–1721

Innocent XIII (Michelangelo Conti), 1721–1724

Benedict XIII (Pietro Orsini), 1724–1730

Clement XII (Lorenzo Corsini), 1730–1740

Benedict XIV (Prosper Lambertini), 1740–1758

Clement XIII (Carlo Rezzonico), 1758–1769

Clement XIV (Giovanni Ganganelli), 1769–1774

Pius VI (Giovan-Angelo Braschi), 1775–1799

Pius VII (Gregorio Chiaramonte), 1800–1823

Leo XII (Annibale della Genga), 1823–1829

Pius VIII (Francesco X. Castiglione), 1829–1830

Gregory XVI (Mauro Capellari), 1831–1846

Pius IX (Count Giovanni Mastaï-Ferretti), 1846–1878

Leo XIII (Joachim Pecci), 1878–1903

Pius X (Giuseppe Sarto), 1903–1914

Benedict XV (Giacomo della Chiesa), 1914–

PORTUGAL

Emmanuel (Manoel) I, 1495–1521
John III, 1521–1557
Sebastian, 1557–1578
Henry, 1578–1580
Same Sovereigns as in Spain,
1580–1640
John IV, 1640–1656
Alfonso VI, 1656–1667
Pedro II, 1667–1706
John V, 1706–1750
Joseph, 1750–1777
Maria I and Pedro III, 1777–1786
Maria I, 1786–1816
John VI, 1816–1826

Pedro IV, 1826 (*I of Brazil,*
1826–1831)
Maria II, 1826–1828
Miguel, 1828–1834
Maria II, 1834–1853
Pedro V, 1853–1861
Luiz I, 1861–1889
Carlos, 1889–1908
Manoel II, 1908–1910
The Republic, 1910–
Manoel Arriaga, *President,* 1911–
1915
Bernardino Machado, *President,*
1915–

PRUSSIA

Electors of Brandenburg
Joachim I, 1499–1535
Joachim II, 1535–1571
John George, 1571–1598
Joachim Frederick, 1598–1608
John Sigismund, 1608–1619
George William, 1619–1640
Frederick William, 1640–1688
Frederick III, 1688–1701 (*as*
Frederick I, King of Prussia,
1701–1713)

Kings of Prussia
Frederick I, 1701–1713
Frederick William I, 1713–1740
Frederick II, 1740–1786
Frederick William II, 1786–
1797
Frederick William III, 1797–
1840
Frederick William IV, 1840–
1861
William I, 1861–1888
Frederick III, 1888
William II, 1888–

RUMANIA

Charles I, *Prince,* 1866–1881,
King, 1881–1914

Ferdinand I, 1914–

RUSSIA

Ivan III, 1462–1505
Basil IV, 1505–1533
Ivan IV, 1533–1584
Theodore, 1584–1598
Boris Godunoff, 1598–1605
Michael, 1613–1645
Alexius, 1645–1676
Theodore II, 1676–1682
Ivan V and Peter I, 1682–1689
Peter I, 1689–1725
Catherine I, 1725–1727
Peter II, 1727–1730

Anna, 1730–1740
Ivan VI, 1740–1741
Elizabeth, 1741–1762
Peter III, 1762
Catherine II, 1762–1796
Paul, 1796–1801
Alexander I, 1801–1825
Nicholas I, 1825–1855
Alexander II, 1855–1881
Alexander III, 1881–1894
Nicholas II, 1894–

Serbia

Karageorge, *Prince*, 1804–1813
Milosh, *Prince*, 1817–1839
Milan, *Prince*, 1839
Michael, *Prince*, 1839–1842
Alexander I. *Prince*, 1842–1859

Michael, *Prince*, 1860–1868
Milan, *Prince*, 1868–1882, *King*, 1882–1889
Alexander, 1889–1903
Peter I, 1903–

Spain

Ferdinand and Isabella, 1479–1504
Ferdinand and Philip I, 1504–1506
Ferdinand and Charles I, 1506–1516
Charles I (*V of Holy Roman Empire*), *alone*, 1516–1556
Philip II, 1556–1598
Philip III, 1598–1621
Philip IV, 1621–1665
Charles II, 1665–1700
Philip V, 1700–1746

Ferdinand VI, 1746–1759
Charles III, 1759–1788
Charles IV, 1788–1808
Joseph Bonaparte, 1808–1813
Ferdinand VII, 1813–1833
Isabella II, 1833–1868
Revolutionary Government, 1868–1870
Amadeo of Savoy, 1870–1873
The Republic, 1873–1875
Alphonso XII, 1875–1885
Alphonso XIII, 1886–

Sweden

Same Sovereigns as in Denmark, 1470–1523
Gustavus I Vasa, 1523–1560
Eric XIV, 1560–1568
John III, 1568–1592
Sigismund, 1592–1604
Charles IX, 1604–1611
Gustavus II Adolphus, 1611–1632
Christina, 1632–1654
Charles X, 1654–1660
Charles XI, 1660–1697
Charles XII, 1697–1718

Ulrica Eleonora, 1718–1720
Frederick I, 1720–1751
Adolphus Frederick, 1751–1771
Gustavus III, 1771–1792
Gustavus IV, 1792–1809
Charles XIII, 1809–1818
Charles XIV, 1818–1844
Oscar I, 1844–1859
Charles XV, 1859–1872
Oscar II, 1872–1907
Gustavus V, 1907–

Turkey

Mohammed II, 1451–1481
Bayezid II, 1481–1512
Selim I, 1512–1520
Suleiman II, "the Magnificent," 1520–1566
Selim II, 1566–1574
Murad III, 1574–1595
Mohammed III, 1595–1603
Ahmed I, 1603–1617
Mustapha I, 1617–1618

Othman II, 1618–1623
Murad IV, 1623–1640
Ibrahim, 1640–1648
Mohammed IV, 1648–1687
Suleiman III, 1687–1691
Ahmed II, 1691–1695
Mustapha II, 1695–1703
Ahmed III, 1703–1730
Mahmud I, 1730–1754
Othman III, 1754–1757

TURKEY — *Continued*

Mustapha III, 1757–1773
Abdul Hamid I, 1773–1789
Selim III, 1789–1807
Mustapha IV, 1807–1808
Mahmud II, 1808–1839

Abdul Medjid, 1839–1861
Abdul Aziz, 1861–1876
Murad V, 1876
Abdul Hamid II, 1876–1909
Mohammed V, 1909–

INDEX

Printed in the United States of America.